SOCIAL RIGHTS JUDGMEN[
POLITICS OF COMPLI

The past few decades have witnessed an explosion of judgments on social rights around the world. However, we know little about whether these rulings have been implemented. *Social Rights Judgments and the Politics of Compliance* is the first book to engage in a comparative study of compliance of social rights judgments as well as their broader effects. Covering fourteen different domestic and international jurisdictions and drawing on multiple disciplines, it finds significant variance in outcomes and reveals both spectacular successes and failures in making social rights a reality on the ground. This variance is strikingly similar to that found in previous studies on civil rights, and the key explanatory factors lie in the political calculus of defendants and the remedial framework. The book also discusses which strategies have enhanced implementation and focuses on judicial reflexivity, alliance building, and social mobilisation.

MALCOLM LANGFORD is Associate Professor at the Faculty of Law, University of Oslo, and Co-Director of the Centre on Law and Social Transformation, Chr. Michelsen Institute and University of Bergen.

CÉSAR RODRÍGUEZ-GARAVITO is Executive Director of the Center for Law, Justice, and Society (Dejusticia) and Associate Professor of Law at the University of the Andes.

JULIETA ROSSI is Associate Professor at the National University of Lanús, at the Centre for Justice and Human Rights, Researcher at the Centre for Justice and Human Rights (University of Lanús) and legal advisor at the Federal Prosecutor´s Office (Ministerio Público Fiscal).

SOCIAL RIGHTS JUDGMENTS AND THE POLITICS OF COMPLIANCE

Making It Stick

Edited by

MALCOLM LANGFORD
University of Oslo

CÉSAR RODRÍGUEZ-GARAVITO
University of Los Andes and Dejusticia

JULIETA ROSSI
National University of Lanús, Argentina

CAMBRIDGE
UNIVERSITY PRESS

CAMBRIDGE
UNIVERSITY PRESS

University Printing House, Cambridge CB2 8BS, United Kingdom

One Liberty Plaza, 20th Floor, New York, NY 10006, USA

477 Williamstown Road, Port Melbourne, VIC 3207, Australia

314-321, 3rd Floor, Plot 3, Splendor Forum, Jasola District Centre, New Delhi-110025, India

79 Anson Road, #06-04/06, Singapore 079906

Cambridge University Press is part of the University of Cambridge.

It furthers the University's mission by disseminating knowledge in the pursuit of education, learning and research at the highest international levels of excellence.

www.cambridge.org
Information on this title: www.cambridge.org/9781316613313
DOI: 10.1017/9781316673058

First published 2017
First paperback edition 2018

A catalogue record for this publication is available from the British Library

Library of Congress Cataloging in Publication data
Names: Langford, Malcolm, editor. | Rodríguez-Garavito, César, editor. | Rossi, Julieta, editor.
Title: Social rights judgments and the politics of compliance: making it stick / Malcolm Langford, University of Oslo; César Rodríguez-Garavito, University of Los Andes and Dejusticia; Julieta Rossi, National University of Lanús, Argentina.
Description: Cambridge, United Kingdom; New York, NY: Cambridge University Press, 2016. |
Includes bibliographical references and index.
Identifiers: LCCN 2016026904 | ISBN 9781107160217 (hardback)
Subjects: LCSH: Social rights. | Executions (Law)
Classification: LCC K1700.C657 2016 | DDC 342.08/5–dc23
LC record available at https://lccn.loc.gov/2016026904
ISBN 978-1-107-16021-7 Hardback
ISBN 978-1-316-61331-3 Paperback

CONTENTS

FIGURES AND TABLES

Figures

Tables

CONTRIBUTORS

CATHY ALBISA is the Executive Director of NESRI and a constitutional and human rights lawyer with a background on the right to health. Ms. Albisa also has significant experience working in partnership with community organizers in the use of human rights standards to strengthen advocacy in the United States. Her publications include *Bringing Human Rights Home: A History of Human Rights in the United States* (Pennsylvania Studies in Human Rights, 2009), edited with C. Soohoo and M. Davis.

THEODOROS ALEXANDRIDIS is a lawyer at Greek Helsinki Monitor. He has handled numerous cases relating to racial discrimination, police ill-treatment, freedom of speech, and freedom of religion before domestic and international tribunals. Between 2007 and 2009, he worked as a staff attorney at the European Roma Rights Centre in Budapest and was involved in a series of landmark cases before international organs. He has also worked as a legal consultant to Albanian human rights NGOs and is a member of the Athens Bar Association.

DANIEL M. BRINKS is Associate Professor of Government and Professor of Law (by courtesy), and co-director of the Rapoport Center for Human Rights and Justice at the University of Texas at Austin. Dan's research focuses on the role of the law and courts in supporting and deepening democracy and constitutional rights. His research appears in journals such as *Perspectives on Politics*, *Comparative Politics*, and the *Texas Law Review*. He has authored and edited books on the judicial response to police violence, the enforcement of the rights to health care and education in the developing world, and the varied experiences of democratic regimes in Latin America. Dan has a Ph.D. in Political Science from the University of Notre Dame, and a J.D. from the University of Michigan Law School.

LUISA CABAL is Chief, Human Rights and the Law, UNAIDS and former Vice President of Programs at the Center for Reproductive Rights where she oversaw all of the organization's legal programs and advocacy efforts in the United States and across the globe. Ms. Cabal is also a Lecturer in Law at Columbia University Law School and a co-founder of the first network of Latin American law professors (RED ALAS) working to integrate a gender perspective and women's rights into law school curricula. She is currently a member of the Lancet Commission on Global Health and the Law, and has served as advisor to the World Health Organization's Reproductive Health Department's Gender Advisory Panel, International Federation of OB/GYN's (FIGO) Sexual and Reproductive Rights Committee, and University of California's Global Health Institute.

BAŞAK ÇALI is Professor of International Law at Hertie School of Governance, Berlin and Director of Center for Global Public Law, Koç University, Istanbul. She has published widely in the field of international human rights law, in particular on the legitimacy and design of international human rights institutions and the effects of human right law on domestic law, politics and civil society action. Her publications include *The Authority of International Law: Obedience, Respect and Rebuttal* (Oxford University Press, 2015), *International Law for International Relations* (Oxford: Oxford University Press, 2009) and *The Legalisation of Human Rights* (London: Routledge, 2006, with Meckled-Garcia).

POORVI CHITALKAR is a Senior Program Officer at the Global Centre for Pluralism. The contents of this paper are the responsibility of the author and do not necessarily reflect the views of the Global Centre for Pluralism.

ANDI DOBRUSHI has been the Executive Director of Open Society Foundation for Albania (OSFA) since March 2009. Prior to joining OSFA, he worked for twelve years at the European Roma Rights Centre in Budapest, promoting public interest law and in combating human rights abuses. A lawyer by training, he is an expert of Roma/minority rights and in the development of legislation, policies, and measures relating to human rights and equality. He has served as an expert on these issues at the national and international level, advising various international and local institutions, including the United Nations High Commissioner for Human Rights, Council of Europe, and the Norwegian Center for Human Rights. He has published various articles and commentaries on issues of discrimination, Roma rights, economic and social rights and civil society developments. Dobrushi has a degree in Law from the University of Tirana, Albania, and a LL.M. in Law from the Central European University, Budapest.

OCTAVIO LUIZ MOTTA FERRAZ is a Reader in transnational law at the Dickson Poon School of Law and an affiliate of the Brazil Institute, both at King's College London. He was formerly a senior research officer to the UN Special Rapporteur on the Right to Health. He has published widely in the field of social and economic rights, in particular on the right to health litigation, including 'Health Inequalities, Rights and Courts: The Social Impact of the 'Judicialization of Health' in Brazil', in *Litigating the Right to Health: Can Courts Bring More Justice to Health Systems?* (edited by Yamin and Gloppen, Harvard University Press, 2011) and 'Harming the Poor through Social Rights Litigation Lessons from Brazil', *Texas Law Review*, Vol. 89 (2011).

VARUN GAURI is a Senior Economist in the Development Research Group, World Bank. He has published papers on a wide variety of topics, including customary law systems, public interest litigation, judicial enforcement of socio-economic rights, the political economy of HIV/AIDS, the strategic choices of NGOs, the use of education vouchers, and immunization in developing countries. He has held positions as Visiting Lecturer in Public and International Affairs at Princeton University and as Visiting Professor in the Department of Economics at ILADES in Santiago, Chile. He recently published *Courting Social Justice* (co-edited with Daniel Brinks, Cambridge University Press, 2008) and 'The Cost of Complying with Human Rights Treaties', *The Review of International Organizations*, Vol. 6 (2011).

STEVE KAHANOVITZ works in the Cape Town office of South Africa's public interest law group the Legal Resources Centre (LRC). He spent many years representing clients facing an oppressive apartheid state before serving as legal and later national director of the LRC. Since the adoption of the Bill of Rights in a democratic South Africa, he has been primarily litigating cases regarding socio-economic rights, particularly the right of access to housing. He has returned to the LRC having spent 2012 as an acting judge of the Land Claims Court of South Africa.

ANNE KOCH is a researcher and policy consultant at the Stiftung Wissenschaft und Politik (SWP) in Berlin. Prior to joining SWP she held research and lecture positions at the Hertie School of Governance, the European University Viadrina and University College London, and worked for UNHCR's Peace Building, Livelihoods and Partnerships Section as well as for Capacity Building International. From 2010 till 2011, she worked as a researcher in the ESRC-funded project 'The Legitimacy and Authority of Supranational Human Rights Courts'. She wrote her

PhD dissertation at the Freie Universität Berlin about the institutional and normative underpinnings of migrant return policies in Germany and the United Kingdom. Her work has been published in the *Journal of Ethnic and Migration Studies, Forced Migration Review, Human Rights Quarterly, and Human Rights Law Review*.

MALCOLM LANGFORD is an Associate Professor, Faculty of Law, University of Oslo and the Co-Director of the Centre on Law and Social Transformation, Chr. Michelsen Institute (CMI) and University of Bergen. He is also an affiliate researcher at the Pluricourts Centre of Excellence. He has been an advisor to the Office of the UN High Commissioner of Human Rights, UN-Habitat, WHO, and UN CESCR and a visiting fellow and professor at a number of universities. He has published on a wide range of topics on human rights, international development, and international investment in the fields of law, economics, and political sciences. His books include *Symbols or Substance? The Role and Impact of Socio-Economic Rights Strategies in South Africa*, edited with B. Cousins, J. Dugard, and T. Madlingozi (Cambridge: Cambridge University Press, 2013) and *Social Rights Jurisprudence: Emerging Trends in International and Comparative Law*.

DIEGO MORALES is an Associate Professor at National University of Lanus, Palermo, and University of Buenos Aires, Argentina. Previously, he was the Director of Social, Economic, Cultural Rights, and Social Inclusion Area at Centro de Estudios Legales y Sociales (CELS) (www.cels.org.ar) as well as its Director of Litigation and Legal Defense from 2003 to 2010. He has published research papers about economic, social, and cultural rights, and migrants rights.

SUZANNAH PHILLIPS is the Senior Legal Advisor for Women Enabled International. She was previously the Legal Adviser for International Advocacy at the Center for Reproductive Rights and a clinical teaching fellow and staff attorney with the Human Rights and Gender Justice Clinic at the City University of New York School of Law (CUNY). She has co-authored a number of institutional research publications, including *Dignity Denied: Violations of the Rights of HIV-Positive Women in Chilean Health Facilities* (Center for Reproductive Rights: 2010) and *Clearing the Slate: Seeking Effective Remedies for Criminalized Trafficking Victims* (CUNY School of Law, 2014).

BRUCE PORTER is the Executive Director of the Social Rights Advocacy Centre in Canada, the Co-Director of a major research project into 'social rights practice' in Canada, a Commissioner of the Ontario Human Rights Commission and Senior Advisor to the UN Special Rapporteur on the Right to Adequate Housing. Internationally, he has been active for many years in promoting improved monitoring and adjudication of ESCR. A founding member of ESCR-Net, he has been active in promoting the Optional Protocol to the ICESCR and in strategic litigation. He has published extensively in the field and his writings include *Advancing Social Rights in Canada* (Toronto: Irwin Law, 2014, edited with M. Jackman) and 'Inclusive Interpretations: Social and Economic Rights and the Canadian Charter' in *Social and Economic Rights in Theory and Practice: Critical Inquiries* (London and New York: Routledge, 2015).

OLMAN A. RODRÍGUEZ has served as a *letrado* (clerk) to the Costa Rican Constitutional Chamber since 1991; and a Liaison Officer for the Venice Commission – European Union. He has been an integral part of several collaborative projects to enhance the judicial process in Costa Rica including the National Commission for the Enhancement of the Administration of Justice and the Popular Legal Education Commission. He has also worked on several bilingual editions of the *Constitution of the Republic of Costa Rica* and published his research on Costa Rican Constitutional Court's jurisdiction in the *Duquesne Law Review*.

CÉSAR RODRÍGUEZ-GARAVITO is Associate Professor and founding Director of the Program on Global Justice and Human Rights at the University of the Andes (Colombia). He is a founding member and the Executive Director of the Center for Law, Justice, and Society (Dejusticia). He has been a visiting professor at Stanford University and Brown University, and was appointed as a Global Professor of Law at New York University (2018). He is an Adjunct Judge of the Constitutional Court of Colombia and a Master of the Court on the right to health. His degrees include a PhD and an MS (Sociology) from the University of Wisconsin-Madison and an MA from New York University's Institute for Law and Society. His publications include *Radical Deprivation on Trial: The Impact of Judicial Activism on Socioeconomic Rights in the Global South* (co-authored, Cambridge: Cambridge University Press); *Balancing Wealth and Health: The Battle over Intellectual Property and Access to Medicines in Latin America* (Oxford: Oxford University Press, 2015 – co-edited); and *Globalization from Below: Toward a Cosmopolitan Legality* (Cambridge: Cambridge University Press, co-edited).

JULIETA ROSSI has a law degree from the Universidad de Buenos Aires (1997), an LLM from New York University Law School (2005), and was also a Fullbright Scholar (2005). She is currently a legal advisor at the Federal Prosecutor's Office (Ministerio Público Fiscal), Associate Professor at the National University of Lanús and researcher at the Centre for Justice and Human Rights at the same university. She also teaches graduate and postgraduate courses at the University of Buenos Aires and at the National Universities of San Martín and Tres de Febrero. She was director of the International Network for Economic, Social and Cultural Rights (ESCR-Net), director of the Program on Economic, Social and Cultural Rights and member of the Board of Directors at the Centre for Legal and Social Studies (CELS). She has published articles and research papers about human rights law, in particular on economic, social, and cultural rights and human rights-based approaches.

AMANDA SHANOR is a Fellow, Center for National Security & the Law, Georgetown University Law Center. She previously clerked in the Southern District of New York and next the DC Circuit. Previously, Amanda was a fellow at the Georgetown University Law Center, where she litigated and wrote on national security and constitutional law. For several years, she was the US Program Officer at the Robert F. Kennedy Center for Human Rights, where she worked on the implementation of international human rights standards in the United States. Her publications include *Counterterrorism Law: Cases and Materials* (with C. Shanor, Foundation Press, 2011) and 'Beyond Humanitarian Law Project: Promoting Human Rights in a Post-9/11 World', *Suffolk Transnational Law Review*.

MARTÍN SIGAL is a lawyer educated at the Universidad de Buenos Aires (1999), with a LLM from Columbia Law School (2006), and was a Fullbright Scholar (2005). He was Co-founder and Co-director of Asociación Civil por la Igualdad y la Justicia (www.acij.org.ar). Sigal has published on class action litigation and their relation to the defense of right to health, right to education, and consumer rights. He is co-author of the book *Las Acciones Colectivas* (Lexis Nexis, 2005), and he has participated as lawyer in several leading cases in collective litigation in Argentina. He has also served as professor in undergraduate and LLM degree courses at Universidad de Palermo, Universidad de San Andrés, and Universidad de Buenos Aires, and he has coordinated the public interest law clinic at the Palermo Law School. Currently he is the Director of the Center for Human Rights at Law School at Universidad de Buenos Aires.

FRANS VILJOEN is Professor and Director of the Centre for Human Rights, Faculty of Law, University of Pretoria. He has been involved in advocacy and training in and on the African regional human rights system, and he has published widely on international human rights law, including *International Human Rights Law in Africa* (2nd edn, Oxford University Press, 2012). He is also Editor-in-Chief of the *African Human Rights Law Journal* and Co-Editor of the English and French versions of the *African Human Rights Law Reports*.

BRUCE M. WILSON (PhD, Washington University) is Professor of Political Science at the University of Central Florida, Orlando, Florida, and an associated senior researcher at the Chr. Michelsen Institute, Bergen, Norway. His research has appeared in numerous peer-reviewed journals including *Comparative Political Studies*, the *Journal of Latin American Studies*, *Comparative Politics*, *Journal of Politics in Latin America*, and the *International Journal of Constitutional Law*. His books include *Costa Rica: Politics, Economics, and Democracy* (Lynne Rienner Publishers, 1998) and a co-authored book, *Courts and Political Power in Latin America and Africa* (Palgrave Macmillan, 2010). He is the former co-editor of the *Journal of Political Science Education*.

PREFACE

The maturing of socio-economics rights jurisprudence in diverse jurisdictions prompts questions about its effectiveness. This book is the first comparative and interdisciplinary study that closely analyses the issue of compliance. Not only does it map the degree to which judgments are implemented but it also examines the casual factors and strategies which have proved useful in practice. We hope it provides a valuable resource to scholars and practitioners alike in thinking through the dynamics of compliance and tackling non-compliance.

The origins of this book lie in a meeting organised by the International Network for Economic, Social and Cultural Rights (ESCR-Net) in Bogota together with our respective institutions: the University of Oslo, the University of Los Andes, the Center for Law, Justice and Society (Dejusticia) and the University of Lanús. After generous support from Ford Foundation, a conference was held in Bogota in May 2010, and many of the papers presented have emerged as chapters in this volume.

The book draws together scholars and some advocates from a range of disciplines. The result is that the methods vary from single case studies to the more quantitative, but most deploy a comparative case method. In order to enhance consistency and comparability across the chapters, contributors were asked to address a common set of questions and topics. We would like to deeply thank them for their willingness to take on the challenge, particularly in uncovering new insights and perspectives, and their patience in dealing with endless questions and queries from the editors.

We would also like to deeply thank Rebecca Brown, Deputy Director at ESCR-Net, who served as the managing support to the project, as well as Cheryl Lorens, Elyse Leonard and Natasha Telson at the Norwegian Centre for Human Rights, Tonje Stegavik (IOR) and Daniela Ikawa, Program Officer at ESCR-Net, who provided editing support, and Celeste Kaufmann and Carolina Bernal at Dejusticia who helped organise the original conference.

In the production of the book, we are very grateful to John Berger at Cambridge University Press for his support for the project from its inception, to Siva Prakash Chandrasekaran, Helen Francis and Lisa Sinclair for shepherding the book through its various phases and to Sumathi for the painstaking copy editing of the entire manuscript.

Part I

Overview

Introduction: From Jurisprudence to Compliance

MALCOLM LANGFORD, CÉSAR RODRÍGUEZ-GARAVITO
AND JULIETA ROSSI

In the past two decades, the volume of judgments on economic, social and cultural (ESC) rights has risen dramatically. Despite traditional reservations about justiciability, feasibility, and legitimacy, judicial decisions addressing multiple aspects of these rights can now be found in all regions of the world (see, e.g., Coomans, 2006; ICJ, 2008; Langford, 2008; Rossi and Filippini, 2009). The primary scholarly response to this new phenomenon has been normative and doctrinal. Research has been consumed by the justification of such adjudication in light of democratic and legal theory (e.g., Bilchitz, 2007; Dennis and Stewart, 2004; Fabre, 2000; King, 2012; Vierdag, 1978; Waldron, 2009) or the task of examining, systematising, refining and critiquing the emerging jurisprudence (e.g., Abramovich and Courtis, 2001; Gargarella, Domingo and Roux, 2006; Katherine Young, 2008; Liebenberg, 2010).

The post-judgmental phase of litigation has received comparatively less attention. Yet, both advocates and scholars have raised the alarm that a significant number of judgments on ESC rights remain unimplemented (Berger, 2008; CEJIL, 2003; Wachira and Ayinla, 2006). In reviewing the rise of ESC rights jurisprudence in South Asia, Byrne and Hossain (2008: 143) concluded that, 'Advances in jurisprudence urgently need to be matched by action on the ground to ensure compliance of all concerned authorities with the judgments'. Elsewhere, one can find critiques that ground-breaking judgments were poorly or sluggishly implemented in practice. Whether it is access to vaccines for haemorrhagic fever in

Malcolm Langford is Associate Professor in the Faculty of Law, University of Oslo. He is also Co-Director, Centre on Law and Social Transformation, University of Oslo, and former Co-Coordinator, Adjudication Group, ESCR-Net.

César Rodríguez-Garavito is Associate Professor at the University of Los Andes, and founding member, Dejusticia.

Julieta Rossi is a professor at the National University of Lanus and University of Buenos Aires, and former Director of ESC-Net.

Argentina, the right to emergency housing in South Africa or the right to adequate education in the United States, concerns have been raised that litigants have struggled to transform progressive jurisprudence into progressive outcomes. The same also applies to rulings from regional and international tribunals. This is evidenced by the patchy efforts by Nigeria to regulate the impact of the multinational Shell's activities on the right to food and water within the state (after a decision of the African Commission on Human and Peoples' Rights), the Czech Republic's failure to ensure equal access to schools for Roma children (following a judgment of the European Court of Human Rights) or Peru's sluggish approach to compliance with approved settlements and decisions on reproductive health (from the Inter-American Commission on Human Rights and the UN Human Rights Committee).

To this emerging narrative of poor or partial compliance we can find various scholarly responses. Some are pro-active, seeking to identify how enforcement may be improved in practice (Mbazira, 2008a; Roach and Budlender, 2005). Others are critical. Poor enforcement confirms some longstanding doubts over the appropriateness of social rights adjudication. Concerns with the justiciability, democratic legitimacy and the institutional competence of judges may account for governmental reluctance to comply. As Cavanagh and Sarat (1980: 372) put it, 'the more courts do, the less they do well'. Critics also seize on such evidence in order to cast doubt on the relevance and effectiveness of social rights adjudication as a framework for ensuring social justice (Hirschl and Rosevear, 2012; Thompson and Crampton, 2002), raising the spectre of Hazard's (1969: 712) prediction that the contribution of courts to social change will be 'diffuse, microcosmic, and dull'.

The truth is, however, that beyond some anecdotal evidence, we do not know the extent to which compliance is a problem in comparative and international perspective. Nor do we have a clear grasp of why levels of compliance vary. Yet, such an understanding is surely essential for any informed debate on the utility or reform of the practice of social rights adjudication. While it is common to hear that the type of right adjudicated (social, civil or political) determines the level of compliance, is this necessarily correct? Could compliance instead be a function of broader factors that are also relevant for civil and political rights? These might include the responsiveness of defendants, courts and public opinion, the influence of civil society groups and their allies and a host of contextual specificities that mark the trajectory of each case.

Until recently, the literature on the post-judgment aspects of litigation was primarily limited to the United States. Initially, it was the subject of specific compliance studies (Horowitz, 1977; Spriggs, 1997), although increasingly it has been subsumed by a surfeit of literature on the broader material, political and symbolic effects of judgments (e.g., Baas and Thomas, 1984; Hoekstra, 2000; Johnson and Martin, 1998; Linos and Twist, 2013; McCann, 1994; Muir, 1973; Rosenberg, 1991; Ura, 2014). The focus has largely been on civil and political rights with the exception of significant, but often overlooked, research on the implementation and impact of school finance litigation (e.g., Berry, 2007; Hickrod et al., 1992; Thompson and Crampton, 2002) – all US state constitutions provide varying degrees of recognition of the right to education.

When we move beyond the United States, the pattern is similar. Emerging research on the judgments of domestic and international courts has been largely confined to civil and political rights. This is the case whether it concerns compliance (Çali and Wyss, 2011; Ginsberg and McAdams, 2004; Goldsmith and Posner, 2005; Hillebrecht, 2014; OSJI, 2010) or broader impacts (Helfer and Voeten, 2014; Hillebrecht, 2014; Keller and Sweet, 2008; OSJI, 2010). Nonetheless, the past few years have witnessed a growth in the studies on the impact of ESC rights judgments. This includes cross-country studies (Gauri and Brinks, 2008; Yamin and Gloppen, 2011), in-depth single-country studies (Langford et al., 2014; Rodríguez Garavito and Rodríguez-Franco, 2015), and single-case studies (e.g., Heywood, 2009; Rodríguez-Garavito, 2011; Wilson, 2011).

However, by and large, these studies on ESC rights either ignore the specific compliance dimension of impact or note it without theorising or analysing it in any detail. Yet, compliance deserves particular consideration on instrumental and methodological grounds. As Kapiszewski and Taylor (2013: 803) argue, compliance may not only 'influence broader policy and political outcomes', it is also central to the rule of law, 'undergirding and reinforcing the institutional framework for legality and constitutionality', and can have 'powerful feedback effects on judicial decision making, independence and power'. Moreover, there are a host of specific challenges in measuring and explaining compliance, determining 'when and why' defendants conform to judicial mandates (Kapiszewski and Taylor, 2013: 804). To this we would add the challenge of identifying which type of reforms or changes would improve compliance. In other words, there is a need to transform explanatory theories into workable policy policies and advocacy strategies in order to improve implementation?

This book therefore sets out to shed light on the degree and causes of compliance with ESC rights judgments and helps shape the growing policy discussions on improving the rule of law. It poses three distinct questions in comparative and international perspective. The first is *empirical:* What is the current level of enforcement of ESC rights judgments, including international quasi-judicial decisions? The second is *explanatory:* What is the reason for the level of compliance with a given ruling (or set of rulings) on ESC rights? The third is *strategic* and forward looking: What legal and political arrangements and strategies help promote the implementation and the impact of ESC rights judgments?

The authors in this book are drawn from law, political science and sociology; they are mostly scholars but some are practitioners with in-depth knowledge of the particular cases. All authors were asked to combine social science methods of research (e.g., interviews, focus groups, generation or analysis of quantitative data) with a solid understanding of the legal arc and remedial framework of their cases.

The remainder of this Introduction proceeds by first outlining the methodology behind this book in the context of the broader literature on compliance (Section 1.1), which is followed by an overview of the various chapters in the volume (Section 1.2), a synthesis of the key themes concerning measurement and particularly explanation of compliance (Section 1.3) and some practical suggestions on how enforcement might be improved (Section 1.4).

1.1   Methodology in Context

1.1.1   *Measuring the Level of Compliance*

Determining the level of compliance involves a standard but not uncontroversial or unproblematic task of selecting a set of judgments, defining the relevant baseline (*what* is to be done, by *when* and by *whom*) and comparing it against the outcomes in practice. For the most part, authors have chosen a comparative case method of tracing implementation of three to ten cases within a select jurisdiction in order to generalise at some level of abstraction. Some authors go further and adopt a large N approach, drawing on a broader sample of judgments and systemic surveys of implementation.

The cases principally deal with rights concerning health, education, housing, social security and food at both the domestic and international level. While the bulk of the judgments come from a cross-regional selection of national courts, this domestic sample is complemented by decisions from the European Court of Human Rights, European Committee on Social Rights and African Human Rights Commission together with a number of cases from the Inter-American and UN human rights treaty body system. The inclusion of the latter may seem unusual. The field of compliance studies is strongly bifurcated between domestic and international adjudication. This may be partly because international adjudication presents an additional wrinkle: adjudicators often lack the remedial and enforcement powers of their domestic counterparts. However, it is doubtful whether formal remedial power should be considered a scope condition – it may function better as an independent variable. This is because the coercive power of the judiciary is rarely the solely determinative cause of compliance. Moreover, the debate over compliance often takes the same course, regardless of whether the adjudicatory institution is national or supranational. Thus, in our view, there is much to be gained from a multilevel analysis that draws on the similarities in compliance behaviour rather than the differences.

One of the most difficult aspects of this research question is defining what constitutes full, or even partial, compliance. As Hillebrecht (2014: 11) laments, 'The domestic politics of compliance can be murky and difficult to navigate, and almost always contentious'. The meaning of a judicial remedy may be highly contested, the order may be complex or multi-level, or intervening events may confound the scope or sequencing of compliance steps. To this we could add further complexity such as multiple petitioners and defendants or government responses that meet the spirit but not the letter of the remedy (Kapiszewski and Taylor, 2013: 815–816). Thus, as some of the studies make clear, measuring compliance is as much an exercise in interpretation as one in data gathering.

Importantly, this book largely avoids a binary understanding of compliance and distinguishes between partial and full implementation. While this distinction is harder to sustain in quantitative studies (Hillebrecht, 2014; Voeten, 2012: 45–47), the qualitative thrust of this books allows us to describe a richer picture of post-judgment implementation. This is particularly important from the perspective of the litigant or respondent: partial compliance may be respectively significant or costly. Moreover, some courts may be less reflexive in their remedial orders, requiring an unrealistic number of actions within a short period of time. Compare, for example, the anaemic and thin orders of the European Court of Human Rights with the expansive and multi-pronged remedies of the Inter-American Court of Human Rights. With the lens of partial compliance, we can track important behavioural changes by respondents as a consequence of an ambitious judgment.

At the same time, the book seeks to avoid conflating compliance with impact. Impact means the total influence or effect of a decision, which may be greater than mere implementation of the order (e.g., through additional indirect effects) or even 'net negative' due to unintended consequences. The chapter by Rodríguez-Garavito provides an analytical framework with which to specify the relationship between the two concepts in theory and practice. Comparing the possible results for implementation and impact, he distinguishes four possible combinations: non-implemented rulings with no impact; non-implemented rulings with significant impact; implemented rulings with little or no impact and implemented rulings with significant impact.

A good example of the dangers of conflating compliance and impact is the common analysis of the iconic South African *Grootboom* judgment on the right to housing. Drawing on a single newspaper article,[1] scholars often describe the passing away of the lead applicant without a home as an illustration of the court's inability to ensure implementation with its decisions on socio-economic rights. Yet, Liebenberg (2008: 99) points out though that 'a widely misunderstood feature' of the case is that it was partly settled at an earlier stage by the parties. The community were saved from eviction and secured access to basic services and basic building materials. Moreover, the Constitutional Court's judgment did not address an immediate right to *permanent housing* for the community but rather the broader obligation of the state to develop an *emergency housing* programme with earmarked funding (which it did four years later). In any case, as this book shows, the community itself achieved permanent housing on account of the local interpretation of the judgment.[2]

However, this is not to deny the importance of analysing the impact of judgments. The broader impact of a court's decision in setting a jurisprudential standard for other cases, catalysing state action, or fostering political and attitudinal change is commonly invoked in justifications for judicial review or the practice of public interest litigation. For instance, Howse and Teitel (2010) decry a recent turn in international law

---

[1] Joubert (2008).
[2] See also Langford (2014).

scholarship to compliance as it hollows out our understanding of law's functions. They claim that such research ignores the 'centrality of interpretation to the generation of legal meaning' and the role of law in managing the relations 'between diverse norms and regimes', setting 'benchmarks' for decision making, bargaining and institutional access for actors, transforming perceptions of political conflicts and problems and catalysing ultra-compliance by producing 'normative effects that are greater or more powerful or different' than intended or envisaged (Howse and Teitel, 2010: 128, 30, 31, 33).

Importantly, key actors in litigation often have their eye on such impacts. Applicants may seek, or courts may order, very narrow remedies in the expectation that they will be sufficient to generate broader effects. A straight-jacketed compliance analysis will miss such strategic nuances and potentially inflate the effects of the decision if the strategy fails; or under-count a judgment's importance if the effects go beyond the realm of compliance. A mere focus on compliance may also under-estimate the substantial impacts that flow from partial or even minimal implementation. In some instances, divorcing the two concepts is rather challenging. In the literature, there is methodological divergence in examining the *erga omnes* effects of decisions. Some see failure by the state to abide by the precedent set in a judgment in subsequent analogous cases as one of compliance (e.g., Mbazira, 2008a) while others view it as a lack of impact. As a consequence, while the book's chapters focus primarily on compliance, it remains open to the analysis of other types of effects. The result is that a number of authors consider broader impacts, including in cases in which compliance has been partial.

1.1.2   Explaining Compliance

Why do states and other respondents comply or not comply with judgments? This is the subject of a long and contested methodological and theoretical debate in both law and social science. We agree with Kapiszewski and Taylor (2013: 819) that the different theories of compliance can be broadly and roughly classified as *instrumental* and *norms based* although we describe them somewhat differently and introduce social rights in to this explicatory terrain.

Instrumental Theories

Instrumental theories focus on the costs and benefits of compliance, whether material or political in nature. The traditional instrumental approach, for many lawyers and their critics, has been based on the assumption that the potency of law, and by extension courts, stems from its *coercive* power (OSJI, 2010). Thus, consequences compel non-compliance. If the judiciary possess the authority to constrain the options of any actor, and thus force them to do something contrary to their will,[3] implementation of judgments should, *ipso facto*, follow. This classical conception of law involves both the power to *order* sanctions and *enforce* them (Yankah, 2008).

Domestic courts (and to a much lesser extent international courts) are usually empowered to punish recalcitrant defendants ('contempt powers'), secure property and monies ('execution powers') or establish continuing supervision over implementation. Such powers have been exercised in social rights adjudication. For instance, in India, the Supreme Court threatened, with some success, to imprison officials if they failed to implement its order to convert motor vehicles to cleaner fuels in order to protect the right to environmental health;[4] a survey of sixty right to health cases in Argentina found that a quarter of the judgments were implemented only after courts imposed fines on various health insurers, providers and authorities (Bergallo, 2011); and in South Africa, the Constitutional Court opened the door to money-based claims being made against the assets of the state in a case concerning medical negligence.[5]

However, this conception of compliance is open to challenge in various ways. First, although *realists* accept this classical understanding and expectation of law, they doubt whether it fits with practice. Contrary to the democratic concern that the judiciary will overstep its boundaries, the assumption is that the judiciary is weak. In the face of resistant politicians, government officials or private defendants, judges remain powerless in their ability to enforce effectively their orders. Judicial institutions are mere 'epiphenomena or surface manifestations of deeper forces operating in society', and social change occurs only when 'the balance of these deeper forces shifts' (Young, 2001: 117–118). For instance, Rosenberg (1991) doubts whether the US Supreme Court's *Brown v. Board of Education* was responsible for progress on school desegregation. In his opinion, it

---

[3] Wertheimer (1987: 172) defines coercion as creating a 'choice situation' in which a person or entity has 'no reasonable alternative' but to accept the coercive proposal. Quoted in Edmundson (1995: 82).

[4] *M. C. Mehta v. Union of India* (1998) 6 SCC 63 (Supreme Court of India). See discussion in Muralidhar (2008), Shankar and Mehta (2008) and Gauri (2010).

[5] *Nyathi v. Member of the Executive Council for the Department of Health Gauteng & Ors*, 2008 (5) SA 94 (CC) (Constitutional Court of South Africa).

was 'growing civil rights pressure from the 1930s, economic changes, the Cold War, population shifts, electoral concerns, the increase in mass communication' that prompted desegregation. The Court simply 'reflected that pressure; it did not create it' (Rosenberg, 1991: 168).[6] Going further, Rosenburg claims that the use of litigation itself may be an endogenous variable in explaining poor progress, if the turn to legal strategies distracts advocates from potentially more effective political strategies.[7]

However, realist perspectives may underestimate the power of courts and neglect mediating and conditioning variables. We can thus identify a second and alternative instrumental account that we might label strategic. Defendants are assumed to be rational actors, but their calculus is driven by a diverse set of benefits and costs. This calculus may be political: Governments and other powerful actors may be incentivized to comply with a judgment if it is consistent with public opinion, diffuses protest and dissension from activist groups and other states, or legitimates existing but unpopular policies (Helfer and Voeten, 2014; Moravcsik, 2000; Simmons, 2009). It may also be material: Compliance may be financially rewarding. For instance, it may constitute a useful 'signal' to the international community that uses human rights performance as 'conditions on trade, aid, and a seat at the international negotiating table' (Hillebrecht, 2014: 27); or permit corporations access to particular public goods. Alternatively, compliance may be financially costly, a not uncommon claim about social rights. Such a strategic outlook may also be reflexive and diachronic. A state may begrudgingly comply in order that future governments, other states, or other actors will also comply. It seeks to create a culture of compliance or a reciprocal sense of duty.

Despite the eclectivism of the strategic approach in its choice of costs and benefits, it can nevertheless overlook the particular legal, social and institutional *characteristics* of a particular case. Three are particularly worth mentioning. The first is the complexity of the remedy. Some remedies may be particularly difficult to implement (regardless of the material cost). Sometimes change simply takes time (a development of a new policy or practice), and courts lack the necessary levers to hasten it. Melish and Courtis argue that in both civil and social rights cases of the Inter-American Court of Human Rights and Argentinean courts, compensation and individual-based

---

[6] Rosenberg (1991).

[7] '[A] danger of litigation as a strategy for significant social reform is that symbolic victories may be mistaken for substantive ones, covering a reality that is distasteful. Rather than working to change that reality, reformers relying on a litigation strategy for reform may be misled (or content?) to celebrate the illusion of change' (p. 248).

orders were quickly executed while wider and more structural orders often lagged in implementation.[8] Second, the visibility of non-compliance may significantly determine whether a defendant is incentivized to comply (Kagan and Skolnick, 1993). If the behaviour to be regulated is easily identifiable by multiple actors, the likelihood of compliance is greater. Third, there are a greater range of mediating actors between petitioners and the formal defendant, particularly bureaucrats, corporate officials and leading experts. As Epp (2009) argues, 'bureaucratic contingency' or the willingness or ability of officials to comply is one of the most significant determinants of compliance. This is further complicated by the number of intermediating actors. In her study of one regional court, Huneeus (2011: 509–510) found that the level of compliance by states was inversely related to the number of state organs that were addressed by a remedial order.

Norms Based

These instrumental views of law and courts have been strongly challenged on the grounds they neglect law's ideational power. Responding to coercive accounts, Hart (1961) argued that the role of law is primarily normative, providing reasons to act: rules provide the 'reason and justification' for any use of coercive authority. Raz (1994) has claimed that law is essentially an authoritative social institution that affects the calculus of our practical reason and action: 'The authority does not merely add to or provide sufficient reasons to act in a particular way, but rather alters the domain of reason on which one may act at all'.[9] While coercion may be an element of establishing the peculiarity and force of the authoritative institution of law, it may not primarily account for all of its influence on behaviour. This account sees law as *persuasive*. We grant law significant respect in deliberating over whether to comply or not.

Persuasive theories ascribe significant moral agency to individuals and political actors. However, there may be significant doubts as to its determinative value and consistency under different conditions. An alternative norms-based account is sociological, which points to the *cultural* function of law. The expressive role of law may change social meanings of acceptable behaviour (McAdams, 2000),[10] and legal norms may be acculturated

---

[8] Courtis (2008) and Melish (2008).

[9] As summarised by Yankah (2008).

[10] In her discussion of the decline of pederasty in classical Athens, Lanni (2010: 45) argues that, 'By changing the *social meaning* of homosexual pederasty, these [Athenian] laws influenced norms regarding purely private conduct and reached beyond the limited number of politically active citizens likely to be prosecuted under the law.'

(Goodman and Jinks, 2008).[11] How this function works is a matter of debate, but law may particularly affect prevailing 'civility norms', which exert significant social and psychological power. It may be particularly powerful through the process of double institutionalisation, whereby law 'reinforces an already existing normative order' or an emergent one (Kagan and Skolnick, 1993: 85).

Some norm-based accounts are more dynamic and eclectic and suggest a dialectic relationship between persuasive and cultural mechanisms. In discursive institutionalism, norms are not only a construction but are simultaneously an independent phenomenon. They may shape the 'background ideational abilities' of agents as much as their 'foreground discursive abilities', which 'enable them to communicate critically about those institutions, to change (or maintain) them' (Schmidt, 2008: 4).

That being said, one needs to be quite careful about assuming that courts can leverage significant attitudinal effects. The survey and experimental evidence on the influence of courts on public opinion reveals effects that are modest and contingent.[12] For example, landmark cases tend to have a more significant impact while educated elites are more susceptible to influence than others.

Whether judgments of social rights can exert such normative influence is an open question. On the one hand, the use of law and rights-based reasoning may exert particular persuasive and cultural pressure on reluctant actors and officials to comply. Arguably, the influence is likely to be greatest when litigation exposes a clear dissonance between a well-accepted social right and a non-compliant policy. A good example is Portugal's swift and dramatic response to a quasi-judicial finding of the European Committee on Social Rights on its failure to take effective steps to prevent child labour.[13] Notably, the adjudicative body carries no coercive authority, and the degree of political mobilisation on the issue by civil society organisations was not significant. However, as the issue is generally considered completely unacceptable, at least amongst the states to which Portugal compares itself, norm-based effects may explain much of the efforts to comply.

[11] 'By acculturation, we mean the general process by which actors adopt the beliefs and behavioural patterns of the surrounding culture' (Goodman and Jinks, 2008: 726).

[12] See, e.g., Baas and Thomas (1984); Blake (1977); Franklin and Kosaki (1989); Helfer and Voeten (2014); Hoekstra (2000, 2003); Johnson and Martin (1998); Linos and Twist (2013); Muir (1973); Stoutenborough, Haider-Markel and Allen (2006); Ura (2014); Vecera (2014); Wlezien and Goggin (1993).

[13] *ICJ v. Portugal*, Complaint No. 1/1998, Decision on the Merits (ECSR).

On the other hand, attitudes on social rights and towards particular claimant groups may operate as a significant brake on compliance. Any normative power of a judgment may be neutralised completely by opposition amongst the public or key actors. While this is a challenge for all rights (e.g., on LGBT rights see Helfer and Voeten, 2014), its effect may be even greater for social rights in contexts where these rights or their adjudication are viewed less favourably than civil and political rights. Although social rights that clearly overlap with civil rights, particularly the right to life, may carry more weight in implementation (Cavallaro and Brewer, 2008). Such instances could include failure to treat HIV patients or failure to prevent precarious housing from flooding.

Analytical Framework

For the purposes of this book, we have not narrowed the theoretical palette of explanatory factors or developed a deductive frame in which authors must conduct their research or test particular hypotheses. Instead, we have developed a broad analytical framework as an inductive starting point for authors. In addressing the explanatory question, authors were asked to consider four broad clusters of potential independent variables.[14] The factors are set out in a quadrant form in Table 1.1 and were:

- *Legal variables* such as the nature of the right (e.g., social rights vs. civil rights), litigants (e.g., individual or collective action and number affected), remedies and court monitoring (type and strength), legal system (e.g., common law vs. civil law) and judicial culture.
- *Political variables* that concern the characteristics of the state and political system, such as: capacity of the state apparatus to implement ESC rights rulings; type of political system; institutional arrangements between the branches of government; the type of defendant (e.g., national, provincial, local or non-state actor).
- *Socio-economic variables* that cover broader country characteristics such as levels of wealth, social inequality and ethnic fractionalisation as well as degree of public and majoritarian support for particular cases or litigants.
- *Civil society variables* that are agent-centred but extra-institutional. These particularly include the structure and cohesion of the partnership between litigants and lawyers and broader civil society coalitions;

---

[14] The second and third variables were original combined but we have seprated out the more institutional factors from the broader parameter-like ones.

Table 1.1 *Factors affecting compliance*

	Supply side	Demand side
Institutional	Legal variables • Type and strength of remedies • Follow-up of remedy by court • Complexity of remedies • Individual/collective case; positive or negative duties • Status of social rights in courts • Admissibility requirements	Political variables • Type of actor (executive, legislature, local authority, non-state, international) • Capacity of the state or other apparatus to implement or be transformed • Affective interests of actors and their staff in complying • Type of political system (degrees of democracy/federalism) • Institutional relations of actors with judiciary
Non-Institutional	Socio-economic parameter variables • Characteristics of litigants • Attitudinal preferences of population • Whether judgment was pro- or anti-majoritarian in public opinion • Budgetary, economic, natural and human resources available • Level of social inequality and structure of economy	Civil society variables • Structure and level of cohesion of civil society coalitions in litigation • Repertoire of accompanying strategies (direct action, media, advocacy, etc) • Degree of alliance-building • Type of lawyers (public/private) • Level of participation of affected people/social movements in the case • Access to funding

the trajectory and nature of legal mobilisation and the available reper-
toire of contention; transnational collaboration with similar civil society
actors; and access to donor funding.

The list of potential variables is long and was intentional for the purposes
of this volume. The danger of adopting a too narrow analytical framework
is that it can quickly advantage one theory or assumption over another. For
instance, a focus on agent-centric variables (political, civil society) may
obfuscate the particular economic and attitudinal incentives/constraints
or the particular legal character of the case (Kapiszewski and Taylor,
2013: 824) and vice versa. Thus we are eclectic, setting out a wide range of
potential factors for investigation. And, in Section 1.3, we provide an analysis of these factors which tend to emerge more consistently across the studies. They suggest potential necessary conditions for compliance although
locating sufficient conditions for compliance is more difficult if not elusive.

However, this does not mean that we are averse to more focused and
constrained theoretical approaches. Unlike Kapiszewski and Taylor (2013:
824–825), we believe there can be value in trying to develop coherent theories in order to test particular hypotheses or highlight salient features of
compliance. As much as 'unified theory seeking to explain *all* such action
would necessarily be too abstract to be useful' (Kapiszewski and Taylor,
2013: 824), attempting to include *every* explanation is likely to produce
conclusions of equally low utility, even if they fully explain compliance
in a particular case. Notably, a number of contributors use theoretical
frameworks through which to develop specific hypotheses that focus on
the interaction of some variables. This includes the interactional account
by Çali and Koch in the subsequent chapter and the concluding chapter by
Brinks which analyses the book's empirical analysis in the framework of
'cost inequality', where the degree of enforcement is a function of the cost
of compliance versus the cost of non-compliance.

1.2   Overview of the Book

The book begins by asking what can be learnt from the implementation
of civil and political rights judgements and whether there are any significant differences between the two sets of rights as concerns compliance.
Çali and Koch propose an interactional account of compliance, with a
particular focus on international rulings in which the speed and comprehensiveness of rights implementation is intertwined with the relationship
between supranational human rights bodies and national decision makers.
After putting in question the categorisation of human rights into different

'generations', they argue that, just as in the realm of civil and political rights, compliance with international ESC rights rulings hinges on who decides on compliance requirements (and how) at the supranational level and who responds to compliance requirements (and how) at the national level.

Based on an analytical framework for assessing the enforcement and the broader effects of court decisions, *Rodríguez-Garavito* argues that, in order to capture the full range of effects of rulings, impact studies need to enlarge the conventional theoretical and methodological field of vision, to include not only direct material effects (i.e., those following immediately from the enforcement of the rulings), but their broader impact, which includes equally important indirect and symbolic effects. Drawing on a study of the impact of major ESC rights rulings handed down by the Colombian Constitutional Court, he further argues that the key court-controlled factors explaining the level of enforcement and impact are the types of remedies and the existence and nature of mechanisms for monitoring their implementation. He closes the chapter by making a case for 'dialogic judicial activism', which encourages participatory monitoring mechanisms that both deepen democratic deliberation and enhance the impact of courts' interventions.

The book then turns to focused country studies. *Wilson and Rodríguez* quantitatively and qualitatively analyse compliance with judgments of the Costa Rican Supreme Court with a focus on which institutions generally comply with court orders, and which types of ruling engender higher levels of compliance. Contrary to findings in the literature that point simply to the influence of well-organised and well-funded civil society organisations movements, they find that, in highly accessible judicial systems like Costa Rica's, the key factors determining the enforcement of ESC rights decisions are the nature of the defending institution and the length of time granted by the court to comply. Court decisions that demand immediate action on the part of the government have a higher likelihood of enforcement, as are those that are targeted at specific, decentralised institutions with autonomy to implement the remedies set by the court. However, they concede that efforts to improve compliance with progressive orders against larger institutions will require enhanced civil society mobilisation.

Sigal, Rossi and Morales examine a slightly wider range of variables that might explain enforcement, such as the size of the case, complexity of the remedy, court's stance, institutional strength, political will to comply. Based on the study of thirteen social rights judgments in Argentina, the chapter highlights the particular role of the size of the litigant group, the receptiveness of the particular judge and the broader political will, and concludes by advancing some strategies that would inflect these particular variables.

Ferraz's chapter on Brazil focuses on a feature of ESC rights litigation that is particularly observable in Latin America: the explosion of individual claims that are decided on a case-by-case basis and, in the case of Brazil, the corresponding scarcity of collective suits addressing the underlying structural policy flaws that catalyse such individual legal action. Based on a study of health rights litigation, Ferraz seeks to demonstrate that the courts are highly, if not excessively, reflexive, in their expectations of compliance. He hypothesises that the high success rates for individual litigation and the low success rate of collective litigation are explained by both legal and factual obstacles to enforcement. The reluctance of Brazilian courts to entertain collective suits and remedies – together with their openness to individual claims – creates strong institutional incentives for patients to claim medicines and treatments through a myriad of individual suits according to Ferraz. While Ferraz's study does provide some evidence of different compliance levels in practice (where collective remedies have been ordered), his main contribution is to highlight the importance of compliance expectations within the legal community. Such expectations may have significant feedback effects on jurisprudence, success rates and remedies.

The next two chapters concern North America. Analysing Canadian litigation, *Porter* puts the spotlight on the role of remedies: he argues that more open, dialogical and softer remedies would have greater impact even if they are more difficult to enforce. Like Ferraz, Porter he argues that judicial perception of the likelihood of enforcement influences the nature of decisions and remedies but that a more systemic vision of the role of judicial intervention is required. Nonetheless, through a series of case studies, Porter also shows how a series of narrow traditional cases can have a transformative effect over time.

Albisa and *Shanor* examine selected cases from four decades of widespread school finance litigation in the United States (at the state level). Focusing on the demand side, they explore how social mobilisation and the type of civic engagement have influenced levels of compliance and impact. The chapter highlights how the level of civil society activity – particularly of social movements – and commitment before, during and following a judicial decision has a significant, if not dispositive, impact on the effectiveness of a court's decision.

Moving further afield, *Chitalkar and Gauri* examine the long-running structural right to food litigation before the Supreme Court of India.

Compared to earlier decisions, they argue that the 2001 judgment and the more than fifty orders that followed engendered higher levels of compliance. Not only did the Court declare the right to food a fundamental right, it went on to give it meaning by spelling out the specific entitlements provided by the right, created an institutional mechanism to monitor compliance with its orders, and remained engaged in the litigation. This was further complemented by the court's collaboration with key allies in civil society and a decisive shift in public opinion about the chronic hunger crisis.

Langford and Kahanovitz scrutinise South African judgments and prevailing empirical and causal narratives of compliance. The bulk of the chapter is devoted to a close analysis of six case studies in South Africa concerning the right to housing in urban areas which are also contrasted with the existing literature on enforcement of health and social security rights judgments. Their account provides a picture of dramatic variation in levels of compliance and the salience of civil society mobilisation; but they suggest that improving levels of compliance for the hard cases will require more reflexive and experimental courts.

The final case studies concern the international arena. *Viljoen* reflects on the domestic enforcement of the recommendations of the African Commission on Human and Peoples' Rights using both quantitative and qualitative methods. By postulating a number of hypotheses, he suggests some factors (related to the litigants, civil society, international community, the African Union and relevant body or tribunal) as possible predictors of domestic enforcement. *Cabal* and *Philips*'s chapter evaluates how successfully some of the groundbreaking international judicial decisions on reproductive rights have been implemented, identifying key factors – institutional design, the nature of the remedies awarded, public attention to the case, and the social, political and institutional environment that enhance or hinder these decisions by national, regional and international bodies. *Dobrushi* and *Alexandridis* provide an overview of the judgments and decisions by United Nations and Council of Europe bodies pertaining to the right of housing of Roma/Travellers. They trace the evolutionary nature of the case law on housing issues and the challenges of implementing the decision on the ground. The authors note that widespread racial prejudice makes implementation extremely difficult, suggesting that the status of the group is a crucial factor.

The concluding chapter by *Brinks* brings together the analysis in the framework of 'cost inequality'. Costs include political costs (public disapproval); financial costs; and affective costs (the distance between the objective of the litigation and the expressed normative commitments and values of the organisation in question). The relationship between these different costs and the variables discussed is not always obvious. For instance, we would normally expect that, the greater the number of beneficiaries, the higher the political cost of non-compliance and thus the greater likelihood of compliance. But if benefits are greatly diffused across society, collective action problems make it hard to mobilise enough directly affected people to create pressure. Implementation may be easier when there are positive affects – where a judgment has high symbolic value or there is a regime change that more closely aligns the values of the government with that of the litigants. But it can be extremely difficult in cases of negative affect: in cases that involve deeply unpopular groups it may not even matter what the assigned task is, as the opposition is value-based rather than built on a rational cost-benefit calculus. In negative affect cases, moreover, politicians are often able to gain political capital by defying the court order.

1.3   Common Themes in Measurement and Explanation

Despite the use of different methodologies and the deployment of an open-ended explanatory framework, particular patterns emerge across the book. When we look at the studies together, five themes appear particularly salient. The first two relate to the nature of the case, particularly its complexity and size, although the evidence of their relevance is ambiguous. The three other factors are more consistent in their salience: they are social mobilisation, the nature of judicial remedies, and the status of affected groups. We find that as the material or (particularly) political costs of implementation increase, the positive presence of one or more of these final factors becomes crucial for ensuring significant and/or swift compliance. We discuss each of the five factors in turn.

1.3.1   Levels of Compliance and the Nature of Rights

The chapters reveal widely differing levels of compliance (minimal, partial and full) and speed of compliance (immediate, moderate, and sluggish). Pertinently, and contrary to some literature, the evidence does not suggest that implementation of ESC rights decisions is more difficult than those on civil and political rights. The overall pattern for both sets of rights is one of tremendous variation.[15] Such a pattern in

---

[15] Grewal and Voeten (2012: 3) employ the same adjective in describing the speed of compliance with ECtHR judgments.

civil and political rights decisions is demonstrated by Çali and Koch and Viljoen in this volume; aggregative studies on international courts (Hillebrecht, 2014; Voeten, 2014); and studies on domestic courts from the United States to Nepal (Langford and Bhatterai, 2011; Songer and Sheehan, 1990).

It might be equally thought that variation lies in the nature of the obligations or, more precisely, the nature of the orders. We know that social rights *and* civil and political rights can carry both complex and positive obligations and straightforward negative obligations (Eide, 1987; Shue, 1980). Thus, we might presume that the greater the complexity of the order (in terms of its scope and range of respondents), the greater the likelihood of speedier or eventual compliance. The volume does provide evidence in this regard with a a significant number of authors noting swift payment of compensation but delayed progress on mandated policy changes. *Cabal's and Phillip's* comparative and international overview of reproductive rights decisions is not notable in this regard while in the case of Costa Rica, *Wilson and Rodríguez* conclude quantitatively that where ESC rights rulings are to be enforced with some immediacy, the compliance rate appears significantly higher.

However, complexity is only one factor. In some instances, complex remedies were implemented more quickly than simpler ones. This occurred in cases where the political or even material costs were lowered. Langford and Kahanovitz reveal how the Modderklipp judgment, which required a housing solution for 40,000 informal settlers, was implemented rapidly on account of the economic incentives that were integrated within the remedial order. Rodriguez-Garavito charts the dramatic upscaling of financial support for internally displaced persons in Colombia after a structural judgment, possibly because the political costs of noncompliance were high (and because of the nature of the remedial order – see the section that follows). Thus, greater complexity may bear a probabilistic relation with low levels of compliance but it is neither a necessary nor sufficient condition.

1.3.2   Size of the Case

A number of contributors tie the level of enforcement to the size of the case (in terms of litigant numbers), which can be classified as individual, medium and collective/structural. However, the relationship between the degree of compliance and the size of the case is neither linear nor unidirectional across the chapters.

Sigal, Morales, and Rossi argue that the challenge of enforcement rises with the size of the case. Through their analysis of all three types of cases they find that a combination of increasing costs (political and financial) and greater remedial complexity makes full compliance significantly less likely. However, they claim that the problem may be offset by the presence of an active court and specific execution procedures, which pushes or nudges a defendant towards compliance. In his chapter on Brazil, *Ferraz* comes to a similar position. Even when a few large-scale structural cases resulted in positive decisions, enforcement did not follow; petitioners had to return to the courts as individual litigants, a strategy which met with greater success. Collective orders were essentially converted into individual orders, which do not require the political and financial resources necessary to undertake structural reforms. Courts found themselves less willing and capable of translating the abstract provisions of the constitution into specific orders for the state when the issue involved is of a more complex nature and larger scale; while, on the contrary, individual orders were clearly less complex to enforce. At the regional level, *Viljoen* also found that cases involving a single complainant lead to greater compliance than cases dealing with violations on a massive scale.

By contrast, a number of chapters suggest the opposite conclusion: Structural litigation was a particularly effective weapon in overcoming barriers faced by individuals in accessing their rights. In the case of the rights of the internally displaced in Colombia, *Rodríguez-Garavito* contends that repeat individual litigation resulted in poor levels of compliance and the failure by the state to address the underlying causes of deprivation. The Constitutional Court's decision to approach the case using dialogical activism in order to increase political and affective costs of non-enforcement was dispositive. It transformed the case into a structural judgment that targeted the millions of internally displaced persons in Colombia, a decision which has achieved significant impact. Likewise the chapter on India highlights the effectiveness of the structural and nation-wide right to food litigation while the chapter on South Africa reveals the greater overall success of nationally-organised structural cases (such as *Treatment Action Campaign)* over individual and medium cases (such as urban housing litigation).

A third position is staked out by authors who challenge the dichotomy between individual and collective cases. Some individual cases are precedent-setting. A court *or* respondent effectively transforms an order affecting a particular individual into a collective judgment with *erga omnes* effects. While the degree and speed of compliance (or impact) can vary with such orders, a number of these cases have ushered in significant reforms in policy and practice. This was particularly common in HIV/AIDS health litigation in Costa Rica and arguably occurred earlier in Brazil on access to anti-retroviral medicines (Hoffmann and Bentes, 2008). *Porter* discusses explicitly how some individual cases in Canada such as *Eldridge*, which concerned access of deaf patients to interpretive services in hospitals, have generated significant systemic effects.

A final position is diachronic and focuses on the long-term dynamics of compliance across different types of cases. For instance, in Colombia, individual litigation regarding health rights, while successful in each individual case, had overwhelmed the courts and the health system by the mid-2000s. *Sustainable* compliance was possible only through some form of structural intervention to redress this fallacy of composition. The dilemma can be considered through *Brinks'* typology of costs. The affective costs associated with non-enforcement in an individual case were large while the financial costs of compliance were low (although in aggregate they are enormous).[16]

Thus, we are unable to make any definite conclusions concerning the causal role of the size of a case. However, in section 1.4 we outline various circumstances that might guide advocates in their choices in this regard.

1.3.3   Social Mobilisation around the Case

Of the factors that increase the likelihood of compliance, the degree of social mobilisation was the most cited. As *Brinks* puts it, social mobilisation increases the political and affective costs of non-enforcement. Nearly all of the chapters point to the importance of this 'demand-side' dimension of compliance.

At the international level, social mobilisation is obviously critical. International courts and quasi-judicial bodies are hamstrung in their ability to order coercive measures for non-compliance. In addressing the implementation of decisions within the African human rights system, *Viljoen* concludes that 'there are strong indications that implementation is enhanced by the continuous engagement by and involvement of

---

[16] At the same time, advocates have been unable to find strategies that successfully reduce the political and financial costs of the necessary structural reforms in order to stem the flow of individual health cases (Rodríguez Garavito, 2014).

domestically located and embedded NGOs and community groups, acting with the support of international civil society'. *Cabal and Phillips* find
that, in the context of reproductive rights cases from international courts,
domestic partners play a 'significant role in mobilising public attention
to these issues through strategic use of the media, coalition-building, and
other awareness-raising strategies'. *Çali and Koch* attribute great significance to participation of non-governmental actors in the implementation
process of international decisions: 'Through monitoring and publicising
the measures taken by governments in response to supranational human
rights judgments, non-governmental organisations can furthermore
expose states that try to limit the implementation process to a superficial
engagement with the issues at hand.' In addition, they argue that increased
participation of non-governmental organisations in the enforcement of
judgments phase, including in the formulation and monitoring of remedies, is central for influencing domestic compliance processes. This is
especially important, they claim, when litigation concerns marginalised communities and disadvantaged groups that tend to be ignored by
respondent states, or when remedies involve high compliance costs that
are not obvious to the general public.

   Social mobilisation emerges as an equally critical factor at the domestic
level, despite the greater coercive power of national courts. *Chitalkar and
Gauri* identify the emergence of a social movement on the right to food
in the 2000s as a key factor in explaining the greater effectiveness of litigation on hunger in comparison to earlier decades. According to *Shanor
and Albisa*, the variation across US states in compliance with education
rights litigation is largely a function of the capacity of the petitioners to
sustain political pressure over time. Litigation without broader social
movements, as in Texas, is not necessarily unhelpful but does not catalyse
significant changes, while litigation that driven or supported by professional organisers can turn rulings into legislated policy, as in New York,
and in the presence of broad well-organised movements very significant
change, as in Kentucky. The Argentinean case study highlights the critical role of active involvement of petitioners and support from strategic
alliances among prestigious human rights organisations, research centres,
religious organisations or other social organisations with advocacy and
mobilisation capacities.

   One particular feature of the chapters is a fine-grained approach to
what we mean by social mobilisation. The archetype of large-scale national
social movements, trade unions or professional/social associations mobilising around iconic judgments is not always feasible or always necessary

in ensuring compliance.[17] The chapters on domestic courts thus place great emphasis on the quality of the different dimensions of the civil society side of the equation. Particularly important appears to be the degree and extent of *internal mobilisation* amongst litigants, the *strength of leadership* in affected communities and the *types of alliances* in the enforcement phase.

The chapter on South Africa places particular emphasis on the organisational quality of both litigants and allies, particularly in the absence of a relevant centralised national social movement. Well-organised communities, with strong leadership and staying power, and alliances with some social movements or elites (e.g., academics, public interest lawyers, and politicians) secured the greatest benefits from their wins in the courtroom (*Langford and Kahanovitz*, this volume).

1.3.4   Judicial Remedies and Monitoring

Many chapters point equally to the 'supply side' of the compliance formula. This encompasses the judicial choice of remedies and the broader enforcement powers of courts and quasi-judicial bodies. Many legal scholars and organisations have called for the enhanced use of coercive remedies and continuing supervision in order to ensure compliance with decisions on both civil and political rights and ESC rights (Mbazira, 2008b; OSJI, 2010). A number of authors report the importance of judicial penalties, such as threats to imprison public officials for non-compliance, but emphasise the role of judicial monitoring of implementation in collective cases. Interestingly, judicial monitoring was seen as relevant not only where political will was lacking, but also where states lacked capacity to implement, particularly where there were coordination problems posed by the presence of multiple respondents. Moreover, post-judgment court involvement was also a feature of cases in which social mobilisation was particularly strong, suggesting that judgments were rarely self-executing and that demand and supply-side strategies were simultaneously reinforcing.

Strong forms of ongoing supervisory jurisdiction of a managerial nature were relatively rare in the case studies. It seems that the use of regular structural injunctions, detailed orders and special masters has moved only partly beyond the United States. The most notable exception is India. In the right to food litigation, Chitalkar and Gauri demonstrate that the use of ongoing hearings (which engendered fifty-five-plus interim orders), close

---

[17] For an in-depth discussion on this point, see Dugard and Langford (2011).

judicial engagement, the appointment of commissioners was essential in the court securing a relatively high degree of compliance and even the quality of orders over time through the embedded feedback mechanism. In South Africa, the model has not been embraced by the Constitutional Court but lower courts have used the approach with varying degrees of success as shown by Langford and Kahanovitz in some cases on housing and social security rights.

However, authors were able to point to high levels of compliance where remedies were more reflexive, experimental and dialogical.[18] This ranged from simple delayed declarations of validity that provided a respondent a certain period of time to propose the remedy through to the use of broad-brush remedies which were only given content though regular consent orders negotiated amongst the parties. Delayed declarations of invalidity were used regularly in Canada; ongoing monitoring was more common in Colombia and Argentina, while both forms have been used by US courts in the right to education cases.[19] In South Africa, both the apex and lower courts have endorsed milder forms of experimentalism, which occur within the initial proceedings, which have resulted in consent orders and settlements that have triggered various policy innovations.

The authors identify two reasons why open-ended, dialogical or deliberative remedies were regularly (but *not always*) effective. The first is that they permit the defendant to design more efficient, lower-cost ways to achieve the goals of the litigation than could be designed by a court with limited experience and information in the policy area. Thus, a reflexive approach which acknowledges differentiated institutional competences is not only likely to help address concerns over a court's legitimacy and competence to rule on ESC rights, it may also enhance compliance. If an agency has a hand in designing the solution to the problem identified in the litigation, it may be more likely to implement the judgment rather than resist it. *Shanor and Albisa* show specifically how education reform efforts are more likely to succeed when courts give local officials a role in designing the reforms.

This experience with ESC rights thus mirrors that of some civil and political rights-focused courts. *Çali and Koch* describe such a deliberative process, administered by states themselves, that leads to significant compliance in the case of ECtHR judgments. The monitoring process

---

[18] For a discussion of these forms of remedies, see Dorf (2003), Roach (2004) and Sabel and Simon (2004).
[19] On the latter, see Heise (1995).

has a constitutive impact on domestic compliance dynamics, because it 'allows states to realistically assess what measures need to be taken to remedy rights violations', affords 'states more ownership of compliance decisions' it furthermore increases the legitimacy of the process in the eyes of respondent states', and provides a safeguard to 'offset' domestic 'backlashes against enforcement'. The Court also adjudicates a number of express and implied social rights and *Dobrushi and Alexandridis* highlight the important role of the ECtHR compliance process in following up the generally very poor implementation of international and domestic decisions on Roma rights.

The second reason for the success of some reflexive and dialogical remedies is that the monitoring process provides a clear space for social mobilisation. As *Brinks* points out, affected groups are able to use these processes as a focal point and platform for continued organised political activity. In Colombia, the monitoring phase permits the representatives of the affected parties to develop information, produce proposals (and ultimately solutions) that are most likely to succeed, while allowing a periodic re-examination of compliance and publicity and the imposition of costs for delays and failures to comply *(Rodríguez-Garavito)*. And after the *Doucet-Boudreau* decision in Canada, *Porter* notes that 'the claimant communities relied on the reporting sessions as democratic accountability mechanisms to ensure the timely implementation of their fundamental rights, such that the judicial remedy operated to enhance democratic accountability'.

According to *Brinks*, when continued monitoring failed, most notably in the Roma cases, it is because the monitoring entity was weak if not complicit, and thus the affected community was unable to create political opportunities out of a supervised compliance process. For instance, while the European Committee of Social Rights found a violation of Roma housing rights on the part of Greece, the Council of Ministers, which is supposed to be the monitoring/implementing entity for the ECSR, failed to take any real action to follow up on the ruling. Greece consequently failed to make any real changes to its policies beyond repealing the most offensive of the regulations in question (Dobrushi and Alexandridis, this volume). Continued monitoring also failed in some instances in South Africa, when the affected community lacked the organisational resources to capitalise on continued court involvement in their plight (Langford and Kahanovitz). It seems likely, therefore, that continued compliance monitoring by a court would work best for proponents with some organisational capacity, in a political context in which it is possible that political actors could suffer costs for failing to attend to the needs identified in the litigation.

1.3.5   Status of the Affected Group

One underlying yet somewhat immutable factor is the public status of the litigants. Implementation of judgments that must overcome prejudices against ethnic minorities and other highly stigmatised groups represent a particular challenge. As Brinks put it 'when the litigants are poor, excluded from the political process, or otherwise less capable of exerting political pressure, we should expect a lower likelihood of compliance regardless of the cost of compliance, simply because these plaintiffs have less collective political capital'.

Dobrushi and Alexandridis believe that the main reason at play behind the persistent and recurring failure to implement favourable decisions concerning the Roma is simply the very ethnic identity of the applicants. Deeply-embedded discrimination means that European politicians face backlash if they seek to implement pro-Roma decisions while the number of supportive political allies in civil society is limited. In some instances, as *Cabal and Phillips* show, the combination of a group (e.g., women) with a particular issue (e.g., abortion) can generate significant counter-mobilization and backlash – and litigation requires careful planning with that in mind.

A striking example of the role of claimant status is the litigation by the Treatment Action Campaign in South Africa for anti-retroviral medicines for prisoners. In many respects, the *Westville* litigation ticked off many of the criteria discussed. The case was backed by the country's one of the strongest social movement, the High Court issued strong and repeated orders, and the remedy was not particularly complex or financially costly. Yet, as Langford and Kahanovitz point out, prison officials continued to refuse to comply. The political costs of non-compliance for failing to protect this group appeared to be particularly low or the normative climate for the rights of this group was rather weak and thin.

Nonetheless, some authors point to litigation that succeeded despite the significant unpopularity of the petitioners. As *Wilson and Rodríguez* explain, LGBT persons in Costa Rica in the 1990s were one of the most stigmatised groups in the country; but the Constitutional Court backed their demands for HIV/AIDS medicines, and compliance was forthcoming. This suggests that for marginalised groups which find little traction in democratic processes, courts may provide a more receptive and even an effective forum for the advancement of social rights. However, *Wilson and Rodriguez* argued that compliance was helped by the Court's gradualist approach to jurisprudential development and the immediacy embedded in the Court orders.

1.4   Improving Enforcement

These explanatory results point to some strategies that could be adopted to improve enforcement, although there are some clear feasibility constraints. Some of these strategies are internal to the litigation itself. Authors examine particular and conscious strategies by litigants, courts and governments to improve the level of enforcement. Many litigants seek to structure the orders in ways that are more or less coercive, cohere with political or bureaucratic incentives or dominant normative frames, are reached through more dialogical/persuasive process, and thus seek to maximise overlapping interests with the elites that are tasked with compliance. Other strategies are external to the litigation. They include attempts to shape a conducive framework for enforcement, develop new legal frameworks that enhance the likelihood of compliance or construct monitoring and enforcement institutions.

The broad array of solutions tried in jurisdictions around the world is likely to be an important resource for practitioners trying to solve the same problem in their own cases (see also OSJI, 2010, 2013; Rodríguez Garavito and Kauffman, 2014). At the same time, the strategies also respond to factors and challenges specific to the case and country in question. Moreover, a single strategy is unlikely to be effective on its own. For instance, while Sigal, Morales, and Rossi consistently examine the size and complexity of each case, judicial posture and social mobilisation, they rarely give complete priority to one over the other. Although the variables and strategies were examined independently of one another, it is clear that they interact, and the combination of variables and strategies may have results that are not anticipated when considered in isolation.

From this reflection and others in the book, an important lesson is that before commencing litigation, it is essential to consider the relevant factors that will likely affect the enforcement of an eventual decision - e.g., budgetary considerations, political costs, the public perception of the case, ideological alignments of the government regarding the issue, and level of complexity of the decision – and focus on which factors will translate into challenges to enforcement. Another way of putting it is that the strategies covered in this book were often designed to address: the necessary level and form of social mobilisation and public participation, in particular the participation of those whose rights have been violated, in the proceedings; the appropriate type of litigation in terms of size and complexity of the remedies sought, and how to ensure that the multiplicity of costs of enforcement (financial, political, affective) favour enforcement. Some of these strategies are considered individually, while several of the strategies attempt to tackle several of these challenges at once. In addition, enforcement challenges at the international level are distinct, and require different enforcement strategies. We take up four of these general themes as follows.

1.4.1   Mobilising Civil Society to Improve Enforcement

A primary factor that many of the authors of this book identified as important, if not dispositive, in the implementation of certain ESC rights cases, is the work and activism of social movements. Porter argues that 'social rights violations are usually the result of failures of democratic accountability and inclusiveness; thus, If social rights remedies are to actually bring about the enjoyment of social rights, the remedies will have to be based on ... the empowerment of marginalised communities to be involved in that process.'

Assuming that we *do* want social mobilisation in order to increase the political and affective costs of non-enforcement, Langford and Kahanovitz argue that 'sometimes, it is not a question of *more* civil society but *better* civil society'. *Shanor and Albisa* unpack this further and identify 'robust networks, committees, leadership development and recruitment of skilled and respected members of society, strategy, resources, tactics, rights consciousness and understanding of the social problem, as well as relationship to the media' as critical to effective social mobilisation – and which are ideally part of a broader pre-litigation political strategy.

However, as Langford and Kahanovitz note, social mobilisation is not a silver bullet to ensuring enforcement of social rights decisions, and should be considered in conjunction with other strategies. Even this book's foremost proponents of social mobilisation, Shanor and Albisa, note that the success of social mobilisation is dependent on external factors, including media response, public receptivity and pre-existing understandings of the issue, and the political and economic landscape, among others. For example, in considering whether and how to adopt a social movement strategy to improve enforcement, Langford and Kahanovitz suggest that various factors of the specific case should be taken into consideration. In remote or local cases, mobilisation may be unfeasible, and ongoing judicial or political support will be often necessary.

1.4.2   Matching Litigation Strategy with Case Size and Complexity

Many contributors drew attention to the differing effects produced by the size of the case, often with competing answers to the question of which type of case is most like to be enforced. Sigal, Morales, and Rossi and Ferraz argue that enforcement becomes more challenging as the size of the case increases; while Wilson and Rodríguez and Rodríguez-Garavito found the contrary. In any event, the reasons they identify are useful in designing strategies for improving enforcement in individual cases.

Porter advises advocates to think about the concrete goals and results for the short, medium and long term when designing a legal strategy. Considering these goals, in conjunction with how different cases (individual, medium, structural) fare in a specific country's legal system, should lead to a solid legal strategy. Thus, for example, according to Sigal, Morales and Rossi, 'if the expected result is solving the problem in the short/medium term for an individual or a group of persons, the most adequate choice will [be] a medium case. If the objective is to influence public policy in respect to a given issue, we should assume that in countries of low institutional quality, in the short/medium term, efforts should probably be mainly devoted to generating the necessary institutional preconditions, and later to the reparation of the rights violated in the longer term.' By contrast, in countries with strong, activist courts, capable of monitoring the implementation process, a structural case may be successful at changing public policy with respect to an issue.

For cases that fall into the final category described by Sigal, Morales, and Rossi (cases with far-reaching goals, but low institutional quality to enforce court decisions to reach those goals), Brinks offers a strategy to ensure that political costs favour enforcement. He suggests beginning with individual cases 'until a right is well established and accepted by the public'. Thus, 'narrow, targeted orders and the threat of small court-ordered penalties aimed at lower level bureaucrats' can be used to raise the cost of non-compliance in early cases; and 'once the right is broadly accepted, one can attempt a more important collective case with a far higher budgetary cost, trusting that publicly defying a well-established right in an important instance can generate much higher political costs'.

1.4.3   Reflexive Remedies

According to Dorf (2003: 397), reflexive approaches to adjudication are 'best suited to questions as to which there is consensus on broad goals or principles, but uncertainty about means'. His account also emphasises the adaptive element of litigation and the space for dialogue and experimentalism: '[P]erformance standards are continually ratcheted up as local experimentation reveals what is possible' (Dorf, 2003: 399).

In his chapter, Rodríguez-Garavito proposes such a strategy but with the aim of improving the enforcement of ESC rights, an approach which the Colombian Constitutional Court has used in various cases with success. He terms it 'dialogic activism', and describes its three defining characteristics: a strong declaration of the rights in questions; a clear goal that the government must achieve, while laying out clear roadmaps for measuring compliance, but leaving policy decisions regarding how to reach those goals to the elected branches of power; and active court monitoring of the implementation of its orders through participatory mechanisms, which include ample opportunity for all relevant stakeholders to participate in the implementation process, and deepen democratic deliberation and enhance the impact of courts' interventions.[20]

Such an approach to litigation and monitoring yields potentially greater enforcement and impact of court decisions. As discussed, it overcomes two important obstacles to enforcement: (1) ensuring social mobilisation and participation by those who have had their rights violated, and (2) increasing political and affective costs of non-enforcement. However, using soft or moderate remedies has its risks, as *Brinks* notes, and he offers some strategic considerations regarding their use. He considers that principle-based orders should be used only when the case generates affective costs that favour enforcement (which conforms to Dorf's argument that experimental remedies are appropriate when there is broad agreement on the goals). By contrast, specific mandates may be more effective in cases with strongly negative affective costs associated with enforcement.

A second challenge is convincing courts to move towards more reflexive and experimental modes of adjudication. Willingness to reform court

---

[20] See also Rodríguez-Garavito and Rodríguez-Franco (2015).

procedure varies dramatically across countries and is partly a product of path dependency. Some courts have been forced to develop new remedial forms out of necessity. The development of structural injunctions in the United States was partly a product of nineteenth-century bankruptcy litigation (Sabel and Simon, 2004). Likewise, there is variance within and across courts concerning their willingness to learn from experimental approaches elsewhere.[21] This is partly because judges diverge considerably in their readiness to invest judicial energy and capital in innovation and follow-up, as experiences from South Africa, Nepal and even Colombia demonstrate. Thus advocates should be careful with the frequency with which they demand this remedy and the frequency of follow-up hearings.

1.4.4 Strategies to Improve Enforcement of International Decisions

Many of the obstacles to the implementation of ESCR decisions at the international and regional level are different from those at the domestic level. At the international level, obstacles present at the domestic level may be irrelevant, heightened or play out differently. As noted by *Viljoen*, high-level officials may feel fewer qualms about publically rejecting international court decisions given that may have less democratic legitimacy from a domestic perspective.

Such differences in obstacles to enforcement lend themselves to different strategies to improve enforcement, although some domestic strategies may be adapted to the international level. Several of the findings of *Viljoen* regarding the factors most likely to influence compliance provide a useful bridge from identifying the problem to developing concrete strategies to increase enforcement of international ESC rights decisions. According to Viljoen as well as Çalı and Koch, a stable, open and democratic system of government is conducive to compliance. Civil society efforts to monitor compliance also tend to result in greater enforcement levels.

While establishing a free and open democracy as a precondition to implementation is beyond the capacity of most (or all) human rights advocates, they can take advantage of the other factors. Thus, advocates should consider how best to make use of social mobilisation, as discussed,

---

[21] Compare the recent attempts by Kenyan judges to apply dialogical remedies after an exchange to Colombia with the significant reluctance of the South African Constitutional Court to innovate with post-judgment remedies.

as well as how their goals relate to considerations regarding the size and complexity of the case and remedies sought during case selection. In addition, Viljoen's findings suggest that in human rights systems that suffer from low enforcement levels, those bodies should adopt an active, creative monitoring role. By contrast, Çalı and Koch suggest that in contexts where the legitimacy of the human rights body is not in question, a more deliberative approach that grants states freedom to remedy violations on their own terms may be more effective.

In addition, as mentioned, states often separate their foreign policy from their domestic policy, which complicates the implementation of regional or international court orders. The state agents who appear before regional or international bodies often represent the foreign policy ministries, which are usually part of the executive branch. Therefore, when an international human rights body issues orders to change domestic policy, these very state agents who appear before these tribunals often have no capacity to enact such changes. It is crucial for states to connect the officials representing the state before regional courts and the national officials who have the authority to make the necessary domestic policy changes to implement the decisions. These mechanisms can take various forms and can vary in their level of comprehensiveness and permanency, ranging from comprehensive models of implementation, such as norms adopted by Peru and Colombia, to programs designed to increase coordination among relevant government actors, as the United Kingdom has done, or even using ad hoc inter-ministerial committees to implement decisions in specific cases, as Poland and Romania have done.[22]

Other enforcement strategies stem from Viljoen findings regarding civil society participation and involvement of the international body during the monitoring phase. Abramovich (2015) describes several implementation strategies the Inter-American Court has used that make use of these findings.[23] First, the Inter-American Court issues compliance orders in order to set deadlines for state action, require parties to take actions that it deems necessary to achieve compliance with a decision, and to focus on issues of particular concern. Such orders are often based on information and requests made by the litigants, and thus provide an excellent opportunity for petitioners to be involved in the monitoring phase and pressure

---

[22] For a set of systemic recommendations in this regard, see OSJI (2013).
[23] This chapter appears in the forthcoming Spanish version of this volume.

the state to comply with the Court's decision. The Court also uses compliance hearings, which partly reflects dialogic activism at the domestic level, in that the Court provides a space for negotiation between the state and the petitioner, while the Court's presence remedies potential power imbalances between the parties.

1.5 Conclusion: Towards Transformative Impact?

From the perspective of strategic rather than individual-based litigation, impact is the ultimate prize. Interestingly, many of the chapters reveal significant direct and indirect impacts which were generated despite minimal or partial compliance with the actual order. Litigation is a political act and can have multiple consequences for policy, politics and perceptions. As far as possible, it is important that advocates are oriented to maximising broader impacts as much as compliance in individual cases.

Paradoxically, some authors express the concern that full compliance does not always lead to transformative and redistributive effects. As Porter says, 'it is critical that litigation strategies develop enforceable remedies that engage with the need for a transformative social rights practice, rather than one that relies solely on judicial remedies framed within the existing entitlement system'. Similarly, in light of the Brazilian experience with health rights adjudication, Ferraz questions the individual non-precedential model of litigation because it can enhance rather than diminish social inequalities. While the extent to which there is a systemic and problematic middle-class bias in adjudication in some Latin American countries is contested (Brinks and Gauri, 2014; Rodríguez Garavito, 2014), in the context of a civil law system, collective suits should possess in principle a greater potential to tackle structural inequalities.

In any case, for social rights adjudication to contribute to social transformation it must engage with both the 'most critical issues of exclusion and deprivation' and the 'transformative dimension of policy and program design and implementation' (Porter, in this volume). Litigating such cases is challenging from a jurisprudential, remedial and enforcement perspective given the complex interactions amongst relevant policy domains. Yet, various cases in this volume demonstrate that a combination of creative but nuanced jurisprudence, reflexive remedies and the presence of engaged and grounded social actors can help realise this transformative project.

References

Abramovich, Victor and Christian Courtis (2001), *Los derechos sociales como derechos exigibles* (Madrid: Trotta).

Baas, Larry and Dan Thomas (1984), 'The Supreme Court and Policy Legitimation: Experimental Tests', *American Politics Quarterly*, 12(3), 335–360.

Bergallo, Paula (2011), 'Argentina: Achieving Fairness Despite "Routinization"?', in Alicia Ely Yamin and Siri Gloppen (eds.), *Litigating Health Rights: Can Courts Bring More Justice to Health?* (Cambridge, MA: Harvard University Press), 43–75.

Berger, John (2008), 'Litigating for Social Justice in Post-apartheid South Africa: A Focus on Health and Education', in Varun Gauri and Daniel Brinks (eds.), *Courting Social Justice: Judicial Enforcement of Social and Economic Rights in the Developing World* (Cambridge: Cambridge University Press), 38–99.

Berry, Christopher (2007), 'The Impact of School Finance Judgments on State Fiscal Policy', in Martin R. West and Paul E. Peterson (eds.), *School Money Trials: The Legal Pursuit of Educational Adequacy* (Washington, DC: Brookings Institution), 213–240.

Bilchitz, David (2007), *Poverty and Fundamental Rights: The Justification and Enforcement of Socio-Economic Rights* (Oxford: Oxford University Press).

Blake, Judith (1977), 'The Abortion Decisions: Judicial Review and Public Opinion', in Edward Manier, William Liu and David Solomon (eds.), *Abortion: New Directions for Policy Studies* (Notre Dame: University of Notre Dame Press).

Brinks, Dan and Varun Gauri (2014), 'The Law's Majestic Equality? The Distributive Impact of Judicializing Social and Economic Rights', *Perspectives on Politics*, 12(2), 375–393.

Byrne, Iain and Sara Hossain (2008), 'South Asia: Economic and Social Rights Case Law of Bangladesh, Nepal, Pakistan and Sri Lanka', in Malcolm Langford (ed.), *Social Rights Jurisprudence: Emerging Trends in International and Comparative Law* (Cambridge: Cambridge University Press), 125–143.

Çali, Başak and Alica Wyss (2011), 'Why Do Democracies Comply with Human Rights Judgments? A Comparative Analysis of the UK, Ireland and Germany', Working Paper.

Cavallaro, James and Stephanie Brewer (2008), 'The Virtue of Following: The Role of Inter-American Litigation in Campaigns for Social Justice', *SUR-International Journal on Human Rights*, 5(8), 8–85.

Cavanagh, Ralph and Austin Sarat (1980), 'Thinking about Courts: Towards and Beyond a Jurisprudence of Judicial Competence', *Law & Society Review*, 14(2), 371–420.

CEJIL (2003), 'Unkept Promises: The Implementation of the Decisions of the Commission and the Court', *Gazette*, 10.

Coomans, Fons (ed.) (2006), *Justiciability of Economic and Social Rights: Experiences from Domestic Systems* (Antwerpen: Intersentia and Maastrict Centre for Human Rights).

Courtis, Christian (2008), 'Argentina: Some Promising Signs', in Malcolm Langford (ed.), *Social Rights Jurisprudence: Emerging Trends in International and Comparative Law* (Cambridge: Cambridge University Press), 163–181.

Dennis, Michael and David Stewart (2004), 'Justiciability of Economic, Social, and Cultural Rights: Should There Be an International Complaints Mechanism to Adjudicate the Rights to Food, Water, Housing, and Health?', *American Journal of International Law*, 98, 462–515.

Dorf, Michael (2003), 'The Domain of Reflexive Law', *Colombia Law Review*, 103(384–401).

Dugard, Jackie and Malcolm Langford (2011), 'Art or Science? Synthesising Lessons from Public Interest Litigation and the Dangers of Legal Determinism', *South African Journal on Human Rights*, 26(3), 39–64.

Edmundson, William (1995), 'Is Law Coercive?', *Legal Theory*, 1(1), 81–111.

Eide, Asbjørn (1987), *The Right to Food (Final Report)* (Geneva: UN).

Epp, Charles (2009), *Making Rights Real: Activists, Bureaucrats, and the Creation of the Legalist State* (Chicago: University of Chicago Press).

Fabre, Cécile (2000), *Social Rights under the Constitution* (Oxford: Oxford University Press).

Franklin, Charles and Liane Kosaki (1989), 'Republican Schoolmaster: The US Supreme Court, Public Opinion, and Abortion', *American Political Science Review*, 69(3), 7517–7571.

Gargarella, Roberto, Pilar Domingo and Theunis Roux (2006), *Courts and Social Transformation in New Democracies: An Institutional Voice for the Poor?* (Aldershot/Burlington: Ashgate).

Gauri, Varun (2010), 'Public Interest Litigation in India: Overreaching or Underachieving?', *Indian Journal of Law and Economics* 1, 71–93.

Gauri, Varun and Daniel Brinks (2008), *Courting Social Justice: Judicial Enforcement of Social and Economic Rights in the Developing World* (New York: Cambridge University Press).

Ginsberg, Tom and Richard McAdams (2004), 'Adjudicating in Anarchy: An Expressive Theory of International Dispute Resolution', *William and Mary Law Review*, 45(4), 1229–1330.

Goldsmith, Jack and Eric Posner (2005), *The Limits of International Law* (New York: Oxford University Press).

Goodman, Ryan and Derek Jinks (2008), 'Incomplete Internalization and Compliance with Human Rights Law', *European Journal of International Law*, 19(4), 725–748.

Grewal, Sharanbir and Erik Voeten (2012), 'The Politics of Implementing European Court of Human Rights Judgments', SSRN Working Paper.

Hart, H.L.A. (1961), *The Concept of Law* (Oxford: Oxford University Press).

Hazard, G. (1969), 'Social Justice through Civil Justice', *University of Chicago Law Review*, 36, 699–712.

Heise, Michael (1995), 'State Constitutions, School Finance Litigation, and the Third Wave: From Equity to Adequacy, Heise, Michael', *Temple Law Review*, 68, 1151–1176.

Helfer, Laurence and Erik Voeten (2014), 'International Courts as Agents of Legal Change: Evidence from LGBT Rights in Europe', *International Organization*, 68(1), 77–110.

Heywood, Mark (2009), 'South Africa's Treatment Action Campaign: Combining Law and Social Mobilization to Realize the Right to Health', *Journal of Human Rights Practice*, 1(1), 14–36.

Hickrod, A., Edward Hines, Gregory Anthony, John Dively and Gwen Pruyne (1992), 'The Effect of Constitutional Litigation on Education Finance: A Preliminary Analysis', *Journal of Education Finance*, 18(2), 180–210.

Hillebrecht, Courtney (2014), *Domestic Politics and International Human Rights Tribunals: The Problem of Compliance* (Cambridge: Cambridge University Press).

Hirschl, Ran and Evan Rosevear (2012), 'Constitutional Law Meets Comparative Politics: Socio-Economic Rights and Political Realities', in Tom Campbell, K. D. Ewing and Adam Tomkins (eds.), *The Legal Protection of Human Rights – Sceptical Essays* (Oxford: Oxford University Press), 207–228.

Hoekstra, Valerie (2000), 'The Supreme Court and Local Public Opinion', *American Political Science Review*, 94(1), 89–108.

    (2003), *Public Reaction to Supreme Court Decisions* (Cambridge: Cambridge University Press).

Hoffmann, Florian and Fernando Bentes (2008), 'Accountability for Social and Economic Rights in Brazil', in Varun Gauri and Daniel Brinks (eds.), *Courting Social Justice: Judicial Enforcement of Social and Economic Rights in the Developing World* (Cambridge: Cambridge University Press), 100–145.

Horowitz, Donald (1977), *The Courts and Social Policy* (Washington, DC: The Brookings Institution).

Howse, Robert and Ruti Teitel (2010), 'Beyond Compliance: Rethinking Why International Law Really Matters', *Global Policy*, 1(2), 127–136.

Huneeus, Alexandra (2011), 'Courts Resisting Courts: Lessons from the Inter-American Court's Struggle to Enforce Human Rights', *Cornell International Law Journal*, 44, 493–533.

ICJ (2008), *Courts and the Legal Enforcement of Economic, Social and Cultural Rights: Comparative Experiences of Justiciability* (Geneva: International Commission of Jurists).

Johnson, Timothy and Andrew Martin (1998), 'The Public's Conditional Response to Supreme Court Decisions', *American Political Science Review*, 92(2), 299–309.

Joubert, Pearlie (2008), 'Grootboom Dies Homeless and Penniless', *Mail & Guardian*, 8 August.

Kagan, Robert A. and Jerome Skolnick (1993), 'Banning Smoking: Compliance without Coercion', in Robert Rabin and Stephen Sugarman (eds.), *Smoking Policy: Law, Policy and Politics* (Oxford: Oxford University Press), 69–94.

Kapiszewski, Diana and Matthew Taylor (2013), 'Compliance: Conceptualizing, Measuring and Explaining Adherence to Judicial Rulings', *Law & Social Inquiry*, 38(4), 803–835.

Keller, Helen and Alec Stone Sweet (eds.) (2008), *A Europe of Rights: The Impact of the ECHR on National Legal Systems* (Oxford: Oxford University Press).

King, Jeff A. (2012), *Judging Social Rights* (Cambridge: Cambridge University Press).

Langford, Malcolm (ed.), (2008), *Social Rights Jurisprudence: Emerging Trends in International and Comparative Law* (Cambridge: Cambridge University Press).

Langford, Malcolm (2014), 'Housing Rights Litigation: *Grootboom* and Beyond', in Malcolm Langford, Ben Cousins, Jackie Dugard and Tshepo Madlingozi (eds.), *Symbols or Substance? The Role and Impact of Socio-Economic Rights Strategies in South Africa* (Cambridge: Cambridge University Press), 187–225.

Langford, Malcolm and Ananda Bhatterai (2011), 'Constitutional Rights and Social Exclusion in Nepal', *International Journal on Minority and Group Rights*, 18(2), 387–411.

Langford, Malcolm, Ben Cousins, Jackie Dugard and Tshepo Madlingozi (eds.) (2014), *Socio-Economic Rights in South Africa: Symbols or Substance?* (Cambridge: Cambridge University Press).

Lanni, Adriaan (2010), 'The Expressive Effect of the Athenian Prostitution Laws', *Classical Antiquity*, 29(1), 45–67.

Liebenberg, Sandra (2008), 'South Africa: Adjudicating Social Rights under a Transformative Constitution', in Malcolm Langford (ed.), *Social Rights Jurisprudence: Emerging Trends in International and Comparative Law* (Cambridge: Cambridge University Press), 75–101.

(2010), *Socio-Economic Rights: Adjudication under a Transformative Constitution* (Claremont: Juta).

Linos, Katerina and Kimberley Twist (2013), 'Endorsement and Framing Effects in Experimental and Natural Settings: The Supreme Court, the Media and the American Public', *UC Berkeley Public Law Research Paper No. 2223732*.

Mbazira, Christopher (2008a), *You Are the "Weakest Link" in Realising Socio-economic Rights: Goodbye – Strategies for Effective Implementation of Court Orders in South Africa* (Research Series 3; Cape Town: Community Law Centre, University of the Western Cape).

(2008b), 'Non-Implementation of Court Orders in Socio-Economic Rights Litigation in South Africa', *ESR Review*, 9(4), 2–7.

McAdams, Richard (2000), 'An Attitudinal Theory of Expressive Law', *Oregon Law Review*, 79, 339–390.

McCann, Michael (1994), *Rights at Work: Pay Equity Reform and the Politics of Legal Mobilization* (Chicago: University of Chicago Press).

Melish, Tara (2008), 'Inter-American Court of Human Rights: Beyond Progressivity', in Malcolm Langford (ed.), *Social Rights Jurisprudence: Emerging Trends in International and Comparative Law* (Cambridge: Cambridge University Press), 372–408.

Moravcsik, Andrew (2000), 'The Origin of Human Rights Regimes: Democratic Delegation in Postwar Europe', *International Organization*, 54(2), 217–252.

Muir, William (1973), *Law and Attitude Change* (Chicago: University of Chicago Press).

Muralidhar, S. (2008), 'India: The Expectations and Challenges of Judicial Enforcement of Social Rights', in Malcolm Langford (ed.), *Social Rights Jurisprudence: Emerging Trends in International and Comparative Law* (Cambridge: Cambridge University Press), 102–124.

OSJI (2010), *From Judgment to Justice: Implementing International and Regional Human Rights Decisions* (London: Open Society Justice Initiative).

(2013), *From Rights to Remedies: Structures and Strategies for Implementing International Human Rights Decisions* (New York: Open Society Foundation).

Raz, Joseph (1994), 'Law, Authority and Morality', in Joseph Raz (ed.), *Ethics in the Public Domain* (Oxford: Oxford University Press).

Roach, Kent (2004), 'Dialogic Judicial Review and Its Critics', *Supreme Court Law Review*, 23(2), 49–104.

Roach, Kent and Geoff Budlender (2005), 'Mandatory Relief and Supervisory Jurisdiction: When Is It Appropriate, Just and Equitable', *South African Law Journal*, 122, 325–351.

Rodríguez Garavito, César (2014), 'The Judicialization of Health Care: Symptoms, Diagnosis, and Prescriptions', in Randall Peerenboom and Tom Ginsberg (eds.), *Law and Development of Middle-Income Countries: Avoiding the Middle-Income Trap* (New York: Cambridge University Press), 246–269.

Rodríguez Garavito, César and Celeste Kauffman (2014), *Making Social Rights Real: Implementation Strategies for Courts, Decision Makers and Civil Society* (Bogota: Dejusticia).

Rodríguez Garavito, César and Diana Rodríguez-Franco (2015), *Radical Deprivation on Trial: The Impact of Judicial Activism on Socioeconomic Rights in the Global South* (Cambridge: Cambridge University Press).

Rodríguez-Garavito, César (2011), 'Beyond the Courtroom: The Impact of Judicial Activism on Socioeconomic Rights in Latin America', *Texas Law Review* 89, 1669–1698.

Rosenberg, Gerald (1991), *The Hollow Hope: Can Courts Bring About Social Change?* (Chicago: University of Chicago Press).

Rossi, Julieta and Leonardo Filippini (2009), 'El derecho internacional en la justiciabilidad de los derechos sociales en Latinoamérica', in P. Arcidiácono, N. Espejo and C. Rodríguez-Garavito (eds.), *Derechos sociales: Justicia, política y economía en América Latina* (Bogotá: Siglo del Hombre).

Sabel, Charles F. and William Simon (2004), 'Destabilization Rights: How Public Law Litigation Succeeds', *Harvard Law Review*, 117, 1015–1101.

Schmidt, Vivien (2008), 'Discursive Institutionalism: The Explanatory Power of Ideas and Discourse', *Annual Review of Political Science*, 11, 303–326.

Shankar, Shylashi and Pratap Bhanu Mehta (2008), 'Courts and Socio-Economic Rights in India', in Varun Gauri and Daniel Brinks (eds.), *Courting Social Justice: Judicial Enforcement of Social and Economic Rights in the Developing World* (Cambridge: Cambridge University Press), 146–182.

Shue, Henry (1980), *Basic Rights: Subsistence, Affluence and US Foreign Policy* (Princeton: Princeton University Press).

Simmons, Beth (2009), *Mobilizing for Human Rights: International Law in Domestic Politics* (New York: Cambridge University Press).

Songer, Donald and Reginald Sheehan (1990), 'Supreme Court Impact on Compliance and Outcomes: Miranda and New York Times in the US Court of Appeals', *The Western Political Quarterly*, 43(2), 297–316.

Spriggs, James F. II (1997), 'Explaining Federal Bureaucratic Compliance with Supreme Court Opinions', *Political Research Quarterly*, 50(3), 567–93.

Stoutenborough, James, Donald Haider-Markel and Mahalley Allen (2006), 'Reassessing the Impact of Supreme Court Decisions on Public Opinion: Gay Civil Rights Cases', *Political Research Quarterly*, 59, 419–433.

Thompson, David C. and Faith E. Crampton (2002), 'The Impact of School Finance Litigation: A Long View', *Journal of Education Finance*, 28(1), 133–172.

Ura, Joseph Daniel (2014), 'Backlash and Legitimation: Macro Political Responses to Supreme Court Decisions', *American Journal of Political Science*, 58(1), 110–126.

Vecera, Vincent (2014), 'The Supeme Court and the Social Conception of Abortion', *Law & Society Review*, 48(2), 345–375.

Vierdag, E. W. (1978), 'The Legal Nature of the Rights Granted by the International Covenant on Economic, Social and Cultural Rights', *Netherlands Yearbook of International Law*, 9, 69–105.

Voeten, Erik (2012), 'Does a Professional Judiciary Induce More Compliance? Evidence from the European Court of Human Rights', SSRN Working Paper, http://papers.ssrn.com/sol3/papers.cfm?abstract_id=2029786) forthcoming.

(2014), 'Domestic Implementation of European Court of Human Rights Judgments: Legal Infrastructure and Government Effectiveness Matter: A Reply to Dia Anagnostou and Alina Mungiu-Pippidi', *European Journal of International Law*, 25(1), 229–238.

Wachira, George and Abiola Ayinla (2006), 'Twenty Years of Elusive Enforcement of the Recommendations of the African Commission on Human and Peoples' Rights: A Possible Remedy', *African Human Rights Law Journal*, 6(2), 465–492.

Waldron, Jeremy (2009), 'Socio-Economic Rights and Theories of Justice', in Thomas Pogge (ed.), *Freedom from Poverty as a Human Right*, Vol. 2 (Paris: UNESCO).

Wertheimer, Alan (1987). *Coercion*, Princeton: Princeton University Press.

Wilson, Stuart (2011), 'Litigating Housing Rights in Johannesburg's Inner City', *South African Journal on Human Rights*, 27(3).

Wlezien, Christopher and Malcolm Goggin (1993), 'The Courts, Interests Groups, and Public Opinion about Abortion', *Political Behaviour*, 15(December), 381–405.

Yamin, Alicia Ely and Siri Gloppen (2011), *Litigating Health Rights: Can Courts Bring More Justice to Health?* (Cambridge, MA: Harvard University Press).

Yankah, Ekow N. (2008), 'The Force of Law: The Role of Coercion in Legal Norms', *University of Richmond Law Review*, 42, 1195–255.

Young, Katherine (2008), 'The Minimum Core of Economic and Social Rights: A Concept in Search of Content', *Yale Journal of International Law*, 33, 113–175.

Young, Oran R. (2001), 'Inferences and Indices: Evaluating the Effectiveness of International Environmental Regimes', *Global Environmental Politics*, 1(1), 99–120.

Explaining Compliance: Lessons Learnt from Civil and Political Rights

BAŞAK ÇALI AND ANNE KOCH

2.1 Introduction

The enforcement of economic, social and cultural (ESC) rights judgments is often considered to present challenges that are different from those encountered in the realm of civil and political (CP) rights.[1] Linking in with a growing literature on the judicial enforcement of ESC rights (Merali and Oosterveld, 2001; Dixon, 2007; Gauri and Brinks, 2008; Gloppen, 2009; Langford, 2008; Rodríguez-Garavito, 2011), this edited volume as a whole is based on the assumption that there is something particular about the implementation of ESC rights that is worth investigating. Notwithstanding the well-founded claims underlying this assumption, this chapter takes a step back and asks what lessons from the implementation of international CP rights judgments might be generalised and fruitfully applied to the broader field of international human rights implementation, including the realm of ESC rights.[2]

---

[1] In this chapter we shall use the terms 'enforcement' and 'implementation' interchangeably.

[2] Rodríguez-Garavito (2011) has identified the implementation stage of socioeconomic rights as an 'analytical and practical blind spot' and a 'black box' that needs to be elucidated in order to further our understanding of the justiciability of these rights.

Başak Çalı is Professor of International Law at Hertie School of Governance, Berlin, and Director of Center for Global Public Law, Koc University, Istanbul.

Anne Koch is a researcher and policy consultant at the Stift ung Wissenschaft und Politik (SWP), Berlin.

We would like to acknowledge the financial support of the research project titled 'The Judicial Legitimacy and Authority of Supranational Human Rights Courts: A Comparative Analysis of the Perception of the European Court of Human Rights in Bulgaria, Germany, Ireland, Turkey and the United Kingdom', Economic Social Research Council (United Kingdom) Grant No: RES-061-25-0029. For comments on earlier drafts, we are grateful to the participants of the Symposium on Enforcement of ESCR judgments that took place in Bogota on 6–7 May 2010 and in particular to Malcolm Langford, Daniel Brinks, Damon Hewitt, César Rodríguez-Garavito and Varun Gauri.

The chapter's key contribution to the discussion of enforcement is achieved through a shift of focus: rather than concentrating on the type of judgment to be enforced and presuming that the *content* of the right in question will determine the success or failure of its enforcement, this chapter looks at the *process of human rights judgment implementation* as such – taking into consideration the costs of compliance and how these costs can be moderated by the institutional design of enforcement regimes.[3] The analysis focuses on international adjudication but draws partly on comparative research, and its findings are relevant to the national level. It proposes an interactional framework for understanding human rights judgment implementation in which the speed and comprehensiveness of domestic human rights judgment enforcement is determined by the interaction between international human rights bodies and national decision makers, and argues that the process through which the terms of implementation are defined is of crucial importance. The chapter illustrates this argument through the analysis of the enforcement regime in place for the judgments of the European Court of Human Rights, where a 'deliberative enforcement model' is used to mitigate the domestic costs of compliance with complex CP rights remedies. The overall analysis suggests that the realm of CP rights enforcement offers important lessons for identifying and overcoming challenges to the enforcement of ESC rights. This is all the more pertinent as the Optional Protocol for the International Covenant on Economic and Social Rights is now in force and the cases decided by the Committee on Economic Social and Cultural Rights are growing.

The chapter has three parts. First, it takes issue with the widespread view that the categorisation of human rights into different categories or 'generations' tells us something about the likelihood of implementation. It briefly summarises the discussion surrounding the differences between ESC rights and CP rights and identifies the challenges specific to the enforcement of ESC rights that have been deduced from this. It queries the widespread idea that enforcement of CP rights is inherently easier and less costly than the implementation of ESC rights by drawing on examples from the experience of the enforcement of CP rights at the European level. Instead, it shows that the enforcement of international CP rights judgments has much in common with the enforcement of international

---

[3] In this chapter we employ the concept of 'costs' not in purely material and strategic terms, but in a wider sense, also including social costs, such as betraying shared ideals, harming one's standing and self-esteem, or damaging relationships.

ESC judgments and that lessons learnt in the realm of CP rights enforcement regimes provide important insights for improving the design of ESC enforcement and for making the interventions of litigators and ESC rights activists more effective.

Second, the chapter turns to the process of enforcement of international human rights judgments. On the basis of a review of human rights compliance literature, evidence from a qualitative dataset of 137 interviews with elites involved in the Council of Europe human rights architecture and publicly available documents from different international human rights adjudication bodies, it argues that the configuration of costs by those involved in enforcing judgments and the design of international enforcement regimes constitute the two key factors that influence the processes of implementation with international human rights judgments, regardless of the type of right in question.

The chapter's third and final section expands upon the institutional design features of the European human rights system. While the European Court of Human Rights does not shy away from adjudicating ESC rights (Palmer, 2009), it is primarily an example of a CP adjudicating institution that is instructive due to its relative success in comparison to other regional or international human rights bodies. The final section discusses how the design of the enforcement system in Europe influences domestic motivations for enforcing human rights judgments. It uses what we term as the 'European deliberative enforcement model' as an example to illustrate the analytical value of the proposed interactional framework for understanding enforcement. Finally, the chapter discusses what kinds of lessons can be learnt from the European deliberative enforcement model and to what extent these lessons may be relevant for other regional or United Nations (UN) bodies and provide guidance for civil society activism.

2.2 Common Challenges to the Implementation of CP and ESC rights

CP and ESC rights have commonly been discussed as two separate and, at times, incompatible paradigms. The creation of two separate treaties and interpretation regimes under the umbrella of the UN – the International Covenant on Civil and Political Rights (ICCPR) and the International Covenant on Economic, Social and Cultural Rights (ICESCR) – has contributed to this distinction. Both covenants have been widely ratified. Nonetheless, this historical separation of basic human rights into two treaties is indicative of a distinction that is still prevalent in many discussions regarding the enforcement of human rights judgments today. CP rights and ESC rights are often named 'first generation' and 'second generation' rights respectively, with reference to the order in which they were accepted by Western European and North American states (Alston, 1982; Meron, 1986; Saito, 1996; Mutua, 1999). Alston and Quinn (1987: 158) recall how the United States 'maintained that economic, social, and cultural rights belong in a 'qualitatively different category' from other rights, that they should be seen not as rights but as goals of economic and social policy, and that, as rights, they are too easily abused by repressive governments as justifications for violations of civil and political rights.' This deeply held distinction between the two types of rights often entails a fundamental contestation of the status of ESC rights as justiciable rights.

International law has moved in a direction in which both CP rights and ESC rights have equal formal standing. Yet significant institutional differences remain. While the ICCPR's monitoring body, the Human Rights Committee, has held the power to examine individual complaints since 1985, an optional protocol stipulating the equivalent powers of the Committee on Economic, Social and Cultural Rights only came into force in 2013. The ICCPR has therefore been backed up by a functioning international adjudicatory body (however weak its influence) and a growing body of case law, while the ICESCR adjudication only started in 2013. The Committee on Economic Social and Cultural Rights delivered its first decision in the case of *IDG v. Spain* in 2015. Regional adjudication of ESC rights, too, has been patchy, compared to CP rights adjudication. Owing to this, remedies for CP rights violations are much further developed than remedies for ESC rights violations (Roach, 2008).

There are three widely held assumptions regarding the enforcement of ESC rights that may be held individually or in combination: (1) CP rights remedies are easier to enforce than ESC rights. (2) CP rights enforcement is almost free of cost, whereas the enforcement of ESC rights is very resource-intensive. (3) CP rights violations are not subject to ideological contestation and can easily attract public support, whilst ESC violations are subject to deep ideological contestation. Whilst the lack of widespread adjudication of ESC rights has contributed to these assumptions, we also find that they are perpetuated by a lack of careful analysis of the implementation processes of CP rights.

Empirical research on the implementation of international CP rights judgments indicates that there are considerable challenges to the enforcement of judgments issued by human rights bodies at the UN or in different regional contexts – in Africa and the Americas as well as in Europe (Anagnostou 2010; Baluarte and Vos, 2010; Hillebrecht 2014; Murray and Long, 2015). It is hard to sustain, based on these insights, the simplified views on CP rights enforcement outlined earlier. Instead, the situation can be presented as follows:

(1) The CP rights enforcement realm is abundant with examples of cases that can be realised only through active, lengthy and complex state engagement. Contrary to the belief that CP rights require only future non-intervention, and at most payment of compensation, the doctrine of positive obligations implies that all rights have some corresponding positive duties for their realisation (Mowbray, 2004). Enforcement of the violations of procedural obligations with respect to the protection of the right to life may for instance depend on developing effective investigation and prosecution capacities, often amounting to a complex and lengthy process of domestic reform.[4] The customary international law obligation to prevent future violations (Crawford, 2002) further undermines the stereotype concerning easy remedies for CP rights as opposed to complex remedies for ESC rights. Whilst it is true that remedies for ESC rights violations that entail progressive realisation are likely to require complex remedies that are subject to negotiation and consultation by a multiplicity of actors, remedies for gross and systematic CP rights violations also face similar problems.[5] For instance, the measures that governments have to take to fulfil the right to truth in the aftermath of gross CP rights abuses demand a longer-term process rather than one-off remedies, involving creative – and often not pre-determined – measures.[6]

---

[4] See, for example, the length and complexity of the enforcement of six cases concerning the actions of the security forces in the United Kingdom, which involved the duty to effectively investigate killings in Northern Ireland. The implementation of these cases has been on-going since 2001 before the Committee of Ministers of the Council of Europe, the body that is responsible for overseeing the enforcement of judgments in the European System. *McKerr v. UK* (App No 28883/95), judgment of 4 May 2001, *Shanaghan v. UK* (App No 37715/97), judgment of 4 May 2001, *Hugh Jordan v. UK* (App No 24746/94), judgment of 4 May 2001, *Kelly and others v. UK* (App No 30054/96), judgment of 4 May 2001, *McShane v. UK* (App No 43290/98), judgment of 28 May 2002, *Finucane v. UK* (App No 29178/95), judgment of 1 July 2003.

[5] See, for example, The Committee of Ministers, 2007. Actions of Security Forces in Turkey: Progress Achieved and Outstanding Issues. https://wcd.coe.int/ViewDoc .jsp?Ref=CM/Inf/DH(2006)24&Language=lan English&Ver=rev2&Site=CM&BackColo rInternet=9999CC&BackColorIntranet =FFBB55&BackColorLogged=FFAC75 (accessed 21 April 2015).

[6] *Kurt v. Turkey* (App No 24276/94), judgment of 25 May 1998, *Tas v. Turkey* (App No 24396/ 94), judgment of 14 November 2000 and *Cyprus v. Turkey* (App No 25781/94), judgment

This directly links in with point (2) mentioned: Remedying certain
CP rights violations may involve significant material costs (Tushnet,
2003a: 1896), for example, in cases which require institutional reform, the
training and hiring of additional staff or consultations with marginalised
groups in society. Several countries in Europe have struggled to comply
with European Court of Human Rights judgments that found instances
of excessive length of proceedings[7] or that called for an improvement of
conditions in prisons[8] or asylum seeker detention centres.[9] Remedying
violations of classical CP rights like freedom from arbitrary detention, torture and inhuman and degrading treatment, therefore, depends crucially
on the availability of resources, and may require budgetary decisions that
prioritise one policy area over another – a requirement often criticised by
opponents of ESC rights adjudication.

(3) The contention that CP rights implementation attracts less ideological contestation does not withstand close scrutiny. The experience of the
CP rights implementation shows that standard CP cases such as discrimination,[10] conscientious objection,[11] non-refoulement,[12] and discrimination based on sexual orientation[13] constitute sites of strong ideological
contestation amongst various political factions within states. There is no
evidence to suggest that ideological contestation on cultural, political,
social or moral grounds is less significant than that on political economy
grounds.

The enforcement of both CP and ESC rights involves positive obligations and the duty to prevent future rights violations of a similar kind.
This forward-looking concern that underpins the enforcement of both
types of rights leads us to investigate the institutional mechanisms

of 10 May 2001. See also Views of 3 April 2003, *Lyashkevich v. Belarus*, Communication
No 887/1999, UN Doc. CCPR/C/ 77/D/950/2000, para. 9.2; Inter-American Commission,
Report No. 136/99, 22 December1999, *Ignacio Ellacriaetal. v. El Salvador*, para. 221.

[7] *A. B v. Italy* (App No 37874/97), judgment of 5 May 1998, is a case pending for enforcement
in Europe since 1997 together with 2,183 identical cases concerning the structural problem
of the length of proceedings in the Italian legal system.

[8] *Kalashnikov v. Russia* (App No 47095/99), judgment of 15 July 2002.

[9] *Mamatkulov v. Turkey* (App No 46827/99), judgment of 4 February 2005.

[10] *Nachova v. Bulgaria* (App No 43577/98 and 43579/98), judgment of 7 July 2005.

[11] *Ulke v. Turkey* (App No 39437/98), judgment of 24 April 2006; *Ercep v. Turkey* (App No
43965/04) judgment of 22 November 2011.

[12] *Omar Othman (AbuQatada) v. United Kingdom* (App No 8139/09), judgment of 17
January 2012.

[13] *X v. Columbia*, Communication No. 1361/2005, UN Doc. CCPR/C/89/D/1361/2005 of 14
May 2007.

through which international courts formulate general remedies, and the conditions under which these remedies can be successfully implemented by domestic actors.

2.3   Factors Influencing the Implementation Process: Domestic Reception versus the Design of Enforcement

In shifting the focus of analysis away from the type of right adjudicated and towards the enforcement process as such, we consider the domestic factors influencing compliance and the design of enforcement processes to constitute key factors influencing enforcement. Their interaction is shaped by the degree of leeway that an international human rights adjudication body leaves to a respondent state in determining the content of remedies. How demanding and how narrowly defined are remedies addressed at states, how much of a say do state authorities have in proposing and designing suitable remedies themselves, and how do the relevant agents – that is, domestic politicians and judges – perceive the costs and benefits associated with the enforcement of human rights judgments?

2.3.1   *The Domestic Setting: Thinking about Enforcement in Terms of Its Political, Institutional, and Normative Dimensions*

Domestic contexts are central to the implementation of human rights law, and a steady stream of political science research has studied the impact of domestic political and legal processes on compliance with international human rights treaties through both large-N and case study research (Dai, 2005; Cardenas, 2007; Simmons, 2009). In contrast to this there is comparatively little work on the enforcement of *specific* human rights judgments, particularly outside the United States (Anagnostou, 2010; Hillebrecht, 2014). The enforcement of specific human rights judgments is different from the enforcement of human rights law as such because costs and benefits of enforcement for the former are identified based both on ideas that take into account long-term advantages and disadvantages of enforcement of judgments in general, and the ideas that are introduced by particular characteristics of each judgment. In other words, individual human rights judgments trigger more multi-dimensional and nuanced cost and benefit considerations. Reasons for complying with human rights law in general inform, but do not determine, compliance behaviour at the individual judgment level. Having said this, lessons from the research on human rights law enforcement can be fruitfully built on when considering human rights judgment enforcement. An important lesson from these studies is that conditional theories are better equipped to explain enforcement. According to these, enforcement depends on the absence or presence of various factors in a particular context at a given time. In this section, we draw on this insight when analyzing our original qualitative dataset that comprises interviews with domestic decision makers on why they comply with human rights judgments. In order to map the domestic factors pertinent for the enforcement of human rights *judgments*, we need to disaggregate domestic contexts both in terms of actors and in terms of the kinds of cost and benefit perceptions that relevant actors hold.

Direct and Indirect Enforcement Actors

A diverse range of actors have an active role in the enforcement of both CP and ESC rights judgments. We may categorise the involvement of actors based on their functions in the enforcement process: direct enforcers of human rights judgments, pro-enforcement constituents (e.g. human rights NGOs, national human rights institutions, other states, international organisations) and anti-enforcement constituents (e.g. political groups, civil society, other states).

Direct enforcers of international human rights judgments can further be categorised based on the kind of decision-making powers they have. First, there are political actors with action-defining decision-making powers, such as government ministers, who have the power and authority to push through policies and reforms and alter the negative consequences of human rights violations for individual applicants. Second, there are members of parliament, who have action-guiding powers, such as the authority to repeal, amend or introduce legislation. Third, there are domestic judiciaries, who are responsible for remedying human rights violations procedurally, for example, by reopening an unfair trial, or for internalising the international case law of human rights courts by applying the case law in future cases. Finally, there are domestic bureaucracies and regulatory agencies, whose task it is to bring policy in line with the actions of the government and the parliament. This, however, is only a simplified sketch. Other independent institutions at the local, state, federal or supranational level may be equipped with powers to implement international human rights judgments, for example, elected local authorities or supranational authorities like the European Union. The enforcement of any individual international human rights judgment may therefore require the involvement of a broad array of actors with powers to implement different aspects of the judgment.[14]

Pro-enforcement constituents are those groups who are not direct compliers themselves, but who seek to bring about the enforcement of human rights judgments. These constituents typically do not only comprise the applicants themselves, but also non-governmental organisations and other members of the civil society who support the applicants' causes and claims. Similarly, anti-compliance constituents comprise individuals and groups who oppose the enforcement of a specific international judgment.

Enforcement Motivations

Actors involved in the implementation of international human rights judgments are situated in specific social and institutional contexts from which they draw both social and material motivations influencing their decisions to enforce a human rights judgment. On the basis of these motivations, actors choose either to promote or to obstruct the implementation of a specific human rights judgment. While each judgment – unless explained by habitual enforcement (Hopf, 2010)– will have its own unique sequence of events that will explain what ultimately was decisive for bringing about a particular enforcement outcome, an empirically informed mapping of the typology of motivations is helpful to establish a framework of analysis for organising potential enforcement hurdles or opportunities in specific cases. The mapping of the kinds of anti-enforcement motivations, in particular, is of paramount importance since instances of non-enforcement constitute a systemic and widespread problem across international human rights systems.

The literature on compliance in general is highly relevant to the enforcement of human rights judgments (Downs and George, 2002; Raustiala and Slaughter, 2002; Tallberg, 2002; Wiener, 2004; Dai, 2005). This literature approaches compliance with international law as a matter of the strategic or normative reasons – or combinations thereof – that actors have. Drawing on our empirical investigation of actor-level enforcement motivations for human rights judgments in five different countries, we propose to distinguish between perceived 'audience costs', 'governance costs' and 'normative enforcement motivations' as a typology of motivations relevant for the enforcement of human rights judgments. These costs have material

---

[14] For an example that required the involvement of all 'direct compliers' listed here, cf. the roadmap developed by the Committee of Ministers in the *Aydin v. Turkey* judgment that found systematic torture by police officers (App No. 23178/94), judgment of 25 September 1997 at https://wcd.coe.int/ViewDoc.jsp?id=472455&Site=COE (accessed 30 March 2015).

and social dimensions. They also come with human rights case-specific and general characteristics. In the following we will outline what each of the three sets of motivations comprises.

Audience Costs

In domestic settings with regular democratic elections, strategically defined costs and benefits related to the implementation of international human rights judgments typically take the form of audience costs – that is, the political saliency of the issue area in question determines how enforcement will affect the support political actors receive from dominant domestic groups and voters. At the heart of audience costs in a democratic context is the idea that enforcers want to stay in office (Fearon, 1994; Gaubatz, 1996; Dai, 2005). In the case of some human rights judgments, audience costs can include social costs (i.e., concerns for losing reputation) and extend beyond the domestic polity. In our research in Bulgaria, a country that joined the European Union in 2007 and aims to break with its communist past, for example, we have found that approval from EU authorities was identified as an important factor in decisions relating to the enforcement of human rights judgments.[15] In cases where the social or material benefits from international actors are negligible, however, domestic audience costs would be central. In this respect, regional human rights courts may exert more audience costs than the UN treaty bodies.

Audience costs also depend on the country-specific perception of the issue a judgment raises. Dominant political cultures may be hostile to different kinds of groups. In the European context with established democracies, decision makers are typically more reluctant to comply with human rights judgments that concern the protection of the rights of noncitizens due to fear of backlash from citizens (Dembour, 2003). There are also studies that find countries with ethnic-nationalist ideologies to be more reluctant to enforce human rights judgments concerning minorities (Anagnostou, 2010). In our interviews in Turkey, for example, a government politician identified complying with a judgment on gay rights as incurring significant audience costs compared to other civil and political rights judgments.[16] Conversely, in the United Kingdom, decision makers identify non-compliance with gay rights judgments as incurring important audience costs.[17] In countries where the political culture is generally

---

[15] Authors' interview (Bulgarian lawyer), Sofia, 16 October 2008.

[16] Authors' interview (Turkish politician), Ankara, 6 November 2008.

[17] The enforcement of *Smith and Grady v. United Kingdom* is often explained in terms of the domestic audience costs that would have occurred in the case of non-compliance.

responsive to pressure from civil society, and allows for the active participation of civil society in decision-making mechanisms, civil society actors
(be they pro- or anti-compliance) can significantly alter the audience costs
for decision makers (Simmons, 2009).

Governance Costs

We define governance costs as those costs that arise from domestic
decision-making elites' concern to effectively govern in their sphere of
activity. Governance costs primarily concern maintaining good relationships with other branches of the state. Judges do not want to upset parlia-
ments. Executives do not want to upset judges. Different ministries and
agencies do not want to step onto one another's toes by proving to be too
keen or too obstructive in the implementation of a human rights judgment
that affects the ideologies, practices and policies in place in other parts of
the governance apparatus.

Governance costs, too, can be social or material. Actors may fear for
their reputation and standing within the state apparatus (i.e. judges in relation to politicians, Ministry of Interior in relation to Ministry of Justice),
and worry about a backlash from institutions that disagree with complying with a particular human rights judgment. Governance costs are more
pronounced when spheres of influence within different parts of the state
apparatus overlap and have competing interests or viewpoints on a human
rights case. Unlike domestic audience costs and benefits, which arise due
to the stance that the electorate or interest groups take towards an individual human rights judgment, governance costs and benefits arise from
the need to manage the interests of those who make up the respective state
institutions. Enforcement of human rights judgments may empower one
branch of the state apparatus vis-à-vis another (Benevisti and Downs,
2009). In some cases, the enforcement of international human rights judgments thus amounts to a shift of power, for example, from the executive
branches, such as the Ministry of Interior, to the judiciary.[18] In other cases,
politicians may be reluctant to enforce judgments because of an anticipated backlash due to long-established legal or bureaucratic traditions.
In our interviews with Irish judges, for example, we found that domestic judges were concerned about the implications of taking into account
the case-law of the Strasbourg court in instances in which they believed
it would encroach upon the mandate of the Parliament.[19] In Turkey, on

---

[18] *Othman (Abu Qatada) v. United Kingdom* (App No 8139/09), judgment of 12 January 2012.
[19] Authors' interview (Irish judge), Dublin, 13 May 2009.

the other hand, we found evidence that the Ministry of Justice and the prosecutor's office were unwilling to prosecute members of the Ministry of Interior for their involvement in crimes of torture and unlawful killings (Çalı, 2010).

Normative Enforcement Motivations

Unlike audience costs and governance costs, normative enforcement motivations primarily concern social costs and benefits. They arise from the ideational commitments of enforcers, and from what they consider to be appropriate behaviour. They are, therefore, based on the norms, ideas and values that enforcers hold. Normative motivations may overlap with the audience and governance costs actors perceive. They may also run counter to them, pulling the decision maker in an opposite direction. Decision-makers' normative motivations vary depending on the political regime in power or the judicial culture in place. They can either support the implementation of international human rights judgments (e.g., commitment to the rule of law, human rights, integration, non-discrimination, respect for Court judgments),[20] or be opposed to it (e.g., commitment to national sovereignty, national identity or the primacy of domestic democratic processes).[21] The implementation of individual human rights cases is also shaped by decision makers' normative considerations both at the substantive case level and at the level of general ideas about enforcing human rights judgments. For example, human rights cases that advance women's rights can be resisted both on grounds of family values (a substantive normative objection) and on grounds of state sovereignty (a generic objection to enforcing international court judgments).[22] In domestic contexts where general pro-enforcement normative motivations are not securely anchored, the normative implications of an individual case can become more pronounced and would play a decisive role in an enforcer's attitude towards implementation.

This three-dimensional account of enforcement motivations depicts domestic enforcers of human rights judgments as actors embedded in

---

[20] See, for example, the Parliamentary Debate on the Enforcement of the *Hirst v. UK* Judgment, at www.parliament.uk/business/news/2011/february/mps-debate-voting-by-prisoners/ (accessed 25 April 2012).

[21] See, for example, the reasoning of the Turkish Constitutional Court on the refusal to follow the European Court of Human Rights case law on women's right to identity based on traditional family values of the Turkish society at www.resmigazete.gov.tr/eskiler/2011/10/20111021-8.htm (accessed 1 April 2014).

[22] Ibid.

national contexts who are both carriers of ideas and responsive to the constraints imposed by their environment. While this view assumes that standards of appropriate behaviour are gained through acting in social environments (conceived of having both domestic and international dimensions), it does not hold that the behaviour of actors can be reduced to an examination of the environment itself. Recognising this gap between decision makers' perceptions of the environment and the systematic features of the environment itself (Berman, 1998) makes it possible to develop a more nuanced view about how the remedies required to enforce international human rights judgments have an impact on the perceived costs and benefits of compliance. In the following section we provide an overview of different remedy models and discuss how they interact with the motivations to enforce human rights judgments.

2.3.2   The International Setting: The Institutional Design of International Human Rights Adjudicating Bodies

A broad array of institutions and instruments exist that oversee and induce states' compliance with human rights judgments. There are judicial or quasi-judicial mechanisms and institutions that deliver decisions on individual cases. Mainstream analyses of these international bodies have traditionally focused on whether they deliver legally binding or non-binding judgments. There is, however, no authoritative evidence with regard to whether the binding authority of such judgments makes any significant difference in terms of compliance outcomes (Guzman, 2009;): Some of the non-binding decisions of the Human Rights Committee have been complied with, while other – legally binding – judgments of the European Court of Human Rights and the Inter-American Court of Human Rights have not (Cavallero and Brewer, 2008; Hillebrecht, 2009; Çalı, 2010). While the legally binding nature of judgments is likely to be one factor among others that changes domestic decision makers' compliance calculus and increases the overall likelihood of compliance, it does not necessarily determine the outcome in any one individual case. Instead, any analysis of enforcement processes should take into account the full range of motivations that vary from one setting to the next, and impact on domestic actors' enforcement decisions.

Irrespective of the binding or non-binding nature of international human rights judgments, the international settings within which these judgments are formulated are important for understanding enforcement processes. Different international human rights bodies have different ways of formulating their decisions, and both the form and the content of these implementation recommendations or requirements delineate what is considered as an 'acceptable level' of implementation (Chayes and Chayes, 1993: 201). This is the benchmark against which domestic actors formulate the costs and benefits of enforcement. This perspective relegates the binding/non-binding divide to one factor among others that influence actors' enforcement decisions and instead puts a spotlight on the extent to which the institution delivering the judgment specifies the remedies, and on whether there is a follow-up monitoring mechanism in place that creates opportunities for exerting pressure on decision makers.

An analysis of compliance processes that focuses on the types of remedies international human rights bodies stipulate, as well as on their monitoring powers, echoes academic debate on the types of judicial review at the domestic level. Gardbaum (2001: 743) and Tushnet (2003b: 820; 2008) have pioneered the comparative study of domestic constitutional courts in terms of the strength of their judicial review powers. In their writing, they show that judicial review is a matter of degree in terms of the extent to which the judiciary interferes with the decision-making domains of the legislative and the executive. Judicial review is strongest when courts spell out the terms of compliance in detail, leaving no leeway to implementing actors, and furthermore have the power to enforce these stipulations. Judicial review is regarded as weak when courts do not have the authority to stipulate specific remedies, but instead provide overall guidance to legislatures or to the executive regarding which form of action would be most appropriate. Domestic judiciaries can thus be ranked according to their strength of judicial review, with different types of review offering different advantages and disadvantages for the implementation of domestic judgments.

By analogy, we can make use of this domestic-level continuum between weak and strong types of judicial review to make sense of the different types of human rights adjudication at the international level. International human rights courts or quasi-judicial bodies, however, typically do not have the power to enforce their judgments or to strike out domestic legislation the way their domestic counterparts have. At the international level, models matching the strong version of domestic judicial review therefore do not exist, and any comparative scale has to be adjusted accordingly.

According to Tushnet's classification, weak types of domestic judicial review encompass both mere declarations of rights violation and instances in which courts stipulate 'a requirement that government officials develop plans that hold out some promise of eliminating the constitutional violation within a reasonably short, but unspecified time period' (Tushnet 2003a: 1910). At the international level, the difference between merely declaring a human rights violation, or instead outlining desirable – albeit non-binding – remedial measures is significant in mobilising support for or against implementation. In order to account for these differences, we propose to distinguish between weak, intermediary and strong forms of *international judicial review*:

(1) Weak international judicial review: An international human rights adjudicating body states a rights violation but is not engaged in discussions regarding potential remedies. It does not monitor the reparation of the violation.
(2) Intermediate international judicial review: An international human rights adjudicating body states a rights violation and demands an effective remedy to repair this violation and to prevent violations of the same kind without specifying the type of remedy required. There is a non-judicial system in place monitoring the implementation of the decision.
(3) Strong international judicial review: An international human rights adjudicating body states a rights violation and specifies the type of remedy required to repair this violation, and to prevent future violations of the same kind. The implementation of these remedies is monitored by judicial means.

International Instruments Featuring Weak Judicial Review

At the domestic level, weak systems of judicial review 'openly acknowledge the power of legislatures to provide constitutional interpretations that differ from [...] interpretations provided by the courts' (Tushnet, 2003b: 818). Instruments falling under this category are typically not binding.[23] At the international level, weak forms of judicial review are typically

---

[23] Since the adoption of the Human Rights Act in the United Kingdom and the overall spread of bills of rights, it is difficult to find a national system that consistently features the legislative supremacy described in this statement. However, certain individual elements of national constitutions qualify. The 'Directive Principles of Social Policy' that form part of the Irish Constitution are a case in point: While being included in a written constitution, the rights set out in these principles are merely declaratory: Courts can refer to them in their reasoning regarding other rights, but they are not by themselves justiciable. See also Tushnet (2003a: 1898).

found in the UN treaty monitoring system. The decisions issued by UN treaty bodies in response to individual complaints are not legally binding. Furthermore, these bodies are not engaged in a discussion of what the reparation of a specific rights violation should entail, but merely declare that the respondent state should provide a remedy. This approach leaves a wide margin of discretion to the domestic actors in terms of what implementation measures to take. In this set-up, the preferences of domestic decision makers, and the existing leverage of established pressure group will determine whether and to what extent a decision is enforced. The international human rights adjudicating body therefore does not significantly alter the calculus of domestic decision makers: Implementation remains tied to existing domestic power structures.

There are indications that most international human rights bodies are abandoning a strict weak-review approach to remedies by introducing soft follow-up procedures of their decisions. In response to criticisms from non-governmental organisations, the UN Human Rights Committee, for example, has started to impose a time limit of 180 days following a violation decision to receive information regarding planned remedies from the state concerned. The committee, however, 'wishes' to receive this information rather than demanding it as part of its institutional design.[24] It is left to the state to decide by what means and at what point in time the violation found by the treaty monitoring body will be remedied.[25] This indicates that the UN Human Rights Committee retains its hands-off approach with regard to implementation, and that states that fail to provide the required information will not be ousted from the system.

The African Commission on Human and Peoples' Rights has also originally started as a weak judicial review in line with the view that the duty to ensure the protection of human rights falls on the state authorities (Musila, 2006: 460).[26] That said, the African Commission system,[27] too,

---

[24] See, for example, Views of the Human Rights Committee with respect to Communication No. 1799/2008, CCPR/C/99/D/1799/2008.

[25] The Human Rights Committee (HRC), the Committee Against Torture (CAT), the Committee on the Elimination of Racial Discrimination (CERD) and the Committee on the Elimination of Discrimination Against Women (CEDAW) offer the possibility of individual and interstate complaints.

[26] NGOs holding observer status at the African Commission for Human and Peoples' Rights have the chance to provide input regarding the human rights situation in their respective countries. However, due to the lack of concrete remedies being developed by the Commission, this does not amount to NGOs having a say in rights enforcement.

[27] Rules of Procedure of the African Commission on Human and Peoples' Rights, Rule 112 (2011).

is evolving towards a more intermediate form of judicial review. Under its revised Rules of Procedure, the African Commission on Human and People's Rights has defined a follow-up procedure with regard to the decisions it delivers.

International Instruments Featuring Intermediate Judicial Review

Rather than issuing decisions that leave full discretion to the respondent state in terms of what measures need to be taken to remedy a given human rights violation, some international human rights adjudicating bodies have adopted models of adjudication and enforcement that we refer to as intermediate forms of judicial review.[28] Intermediate forms of judicial review are characterised by the fact that they seek to strike a balance between dictating what enforcement of a right requires, and leaving some 'breathing space' to domestic decision makers by allowing them to choose mechanisms of enforcement that match the requirements of the national or local context. With regard to domestic judicial review, Gardbaum refers to Canada as an example of a country that seeks to find a middle ground between legislative supremacy and effective judicial protection of human rights.[29] In the international context, the equivalent balancing exercise requires finding a middle ground between ensuring effective international rights protection while at the same time respecting the decision-making authority of the domestic judiciaries, legislatures, executives, with meaningful participation from civil society actors.

At the international level, the European human rights system stands out as operating an intermediate form of judicial review. This is discussed in more detail in the section that follows. In Europe, a judicial body (the European Court of Human Rights) and a political body (the Committee of Ministers that is made up of government representatives from each of the forty-seven member states of the Council of Europe) cooperate with each other and with respondent states in order to specify appropriate remedies for a human rights violation. The enforcement process is exclusively

---

[28] See also Rodríguez-Garavito's (2011) concept of 'dialogic activism' that refers to a similar development domestically.

[29] With the introduction of the Charter of Rights and Freedoms in 1982, Canada departed from its earlier model of UK-style parliamentary sovereignty to adopt a system in which the Supreme Court's power of judicial review were significantly expanded. The model does, however, retain a provision that 'allows a legislature to respond to judicial decisions enforcing a constitutional constraint by re-enacting the challenged statute.' The provision authorises legislatures to make statutes effective 'notwithstanding' rights-protective provisions of the Charter. See also Tushnet (2003c: 354) and Porter in this volume.

monitored by the political arm, the Committee of Ministers (Çalı and Koch, 2014). This body has the power to officially declare a case 'closed', thereby marking the end of the implementation process once a judgment has been complied with to the full satisfaction of the Committee of Ministers.[30]

This institutional set-up differs from the early days of the African commission system as well as from the UN treaty monitoring mechanisms in that the mere declaration of a violation and the unspecified call for remedies is replaced by more demanding requirements. In the European system, court judgments limit the range of options the state may choose from in its implementation activities, and an intergovernmental peer review mechanism monitors the implementation process.[31] There is often a space for continuous deliberation for deciding how to implement a human rights judgment. The Department of the Execution of Judgments (which acts as the Secretariat of the Committee of Ministers) asks the respective state to prepare an action plan setting out how it will comply with the judgment, or submit an action report detailing the measures already taken. The action plan has to be agreed upon by the Committee of Ministers before it becomes the definitive road map of implementation. The agreed-upon action plan remains on the agenda of the Committee of Ministers' quarterly monitoring meetings until all provisions it entails are implemented. Individual applicants and non-governmental organisations have access to the whole enforcement process and may provide input to these discussions in the form of written submissions to the Committee of Ministers.[32]

International Instruments Featuring Strong
International Judicial Review

In the domestic context, strong judicial review is often associated with the US Supreme Court (Tushnet, 2003c). This court is equipped with the power to strike down any statute or treaty that it deems to be unconstitutional.

---

[30] See paragraphs 1 and 2 of art. 46 of the European Convention on Human Rights and Fundamental Freedoms: 'The High Contracting Parties undertake to abide by the final judgment of the Court in any case to which they are parties. The final judgment of the Court shall be transmitted to the Committee of Ministers, which shall supervise its execution.'

[31] We elaborate on this in Çalı and Koch 2014.

[32] Rules of the Committee of Ministers for the supervision of the execution of judgments and of the terms of friendly settlements, Adopted by the Committee of Ministers on 10 May 2006 at the 964th meeting of the Ministers' Deputies: https://wcd.coe.int/ViewDoc.jsp?id=999329&BackColorInternet=9999CC&BackColorIntranet=FFBB55&BackColorLogged=FFAC75 (accessed 30 January 2009).

As mentioned before, no international court has powers to strike down domestic legislation, policy or decisions, and the concept of strong judicial review therefore has to be defined by different characteristics at the international than at the domestic level. We propose that the Inter-American regional system, and in particular, the Inter-American Court of Human Rights constitutes an institution that comes closest to an international version of strong judicial review. Why is this the case? Different from the international institutions discussed earlier, the Inter-American Court of Human Rights spells out the measures states have to implement in order to remedy a given violation in an exceptionally detailed manner, thereby leaving no room for any further deliberation as to what the appropriate form of implementation might be.[33] Examples include judgments that require reopening of village schools, medical and psychological treatment for victims or repealing specific pieces of legislation.[34] Based on this, Basch (2007: 14) concludes that the Court has the de facto function of an appellate court. In the context of our argument, it is important to point out that the lack of potential deliberation regarding the exact form of implementation raises the cost of enforcement for reluctant compliers. The system, however, offers particular advantages from the perspective of 'willing compliers' since it allows them to pass far-reaching reforms while diverting any potential criticism to the Inter-American Court of Human Rights.

2.4 Lessons Learnt from the European Context: Domestic Compliance Motivations and International Institutional Design

It is often assumed that the European Human Rights System has a good enforcement record and that this is due to the fact that the court deals with civil and political rights in a region that is characterised by engrained democratic values and generally human rights respecting state authorities (Cavallero and Brewer, 2008). This implies that European states do not have to take demanding measures to enforce the judgments of the European Court of Human Rights. However, a closer look at the European human rights system shows that its member states include a wide range of political regime types, the European Court of Human Rights' CP judgments often

---

[33] This is set out in the text of the Inter-American Convention on Human Rights. See, in particular, art. 1, 2, 50, 51, 63 and 68 of the American Convention on Human Rights.

[34] See, for example, Aloeboetoe v. Suriname, 1993 Inter-Am. Ct. H.R. (ser. C) No. 11, ¶¶ 11–15 (10 September 1993); Plan de Sáánchez Massacre v. Guatemala, Inter-Am. Ct H.R. (ser. C) No. 116, ¶ 32 a)-b), 38, 49.2–49.4 (19 November 2004); *lmonacid-Arellano et al. v. Chile*, Judgement of 26 September 2006 (ser. C) No. 154.

require complex and demanding remedies, and enforcement takes a long
time in old and new members alike (Committee of Ministers, 2009, 2015).
This suggests that motivational alliance with human rights ideas, whilst
part of the story, does not adequately explain human rights compliance
dynamics in Europe.

In our qualitative investigation of actor-level enforcement motivations
we found strong system-level support for implementing human rights
judgments meshed with anti-enforcement motivations. Our interviews in
Germany, Ireland and the United Kingdom demonstrate that the decision
makers in the older European democracies view the Council of Europe both
as a way to affirm their social identities as human rights respecting states
and as a way to spread human rights, democracy and the rule of law among
the Council's newer members and beyond. The judgments of the European
Court of Human Rights are regarded as non-partisan and objective ways of
pressuring other states to implement human rights law. In aiming to encourage the newcomers to develop structures that respect human rights, these
older democracies feel compelled to set an example and enforce the judgments against themselves. For older European democracies, therefore, there
are both normative costs and international audience costs involved in *not*
enforcing judgments against themselves. The interviews we conducted in
2010 in Turkey and Bulgaria, two transitional states at the Eastern periphery
of Europe, on the other hand, show that, at the time, actors in these countries
were motivated to improve domestic governance and replacing previous
communist or authoritarian traditions. More generally they strove to belong
to a zone of democracy and rule of law and regard enforcement of human
rights judgments as means of achieving this regional belonging. They too
saw normative and audience costs in not respecting the judgments.

Decision makers in both established and newer democracies, however,
also hold anti-compliance motivations. Elites in old democracies with
well-established rule of law systems typically have a high degree of trust
in their own systems and tend to view the European Court of Human
Rights as intruding into well-established domestic decision-making procedures.[35] This perception increases the governance costs of complying
with human rights judgments. Along similar lines, democratic decision
makers contest the decisions of the European Court of Human Rights

[35] Hoffmann, Lord (2009) 'The Universality of Human Rights', Judicial Studies Board Annual
Lecture. London: Judicial Studies Board. Available at: www.judiciary.gov.uk/media/
speeches/2009/speech-lord-hoffman-19032009. Hale, Baroness (2011) 'Common Law and
Convention Law: The Limits to Interpretation', *European Human Rights Law Review*, 5,
534–543.

on normative grounds by arguing that the Court lacks the legitimacy to initiate far-reaching changes in democratic domestic settings.[36] This is especially the case when Court judgments stipulate complex remedies that require policy changes that would normally be decided upon by domestic legislatures. In the case of transitional states, anti-enforcement motivations tend to be rooted in arguments concerning the need to protect either national identity or ideologies that are entrenched in the domestic political, judicial or bureaucratic culture.

In both democratic and transitional contexts in Europe, therefore, audience, governance and normative costs for enforcing judgments at the system level are not uniformly pro-enforcement. To this, one also has to add costs that are triggered by specific cases. As we discussed in the earlier section, the policy issues behind a specific judgment may accentuate the audience and governance costs or give rise to anti-enforcement normative motivations. The institutional design of the European human rights system impacts upon these perceived costs and benefits both through its delineation of enforcement requirements and its monitoring: On the one hand, its dialogic way of arriving at enforcement requirements tends to build domestic ownership of the agreed-upon implementation measures. On the other hand, keeping the unimplemented cases on the agenda of an intergovernmental peer review mechanism for an indefinite period of time prevents any case from 'falling under the radar' and constitutes a continuous lobbying opportunity for domestic rights proponents. The next section discusses these mechanisms in more detail.

2.4.1 The Deliberative Compliance Model and the Enforcement of CP Rights in the European Context

In Europe, the judicial review carried out by the European Court of Human Rights plays an important role in influencing the perceived normative and governance costs of compliance by creating a certain 'breathing space' for domestic governments, especially in cases that require complex and demanding remedies. Examples include judgments that require changes

---

[36] For example, see the debates in particular in the United Kingdom: 'European Judges have no right to rule on prisoner voting, says Grieve', *The Guardian*, 2 November 2011; and Lord Hoffman's Foreword to *Bringing Rights Back Home* (Policy Exchange, February 2011); (Judicial Studies Board Annual Lecture 2009, *The Universality of Human Rights*). Jack Straw, former UK Home Secretary: House of Commons Debate, 10 February 2011, Hansard Col 504; Dominic Raab, (2011) Strasbourg in the Dock: Prison Voting, Human Rights and the Case for Democracy (London Civitas).

to nationalisation or housing policy, or judgments demanding prison reforms.[37] By not dictating the exact terms of these policy changes but instead providing both expertise (the Secretariat of the Committee of Ministers) and a forum for discussion (the quarterly human rights meetings), the European system recognises the value of arriving at appropriate remedies through domestic democratic processes and encourages ownership of implementation measures by domestic actors. For this reason, we propose to call the enforcement model in Europe, which we categorised as entailing an intermediary form of judicial review, the 'deliberative compliance model'.

In order to assess how domestic ownership of judgments is created in the European context, we need to provide a more detailed account of the implementation mechanisms in place. Formally, there are three types of compliance requirements in the European human rights system: payment of compensation, individual measures and general measures. These become more demanding in the order listed here, and the more demanding they are, the higher are the compliance costs they entail. The payment of compensation aims to remedy the financial and emotional damage suffered by an applicant as a result of a human rights violation. States are required to pay compensation within three months of the final decision. *Individual measures* aim to reinstate the status of the applicant to her position prior to the relevant human rights violation, or to erase the on-going consequences of a violation for the applicant herself. They are case-specific. They may include the erasure of criminal charges from records, the halting of deportation orders, the permission of a parent to have access to her child, or the reopening of domestic proceedings before domestic courts. *General measures* aim to prevent the recurrence of similar violations in the future. The court resorts to general measures when a given violation is considered to not be a 'one-off' incident, but rather part of a systemic problem.[38] Such problems may require changes in legislation, regulation or administrative practice and policy, as well as institutional reform, training of public authorities and awareness-raising of human rights judgments

---

[37] Cf. *Sarica and Dilaver v. Turkey* (no. 11765/05, 17 May 2010) (nationalization of property), *Saghinadze and others v. Georgia* (no. 18768/05, 27 May 2010), *Dokic v. Bosnia Herzegovina* (no. 6518/04, 27 May 2010) (housing policy), *Kalashnikov v. Russia* (no. 47095/99, 15 October 2002) (reform of prison conditions).

[38] In the language of the Committee of Ministers, the former are called 'isolated cases' and the latter are called 'lead cases'. Lead cases point to the fact that other similar violations are imminent due to systemic shortcomings of the domestic system, and that the state has to address these systemic problems in order to comply with the judgment.

through their translation and dissemination, all of which have financial implications.

The most significant feature of European Court of Human Rights judgments with regard to enforcement is that the Court does not have to spell out the compliance requirements for each and every case. Judgments come in three different ways: First, many of the human rights judgments in Europe are 'declaratory' judgments. In these cases, the Court establishes that there has been a rights violation and determines the amount of compensation and legal costs to be paid to the applicant. It leaves it to the state to decide on the best means to remedy the broader consequences of the violation, and to prevent its recurrence through appropriate individual and general measures.[39] Second, alongside awards for compensation, the European Court of Human Rights goes a step further and indicates what other individual or general measures should be taken. For example, it stipulates that a particular law should be changed or that an applicant should be provided with a specific remedy, such as reinstitution or recognition of status.[40] Third, and most recently, the Court has adopted what is called the 'pilot judgment procedure'.[41] Under this procedure, the Court not only identifies a violation of the Convention, but also an underlying systemic problem that leads to a large number of identical cases from a single country.[42] In the judgment, it offers assistance to the state and the Committee of Ministers in finding an appropriate general solution that would address the entire group of cases. It allows for a reasonable amount of time for the state to set up a generally effective remedy and for the Committee of Ministers to monitor it. During this period it adjourns the litigation of identical

---

[39] It is also common for the Court to declare that the finding of a violation in itself is just satisfaction for the applicant. See, for example, *Castells v. Spain* (11798/85, 23 April 1992).

[40] See, for example, *ÜnalTekeli v. Turkey* (29865/96, 16 November 2004) which indicates that the Civil Code needs to be amended to ensure equality between men and women in choosing their names in marriage and *Gorgulu v. Germany* (no. 74969/01, 26 May 2004) indicating that a father who was denied custody of his child by domestic proceedings should be given access to his child to remedy the violation of his right to family life.

[41] The first case in which the pilot judgment procedure was applied was *Broniowski v. Poland* (31443/96, 28 September 2004).

[42] The pilot judgment procedure has been applied to identical cases that reveal systemic problems in a number of countries. Examples include access to property in Northern Cyprus (*Xenides-Arestis v. Turkey*, no. 46347/99, 22 December 2005), length of proceedings and de facto expropriation in Italy (*Scordino v. Italy*, no. 36813/97, 29 March 2006), the system of property restitution in Albania (*Driza v. Albania*, no. 33771/02, 13 November 2007), compulsory letting and compulsory sale of property in the Slovak Republic (*UrbárskaObe cTrenčianskeBiskupice v. Slovakia*, no. 74258/01, 27 November 2007), and inadequate procedures in prison discipline regimes in Turkey (*Gülmez v. Turkey*, no. 16330/02, judgment, 20 May 2008).

cases and waits for domestic remedies to be installed and implemented. However, it retains the right to reopen adjourned applications if the state fails to provide an adequate remedy for such cases at the national level.

2.4.2 *Advantages and Drawbacks of the Deliberative Compliance Model*

All three forms of judgments that have been outlined leave a certain leeway for the state and the Committee of Ministers in their respective implementation and monitoring tasks in that they allow for the deliberation of what remedies would be appropriate both at the national level and in the context of the Committee of Ministers peer review system. This institutional practice is based on the idea that supranational human rights protection in Europe is subsidiary to national human rights protection and that (democratic) states are better able to assess human-rights-related compliance requirements than an international body (Leach, 2001: 93; Carozza, 2003). Under a strictly juridical model of enforcement, there are obvious difficulties with this set-up. The discretion left to the state and the peer review body contains the risk of 'watering down' the real effects of the judgments and may encourage backdoor diplomatic negotiations about appropriate remedies. When compliance requirements are left ambiguous, states that aim to limit the domestic effects of supranational human rights judgments can use this system to their advantage.

That said, even though the European Human Rights system allows for a space to deliberate how a judgment should be complied with, this does not amount to a purely political compliance process marked by interstate bargaining and diplomatic negotiations. Instead, the combination of well-reasoned human rights judgments and political deliberations often amounts to a predictable process where similar cases against all countries are treated alike.[43] In stipulating compliance requirements, the Committee

---

[43] The Committee of Ministers issues resolutions on compliance requirements regarding repetitive problems and publishes 'best practice' documents outlining compliance requirements in similar cases. See, for example, Recommendation No. R (2000)2 of the Committee of Ministers to member states on the re-examination or reopening of certain cases at the domestic level following judgments of the European Court of Human Rights(*Adopted by the Committee of Ministers on 19 January 2000 at the 694th meeting of the Ministers' Deputies)*; Recommendation CM/Rec(2004)6 of the Committee of Ministers to member states on the improvement of domestic remedies *(adopted by the Committee of Ministers on 12 May 2004 at its 114th Session)*; CM/Inf/DH(2007)33 Information Document 'Round Table on "Non-enforcement of domestic courts decisions in member states: general measures to comply with European Court Judgements"' *(Document prepared by the Department for the Execution of the Judgements of the European Court of Human Rights)*; Recommendation CM/Rec(2008)2 of the Committee of Ministers to member states on

of Ministers is constrained by the texts of the judgments in which the Court identifies failures in human rights protection. In the European context, the space of deliberation left to state authorities and to the Committee of Ministers can therefore be seen in a positive light. It ensures that the compliance process sets out realistic requirements that lead to eventual and in most cases effective implementation. The lack of a top-down approach to complex and demanding remedies increases the legitimacy of the Court in the eyes of respondent states (Cali et al. 2013). The active involvement in the process of identifying suitable compliance requirements allows state authorities to develop a sense of ownership of this process, and this in turn increases the likelihood of effective compliance. Furthermore, cases are officially closed only when a state has fulfilled the agreed-upon compliance requirements. This makes it impossible for a state to simply 'sit out' unpopular court judgments – through recurring discussions of open cases at the level of the Committee of Ministers, compliance pressure is kept up for an unlimited period of time.

Despite these positive features, the danger of extremely slow or negligent compliance still exists in this system,[44] and there is no highly developed toolbox of sanctions to react to such instances. It is possible to expel a state from the Council of Europe by majority vote, but this constitutes an extreme measure that has never been reverted to in the history of the organisation. The only practical pressurising tool available to the Committee of Ministers is therefore the public exposure of states that are guilty of slow or negligent implementation processes at the Committee's regular quarterly meetings. These tools are aimed at normatively persuading the reluctant compliers and increasing the audience costs for not complying. The Committee of Ministers undertakes this public exposure by issuing 'interim resolutions' that point to its dissatisfaction with specific aspects of a given compliance process.[45] Protocol 14 to the European Convention

---

efficient domestic capacity for rapid execution of judgments of the European Court of Human Rights *(Adopted by the Committee of Ministers on 6 February 2008 at the 1017th meeting of the Ministers' Deputies).*

[44] Report of Committee of Ministers on Slow and Negligent Judgments. *Activity Report: Sustained action to ensure the effectiveness of the implementation of the ECHR at national and European levels* (as adopted by the CDDH at its 66th meeting, 25–28 March 2008). www.coe.int/t/e/human_rights/cddh/3._committees/01.%20steering%20 committee%20for%20human%20rights%20%28cddh%29/05.%20meeting%20reports/ 66thAddI_en.asp (accessed 9 April 2010).

[45] For a compilation of interim resolutions by the Council of Europe, see, Collection of Interim Resolutions: 2009-2015: Document prepared by the Department for the Execution of Judgments of the European Court of Human Rights

on Human Rights constitutes a relatively recent innovation that complements the traditional tools of diplomatic pressure and public shaming by new institutional procedures. It allows the Committee of Ministers to take 'infringement proceedings' against a state that fails to cooperate with it.[46] These proceedings enable the European Court of Human Rights to play a more direct role in the compliance process by empowering it to determine to what extent a state has complied with a court judgment. Given that the procedure has only recently been introduced, it is difficult to assess its effectiveness in inducing compliance.

The on-going monitoring process at the Committee of Ministers encourages eventual compliance with court judgments. The lack of time pressure further allows domestic authorities to come to terms with judgments that are particularly difficult to implement due to particularly high audience, governance or normative costs. Dorf and Sabel's account of subnational mechanisms that they describe as 'democratic experimentalism' shows important procedural similarities to the European deliberative compliance model:

> Democratic experimentalism requires the [subnational] social actors, separately and in exchange with each other, to take constitutional considerations into account in their decision making. The administrative agency assists the actors even while monitoring their performance by scrutinising the reactions of each to relevant proposals by the others. The courts then determine whether the agency has met its obligations to foster and generalise the results of this information pooling. (Dorf and Sabel, 1998: 268)

Irrespective of the different fields and levels of application, these striking conceptual parallels support our argument that the relative success of the European model can best be explained by pointing to the space it leaves for deliberation, cooperation and continuous information exchange between the adjudicatory body and the respondent actors, all of which taken together plays a role in the constitution of the costs of enforcement.

When thinking about the application of lessons learnt from the European context to other regional contexts, it is important to note that the European Court of Human Rights' reputation remains largely undamaged by instances of delayed or slow enforcement. This is due to the fact that the Court's judgments themselves are not intrusive in

https://rm.coe.int/CoERMPublicCommonSearchServices/DisplayDCTMContent? documentId=090000168059ddb0 (accessed 14 September 2016).

[46] See Art. 16 of Protocol No. 14 to the Convention for the Protection of Human Rights and Fundamental Freedoms, amending the control system of the Convention http:// conventions.coe.int/Treaty/EN/Treaties/html/194.htm (accessed 9 April 2015).

terms of the remedies they impose, and that the Court does not have any formal responsibility to monitor compliance with its own judgments. For this juri-political task-sharing to work in other regions of the world or internationally, the supranational judicial body in question has to be held in high esteem by the intergovernmental body so that the decisions handed down by one institution are not compromised by the other. In addition, judgments issued by the court have to be clear and well-reasoned enough to allow for a reasonable assessment of compliance requirements. Admittedly, the rich case law of the European Court of Human Rights, with more than ten thousand judgments in the past fifty years, also contributes to the process of identifying adequate remedies. We must note, however, that the institutional space for ownership and deliberation for compliance with judgments does not always ensure compliance. That is, a clear unwillingness to comply with a human rights judgment due to a combination of hostile motivations cannot at all times be altered. This would lead to unimplemented judgments. Those judgments, however, remain on the agenda of the Committee of Ministers.

2.5 Conclusion

This chapter has argued that the challenges inherent in the implementation of CP and ESC rights share more commonalities than is currently acknowledged in the literature. In arguing that the respective strength of judicial review is a defining feature of international human rights enforcement mechanisms, it holds that both the design of international enforcement systems and the dynamics of domestic enforcement motivations – with the former impacting upon the latter – constitute two crucial factors influencing compliance processes and outcomes, irrespective of the type of rights violation being adjudicated. The design of the international enforcement system, in particular, influences the degree of ownership of the enforcement process by governments and the degree of participation by non-governmental organisations in the specification of appropriate remedies and monitoring activities.

The European example illustrates that the design of a given international (or in this case regional) system can have a constitutive impact on domestic compliance dynamics. The design of the European deliberative model grants states a margin of discretion in the specification of remedies. This tends to increase domestic actors' ownership of the implementation process. In the case of Europe, the potential disadvantages of having states participate in the specification of remedies are offset by the institutional design of the implementation and remedy regime. The European system further features an increasing array of opportunities for non-governmental organisations to participate in the specification of compliance requirements. Such participation has the potential of influencing audience costs as well as preventing risks of under-compliance.

When thinking about the enforcement of economic and social rights, the deliberative model we presented has some important advantages: It allows states to realistically assess what measures need to be taken to remedy rights violations and provides non-governmental organisations with entry points to influence early stage decisions regarding suitable remedies. By affording states more ownership of compliance decisions it increases the legitimacy of the process in the eyes of respondent states and has the potential to offset backlashes against enforcement. However, it is important to bear in mind that the European Court of Human Rights' well-developed and well-reasoned jurisprudence regarding CP rights acts as a safeguard against domestic actors obstructing the enforcement process. In the case of ESC rights adjudication, too, well-reasoned judgments with adequate guidance regarding suitable remedies would be crucial.

The design of supranational compliance regimes and the perceived costs of compliance need to be taken into account together when assessing the relative merits of different compliance-inducing strategies for non-governmental organisations. Regime design plays a role in whether and to what extent governmental and non-governmental actors can participate in the specification of remedies. The participation of non-governmental organisations in this process should be encouraged both by adjudicatory bodies and by respondent states. Through monitoring and publicising the measures taken by governments in response to supranational human rights judgments, non-governmental organisations can furthermore expose states that try to limit the implementation process to a superficial engagement with the issues at hand.

In terms of influencing domestic compliance processes, the key lesson of this chapter is that non-governmental organisations should move from a paradigm of strategic litigation to one focusing on the enforcement of judgments. Increased participation in the formulation and monitoring of remedies is central to this paradigm change. This is especially important when litigation concerns marginalised communities and disadvantaged groups that tend to be ignored by respondent states, or when remedies involve high compliance costs that are not obvious to the general public.

In such cases, rather than expecting the judicial decision to directly bring about enforcement, it is advisable to factor in compliance strategies even before the judicial litigation process starts.

References

Alston, Philip (1982), 'A Third Generation of Solidarity Rights: Progressive Development or Obfuscation of International Human Rights Law?', *Netherlands International Law Review*, 29(3), 307–322.

Alston, Philip and Gerard Quinn (1987), 'The Nature and Scope of States Parties' Obligations under the International Covenant on Economic, Social and Cultural Rights', *Human Rights Quarterly*, 9(2), 156–229.

Anagnostou, Dia (2010), 'Does European Human Rights Law Matter? Implementation and Domestic Impact of Strasbourg Court Judgments on Minority-Related Policies', *International Journal of Human Rights*, 14(5), 721–743.

Baluarte, David and Christian De Vos (2010), *From Judgment to Justice: Implementing International and Regional Human Rights Decisions* (New York: Open Society Foundations).

Basch, Fernando Felipe (2007), 'The Doctrine of the Inter-American Court of Human Rights Regarding States' Duty to Punish Human Rights Violations and Its Dangers', *American University International Law Review*, 23(1), 195–230.

Benvenisti, Eyal, and George W. Downs (2009), 'National courts, domestic democracy, and the evolution of international law', *European Journal of International Law* 20(1), 59–72.

Berman, Sheri (1998), *The Social Democratic Moment: Ideas and Politics in the Making in Interwar Europe* (Cambridge, MA: Harvard University Press).

Beyers, Jan (2005), 'Multiple Embeddedness and Socialization in Europe: The Case of Council Officials', *International Organisation*, 59(4), 899–936.

Çalı, Başak (2010), 'The Logics of Supranational Human Rights Litigation, Official Acknowledgment, and Human Rights Reform: The Southeast Turkey Cases before the European Court of Human Rights, 1996–2006', *Law and Social Inquiry*, 35(2), 311–337.

Çalı, Başak, Anne Koch and Nicola Bruch (2013), 'The Legitimacy of Human Rights Courts: A Grounded Interpretivist Analysis of the European Court of Human Rights', *Human Rights Quarterly* 35(4), 955–984.

Çalı, Başak and Anne Koch (2014), 'Foxes Guarding the Foxes? Peer Review of Human Rights Judgments by the Committee of Ministers of the Council of Europe', *Human Rights Law Review*, 14 (2), 301–325.

Cardenas, Sonia (2007), *Conflict and Compliance: State Responses to International Human Rights Pressure* (Philadelphia, PA: Pennsylvania University Press).

Carozza, Paolo G. (2003), 'Subsidiarity as a Structural Principle of International Human Rights Law', *American Journal of International Law*, 97, 38–79.

Cavallaro, James and Stephanie Erin Brewer (2008), 'Re-evaluating Regional Human Rights Litigation in the Twenty First Century: The Case of the Inter American Court', *American Journal of International Law*, 102, 768–827.

Chayes, Abram, and Antonia Handler Chayes (1993), 'On compliance', *International organization* 47(2), 175–205.

Council of Europe Committee of Ministers (2009), *Supervision of the Execution of Judgments of the European Court of Human Rights: 3rd Annual Report* (Strasbourg: Directorate General of Human Rights and Legal Affairs).

(2015), *Supervision of the Execution of Judgments of the European Court of Human Rights: 9th Annual Report* (Strasbourg: Directorate General of Human Rights and Legal Affairs).

Crawford, James (2002), *The International Law Commission's Articles on State Sovereignty* (Cambridge: Cambridge University Press).

Dai, Xinjuan (2005), 'Why Comply? The Domestic Constituency Mechanism', *International Organization*, 59(2), 363–398.

(2007), *International Institutions and National Processes* (Cambridge: Cambridge University Press).

Dembour, Marie-Benedicte (2003), 'Human Rights Law and National Sovereignty in Collusion: The Plight of Quasi-Nationals at Strasbourg', *Netherlands Quarterly of Human Rights*, 21(1), 63–98.

Dixon, Rosalind (2007), 'Creating Dialogue about Socioeconomic Rights: Strong-Form versus Weak-Form Judicial Review Revisited', *International Journal of Constitutional Law*, 5(3), 391–418.

Dorf, Michael C. and Charles F. Sabel (1998), 'A Constitution of Democratic Experimentalism', *Columbia Law Review*, 98(2), 267–473.

Downs, George W. and Michael A. Jones (2002), 'Reputation, Compliance and International Law', *Journal of Legal Studies*, 31(1), 595–115.

Fearon, James D. (1994), 'Domestic Political Audiences and the Escalation of International Disputes', *American Political Science Review*, 88(3), 577–592.

Gardbaum, Stephen (2001), 'The New Commonwealth Model of Constitutionalism', *American Journal of Comparative Law*, 49, 707–760.

Gaubatz, Kurt Taylor (1996), 'Democratic States and Commitment in International Relations', *International Organization*, 50(1), 109–139.

Gauri, Varun and Daniel Brinks (eds.) (2008), *Courting Social Justice. Judicial Enforcement of Social and Economic Rights in the Developing World* (Cambridge: Cambridge University Press).

Gloppen, Siri (2009), 'Legal Enforcement of Social Rights: Enabling Conditions and Impact Assessment', *Erasmus Law Review*, 2(4), 465–480.

Goodman, Ryan and Derek Jinks (2008), 'Incomplete Internationalization and Compliance with International Law', *European Journal of International Law*, 19(4), 725–748.

Guzman, Andrew (2009), *How International Law Works: A Rational Choice Theory* (Oxford University Press).

Hillebrecht, Courtney (2014), *Domestic Politics and International Human Rights Tribunals: The Problem of Compliance* (Cambridge: Cambridge University Press).

Hopf, Ted (2010), 'The logic of habit in international relations', *European Journal of International Relations* 16(4), 539–561.

Langford, Malcolm (ed.) (2008), *Social Rights Jurisprudence. Emerging Trends in International and Comparative Law* (Cambridge: Cambridge University Press).

Leach, Philip (2001), *Taking a Case to the European Court of Human Rights* (London: Blackstone Press).

Merali, Isfahan and Valerie Oosterveldeds (2001), *Giving Meaning to Economic, Social, and Cultural Rights* (Philadelphia: University of Philadelphia Press).

Meron, Theodor (1986), 'On a Hierarchy of International Human Rights', *American Journal of International Law*, 80, 1–23.

Mowbray, Alastair (2004), *The Development of Positive Obligations under the European Convention on Human Rights by the European Court of Human Rights* (Oxford: Hart Publishing).

Murray, Rachael and Debra, Long (2015), *The Implementation of the Findings of the African Commission on Human and Peoples Rights* (Cambridge University Press).

Musila, M. Godfrey (2006), 'The Right to an Effective Remedy under the African Charter on Uman and Peoples' Rights', *African Human Rights Law Journal*, 6(2), 442–464.

Mutua, Makau (1999), 'The African Human Rights Court: A Two-Legged Stool?', *Human Rights Quarterly*, 21(2), 342–363.

Palmer, Elizabeth (2009), 'Protecting Socio-Economic Rights through the European Convention on Human Rights: Trends and Developments at the European Court of Human Rights', *Erasmus Law Review*, 2(4), 397–425.

Raustiala, Kal and Anne-Marie Slaughter (2002), 'International Law, International Relations and Compliance', in Walter Carlsnaes, Thomas Risse and Beth A. Simmons (eds.), *Handbook of International Relations* (London: Sage Publications), 538–558.

Roach, Kent (2008), 'The challenges of crafting remedies for violations of socio-economic rights' in Malcolm Langford (ed.) *Social Rights Jurisprudence: Emerging Trends in International and Comparative Law* (New York: Cambridge University Press), 46–58.

Rodríguez-Garavito, César (2011), 'Beyond the Courtroom: The Impact of Judicial Activism on Socioeconomic Rights in Latin America', *Texas Law Review*, 89(7), 2011.

Saito, Natsu Taylor (1996), 'Beyond Civil Rights: Considering "Third Generation" International Human Rights Law in the United States', *The University of Miami Inter-American Law Review*, 28(2), 387–412.

Simmons, Beth (2009), *Mobilising Human Rights: International Law in Domestic Politics* (New York: Cambridge University Press).

Tallberg, Jonas (2002), 'Paths to Compliance: Enforcement, Management and the European Union', *International Organisation*, 56(3), 609–643.

Tushnet, Mark (2003a), 'Forms of Judicial Review as Expressions of Constitutional Patriotism', *Law and Philosophy*, 22(3/4), 353–379.

(2003b), 'Social Welfare Rights and the Forms of Judicial Review', *Texas Law Review*, 82, 1895–1919.

(2003c), 'New Forms of Judicial Review and the Persistence of Rights- and Democracy-Based Worries', *Wake Forest Law Review*, 38, 813–838.

(2008), *Weak Courts, Strong Rights: Judicial Review and Social Welfare Rights in Comparative Constitutional Law* (Princeton, NJ: Princeton University Press).

Wiener, Antje (2004), 'Contested Compliance: Interventions on the Normative Structure of World Politics', *European Journal of International Relations*, 1(2), 189–234.

Beyond Enforcement: Assessing and Enhancing Judicial Impact

CÉSAR RODRÍGUEZ-GARAVITO

3.1 Introduction

At approximately 2 p.m. on October 20, 2016, Justice Jorge Iván Palacio, a judge of the Constitutional Court of Colombia, approached the podium to open a remarkable public hearing in a remarkable place. The hearing was a continuation of the monitoring process of one of the most important rulings of one of the most activist courts regarding economic and social rights (ESR). In handing down this decision in 2008, the court ordered structural injunctions and undertook the long process of monitoring compliance with its orders, in order to address the structural causes of failures in the healthcare system. The hearing took place in Quibdó, on the Pacific Coast the capital of the poorest province of Colombia whose hospital was falling to pieces, as we had confirmed in a visit with the court the same day.

In spite of the evidence that demonstrated how much was left to be done to fulfill the right to health, the hearing also made clear to all of us in attendance the impact that eight years of court intervention had had. The decision and monitoring process set off legislative and administrative reforms that substantially improved health services, as the minister of health recognized in his presentation. In addition, it placed the issue

César Rodríguez-Garavito is Executive Director of Dejusticia and Associate Professor of Law at the University of los Andes (Colombia).

This chapter is a revised version of Rodríguez-Garavito (2011a). I am grateful to Camila Soto and Carolina Bernal for superb research assistance. For comments on earlier drafts of this chapter, I would like to thank Daniel Brinks, Jackie Dugard, Siri Gloppen, Malcolm Langford, and Rodrigo Uprimny. I am particularly indebted to my colleague Diana Rodríguez-Franco for her decisive contribution to the coauthored case study that laid the empirical foundation for the broader research project presented in this chapter (see Rodríguez-Garavito and Rodríguez-Franco 2015). I gratefully acknowledge permission from the Texas Law Review Association to reprint excerpts from Rodríguez-Garavito (2011a).

of health crisis at the center of media and public policy debate, as analysts and special masters appointed by the court for the case highlighted in our presentations, and as the presence of cameras and important media outlets in the event demonstrated. Also, the court managed to create a dialogue between diverse social and professional sectors involved in the health system, from doctors to patients and human rights nongovernmental organizations (NGOs), who presented themselves before the court during the long day.

Although the Colombian Constitutional Court (CCC) in general, and its ruling on the right to health in particular, embodies an especially visible and ambitious form of judicial activism on ESR, the court's actions can be viewed as part of a broader trend evident in other countries of the Global South, toward the judicial enforcement of such rights in contexts of stark deprivation and inequality (Bilchitz, 2013; Bonilla, 2013; Rodríguez-Garavito and Rodríguez-Franco, 2015). A variety of constitutionalism that has developed largely in the Global South expands the concept of human rights and the role of courts in protecting them, so as to include ESR alongside civil rights as justiciable legal provisions. Although initially raising doubts among scholars (Sunstein, 1996) and advocates (Roth, 2004), such "Southern constitutionalism" has gradually been transnationalized (Rodríguez-Garavito, 2011a). As evident in the chapters in this volume, numerous governments, courts, and NGOs in both the North and the South have promoted legal instruments, doctrines, and strategies to make ESR justiciable. In a reverse legal transplant, the idea of enforceable ESR has been embraced by some of its former critics and incorporated into debates in US and European constitutional theory (Dixon, 2007; Fredman, 2008; Michelman, 2009; Sunstein, 2004). Among the best-known examples of this trend is the jurisprudence of India's Supreme Court, which has addressed structural social problems such as hunger and illiteracy and has been accompanied by the appointment of commissioners that monitor the judgments' implementation (Chitalkar and Gauri in this volume; Muralidhar, 2008; Rodríguez-Garavito, forthcoming; Shankar and Mehta, 2008). Similarly, the South African Constitutional Court has become a central institutional forum for promoting rights such as housing and health and for nudging the state to take actions against the economic and social legacy of apartheid (Langford and Kahanovitzs in this volume; Langford et al., 2013; Liebenberg, 2010).

In Latin America, judicial activism on ESR has become increasingly prominent over the past two decades. In countries as different as

Brazil and Costa Rica, courts have decisively shaped the provision of fundamental social services such as healthcare (Ferraz, 2011; Wilson, 2011). In Argentina, some courts have undertaken structural cases and experimented with public mechanisms to monitor the implementation of activist judgments such as *Verbitsky* (on prison overcrowding) and *Riachuelo* (on environmental degradation) (CELS, 2008; Fairstein, Kletzel, and García, 2010; Sigal, Morales, and Rossi in this volume). In Colombia, a particularly activist and innovative constitutional court has stretched the limits of the civil law tradition by aggregating, on its own initiative, thousands of individual constitutional complaints (*tutelas*) on ESR violations and handing down collective rulings with long-term, structural injunctive remedies to attend to them. By declaring such situations as "unconstitutional state of affairs," the Colombian Court has launched multiyear participatory processes to monitor compliance with its rulings on the rights of, among others, prisoners in overcrowded detention facilities, patients seeking treatments and medicines from the dysfunctional healthcare system (Lamprea, 2015; Rodríguez-Garavito, 2013; Yamin, Parra, and Gianella, 2011), and millions internally displaced persons (Rodríguez-Garavito and Rodríguez-Franco, 2015).

The literature on the justiciability of ESR has multiplied apace with the proliferation of activist rulings. Two angles of analysis have dominated this scholarship. First, some key contributions have concentrated on making a theoretical case for the justiciability of ESR, in light of the demands of democratic theory and the reality of social contexts marked by deep economic and political inequalities (Arango, 2005; Bilchitz, 2007; Gargarella, 2011). Second, a number of works have entered into discussion from the perspective of human rights doctrine, in order to give greater precision to judicial standards for upholding ESR, and to boost their utilization by judicial organs and supervisory bodies at both the national and international level (Abramovich and Courtis, 2004; Coomans, 2006; International Commission of Jurists, 2008; Langford, 2009).

These perspectives have advanced considerably in the conceptual elucidation and practical impetus of the justiciability of ESR. Nevertheless, their emphasis on the production phase of judgments has created a blind spot, both analytical and practical: the implementation stage of rulings. For this reason, there is a paucity of systematic studies on the fate of judicial decisions on ESR rights such as the above-mentioned ruling of the CCC on the healthcare system. Beyond the courtroom, what happens to the orders contained in these judgments? To what extent do public officials adopt the conduct required by courts to protect a given ESR? What impact do the rulings have on the state, civil society, social movements, and public opinion? Ultimately, do they contribute to the realization of ESC rights?

A budding area of scholarship seeks to tackle these questions. Some contributions to this literature have offered domestic or comparative quantitative assessments of the effects of ESR rulings (Gauri, 2010; Gauri and Brinks, 2008). Others have zoomed in on rulings on a specific right – notably the right to health – in order to offer detailed comparisons of effects across jurisdictions (Yamin and Gloppen, 2011). Yet others have surveyed national and international courts' practice (Rodríguez-Garavito and Kauffman, 2014) or detailed case studies to extract analytical conclusions on the implementation and efficacy of ESR rulings (see the chapters in this volume as well as Dugard and Langford, 2011; Langford, 2003; Rodríguez-Garavito, 2011a; Rodríguez-Garavito and Rodríguez-Franco, 2015; Uprimny and García, 2004).

3.1.1   Enforcement and Impact

Some of these contributions, however, tend to conflate two analytically distinct issues: (1) whether or not the government and other actors targeted by a given ruling on ESR actually comply with the court's orders, and (2) whether or not the ruling contribute to the fulfillment of the right in question. In other words, they oftentimes lump together the questions on the *enforcement* of a ruling and the one on its broader *impact*.

The fact that these questions are analytically separate becomes evident if we examine the four possible combinations of answers to them, as shown in Figure 3.1. From left to right, combination I entails a ruling that is not implemented and has no other effects. These cases are victories on paper for the litigants who run into implementation obstacles (typically lack of government will or capacity to provide the good or service ordered by the court) that render them ineffectual. Precisely because of their fate, these cases tend to be invisible and constitute silent defeats in practice for litigants and courts alike.

As I posit later, lack of enforcement does not necessarily mean that a given ruling is fruitless. For the latter can have indirect effects, such as the formation of a coalition of NGOs and social movements that, after coming together around the case, advance the right under question through new political and legal strategies. This is the second combination

Enforced?	Positive impact? No	Positive impact? Yes
No	I. Paper ruling	II. "Winning by losing"
Yes	III. Zero-sum litigation	IV. Positive-sum litigation

Figure 3.1 Combinations of enforcement and impact of ESR rulings

("winning by losing") portrayed in the table. The well-known *Joseph* decision by the South African Constitutional Court is a case in point. The court's ruling in favor of low-income residents of Johannesburg whose electricity service had been arbitrarily disconnected was never implemented, as vandals had stripped off the building of its electrical wiring while the case went through the judicial system and reached the court. However, Dugard and Langford (2011: 46) showed that the unenforced decision indeed had important effects, as new litigation achieved the reconnection of electricity to the low-income residents of Johannesburg by using *Joseph* as precedent, and that "the case defined electricity as a rights issue and publicised systemic problems in municipal services billing and services."

The third possibility entails the opposite scenario, that is, one in which the implementation of an ESR ruling has broader impacts that are deleterious to the fulfillment of the right in question. Individual cases in which patients ask for specific treatments or medicines –which are by far the most common type of litigation in Latin America and other regions (Rodríguez-Garavito, 2013; Yamin and Gloppen, 2011) – offer the clearest illustration of this zero-sum combination. Given finite public budgets for healthcare, the enforcement of case-by-case allocation of treatments and medicines by judges may actually reduce the enjoyment of the right to health by marginalized sectors of the population if litigants are disproportionately middle- or upper class (Mœstad, Rakner, and Ferraz, 2011).

This seems to be the case in countries such as Brazil, where judicial decisions on the right to health has benefitted mostly middle-class citizens and has possibly diverted public funds away from health case provision for the poor (Ferraz, 2011).

Finally, combination IV entails a positive-sum scenario in which the effective enforcement of the court's order also has broader, favorable repercussions for the fulfillment of a socioeconomic right. As we will see, this is the case of another decision of the Constitutional Court of Colombia that offers the bulk of the empirical evidence for this chapter, that is, ruling ordering the government to design and carry out public policies aimed to protect the basic ESR of the over five million internally displaced persons (IDPs) in the country.

3.1.2   *The Organization and Arguments of the Chapter*

In what follows, I aim to further unpack the relationship between enforcement and impact, and, more generally, to contribute to opening the black box of the postjudgment phase of ESR litigation. To that end, I begin by laying out an analytical framework for assessing the enforcement and the broader effects of such decisions. Thus, in the second section of the chapter, I offer a typology of effects and discuss its methodological implications for sociolegal studies on judicial impact.

Against this analytical background, in the third section I focus on the broader issue of impact and turn to an explanatory question: What accounts for the different levels of impact of ESR rulings? Why do some decisions have deep and multifarious effects, while others remain on paper? Since the fate of judicial decisions hinges on responses from a wide array of actors – for example, activists' and litigators' postjudgment strategies, governmental reactions to the court's orders, and the court's role in the implementation phase – multicausality makes these questions intractable unless the analysis is restricted to a specific set of factors. I thus focus on those that are within the court's purview. Everything else being equal, the question that concerns me is: What types of judicial decisions are more likely to have a broader positive impact on the fulfillment of ESR? What kind of judicial interventions may foster positive-sum relations between enforcement and overall effects? Put in prescriptive terms, what can courts do to enhance the positive impact of their rulings on ESR?

To empirically ground my analysis, I draw on evidence from a larger comparative study of the impact of CCC's rulings in structural cases (Rodríguez-Garavito, 2011b). The pivotal case study, on decision

T-025 of 2004 on IDPs,[1] results from a collaborative project with Diana Rodríguez-Franco, which examined in detail both the enforcement and broader impact of such a ruling (Rodríguez-Garavito and Rodríguez-Franco, 2015). As we will see, the case stemmed from the court's decision to aggregate 1,150 constitutional complaints (*tutelas*) initiated by forcefully displaced families, and to declare that the humanitarian emergency of displacement constituted an "unconstitutional state of affairs," that is, a massive human rights violation associated with systemic failures in state action. As the complaints that had reached the court from all corners of the country showed, there was no serious and coordinated state policy for offering emergency aid to IDPs; nor was there reliable information on how many IDPs there were and the situations they were facing. Moreover, the budget allocated to the issue was clearly insufficient. To eradicate the root causes behind this "state of affairs," the court ordered a series of structural measures that, as we will see, spawned a long implementation and follow-up process that continues today.

I contrast the relatively high impact of IDPs with the more modest effects of two other structural rulings. On the one hand, the 1998 decision whereby the CCC declared that the dire situation of detainees in overcrowded prisons also amounted to an unconstitutional state of affairs (heretofore *Prison Overcrowding* case).[2] Although the court issued a number of short-term orders aimed to address the gravest administrative and budgetary flaws underlying prison overcrowding, it stopped short of establishing any meaningful monitoring mechanism. This omission helps explain the decision's overall low impact and the fact that, due to worsening prison conditions, the court decided to re-open the case in 2015. On the other hand, I inquire into the above-mentioned ruling on the right to health (T-760 of 2008, heretofore *Healthcare Crisis*). Albeit not formally using the doctrine of unconstitutional states of affairs, the court issued a set of structural injunctive remedies and launched an ambitious monitoring process not unlike those of IDPs, in order to nudge the government to address long-standing administrative and legislative bottlenecks that crippled the healthcare system and overwhelmed courts with thousands of patients' petitions for basic medicines and treatments. As we will see, monitoring has lost steam, and the

---

[1] Corte Constitucional [C.C.] [Constitutional Court], Sentencia T-025/04 (Colom.)
[2] Corte Constitucional [C.C.] [Constitutional Court], Sentencia T-153/98 (Colom.).

decision has had a moderate level of impact, thus ranking in between IDPs and *Prison Overcrowding*.

In line with the structure of the paper, my argument is twofold. First, I claim that, in order to capture the full range of effects of court decisions, impact studies need to enlarge the conventional theoretical and methodological field of vision. In addition to the direct material effects of court orders (i.e., those following immediately from the *enforcement* of the latter), attention should be paid to their broader *impact*, which includes equally important indirect and symbolic effects. On the basis of case study evidence, I posit that the potential range of relevant effects include (in addition to governmental action specifically mandated by the court), the reframing of socioeconomic issues as human rights problems, the strengthening of state institutional capacities to deal with such problems, the formation of advocacy coalitions to participate in the implementation process, and the promotion of public deliberation and collective search for solutions on the complex distributional issues underlying structural cases on ESR.

Second, with regard to court-controlled factors that may enhance a given ruling's overall effects and foster a positive-sum relationship between enforcement and impact, I single out the scale of the decision, the type of orders, and the existence and nature of monitoring. I argue that impact is likely to be higher when courts engage in "dialogic activism" (Dixon, 2007; Gargarella, 2011; Rodríguez-Garavito, 2011b), through three institutional mechanisms. First, dialogic rulings favor a structural approach to the conditions underlying violations of ESR. Instead of focusing exclusively on solving thousands of individual complaints, dialogic courts decide a given case while bearing in mind the existence of similar cases and the broader effects of their rulings on the ESR of nonlitigants. This entails a preference for decisions with collective effects, in which reasons and arguments are considered in light of the needs of a collectivity of similarly situated individuals (for instance, all individuals in need of healthcare), as opposed to only the claim of an individual litigant (for instance, the request for a specific, high-cost treatment or medicine). In common law countries, this is facilitated by the system of binding precedents and the use of class actions. In civil law countries where most of ESR litigation takes place, translating individual claims into structural rulings requires constitutional innovations, such as CCC's aggregation of individual cases in unconstitutional state of affairs rulings, or the Argentinian *Riachuelo* court's recognition of all inhabitants of a polluted river's bank as collective litigants in the case.

While structural rulings reduce the risk of negative societal effects of ESR litigation, they are also more difficult to enforce than individual decisions. Herein lies the tension between enforcement and impact: individual rulings are easier to enforce, but may have counterproductive effects for the enjoyment of ESR; collective rulings may avoid those effects, but are harder to enforce and are more likely to encounter political resistance on the part of governments.

Dialogic courts tackle this trade-off through the other two institutional features that I highlight in my analysis. As for the type of orders, dialogic courts tend to set broad goals and a clear implementation path (e.g., through deadlines and progress reports), while leaving substantive decisions and detailed outcomes to governmental agencies. Orders of this nature are not only compatible with the separations of powers principle, but also can bolster the overall efficacy of a given decision. Also, a dialogic approach to ESR cases encourages participatory follow-up mechanisms (e.g., public hearings, court-appointed monitoring commissions, and invitations to civil society and government agencies to submit relevant information and participate in court-sponsored discussions), which both deepen democratic deliberation and enhance the impact of courts' interventions.

3.2   The Blind Spot in the Justiciability Debate: Rights: The Impact of Rulings

3.2.1   The Effects of ESR Rulings: An Analytical Framework

A well-established interdisciplinary literature on courts and social transformation offers useful conceptual and methodological clues to assess the effects of the recent wave of litigation and judicial activism on ESR. The literature has explored the impact of prominent judicial decisions on a variety of topics, including gender equality in the job market (McCann, 1994), racial discrimination (Klarman, 2007; Rosenberg, 1991), and prison overcrowding (Feeley and Rubin, 1998). From different perspectives, these studies have theorized and empirically evaluated the outcomes of the "rights revolution" (Epp, 1998) and the corresponding "juristocracy" (Hirschl, 2004) embodied by judges' growing intervention in fundamental political and social questions.

Judicial impact studies can be classified into two groups, depending on the type of effects on which they focus. On the one hand, some authors concentrate their attention on judicial decisions' direct and palpable effects.

Adopting a neorealist perspective – which views law as a set of norms that shapes human conduct – they apply a strict causality test to measure the impact of judicial interventions: a judgment is effective if it has produced an observable change in the conduct of those it directly targets. For example, the question of determining the effects of IDPs would be resolved by analyzing its impact on the conduct of government authorities in charge of public policy on forced displacement and, ultimately, by evaluating its consequences for the situation of internally displaced persons.

The seminal work of this approach is that of Rosenberg (1991), on the effects of the US Supreme Court's decision in *Brown vs. Board of Education*. Contrary to the conventional view on *Brown* – which sees the decision as revolutionizing race relations in the United States and as contributing to the birth of the civil rights movement in the 1960s – Rosenberg's empirical study concluded that the judgment had had little effect, and that the faith placed in courts as mechanisms for social change was a "hollow hope." In his view, it was the political mobilization of the 1960s and its resulting antidiscrimination legislation (and not the structural judicial decision) that achieved racial desegregation.

On the other hand, authors inspired by a constructivist conception of the relationship between law and society (Bourdieu, 2000) have criticized Rosenberg and the neorealists for focusing only on judgments' direct, material effects. According to these critics, law and judicial decisions generate social transformation not only when they induce changes in the conduct of groups and individuals directly involved in the case, but also when they produce indirect transformations in social relations, or when they alter social actors' perceptions and legitimate the litigants' worldview. Returning to the example of IDPs, beyond its direct, material effects, it is possible that the decision has generated equally important indirect or symbolic effects. For example, it may have contributed to changing public perception of the urgency and gravity of forced displacement in Colombia, or it may have legitimated claims and reinforced the negotiating power of human rights NGOs and international human rights agencies that have been pressuring the Colombian government to do more for IDPs.

The eminent work employing the constructivist approach is McCann's study on the effects of legal strategies used by the feminist movement in fighting for wage equity in the United States (McCann, 1994). Its findings suggest that litigation and judicial activism's indirect effects may be more important than the direct effects that neorealists focus on. Thus, "although judicial victories often do not translate automatically into desired social change, they can help to redefine the terms of both immediate and long-term struggles among social groups" (McCann, 1994: 285).

These conceptual differences go hand in hand with methodological disagreements. Neorealists' epistemological positivism implies a nearly exclusive emphasis on quantitative research techniques that allow measurement of direct material effects. This is evident in impact studies inspired by the law and economics movement, whose conclusions tend to share Rosenberg's skepticism, as shown by the economic literature on CCC's activism.[3]

In contrast, the constructivist approach widens the range of research strategies to include qualitative techniques that capture a given decision's indirect and symbolic effects (e.g., in-depth interviews with public officials, activists and members of the beneficiary population to examine the judgment's impact on their perception of their situation and the strategies to address it), on an equal footing with quantitative techniques (e.g., analysis of social indicators for the beneficiary population, and measurement of press coverage before and after the decision).

To clarify and highlight the difference between these two perspectives, I construct a typology of the effects under consideration (Figure 3.2).

On the one hand, as shown by the horizontal axis of Figure 3.2, rulings can have direct or indirect effects. The former consists of court-mandated actions and affects participants in the case, be they the litigants, the beneficiaries or the state agencies that are the target of the court's orders. In the cases under consideration, direct effects of the CCC's structural rulings include the government's decision to declare the state of economic emergency in late 2009, so as to be able to issue a series of decrees ostensibly aimed to conjure the crisis of the healthcare system and comply with some of the court's orders in *Healthcare Crisis*.[4] Similarly, to comply with *Prison Overcrowding's* main order, the government's planning council issued a document laying out a policy strategy for dealing with prison overcrowding.[5]

---

[3] See Clavijo (2001), Kalmanovitz (2001). For an analysis of the confrontation between economists and constitutional lawyers on judicial activism in Colombia, see Rodríguez-Garavito (2011a).

[4] Interestingly, the government's decree declaring the emergency (and the resulting decrees reforming key components of the health care system) were subsequently struck down by the CCC on grounds that the administration could not resort to state of emergency legislation to fix policy failures that had been brought about by its own negligence (including its inaction vis-à-vis the structural injunctions of ruling T-760). See Corte Constitucional [C.C.] [Constitutional Court], Sentencia C-252/10 (Colom.).

[5] Consejo Nacional de Política Económica y Social [National Council on Economic and Social Policy], Conpes Document No. 3086 of 2000.

	Direct	Indirect
Material	Designing public policy, as ordered by the ruling	Forming coalitions of activists to influence the issue under consideration
Symbolic	Defining and perceiving the problem as a rights violation	Transforming public opinion about the problem's urgency and gravity

Figure 3.2 Types and examples of effects of judicial decisions
Source: Rodríguez-Garavito (2011a).

Indirect effects include all kinds of consequences that, without being stipulated for in the court's orders, nonetheless derive from the decision. They affect not only the parties to the case, but also other social actors. For instance, structural injunctive remedies often prompt sympathetic state agencies and NGOs to seize the opportunity opened up by the decision, and to become involved in the follow-up process above and beyond what the court had initially contemplated. For instance, a proactive Ombudsman's Office in Colombia took it upon itself to put pressure on the government to undertake prison reform in the aftermath of the decision on prison overcrowding,[6] while several NGO coalitions have been formed to advocate healthcare reform along the lines of *Healthcare Crisis*.

On the other hand, as represented by the table's vertical axis, judicial decisions can generate material or symbolic effects (García, 2014). The former category entails tangible changes in the conduct of groups or individuals, of the type I have just described. Symbolic effects consist of changes in ideas, perceptions and collective social constructs relating to the litigation's subject matter. In sociological terms, they imply cultural or ideological alterations with respect to the problem posed by the case (Swidler, 1986).

[6] See Defensoría del Pueblo [Colombia's Ombudsman's Office]. Reply to CCC's memo OPT B 397, 2007 (Dossier No. T-1. 644.081).

For instance, when judicial interventions attract media coverage, they may shape the understanding that both the media and the public have of the issue under consideration. This was the case with *Healthcare Crisis*, which prompted the reframing of the issue of healthcare in Colombia. Content analysis of news and opinion pieces published in the country's two main press outlets indicates that, before the CCC's decision, the most frequent frame for speaking about the issue was one of "institutional crisis" (which was dominant in 60 percent of the pieces published between 2004 and mid-2008). The reframing process can be clearly seen at work in the press coverage following the decision: between mid-2008 and late 2014, the press framed the large majority (76 percent) of the pieces in terms of the "right to health."[7]

As the figure portrays, the intersection of these two classifications gives rise to four types of effects: direct material effects (e.g., formulation of a policy ordered by the court); indirect material effects (e.g., intervention of new actors in the debate); direct symbolic effects (e.g., reframing of media coverage); and indirect symbolic effects (e.g., the transformation of public opinion on the matter).

With this typology in mind, let us return to the contrast between neo-realist and constructivist approaches. While neorealists center on direct material effects (i.e., on the ruling's *enforcement*), constructivists consider all four types. This explains why a judgment can be seen as ineffective by the neorealists and as effective by the constructivists, to the extent that what counts as impact for the latter group includes a broader set of effects.

In this vein, a neorealist analysis would conclude that virtually all landmark cases in ESR jurisprudence have had little impact. Consider, for instance, the well-known South African Constitutional Court's ruling in the *Grootboom* case, on the right to housing.[8] The fact that the plaintiff, Irene Grootboom, sadly died in a shack while waiting for a decent house eight years after winning the case would suggest that the ruling was in vain, as its expected direct material effects failed to materialize.[9] This conclusion, however, ignores important outcomes of the

---

[7] The two media outlets included in the study were the daily *El Tiempo* and the weekly *Semana*.

[8] *Government of the Republic of South Africa v. Grootboom*, 2000 (11) BCLR 1169 (CC) (finding housing rights of people living in informal settlements in Cape Town had been violated).

[9] Pearlie Joubert, "Obituary: Grootboom Dies Homeless and Penniless," *Mail & Guardian*, August 8, 2008.

case. For instance, it misses the manifold indirect material and symbolic effects produced by the *Grootboom* ruling, from the litigation cascade of similar cases whereby communities in different parts of South Africa managed to fend off eviction to the creation of emergency housing policies (Langford, 2013).

My study of the impact on the CCC's structural decisions finds empirical support for the constructivist approach. Indeed, my case studies suggest that indirect and symbolic effects may have legal and social consequences that are just as profound as the decision's direct, material effects. These various forms of judicial impact have been most visible in the eight-year monitoring process of the IDPs decision, to which I now turn to illustrate the above-mentioned typology.

3.2.2   *The Effects of ESC Rights Rulings: the IDPs Judgment*

In IDPs, the CCC laid down three main orders. First, it mandated the government to formulate a coherent plan of action to tackle IDPs' humanitarian emergency and overcome the unconstitutional state of affairs. Second, it ordered the administration to calculate the budget that was needed to implement such a plan of action, and to explore all possible avenues to actually invest the amount thus calculated on programs for IDPs. Third, it instructed the government to guarantee the protection of at least the survival-level content ("essential core") of the most basic rights (e.g., food, education, healthcare, land, and housing). All of these orders were directed to all relevant public agencies, including national governmental entities and local authorities.

After thirteen years, what effects have these and subsequent orders had? Interviews with key actors, content analysis of press coverage, participatory observation of court-sponsored meetings and hearings, and data from the extensive paper trail left by this case substantiate the existence of five major effects, as represented in Figure 3.3.

Unlocking Effect

IDPs' immediate effect was the shaking up of state bureaucracies in charge of attending to the displaced population. By ordering the government to draft a coherent policy to protect the rights of IDPs and setting deadlines for progress, the CCC used ESR as "destabilization rights" (Unger, 1987), that is, as leverage points for breaking institutional inertia and prompting the government into action. Thus, in terms of this typology, this was a direct material impact of the ruling (see Figure 3.3).

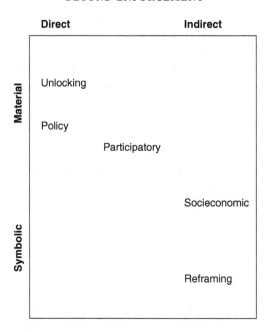

Figure 3.3 Effects of the IDPs judgment
Source: Rodríguez-Garavito and Rodríguez-Franco (2015: 21).

Several interviewees highlighted this effect. For instance, the attorney in charge of IDP issues at the Ombudsman's Office explained how the lingering deadlines to report back to the court served as an effective nudge for the relevant governmental agencies. He recalled that "in inter-agency preparatory meetings prior to follow-up meetings with the Court, national and local law enforcement officials would state that they had to hurry because they were going before the court or because they would miss the court's deadline."[10] As we will see, the court kept the pressure on the government through follow-up orders and meetings, which further nudged the government into action. Thus, as a newspaper editorial put it in 2007, the judgment "was key in energizing the attitude of the government. Periodic orders from the court, which opened the process for contempt complaints against government officials – as well as critical reports from the Attorney General, the Comptroller, and the Ombudsman on the failures of implementation – have kept the pressure on the government to fulfil its obligations."[11]

[10] Interview with Hernando Toro, coordinator of the Ombudsman's Office of Attention to Displacement, January 22, 2009.
[11] *El Tiempo*, "El Año de los Desplazados," April 8, 2007 (author's translation).

The structural policy failures underlying IDPs' humanitarian emergency stemmed not only from the inaction of relevant institutions, but also from the lack of coordination among them. In instructing those institutions to collaborate on the design, financing, and implementation of a unified policy on IDPs, the CCC promoted the requisite coordination, both among agencies directly targeted by the decision and among agencies indirectly related to the case, that helped unlock policy processes.

In the words of a Ministry of Education official, "the ruling told us to put our own house in order. And it allowed us in government to solve who does what, and to determine which tasks need to be carried out collaboratively by everyone."[12] Although far from perfect, the result is a functioning inter-agency coordination committee that meets regularly and reports back to the court.

Policy Effect

IDPs have had a sizable impact on the design of a long-term national policy on IDPs, as well as on the establishment of mechanisms to implement, fund, and monitor it. Indeed, one year after the judgment and directly in response to the court's first order, the government issued a National Plan for the Integral Attention to the Population Displaced by Violence. Further, in 2011, government and Congress worked together to pass a comprehensive Victims and Land Restitution Statute, which turned several of the court's orders into legal mandates. Interestingly, although clearly a direct material effect (thus its location in Figure 3.3), these developments also reveal some symbolic consequences of the ruling, as the government and Congress explicitly adopted the language and the legal frame of the court's "rights approach" *(enfoque de derechos)* in these and subsequent policy documents and regulations. Hence the intermediate location of this effect in Figure 3.2.

Moreover, IDPs had a direct impact on the government allocation of funds for programs for displaced persons, in line with the court's second order. Indeed, the ruling prompted the administration to triple the budget allocated to these programs in 2004, and has had a steady upward effect over time. The 2014 national budget for IDPs programs, albeit still insufficient, was more than ten times that of 2003 (National Planning Department and Ministry of Finance of Colombia, 2014).

---

[12] Interview with Yaneth Guevara, Ministry of Education, February, 2009 (author's translation).

Participatory Effect

The follow-up process to IDPs has opened up judicial proceedings and policymaking to the participation of a broad range of governmental and nongovernmental actors. This key material effect has been partly the direct product of the ruling, and partly an indirect, unexpected consequence of it (see Figure 3.3). From the beginning, the CCC's orders directly involved not only the core governmental agencies responsible for IDPs – for example, the Ministry of the Interior and *Acción Social* (the agency in charge of antipoverty programs) – but also all others with related responsibilities at the international, national, and local levels (e.g., the UN Refugee Agency – UNCHR – the Ombudsman's Office and most national ministries, as well as governors and mayors of localities heavily hit by violence and displacement).

Interestingly, an indirect outcome was the formation of civil society organizations and coalitions to participate in the monitoring process. NGOs such as Codhes, Dejusticia, and Viva la Ciudadanía joined efforts with grassroots organizations as well as sectors of the Catholic Church and academia to found a coalition specifically geared to contribute to the implementation of IDPs: the Monitoring Commission on Public Policy on Forced Displacement. In a striking boomerang effect, the CCC subsequently acknowledged the Commission as party to the follow-up procedures, and relied heavily on the data and recommendations that it has submitted. In this way, although not officially appointed as such by the CCC, the Commission has in practice played a role similar to the commissioners appointed by the Indian Supreme Court to oversee the implementation of its decision. Thus, the participatory effect straddles the direct and indirect threshold as some of its aspects resulted from explicit orders from the court while others emerged unexpectedly (Rodríguez-Garavito and Rodríguez-Franco, 2015: 24).

As explained in the pages that follow, the CCC has encouraged engagement by and dialogue among state agencies and civil society organizations through hearings and periodic petitions for information, thus promoting the type of dialogic judicial activism that, I argue, can enhance the impact of ESC rights rulings.

Socio-economic Effect

Every ESC rights ruling targets specific sectors of the population as beneficiaries, be it homeless citizens vindicating their right to decent housing as in *Grootboom*, disgruntled patients asking courts to make real their right to health as in *Healthcare Crisis*, or detainees in overcrowded prisons going to court to demand decent conditions of incarceration. A key question, therefore, is what effects a given ruling has on the socioeconomic conditions of that specific social sector. In our case, has IDPs contributed to ameliorate the situation of the victims of forced displacement?

There is no definitive answer to this question, as it is riddled with methodological difficulties. Specifically, one of the defining traits of systemic policy failures is the lack of reliable data on the conditions of the victimized population. Indeed, this was one of the reasons why the CCC declared the unconstitutional state of affairs in IDPs. Thus, we lack a baseline for making comparisons with the IDPs' socioeconomic situation after the decision.

However, since the above-mentioned civil society Monitoring Commission on Public Policy on Forced Displacement collects quality survey data, it is at least possible to have a sense of the evolution of the conditions of IDPs after the judgment. The latest figures show that the situation has changed little: although access to education and health has dramatically improved and benefits nearly 80 percent of IDPs, conditions with regard to all other ESC rights continue to be dramatic. To illustrate, 98 percent of IDPs live in poverty, only 5 percent have adequate housing, and only 0.2 percent of displaced families had received the legally mandated emergency humanitarian assistance in the months immediately ensuing their forceful displacement (Comisión de Seguimiento a la Política Pública sobre Desplazamiento Forzado, 2008). Moreover, forceful displacement continues at exorbitant levels: 156,000 people were uprooted in 2013 (El Tiempo, 2014) and came to engross the approximately five million Colombian IDPs, the second largest forcefully displaced population in the world (UNCHR, 2013: 24). As suggested by the location of this type of impact in Figure 3.3, court decisions can also have symbolic effects on the beneficiary social sector, as their members and organizations come to adopt the language of the law to frame their claims. This was evident in interviews and participant observation with leaders of the IDP population, whose discourse is peppered with allusions to the technical language of the court. Terms such as tutela (constitutional action), auto (follow-up injunction), or audiencia (hearing) often become intertwined with personal stories of uprooting and radical deprivation.[13]

---

[13] Interview with leader of Adacho (Association of Displaced Afro-Colombians of the Chocó Province), Quibdó, July 24, 2008; interview with Eusebio Mosquera, founding member of Afrodes (National Association of Displaced Afro-Colombians), Geneva, August 9, 2009.

Reframing Effect

Symbolic reshaping extends beyond the right holders targeted by the ruling. Through IDPs and the follow-up process, the CCC has helped to reframe the issue of forced displacement – which was once considered a side effect of armed conflict – as a human rights problem requiring an immediate reaction. This is an indirect consequence of the ruling, in that it concerns a group of actors much broader than IDPs, from the media to international human rights agencies to public opinion at large.

Content analysis of press coverage on forced displacement offers a hint on the operation of this effect. Whereas in the period prior to the judgment (2000–2003), the press covered displacement mostly through the frame of "armed conflict," in the subsequent period (2004–2014), legal categories have come to dominate press coverage of the issue. Indeed, forced displacement is talked about mostly in pieces whose dominant frame is "human rights violations" or "lack of compliance" with the law (Rodríguez-Garavito and Rodríguez-Franco, 2015).

In sum, beyond the specifics of IDPs, the empirical analysis of its effects illustrates a general point: judicial activism on ESR may have consequential impacts that go well beyond the direct, material consequences following from the court orders. And they become visible with the aid of an expanded analytical and methodological toolkit.

This is not to suggest, of course, that structural rulings on ESR in general, and *T-025* in particular, produce the whole range of effects, nor that, when they do have an impact, it is substantial. Indeed, the results of IDPs have been mixed. While some of its effects (such as the unlocking and reframing effects) have been profound, others (such as the socioeconomic and coordination effects) have been moderate.

Nonetheless, the breadth and depth of the IDPs decision effects remain striking when compared to those of other structural rulings by the CCC and other tribunals. What accounts for this variation? Why do some decisions (e.g., IDPs) have greater impact than others (e.g., *Prison Overcrowding* and *Healthcare Crisis*)? In the following section, I claim that institutional mechanisms associated with dialogic judicial activism provide useful clues to answer these questions.

3.3 Judicial Impact and Dialogic Activism

3.3.1 An Empirical Case for Dialogic Activism

Inspired by decisions like IDPs and *Grootboom*, a growing literature in comparative constitutionalism has extolled rulings that, in addition to protecting ESR, promote democratic deliberation. Proponents of this type of dialogic activism aim for an intermediate path between judicial restraint and juristocracy. While defending the justiciability of ESR, they criticize rulings that, by imposing detailed policies and programs, encroach upon the purview of the executive and legislative branches, and close off opportunities for public debate on the underlying socioeconomic issues.[14]

Thus far, the case for dialogic activism has rested on democratic theory and constitutional law. In response to the classic objection against judicial activism for allegedly lacking democratic legitimacy and violating the separation of powers principle, constitutional scholars and theorists of deliberative democracy have cogently demonstrated the democratic credentials of judicial interventions that elicit collaboration among the different branches of power, and promote deliberation on public issues (Abramovich, 2005; Gauri and Brinks, 2008; Nino, 1996; Uprimny, 2006). On the other hand, in critical engagement with overly expansive understandings of the role of courts, they have pointed out the shortcomings of court-imposed policies that circumvent the channels of democratic representation and deliberation (Gargarella, 2011; Rodríguez-Garavito, 2011a; Sabel and Simon, 2004). Together, these and other contributions have made a case for dialogic activism on grounds that it deepens democratic *legitimacy* in constitutional regimes committed to decent standards of economic well-being.

Here I want to make a different yet complementary case for dialogic activism, based on the potential of the latter to enhance courts' *impact* on the fulfillment of ESR. This argument addresses the other classical objection against activism, according to which courts lack the requisite institutional capacity to deal with complex socioeconomic issues and enforce their rulings (see Rosenberg, 1991).

Upon close examination, it becomes clear that this line of critique identifies judicial activism with a specific variety of court interventions. In terms of Tushnet's (2008) criteria for distinguishing "strong" judicial remedies from "weak" ones – that is, the breadth of orders and the extent to which orders are compulsory and peremptory – the critique assumes that activist courts opt for strong remedies that not only set a course for addressing policy failures, but also determine the minutiae of the new policies. What the critics have in mind is the kind of activism that marked US jurisprudence in the 1950s through the 1980s, characterized by rulings ordering particular policy and institutional reforms. As exemplified

---

[14] For a review of the literature on dialogic activism, see Dixon (2007).

by many judicial interventions seeking to reform the dysfunctional US prison system, judges not only declared the existence of a structural violation of prisoners' rights, but also sought to address it through detailed orders on matters as specific as the number of guards that should be hired and the details of the designs of prison facilities (Feeley and Rubin, 1998). This is the same variety of activism seen in some of the CCC's rulings of the 1990s. For instance, in a 1999 decision, the CCC not only declared unconstitutional the national system of housing finance but also set detailed parameters of new legislation which the court ordered be issued by Congress to replace the extant system.[15]

Further, critics tend to take for granted the process of implementation that is predominant in these rulings. It is a closed and top-down process, which tends to feature courts imposing specific policy alternatives on impermeable bureaucracies and interest groups resistant to change. Under these conditions, it is unsurprising that the courts' institutional capacity is insufficient to enforce their judgments, as demonstrated by empirical studies on this type of monologic activism.

In practice, detailed top-down orders generated transformations much less ambitious than those envisioned by the courts, largely because of resistance from vested interests and courts' legal and technical limitations to deal with structural social problems (see Feeley and Rubin, 1998). A telling case is the above-mentioned CCC ruling (C-700/99), which sought to replace the national system of housing finance with a court-designed one. Although the Colombian Congress complied with the court's order to pass a bill establishing a new mortgage system, the myriad technical complexities involved in implementing it, coupled with organized resistance from the financial sector, diluted the ruling into thousands of individual suits that mortgage debtors have fruitlessly brought before civil courts to have their debts refinanced as ordered by the CCC. In light of this, the CCC itself has backtracked in its more recent jurisprudence on housing finance, which has further eroded the implementation of its original decision.

Evidence of the limited effects of monologic activism and concerns about the latter's democratic credentials do not undermine judicial activism *tout court*, as defenders of judicial restraint would have it. Nor do they question the justiciability of ESR at large. However, they do call for a reconstruction of the theory and practice of court interventions in structural socioeconomic issues, so as to address the above-mentioned objections through dialogical activism.

[15] Corte Constitucional [C.C.] [Constitutional Court], Sentencia C-700/99 (Colom.)

3.3.2   The Workings of Dialogic Activism

Whether a given ESR judgment is more or less dialogic depends on the
court's choices with regard to three components of the ruling: substantive
content, remedies, and monitoring mechanisms. The decision's *substantive content* relates to whether, and to what extent, the court declares that
there has been a violation of a justiciable ESR. As explained, this declaratory stage is the focus of most of the jurisprudence and the literature on
the justiciability of ESR. In terms of Tushnet's (2008) typology of judicial
approaches to ESR, the choice that a court faces at this juncture is whether
to affirm the justiciability of an ESR in the case at hand, and – if it finds
for the plaintiff – how strongly to interpret the scope of the latter's rights.
Thus, activist rulings, of both the monologic and the dialogic varieties,
entail the affirmation of "strong rights."

With regard to *remedies*, whereas monologic judgments involve precise, outcome-oriented orders, dialogic ones tend to outline procedures
and broad goals, and place the burden on governmental agencies to design
and implement policies, in line with the separations of powers principle.
In terms of Tushnet's (2008) criteria to distinguish "strong" judicial remedies from "weak" ones – that is, the breadth of orders and the extent to
which orders are compulsory and peremptory – dialogic remedies tend to
be weaker.[16]

Missing from Tushnet's typology is a third component – *monitoring* –
which is factually and analytically distinct from remedies. Regardless of
the strength of rights and remedies of the decision, courts face the choice
of retaining supervisory jurisdiction over its implementation. Dialogic
decisions tend to open a monitoring process that encourages discussion
of policy alternatives to solve the structural problem detected in the ruling. Unlike in monologic judicial proceedings, the minutiae of the policies arise in the course of the monitoring process, not the judgment itself.
Dialogic courts often issue new decisions in light of progress and setbacks
in the process and encourage discussion among actors in the case through
deliberative public hearings. As noted, this constitutional dialogue
involves a broader spectrum of stakeholders in the monitoring process. In

---

[16] Given my focus on structural rulings that mandate positive actions on the part of the executive or the legislature, I do not dwell on negative remedies here – i.e., those that order
elected authorities to *abstain* from a given course of action found to violate an ESR (e.g.,
disproportionately taxing the poor). An insightful discussion of positive and negative remedies on ESC rights, as well as other factors impinging on the enforcement of ESR rulings,
can be found in Uprimny (2006).

addition to the court and state agencies directly affected by the judgment, implementation involves victims whose rights have been violated, relevant civil society organizations, international human rights organizations, and other actors whose participation is useful for the protection of the rights at issue, from grassroots organizations to academia.

This threefold characterization allows for an assessment of the mono-logic or dialogic character of a given ruling or court. The most dialogic decisions in structural cases involve a clear affirmation of the justiciability of the right in question (i.e., strong rights), leave policy decisions to the elected branches of power while laying out a clear roadmap for measuring progress (i.e., moderate remedies), and actively monitors the implementa-tion of its orders through participatory mechanisms (i.e., strong monitor-ing through public hearings, progress reports, and follow-up decisions).

There are stark differences among activist courts (and among deci-sions of the same court) on each of the three dimensions.[17] As we will see, although in IDPs the CCC has explicitly adopted a dialogic approach, in previous structural rulings such as *Prison Overcrowding* it leaned toward a monologic combination of strong rights, strong orders, and no monitor-ing. Yet in other structural decisions such as *Healthcare Crisis*, it has stood somewhere in between monologic and dialogic approaches.

The South African Constitutional Court has tended to adopt a combi-nation of moderate rights, weak remedies, and no monitoring. In cases like Soobramoney[18] (on the right to health) and Mazibuko[19] (on the right to water), its moderate-rights approach has led it to reject ESR claims on the basis that the state had not breached the reasonableness standard in refusing to provide, respectively, kidney dialysis to a terminally ill patient, and sufficient amounts of free water to impoverished citizens (Dugard, 2013). In other cases such as Grootboom, it has found for the plaintiff but chosen not to set deadlines or follow-up proceedings for enforcement. In the exceptional case of Treatment Action Campaign,[20] it handed down a strong remedy (i.e., an order for the state to provide nevirapine to preg-nant mothers across the country to avoid mother-to-child transmission of HIV at birth), but reaffirmed its preference for moderate rights (through the reasonableness test) and no monitoring. A more dialogic approach is

---

[17] For a more thorough comparison of the South African, Indian and Colombian courts, see Rodríguez-Garavito and Rodríguez-Franco (2015, ch. 8), from which this section is partially taken.

[18] *Soobramoney v. Minister of Health, KwaZulu-Natal* (1) SA 765 (CC) (1998).

[19] *Mazibuko v. City of Johannesburg* (4) SA 1 (CC) (2010).

[20] *Minister of Health v. Treatment Action Campaign* (5) SA 721 (CC) (2002).

evident in the Olivia Road case,[21] where the court directed the state and the applicants to engage meaningfully with each other in order to find an adequate housing alternative in the face of the need to relocate the applicants from their informal dwellings (Pillay, 2012).

The Indian Supreme Court's jurisprudence has oscillated among different understandings of rights, remedies, and monitoring (Pillay, 2014). It has oftentimes resorted to a monologic mixture of strong rights, strong remedies, and strong monitoring mechanisms (Muralidhar, 2008). Its strong-rights approach is noteworthy given that the 1949 Constitution did not enshrine SERs as enforceable rights, but rather as directive principles of state policy. The court has thus built its approach by interpreting the constitutional provisions on the protection of the right to life as including the right to livelihood, in cases like *Francis Mullin*[22] and *Olga Tellis.*[23] However, its recent jurisprudence can be better characterized as dialogic (Chandrachud, 2009; Chitalkar and Gauri in this volume), as the court has taken up the role of an "embedded negotiator in facilitating the dialogue between the state and citizens" through strong rights, moderate remedies, and strong monitoring (Shankar, 2013: 103). This has notably been its approach in the *PUCL* case on the right to food (Rodríguez-Garavito, forthcoming). Nonetheless, the court has at times reverted toward a weak rights approach in key cases like *Narmada Bachao Andolan*, where it failed to find violations of the rights of 41,000 families displaced from their homes as a result of the building of a dam (Rajagopal, 2005, 2007).

Do these differences have a bearing on judicial impact? Evidence from the comparative case study of CCC's rulings suggests that they do. I turn to this evidence in closing.

3.3.3   *The Impact of Dialogic Activism*

The three key structural rulings of the CCC share a "strong rights" approach. The foundational decision, T-153/98, entailed a strong condemnation of prison overcrowding for violating basic detainees' rights, whose justiciability the court also decisively affirmed. A similarly painstaking documentation and severe judgment of massive ESR violations can

---

[21] *Ocuppiers of 51 Olivia Road, Berea Township and 197 Main Street Johannesburg v. City of Johannesburg* (3) SA 208 (CC) (2008).

[22] *Francis Mullin v. The Administrator*, 1 SCC 608 (1981).

[23] *Olga Tellis v. Bombay Municipal Corporation*, 3 SCC 545 (1985).

be found in the subsequent rulings on IDPs (T-025/153) and healthcare (T-760/08).

With regard to remedies, however, a sharp turn is evident between the earlier ruling and the more recent jurisprudence. In *Prison Overcrowding*, the CCC adopted the strong-remedies approach by handing down detailed orders for the government to immediately suspend a contract for the renovation of one of the largest prisons in Bogotá; to formulate, in three months, a comprehensive plan for the renovation of existing prisons and the construction of new ones, which was to be executed within a four-year period; and to put an end, in four years, to the confinement of detainees under trial in the same prisons as convicted detainees.

As noted, the IDPs court adopted a more procedural, dialogic approach by leaving it to the government to decide the content of programs on IDPs and the requisite funding carrying them out. At the same time, however, it set stringent deadlines and handed down an outcome-oriented order requiring the government to protect the most basic rights of IDPs in the short term (six months). Thus, in terms of the mentioned classification, this decision entailed moderate remedies.

A similarly moderate, intermediate approach to remedies is evident in the more recent decision on healthcare. Most of its orders are means-oriented, mandating the government to formulate a contingency plan to deal with the impending bankruptcy of the healthcare system, create administrative protocols for resolving patients' complaints, and put in place mechanisms for efficiently overseeing private healthcare providers. The relative weakness of these orders is offset by stringent deadlines and a strong injunction ordering the government to unify the basic coverage for patients in the private and the public healthcare systems, as mandated by a 1993 law that had remained on paper.

Finally, with regard to monitoring, IDPs stands apart from the other rulings. Over the course of 11 years (2004–2015), it has entailed 22 follow-up public hearings involving a wide array of governmental and nongovernmental actors, as well as 289 follow-up decisions whereby the CCC has fine-tuned its orders in light of progress reports. The CCC has thus put in place a remarkably strong monitoring process.

In contrast, the earlier approach of *Prison Overcrowding* did not include any court-sponsored monitoring mechanism. Instead, the court limited itself to asking the Ombudsman's Office and the Comptroller's Office to oversee the decision's enforcement. Likewise, the *Healthcare Crisis* Court, despite having outlined in the decision a monitoring mechanism akin

Table 3.1 *A comparison of CCC's structural rulings*

	Rights	Remedies	Monitoring	Impact
T-025/2004	Strong	Moderate	Strong	High
T-760/2008	Strong	Moderate	Weak	Moderate
T-153/1998	Strong	Strong	Weak	Low

to that of IDPs, has largely remained passive: It has held only two public hearings, failed to promote meaningful citizen participation, and largely limited its follow-up injunctions to petitions for information from the government.[24] Weak monitoring, therefore, has marked these two cases.

Table 3.1 sums up the comparison among the three cases, as well as the results of above-mentioned impact analysis.

Although a larger sample of cases would be needed to extract firm conclusions, this comparison offers useful hints on the relationship between dialogic activism and judicial impact. The results suggest that dialogic rulings such as IDPs hold out the prospect for greater overall impact[25] on the fulfillment of ESR, whereas monologic rulings such as *Prison Overcrowding* are likely have lower impact. In between are different combinations of rights, remedies, and monitoring that are likely to have a moderate impact.

Interestingly, the CCC seems to have extracted similar lessons from the contrasting trajectory of its structural rulings. At the time of writing (late 2015), the court was gradually shifting its approach to both *Prison Overcrowding* and *Healthcare Crisis* in a dialogic direction. Evidence that dire prison conditions have not improved led the court to reactivate its supervisory jurisdiction in the former case in 2015, as well as to convene a civil society follow-up commission modeled after the one in the IDPs case. In the *Healthcare Crisis* case, the court decided to appoint expert witnesses and work with civil society and academic organizations that can provide independent opinions on the government's compliance with the ruling's order. It has also convened fruitful "technical sessions" among government officials, members of the court, and masters of the court (including the author of this chapter), whereby a more dialogic and interactive

---

[24] An exception to the Court's passivity follow-up decision (Auto) 342 of 2009, which orders the government to immediately comply with the Court's order to unify coverage for underage patients in the public and the private health care systems.

[25] I use here a synthetic assessment of rulings' impact, which aggregates the four types of direct, indirect, material, and symbolic effects discussed earlier.

monitoring process has gradually emerged that holds out the prospect of improving enforcement and maximizing the positive impact of the court's intervention.

Additional research would also be needed to unpack the specific mechanisms underlying judicial impact of dialogic rulings. I hypothesize that dialogic rulings have greater impact because they address the two key practical obstacles to the implementation of structural decisions: political resistance and institutional capacity. As for the former, structural injunctions on ESR naturally elicit resistance from powerful sectors with vested interests in the status quo. In the cases under consideration, they included private healthcare providers and pharmaceutical companies reaping huge profits from thousands of lower-court rulings ordering the government to pay for brand-name medicines, indifferent public officials in sclerotic bureaucracies responsible for programs on IDPs, and negligent or corrupt personnel in the overcrowded prison system.

By empowering a broader range of stakeholders to participate in monitoring, courts unleash direct and indirect effects that may help them overcome political resistance. The main effect is the direct involvement of political actors (e.g., human rights NGOs, reform-oriented public agencies, and grassroots organizations) that are likely to adopt the ruling's implementation as part of their own agenda, and thus become a source of countervailing power against the status quo. Moreover, orders of this nature may prompt the formation of political coalitions in support of the court, as well as elicit media coverage that magnifies the material and symbolic effects of the case. As noted, this is the case of IDPs, which prompted the foundation of a civil society monitoring commission that has turned into a key ally of the court as well as a provider of valuable information and recommendations.

Second, the mechanisms of dialogic activism may help courts address their institutional shortcomings in dealing with complex socioeconomic issues. One does not have to be a legal formalist to concede that courts lack the technical knowledge, personnel, and resources (let alone the legitimacy) to find and implement solutions to problems as complicated as forceful displacement or lack of access to essential medicines.

This does not mean, however, that courts cannot provoke and moderate a dialogue among public authorities and civil society actors on those issues, in the face of massive policy failures and violations of ESR. By calling not only on government officials but also on a wide variety of actors with relevant knowledge – for example, leaders and members of the beneficiary population, academic experts, and international human rights agencies – dialogic courts may promote a collaborative search for solutions, or at least a public discussion on alternative courses of action (Sabel and Simon, 2004). Direct and indirect effects potentially stemming from this dialogue include the unlocking of policy processes, improved coordination among hitherto disconnected state agencies, and the creation of public policies framed in the language of rights.

IDPs provide an interesting illustration of these effects. A particularly useful feature of the monitoring process has been the collaborative formulation of progress indicators on the fulfillment of IDPs' rights. Through an iterative, multiyear process that has included numerous follow-up court orders and proposals by governmental and nongovernmental agencies, the CCC adopted a list of quantitative, rights-based indicators to assess progress. These indicators have provided a shared monitoring framework for all the stakeholders, as well as a tool for the court to fine-tune its follow-up injunctions in response to evidence on the evolution of policies and the situation of IDPs.

In sum, by combining the rights, remedies, and monitoring mechanisms of dialogic activism, courts may offset some of the political and institutional shortcomings that render ineffectual their interventions in complex distributional issues and enhance their overall impact on the fulfillment of ESR.

3.4   Conclusion

Over the past two decades, courts, activists, and scholars have developed legal theories, strategies, and doctrines aimed to make real the promise of social and economic rights, in contexts marked by massive deprivation and inacceptable inequalities. Missing from the literature and the jurisprudence is a systematic reflection on the enforcement and the actual impact of ESR rulings. In this chapter, I have sought to contribute to addressing these questions by tackling them from two angles. First, I offered an analytical and methodological framework aimed to capture the full range of effects of court rulings. I argued that, in addition to the direct material outcomes that courts and analysts tend to focus on, judicial impact includes a broader array of indirect and symbolic effects that can be as consequential for the fulfillment of ESR as those directly stemming from court orders. I illustrated this broader typology of effects with evidence on the multifarious impacts of the most ambitious structural ruling of the CCC (IDPs, on the rights of internally displaced people).

Second, I inquired into the features of courts' decisions that can have bearing on their overall impact. I singled out (1) the scale of the cases (individual vs. collective) as well as the strength of judgments, (2) declaration of rights, (3) remedies, and (4) monitoring. I further hypothesized that dialogic rulings – characterized by strong rights, moderate remedies, and strong monitoring – are likely to have the greatest overall impact on the fulfillment of ESR. I illustrated this hypothesis with findings from a comparative study of the impact of CCC's three key structural decisions on ESR.

Additional research is needed to test these findings and hypotheses. Promising avenues are studies on a larger sample of cases, as well as cross-national comparisons (Rodríguez-Garavito, forthcoming). These and other research strategies hold out the promise of opening the black box of the postjudgment phase of ESR cases.

The need for this type of analysis is particularly pressing because the issue of impact ranks high on the minds of litigators and judges alike. After all, having a concrete impact on improved access and quality of goods and services such as decent housing or healthcare is what drives litigators and activists to resort to the courts in the first place. Similarly, if their rulings had no practical consequences, courts would be ill-advised to incur the considerable institutional costs associated with their activists rulings on ESR, especially in structural cases that entail protracted negotiations and tensions with governmental agencies responsible for implementing them. Once the dust has settled from a case, a question lingering on everyone's mind is: Was it worth the effort?

References

Abramovich, Víctor (2005), "Líneas de trabajo en derechos económicos, sociales y culturales: herramientas y aliados," in Sur: Revista Internacional de Derechos Humanos 2(2), 188–223.

Abramovich, Víctor and Christian Courtis (2002), Los derechos sociales como derechos exigibles (Madrid: Trotta).

Abramovich, Víctor and Laura Pautassi (eds.) (2009), La revisión judicial de las políticas sociales: estudios de caso (Buenos Aires: Editores del Puerto).

Arango, Rodolfo (2005), El concepto de derechos sociales fundamentales (Bogotá: Legis-Uniandes).

   (ed.) (2007), "¿Los partidarios de la democracia deliberativa deben defender la protección judicial de los derechos sociales?" in Filosofía de la democracia. Fundamentos conceptuales (Bogotá: Siglo del Hombre Editores), 377–408.

Berger, Jonathan (2008), "Litigation for Social Justice in Post-Apartheid South Africa: A Focus on Health and Education," in Varun Gauri and Daniel Brinks (eds.), *Courting Social Justice. Judicial Enforcement of Social and Economic Rights in the Developing World* (New York: Cambridge University Press), 38–99.

Bilchitz, David (2007), *Poverty and Fundamental Rights: The Justification and Enforcement of Socio-Economic Rights* (Oxford: Oxford University Press).

Bilchitz, David (2013), "Constitutions and Distributive Justice: Complementary or Contradictory?" In Daniel Bonilla (ed.), *Constitutionalism of the Global South: The Activist Tribunals of India, South Africa, and Colombia* (New York: Cambridge University Press), 41–94.

Bourdieu, Pierre (2000), "Elementos para una sociología del campo jurídico," [La fuerza del derecho: Elementos para una sociología del campo jurídico]. In *Pierre Bourdieu and Gunther Teubner the Force of Law* [La fuerza del derecho]. Bogotá: Uniandes y Siglo del Hombre Editores.

Bonilla, Daniel (ed.) (2013), *Constitutionalism of the Global South: The Activist Tribunals of India, South Africa, and Colombia* (New York: Cambridge University Press)

Bourdieu and Gunther Teubner (eds.), *La fuerza del derecho* (Bogotá: Uniandes and Siglo del Hombre Editores), 153–220.

CELS (Centro de Estudios Legales y Sociales) (2008), *La lucha por el derecho. Litigio estratégico y derechos humanos* (Buenos Aires: Siglo Veintiuno Editores).

Chandrachud, Abhinav (2009), "Dialogic judicial activism in India," *The Hindu*, July 18, www.thehindu.com/2009/07/18/stories/2009071852820800.htm.

Chayes, Abram (1976), "The Role of the Judge in Public Law Litigation," *Harvard Law Review*, 89(7), 1281–1316.

Clavijo, Sergio (2001), *Fallos y fallas de la Corte Constitucional* (Bogotá: Alfaomega).

Codhes (Consultoría para los Derechos Humanos y el Desplazamiento) (2011), *¿Consolidación de qué? Informe sobre desplazamiento, conflicto armado y derechos humanos en Colombia en 2010* (Bogotá: Codhes).

Comisión de Seguimiento a la Política Pública sobre Desplazamiento Forzado (2008), *Séptimo Informe de verificación sobre el cumplimiento de derechos a la población en situación de desplazamiento* (Bogotá: Comisión de Seguimiento).

Coomans, Fons (ed.) (2006), *Justiciability of Economic Rights* (Intersentia).

Dixon, Rosalind (2007), "Creating Dialogue about Socioeconomic Rights: Strong-Form versus Weak-Form Judicial Review Revisited," *International Journal of Constitutional Law*, 5 (3), 391–418.

Dugard, Jackie (2013), "Urban Basic Services: Rights, Reality and Resistance," in Malcolm Langford, Ben Cousins, Jackie Dugard, and Tshepo Madligozi (eds.), *Socio-Economic Rights in South Africa: Symbols or Substance?* (New York: Cambridge University Press), 275–309.

Dugard, Jackie and Malcolm Langford (2011), "Art or Science? Synthesising Lessons from Public Interest Litigation and the Dangers of Legal Determinism," *South African Journal on Human Rights*, 27(1), 39–64.

El Tiempo (2014), "Colombia es el segundo país del mundo con más desplazados, tras Siria," May 14, www.eltiempo.com/mundo/latinoamerica/desplazamiento-en-colombia-segun-consejo-noruego-para-los-refugiados-/13989688.

Epp, Charles (1998), *The Rights Revolution: Lawyers, Activists and the Supreme Courts in Comparative Perspective* (Chicago: Chicago University Press).

Fairstein, Carolina, Gabriela Kletzel and Paola García Rey (2010), "En busca de un remedio judicial efectivo: Nuevos desafíos para la justiciabilidad de los derechos sociales," in Pilar Arcidiácono, Nicolás Espejo and César Rodríguez Garavito (eds.), *Derechos sociales: justicia, política y economía en América Latina* (Bogotá: Ediciones Uniandes, CELS, Universidad Diego Portales and Siglo del Hombre Editores), 25–80.

Feeley, Malcolm and Edward Rubin (1998), *Judicial Policymaking and the Modern State: How Courts Reformed America's Prisons* (Cambridge: Cambridge University Press).

Ferraz, Octavio (2011), "Brazil, Health Inequalities, Rights and Courts: The Social Impact of the Judicialization of Health," in Alicia Yamin and Siri Gloppen (eds.), *Litigating Health Rights: Can Courts Bring More Justice to Health?* (Cambridge, MA: Harvard University Press), 76–102.

Fredman, Sandra (2008), *Human Rights Transformed. Positive Rights and Positive Duties* (Oxford: Oxford University Press).

García-Villegas, Mauricio (2014), *La eficacia simbólica del derecho* (Bogotá: Debate).

Gargarella, Roberto (2011), "Dialogic Justice in the Enforcement of Social Rights," in Alicia Yamin and Siri Gloppen (eds.), *Litigating Health Rights: Can Courts Bring More Justice to Health?* (Cambridge, MA: Harvard University Press), 232–245.

Gauri, Varun (2010), "Fundamental Rights and Public Interest Litigation in India: Overreaching or Underachieving?" *Indian Journal of Law and Economics* 1 (1): 71–93.

Gauri, Varun and Daniel Brinks (eds.) (2008), *Courting Social Justice: Judicial Enforcement of Social and Economic Rights in the Developing World* (New York: Cambridge University Press).

González, Felipe (2004), *El trabajo clínico en materia de derechos humanos e interés público en América Latina* (Bilbao: Universidad de Deusto).

Hirsch, Danielle (2007), "A Defense of Structural Injunctive Remedies in South African Law," *Oregon Review of International Law*, 9(1), 1–66.

Hirschl, Ran (2004). *Towards Juristocracy: The Origins and Consequences of the New Constitutionalism*. Cambridge: Harvard University Press.

International Commission of Jurists (2008), *Courts and the Legal Enforcement of Economic, Social and Cultural Rights, Human Rights and Rule of Law Series No. 2* (Geneva: CIJ).

Kalmanovitz, Salomón (2001), *Las instituciones y el desarrollo económico en Colombia* (Bogotá: Editorial Norma).

Klarman, Michael (2007), *Brown v. Board of Education and the Civil Rights Movement* (Oxford: Oxford University Press).

Lamprea, Everaldo (2015), *Derechos en la práctica: Políticas de salud, litigio y cortes en Colombia (1991–2014)* (Bogotá: Uniandes).

Langford, Malcolm (ed.) (2003), *Litigating Economic, Social and Cultural Rights: Achievements, Challenges and Strategies* (Geneva: Centre on Housing Rights and Evictions).

(ed.) (2009), *Social Rights Jurisprudence. Emerging Trends in International and Comparative Law* (New York: Cambridge University Press).

Langford, Malcolm (2013), "Housing Rights Litigation: Grootbom and Beyond," in Malcolm Langford, Ben Cousins, Jacky Dugard, and Tshepo Madlingozi (eds.) (2013), *Symbols or Substance: The Role and Impact of Socio-Economic Rights Strategies in South Africa* (New York: Cambridge University Press), 187–225.

Langford, Malcolm, Ben Cousins, Jacky Dugard, and Tshepo Madlingozi (eds.) (2013), *Symbols or Substance: The Role and Impact of Socio-Economic Rights Strategies in South Africa* (New York: Cambridge University Press).

Liebenberg, Sandra (2010), *Socio-Economic Rights: Adjudication under a Transformative Constitution* (Claremont: JUTA).

Maurino, Gustavo, Ezequiel Nino, and Martín Sigal (2005), *Las acciones colectivas. Análisis conceptual, constitucional y comparado* (Buenos Aires: LexisNexis).

McCann, Michael (1994), *Rights at Work: Pay Equity Reform and the Politics of Legal Mobilization* (Chicago: Chicago University Press).

Michelman, Frank (2009), "Economic Power and the Constitution," in Jack Balkin and Reva Siegel (eds.), *The Constitution in 2020* (Oxford: Oxford University Press).

Muralidhar, S. (2008), "India," in Malcom Langford (ed.), *Social Rights Jurisprudence. Emerging Trends in International and Comparative Law* (New York: Cambridge University Press), 102–124.

National Planning Department and Ministry of Finance of Colombia (2014), "Report on Resources Assigned and Spent in the Framework of the Public Policy for the Population of Victims of Internal Displacement – Response to Order 5 of Decision 219 of 2011," Bogotá: DNP y MHCP. February 28.

Nino, Carlos Santiago (1996), *The Constitution of Deliberative Democracy* (New Haven, CT: Yale University Press).

Ottar Moestad, Lise Rakner, and Octavio Ferraz (2011), "Assessing the Impact of Health Rights Litigation: A Comparative Analysis of Argentina, Brazil, Colombia, Costa Rica, India, and South Africa," in Alicia Yamin and Siri Gloppen (eds.), *Litigating Health Rights: Can Courts Bring More Justice to Health?* (Cambridge, MA: Harvard University Press), 273–303.

Pillay, Anashri (2012), "Toward Effective Social and Economic Rights Adjudication: The Role of Meaningful Engagement," *International Journal of Constitutional Law* 10 (3), 732–755.

(2014), "Revisiting the Indian Experience of Economic and Social Rights Adjudication: The Need for a Principled Approach to Judicial Activism and Restraint," *International and Comparative Law Quarterly*, 63, 385–408.

Rajagopal, Balakrishnan (2005), "Limits of Law in Counter-Hegemonic Globalization: The Indian Supreme Court and the Narmada Valley Struggle," in Boaventura Santos and César Rodríguez Garavito (eds.), *Law and Globalization from Below: Toward a Cosmopolitan Legality* (New York: Cambridge University Press).

(2007), "Pro-Human Rights but Anti-Poor?: A Critical Evaluation of the Indian Supreme Court from a Social Movement Perspective," *Human Rights Review* 18 (3), 157–186.

Rodríguez-Garavito, César (2011a), "Beyond the Courtroom: The Impact of Judicial Activism on Socio-Economic Rights in Latin America," *Texas Law Review*, 89(7), 1669–1698.

(2011b), "Toward a Sociology of the Global Rule of Law Field: Neoliberalism, Neoconstitutionalism, and the Contest over Judicial Reform in Latin America," in Bryant Garth and Yves Dezalay (eds.), *Lawyers and the Rule of Law in an Era of Globalization* (New York: Routledge), 156–182.

(2013), "The Judicialization of Health: Symptoms, Diagnosis, and Prescriptions," in Randall Peerenboom and Tom Ginsburg, *Law and Development of Middle-Income Countries* (Cambridge: Cambridge University Press), 246–269.

(forthcoming), "Empowered Participatory Jurisprudence: Experimentation, Deliberation and Norms in Socioeconomic Rights Adjudication," in Katharine Young (ed.), *The Future of Economic and Social Rights* (Cambridge: Cambridge University Press).

Rodríguez-Garavito, César and Celeste Kauffman (2014), *Making Social Rights Real. Implementation Strategies for Courts, Decision Makers and Civil Society* (Bogotá: Dejusticia).

Rodríguez-Garavito, César and Diana Rodríguez-Franco (2015), *Radical Deprivation on Trial: The Impact of Judicial Activism on Socioeconomic Rights in the Global South* (Cambridge: Cambridge University Press).

Roth, Kenneth (2004), "Defending Economic, Social and Cultural Rights: Practical Issues Faced by an International Human Rights Organization," *Human Rights Quarterly*, 26(1), 63–73.

Rosenberg, Gerald (1991), *The Hollow Hope. Can Courts Bring About Social Change?* (Chicago: University of Chicago Press).

Sabel, Charles and William Simon (2004), "Destabilization Rights: How Public Law Litigation Succeeds," *Harvard Law Review*, 117(4), 1015–1101.

Shankar, Shylashri (2013), "The Embedded Negotiators: India's Higher Judiciary and Socioeconomic Rights," in Daniel Bonilla (ed.), *Constitutionalism of the Global South: The Activist Tribunals of India, South Africa, and Colombia* (New York: Cambridge University Press), 95–128.

Shankar, Shylashri and Pratap Bhanu Mehta (2008), "Courts and Socioeconomic Rights in Brazil," in Varun Gauri and Daniel Brinks (eds.), *Courting Social Justice: Judicial Enforcement of Social and Economic Rights in the Developing World* (New York: Cambridge University Press), 100–145.

Swidler, Ann (1986), "Culture in Action: Symbols and Strategies," *American Sociological Review*, 51(2), 273–286.

Sunstein, Cass (1996), "Against Positive Rights," in András Sajo (ed.), *Western Rights? Post-Communist Applications* (The Netherlands: Kluwer Law International), 225–232.

(2004), *The Second Bill of Rights* (New York: Basic Books).

Tushnet, Mark (2008), *Weak Courts, Strong Rights: Judicial Review and Social Welfare Rights in Comparative Constitutional Law* (Princeton: Princeton University Press).

Unger, Roberto (1987), *False Necessity: Anti-Necessitarian Social Theory in the Service of Radical Democracy* (New York: Verso).

UNHCR (2013), "War's Human Cost: UNHCR Global Trends 2013," http://www .unhcr.org/statistics/country/5399a14f9/unhcr-global-trends-2013.html.

Uprimny, Rodrigo (2006), "Should Courts Enforce Social Rights? The Experience of the Colombian Constitutional Court," in Fons Comans (ed.), *Justiciability of Economic and Social Rights: Experiences from Domestic Systems* (Antwerpen: Intersentia), 355–388.

Uprimny, Rodrigo and Mauricio García-Villegas (2004), "Corte Constitucional y emancipación social en Colombia," in Boaventura Santos and Mauricio García (eds.), *Emancipación social y violencia en Colombia* (Bogotá: Editorial Norma), 463–516.

Wilson, Bruce (2005), "Changing Dynamics: The Political Impact of Costa Rica's Constitutional Court," in Rachel Sieder, Line Schjolden and Alan Angell (eds.), *The Judicialization of Politics in Latin America* (London: Palgrave Macmillan), 47–66.

(2011), "Costa Rica: Health Rights Litigation: Causes and Consequences," in Alicia Yamin and Siri Gloppen (eds.), *Litigating Health Rights: Can Courts Bring More Justice to Health?* (Cambridge, MA: Harvard University Press), 132–154.

Yamin, Alicia, Oscar Parra and Camila Gianella (2011), "Judicial Protection of the Right to Health: An Elusive Promise?" in Alicia Yamin and Siri Gloppen (eds.), *Litigating Health Rights: Can Courts Bring More Justice to Health?* (Cambridge, MA: Harvard University Press), 103–131.

Yamin, Alicia and Siri Gloppen (eds.) (2011), *Litigating Health Rights: Can Courts Bring More Justice to Health?* (Cambridge, MA: Harvard University Press).

Part II

Case Studies

Costa Rica: Understanding Variations in Compliance

BRUCE M. WILSON AND OLMAN A. RODRÍGUEZ

4.1 Introduction

After many years of judicial inactivity, a new Constitutional Chamber of the Supreme Court was created in Costa Rica in 1989, the Sala Constitucional, commonly called the Sala Cuarta or Sala IV.[1] In the subsequent twenty years the Sala IV decided over 230,000 cases addressing virtually every article of the country's constitution including many economic, social, and cultural (ESC) rights. While a great deal is known about the creation of the Sala IV, how and why it became active, and the nature of its jurisprudence, little is known about the central question posed in this book: Under what conditions do court-mandated ESC rights decisions stick? This chapter examines this question by first detailing the transformation of the Costa Rican superior court system into one of the most assertive courts in the Americas, routinely deciding constitutional and rights-based cases. The following sections briefly examine the rapid expansion of the Court's caseload during its first twenty years of operation, while the body of the chapter addresses the book's central questions: What happens once a court makes a favourable ruling on ESC rights? Are its orders implemented or ignored by the government and other state and non-state actors? And which factors help, hurt, or hinder compliance with those decisions? We use new preliminary data from the Constitutional Chamber of the Supreme Court to examine which institutions generally comply with Court orders and which ones fail to comply,

---

[1] Prior to the creation of the Sala IV, the Costa Rican Supreme Court consisted of three Chambers that specialized in different areas of the law. In 1989, the Sala IV became the fourth chamber and specialized in constitutional issues; the original three chamber retained their function as Courts of Cassation in their specific field of law.

Bruce M. Wilson is a professor at the University of Central Florida, and Associated Senior Researcher, Chr. Michelsen Institute, Bergen Norway.

Olman A. Rodríguez L. is a *Letrado* in the Sala Constitucional, San José, Costa Rica.

and which types of ruling are more likely to be complied with. We also examine some specific successful ESC rights cases to tease out the conditions under which they are likely to be met with compliance or resistance by the defendant institutions. The cases help illuminate the positive impact some of these cases have had on the individual litigants and reveal the extent to which they have mitigated inequality and social injustice in Costa Rica. The final sections of the chapter examine the empirical evidence of the compliance or non-compliance with the Costa Rican Constitutional Court's ESC rights decisions.

4.2   Judicial Context: Animating a Rights-Rich Constitution

Costa Rica's Constitutional Chamber of the Supreme Court is generally recognised as one of the most powerful and assertive courts in the Americas, exercising both a significant accountability function and routinely enforcing a wide range of economic social and cultural rights (Navia and Ríos-Figueroa 2005; Gloppen et al. 2010; Helmke and Ríos-Figueroa 2011). Before the 1989 creation of the Constitutional Chamber of the Supreme Court, the country's rights-rich Constitution was largely ignored, and the significant powers mandated to the Court by the 1949 Constitution were rarely used to hold the other branches of state to account.[2] Historically, Costa Rica's Superior Court[3] was a typical Latin American superior court that rarely heard or ruled on cases seeking protection of any fundamental rights enumerated in the Constitution. Rodríguez Cordero (2002: 43) notes that in 1980 the Supreme Court dealt with just eleven rights-based *amparo* cases (writs of protection). The Supreme Court magistrates' view of their own powers and function was

---

[2] Among the historical developments of the many fundamental rights enshrined in the Costa Rican Constitution, it regulates those rights related to Civil and Political rights (first generation), the Economic, Social, and Cultural Rights (second generation), and those relating to Solidarity Rights (third generation). The 1949 Constitution holds those rights associated to a liberal constitution such as the right to freedom of expression (art. 29), of religion (art. 75), and to political rights (art. 90–98). It also regulates rights associated to a social constitution including housing rights (art. 65) or social security rights (art. 73), and finally those rights based on a solidarity concept such as the right to a healthy and ecologically balanced environment (art. 50), rights of the consumer (art. 46), among others. These and other rights are expanded through art. 48 of the Constitution, as it incorporates international human rights instruments (*Constitución de la República de Costa Rica, 1949*).

[3] The Supreme Court plays a second function as the administrative body of the Judicial branch (Poder Judicial) and prior to the 1989 constitutional reforms, it also acted as a constitutional court.

very limited; they 'exercised constitutional control with excessive timidity' (Gutierrez 1999: 49), and presumed the 'constitutionality for all laws' passed by the legislative assembly (Cruz Castro 2007: 557).

With the promulgation of a new constitution in 1949, political power was delineated among three independent branches of state: executive, legislature, and Supreme Court.[4] In the following forty years, the executive and legislative branches and the Supreme Elections Tribunal (TSE, Tribunal Supremo de Elecciones) solidified their institutional positions, while the Supreme Court maintained its pre-war deference to the popular branches and continued to demonstrate a lack of concern for constitutional rights. The Supreme Court was largely an irrelevance in the day-to-day political life of Costa Rica until after 1989 (Wilson 2007, 2009; Wilson and Rodríguez Cordero 2006).

4.2.1 Enabling an Assertive Court

The motivations for the judicial reform that created the Sala IV and the specific laws that created the new chamber of the Supreme Court have been discussed elsewhere (see, for example, Murillo 1994; Rodríguez 2011; Wilson 2011). In short, a legislative commission, established in the mid-1980s to investigate corruption in the Supreme Court, highlighted the Court's institutional shortcomings and recommended a more modern, efficient form of constitutional adjudication (Hernández 2007). The philosophical underpinnings of the 1989 constitutional amendments, then, were to give juridical life to the 1949 Constitution; one of the architects of the reforms, Rodolfo E. Piza Escalante, notes 'the cornerstone of our entire political system resides in the supremacy of the Constitution, which for us is the guarantee of democracy, freedom, the rule of law. So everything we do should tend toward the constitutionality of the actions of all public authorities and individuals, all that being conducive to getting things done under the Constitution, should be welcomed and everything that harms it must be rejected' (quoted in Castillo and Sansonetti, undated, 334). For Piza, a democratic constitution requires open access to the Court to protect the constitution and fundamental rights contained in international human

---

[4] Constitution Article 9, 'The Government of the Republic is popular, representative, participatory, alternative and responsible. It is exercised by three distinct and independent branches: Legislative, Executive, and Judicial. None of these Branches may delegate the exercise of their own functions' (as amended by law No. 8364, 1 July 2003). A quasi-fourth branch, the TSE was also created 'to interpret, with exclusive and compulsory effect, all constitutional and legal provisions on electoral matters' (art. 102).

rights instruments. A complete account of the constitutional changes that created the Constitutional Chamber of the Supreme Court is contained in Castillo and Sansonetti (undated), Hernández (2007), Wilson (2007, 2011), and Rodríguez (2011). Here we offer a brief summary of those changes and outline the most significant of the enabling laws that facilitated the Court's new assertiveness and subsequent jurisprudence.

The Sala IV has, since its creation, routinely exercised a broad account-ability function with respect to other branches of government, jettisoned the pre-reformed Supreme Court's long-standing adherence to legal for-mality, and opened a legal opportunity structure[5] that allowed even the poorest, most marginalised individuals to seek protection of their consti-tutional rights from the Court (Wilson 2007, 2011; Gloppen et al. 2010). The stark difference in judicial behaviour before and after the reforms of 1989 is often referred to as a 'judicial revolution' (Murillo 1994; Solis Fallas quoted in Martínez 2009). The rest of this chapter speaks to this 'revolu-tion' and examines the extent to which the Court's decisions stuck and made tangible differences to the litigants involved.

The *Ley No. 7128*,[6] (the law that amended the 1949 Constitution), man-dates the creation of a Constitutional Chamber of the Supreme Court, whilst the *Ley de la Jurisdicción Constitucional*[7] (*Law of the Constitutional Jurisdiction*) requires the Sala IV to 'guarantee the supremacy of the norms and constitutional principles, international law, and community law in force in the Republic, their uniform interpretation and application of fundamental rights and freedoms consecrated in the constitution or in international instruments in force in Costa Rica' (LJC 1989, art. 1). The LJC centralises judicial review, *habeas corpus*, *amparo*, etc. in the Sala IV. The writ of *amparo*, the most commonly filed case, is a 'summary pro-ceeding designed to discuss claims involving fundamental rights breaches (individual and social rights), it provides for an injunction relief with the exception of those rights relating to personal liberty, that are protected by the writ of *habeas corpus*' (Rodríguez 2011: 250). The writ of *amparo* can be viewed as a very malleable procedure, significantly different from the

---

[5] We use the term 'legal opportunity structure' to denote the structures and rules of the newly invigorated courts that created a new institutional avenue that individuals and groups can harness and utilise to seek protection of their rights or to demand other branches of the state be held to account for the constitutionality of their actions (Hilson 2002; Wilson and Rodríguez 2006).

[6] Law 7128, 18 August 1989, amended the 1949 Constitution's arts. 10, 48, 105 and 128.

[7] Ley de la Jurisdicción Constitucional [Law of the Constitutional Jurisdiction] Ley 7135, 11 October 1989, art. 1.

pre-reformed Supreme Court's high level of legal formality and restrictive standing, that allows any person regardless of gender, citizenship, or age, to file an *amparo* case, 24 hours a day, 365 days a year without the need for legal representation, legal knowledge, or filing fees. The lack of formality is reflected in the Court's willingness to accept even *amparos* hand-written on bread- wrapping paper, or in Braille (Terra 2009).

The new chamber of the Supreme Court transformed the Court from an inactive, institutionally weak, formal rule-bound institution to one of the most powerful and assertive superior courts in Latin America (Gloppen et al. 2010; Helmke and Ríos-Figueroa 2011). The Court has the power to adjudicate conflicts between government branches; exercise judicial review *a priori* and *a posteriori* and a dispute is not always necessary to ground jurisdiction, as abstract review can also be used. All the Court's precedents are binding jurisprudence, except on the Court itself, which is an unusual situation given that most *amparo* and *habeas corpus* decisions are motivated by individual claims. Indeed, according to former president of the Sala IV Magistrate Luis Fernando Solano 'there is no other tribunal in the world that has the competencies of the Sala IV' (Vizcaíno 2006; see also Hernández 2008). While none of these rules or powers guarantee their exercise by the Court, Wilson and Rodríguez Cordero (2006) demonstrate how taken together they created a low-cost legal opportunity structure that previously did not exist. As Sala IV Magistrate Eduardo Sancho notes, the Sala IV was not 'an institution created to be at the service of the executive branch, but quite the reverse: to protect the rights of people' (Corte Suprema de Justicia 1999). As the sections that follow show, this new legal opportunity structure has been widely used by groups and individuals from virtually every sector of society including the weakest, most marginalised individuals and groups from prisoners, homosexuals, and AIDS patients to women and labour.

4.2.2   The Sala IV's First Twenty Years

The darker area of Figure 4.1 illustrates the dramatic increase in the Court's total caseload since its inception, from approximately 2,300 cases in its first full year of operation (1990) to almost 19,000 in 2009.[8] The lighter area in Figure 4.1 shows the rapid growth in *amparo* cases (many

---

[8] While the growth in the number of cases filed is very real, fluctuations in the number from one year to the next need to be treated with some caution. On any given day the number of cases filed might jump by hundreds due to the filing of 'casos masivos' by unions or professional associations on behalf of their members.

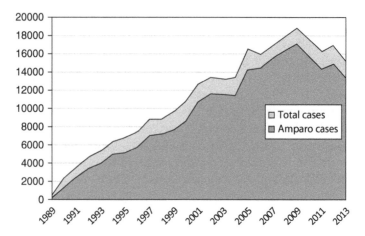

Figure 4.1 Cases filed with the Sala IV, 1989–2013
Source: Sección de estadísticas, departamento de planificación, Poder Judicial, 2015.
http://sitios.poder-judicial.go.cr/salaconstitucional/estadisticas.htm

of which involve ESC rights), which constitute the overwhelming majority of the caseload. Unfortunately, the limited nature of the Sala IV's study
on compliance does not reveal any concrete information on the percentage of the writs of *amparo* that directly involve ESC rights. What we do
know, both anecdotally[9] and from the Court's published list of leading
cases (Poder Judicial 2012), is that the number of ESC rights cases has
similarly increased over the years. To overcome the limitations of the
data, we use a series of examples of successful ESC rights claims to illustrate compliance levels of the Constitutional Chamber of the Supreme
Court's decisions. The level of informality, accessibility, and prioritised
proceedings makes the Sala IV an attractive and effective avenue for
individuals or groups to harness the power of the Court to establish or
protect their constitutional rights. Figure 4.2 illustrates that the rush to
harness the easy, low-cost access to the new court generated a caseload
that almost swamped the Court's capacity to decide the cases. In the early
years of the Court, as the caseload grew, so too did the time required to
decide cases, from approximately eleven weeks in the first years to almost
forty weeks by the mid-1990s. The Court finally caught up with its caseload and gradually reduced the time between the filing of the case and the

---

[9] One of the authors of this chapter, Olman Rodríguez, has worked as a *letrado* (clerk) on the
Sala IV for more than twenty years.

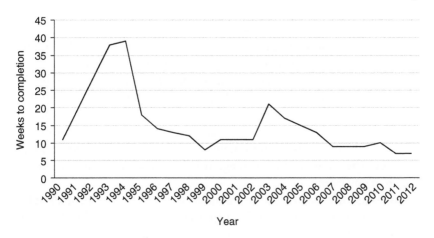

Figure 4.2 Average time to resolve a writ of Amparo by the Sala IV, 1990–2012
Source: Sección de estadísticas, departamento de planificación, Poder Judicial, 2015.

rendering of a decision, which declined to the current level of less than nine weeks. The increase in the speed of the judicial process coupled with the legal opportunity structure's low-cost access perhaps encouraged still more cases.

But as Sieder et al. (2005: 3) note, 'greater activism on the part of the Courts does not necessarily or automatically signal the strengthening of individual or group rights'. That is, just because there is a clear judicialisation of ESC rights claims, it does not follow that the Court would necessarily support those rights claims. And, even if the Court does decide in favour of the rights claims, there is no guarantee the Court's decisions would automatically be complied with.

The extent of the Court's willingness to support and protect individual rights is documented in Wilson (2007, 2009, 2011, 2014); here an examination of some notable, early rights cases provide a clear picture of the Sala IV's jurisprudence enforcing the constitutional rights of weak, marginalised individuals and groups. Critics of the Court's caseload claim that the Court is 'occupied with cases of little importance', but Magistrate Rodolfo Piza Escalante (quoted in Méndez 1999) argues that they are missing the significance of the Court's jurisprudence. He notes that in these cases 'everything depends on for whom it is important'. By way of an example, he references one of the Court's earliest decisions (Resolution No. 75–89) in favour of 'Don Trino', a humble shaved-ice vendor. In 1989, President Oscar Arias (PLN 1986–90), minister for security, argued that 'Don Trino' would be a security risk if he continued to sell his wares in his usual location outside the Legislative Assembly building during a meeting of Latin American Heads of State that was to be held nearby. But the Sala IV stated 'Don Trino' had a right to work unimpeded by the state and should be allowed to ply his trade in his usual location; for him 'the most important thing was to eat and to bring sustenance back to his family'. This early decision set the tone for many subsequent cases involving marginalised, weak sectors of society seeking to protect their ESC rights even against the decisions of the executive branch of government.

Subsequent decisions included rulings in favour of disabled people's right of access to public buildings and transportation (Resolution No. 4576–96) and protection for prisoners from poor living conditions and overcrowding (Resolutions No. 7484-00). Both these decisions were complied with and resulted in major improvements in the lives of the plaintiffs, improved access for disabled people and the renovation and building of new jails to reduce overcrowding (US Department of State 2001). Homosexuals, another socially and politically marginalised group, won the right to legal recognition for their organisations and subsequently won protection from police brutality as a result of a Sala IV decision (Resolution No. 4732–94). Similarly, journalists and workers have won Court decisions protecting their economic rights: in 1995, the Sala IV declared that a mandatory state license for journalists was an unconstitutional limitation on journalists' right to work (Resolution No. 2313–95); in 1998 labour unions won the right to strike (Resolution No. 1317–98), which had been severely restricted by the state since the end of the Civil War in 1949 (Wilson 2009). In all these cases the Court's decisions were accepted and complied with by the relevant government agencies and significantly enhanced the lives of all people in similar situations, not just the unions and individuals who filed the cases.

The Sala IV has not limited itself to enforcing only individual rights contained explicitly in the Constitution. Rather the Court has, on occasion, also constructed new ESC rights or expanded existing ones by combining constitutional articles and international legal instruments, including, for example, a new fundamental right to health, discussed in later pages. Since its inception, the Sala IV has cited international human rights treaties and instruments, such as the Universal Declaration of Human Rights, to deepen the reach of constitutional rights on Costa Rican society. In 1990, for example, the Court resolved a conflict between domestic legislation and the Inter-American Convention of Human

Rights in a habeas corpus case (Resolution No. 1990–00282). The Court argued international instruments should be treated according to art. 7 of the Constitution, which states 'public treaties, international agreements and concordats duly approved by the Legislative Assembly shall have a higher authority than the laws upon their enactment or from the day that they designate'. This decision quickly became a leading case and has been widely used in subsequent Court decisions allowing human rights instruments to prevail over Costa Rican law, a clear reversal of the pre-reformed Supreme Court's view of international human rights treaties. Four subsequent decisions (Resolution Nos. 1992–3435, 1993–5759, 1995–2313, 2000–9685) rely on art. 48 to expand this important legal principle to recognise that international human rights instruments prevail over the Constitution as long as they grant more protection than the Constitution.[10]

4.3   Making ESC Rights Decisions Stick

Although a huge and growing number of *amparo* cases are filed each year, only a small percentage actually win favourable decisions from the Sala IV. Even with only a low proportion of *amparo* cases winning at the Court, this still produces a large absolute number of successful cases due to the massive caseload. For example, in 2009 almost 19,000 cases were filed at the Sala IV, 90 per cent (17,000) of which were *amparo* cases; 25 per cent of those cases won favourable decisions from the Court creating approximately 4,000 successful litigants. The success of *amparo* cases, though, is not uniform across all subcategories of *amparo* cases. Indeed, if we consider the success rate just for health rights cases, it is revealed that over 60 per cent of cases are successful, significantly higher than the average for all *amparos* (Doryan Garron 2008). The question of what happens once a case is successful at the Court was, until recently, unknown. Historically, the Court collected no systematic data on levels of compliance with its decisions, which led Costa Rican Political Scientist, Vargas Cullell (2010), to conclude, 'it is possible to have faith in the system of judicial administration', but what happens after a ruling is made 'in many cases, is a real

---

[10] Article 48 states, 'Every person has the right to present writs of *habeas corpus* to guarantee his freedom and personal integrity and writs of amparo to maintain or reestablish the enjoyment of other rights conferred by this Constitution as well as those of fundamental nature established in international instruments on human rights, enforceable in the Republic. Both writs shall be within the jurisdiction of the Chamber indicated in Article 10' (as amended by Law No. 7128 of 18 August 1989).

mystery and, probably, an ordeal for many who received a favorable but ineffective decision'.

While the Court lacked any formal mechanism to track what happened to its decisions once a case had been decided, it does, on the surface, appear to have some strong tools to enforce compliance with its decisions, including the power to review cases for compliance and to initiate prosecutions of non-compliant defendants.[11] Also, to encourage compliance with Court decisions, Sala IV issues decisions against named defendants, usually the senior official at the offending agency. If the official does not comply with the Court order, the Sala IV will again order the superior official to comply. If they still fail to comply, criminal charges can be brought against the offending official.[12] Furthermore, when a defendant repeatedly engages in actions that the Court had previously found unconstitutional, another set of criminal penalties apply.[13] But as with other non-compliance cases, the Sala IV relies on Public Prosecutors office to initiate criminal proceedings before lower-level criminal courts, using the special criminal provisions held in the Law of the Constitutional Jurisdiction for dealing with people who defy the Court's orders or are in contempt of Court.[14] Penalties for defendants found guilty for non-compliance range from two to three years in jail or a fine of between twenty to sixty days' income, as determined by the criminal judge based on the defendant's personal income.

It is often thought the Court never closes a file until it is satisfied there is enforcement, the reality, though, is a little more complex. If a defendant fails to comply with a Court order, the principal mechanism for alerting the Court comes from the unsatisfied successful plaintiff. If the failure to comply is due to an inborn problem in the nature of the Court's original decision, the Court may respond to a plaintiff or a defendant's request to adapt its decision, taking into account the difficulties of complying with the original decision. It should be noted that the framers of the LJC left open the possibility for the Court to act *sua sponte* (to act on its own authority and independent from the parties involved) to implement the decision or to guarantee full compliance with the constitutional decision (see art. 12 of

---

[11] Law of the Constitutional Jurisdiction, arts. 56, 71.

[12] Law of the Constitutional Jurisdiction, art. 53. The law establishes the obligation to comply to a ruling without delay, nevertheless if within forty-eight hours the defendant does not do so, the Constitutional Chamber will order the superior to comply and to initiate disciplinary proceedings against the defiant conduct.

[13] Ley de la Jurisdicción Constitucional, art. 72.

[14] For other judicial proceedings different from the Constitutional Jurisdiction, the Código Penal Ley No. 4573 del 4 de mayo de 1970, art. 307, or if no other special legislation applies to the case.

the LJC). The Sala IV, then, needs either party to make it aware of the compliance problem, unless it is apparent to the Court that it needs to modify its own decision in order for it to be complied with.

In general, though, it is primarily the responsibility of the plaintiff to pursue recalcitrant defendants and request the Constitutional Chamber to summon them, hear their responses, and rule on the non-compliance in a summary fashion. While this could be viewed as an effective monitoring system, it is perhaps a cumbersome method of responding to instances of non-compliance, especially when the judicial informality and open access to the Court was specifically designed to allow even the poorest, most marginalised people in society to use the legal opportunity structure afforded by the Court. Daniel Brinks (2011), though, takes a more positive view of the original compliance mechanism, noting that it was perhaps an effective, 'good system' that acted as 'a fire alarm rather than a police patrol – more efficient and in the care of the most directly affected'.

In 2009, the Sala IV in conjunction with the Estado de la Nación, a leading Costa Rican think tank, created a monitoring mechanism to trace what happens once the Court issues its decisions (Gauri et al. 2015). Owing to the huge number of cases and paucity of resources devoted to the study,[15] the investigators elected to follow the progress of successful cases decided over a thirteen-month period from 1 October 2009 and 31 October 2010 in which a concrete order was issued. During the period covered by the study, 20,205 cases were decided of which 4,333 were successful cases with concrete orders. The investigators phoned the litigant to ascertain their view of what the defendant did in response to the Court's order. If the litigant was satisfied with the defendant's level of compliance, the investigators recorded it as 'complied with', but if they were not satisfied, then the investigators contacted the defendants for their explanation. The results were then registered and communicated to the magistrate in charge of the case for further judicial scrutiny.

The preliminary results reveal that a favourable ruling from the Court does not guarantee compliance from the defendant or that the plaintiff will actually benefit from the ruling. Rather, the study shows 'levels of compliance with the resolutions of the Constitutional Chamber are low' with many defendants not complying with the Court's rulings (PEN 2011: 264). While the monitoring is ongoing and has, at the time of writing, only

---

[15] Currently only two members of the Sala IV's staff are engaged in the laborious task of phoning plaintiffs and defendants from thousands of court decisions to determine the level of compliance and the reasons for the compliance or lack thereof (PEN 2011: 264).

ascertained the outcome of 2,355 of the 4,333 cases, it reveals some clear compliance patterns with Court decisions and hints at the conditions under which successful litigants are more likely to see their judicial victory enforced. Although the monitoring mechanism does not distinguish between ESC rights and other cases, the study still sheds some light on the conditions under which the Court's decisions stick.[16] The compliance study divides the Sala IV cases by the type of defendant and the general subject matter of litigation. The study shows that, in general, 'the levels of compliance with the resolutions of the Constitutional Chamber are low, though with differences depending on the defendant institution and the deadlines for compliance with the ruling' (PEN 2011: 227).

The provisional nature of the Sala IV's compliance study necessarily makes any conclusions drawn from the data tentative. Furthermore, we have less concrete evidence to explain the motivation of the defendants in these cases, but it is perhaps possible to suggest some plausible explanations for the different patterns of compliance that have been observed. First, different levels of constitutional independence and autonomy afforded to government institutions and agencies appear to affect the level of compliance with Court decisions. Government ministries, for example, due to their close political ties and institutional role as part of the executive branch enjoy a stronger, more buttressed legal position when the Court rules against them. This may explain why these institutions are less likely to comply with Court decisions compared to smaller state institutions such as decentralised institutions including autonomous institutions and municipalities. It is also plausible that autonomous institutions and municipalities are able and will respond to Court orders more quickly than the centralised governments due to their size and their ability to utilise important legal instruments. We now examine these two factors that have a significant impact on compliance with the Sala IV's rulings: the nature of the defendant and the required time limits for compliance.

4.3.1   Nature of the Defendant

Table 4.1, based on the data produced in the compliance study, reveals some key insights into the puzzle of which defendants comply with the Court's rulings and when they do so. A major factor in the level of compliance

---

[16] Gauri et al. (2015: 774) conclude that 'vague orders, and orders issued without definite time frames for compliance, were associated with delayed implementation' and that once it became widely known the court was, for the first time, monitoring compliance with its decisions, the time to implementation declined by up to two months.

Table 4.1 *Compliance with Sala IV Orders by Sector, 1 October 2009–31 October 2010*

Institutional Sector	Complied	Not Complied	Total
Centralised Public Sector	427 (24%)	1,340 (76%)	1,767 (100%)
Decentralised Public Sector	370 (88%)	49 (12%)	419 (100%)
Non-state Public +Entities	3 (100%)	0 (0%)	3 (100%)
Municipalities	108 (78%)	31 (22%)	139 (100%)
Private Organisations or Persons	23 (85%)	4 (15%)	27 (100%)
Total	931 (40%)	1,424 (60%)	2,355 (100%)

Note: These data do not include the 1,900 sentences that have not been followed up on by the Centro de Jurisprudencia Constitucional. Decentralised state sector includes the state's autonomous institutions such as CCSS, AyA, ICE. Centralised state sector are the state ministries, non-state public entities include professional associations. 'Complied' includes all sentences classified as 'cumplidas' by the Centro de Jurisprudencia Constitucional; 'Not Complied' includes all sentences classified as 'cumplimiento parcial', 'cumplimientos no probados' and 'sin respuesta por la entidad recurrida'.
Source: Programa Estado de la Nación elaborated from the database of the seguimiento de sentencias, Centro de Jurisprudencia Constitucional, Sala IV.

depends, in large part, on the nature of the defendant. For example, centralised public agencies are the least likely state institutions to comply with Sala IV decisions. In the period covered by the study, the centralised agencies (primarily the various ministries) complied with just 24 per cent of the 1,767 decisions they lost at the constitutional court, failing to comply with a full 76 per cent of the rulings.[17] That is, litigants who file claims against the centralised state agencies might win a case at the Sala IV, but they are unlikely to benefit from their successful litigation.

[17] Recently, the Ministry of Education (MEP), a centralised state agency, became aware of its poor compliance record and has decided to voluntarily report back to the Court when it has complied with the Constitutional Chamber's rulings. This information will be added to the Sala IV's compliance database under a new category "*Cumplimiento no comprobado*" "unverified compliance"). Sonia Villegas Grijalba, Interview with the coordinator of the Centro de Jurisprudencia Constitucional on 9 September 2011.

At the other end of the compliance scale are decentralised public institutions that comply with Sala IV decisions in over 88 per cent of the cases
they lose. Similarly, private individuals and organisations have a relatively
high compliance rate with Court decisions (85 per cent of the time) as have
the country's municipal governments which complied with almost 78 per
cent of the cases in which they received a negative ruling (108 out of 130).[18]

4.3.2   Time Granted for Compliance

Another major factor affecting defendants' compliance levels is the length
of time given by the Sala IV to comply with its decisions. Table 4.2 shows
that the overall compliance rate is 40 per cent, but this figure, however,
hides some significant variation in compliance rates depending on the
length of time the Court allowed for implementation. To illustrate, over
94 per cent of all cases containing an order for immediate implementation are in fact complied with. For decisions allowing up to a month for
compliance, the rate decreases to 39 per cent and to 25 per cent for cases
where the decisions allowed more than a month to over a year. For decisions not specifying a time limit, compliance rates were similarly low at 27
per cent.[19] Thus, Table 4.2 illuminates that decisions ordering immediate
execution of the Court's order are significantly more likely to be complied
with than any other judicial order with a more relaxed time or no time
requirement.

Because of the preliminary nature of the Sala IV's compliance study, it
remains unclear if the time period allocated to comply with the Court's
decisions is itself the driver of non-compliance or if it is the complexity
and nature of the order to be executed that results in the Court offering longer time limits that foster non-compliance. For example, a health
rights case requiring immediate action on a Court decision to keep
a patient alive would likely be complied promptly and in full. On the
other hand, decisions requiring the construction of public infrastructure
(new street lamps, retro-fitting buildings for handicap access, etc), or
where individual circumstances of cases necessarily require more time

[18] Professional associations are reported to have complied at a rate of 100 per cent, but this is
based on only three cases in which they were unsuccessful defendants during the period of
the study.
[19] The paucity of cases in the mid-time periods required them to be combined into a single
category of 'more than a month to over a year'.

Table 4.2 *Compliance with Sala IV Orders by Time, 1 October 2009–31 October 2010*

Nature of decision	Complied	Not complied	Total
Immediately	289 (94%)	17 (6%)	306 (100%)
Up to one month	275 (39%)	423 (61%)	698 (100%)
Between one month and more than a year	39 (25%)	118 (75%)	157 (100%)
No time limit	327 (2)%	866 (73%)	1,193 (100%)
Total	930 (40%)	1,424 (60%)	2,354 (100%)

Source: Programa Estado de la Nación elaborated from the database of the seguimiento de sentencias, Centro de Jurisprudencia Constitucional, Sala IV

for planning, public hearings, permits, site preparation and execution, might offer a plausible explanation for the lack of compliance with the Court's order.

What we do know is that decentralised institutions tend to be given less time to comply with the Court's rulings; 'immediate orders for execution' account for over 40 per cent of all the decisions affecting that sector; a further 25 per cent granted up to a month and only few decisions (less than 5 per cent) fall in the medium-term range of 'between one month and more than a year', with the remainder of the rulings having no time period specified. Rulings against the centralised institutions as defendants rarely order immediate action (4.4 per cent), but often (33 per cent of the time) require compliance within a month. The majority of the rulings, though, include no time limit to meet the Court's orders. Similar patterns of time limits are given for rulings against non-state, public entities (56 per cent) and municipalities (45 per cent). The vast majority of decisions against private persons or organisations (over 70 per cent) have no specified time limit for compliance. The data presented, then, show a very clear picture of when Sala IV decisions are complied with. Without needing to know the nature of the case or the likely costs of the judgment's implementation, or the extent of the litigant's support groups, it is possible to predict with a fairly high level of accuracy whether or not the successfully litigated claim will be complied with. The two key elements are the nature of the defendant institution and length of time the Court gives the defendant to comply. Thus, a Sala IV decision with an order of immediate application issued against a decentralised state agency has an extremely high likelihood of compliance. On the other hand, a decision against a centralised state agency with a mid-range time requirement is unlikely to be complied with.[20]

4.4   When ESC Rights Do Not Stick

Before examining the conditions under which successfully argued ESC rights are implemented, it is helpful to briefly discuss an example of where a defendant did not comply with the Court's decision. Here we look at a constitutionally protected employees' right to the timely payment of severance pay. Although it has been repeatedly affirmed in numerous Sala IV decisions, it remains a frequently infringed ESC right. These cases help illustrate under what conditions Sala IV decisions protecting ESC rights are difficult to enforce.

Article 56 of the Constitution[21] requires the state to actively ensure all forms of labour are legal and properly remunerated, to preserve workers' freedom of choice of work, and enforce the prohibition of slavery and any form of labour that undermines human dignity. One aspect of the labour legislation[22] that has been repeatedly brought to the Court concerns workers' entitlement to severance payments if they are dismissed from their job. If an employer unilaterally dismisses a worker without due cause, the worker is entitled to full severance payment. If, on the other hand, the worker is terminated for malfeasance, then he or she is not entitled to severance payments. The idiosyncratic nature of the individual employee's dismissal perhaps makes the general application of the jurisprudence more difficult. In addition, since there are many different employers, even within the state sector, and many different people involved in the processing of

[20] The Sala IV in its rulings weighs and ponders all the circumstances at stake in a particular case including the ease with which the defendant could realistically comply with the ruling. Moreover the Court has to establish the nature and feasibility of a ruling being complied with under a particular setting in order to protect an individual fundamental right.

[21] Constitución de la República de Costa Rica (1949) art. 56. 'Work is a right of the individual and an obligation to society. The State shall seek to ensure that everyone has lawful, useful and properly remunerated employment, and to prevent the establishment of conditions that in any way curtail human freedom or dignity or degrade labor to the status of mere merchandise. The State guarantees the right to free choice of work.'

[22] Código de Trabajo (1949) arts. 28, 29, 31.

severance payments, it may be more difficult to routinely avoid the rights infringement.

Throughout the 1990s and continuing in the 2000s, the Sala IV consistently argued that severance pay must to be paid to terminated employees within a reasonable timeframe, with any excessive delay deemed unconstitutional. In spite of the consistency of the Court's jurisprudence on the question of delays in making severance payments, there remains a significant volume of very similar cases from public workers suggesting that this particular ESC right is not being followed by public authorities. Even today, there are many cases and claims against public entities, central government, decentralised agencies, and municipalities that have in one way or another overstepped this rule and infringed the Constitutional Chamber's doctrine.[23]

By way of an example, in 1996, a police officer was dismissed by the Ministerio de Seguridad Pública (Ministry of Public Security), a centralised state agency. After several months had passed and he had still not received his severance payment, he filed a case with the Sala IV. The Court decided (Resolution No. 1997–0942) in his favour and argued the role of the state is to protect, not undermine the policeman's liberty and human dignity. The Court ordered the ministry to pay the severance money in a timely manner without infringing the former police officer's human dignity and the universal right to human life. What is interesting in this case is that a number of similar cases[24] were previously decided by the Court in response to a series of claims from public workers who were laid off as part of a government state employment reduction policy. The state offered workers extraordinary payments, benefits, and indemnities to voluntarily leave public employment, but only made those severance payments after considerable delay and a torturous claims procedure.

In these severance payment cases, Court jurisprudence has *erga omnes* effect and has been consistent in resolving similar cases on how the centralised and decentralised agencies must conduct their business operations to avoid infringements of constitutional rights (of their employees and the public in general). Yet, the defendant agencies tend not to curtail their unconstitutional behaviour until a claimant files a case with the Court and

---

[23] See, for example, resolutions 2011–2896; 2011–2813; 2011–1754; 2011–1751 decided against the Ministry of Education; resolution 2011–1901 against MINAET; resolutions 2010–16305 and 2011–2909 against the CCSS; resolution 2011–2916 against the municipality de Moravia.

[24] SCCSJ, 1 March 1996, SCIJ, No. 1996-01064; (Costa Rica); SCCSJ, 27 September 1995, SCIJ, No. 1995–05312 (Costa Rica). These cases were cited in the 1997-0942 case.

they are summoned with the threat of criminal penalties. Although we lack sufficient information to draw generalised conclusions concerning the degree to which different government institutions routinely adhere to the doctrine of the Sala Constitucional, it is clear that some agencies follow the Court's decisions only after there has been a specific concrete warning directed at them to comply and do so merely on a case-by-case basis rather than as an expansive application of the Court's decision.[25] In cases like these, it seems that the Court's clear rulings on the constitutionality of timely severance payments does not alter the behaviour of employers, public and private, until a specific case is filed with the Court. If the Court decides in favour of the specific litigant, compliance tends to follow.

4.5   When ESC Rights Decisions Stick

This section discusses some illustrative ESC rights cases that won favourable rulings from the Sala IV and where the defendant complied with the Court's order in a timely fashion. Our motive for selecting cases affecting some of the weakest, most socially marginalised, and politically disenfranchised groups in society is to highlight the far-reaching impact of the Court's ESC rights decisions and illustrate the ease of access to the Court. If the weakest groups in society are able to harness the powers of the Court to protect their constitutional rights, it is logical that more privileged sectors of society are similarly able to seek its protection.

An early example of an ESC rights decision that imposed positive obligations on the state and had a significant impact on both the individual litigant and a wider class of persons was handed down by the constitutional court in its first year of existence. The Sala IV ordered an end to years of state agencies' discriminatory practice and neglect of blind people's employment rights (Resolution No. 1990–0567). The case illustrates the capacity of a superior court ruling to have a major impact on the lives of the litigants, with the enforcement of its ruling going beyond what had been possible through the promulgation of a law by the Legislative Assembly. It further demonstrates the importance of the new and more

---

[25] There are two types of resolution of these severance cases, those where the defendant complies (satisfying the plaintiff's petition) once the amparo proceeding started, which will result in a favourable decision awarding the plaintiff only damages caused. When this does not happen, the Sala IV will order the defendant to immediate pay the severance money (and damages) and will be given up to fifteen days to comply with the ruling. See, for example, the recent Sala IV decisions No. 2011–2896, 2011–2813, 2011–1901, 2011–1754, and 2011–1751.

accessible legal opportunity structure for the politically weak, marginalised, and unorganised individuals and groups. A 1957 law clarified
the state's legal obligations to blind employees and specified remedies
to remove the barriers impeding the advancement of their careers. This
law, however, was largely ineffectual.[26] State agencies did little to enforce
the law and efforts by the Civil Service Office, and the Commission also
failed to resolve the problem. As a result, sight-impaired people were
unable to effectively and practically sit promotion exams required for
the advancement of their careers in the same manner as their sighted
colleagues.

The Constitutional Chamber's ruling opened up new opportunities to blind people seeking careers in public administration by forcing
state agencies to provide braille versions of promotion exams, which are
now routinely available to blind people seeking to advance their careers
(Resolution No. DG-234-2008). The Court's decision, though, had a much
broader impact. In subsequent years, the Civil Service Office adopted the
sentiment of the Court's ruling by recruiting persons with disabilities to
fill up to 5 per cent of all vacant posts (until they constitute 2 per cent of all
jobs in the Central Government). This decision opened up the number of
positions available to persons with disabilities, removed barriers to their
promotion, and led to the Civil Service Office's routine incorporation of
international instruments including the Inter-American Convention to
Eliminate All Forms of Discrimination Against Persons with Disabilities;[27]
the Convention Concerning Vocational Rehabilitation and Employment
(Disabled Persons);[28] and the Law on Equal Opportunities for Persons
with Disabilities.[29]

Costa Rican unions, although not socially marginalised, are another
group that struggled politically for many years, without success, to nul-
lify anti-union laws severely limiting their members' ESC rights. Once

---

[26] Ley del Patronato de Ciegos [Council for the Blind Law], art. 20, Ley No. 2171 del 30 de
octubre de 1957 (Costa Rica).

[27] Convención Interamericana para la eliminación de todas las formas de discriminación
contra las personas con discapacidad [Inter-American Convention on the Elimination
of all Forms of Discrimination Against Personas with Disabilities] Ley No. 7948 de 22 de
noviembre de 1999 (Costa Rica).

[28] Convención sobre la readaptación profesional y el empleo de personas inválidas [ILO
Vocational Rehabilitation and Employment (Disabled Persons) Convention (159)] Ley No.
7219 de 18 de abril de 1991(Costa Rica).

[29] Ley de Igualdad de Oportunidades para las Personas con Discapacidad [Law on
Equal Opportunities for Persons with Disabilities] Ley No. 7600 de 2 de mayo de 1996
(Costa Rica).

the Sala IV was created, organised labour shifted its strategy and sought to harness the power of the Court to impose negative obligations on the state to protect their members' rights. Thus, in one case the unions sought to challenge the laws governing Costa Rican labour relations before the Court. These labour laws found under the 1943 Código de Trabajo Ley No. 2, of 27 August 1943 (Labour Code), which contained language designed, in part, to weaken the economic and political power of organised labour, especially public sector labour unions (Wilson 1998: 69–70), were the main subject of these proceedings. For example, while the Constitution contains a 'right to strike' (art. 61), that right was historically only afforded to non-public sector workers in accordance with the Labour Code.[30] An additional example was art. 376 of the Labour Code, which used a very broad definition of 'public worker' to include the overwhelming majority of the workforce effectively removing the constitutionally protected right to strike from over 60 per cent of the total labour force (Villalobos 1998). This was a clear and significant weakening of unions' ability to threaten or employ strike action as part of their bargaining strategy.

In the 1998 decision, the Sala IV ruled in favour of four public sector unions finding that the Labour Code's definition of 'public worker' was too broad and was consequently unconstitutional (Resolution No. 1317–98).[31] This automatically restored the right to strike not just to members of the four unions that filed the case, but to the vast majority of public workers, essentially strengthening their bargaining power (Villalobos 1998). Since the ruling, only a very narrow definition of 'public sector workers' has been used in determining the legality of strike actions by unions.

This case and others that require the state to adopt new rules and codes to enhance ESC rights or to stop impeding the application of those rights tend to be relatively easy to comply with since the Court's orders are clear and specific and the cost of implementation low. The impact of these relatively low cost compliance actions have, nonetheless, resulted in profound impacts on the plaintiffs' situation and broader society. In the Labour Code decisions, discussed above, it was not just the four public unions filing the case that benefitted, but all unions and their members.

---

[30] Código de Trabajo [Labour Code] Ley No. 2, 29 August 1943 (Costa Rica) art. 61 states: 'The right of employers to lockout and of workers to strike is recognized, except in public services, as determined by law and in accordance with the legal regulations on this subject, which shall prohibit all acts of coercion or violence.'

[31] Articles 376a, 376b, 376e, and art. 389, paragraph 2, of the Labour Code.

4.5.1   Gender Equality

As a result of a ruling by the Sala IV, gender equality in Costa Rica is much more of a reality. An early Court decision on naturalisation (Resolution No. 1992–3435) is another important example of public agencies routinely complying with Constitutional Chamber decisions. Before the Court decision in 1992, art. 14.5 of the Constitution only permitted the naturalisation of foreign-born wives of Costa Rican men; foreign-born husbands of Costa Rican women had no parallel right to naturalisation. Article 14.5 states,

> A foreign woman who, after being married to a Costa Rican for two years, and having resided in the country during the same period, indicates her desire to acquire the Costa Rican nationality.[32]

The Court saw this limitation as discriminatory and ruled that all foreign-born spouses should be treated equally in the naturalisation process. In response, the government agency responsible for processing applications for naturalisation, the Civil Registrar Office within the Supreme Elections Tribunal (TSE) immediately complied with the Court's order and brought equality to the naturalisation process, positively benefitting thousands of mixed-nationality couples who were eligible to acquire Costa Rican citizenship. While the ruling took immediate effect, the Legislative Assembly took another seven years to pass Law No. 7879 eliminating the discriminatory language identified by the Constitutional Chamber.[33]

4.5.2   Imposing Obligations on the State

Health rights cases are qualitatively different from the ESC rights enforcement cases discussed earlier, as they generally impose positive (very expensive) obligations on the state. In successful health rights cases, the order issued by the Court still requires the defendant to correct a constitutional infringement. However, unlike cases leading to administrative rule changes, the imposition of positive obligations nearly always

---

[32] Constitution art. 14.5, 1949.

[33] Reforma del inciso 5) del artículo 14 de la Constitución Política [Amendment to section 5 of article 14 of the Constitution] Ley No. 7879 del 27 de mayo de 1999, publicada en *La Gaceta* No. 118 del 18 de junio de 1999 (Costa Rica). The relevant section on naturalisation in art. 14 reads: 'A foreigner who by marrying a Costa Rican loses their nationality or who after having been married two years to a Costa Rican, and resides in the country in the same period, expresses their desire to acquire Costa Rican nationality.' See www.tse.go.cr/servicio30.htm.

requires action and significant expense on the part of the state. Here, the Court is placed in the centre of a complex budgetary decision-making process.

The explosion in successful health rights cases was somewhat unexpected in Costa Rica because the 1949 Constitution, unlike many other Latin American constitutions, contains no fundamental right to health.[34] Rather, over a number of years, the Court constructed[35] a right to health (Wilson 2011: 141–145; Norheim and Wilson 2014) by drawing on art. 21 and 73 (the protection of human life[36] and the right to social security protection),[37] and various international human rights instruments[38] including the Universal Declaration of Human Rights,[39] the American Declaration of Rights and Duties of Man,[40] the American Convention on Human Rights[41] and the International Covenant on Civil and Political Rights.[42] According to Magistrate Cruz Castro (2007: 506), the Sala IV's magistrates treat these international instruments as if they have 'an almost supra constitutional value'.[43] The Court subsequently moved further in the direction of international and national legal systems, making the right to health a separate and clearly individualized fundamental right.

[34] Even though Brazil, Chile, Colombia, El Salvador, Nicaragua, and Venezuela, for example, have an explicit constitutional right to health (Brewer-Carías 2009), those rights are not always justiciable.

[35] Magistrate Solano (2007, 141–144) details how the Court constructed the right to health.

[36] Constitution art. 21, which states that 'human life is inviolable', was motivated by a desire to ban capital punishment.

[37] Article 73: 'Social security is established for the benefit of manual and intellectual workers, regulated by a system of compulsory contributions by the State, employers and workers, to protect them against the risks of illness, disability, maternity, old age, death and other contingencies as determined by law.'

[38] Solano (2007: 142–143); Vargas (2010: 150). Article 48 gives international rights instruments the same power as domestic constitution

[39] Universal Declaration of Human Rights, G.A. Res. 217A (III), U.N. Doc A/810 at 71 (1948).

[40] American Declaration of the Rights and Duties of Man, O.A.S. Res. XXX, adopted by the Ninth International Conference of American States (1948), reprinted in Basic Documents Pertaining to Human Rights in the Inter-American System, OEA/Ser.L.V/II.82 doc.6 rev.1 at 17 (1992).

[41] American Convention on Human Rights, O.A.S. Treaty Series No. 36, 1144 U.N.T.S. 123, entered into force 18 July 1978, reprinted in Basic Documents Pertaining to Human Rights in the Inter-American System, OEA/Ser.L.V/II.82 doc.6 rev.1 at 25 (1992). Ley 4534 of 23 February 1970 (Costa Rica).

[42] International Covenant on Civil and Political Rights, G.A. Res. 2200A (XXI), 21 U.N. GAOR Supp. (No. 16) at 52, U.N. Doc. A/6316 (1966), 999 U.N.T.S. 171, entered into force 23 March 1976. Ley 4229 of 11 December 1968 (Costa Rica).

[43] Magistrate Gilbert Armijo (2003) discusses the role of international human rights instruments in Sala IV's ESC rights jurisprudence.

Even once the Court identified a constitutional right to health, it treated it as a 'qualified right' and, when making its decisions gave significant weight to the economic costs of the medical treatment sought by the litigant. For example, in 1992 the Court rejected a litigant's claim for state-funded antiretroviral medication, azidothymidine. The Court argued that the cost of providing the medication would be 'a very large sacrifice for [the] socialized medicine' system and also that the medication was not a cure for HIV/AIDS (Resolution No. 280–92). By the late 1990s, though, the Court had incrementally clarified its view of health rights and ultimately rejected cost arguments as a legitimate limitation on that right. Thus in a landmark AIDS medication case that reversed the Court's 1992 decision, it reasoned, 'what good are the rest of the rights and guarantees … [or] the advantages and benefits of our system of liberties, if a person cannot count on the right to life and health assured?' (Resolution No. 5934–97). The Court subsequently noted the right to life and the right to health are evidently related, where the right to health has the purpose of securing life (Resolution No. 2004–07026).

This particular case is significant as it categorically rejected the state-funded health agency's economic arguments, stating the Caja Costarricense de Seguro Social (CCSS, Costa Rican Social Security Fund) cannot reject medications prescribed by a patient's treating physician for 'eminently economic reasons', but rather is 'under the undeniable obligation' to supply those medications (Resolution No. 00043-07). The Court, thus, demonstrated its willingness to impose positive obligations on the state in support of health rights. The case is also interesting as it is an ESC rights case that stuck and established a firm precedent for future cases. More remarkably, CCSS did not delay compliance with the decision or implement a mere narrow reading of the 1997 ruling, but instead took a broad interpretation of the judgment and subsequently supplied antiretroviral medications to every person living with AIDS (PLWA) with a CCSS doctor-issued prescription. Two years after the ruling, the cost of providing anti-retroviral medications to all 680 patients suffering from HIV/AIDS consumed 11 per cent of the CCSS's total medicine budget (*La Nación, 1999*).[44]

What is also striking is that even though the CCSS had argued for much of the 1990s that the medications were expensive, ineffective, and

---

[44] The medications' initial costs declined in subsequent years as did its share of the Caja's medications budget to less than 10 per cent in 2000 and 5.4 per cent in 2002 (quoted in Rodríguez Herrera 2005: 25).

should not be part of the CCSS's medications list, once the 1997 case had been decided, the agency immediately universalised coverage covering the highest percentage of the PLWA in the Americas.[45] This decision immediately stuck and was expanded to all PLWA, a highly marginalised, socially ostracised, unorganised group of people while simultaneously imposing high costs on a reluctant defendant. The impact of this decision was remarkable and fast; morbidity rates for PLWAs declined significantly after the 1997 decision, reversing the trend of the 1980s and 1990s (Wilson 2011).

Since this 1997 decision, the Court's judicial health rights arguments have been successfully used to litigate access to expensive medications for other chronic illnesses that the CCSS had routinely denied on the basis of costs. For example, shortly after the HIV/AIDS decision, thirty-two multiple sclerosis and nineteen amyotrophic lateral sclerosis patients won cases that absorbed almost 1 and 0.4 per cent of the CCSS's medicine budget (*La Nación* 1999). While compliance with the above-mentioned cases might be explained in the individual nature of the claims, the Court's decisions, although *inter partes* in intent, have often had an *erga omnes* impact. The HIV/AIDS case was initially designed to offer relief to individual patients, but was soon extended to all people in a similar situation. When the Court makes health rights decisions for a class of people, the compliance outcome is the same. For example, in 2009, the Court ruled (Resolution No. 2009–8339) against the CCSS ordering pneumococcus vaccinations should be given to all people over sixty-five years of age (Oviedo 2009) at a total cost of US$8 million (Ávalos 2008).

In spite of the complaints and objection of the CCSS directors to the medical rulings of the Sala IV, the CCSS has one of the highest compliance rates with Constitutional Chamber's decisions. The amendment to radiotherapy treatment and linear accelerator is a dramatic example, but it is possible to demonstrate that tendency globally. Court personnel have been able to verify the outcome in 617 of the 665 cases where the Sala IV ruled against CCSS.[46] Of those 617 cases, the CCSS has complied with 607 (98 per cent) of the rulings, whilst in less than 2 per cent of cases, the CCSS has failed to comply. The CCSS's ready compliance with the Sala IV's health rights decisions fits with the general pattern observed for all compliance rates discussed above – it is a

---

[45] Chile, at 82 per cent, has the second highest levels of coverage, while Costa Rica's Central American neighbours are very weak (Avert 2009).

[46] No data exist for approximately 8 per cent of the cases (forty-eight) as their status had not been verified when the compliance data were published.

decentralised state agency and the majority of the health rights decisions from the Court contain requirements for immediate action on the part of the CCSS.

4.6 Conclusion

Since its inception in late 1989, the Constitutional Chamber of the Costa Rican Supreme Court has made over 230,000 decisions. Of those cases approximately 90 per cent are writs of *amparo*, many involving constitutional questions related to ESC rights, implying a successful judicialisation of ESC rights issues. This large number of cases, however, tells only part of the story. First, only a small percentage of these cases (roughly 25 per cent) are successfully litigated at the Constitutional Chamber of the Supreme Court, while the vast majority fail. Second, even when a case is successfully litigated, there is no guarantee that the Court's order will be complied with by the defendant. Indeed, at the time the Court-sponsored monitoring system was introduced in 2009, only a small percentage of the Court's orders are in fact complied with. These conclusions appear to support a large body of literature that rejects the possibility that Court orders on their own can transform societies and enhance individual and collective rights. WhileRosenberg (1991; 2008) argues that courts are incapable of bringing about meaningful social change, Epp (1998) notes meaningful social change is possible, but only if other preconditions are present including well-organised, deep-pocketed advocates. None of these preconditions exists in Costa Rica.

However, contrary to Epp or Rosenberg's expectations there is clear evidence, some of it presented in this chapter, that illustrates that profound change in specific ESC rights has been possible in Costa Rica as a result of the implementation of Court decisions. Indeed, the evidence also suggests the possibility of compliance with Court ESC rights decisions even in the absence of collective action and/or well-financed social movements which are willing and able to fund litigation for those rights. We have argued that it is the openness of the Costa Rican Constitutional Chamber of the Supreme Court that reduces the need for well-financed supporter groups to push ESC rights cases through the Court system. Epp's argument that civil society organisations are pivotal players in forcing state agencies' compliance with Court ESC rights decisions is supported by some case studies in this book, but this has not been part of the central explanation for cases that are complied with in Costa Rica. It is entirely possible, although untestable, that a significant number of Court orders that were not complied with might have resulted in a different outcome if deep-pocketed, well-organised social movements existed in Costa Rica.

Court orders on gender equality or the protection of homosexual rights might appear straightforward and involve low compliance costs to the state, in contrast to medication cases which frequently concern small groups of politically powerless people with very expensive Court-ordered treatments and/or prescriptions. However, as compliance is observed across these groups, we can exclude the financial burden on the state as a major explanatory variable.

Thus, Daniel Brinks's conclusion (this volume), 'when the beneficiaries are one or a few individuals, they can exert very little political pressure, so compliance is weak, even if the overall cost of compliance is low', makes intuitive sense and can explain the original 1992 HIV/AIDS decision, where a small number of politically and socially marginalised PLWA were denied access to antiretroviral medications, in large part due to the cost. This argument, though, cannot account for the 1997 successful HIV/AIDS anti-retroviral case, a case that appears to conflict with Brinks's conclusion. In medical rights cases, the Court's jurisprudence became clearer over the years and compliance levels enhanced by both the immediacy embedded in the Court orders and by the fact that the defendant institution was a centralised institution. These two factors, immediacy required by the order and the nature of the institution, were identified by the Court's compliance study as the two strongest predictors of defendants' compliance with Court orders. While the relationship between these two factors and the likelihood of compliance is very high, a lack of information concerning the nature of the individual cases decided prevent us from drawing more concrete explanations or illuminating the direction of causality. One plausible explanation is that cases that the decentralised state agencies tend to lose are generally ones with orders for immediate application of the rulings. In this case, the immediacy in implementation of the ruling provides added weight in accounting for the variation in compliance with Court rulings.[47]

In sum, initial evidence suggests that in the Costa Rican case, which is characterised by open access to the Court and an abundance of rulings, the resources of those filing the case are less crucial than in other situations.

---

[47] The recent study by Gauri et al. (2015) shows that the mere fact the Court established a compliance monitoring system and publicised it through press conferences resulted in more rapid compliance with the Court's decisions.

Instead, it appears the stipulations on implementation of the rulings, in particular how quickly a decision has to be implemented and by whom, are of greater significance. Where rulings are to be enforced with some immediacy, the compliance rate appears significantly higher. These initial findings provide a solid base for the interpretation of compliance rates and lend themselves for further testing and refinement as more data become available.

References

Armijo, Gilbert (2003), 'La tutela supraconstitucional de los derechos humanos en Costa Rica', *Revista Ius et Praxis*, 9(1), 39–62.

Ávalos, Ángela (2005), 'Costosa oleada de amparos', *La Nación*, 6 June, www.nacion.com.

(2008), 'Sala IV ordena vacunar contra neumococo y rotavirus', *La Nación*, 22 October, www.nacion.com.

AVERT (2009), 'HIV and AIDS in Latin America', www.avert.org.

Brewer-Carías, Allan. R. (2009), *Constitutional Protection of Human Rights in Latin America: A Comparative Study of Amparo Proceedings* (New York: Cambridge University Press).

Castillo Víquez, Fernando and Giulio Sansonetti H. (undated), 'Ley de la Jurisdicción Constitucional', unpublished manuscript, on file with the author.

Constitución de la República de Costa Rica (1949), English language version, www.costaricalaw.com/.

Corte Suprema de Justicia–Sala Constitucional (1999), 'Reseña Histórica', www.poder–judicial.go.cr.

Cruz Castro, Fernando (2007), 'Costa Rica's Constitutional Jurisprudence, Its Political Importance and International Human Rights Law: Examination of Some Decisions', *Duquesnse Law Review*, 45(3), 557–576.

Epp, Charles R. (1998), *The Rights Revolution: Lawyers, Activists, and Supreme Courts in Comparative Perspective* (Chicago: University of Chicago Press).

Gauri, Varun, Jeffrey K. Staton, and Jorge Vargas Cullell (2015), 'The Costa Rican Supreme Court's Compliance Monitoring System', *The Journal of Politics*, 77(3), 774–786.

Gloppen Siri, Bruce M. Wilson, Roberto Gargarella, Elin Skaar, and Morten Kinander (2010), *Courts' Accountability Functions: Lessons from Latin America, Africa, and Eastern Europe* (New York: Palgrave).

Gutiérrez Gutiérrez, Carlos José (1999), 'La constitución 50 años después', in Carlos José Gutiérrez Gutiérrez et al (eds.), *Temas claves de la constitución política* (San José: Investigaciones Jurídicas), 25–52.

Helmke, Gretchen and Julio Ríos-Figueroa, (eds.). (2001), *Courts in Latin America*, (New York: Cambridge University Press).

Hernández Valle, Rubén (2007), Tribunales Constitucionales y consolidación de la Democracia. La evolución de la justicia constitucional y sus retos en Costa Rica. 324 Suprema Corte de Justicia de la Nación 2007. México D.F.

(2008), 'Constitución Política de la República de Costa Rica. Actualizada comentada, anotada y con citas jurisprudenciales 40', Editorial Juricentro 2008.

Hilson, Chris (2002), 'New Social Movements: The Role of Legal Opportunity', *Journal of European Public Policy*, 9(2), 238–255.

Jinesta Lobo, Ernesto (2009), *Tratado de Derecho Administrativo 39–40 ed., 2nd edn.* (San José: Editorial Jurídica Continental).

La Nación (1999), 'Cuestión de números', www.nacion.com.

Martínez Barahona, Elena (2009), *Seeking the Political Role of the Third Government Branch: A Comparative Approach to High Courts in Central America* (Saarbrücken: VDM Verlag).

Méndez G., William (1999), 'Sala IV da sentencia' 11 October 1999, www.nacion .com.

Murillo Víquez, J. (1994), *La sala constitucional: Una revolución político-jurídica en Costa Rica* (San José, Costa Rica: Editorial Guayacán).

Navia, Patricio and Julio Ríos-Figueroa (2005), 'The Constitutional Adjudication Mosaic of Latin America', *Comparative Political Studies*, 38(2), 189–217.

Norheim, Ole F. andBruce M. Wilson (2014), 'Health Rights Litigation and Access to Medicines: Priority Classification of Successful Cases from Costa Rica's Constitutional Chamber of the Supreme Court', *Health and Human Rights: An International Journal*, 16(2), 47–61.

Oviedo, Esteban. (2009). "Sala IV ordena vacunar a ancianos contra neumococo." *La Nación*, June 23. http://wvw.nacion.com/ln_ee/2009/junio/23/pais2005122 .html.

PEN (2010), *Programa Estado de la Nación en Desarrollo Humano Sostenible (Costa Rica), Decimosexto Informe, 16th edn.* (Guilá: PEN).

Poder Judicial (2010), 'Sección de estadísticas, departamento de planificación', www .poder-judicial.go.cr.

(2012), 'Votos por tema', www.poder-judicial.go.cr.

Rodríguez, Olman (2011), 'The Costa Rican Constitutional Jurisdiction', *Duquesne Law Review*, 49(2), 243–292.

Rodríguez Cordero, Juan Carlos (2002), *Entre Curules & estrados: La consulta preceptiva de las reformas constitucionales en Costa* (San José, Costa Rica: Investigaciones Jurídicas).

Rodríguez Herrera, Adolfo (2005), *La reforma de salud en Costa Rica* (Santiago de Chile, Chile: United Nations).

Rosenberg, Gerald N. (1991), *The Hollow Hope: Can Courts Bring About Social Change?* (Chicago: University of Chicago Press).

(2008), *The Hollow Hope: Can Courts Bring About Social Change?* (Chicago: University of Chicago Press). 2nd edition.

Solano Carrera, Luis Fernando. 2007. 'Derecho fundamental a la salud.' *Gaceta Médica de Costa Rica* 9 (2): 141–150.

Terra.com (2009), 'Sentencias de Sala Constitucional de Costa Rica serán transcritas a braille', http://noticias.terra.com/articulos/act1634911/Sentencias_de_ Sala_Constitucional_de_Costa_Rica_seran_transcritas_a_braille/.

Vargas Cullell, Jorge (2010), 'Enfoque', *La Nación*, www.nacion.com.

Vargas López, Karen. (2010). 'El desarrollo del derecho a la salud por parte de la Sala Constitucional y su influencia en el sistema público de salud en Costa Rica.' MA Thesis, Universidad de Costa Rica.

Villalobos, Carlos. A. (1998), 'Sala IV modifica artículos del Código de Trabajo: Amplían derecho a huelga', *La Nación*, www.nacion.com.

Vizcaíno, Irene (2006), 'Luis Fernando Solano: Hay "fariseísmo" contra Sala IV', *La Nación*, www.nacion.com.

Wilson, Bruce M. (1998), *Costa Rica: Politics, Economics, and Democracy* (Boulder, CO: Lynne Rienner).

(2007), 'Claiming Individual Rights through a Constitutional Court: The Example of Gays in Costa Rica', *I•CON, International Journal of Constitutional Law*, 5, 242–257.

(2009), 'Rights Revolutions in Unlikely Places: Costa Rica and Colombia', *Journal of Politics in Latin America*, 1(2), 59–85.

(2010), 'Enforcing Rights and Exercising an Accountability Function: Costa Rica's Constitutional Court', in Gretchen Helmke and Julio Rios-Figueroa (eds.), *Courts in Latin America* (New York: Cambridge University Press), 55–80.

(2011), "The Causes and Consequences of Health Rights Litigation in Costa Rica." In Alicia Yamin & Siri Gloppen (eds). Litigating Health Rights: Can Courts Bring More Justice to Health? (Cambridge: Harvard University Press). Pp132–154.

Wilson, Bruce M. and Juan Carlos Rodríguez Cordero (2006), 'Legal Opportunity Structures and Social Movements: The Effects of Institutional Change on Costa Rican Politics', *Comparative Political Studies*, 39(3), 325–351.

Zamora Zamora, Carlos (2007), 'Los recursos de amparo y recursos de inconstitucionalidad contra la CCSS Costarricense de Seguro Social de 1989 a 2005', *Gaceta Médica de Costa Rica*, 9(2), 130–134.

5

Argentina: Implementation of Collective Cases

MARTÍN SIGAL, JULIETA ROSSI AND DIEGO MORALES

5.1   Introduction

In Argentina today, the question of implementation of collective cases concerning economic, social and cultural rights (ESC or social rights) requires critical consideration, in both scholarship and practice. Strategic ligation that seeks systemic changes has gained momentum in the last decade and has achieved a certain degree of success in the courtroom. Courts of various levels and in different jurisdictions have recognised the justiciable nature of ESC rights, found violations in a significant number of decisions of varying scope and ordered a range of remedies.

A key question is how those legal successes have been translated *post-judgment*. The implementation of many court decisions, in particular decisions issued in structural cases, has been partial or deficient. In many cases, there has been no implementation at all. Within this framework, we consider it relevant to examine the effectiveness and transforming power of court interventions in order to facilitate a better understanding of the possibilities and limitations faced by the judiciary when attempting to achieve the realisation of fundamental rights and to transform unjust social conditions.

Martín Sigal is a lawyer and co-founder of the Asociación Civil por la Igualdad y la Justicia (ACIJ). He is also Director of Human Rights Center at Law School of the Universidad de Buenos Aires.

Julieta Rossi is a lawyer; Associate Professor and Researcher at the National University of Lanús (UNLa) and legal advisor at the Federal Prosecutor Office in Argentina; former Director of the International Network on Economic, Cultural and Social Rights (ESCR-Net) and Board member at the Centro de Estudios Legales y Sociales (CELS).

Diego Morales is a lawyer and Litigation Director of the Centro de Estudios Legales y Sociales (CELS) and Associate Professor and Researcher at the National University of Lanús (UNLa).

The authors would like to specially thank Karina Kalpschtrej, Pilar Arcidiácono, Laura Pautassi, Malcolm Langford, Gustavo Maurino, Ezequiel Nino, Gabriela Kletzel, Carolina Fairstein, Paula Litvachky, Rodrigo Borda and Anabella Museri for their valuable contributions to this chapter.

The objective of this chapter is to identify and elucidate the challenges in the implementation phase of decisions in collective social rights cases in Argentina. In particular, we would like to account for some of the factors that may have an effect on the level of compliance, as well as their potential strategic implications. In particular, we consider whether the relatively complex nature of some social rights obligations and remedies is salient or whether other factors are at play.

The chapter is structured as follows: First, we make a number of methodological comments regarding the conduct of our survey and introduce the sample of cases (Section 5.2). Second, we examine several variables related to a higher or lower probability of decisions being effectively enforced and capable of remedying the violation of the rights at stake (Section 5.3). We conclude by offering some thoughts on the potential strategic implications of the analysis for litigation and related actions aimed at claiming fundamental rights.

5.2   Methodology and Overview of Cases

5.2.1   Defining Implementation

In examining the process of the implementation of judgments, we focus primarily on both the *direct* and *material* effects of court decisions. These effects involve a material change in the situation or conduct of individuals or groups and are *direct* in the sense that they were required by a judgment and involve the relevant actors in the case, including the parties, beneficiaries and any other targets of the orders (Rodríguez Franco and Rodríguez Garavito, 2010).

Among direct material effects, we have been specifically interested in observing any concrete transformations brought about by court decisions concerning social rights violations experienced by those identified in the judgment as affected individuals, including any changes in their environment. In our view, the question related to changes in the life situation of those affected by rights violations is central when considering the impact of court interventions. Furthermore, this question provides a clear framework and context for any subsequent research on other types of effects.

Regarding methodology, we have based our research on a multiple case study approach (Macluf et al., 2008). Although we do not attempt to make definitive generalisations or identify universally applicable patterns, we consider that the results may be valuable for generating broader conclusions that may be relevant for different scenarios (Araluz, 2005: 115).

Within this methodological framework, we have conducted a detailed analysis of the characteristics of the compliance process in the cases chosen. Subsequently, we have compared these characteristics in order to develop explanations regarding the probability of a court decision being implemented (Merlinsky, 2011: 5).

The independent variables we analyse represent only a selection of those relevant to the degree of implementation. Yet, while we have analysed these factors in an isolated manner, we find that they consistently interact and affect each other. The most important dimensions found while examining the cases are categorised by the largely 'constitutive' elements of a court case, although our perspective remains socio-legal. Thus, it is generally accepted that all court cases consist of (1) a procedural subject matter and the case on which it is based – which is defined by the remedy sought, the law invoked and the affected interest; (2) a court of law; (3) a defendant and (4) a plaintiff, i.e. the party that files the legal action.

Within the procedural subject matter (1) variable, we have focused our analysis on case size and characteristics, in particular the scope of the violations claimed, the number of people affected, the type of conduct required by public authorities or individuals to redress the violation, and the geographic extension of the situation of violation, among others. Regarding the court of law (2), we have examined the type of attitude the court adopted when facing the implementation process, i.e. whether it adopted a diligent, sensitive stance towards the claim or behaved in a passive, formalistic manner.[1] As regards the defendant (3), we have focused on the willingness to comply with the court order. Finally, regarding the plaintiff (4), we analyse the type and characteristics of involvement by those affected in both the general proceedings and the implementation process, as well as on the modalities and dynamics of any alliances among various claimants arising in the cases.

5.2.2   Case Selection

Our survey consists of thirteen judgments or agreements reached between the parties within a judicial proceeding that have been recently heard by Argentine courts.[2] The cases all concern social rights although the case concerning detention conditions can be equally characterised as

---

[1] For example, through embracing procedural codes rules which have still not included robust access to justice notions established by the 1994 constitutional reform.
[2] The last empirical evidence for this chapter was gathered in November 2013.

a civil rights case. Our selection was based on two criteria. The first was that the cases were collective. By collective we mean litigation that is not instigated by a single individual and specify further in Section 5.3 the different types of collective cases. We note that many of these cases were prominent in Argentina (Merlinsky, 2011: 3, 4) and have opened up new litigation paths. They can be described as model or paradigmatic cases. They are marked by novel arguments, a strategic attempt to shift particular policies through litigation, or innovative proceduralism, particularly in the type and scope of remedies. More generally, the cases have catalysed the discussion of new issues in the public sphere (CELS, 2008: 17, 18). This paradigmatic and collective litigation also provides a particular methodological perspective: it represents potentially the 'hard case' for compliance, given the complexity, ambition and novelty of any order. We also note that the judgments emerge from various jurisdictions and courts at different levels in Argentina but that the unifying dimension is their collective nature.

A second major determinant of case selection is that we, as the authors of this chapter, have been directly or indirectly involved in them, either as representatives for the litigants or as members of the organisation leading the case. We have been actively involved in developing the cases from their very beginning until the phase of court decision implementation, and have witnessed directly the complexities arising in this final phase. This first-hand knowledge has permitted us to develop a unique, committed and sensitive understanding of the difficulties faced at this stage of the litigation process. In such roles, we have secured access to empirical evidence that is valuable when conducting a qualitative analysis of the cases and on which we have based our observations. This information was complemented with interviews with some of the key players in the cases and an analysis of relevant case documentation (court decisions, court orders issued during the implementation process, briefs filed by the parties, etc.).

Finally, while in some cases the degree of implementation was easy to verify and no difficulties were faced, it is worth emphasising that in other cases the need for more accurate indicators or parameters became apparent. In some cases, it is clear that a judgment has been significantly enforced (e.g., a previously non-existent service is introduced in a given community) or not enforced (e.g., there is a total failure to act by the state). In other cases, determining the level of compliance is complex, making it difficult to fit the analysis within a binary 'all-or-nothing' framework. For example, the state may have initiated some activities, but not enough to fully comply with the decision; a negotiation process may have commenced but there is no significant progress in reaching a solution; or implementation is obstructed by the emergence of new issues, which require fresh court action or a longer period for implementation.[3]

Ultimately, our survey shows the need – particularly in collective rights cases where the design or implementation of general public policies is at stake – for developing indicators to measure and track compliance, both efforts and results. In other words, to measure the effects of this type of decisions, a new conceptual framework is needed which avoids binary, categorical definitions that follow a pattern of compliance/non-compliance, success/failure (Filippini, 2007).

5.2.3   Overview of Cases

Table 5.1 provides an overview of the thirteen cases under selection. It lists the relevant court, litigants, relevant facts and remedy.[4]

5.3   Analysis of Main Variables that Impact Decision Implementation

5.3.1   The Structural Nature of the Case

One major variable we have identified when analysing difficulties in implementation concern a case's degree of structurality. We understand structurality to be an issue that can be measured in degrees depending on the presence (or absence) of certain elements (discussed later). Thus, we can speak of a structurality that increases in intensity from highly individualised and simple cases through to complex and systemic collective cases – in which all elements defining structurality are present.

All cases selected for this analysis possess varying degrees of structurality. We have classified them in a binary fashion, *collective cases* and *structural collective cases*; with the latter possessing all elements of structurality. We have excluded purely individual cases,[5] as we assume that they follow

---

[3] Also, it should be noted that the conclusions about the degree of implementation depend to a large extent on the observer's interpretation of facts, the methodology used to assess them, the particular moment in which the analysis is made and other relevant factors which may lead to different conclusions about the implementation of the same decision.

[4] For a more detailed development of the cases, see CELS (2008), and Maurino and Nino (2009).

[5] We consider *individual cases* those in which the claim deals with an individual violation of a right, i.e. of one person in particular, and focus is made on requesting a specific solution for the affected person.

Table 5.1 *Overview of the cases*

Riachuelo Contamination (Case 1)[a]

Date	Court	Parties	Facts/Decision	Remedy
July 2008	Supreme Court of Argentina (CSJN)	Plaintiff: A group of seventeen residents of the contaminated area and health workers of the same area. Defendant: forty-four companies, National State, the Province of Buenos Aires and the City of Buenos Aires and fourteen municipalities.[b]	The Court found that the defendants were responsible for environmental degradation in the Matanza Riachuelo basin, which was having a serious impact on the health of nearby residents. It took into account that this basin is the most contaminated area in Argentina, affects at least three million people, and covers fourteen municipalities in the Province of Buenos Aires and 34 per cent of the territory belonging to the City of Buenos Aires. The Court determined that there was a collective rights violation and a legal obligation to effectively respond to the issue of basin contamination. The violation of the rights of residents was found to be closely related to the fragmentation and overlapping of governmental jurisdictions, limited or negligible political willingness by bureaucratic authorities to face the issue in a coordinated and integrated manner, and the absence of adequate participation and accountability mechanisms.[c]	The Court finding implied a response of a multijurisdictional nature with an integrated, structural approach. The Court ordered an administrative authority (ACUMAR)[d] to implement an intervention programme, declaring it fully responsible for any failure to comply with or delays in execution. The programme must aim at simultaneously: (1) improving the quality of life of basin residents; (2) cleaning up the environment; and (3) preventing damages.[e] For the purposes of measuring compliance, the Court ordered ACUMAR to adopt 'any of the international measurement systems available'.[f] The programme included a detailed schedule of activities and obligations. These included: (1) organising an Internet-based public information system to report on programme progress; (2) conducting actions aimed at controlling industrial pollution;

(continued)

Table 5.1 (*cont.*)

Date	Court	Parties	Facts/Decision	Remedy
				(3) protecting and providing healthcare for the population; cleaning up landfills; (4) cleaning river shores; expanding the drinking water network; and (5) adopting measures aimed at controlling storm water drainages and sewage treatment. The Court also established time limits and stated that, in case of failure to comply with the schedule, personal fines may be imposed on the person heading ACUMAR. The Court appointed a Board,[g] which is in charge of overseeing the implementation of all court orders.
Buenos Aires Prisons (Case 2)[h]				
May 2005	Supreme Court of Argentina (CSJN)	Plaintiff: Centre for Legal and Social Studies (CELS) Defendant: Government of the Province of Buenos Aires	The Court reviewed the situation of approximately 6,000 detainees awaiting criminal trial in police stations in the Province of Buenos Aires. It also analysed the situation of *prison overcrowding* in the Province of Buenos Aires and the rights violation claimed by the petitioner. Between 1990 and 2005, the prison population had increased exponentially: almost 80 per cent since 1999. This had led to claims that detainees were provided accommodation under inhuman conditions at police stations, which had practically turned into accommodation facilities.[i] The increase in imprisonment rates and the worsening of detention conditions were a consequence of Law 12405 (passed in March 2000, which made prison release schemes more complex, and the Buenos Aires Province Penal Execution Law (which limited access to temporary prison releases by persons convicted of certain crimes).	The Court required the provincial government to report every sixty days the measures adopted to adjust the situation of detainees to the United Nations Standard Minimum Rules for the Treatment of Prisoners, which the Court considered to be fundamental guidelines to be met by all types of detention. In addition, the Court ordered the Supreme Court of the Province of Buenos Aires and lower courts to put an immediate end to any situation of detention involving cruel, inhuman or degrading treatment and to adopt milder measures based on information provided by the provincial executive branch regarding actual detention conditions (type of cell, number of beds, hygiene conditions and access to sanitation facilities).

		The Court found that the situation represented a violation on constitutional and international human rights and declared that in part the situation was due to these reforms, which in addition did not satisfy relevant constitutional and international standards. The Court also affirmed that it is not permissible that children and ill people be detained at police stations.	Effective immediately, the Court prohibited that minors and sick persons be detained at police stations. The Court also urged the governor and legislature of the Province of Buenos Aires to reform the prison release system, as well as regulations referring to penal execution and prisons.
School Availability (Case 3)[j] March 2008	Court of Appeals dealing with Administrative and Tax Matters of the City of Buenos Aires	Asociacion Civil por la Igualdad y la Justicia (ACIJ)/Defendant: City Government of Buenos Aires	The Court found that there were an insufficient number of early childhood education institutions, particularly in disadvantaged areas in the City of Buenos Aires. The defendant was ordered to develop and submit a plan aimed at solving the lack of early childhood education centres. The Court requested detailed information on all construction projects already in progress and new construction projects aimed at meeting the demand for new school openings.	However, before the highest court in the jurisdiction (Superior Tribunal) issued a final decision, the parties reached an agreement that included guidelines to build new schools, submit reports, create a follow-up mechanism for the implementation of the agreement, as well as specific budgetary commitments, among other provisions.
Drinking Water/Villa 31bis (Case 4)[k] July 2007	Buenos Aires City Administrative and Tax Court	Plaintiff: Asociacion Civil por la Igualdad y la Justicia (ACIJ)/Defendant: City Government of Buenos Aires	The Court addressed the lack of drinking water affecting approximately 400 families living in a specific area formed by four blocks by four blocks – inside the urban slum known as Villa 31bis.	The City of Buenos Aires was ordered the City Government to provide drinking water, seven days a week, until projects to expand the water network were complete.

(continued)

Table 5.1 (cont.)

Date	Court	Parties	Facts/Decision	Remedy
Villa La Dulce (Case 5)[l]				
December 2003	Buenos Aires City Administrative Court	Plaintiff: Eighty-six families of Villa La Dulce with legal representation of Center for Legal and Social Studies Defendant: Government of the City of Buenos Aires	More than 180 families were evicted from a piece of land that they had occupied, which had been abandoned for at least ten years. Without alternative accommodation, they built shacks in an adjacent space. Of the initial group, eighty families lived for eleven months without elementary necessities. After a negotiation process, the government of the City of Buenos Aires agreed to build houses within a period of sixty days. Owing to the breach of the agreement, the families filed a legal action (amparo) against the City of Buenos Aires. A new agreement was reached and validated by the intervening judge, which included a solution to the housing rights' violation.	The City government, under the agreement reached with the affected families, promised both to build the necessary housing units to provide a definitive solution to the claimants and to create a dedicated, affordable credit line for the families to be able to buy housing. The agreement incorporated legal standards of the right to adequate housing such as habitability and affordability.
Nutritional Map (Case 6)[m]				
November 2008	Buenos Aires City Administrative and Tax Court	Plaintiff: Asociación Civil por la Igualdad y la Justicia (ACIJ) Defendant: Government of the City of Buenos Aires	A law issued by the City of Buenos Aires legislature (Law no. 105) established that government should create a nutritional map of the City of Buenos Aires, which was necessary to establish a nutritional policy.	A judge ordered the Buenos Aires City government to comply with Law 105, which required it to map the nutritional status of the population in order to inform new public policies for nutrition. The Court of Appeals decision confirmed the claim and the government was ordered to produce the map within 120 days.
Container Classrooms (Case 7)[n]				
July 2006	Buenos Aires City Administrative and Tax Court	Plaintiff: Asociación Civil por la Igualdad y la Justicia (ACIJ) Defendant: Government of the City of Buenos Aires	As a response to the lack of spaces in public primary schools, the City of Buenos Aires government decided to install modular classrooms (iron-made containers) instead of constructing new schools. The schools in which this solution was adopted were located near slums. This was found discriminatory.	The government was ordered to cease in the use of modular classrooms. The Court confirmed the claim that the City government had to provide a solution to the problem caused by the situation of emergency and uncertainty faced by the children in their access to education, and that the solution of installing modular classrooms was not acceptable.

***Wastebaskets* (Case 8)**[o]				
February 2008	Buenos Aires City Administrative and Tax Court	Plaintiff: Asociación Civil por la Igualdad y la Justicia (ACIJ) Defendant: Government of the City of Buenos Aires	The City of Buenos Aires had started a campaign on urban hygiene by placing wastebaskets in public areas and providing related information and citizen education. The poorest area in the City had, however, been excluded from the programme and this was held to violate the right to non–discrimination of the inhabitants of such area of the City.	The Court ordered an expansion of the campaign coverage to include the excluded area in equal conditions as the campaign that was carried out in other areas of the City.
***School Transportation* (Case 9)**[p]				
March 2010	Buenos Aires City Administrative and Tax Court	Plaintiff: Asociación Civil por la Igualdad y la Justicia (ACIJ) Defendant: Government of the City of Buenos Aires	Children in urban slums 31 and 31bis of the city of Buenos Aires had serious problems to access schools which are distant. Bad conditions of local roads and lack of access to the neighbourhood by public transportation increase such difficulties. Judge ordered the City to determine how many children inhabit in these neighbourhoods and to provide free school transportation for those children.	The Court ordered the establishment of a free transportation programme to guarantee that said children could attend their assigned schools.
***Candid 1 Vaccine* (Case 10)**[q] – *Viceconte*				
June 1998	Federal Court of Administrative Matters	Plaintiff: Center for Legal and Social Studies (CELS) Defendant: National government – Executive Power (Federal Ministry of Health)	In order to address Argentine haemorrhagic fever (a specific epidemic affecting the Pampa region), the national State had decided to manufacture a specific vaccine after production had stopped at a US laboratory. The necessary budget allocations were made to equip a lab and produce the vaccine, but government funds were being used for other purposes. The Court found a violation of the right to health.	The Court ordered that the authorities immediately comply with the vaccine production schedule established by the Health Ministry.

(continued)

Table 5.1 (*cont.*)

Date	Court	Parties	Facts/Decision	Remedy
Drinking Water/San Ignacio (Case 11)[r]				
November 2009	Federal Quilmes Court Ad Hoc Secretary	Plaintiff: Asociación Civil por la Igualdad y la Justicia (ACIJ) Defendant: ACUMAR	The drinking water used by around 6,000 neighbours of 'San Ignacio' in Esteban Echeverría district in the Province of Buenos Aires was polluted and was not apt for human consumption. The judge found this to violate the right to health and ordered the creation of a safe water provision system.	The Court ordered the supply of safe drinking water.
El Vergel Healthcare Center (Case 12)[s]				
March 2008	Juvenile Court No. 3, Moreno, Province of Buenos Aires	Plaintiff: Neighbours of 'El Vergel' neighborhood and Asociación Civil por la Igualdad y la Justicia. Defendant: Municipality of Moreno and Province of Buenos Aires	El Vergel, a 2,000-inhabitants neighbourhood in Moreno, Province of Buenos Aires, was isolated due to the bad conditions of access to roads (when it rained it was impossible to enter or exit the neighbourhood), and had no healthcare centre to respond to inhabitants' basic needs. Access to distant schools was impossible under bad weather. Judge found this situation to violate rights of children in El Vergel.	The Court ordered the Province of Buenos Aires to provide necessary resources to the Municipality of Moreno in order to proceed to the creation of a permanent centre for basic healthcare in El Vergel, and ordered the Municipality of Moreno to grant accessibility to the neighbourhood by repairing roads.
Train Station Ramps (Case 13)[t]				
August 1999	Cámara Federal en lo Contencioso Administrativo Federal, Sala I.	Plaintiff: María Inés Verbrugghe with the legal representation of Center of Legal and Social Studies. Defendant: National State (Ministry of Economy/ Transportation Secretary)	This case was filed with a federal court to demand access for persons with reduced mobility to one of the train lines linking the City of Buenos Aires with the northern area of the Buenos Aires Province. The Supreme Court confirmed the decision of the Court of Appeals that Trenes de Buenos Aires (TBA), the company operating the public railway service, was obliged to reasonably accommodate persons with disabilities or reduced mobility in order that they could 'access the service in equal conditions to other users'.	The Court ordered Trenes de Buenos Aires (TBA), a company operating the public railway service, and the National State to build ramps and to adjust stations to ensure autonomous access by persons with reduced mobility. A period of sixty days was given for compliance. The Court also ordered the National State to 'monitor the effective realisation of the works'.

[a] CSJN, Mendoza, Beatriz Silvia y otros c/ Estado Nacional y otros s/ daños y perjuicios (daños derivados de la contaminación ambiental del Río Matanza – Riachuelo), decision dated 8 July 2008. at www.csjn.gov.ar/confal/ConsultaCompletaFallos.do?method=verDocumentos &id=647639.

b Almirante Brown, Avellaneda, Cañuelas, Esteban Echeverría, Ezeiza, General Las Heras, La Matanza, Lanús, Lomas de Zamora, Marcos Paz, Merlo Morón, Pte. Perón and San Vicente.

c Cfr. CELS (2009), p. 333 et seq.

d Created by Law 26168 and made up of the National Government, the Province of Buenos Aires, and the City of Buenos Aires.

e CSJN, *Mendoza*, decision dated 8 July 2008, item 17, para. I.

f CSJN, *Mendoza*, resolution dated 10 August 2010, item 2.

g The Board (*Cuerpo Colegiado*) is coordinated by the Ombudsman and made up of representatives from the NGOs involved in the case (FARN, CELS, Asociación Vecinos de La Boca, ACDH and Greenpeace). See more information on the Board: www.farn.org.ar/riachuelo/cuerpo_colegiado_descripcion.html.

h CSJN, *Verbitsky, Horacio on Habeas Corpus*, decision dated 5 May 2005 at www.csjn.gov.ar/confal/ConsultaCompletaFallos.do?method=verDocumentos&id=5824.

i Although they do not meet the requirements of facilities where prison sentences or temporary detention pending trial may be served.

j Cámara de Apelaciones en lo Contencioso Administrativo y Tributario de la Ciudad de Buenos Aires (CACAT) [Court of Appeals dealing with Administrative and Tax Matters of the City of Buenos Aires], Court I, *Asociación Civil por la Igualdad y la Justicia v. GCBA on Amparo* (Art. 14, Constitution of the City of Buenos Aires, CCABA), Case 23360.

k CACAT, Court I, *ACIJ v. GCBA on Amparo*, Case 20898/0, 18 July 2007 (available at www.acij.org.ar/wp-content/uploads/Sentencia_Agua_en_la_Villa_31_bis.pdf.

l Juzgado en lo Contencioso-Administrativo de la Ciudad de Buenos Aires [Buenos Aires City Administrative Court] No. 5, *Agüero Aurelio Eduvigio and others v. GCBA on Amparo*, Case No. 4437/0.

m Juzgado en lo Contencioso Administrativo y Tributario de la Ciudad de Buenos Aires [Buenos Aires City Administrative and Tax Court] No. 9, *ACIJ v. GCBA on Amparo*, Case 27599/0; decision confirmed by CACAT Court I, November 16 2008 (available at www.adaciudad.org.ar/sitio/pdfs/fallos/CAYT/sala_2/AsociacionCivilporlaigualdadylaJusticia_CABA_2008.pdf).

n Juzgado CAT [Administrative and Tax Court] No. 11, City of Buenos Aires, *Iglesias, José Antonio v. GCBA on Amparo*, Case 1509/0, 7 July 2006 (available at: www.acij.org.ar/wp-content/uploads/2011/10/Aulas-Container-GCBA-Sentencia.pdf).

o CACAT Court 2, City of Buenos Aires, *Asociación Civil por la Igualdad y la Justicia v. GCBA on Amparo*, Case 18112/0, 7 December 2006. Supreme Court of the City of Buenos Aires, 20 February 2008 Case 5435/07 (available at www.tsjbaires.gov.ar).

(continued)

Table Footnote (*cont.*)

p Juzgado CAT No. 12, *ACIJ v. GCBA on Amparo*, Case 32839/0, 25 March 2010 (available at: www.mercadoytransparencia.org/acij-c-gcba-y-otros-s-amparo.

q Cámara en lo Contencioso-Administrativo Federal [Federal Court of Administrative Matters], Court IV, *Viceconte, Mariela Cecilia v. Estado Nacional on Amparo* (Case 31777/96), 2 June 1998 (*Viceconte*).

r Juzgado Federal de Quilmes Sec. Ad-Hoc [Federal Quilmes Court Ad Hoc Secretary], Case 02/2009, *Asociación Civil por la Igualdad y la Justicia v. ACUMAR on invalidity action.*

s Juzgado de Garantías de Menores Nro. 2, Paso del Rey, *Nino, Ezequiel and others v. Municipio de Moreno on Amparo*, Case 5967, unpublished.

t Cámara Nacional en lo Contencioso Administrativo Federal, Court I, *Verbrugghe María Inés v. National State, Ministry of Economy, Secretariat of Transportation and others on Amparo, Law 16986* (Case 8086/98), 30 August 1999; confirmed by the Supreme Court in September 2000.

the structure of other cases historically handled by the courts in a civil law country and do not present major difficulties in the implementation phase. Generally speaking, traditional rules are applied and the decision only applies to the parties in the case, and this is usually enough to achieve the implementation of the decision. Whenever positive obligations are at stake, duties 'to do', they are relatively simple and similar to obligations in classical cases, familiar to judges. Generally, these remedies do not face resistance by the state and, in any case, the available procedural follow-up remedies, such as fines, are usually enough to overcome resistance by State or private defendants.

Under *structural collective cases* (based in part on the definition given by Rodríguez Franco and Rodríguez Garavito, 2011: 87 and 88), we include cases with the following characteristics: the harm alleged affects a large number of persons spread throughout the territory of a state or in a specific territorial unit that is not easily determined; the rights violations arise from systemic gaps in the design or implementation of public policies or from a sheer lack of public policy; and/or the remedy imposed involves complex execution orders that require the allocation of economic resources and through which the judge instructs several public agencies to adopt coordinated measures to protect the whole of the affected population. We include two cases from the Supreme Court of Argentina – *Riachuelo Contamination* (case 1) and *Buenos Aires Prisons* (case 2) – as prototypes of the structural collective case (see Table 5.1).

Collective cases are those which seek to remedy issues neglected by public policies but possess less elements of structurality than structural collective cases. In this category, the violation of a social right affects a relatively important, easily determined amount of people; the violation is limited to a certain geographic area; and, although a public policy is questioned, its scope is smaller than that of structural cases. Usually, the case can be solved by providing a solution for a problem affecting a determined group of people. Furthermore, the court order is not overly complex, and – since it generally involves a single, concrete and quantifiable measure that is limited in time – its enforcement can be ordered and controlled by means usually used by courts for such purposes.[6] Collective cases may be more or less related to structural or individual cases depending on the presence of the aforementioned characteristics of structurality. Under the collective case definition, we could consider a larger amount of

---

[6] Notwithstanding the fact that the execution of the measure ordered may require previous activities, such as submitting information.

examples since this type of case has been litigated more often in the past few years. These included: *School Openings* (case 3), *Drinking Water/Villa 31bis* (case 4), *Villa La Dulce* (case 5), *Nutritional Map* (case 6), *Container Classrooms* (case 7), *Wastebaskets* (case 8), *School Transportation* (case 9), *Candid 1 Vaccine* (case 10), *Drinking Water/San Ignacio* (case 11), *El Vergel Healthcare Center* (case 12) and *Train Station Ramps* (case 13). See Table 5.1.

During our analysis of the levels of implementation of the thirteen selected cases, we found that this distinction mattered. Although *collective cases* may pose compliance problems, they tend to be implemented, while *structural collective cases* generally faced more difficulties in their implementation. Our findings were as follows.

(a)   Collective Cases

Our analysis of *collective cases* revealed high levels of implementation. Total or partial implementation of decisions or court-approved agreements was common for this category. Court decisions that ordered public services to be supplied to certain communities were implemented fully or to a significant extent. This included:

- Provision of drinking water in Villa 31bis (case 4);
- The expansion of an urban hygiene campaign to the most disadvantaged area in the City of Buenos Aires (case 8);
- Provision (partially) of free school transportation for school-age children in Villa 31 and Villa 31bis (case 9);
- Education policy changes in the City of Buenos Aires, such as creating new early childhood education centres (case 3);
- Revocation of a discriminatory policy which allowed classes to take place in containers at several schools located near slums (case 7);
- Building of housing for families living in the street (case 5);
- Production of public goods, such as vaccines, to prevent a disease affecting one region in Argentina (case 10); and
- Opening of a healthcare centre in a neighbourhood which lacked basic healthcare services (case 12).

Of all the cases analysed, only the *Train Station Ramps* (case 13) has not been implemented at all.

As noted already, these cases share several characteristics, including the possibility to determine the *number* of persons or groups affected by the court decision, e.g. the specific group of children needing free school transportation (case 10) or the eighty-six families in need of housing (case 5). Alternatively, a *territorial* unit to be covered by the decision can be identified, such as the four blocks in Villa 31bis, where drinking water must be supplied (case 4); the most disadvantaged area in the City of Buenos Aires, where a hygiene awareness campaign must be established (case 8); the San Ignacio neighbourhood (case 11); or Villa 31 and Villa 31bis (case 9). Or, they identify a *discrete* part of public policy, such as the prohibition on the use of container classrooms (case 7) or the failure to use budgetary allocations to produce a specific vaccine (case 4). Furthermore, these cases involve judgments which contain relatively concrete orders concerning state action or restraint, or a combination of both (e.g., to supply drinking water, eliminate container classrooms, adopt measures to provide an adequate number of school places) and which set a time limit to comply with the obligation.

On the other hand, as a case approaches *structural collective* status (i.e. involving larger numbers of affected persons or multiple territorial units, raising broader public policy questions and the use of resources, or increasing the number of state actors or the level of complexity), the difficulties in implementation become more profound and visible, as will be discussed in the pages that follow.

(b)   Structural Collective Cases

In *Riachuelo Contamination* (case 1), implementation since the 2008 judgment has been mixed: Some actions have been carried out successfully while others have not been implemented at all or only insufficiently, as the Supreme Court itself has acknowledged.[7] For the purposes of illustration, and with no intention to provide a complete list, we can chart the progress in implementation as follows.

The positive achievements include: (1) progress in cleaning up Riachuelo banks and water surface, including removing 170,000 tons of waste from the banks and 18,600 tons from the water; (2) the exertion of greater state regulation control over industrial facilities located in the area and the eviction of businesses illegally located on the river banks, resulting in a gain of 38,813 metres of the towpath (the 35-metre-wide area along the main course of the river) (FARN, 2013: 2) and (3) start-up of an unprecedented

---

[7] CSJN, 'Mendoza, Beatriz y otros c/ Estado Nacional y otros s/ daños y perjuicios (daños derivados de la contaminación ambiental del Río Matanza-Riachuelo)', decision of 12 December 2012.

process of control and registration of industrial facilities aimed at control-
ling industrial pollution of the basin.[8]

Moreover, measures have been adopted to relocate the population living
along the Riachuelo's towpath. According to FARN, by July 2013, 439 of
the total 2,389 families settled in the towpath had been relocated to houses
built under a Federal Housing Plan. This process should include providing the relocated families with title in the real estate, as well as access to
utilities, which significantly reduces exposure to high environmental
risk (FARN, 2013: 2).[9] However, residents relocated to the City of Buenos
Aires have reported that many of the new housing units have insufficient
infrastructure (no power supply, heating system, or water boiling system,
among other deficiencies) and that they cannot continue attending school
due to lack of openings, among other complaints (FARN, 2013).

One of the major pending problems is that, although the identification
and subsequent inspection of industrial facilities is a precondition to starting the control process, the existing situation concerning pollution will not
improve until a comprehensive policy is developed (Cuerpo Colegiado,
2013). In addition, there is still the need to adopt measures to mitigate
environmental risk in the area known as *Polo Petroquímico Dock Sud*,[10]
the area with the highest environmental damage in the basin (Cuerpo
Colegiado, 2013) which exposes the population to concrete health risks
(ACIJ and Junta Vecinal de Villa Inflamable, 2012).

Regarding the obligation to define an emergency environmental sanitation programme related to environmental health, a few instances of progress are worth noting. These include a sanitation status report based on
the development of a survey of environmental risk factors[11] and a comprehensive environmental health study in risk areas such as Villa Inflamable
(ACIJ and Junta Vecinal Villa Inflamable, 2012). Nevertheless, the implementation of the measure to expand the scope of a comprehensive environmental health survey is still pending. This survey should cover all

---

[8] By September 2013, according to ACUMAR, 23,552 operating facilities were identified, and
     1,650 facilities officially declared 'Polluting Agents,' of which 408 had completed Industrial
     Reconversion Programs (See ACUMAR's official web page: acumar.gov.ar).
[9] See also García Silva and García Espil (2012), 'Causa Matanza Riachuelo. Tiempo de
     debatir escenarios de recomposición', Informe Ambiental Anual 2012. FARN. www.farn
     .org.ar/informe2012.pdf.
[10] Within the framework of the Comprehensive Matanza Riachuelo Basin Plan, Polo
     Petroquímico Dock Sud is considered a priority due to the environmental damage affecting
     the area.
[11] Presentation by the Ombudsman before the Supreme Court at hearing on 1 November 2012.

environmental risk areas, considering both children and adults, in order to produce the court-required basic assessment 'of all diseases aimed at distinguishing between pathologies caused by air, soil and water pollution, from other pathologies not related to the said factors'.[12] Furthermore, no mechanisms have been implemented to inform basin residents about the availability of environmental sanitation services and the conditions to access such services.

Along the same line of criticism, FARN claims that, five years after the decision (by 2013), the population at risk has not been identified and no measures have been adopted to meet their healthcare needs. This situation shows a failure to develop a proactive healthcare policy. Such a policy would enable preventive interventions to identify persons suffering pathologies related to the Riachuelo's contamination, which is clearly a pending issue in this case (FARN, 2013). Additional failures include the fact that drinking water, sewage, and storm drain networks have not been expanded to cover the whole basin in order to help prevent waterborne diseases, and no information has been provided on the progress reached in the related infrastructure works (Cuerpo Colegiado, 2013).

Regarding the clean-up of waste dumps in the basin,[13] one positive step has been a reduction in open-air dumps. However, implementation of a comprehensive waste management strategy aimed at waste minimising, source sorting and differentiated collection remains outstanding (FARN, 2013).

Finally, also pending is the implementation of a policy to meet the needs of those persons now living beyond the 35-metre line of the Riachuelo's towpath. Most of them now live under conditions similar to those of persons subject to relocation (FARN, 2013).

Despite the elapse of several years since the judgment in *Buenos Aires Prisons* (case 2), there has been little substantial improvement in detention conditions. Detainees continue to face a harsh reality of prison overpopulation, overcrowding and violations of fundamental rights. The Supreme Court required a halt in the use of police station cells and the harmonisation of prison conditions with the standards of international human rights law. Thus far, these orders have been hardly followed, and no public policies have been designed or agreed upon to address the serious prison crisis.[14]

---

[12] CSJN, *Mendoza*, Consideration No. 17, para. IX, 1.b.
[13] Ibid., para. IV.
[14] See presentation submitted by CELS to the Supreme Court to report failure to comply with the decision dated May 2005, available at www.cels.org.ar/common/documentos/ DENUNCIA%20INCUMPLIMIENTO%20%20SOLICITA%20AUDIENCIA%20%20 PUBLICA%20FINAL.pdf.

As regards material detention conditions at police stations (the issue which triggered the original petition to the Supreme Court), the Province of Buenos Aires has acknowledged that the practice is absolutely inadequate and adopted a policy to eliminate it permanently. In line with this acknowledgement, the number of detainees at police stations has significantly fallen. In December 2011, there were 1,069 detainees at police stations; this represents a sharp reduction from the approximately 6,000 detainees at the time the case was filed. The Ministry of Justice and Security of the Province of Buenos Aires ordered the progressive closing of cells in 138 police stations and the relocation of the detainees to other facilities in the provincial system, such as prisons built to replace police stations as detention centres.[15] In addition, in line with the court's decision of 2005, no children or teenagers may be detained at police stations, except otherwise required by court order.[16]

Although the progressive removal of detainees out of police stations demonstrates significant progress in the implementation of the Supreme Court's decision, the problem of overcrowding and overpopulation was simply shifted to the penitentiaries or prisons. While the prison population fell initially, in early 2008, and after a new administration took office in the executive branch of the Province, the number of persons in custody rose again to 29,557[17] by 2009. Since then, this figure has stabilised at around 30,000. Therefore, the reduction in the number of detainees at police stations was not achieved through a reduction in the prison population. The structural problem remains: detainees outnumber prison beds.[18] Consequently, the government of the Province of Buenos Aires has not been able to implement an adequate building policy to ensure detainees are held under conditions of minimal dignity.

Another clear implementation deficit is the lack of progress in the work by the Dialogue Table established by the Supreme Court in its 2005 decision. We cannot identify a positive action emerging from the Dialogue Table worthy of mention. According to the court's decision, the Dialogue Table was meant to constitute a framework for discussing the content and effectiveness of a prison intervention plan and penitentiary policy. Instead, provincial government deprived this mechanism of its sense of purpose and institutionally weakened it.

---

[15] Statistical data show that the current administration (October 2013) has used other approaches. See CELS, 2012.

[16] Resolution No. 2672/11 by Ministry of Justice and Security of the Province of Buenos Aires.

[17] Of which 4,507 were detained at police stations.

[18] According to data provided by CELS.

One of the positive effects attributable to the decision was the creation of an 'Undersecretariat of Human Rights of Detainees', ordered by the provincial Supreme Court. In addition, a new prison visitation system for judges was adopted after a public hearing convened by the said court in November 2007. This office, operational since November 2010,[19] is principally in charge of managing prison visitation schemes and detention facilities. It also serves as a monitoring mechanism for the enforcement of the Supreme Court's decisions concerning detention standards and judges' compliance with the resulting obligations.[20] Another key development is the reform of the penal execution law in 2011.[21] This revised code introduced some of the standards included in the UN Standard Minimum Rules for the Treatment of Prisoners, as well as tools both to address more effectively the rights violations of persons held in custody[22] and to design public policies that recognise the scope and seriousness of the issue.

Despite these effects, the structural human rights' violations affecting persons held in custody in the Province of Buenos Aires clearly still exist. Moreover, even though the judgment was very clear in its terms, no detention policies have been significantly reformed. In fact, the underlying assumption – that the solution is to increase detention capacity – has remained completely intact.

(c) Implementation of Institutional Preconditions

Notwithstanding the conclusions related to difficulties in implementing structural judgments, we have observed that the orders and remedies do contribute to several institutional preconditions that are needed to redress the violations at stake. If we adopt a broader perspective, and include in our analysis other results of the cases not directly and immediately related to redressing the rights violated, we can identify very palpable, immediate effects, such as those related to the creation of the institutional infrastructure needed to implement the court decision.

The *Riachuelo Contamination* (case 1) presents a good example. Despite implementation difficulties and the lack of substantive progress in making the systemic modifications necessary to fully address pollution (and leaving aside the various positive steps mentioned), certain preconditions

[19] Resolution by Supreme Court of the Province of Buenos Aires No. 3523/10.
[20] Resolution by Supreme Court of the Province of Buenos Aires No. 3415/08.
[21] Law 14296 of the Province of Buenos Aires.
[22] For example, creating as case-law precedent a corrective habeas corpus of a collective nature, as a mechanism to denounce widespread violations of minimum standards applicable to detention conditions (Borda, 2013).

have arisen from this case that are indispensable to addressing the affected rights. The Supreme Court took into account the seriousness of the environmental damage; the bureaucratic overlap existing prior to the decision; and the series of legal, budgetary, institutional, and social processes required to address it. Therefore, the most relevant aspects regarding the implementation status of the decision are perhaps the establishment of institutional conditions which were absent prior to the decision.

A key institutional condition was the creation of an inter-jurisdictional body (ACUMAR) which directs all compliance-relevant actions and stands accountable for progress in implementation. In other words, the responsibility for enforcing the remedies established in the decision, including the responsibility for designing and implementing the necessary public policies to address the basin conditions, is placed upon one single body, formed by several state agencies.[23] In addition, one remedial precondition contributed to the design of a public policy – Plan Integral de Saneamiento Ambiental de la Cuenca Hídrica Matanza Riachuelo (PISA, Comprehensive Environmental Cleanup Plan for the Matanza Riachuelo Basin). Finally, as a precondition to implementing the decision, new surveys on environmental pollution and the health status of the affected population were conducted. Both the court decision and the implementation process have identified the need to adopt a public information system that provides updated, detailed data in a concise way that is accessible for the general public.

Thus, on the one hand, this case shows the difficulties in implementing decisions and improving the life conditions of Matanza Riachuelo basin residents within a timeframe that reflects the urgency and seriousness of the situation. On the other hand, it widens the implementation stage into an extended process, whose initial axis includes the creation of tools, institutions and mechanisms needed to ensure the affected population's environmental security in the medium or long term. Before the Supreme Court's intervention, this hazardous issue – and, more importantly, those directly affected by it – were abandoned by those institutionally responsible: literally, the state was completely absent. After the commencement of legal action, the apparatus of the state – with its insufficiencies, mistakes, and slow pace – has been catalysed into producing the devices that are necessary to design and provide some kind of response.[24]

---

[23] In its report from January 2013, the Monitoring Committee (Cuerpo Colegiado) identified ACUMAR's strengthened institutional status as one of several significant steps in the implementation of the Supreme Court decision.

[24] This can be characterised as an unblocking effect. See also the Colombian case of internally displaced persons, Rodríguez Garavito and Rodríguez Franco (2009), p. 123.

Its participation in the Monitoring Committee (Cuerpo Colegiado) has led FARN to state that, given this case's complexity and seriousness, its destiny cannot exclusively depend on the actions of judges, control agencies, residents or civil society organisations. Instead, actions must be based on a comprehensive state policy concerning the Riachuelo. So far, no such policy has been developed (FARN, 2013).

Likewise, in *Buenos Aires Prisons*, we can identify the achievement of some institutional preconditions such as the survey of the current status of prisons in the province for building infrastructure as well as the production of information on detention conditions. This data can be used to inform policymaking processes regarding prison overpopulation and overcrowding. Furthermore, the creation of a specific agency to address prison overcrowding, the development of a prison visitation mechanism for court officials, the setting of rules for jurisdictional and institutional visits and the centralisation of the database on habeas corpus cases all provide the basis for progressively realising the rights of persons held in custody, if there is political will to do so. Thus, in both cases (though to a lesser extent in *Buenos Aires Prisons*), the intervention by the court contributed to the creation of some of the institutional preconditions required to provide an adequate response to the rights violation at stake.

It can be argued that systemic issues or conflicts related to rights violations which have not been solved (or have even been aggravated) by political actors cannot realistically be addressed *immediately* through judiciary intervention. According to our analysis, it is necessary to promote the creation of tools and capacities (i.e. the necessary institutions) in order to implement a definitive remedy, as well as to identify, acknowledge and address institutional deficits blocking structural, long-term solutions. Unlike in individual cases (in which the implementation of a decision may be achieved more immediately), in structural cases, it is often necessary to go through a phase that we could call the 'preliminary phase'. This preliminary phase relates to the need to develop previously non-existent state capacities in order to satisfy the actual claims and provide the actual services that will lead to the realisation of the affected rights.

Thus, on occasion, the intervention of a court unveils institutional weaknesses, often tied to a lack of political will, that require attention. While the role of political commitment cannot be diminished, the absence of reliable data concerning a situation requiring transformation, an adequate institutional infrastructure, and smooth interaction between relevant state agencies, hinders the development and implementation of comprehensive, coordinated and sustainable public policies.

When faced with cases with a greater degree of structurality, judges need to promote, therefore, the creation of an institutional architecture that is indispensable to achieve redress for violated rights. This will both act as a catalyst for any actions that other state powers may have to adopt as well as help supervise their execution. Developing such architecture requires much time and effort. It often becomes the focus of the parties related to the litigation, at least during the initial phase of decision implementation. There seems to be no alternative: attempting to address the underlying and fundamental issues in a case without relevant data, focused officials, well-coordinated agencies, an adequately defined action plan and policy coherence, is unlikely to succeed and probably would result in an erratic, unsustainable process. The result, from the perspective of compliance, however, is that institutional weaknesses will amplify the challenges of implementation and lengthen the time for implementation, particularly in a structural collective case.

5.3.2   The Court: Degree of Judicial Commitment

Our case analysis has shown that a court's commitment to a decision's effective implementation is a key explanatory factor. This is particularly important given that procedural regulations in Argentina neither impose clear obligations on judges nor define a course of action aimed at executing collective case decisions, which often involve positive obligations and complex remedies. The consequence is that judges may 'take refuge' in this lacuna and absence of regulation, avoiding responsibilities for which they may be accountable. When this happens, the implementation of decisions – both in *collective* and *structural collective* cases – becomes more difficult.

Consequently, courts committed to addressing in full the demands of such cases must often create ad-hoc proceedings. Such proceedings are permitted within their scope of action but are, in no way, obligatory. In some cases, courts face unprecedented and unusual situations, creating insecurity as to the best judicial technique to adopt. This phenomenon may generate resistance towards the adoption of novel efforts that break the traditional paradigm of court action, especially within a system that lacks effective regulation and procedural clarity. In many cases, this reaction prevails. Judges adopt a conservative attitude, refusing to experiment or to establish ad-hoc mechanisms not in line with historical procedural law principles. Given the current procedural architecture, judges may see their function fulfilled even when they do little to achieve full implementation of their decisions and respond simply to party requests. Moreover, many consider that to act otherwise would stretch the boundaries of proper judicial conduct – or at least *their* understanding of judiciary intervention.

However, it should be noted that tools and techniques offered in the existing procedural codes may be extremely useful or utterly useless, depending on how they are employed. In complex proceedings, some code provisions may be useful when applied in a firm and creative way; such tools include the authority to convene hearings for multiple purposes, to conduct visual inspections, to appoint experts and inspectors, auditors or administrators, and to sanction professionals acting with malicious intent. A court determined to use these tools efficiently – as compared to a court loyal solely to the parties' initiatives and reluctant to re-assessing the tools' value and potential in collective processes – can significantly increase the probability of a decision being implemented.

Some of the cases analysed show how an active role assumed by the court has contributed simultaneously to a successful implementation and a reaffirmation of judicial authority:

- In *Nutritional Map* (case 6), the court conducted a large number of hearings to address the technical difficulties involved in designing a mapping concept (to diagnose the nutritional status) and selecting adequate indicators. During these hearings, the parties were encouraged to overcome disagreements, and dialogue was intensively promoted. Through this dialogue, the need to obtain expert assistance became clear, which helped build the consensus that ultimately led to the implementation of the judgment.
- In *Container Classrooms* (case 7), the attitude of the judge helped in preventing the case's complex nature and partially overlapping proceedings from delaying a decision (Maurino and Nino, 2009: 196). The defendant was threatened with coercive measures and the judge convened an on-site hearing – both factors playing a decisive role in achieving speedy implementation in eliminating container classrooms as an alternative space for educational activities.
- In *Candid 1 Vaccine* (case 10), the court – even before the judgment had been issued – decided to actively supervise the implementation. The court adopted a firm and robust approach. This included visiting the facility where the vaccine was to be manufactured to verify progressive State action; holding hearings with all interested parties to examine the causes and responsibilities of implementation failure and non-compliance with the schedule defined by the political authorities

themselves and summoning the Ministry of Health to request clarifications and to demand accountability for implementation failures. The court also established a control mechanism by ordering the National Ombudsman's office to follow up on the schedule and the execution of the budget. This allowed the court to monitor progress in the production of the vaccine on a regular basis, using periodical reports submitted by the National Ombudsman. By 2006, all necessary steps to manufacture the Candid 1 vaccine were completed.

To turn to the structural collective case of *Riachuelo Contamination* (case 1), the Supreme Court decided to establish follow-up criteria by defining continuous evaluation and supervision mechanisms for the measures adopted and their impact. In this case, the court appointed a federal judge who assumed exclusive control of all matters related to the implementation process. Moreover, a Monitoring Committee (Cuerpo Colegiado) was created which included the National Ombudsman and the NGOs involved in the case as interested third parties; this opened a space for participation and supervision of the implementation process.

In fact, the Supreme Court, in order to ensure compliance with its decision, had to actively intervene from early 2010 onwards, given the lack of actual progress. The court demanded the submission of reports referring to all orders issued in the decision dated 8 July 2008. It required that the reports include precise information, based on quantitative guidelines, on the degree of compliance achieved for each goal set out in the remedial programme.[25] On several occasions, after reviewing the information submitted by ACUMAR, the court emphasised the need for redressing failures to comply and for adopting specifically defined measures.[26]

The ongoing implementation process – including the aforementioned correction made by the court – was supported by continuous calls to public hearings, either before the judge in charge of decision execution or before the Supreme Court. The hearings aimed at discussing potential measures, assessing measures already implemented, and modifying state conduct that might hinder the implementation process.

In addition, the Supreme Court introduced an ad-hoc implementation mechanism, as well as a special system for appeals related to every issue emerging from the implementation process. The objective of this measure was to prevent delays in decision-making by the acting judge,

---

[25] CSJN, *Mendoza*, Resolutions dated 6 April 2010 and 26 May 2010.
[26] CSJN, *Mendoza*, Resolutions dated 10 August 2010 and 19 December 2012.

the scattering of cases among various courts and the potential conflicts resulting from such delays and scattering.[27] In 2012, the court removed the judge in charge of implementing the sentence, due to allegations of corruption.[28]

Summing up, the cases *Nutritional Map* (case 6), *Container Classrooms* (case 7), *Candid 1 Vaccine* (case 10) and *Riachuelo Contamination* (case 1) demonstrate the scope of techniques courts can utilise if and when they are committed to implementation. The success of the implementation becomes significantly more difficult when the court adopts a 'conservative' position – or a position shows little commitment with effective implementation and only with the findings in a judgment. The impact of such a conservative or passive attitude is greater in *structural* cases, where an active approach is a key factor to achieve implementation.

It is true that *collective* cases usually face greater state resistance than individual cases, which may complicate the decision's implementation. Compared with *structural* cases, however, courts can craft an execution process in *collective* cases that is more similar to those used in individual cases. The order can involve adopting a certain action that can be easily identified, despite affecting a group rather than an individual; is time-bound rather than open-ended in duration; is easily measurable; and involves a limited number of state actors. For example, in the *School Transportation* (case 9), although there were hundreds of persons affected and resolution required multiple steps – allocating a non-existent budget, designing a bus route, appointing monitors, hiring a school bus company and creating a sign-up system – the plaintiff was able to identify those responsible, demand a response and put pressure on the authorities to achieve implementation through two court hearings and a request for precautionary measures. A focus on these elements in the case allows the tools provided by procedural codes to facilitate effective compliance.[29] Accordingly, lower levels of judicial commitment or involvement in collective cases could be offset if the parties involved 'adequately' employed the traditional procedural rules in Argentina.

On the contrary, in *structural* cases, the lack of committed court intervention may hardly be offset, and, as already noted, it is closely linked to the

---

[27] CSJN, *Mendoza*, Resolution dated 10 November 2009.

[28] The execution process has now been divided into two courts according to a decision by the Supreme Court dated 19 December 2012.

[29] Including instructive hearings, fines, threatening with charges of failure to comply with public officials' obligations, seizure of budget items, and so on.

degree of satisfactory implementation. In structural cases, active court intervention seems to be a necessary precondition for effective decision execution.
The fact that the court *leads* or *facilitates* the implementation process – and
simultaneously strengthens its own authority to do so – is a *sine qua non* for
a decision to have any chance of materialisation in practice. Implementation
can be achieved by generating spaces of dialogue where the parties may
reach solutions based on mutual consent, courts impose decisions in a more
vertical fashion or courts use the few available procedural tools in a creative and firm fashion. Therefore, in the current institutional framework in
Argentina, judges who are committed to the effective implementation of
their decisions are needed in order to achieve results.: judges who are concerned about enhancing their own authority in the case and who recognise
that the successful implementation of their decisions has an impact on their
own legitimacy and that of the judiciary as a whole. If judges act according to
formalistic criteria or embrace the obsolete design of the procedural codes
in force – codes which have failed to include notions of access to justice in
accordance with the 1994 constitutional reform, the implementation will be
less likely to succeed.

In *Buenos Aires Prisons*, the Supreme Court's intervention was limited instead to the issuing of a decision in 2005. The court did not go
beyond that to define follow-up mechanisms for the measures conceived
to implement the decision. For example, the court has remained mostly
inactive as it witnessed the ups and downs in the work by the Dialogue
Table, a group formed by the Province of Buenos Aires government as
ordered by the court's decision. It also failed to react when the Dialogue
Table stopped working, and failed to do anything to promote its reacti-
vation (Filippini, 2007). Neither did it request the province executive to
report on measures adopted to improve the situation of persons held in
custody in its territory. The parties had made several presentations since
2006, and in 2010, the Supreme Court was faced with the fact that there
had been an increase in prison sentences in the Province of Buenos Aires
from 2008 onwards. In February 2010, the Supreme Court urged the
preservation of 'the physical integrity and security' of those held in custody in the Province of Buenos Aires; and to ensure that this mandate be
taken seriously, the court requested an intervention from the Supreme
Court of the province.[30] It was only after this call to the Province's court
authorities that the Undersecretariat of Human Rights of Detainees
started to work.

---

[30] CSJN, decision dated 23 February 2010.

However, the Supreme Court's decision played no role whatsoever in other processes needed to implement the decision. It did not re-activate the Dialogue Table nor influence the debate in the Province of Buenos Aires legislature regarding criminal procedural code reform.[31] In other words, neither the National Supreme Court nor the Provincial Supreme Court assumed the active and firm role required by the seriousness of the situation faced by persons held in custody in the Province of Buenos Aires; this is undoubtedly linked to the poor progress in the decision's implementation.

5.3.3   *The Defendant: Political Will to 'Non-comply'*

Another variable which impacts the chances of implementation of court remedies is the conduct adopted by the defendant. In particular, when the defendant is the state, the lack of political will to comply, which can even manifest in openly obstructionist conduct before the court, can represent a very significant obstacle, even for courts committed to achieving full compliance. Failure to implement decisions due to a defendant's lack of political will applies both to *collective* and *structural* cases. For example, the absence of political will by defendant proved to be impossible to over-come by the judge in the *Train Station Ramps* case. On the other hand, cases such as *El Vergel Healthcare Center, School Transportation, School Openings* or *Nutritional Map* show a clear change in the degree of imple-mentation depending on the commitment of public officers representing the State; those cases exhibited stagnation or advance as the political will of public officers moved from resistance to cooperation. In individual cases in Argentina, this type of resistance is less common, arguably because compliance is less financially costly and the decision does not have prec-edential consequences (Bergallo, 2011: 86).

In *Buenos Aires Prisons*, the relevant actors exhibited a clear lack of political will to implement the judgment. Prison overpopulation was understood by the administration as a question of insufficient prison capacity (supply); thus, the background criminal justice policies (causing the demand for prison places) were never questioned. Measures aimed at solving the problem have been limited to the construction of new facilities and the expansion of existing prison capacity. Yet, as the Supreme Court found in its 2005 decision, the pace of construction would have never

---

[31] The legislature ultimately approved changes in the system of alternative restraining meas-ures to the preventive detention regulations.

been enough to cover even the predictable rise in prison population.[32] The province's executive branch denied the existence of prison overpopulation, explaining that the system had been expanded by 8,540 beds since December 2007 through the adjustment of existing spaces and the completion of new works. However, other calculations show that only around 3,400 new beds were added. Both the government's unorthodox method for accounting for beds added during its administration and its resistance to establishing constitutional parameters to define standards on 'prison beds' reveal an attempt to conceal a historical problem, and makes it difficult to discuss concrete actions to attain implementation of the decision or address the issues at stake.[33] Therefore, the primary question becomes: Can we conceive of the implementation process as a way to dismantle political positions that both (1) oppose a comprehensive, effective resolution of structural rights violations of certain groups and (2) fail to adopt a cooperative, truthful stance towards addressing the roots of the problem at stake? At least in this case – and in accordance with our conclusions on the previous variable – the answer to the question is one of scepticism.

5.3.4   The Plaintiff: Involvement of Affected Persons and Existence of Support Networks

Implementation obstacles caused by a court's passive attitude or an actor's resistance to comply can be overcome or weakened by the active involvement of those affected by the case, as well as by strategic alliances among prestigious human rights organisations, research centres, religious organisations or other social organisations with advocacy and mobilisation capacities (Abramovich, 2009: 46).

The grey zone surrounding procedural rules – a refuge of sorts for judges reluctant to engage in the intensive leadership required by complex proceedings – underlines the importance of participation by those affected and of strategic alliances in these collective cases and, in particular, the implementation phase. The presence in the courtroom of persons directly affected and of organisations representing various social sectors makes it more difficult for judges to adopt a passive attitude.

First, there is a clear caus–effect relationship between judicial actions and the continued violation of rights, which the court hears directly from those affected by the violation. Formalistic explanations lose

---

[32] CSJN, *Verbitsky*, decision dated May 2005, section 31.
[33] We follow here the analysis made by CELS in its 2012 Annual Report.

argumentative strength in situations where the abuse and rights violations are both serious and palpable. Second, the participation of affected persons or the existence of organisational alliances brings more exposure to the judicial process, which otherwise would go unnoticed. Therefore, the proceedings come to life and the court's attitude becomes more visible, exposed to scrutiny and control by the various players in the case. The active involvement by those affected by the situation and other relevant actors demands more accountability from both courts and political actors. Furthermore, the perceived legitimacy of the claim becomes stronger, as does its relevance for multiple players. This tends to reduce the margin for dilatory tactics or formalistic attitudes.

Thus, the presence of directly affected persons and civil society support structures are significant factors which may have an effect on both the attitude of the court and the conduct of the defendant. They encourage a greater judicial commitment to the case and concern with effective redress and infuse proceedings with a sense of urgency. Similarly, with those affected present in the courtroom, it is more difficult for public officials to adopt evasive attitudes in their public explanations. The judge's presence at any dialogue table – along with the fact that a record is kept of officials' explanations and promises – guarantees a certain level of rationality, coherence and consistency over time to the position of any party. In many of the collective cases under analysis, constructive dialogue was achieved. This contributed to the implementation of the court decision, following the court's leadership which guaranteed a certain level of seriousness and commitment. Although dilatory tactics have been observed, they are more difficult to sustain over time, particularly when the requested remedy is a single, concrete, feasible measure.

In *Drinking Water* (case 4), the presence of those affected at various implementation hearings opened a discussion with the authorities (i.e. the defendant) about the degree of actual compliance with implementation measures based on the needs of the families seeking access to drinking water. Similarly, in the *School Transportation* (case 9), the presence of the affected persons – in particular, the mothers of students – enabled both the court and the responsible state agencies to assess and to define corrections in the new measures in order to ensure transportation for children from homes located a greater distance from their schools. In both cases, direct involvement by the affected persons in the implementation process helped ensure the effectiveness of the court measures.

Moreover, in the cases from the Province of Buenos Aires, the active participation of affected groups was identified as a significant contribution to the implementation process. Examples of this are the collective cases related to creating a healthcare centre (case 12) and supplying drinking water to neighbourhoods in the Greater Buenos Aires area (case 11), in which the direct participation by those affected – who met with the public officials that the court decision had deemed responsible for finding a solution – proved decisive. The affected persons also had the support of major civil society organisations. The meetings, which started in the court and continued elsewhere, reduced the margin for evasive answers; created a direct link between those affected and the public officials, which helped the officials to better delimit and understand the issue; and, finally, led to agreements in terms of compliance benchmarks that considered both the affected persons' needs and the technical feasibility of implementing a solution. Both cases ended with court orders that garnered compliance from municipal governments with no prior history of judicial involvement in public policy – particularly, *social policy* – discussions.

In addition to the presence of those affected in the implementation process, the involvement of strategic alliances between affected persons and prestigious civil society organisations, or between various institutional actors, was pivotal in generating the conditions needed to overcome the state's resistance and to ensure compliance within the City of Buenos Aires. In *Villa La Dulce* (case 7), the housing construction project was achieved largely due to the continuous pressure exerted on political authorities by an alliance between the affected group and various prestigious civil society and state organisations. The alliance included social actors, such as a human rights agency which brought forward the court action, the Catholic Church organisation for social care and State agencies in charge of human rights promotion and protection within the City of Buenos Aires, such as Asesoría Tutelar and the City's Ombudsman. Each of them played a specific role and possessed distinct capacities for pressing on various political actors. The alliance was a key factor in determining and channelling the political will of the city government to comply with the agreement.

Likewise, in *Riachuelo Contamination* (case 1), the inclusion of the housing problems of residents as a theme in the judgment execution process resulted from the involvement of residents. They had requested the right to participate in the execution process[34] and contributed to the reports on the impact of relocation measures. Their involvement in the execution process proved indispensable both in preventing eviction orders of

[34] Eduardo Videla, *Los olvidados de la Cuenca*, Página/12, 17 June 2011, available at www.pagina12.com.ar/diario/sociedad/3-170299-2011-06-17.html.

families who had no alternative housing and in promoting adequate relocation processes and infrastructure development in slums located along the Riachuelo banks. Furthermore, the inclusion of the housing problem in the implementation process was strongly related to the Monitoring Committee´s (Cuerpo Colegiado) repeated claims at public hearings, as well as to the report on living conditions at Villa Inflamable prepared by affected community members and ACIJ.

5.4   Conclusions and Strategic Implications

This chapter on Argentine experience has highlighted the key role of four key variables in explaining the vary levels of enforcement of collective social rights judgments. We would like to emphasise that each of these individual variables provides only a partial explanation. We have considered them in a mostly isolated manner but they often interact with each other on a continuous basis, with reciprocal effects. Thus, for example, a decision issued in a structural collective case may be implemented more rapidly than a decision in a collective case if in the former the court adopts an active attitude and the defendant is willing to cooperate, while in the latter the court is passive and the defendant, reluctant to comply; in a case with a passive court but a strong presence of those affected and cooperative public officials, implementation will be easier than in a case with an active court and a state agency with a strong will to refrain from complying, and so on.

Furthermore, several variables which have not been analysed in the chapter are also relevant and interact with the variables considered here. For example, Media coverage of the case can influence the behaviour of both court and defendant, contributing to speedier and effective implementation. The existence of legislative measures backing the court action may lead to a greater commitment and intensity in the judicial intervention. Career-related aspects may also play a role in the way judges approach this type of cases (e.g., a judge may be conditioned if she is in the middle of an official examination process leading to a promotion), and so on.

Basically, multiple combinations of variables – which also affect the process in different degrees (the degree of commitment, creativity, authority, etc. shown by judges can vary significantly between commitment and apathy) – will affect the chances of implementation of court decisions in complex cases. Owing to the large number of variables involved, and the multiplicity of their possible shades, it is difficult to make an *a priori* assumption of which would be the result of every possible combination.

In spite of this difficulty, identifying the variables and understanding how they function on an isolated basis can be a useful contribution to an improved understanding of the dynamics of these processes and to strategic advocacy efforts in a given case. Therefore, we believe an analysis of the factors affecting the degree of difficulty faced in court decision implementation processes within the current institutional framework – as attempted in this chapter – is a valuable, clarifying contribution for those using litigation to defend basic rights.

For example, the differentiation between *collective* and *structural* cases, and the implementation difficulties they face is useful when having to decide which type of case to file. Upon designing a legal strategy including litigation, it is necessary to think about the concrete goals and results intended to be achieved in the short, medium and long term. If one expects to solve a problem in the short/medium term affecting an individual or a group of persons, a structural collective action is unlikely to be a good choice; instead, a collective case or several individual cases might be more effective.[35] In fact, if the case is of a greater structural nature, it should be assumed that, under conditions of institutional weakness or political apathy, it is highly likely that within the short/medium term, efforts will have to be mainly devoted to generating the necessary institutional preconditions, so that the central issue will have to be approached later; if the case is successful, the affected persons will have their violated rights redressed in the long term or, at best, in the medium term.

Based on the comments made earlier, we need to adjust our expectations related to the timeframe within which court decisions are implemented and the activities involved in such processes. Becoming aware of the fact that collective litigation and, in particular, structural collective litigation requires a change of paradigm in terms of the functions traditionally attributed to the judiciary is not easy – not only for the courts themselves. Litigating parties and civil society organisations should also accept that the time and efforts required to implement certain court decisions are much longer and intensive than those required to implement a court decision in a traditional case; consequently, the tools used to measure success or failure should be developed and adjusted to the nature of these cases. Accordingly, we need to accept that the creation of the preconditions needed to ensure effective implementation of a structural decision

---

[35] This evaluation should equally take into account other considerations, including whether medium cases promote distorting solutions compared to more comprehensive alternatives, and whether they strengthen access to justice inequalities by failing to provide a solution for the most vulnerable sectors, and so on.

takes longer than the time cases normally take, and demand intense and creative involvement by judges and litigants.

Furthermore, litigation of structural collective cases exposes systemic gaps in the way political powers face problems involving violations of the population's rights. Within this framework, the judiciary should not be made accountable for providing instant solutions to long-standing problems which have not been approached by the powers constitutionally responsible to do so. However, it can and should be expected that courts assume an active and committed role, since the implementation of their decisions constitutes a fundamental part of exerting an effective constitutional control to protect fundamental rights. Given the absence of specific regulations, the courts should adopt an active stance of leadership in the process, building up their authority, and using available tools in a creative way in order to advance the implementation of structural decisions.

In complex cases, the defendant's reluctance to comply largely hinders the implementation of court decisions, but this difficulty is worsened or weakened depending on the judges' behaviour. We have argued that public officials are less likely to show reluctance when faced with active courts which demand explanations from them, confront them with those affected and expose their non-complying and delaying behaviour at public hearings, and so on.

Finally, we understand that the behaviour of judges (as well as of defendants) is positively influenced when the persons directly affected participate in the case or when solid alliances have been forged between social actors involved in the judicial process. Such alliances can be leveraged through joint actions, by attending public hearings, submitting *amicus curiae* briefs, contributing relevant technical information, participating in dialogue tables, and so on. The presence of persons directly affected or the existence of robust alliances sets limitations to the discretionary power of judges, positively contributes to their more active behaviour and raises the costs of adopting an arbitrary, obstructionist, reluctant attitude by the defendant, be it a state or private actor. Furthermore, such alliances contribute to generate a more vigorous dialogue in the courtroom, which makes it possible to design remedies considering a larger number of affected interests, and to reach more comprehensive, stable and sustainable agreements with the state.

These considerations highlight the importance of ensuring that the case is supported by the persons directly affected, and of forging alliances with social actors having agendas compatible with or complementary to the litigated cases, in order to influence the behaviour of both courts and defendants. Owing to their work agendas, previous relevant experience, daily work and legal obligations -in the case of state agencies in charge of protecting rights-, many actors are likely to be interested in joining alliances aimed at achieving the implementation of the decision obtained.

References

Abramovich, Victor (2006), 'La articulación de acciones legales y políticas en la demanda de derechos sociales', in Alicia Etly Yamin (ed.), *Derechos económicos, sociales y culturales en América Latina. Del invento a la herramienta* (Mexico: Plaza y Valdés) 149–170.

(2009), 'El rol de la justicia en la articulación de políticas y derechos sociales', in Victor Abramovich and Laura Pautassi (eds.), *La revisión judicial de las políticas sociales. Estudio de casos* (Buenos Aires: Editores del Puerto).

Abramovich, Victor and Christian Courtis (2006), *El umbral de la ciudadanía* (Buenos Aires: Editores del Puerto).

Abramovich, Victor and Laura Pautassi (2009), 'El enfoque de derechos y la institucionalidad de las políticas sociales', in Victor Abramovich and Laura Pautassi (eds.), *La revisión judicial de las políticas sociales. Estudio de casos* (Buenos Aires: Editores del Puerto).

ACIJ and Junta Vecinal de Villa Inflamable (2002), *Villa* Inflamable: *Donde comenzó el caso 'Mendoza' los derechos siguen esperando*, October, accessed 28 July 2014 http://acij.org.ar/wp-content/uploads/2012/12/Villa-Inflamable-Informe-Final-optimizado.pdf.

Araluz Solano, Socorro (2005), 'La utilización del estudio de caso en el análisis local', *Región y Sociedad*, 17(32), 108–144.

Bercovich, Luciana and Gustavo Maurino (Coordinadores) (2013), *Los derechos sociales en la Gran Buenos Aires, Algunas aproximaciones desde la teoría, las instituciones y la acción* (Buenos Aires: Eudeba).

Bergallo, Paola (2011), 'Argentina. Courts and the Right to Health: Achieving Fairness Despite "Routinization" in Individual Coverage Cases?', in Alicia Ely Yamin and Siri Gloppen (eds.), *Litigating Health Rights. Can Courts Bring More Justice to Health?* (Buenos Aires: Siglo XXI Editores – CELS), 43–75.

Borda, Rodrigo Diego (2013), 'El habeas corpus colectivo como mecanismo de protección de las personas privadas de libertad', in Florencia Plazas and Luciano Hazan (eds.), *Garantías constitucionales en la investigación penal. A Critical Review of Case Law.* (Forthcoming).

CELS (ed.) (2008), *La lucha por el Derecho. Litigio Estratégico y Derechos Humanos.* (Buenos Aires: Siglo XXI Editores – CELS).

(2012), 'El modelo de la prisión-depósito. Medidas urgentes en los lugares de detención en la Argentina', in *Derechos Humanos en Argentina* (Buenos Aires: Siglo XXI Editores – CELS).

Colegiado, Cuerpo (2013), Informe Especial sobre el Caso Matanza Riachuelo: bases para un adecuado cumplimiento del fallo de la Corte Suprema de Justicia de la Nación. Defensoría del Pueblo de la Nación, accessed 28 July 2014 www .dpn.gov.ar/riachuelo/rio475801.pdf.

Defensoría del Pueblo de la Nación (2006), *Informe Especial de Seguimiento Cuenca Matanza Riachuelo 2003–2005*, accessed 28 July 2014 http://dpn.gov.ar/ informes/riachuelo2006.pdf.

Escudero Macluf, Jesús, Luís Alberto, Delfín Beltrán and Leonor Gutiérrez González (2008), 'El estudio de caso como estrategia de investigación en las ciencias sociales', *Revista Ciencia Administrativa*, No. 1, Universidad Veracruzana, Instituto de Investigaciones y Estudios Superiores de las Ciencias Administrativas, pp. 7–10.

Fairstein, Carolina (2009), 'En busca de soluciones judiciales para mejorar la calidad de vida de los habitantes de la Cuenca Matanza Riachuelo', in CELS, *Derechos Humanos en Argentina* (Editores: Siglo XXI Editores – CELS), 333–358.

FARN (2013), *Riachuelo a cinco años de la sentencia de la Corte*, accessed 30 July 2014 www.farn.org.ar/wp-content/uploads/2013/07/napoli_riachuelo_ 5anosdelfallo.pdf.

Filippini, Leonardo (2007), 'La ejecución del fallo "Verbitsky". Una propuesta metodológica para su evaluación', in Leonardo G. Pitlevnik (dirección), *Jurisprudencia penal de la Corte Suprema de Justicia de la Nación 3* (Buenos Aires: Hammurabi), 148–175.

García Silva, Leandro and Javier García Espil (2012), 'Causa Matanza Riachuelo. Tiempo de debatir escenarios de recomposición' in FARN, *Informe Ambiental Anual 2012*, accessed 30 July 2014 www.farn.org.ar/informe2012.pdf.

Gouvert, Juan Fernando (2013), *Nuevo órgano de contralor y supervisión de la pena en la provincia de Buenos Aires: entre el acierto y su ardua implementación*, accessed 30 July 2014 http://new.pensamientopenal.com.ar/sites/default/ files/2013/02/ejecucion01.pdf.

Maurino, Gustavo (2008), 'Elementos de un nuevo paradigma de acceso a la Justicia', in Asociación por los Derechos Civiles (ADC), *La Corte y los derechos 2005/ 2007*, (Buenos Aires: Siglo XXI Editores – CELS), 81–95.

Maurino, Gustavo and Ezequiel Nino (2009), 'Judicialización de Políticas Públicas de contenido social. Un examen a partir de casos tramitados en la Ciudad de Buenos Aires', in Abramovich Victor and Pautassi Laura, *La Judicialización de las Políticas Sociales, La revisión judicial de las políticas sociales. Estudio de casos* (Buenos Aires: Editores del Puerto), 173–241.

Merlinsky, María Gabriela (2008), 'Agregando valor a los estudios de caso: reflexiones desde la trastienda de la investigación', presented at I Encuentro Latinoamericano de Metodología de las Ciencias Sociales, accessed 30 July 2014 http://metodos-avanzados.sociales.uba.ar/files/2014/04/MERLINSKY.pdf.

Merlinsky, María Gabriela, Carolina Montera, Eliana Spadoni and Melina Tobías (2014), 'La causa Beatriz Mendoza. Política ambiental y derechos en tensión', en *Marginaciones sociales en el área metropolitana de Buenos Aires. Acceso a la justicia, capacidades estatales y movilización legal*, Buenos Aires, Biblos.

Ministerio de Seguridad de la Provincia de BA (2011), *Informe relativo a la situación de las personas privadas de la libertad, durante el período octubre 2007 diciembre 2011*, accessed 14 September www.mseg.gba.gov.ar/mjysseg/libros/LIBRO%20situacion%20octubre.pdf.

Organization of American States, Executive Secretariat for Integral Development (SEDI) (16 December 2011). *Indicadores de Progreso para medición de derechos contemplados en el Protocolo de San Salvador* OEA/Ser.L/XXV.2.1 GT/PSSI/doc.2/11 rev.2 (2011).

Rodríguez Garavito, César (2011), 'Beyond the Courtroom: The Impact of Judicial Activism on Socioeconomic Rights in Latin America', *Texas Law Review*, 89(7), 1669–1698.

Rodríguez Garavito, César and Diana Rodríguez Franco (2010), 'Un giro en los estudios sobre derechos sociales: el impacto de los fallos y el caso del desplazamiento forzado en Colombia', in Pilar Arcidiácono, Nicolás Espejo Yaksic and César Rodríguez-Garavito (eds.), *Derechos sociales: Justicia, política y economía en América Latina* (Bogota: Siglo del Hombre, Uniandes, CELS and Universidad Diego Portales), 83–154.

Rossi, Julieta and Leonardo Filippini (2010), 'El derecho internacional en la justiciabilidad de los derechos sociales', in Pilar Arcidiácono, Nicolás Espejo Yaksic and César Rodríguez-Garavito (eds.), *Derechos sociales: Justicia, política y economía en América Latina* (Bogota: Siglo del Hombre, Uniandes, CELS and Universidad Diego Portales), 193–234.

Smulovitz, Catalina (2011), 'Petición y Creación de Derechos: la judicialización en Argentina', in Rachel Sieder, Line Schjolden and Alan Angell (eds.), *La judicialización de la política en América Latina* (Colombia: Universidad del Externado de Colombia), 175–199.

Yepes, Rodrigo Uprimny and Nelson Camilo Sánchez (2010), 'El uso de indicadores de derechos humanos por la Corte Constitucional Colombiana', in Víctor Abramovich and Laura Pautassi (eds.), *La medición de las políticas sociales* (Buenos Aires: Editores del Puerto), 295–328.

Yin, Robert K. (2003), *Applied Social Research Methods Series: Investigación sobre estudio de casos. Diseño y Métodos*, 2nd edn, Vol. 5 (London: SAGE).

Brazil: Are Collective Suits Harder to Enforce?

OCTAVIO LUIZ MOTTA FERRAZ

6.1 Introduction

The Brazilian constitution of 1988 is generous in the recognition of justiciable social and economic rights. Article 6 establishes that '[e]ducation, health, work, housing, leisure, security, social security, protection of motherhood and childhood, and assistance to the destitute, are social rights under this Constitution'. Article 7, with 34 subsections, regulates in detail conditions of work, including unemployment insurance (7, iii), the minimum wage (iv) and maximum working hours (xiii). Then follows freedom of association to form trade unions in article 8 and the right to strike in article 9.

After redemocratisation and the establishment of the new constitutional order, moreover, courts have been less reluctant to adjudicate these rights. The good reception by judges of social rights cases in some areas has encouraged new ones to come to court, and litigation soon became a regular strategy of social rights claimants and activists, resulting in some areas in an explosion of litigation that has often been called, with a hint of criticism, 'judicialization'.

There is a notable difference, however, in the volume of litigation in different areas, and even within some areas there is significant variation in the volume of lawsuits according to their object. So, for instance, whereas litigation involving the right to health has all but exploded in the past ten years, the right to education has experienced a much lower volume of litigation (with the exception of litigation for pre-school 'creche' places), and the right to housing has experienced virtually no litigation in comparison with health and education.[1] Within education, litigation focuses

---

[1] There is unfortunately no accurate and comprehensive data on social rights litigation in Brazil. Yet it is possible to presume, from scattered studies, media reports and personal experience that health is the area where litigation has been more voluminous. A simple electronic search on the caselaw database of the Court of Appeals of the State of São Paulo, for instance,

Octavia Luiz Motta Ferraz is a Reader in transnational law at the Dickson Poon School of Law and an affiliate of the Brazil institute, both at King's College London.

overwhelmingly on nursery places rather than primary or secondary schooling. Within housing, most litigants try to stop evictions rather than claim a decent house to live in. Within health, whereas thousands of individualised cases have been reaching the courts demanding medication, operations and other types of individualised treatment, the same does not occur when the issue in question is a comprehensive health programme or measure affecting a larger group of people or the population as a whole (such as basic sanitation, hospital equipment). In a recent survey of right to health cases filed against the federal government, it was found that less than 3 per cent of lawsuits are collective in nature.[2]

What explains these differences? Why do individuals litigate significantly more to guarantee their right to health than they do to enforce their rights to education and housing equally recognised in the constitution? For what reasons even within the same area some claims are much more common than others, despite being equally or more important from a deprivation perspective?

There are of course no simple answers to these questions. There must be several factors that, combined in complex ways, explain the differences in volume of litigation in different areas of social and economic rights. Different levels of organisation of civil society around a certain issue, resources available to potential claimants, their socio-economic status, awareness of their rights are just a few of these factors that would potentially feature in a comprehensive answer.[3]

shows the following. For the expression 'right to health', 69,715 decisions are returned. For 'right to education', 1,698 and for 'right to housing' 7,769. It is fair to say that right to housing litigation is nonetheless much lower in volume because most of these 7,769 cases involve protection of private property of middle-class consumers against banks trying to cease them to guarantee the payment of debts rather than protection of the homeless. Indeed, when one includes 'bem de família' as a search term (a technical term meaning a property cannot be executed as a debt guarantee), 3,643 cases come up. For two interesting recent studies on the right to housing in the courts that confirm the lesser volume of litigation in this area and the weaker protection of the homeless see Coutinho (2010) and Nasser (2011).

[2] See Ferraz (2011). Although a collective suit can in principle involve millions of individuals and therefore have a much more significant impact than all individual lawsuits put together, in practice most collective lawsuits are also focused on a particular health issue, such as diabetes, or autism (see the later pages) which affect a certain group in the population, more or less numerous depending on the epidemiology of the disease and the geographical area covered by the lawsuit. The point here, however, is simply to show that, in health, the volume of individual lawsuits has been much higher than collective ones, for reasons discussed in the text below.

[3] Some authors call these factors 'support structure for legal mobilization' (Epp, 1998, 3) or 'opportunity structure for litigation' (Gloppen, 2006, 27). On socio-economic profile of litigants and related inequalities in access to courts in Brazil see Ferraz (2009a).

In the limited scope of this chapter, however, I shall focus on one potential explanatory factor to these differences in volume of litigation that seems to me significant: *obstacles to enforcement*. My hypothesis is that *difficulties in enforcement* can explain significant differences in volume of litigation even when some of the other important factors remain constant. I shall use collective litigation involving the right to health in the state of São Paulo to test this hypothesis.[4]

The chapter is organised as follows. In Section 6.2 I clarify what I mean by enforcement and distinguish between two meanings of the concept (legal and factual enforcement) which are relevant to the issue I deal with in this chapter. In Section 6.3 I analyse some paradigmatic decisions of the Brazilian Supreme Federal Tribunal (Supremo Tribunal Federal) and others by the São Paulo Court of Appeals that highlight greater obstacles of legal enforcement encountered by collective lawsuits in comparison to individual ones in the field of health. In Section 6.4 I look at the collective lawsuits filed by Ministerio Publico (Public Prosecutors' Office) in the state of São Paulo in the field of health and analyse them in terms of what I call factual enforcement. I focus particularly on the so-called case of the Autistic, one of the most complex cases of structural litigation in the field of health of the past decade in the state of São Paulo. Section 6.5 presents the conclusions of my discussion.

6.2   Defining Enforcement

By enforcement here I mean both compliance with a court order already handed down by a judge (I call this *factual enforcement*) and ability or willingness of a judge to translate a legal norm into a practical and implementable remedy (I call this *legal enforcement*). Factual enforcement is dependent on legal enforcement or, to put it another way, legal enforcement is a precondition of factual enforcement, since without a decision by a judge translating the legal norm into an implementable remedy, there can be no compliance (factual enforcement) with a court order; there is no court order to be complied with. To give an example, imagine a lawsuit based on the right to health sponsored by an NGO aiming to force the state to adopt a comprehensive programme that benefits all individuals

---

[4] I suspect that there is no significant difference between civil and political rights and social and economic rights in terms of the problem I am discussing in this paper. Although it is beyond its scope to do this comparison, anedoctal evidence seems to indicate that civil and political collective lawsuits, such as those demanding improvement in prison conditions, face the same problems as social rights collective suits.

suffering from diabetes in a given region. The claim can fail at two different stages, both related to *enforcement* in the way I am proposing to understand the term. It can succeed in convincing the judge to order government to do so, yet fail due to an inability or unwillingness of government, for whatever reason, to implement the judgment. That would be a problem of factual enforcement. But it can also fail at an earlier stage, due to unwillingness or inability of the judge to determine what policies government should implement to guarantee the right to health. Here I believe the problem is also one of enforcement, i.e. of implementation in the real world of a legal norm. Lawrence Sager helpfully referred to this as judicial underenforcement: 'the idea that a conscientious constitutional court will on some occasions stop short of fully enforcing the Constitution because of particular features of the judicial process' (2010, 580).

In either case, as I suggest in this chapter, the result is a discouragement of litigation as a viable strategy for claiming social and economic rights, whereas the opposite, i.e. a series of rulings that do determine what government should do to implement a particular social right (legal enforcement), and a consistent practice of government to comply with these rulings (factual enforcement) create a favourable environment for social rights litigation. As well observed by Siri Glopen, '[p]eople and organizations are assumed to pursue litigation when doing so is seen as the most promising route, given their available resources and the barriers that they face' (Gloppen, 2008, 27).

In the field of health in Brazil this explanation seems rather plausible. On the one hand, we have a burgeoning volume of litigation by individuals claiming a specific health good (most often drugs, but also operations, equipment etc.). On the other hand, we have a significantly lower number of lawsuits where a collective health measure is at issue (e.g. a vaccination programme, basic sanitation actions, improvements in a hospital). Whereas almost all lawsuits of the former kind are successful in terms of factual and legal enforcement, many of the lawsuits of the latter type fail either at the first enforcement hurdle (legal enforcement) or the second (factual enforcement).

Quantitative data presented later and qualitative interviews conducted with lawyers who represent claimants in the right to health litigation cases confirm that these enforcement difficulties are indeed an important reason preventing them from pursuing the collective route more often.[5]

---

[5] Interviews with public defenders of the state of São Paulo, July 2009. Interview with state attorneys of the state of São Paulo, September 2010; interview with members of Public Prosecutors' Office (Ministerio Publico) in the state of São Paulo, September 2010.

But this profile of litigation, which we might call the 'Brazilian model of litigation', is not a good model for the implementation of social and economic rights. This is because, as I discuss in detail elsewhere, this high prevalence of individualised claims for healthcare often results in more rather than less health inequalities and therefore defeats the purpose of the social and economic rights recognised in the constitution. Appropriately devised collective suits, on the contrary, would have in principle a better potential to tackle health inequalities and further the right to health.[6]

It is important to investigate further, therefore, why collective suits face such greater difficulties in terms of enforcement and whether these difficulties can be overcome. This is what motivates the discussion of enforcement I carry out in this chapter.

6.3   Hurdles of Legal Enforcement

As mentioned already, one of the possible reasons that explain the comparatively fewer number of collective lawsuits based on the right to health in Brazilian courts is related to their poorer prospects of success compared to individual lawsuits.[7] It is not clear, as I shall discuss later on, why judges should deal differently with collective and individual cases, but the fact is that they often do.

In individual cases judges find no difficulty in ordering the state to provide the health benefit claimed by the individual plaintiff, often at extremely short notice (forty-eight, seventy-two hours), in a very assertive way (sometimes under threat of prison; often under threat of pecuniary fines) and often without much consideration of the state's arguments. On the other hand, when collective lawsuits are at issue, judges are often more

---

Interviews with public defenders, state attorneys and members of the Ministerio Publico of the state of Bahia, November 2015.

[6] See Ferraz (2009). I include the caveat 'in principle' because collective lawsuits are not necessarily positive or better than individual ones to protect the right to health. One clear advantage they have is to present the complexities of the health policy involved more clearly. Individual suits can sometimes lead judges to overlook the collective dimensions of the right to health and focus too much on the individual case before them. Yet both collective and individual lawsuits can have negative and positive effects, depending on their object, their beneficiaries and the way they are handled.

[7] Other possible contributory reasons which I cannot discuss in any depth in this chapter are: the stricter rules of standing to bring collective suits (only certain officials and organisations can file them); the small number of public attorneys in charge of social and economic rights in comparison with private lawyers that can represent individual litigants; the comparatively more complex and therefore time consuming process of preparation of a collective suit vis-à-vis an individual one.

reluctant to grant the health measures requested by the plaintiff.[8] Indeed, in collective lawsuits the judiciary rarely grants interim measures without at least hearing the state's arguments beforehand.[9] Moreover, interim injunctions are denied more often in collective lawsuits than in individual ones. When an interim injunction is given by the first instance judge, it is more often overturned by the court of appeal in collective cases than in individual ones. Last but not least, final decisions in collective lawsuits are more often in favour of the state than in individual ones.

Figure 6.1 shows the success rates at all stages of the judicial proceeding for right to health lawsuits filed by the Public Prosecutors' Office (Ministerio Publico, or simply MP) from 1999 to 2008 and the Public Defensory (Defensoria Publica, or simply DP)[10] from 2006 to 2009. Given that the MP in the city of São Paulo files only collective suits, whereas the DP focuses on individual lawsuits, it is possible to test whether the impression voiced by many that collective suits are harder to win is correct or not.

The available data seems to confirm that impression. It shows that an individual plaintiff claiming a specific health good is more likely to succeed in court than the Ministerio Publico in collective lawsuits. The final decision is favourable to the claimant in 77 per cent of the cases in individual lawsuits sponsored by the DP, but only in 47 per cent in collective suits sponsored by the MP. The rate of success in the lower courts is practically the same, around 80 per cent. In the interim injunction stage,

---

[8] There are two main types of collective suits in Brazil, the Popular Action ('Ação Popular', or 'AP', Federal Law 4.717, of 1.965 and Federal Constitution, art. 5, LXXIII) and the Public Civil Action ('Ação Civil Pública', or 'ACP', Federal Law 7.347, of 1.985). The former can be filed by any citizen and has as its scope the protection of *public assets*, here included not only economic goods, but also those of historic and cultural value. The latter has more restricted standing rules. Only the Public Prosecutors' Office (Ministerio Publico), the Public Defensory (Defensoria Publica), government at all spheres, state companies, foundations and associations, and civil society associations in operation for longer than one year can make use of them. Their scope overlaps somewhat with that of APs, but is larger. It includes the protection of the environment, consumers, the 'urbanistic order', goods of artistic, historic, aesthetic and touristic value, and any other collective or so-called diffuse interests (interests so general that cannot be located in any group, but rather on society as a whole). For our purposes, only the ACPs will be of interest.

[9] This is partly due to the fact that article 2 of Federal Law n° 8437, of 1.992, expressly states that, in ACPs, no interim injunction can be given without the hearing of the public body involved. Many judges, however, do not follow that rule, especially in individual cases.

[10] We may refer to the MP and DP together as public attorneys, i.e. attorneys paid by the state to represent the public interest. Although their remit is not identical, it overlaps considerably in the representation of economically disadvantaged individuals, so considered by legislation those who earn less than three times the minimum wage.

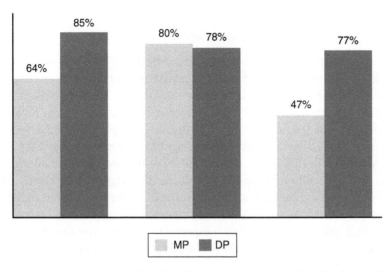

Figure 6.1 Rate of success in right to health cases at three stages of the judicial proceeding (interim decision, first instance decision, and appeal).

it favours the claimant in 85 per cent of the cases in individual lawsuits, and in 64 per cent in collective lawsuits. Given that the final decision can take several years to be handed down, this is an important difference. Interim decisions that are favourable to the claimant can remain in force for several years, sometimes for longer than he or she actually needs the health benefit granted. So, even if the decision is overturned later on at the appeal stage, it should count as a success for the claimant rather than as a failure.[11]

This significantly higher success rate in individual suits is partly due, in my view, to hurdles of what I have called legal enforcement. Courts find themselves less willing and capable of translating the abstract provisions of the constitution into specific orders for the state when the issue involved is of a more complex nature and larger scale. Let us look at a few seminal recent decisions of the Brazilian Supreme Federal Tribunal (Supremo Tribunal Federal, or simply STF), the highest court in the land, to illustrate this point.

---

[11] In some of the collective cases, the Secretariat of Health of the State of São Paulo ended up continuing to provide the health benefit even after winning the appeal. It would be unfair to discontinue treatment after so many years (Interview, September 2010).

6.3.1   The STF and Collective Health Cases

Most reported right-to-health cases decided by the STF are individual and only a few are collective. The former have so far *almost always* been judged in favour of the individual claimant, whereas of the few collective cases reported, several have been judged in favour of the state.[12] Let us look at the reasoning of decisions to find clues that might explain this behaviour.

The first collective case involving the right to health decided by the STF was ADPF 45. In this case, a political party of the opposition challenged the constitutionality of a presidential decree that significantly restricted the funding of the health system. Different from the usual assertiveness showed in individual cases, the STF took a much more deferential role and stated that 'the Judiciary branch – especially this Supreme Court – does not have the institutional function of formulating and implementing public policies'.[13]

This is a clear manifestation of what I called hurdle of legal enforcement. It is virtually impossible (or inadequate, depending on one's view) for courts to determine what type and manner of expenditure in the health system is mandated by the constitutional norm recognising the right to health. According to the decision just quoted, this is something that the political branches of the state, not the judiciary, should decide.

A very similar rationale was applied in all other few collective cases that have reached the STF so far. In STA 185, the lower court judge had ordered the state to take, 'within 30 days, all appropriate measures to enable the realisation of operations in transsexuals' willing to

---

[12] I could find only two individual cases where the plaintiff was unsuccessful, both decided by Justice Ellen Gracie. One was a claim for infertility drugs ('In the present case, looking at the nature of the disease affecting the patient [female infertility associated with anovulation – CID: N97.0] and the high cost of the medicines prescribed for her treatment, which are not included among those of compulsory dispensation in the public system, I believe damage to public order, public health and the public economy are present, since the implementation of decisions such as this one would affect the already undermined public health system. Moreover, absence of treatment until the final decision is taken does not bring risks to the health of the patient'. SS 3263 / GO – GOIÁS SUSPENSÃO DE SEGURANÇA, Judgement: 23 July 2007). The other was a claim for the expensive cancer drug Mabthera (Rituximab), (SS 3073 / RN – RIO GRANDE DO NORTE SUSPENSÃO DE SEGURANÇA, Judgement: 09 February 2007). In this decision, severely criticised, Justice Ellen Gracie warns against the 'potential multiplying effects of the case', 'given the thousands of people potentially in the same situation of the claimant', available at the webpage of the STF, www.stf.gov.br.

[13] ADPF 45-9 – Distrito Federal. Relator: Min. CELSO DE MELLO Judgment: 04 May 2004, available at the webpage of the STF, www.stf.gov.br.

change their sex. The STF decided to suspend the order because 'the enforcement of the order … would impact the budgetary programme of government' and affect the rational administration of the health system 'reallocating resources originally destined to other public health policies'.[14]

In the case STA 424, the federal government, the southern state of Santa Catarina (one of the richest in Brazil) and the municipality of Joinville were jointly condemned in the first instance and in the Court of Appeal to provide three medicines (not included in the official programmes) to all the patients in that municipality suffering from the neuro-developmental condition Microcephaly. The state and municipality appealed to the STF claiming that such decision was inadequate on technical and economic grounds and would cause severe damage to the health services of that locality. The STF, this time led by Justice Gilmar Mendes, took again a deferential stance. The following passage is worth quoting in full:

> Moreover, one must not forget that the management of the Unified Health System (SUS), which is under a duty to respect the constitutional principles of equal and universal access in its health actions and provision of health services, is viable only through the conception of public policies that allocate the resources (naturally scarce) in the most efficient manner. To oblige the public system to fund any existing health action or service would cause grave damage to the administrative order and would lead to the undermining of SUS, harming even more the care of the neediest groups in the population. For that reason, we can conclude that, in principle, *the treatment SUS decided to provide should prevail over a different preference of the patient* whenever it is not proven that the existing health policy is inadequate or inefficient.[15]

In SL 256, the state of Tocantins had been condemned in the first and second instances to cover expenses with transport, food and accommodation for all patients of the municipality of *Araguaína* when receiving treatment outside that municipality.[16] Yet again, the STF, led by Gilmar Mendes, overturned the lower decisions using exactly the same justification given in STA 424 cited earlier.

---

[14] The same rationale was used in STA 91, where the MPF requested medicines for haemodialysis and transplants for all citizens of the state of Alagoas, available at the webpage of the STF www.stf.gov.br.
[15] My free translation from the original in Portuguese and my emphasis.
[16] When a health service provided by SUS is not available in a given municipality the SUS should by law cover the expenses of the patient to be treated in the nearest available unit, including transport, food and accommodation.

Now, this deferential stance of the judiciary, accepting a lack of legal enforceability of the constitutional norms recognising social rights, is not something entirely surprising. In some jurisdictions, such as South Africa, the United Kingdom for example, this is the norm and, for many commentators, the main obstacle for the implementation of these rights.[17] What is surprising about this attitude in Brazil is that it differs significantly, as already mentioned, from the extremely assertive behaviour of the judiciary in individual cases. In individual cases, the STF and most lower courts have rarely accepted the prerogative of the political branches to determine how to spend the limited budget of the health system. On the contrary, they have almost always (with very few notable exceptions) judged in favour of the claimant and have brushed aside any concerns with interference in public policies and resource allocation as secondary and irrelevant.

In a passage that became a kind of de facto precedent for individual cases, surprisingly written by the very same judge who gave the opinion in ADPF 45 cited, in a case where an individual claimed drugs for HIV-AIDS, the following principle was stated:

> Between protecting the inviolability of the right to life, an inalienable Constitutional fundamental right, and a financial and secondary interest of the State, I believe – once this dilemma is established – ethical and legal reasons impose on the judge one single and possible option: unwavering respect for life.[18]

As already mentioned, most of the right-to-health cases that reach the Brazilian judiciary across the country are of this sort, i.e. individual, and the decision is invariably based on this assertive and expansive principle in favour of the plaintiff. No concerns are ever expressed with issues of separation of powers or resource limitations. Whether the Brazilian judiciary is correct in treating collective and individual cases so differently is an important question I will discuss later on. For now I just want to emphasise that what I am calling legal unenforceability affects only collective cases, which might explain to some extent why these cases are not as common as individual ones.

---

[17] See, for instance, the South African cases *Soobramoney* and *Grootboom*, and the fierce discussion it spurred, e.g. Wesson (2004), Dugard and Roux (2006) and Bilchitz (2002).

[18] STF, j. 31.1.97, DJU 13.2.97

6.4   Hurdles of Factual Enforcement – the Diabetes and Autism Cases

Even when the first hurdle of legal enforcement is overcome in collective suits, and it is in several cases (as seen earlier, 47 per cent of the cases in our sample were successful), there is no guarantee that the judicial order is going to be implemented in the real world. Different from individual suits, where virtually all decisions are implemented by the state, collective suits often face major hurdles of factual enforcement.

In some cases, this is the result of the extreme generality in which some of these decisions are necessarily worded. Let us take, as an example, litigation in the field of diabetes, which represents the bulk of right to health litigation in the state of São Paulo and in many other places across Brazil. The government of São Paulo has an official programme to treat the whole diabetic population, which stretches to almost two hundred thousand patients. But the health experts of the Ministry of Health have decided not to offer certain types of insulin (the so-called analogue insulin, much more expensive than the normal type) as the standard treatment for the whole population. Only those who, in the opinion of the health experts of the state, cannot benefit from the regular treatment have access to analogue insulin, on a case-by-case basis. Such policy decision has given rise to a flurry of litigation, most of it individual cases, and a couple of collective lawsuits.

Following the pattern discussed earlier, most individual lawsuits have been judged in favour of the plaintiff. As a result, the Secretariat of State for Health in São Paulo was providing 9.598 doses of analogue insulin for around 6,000 individuals in 2010. On the other hand, none of the two collective suits have so far been successful in extending access to these drugs to the whole of the diabetic population that receives the standard treatment from the state, currently 182,000 people.[19]

Individual orders are clearly less complex to enforce. The judicial order simply grants the individual plaintiff access to the precise drug prescribed by her doctor. There is no leeway for the state to try and avoid compliance. Collective orders are the opposite. The judge is often not equipped to

---

[19]   Interview with Maria Cecilia Correa and Ana Luiza Chieffi, public servants at the Secretariat of Health of the State of São Paulo, 23 September 2010. There have been two collective lawsuits so far against the state of São Paulo, one sponsored by the Public Defensory, already decided in favour of the state, and the other sponsored by the Federal Public Attorney's Office (MPF). In the latter the interim injunction requested was denied in mid-2009 and the final decision can now take years to be taken.

determine, in all the necessary details, how the comprehensive programme ordered should be implemented, and the state can use this to avoid or delay implementation. Let me illustrate this with the order granted in a collective lawsuit in the area of diabetes. In this case, the collective lawsuit (ACP, Ação Civil Pública) was filed in the beginning of 2005 on behalf of all diabetic patients residing in the municipality of São Paulo, i.e. potentially tens of thousands of individuals. In line with the discussion earlier, the interim injunction requested was denied by the lower court and the court of appeal. Almost three years later the case was judged by the lower court in favour of the claimants, ordering the state to:

> provide, free of charge, for all residents of the municipality of Sao Paulo who cannot afford it and who can prove to be suffering from diabetes with a medical prescription, in the dosage and frequency established individually, continuously, regularly and without disruption, in 30 days, all medication for the control and treatment of diabetes.[20]

Exploiting the generality of the decision, the state of São Paulo was able to use strategically a technical procedure (a petition called Embargos de Declaração) asking the judge to specify in more detail how such generic order should be implemented. It questioned, regarding administrative aspects, how they should distinguish between residents of the municipality entitled to treatment and those who are not (i.e. what documents should they require for proof of residency) and whether only prescriptions issued by doctors of the public system should be accepted or also those issued by private doctors. It also questioned the generic wording of the decision, granting 'all treatment', 'all medication' and 'all equipment' necessary, asking the judge (in a slightly provocative move) to specify what exact drugs and equipment she meant.

The judge refused to specify its decision any further claiming that all medical issues should be determined by the patient's doctors on a case-by-case basis and the administrative issues should be decided by the state. This clarification turned in effect what was supposed to be a collective order benefiting thousands of patients into potential future individual ones. Indeed, according to the lower court's decision, each individual in need of diabetes' treatment should henceforth go to the state with a medical prescription for a certain drug and equipment and prove, according to criteria to be established by the state itself, that he or she was a resident of the municipality of São Paulo and could not afford the treatment. If

---

[20] Decision on file with author.

the state was not convinced of any of these conditions (e.g. medical need, residency and poverty) it would be able to deny treatment and the patient would have to go back to court to challenge this administrative decision, just like in any individual case.

But the state decided to appeal (a move that suspends the implementation of the decision until the appeal is decided) and, on 6 October 2009, the court of appeal overturned the lower court's decision precisely for its generality! The following passage of the judgment is worth quoting:

> Can there be a lawsuit whose object is the generic condemnation of the state to provide the necessary medicines for the control of diabetes to all residents of Sao Paulo? In my view, no. This duty is already established in art. 196 of the Federal Constitution, making a judicial decision to that effect unnecessary. It is clear, thus, that the collective protection of health, in this case, has to be necessarily carried out through the protection of individual rights ...[21]

The Brazilian judiciary itself, therefore, seems to be an obstacle to collective lawsuits in the field of health. There is a clear resistance, from their part, even when they grant the request of the plaintiff, to determine with any precision what the state is actually obliged to comply with. They are clearly more comfortable to issue more assertive and determined orders when the case is individual. It is not surprising, thus, that even those who have standing to file collective lawsuits end up preferring to take the individualised route.[22] Collective lawsuits are much more burdensome to prepare, take much longer to be decided and face a much higher risk of failure at both the legal and factual enforcement stages. In this diabetes case, public attorneys waited for almost eight years to have a final decision, and, although the lower court's decision had been favourable, it was too generic to be implemented, and ended up being overturned in the court of appeal.[23]

---

[21] Apelação Cível com Revisão n° 803.640–5/3-00, da Comarca de São Paulo-Faz Pública. The obstacles in this case might be better described as a hybrid of legal and factual enforcement, as there was an attempt by the judge to issue an order translating the norm into an effective measure of implementation, but the order was too generic. The Autism Case discussed in the text is a clearer case of factual enforcement obstacles.

[22] Many public attorneys who have standing to file collective suits have been rather filing multiple individual lawsuits to circumvent the obstacles of legal and factual enforcement mentioned in the text. Interview with state attorneys of the state of São Paulo, September 2010.

[23] In September 2009 the federal MP filed another collective lawsuit against the Federal government and the state of São Paulo asking for diabetes treatment, in this case for the whole population of the state of São Paulo. The lower court denied the interim injunction requested and the case will now run its normal course, i.e. it will likely take several years to

I will go back in the conclusion to the important question of whether judges are justified in treating individual and collective lawsuits differently. Now I want to turn to another collective lawsuit, this time a successful one from beginning to end, to illustrate further what I have been calling the hurdle of factual enforcement.

In this case, the MP filed on 27 October 2000 a Civil Public Action on behalf of all individuals with autism resident in the state of São Paulo to force government to 'fund ... specialised treatment in adequate institutions (private, since no state institution fulfils these conditions)' for them, including education. It requested also that treatment is given in the nearest institution to the patient's residence. Such funding of treatment in private institutions should last, according to the MP, until the state established adequate public institutions, i.e. specialised ones, separate from traditional mental health ones as was the established practice.

In its defence, the state claimed that despite its efforts to give access to specialised treatment to all autistic individuals, resources were insufficient and therefore access had to be rationed and gradually extended, otherwise other important health services and actions would suffer. The lower court rejected, at first, the interim order requested by the MP yet, on 28 December 2001, decided in favour of the claimants and ordered the state to provide everything requested by the MP.

A noteworthy feature of this decision is the way in which the judge dismissed the complexities of the case. For him, the issue was solely legal, i.e. no technical evidence was necessary, in his opinion, to help in his decision. It was a simple case of lack of implementation of the right to health recognised in the constitution which, in his interpretation, puts the state under a duty to treat everyone for any health condition for which there is treatment available. So, for the judge, when the state claimed that it did not have sufficient resources to treat all autistic individuals with the best possible treatment it was simply admitting that it was violating the right to health. Lack of resources could be easily resolved, he claimed, if the state used 'that huge sum wasted with publicity'. In the whole decision, which is eleven pages long, there is a single paragraph on what arguably should be the central issue of the case, i.e. whether the state's policy for the treatment of autism was adequate or not. Yet given that the state admittedly did not offer the best available treatment for all autistic individuals, its policy was quickly dismissed as inadequate by the judge. Most of the decision

be judged in the lower courts and the court of appeal. Decision 2009.61.00.020497-7, on file with author.

is dedicated to a description of what autism is and a discussion of legal aspects of the constitutional right to health.

In mid-2005, the court of appeal upheld the lower court's decision. Yet again, no in-depth discussion was carried out about the policy of the state for the treatment of autism. The decision is focused, as usual, on the legal aspects of the right to health recognised in the constitution, interpreted expansively (also as usual) as a right of all individuals to any treatment available for their condition. Interpreted in such an expansive way, there is (logically) no need to discuss the adequacy of the state's policy at any length. Any policy short of giving the best treatment available to every-one is defective and as a consequence represents a violation of the right to health. The issue of resource limitations is again dismissed without much consideration in the following passage:

> The argument, so typical of the bureaucrats, that the recognition of this essential right of citizens to access to health can undermine other public health policies is unwarranted. All it takes is a rational, efficient and honest management of public assets. No aid should be given [by the state] to big business; no American dollars should be sold at subsidised prices to bank-rupt bankers violating thus the principles of legality and public morality. Taxes proceeds [from CPMF[24]] should be invested in public health pro-grammes. If the state has not yet understood this, it has to be compelled by the Judiciary Power, the guardian of the Constitution, to do so.[25]

On the argument that the judiciary should not determine what and how public policies should be implemented, the decision reiterates the stand-ard response that the constitution does not give a 'blank cheque' to the political powers. On the contrary, the public administration has to operate within the 'axiological vectors' of the constitution, especially the 'principle of human dignity'.

No attempt is made, therefore, to get into the complex issues of *how* to offer adequate treatment to the whole autistic population of the state of São Paulo, yet not because this would represent an undue interference of the judiciary on political matters. Rather, because for the judiciary the matter is very simple: the best available treatment should be given. But even under such expansive interpretation of the right to health, a great

---

[24] CPMF (Contribuição Provisória sobre Movimentaçãoes Financeiras) was a provisional tax created in 1994 on financial transactions whose proceeds should be invested in the pub-lic health system yet, as often happens with this type of earmarked taxes, was gradually diverted from health to other areas, most notably to pay state debt, until it was abolished in 2007.

[25] Apelação Cível n.o 278.801.5/8-00

deal of uncertainty is left about its concrete implementation. What is best available treatment for persons with autism? This case is clearly different from the Diabetes case discussed earlier, where the issue can be resolved on a case-by-case basis through the prescription of certain drugs by the doctor to his individual patient. In the Autism case, we are concerned with the creation of medical institutions equipped to cater for the complex health and educational needs of the person with autism. How should these facilities be equipped, in terms of material and human resources, so as to be considered adequate for the treatment of autism? How many employees should there be per patient? How many doctors, nurses, nutritionists, psychologists etc? How large, light, clean should the rooms be? The issues involved are much more complex than in the medication cases such as the Diabetes' one. Taking again advantage of this problem, the state made use of the clarification proceeding already mentioned (the Embargos de Declaração petition) and managed to get the following clarification from the court of appeal:

> It is the state's role, within a framework of reasonableness, to set the technical criteria, medical and educational, for an institution to qualify as adequate for the treatment of autism.[26]

It is not difficult to imagine the complexities that arose (and still do) for the factual enforcement of that decision. Since no determination was made for the state to produce a study of autism in the state of São Paulo with the estimate number of individuals in need of treatment, and a plan to provide adequate treatment to all of them, enforcement of the decision was left to the initiative of autistic individuals (through their guardians) who, knowing about the court ruling, went to the state to request treatment. These individual administrative requests for treatment were then analysed by the state on a case-by-case basis. The state could either reject the request (e.g. for lack of evidence of autism) or accept it and allocate the patient to a clinic that it deemed suitable for the treatment of that individual.

This individualised format to enforce a collective, complex and comprehensive decision ended up causing a series of enforcement problems. It gave the state a great opportunity to control the pace and scope of the enforcement of the decision, which, in turn, spurred a myriad of further, individualised lawsuits (something the collective lawsuit was supposed to prevent rather than encourage). Indeed, many autistic claimants,

---

[26] Embargos de Declaração n.o 278.801.5/0–01.

unsurprisingly, disputed the administrative decision of the state, even when they were given a place in a clinic (either because of location or because of their alleged inadequacy). Each administrative conflict of this sort gave (and continues to give) rise to an individual lawsuit (called 'habilitação', an individual enforcement procedure subsidiary to the main collective lawsuit), which has to be decided by the judiciary. The judiciary becomes thus a *micromanager* of the delivery of health services. There have been hundreds of such individual lawsuits so far, and they keep coming to court on a daily basis.[27] Let us look at a couple of such cases to see in more detail how this works.

On 19 February 2009, the minor L.P.A., represented by a private lawyer, filed an individual lawsuit claiming that the clinic in which he was being treated, chosen by the state, was inadequate. He asked the judge to order the state to fund his transfer to and treatment in a private clinic of his choice. The judge heard the MP (the sponsor of the collective lawsuit as you will remember), whose opinion was that the claim should be rejected since the state had complied with his duty. The lower court judge accepted this opinion and decided in favour of the state. The claimant appealed, and the court of appeal decided, on 13 April 2010, to overturn the lower court's decision. It stated that it was not sufficient for the state and the MP to say that the clinic was adequate for the needs of that individual patient. They also had to prove, through expert witnesses, that this was the case. It ordered, thus, that such evidence be brought to the court and that, while it was not available, the state should fund the treatment at a clinic of the claimant's choice. Recall, now, that such cases are already up in the hundreds and growing daily.

In addition to the administrative chaos that this 'individualisation' has caused in the lower court that decided the original collective lawsuit (by laws each new subsidiary case has to be processed by the same court), it is also potentially unfair. Indeed, as we have claimed earlier, one of the proclaimed advantages of the collective lawsuits in the enforcement of social rights is the potential avoidance of the regressive effects that individual lawsuits can produce due to inequalities in access to courts. But the individualisation of the enforcement of collective decisions produces exactly

---

[27] Interview with state attorneys, September 2010. It was not possible to establish the exact number of such offshoot individual lawsuits. A search in the database of the Court of Appeal of the state of São Paulo for decisions with the terms 'autistas' and 'ação civil pública' turns up 227 incidents. Considering that the database and searching methods are not fully comprehensive, and do not include lower court cases that have not reached the Court of Appeal, the volume must be considerably higher.

the same risk. It gives a clear advantage for those patients whose families were well-informed and well-resourced enough to have heard of the decision, to be capable of filing an appropriately documented administrative request, and to be able to go to court to dispute an unfavourable administrative decision.

Such enforcement problems and potential unfairness did not escape the lower court judge entrusted with the hundreds of individual enforcement lawsuits. In an unorthodox decision, oozing frustration in every other sentence, he decided, eight years after the original decision that he had enough of micromanaging the delivery of treatment for hundreds of individuals and (to a great extent, still privileged) patients. Fiercely criticising the state for its delaying tactics and the MP for its passive stance, he decided not to accept individual claims any longer and to determine (with some impracticality it must be said) that the MP and the state should combine efforts to deliver, once and for all, adequate treatment to all autistic individuals within ninety days.[28] The following longish extract of this rare decision is worth quoting:

> 6. Numerous relatives of autistic individuals come to the court building, often poor people coming from all over the state, to demand from the judge to make a personal effort so that they receive the money or for their relatives to be admitted to a private clinic. From now on this will change (those relatives and their lawyers should go directly to the state's health secretary or the MP). 7. Due to the tiny number of employees in my court ('6º Ofício da Fazenda Pública da Capital') (around 14) and the news that the Court of Appeal ('Tribunal de Justiça') wants to relocate 450 employees from the lower courts to serve in the offices of illustrious appeal judges, there is no personnel to attend to the relatives of the autistic who come to my court with the hope to get the judicial decision enforced. 8. It is not the judge's duty, according to the wording of the decision, to verify the personal situation of each autistic person.... 9. According to the ruling in the judicial decision, it is the state's Health Secretary who, on a request by the family of the autistic person, should verify, individually, and on the basis of the evidence of a medical report, which is the best institution to send the patient to, as close to her relatives as possible, or to another one as long as there is valid justification for this. 10. Nothing in the judicial decision determines that the enforcement judge should replace the Health Secretary in his duties (the judge is not a doctor to diagnose autism, he is not capable of choosing the adequate institution for each specific case and has no technical knowledge to analyze the medical prescription to determine which treatment is the most suitable for each specific situation). 11 ...

[28] For a similar development in Colombia see the famous decision T-760/08 of the Constitutional Court, and the discussion in Yamin, Parra-Vera and Gianella (2011).

it is noticeable that only those few autistic individuals (considering a population of millions of people in the state of São Paulo) are benefiting since only those who hire private lawyers are receiving assistance through individual enforcement orders from this court ... 13. For this reason, I determine that the state, who has to keep a register of all autistic individuals who seek treatment, deal directly with their relatives and lawyers claims, as determined in the original judicial decision, when accompanied by a medical prescription proving the patient's condition, providing the claimant, within 30 days, an adequate institution for their treatment, according to the wording of the original decision, providing relatives with all the information needed for the beginning of treatment, paying directly the clinics, subject to a daily fine of R$ 50,000,00 [then US$ 30.000,00]. 14. If the state fails to comply with this determination, the MP shall call, simultaneously, the legal guardians of all autistic people, and a leading newspaper, or television network, to hand in the medical documents to the state Health Secretariat in view of enabling the fast provision of educational assistance to the patients, i.e. the full enforcement of the judicial decision, once and for all, within 90 days.

The judge carries on, determining that the MP, the DP and the Court of Appeal publicise the judicial decision across the state of São Paulo so as to reach all autistic individuals and, due to the expected increase in demand, allocate more public prosecutors, public defenders and court employees to attend the autistic claimants. He also determines that the health secretary should increase personnel to attend the expected increased number of autistic patients coming to the state for treatment.

In the end, he determines that, for the sake of fairness to those who cannot come individually to the judiciary to enforce the decision, individual enforcement procedures will no longer be accepted, and finishes with a rather triumphal statement: '21. Courage is needed to determine the enforcement of the judicial decision; the decisions of the Judiciary Power cannot be symbolic.'

I believe the lower court judge's frustration is justified, and the thrust of his argument (leaving aside some peculiar passages) is correct. The individualisation of enforcement ends up defeating the whole purpose of collective suits. As I shall discuss in further detail in the concluding section, I am not sure whether collective enforcement is indeed possible or desirable. But the fact is that individualised enforcement, despite its problems of fairness and micromanagement involvement of the judiciary, is clearly less difficult. The crude truth is that the hundreds of individuals with the resources to resort to the court through individualised enforcement procedures are now receiving treatment in a clinic of their choice, whereas the thousands who cannot come to the court individually, either for lack of awareness, or for lack of resources (or both), depend solely on the more standardised services provided by the state, and often have to go without.

Moreover, most lower court judges (with rare exceptions like this one) and higher courts are more comfortable with individualised enforcement. We have already seen an example of this tendency in the STF decisions and the Diabetes case discussed earlier. The same happened in the present case. The lower court judge's decision just cited was promptly overturned by the Court of Appeal as inadequate. Individualised enforcement, the Court of Appeal said, is not only the adequate method according to procedural rules, but also a fundamental constitutional right of individuals (the right to access to courts, art. 5, XXXV of the Federal Constitution).

6.5   Conclusion

I have discussed in this chapter why collective lawsuits involving claims for social and economic rights are so much fewer in Brazil than individual lawsuits. I suggested that one important explanatory factor is the greater difficulties that collective lawsuits face in terms of enforcement. By enforcement I meant not only the actual implementation of a decision in favour of the claimant (I called this factual enforcement) but also the ability of a court of law to translate the generic constitutional norms recognising social and economic rights into specific orders that can be implemented in the real world (I called this legal enforcement). To test my hypothesis, I looked at the constitutional right to health, recognised in articles 6 and 196 of the Brazilian constitution, which has experienced an explosion of litigation, often called the 'judicialization of health'. As with other social and economic rights, collective lawsuits in the health field are also a small minority in Brazil.

The explanation for this difference in volume has to do, of course, with a complex mix of variables which I did not explore in this chapter. One obvious one is simply mathematical (individuals are logically more numerous than groups formed by the same individuals!). Another is the huge number of private lawyers who are able to file individual lawsuits, in comparison with the few public attorneys who can file collective lawsuits.[29] Yet these cannot alone explain, I suggest, the enormous gap between collective and individual lawsuits. Such gap can also not be explained by other legal,

---

[29]   D. Wang, *Poder Judiciário e participação democrática nas políticas públicas de saúde*, MPhil thesis (University of São Paulo, 2009) and interview with Public Defenders in São Paulo (29 July 2009).

political and social variables commonly mentioned in the literature. There are no significant procedural barriers, for instance, to the filing of collective lawsuits in the Brazilian legal system, apart from the standing rules already mentioned. On the contrary, the constitution and ordinary laws do establish such procedures, such as the Ação Civil Pública (the 'Civil Public Action', Federal Law No. 7.347, from 24.7.1985), which can be easily operated by the Public Prosecutors' Office and other actors. The rules and practices regarding remedies cannot be regarded as a significant barrier either. Brazilian judges are reasonably free to fashion remedial orders which are suitable to the case at hand (ranging from compensation, to prohibitory and mandatory injunctions) and have effective instruments of contempt of court to make their decisions effective, e.g. fines and even threat of prison. The same is true of rules and practices regarding court's supervisory jurisdiction (e.g. court's continued competence to follow-up on ruling implementation). As we have seen in the Autism case, courts are able to follow up on implementation indefinitely, through enforcement procedures, so long as they are prompted by the parties of the case.

As regards so-called political variables, such as capacity of the state apparatus to implement social and economic rights rulings, and institutional arrangements between the judiciary, the executive and the legislature, they also seem to present no significant hurdle in terms of enforcement of social and economic rights in Brazil. Especially in the developed states of the southeast, where litigation is more extensive, the state is by and large capable of implementing most judicial decisions. Moreover, claims of usurpation of power are easily dismissed by courts on grounds that the constitution itself mandates judicial interference for the protection of those rights.

Finally, Brazilian civil society is reasonably well organised in the field of rights' advocacy, especially in health. According to the research of the Brazilian Institute of Geography and Statistics (IBGE), in 2005 there were 60,250 non-governmental organisations of that sort.[30] Many of them are well versed in using the judiciary as a strategy to pursue their interests in the field of health, either directly as in the field of HIV-AIDS or indirectly, via the Ministério Público, as in the cases of diabetes and autism discussed in this chapter.[31]

---

[30] As Fundações Privadas e Associações sem Fins Lucrativos no Brasil 2005, IBGE, available at www.ibge.gov.br/home/estatistica/economia/fasfil/2005/defaulttab.shtm (accessed 25 September 2010)

[31] Ministry of Health, Brazil. 2005. O remédio via justiça: Um estudo sobre o acesso a novos medicamentos e exames em HIV/AIDS no Brasil por meio de ações judiciais.

So, even though no in-depth exploration of all potential variables was carried out in the limited space of this chapter, it seems fair to say that the most common political, legal and social variables usually mentioned as explanatory of levels of litigation and enforcement are not likely to be very significant in Brazil, although they may well play a secondary role worth of further research.

A crucial and perhaps the most important variable, as I have tried to show in this chapter, seems therefore to be obstacles of enforcement (legal and factual) faced more fiercely by collective suits in comparison with individual ones. A qualitative analysis of the decisions in the few collective right to health cases that reached the Supreme Federal Tribunal shows that there is a fierce reluctance on the part of that court to accept collective cases. Whereas almost all individual cases have been judged in favour of the claimant, no collective case has so far been successful in that court. The same reluctance is to be found, though with less intensity, in the states' courts of appeal and the lower courts. Indeed, most interviewees expressed the opinion that collective suits are received more reluctantly by the judiciary. This opinion is consistent with the results of a quantitative survey carried out in all collective cases sponsored by the Ministerio Publico of the state of São Paulo between 2000 and 2008. As shown earlier, the rate of failure of collective suits, at 53 per cent, is much higher than that found in several studies of individual suits (ranging from 17 per cent to 0 per cent). I tried to explain this discrepancy by the greater difficulty of the judiciary to translate the generic norms of the constitution into specific orders for the state when the suit is collective and requires structural measures (I called that the hurdle of legal enforcement). But even when collective suits are successful in the courts, their factual enforcement faces significant hurdles. The Autism case, which I used as a case study in this chapter, provides a clear illustration of the problems. The judicial decision was so comprehensive (the state was condemned to provide adequate treatment to all autistic individuals in the state of São Paulo) that it became virtually unenforceable. The 'solution', as we have seen, was to convert that structural order into individual enforcement orders, leaving for the initiative of interested individuals to come back to court one by one to claim the benefit granted by the original collective decision.

It remains open for debate whether collective suits are indeed unenforceable and whether they should be treated so differently by the judiciary. In my view, it is clearly more complex to implement a collective order of the sort handed down in the Autism case, or in other structural cases such as basic sanitation ones, than in individual ones granting medication or other forms of treatment to a single individual.[32] But the 'solution' is not, in my view, in rejecting collective cases altogether (legal underenforcement) or turning them, at the enforcement stage, into individual ones.

The issue at stake in both individual and collective cases is the same: who should get what in terms of health care (or other social and economic goods, e.g. education, housing etc) within the limited resources of the state. It is an intractable moral and political matter of distributive justice which courts,alone, are neither capable nor legitimised to decide. Collective cases simply make the dilemma more visible.

References

Arantes, Rogério Bastos (2002), *Ministério Público e Política no Brasil* (São Paulo: EDUC, Editora Sumaré and Fapesp).

Barcellos, Ana Paula de (2014), 'Sanitation Rights, Public Law Litigation, and Inequality: A Case Study from Brazil', *Health and Human Rights*, 16(2), 35–46.

Bilchitz, David (2002), 'Giving Socio-Economic Rights Teeth: The Minimum Core and Its Importance', *South African Law Journal* 119, 484–501.

Coutinho, Maria Laura de Souza (2010), 'Ativismo Judicial. Uma Análise a Partir do Direito à Moradia', Masters Dissertation (São Paulo: Fundação Getúlio Vargas).

Dugard, Jackie and Theunis Roux (2006), 'The Record of the South African Constitutional Court in Providing an Institutional Voice for the Poor 1995–2004', in Roberto Gargarella, Pilar Domingo and Theunis Roux (eds.), *Courts and Social Transformation in New Democracies: An Institutional Voice for the Poor?* (Aldershot/Burlington: Ashgate), 107–125.

Epp, Charles R. (1998), The Rights Revolution: Lawyers, Activists and Supreme Courts in Comparative Perspective (Chicago: University of Chicago Press).

Ferraz, Octavio Luiz (2009), 'The Right to Health in the Courts of Brazil: Worsening Health Inequities?', *Health and Human Rights: An International Journal*, 11(2), 33–45.

Ferraz, Octavio Luiz and Fabiola Sulpino Vieira (2009), 'Direito à saúde, recursos escassos e equidade: Os riscos da interpretação judicial dominante', *Dados: Revista de Ciências Sociais*, 52(1), 223–251.

Fuller, Lon (1978), 'The Forms and Limits of Adjudication', *Harvard Law Review*, 92(2), 353–409.

Gauri, Varun and Daniel M. Brinks (2008), *Courting Social Justice: Judicial Enforcement of Social and Economic Rights in the Developing World* (Cambridge: Cambridge University Press).

---

[32] See Barcellos (2014), analysing 258 collective cases demanding construction of basic sanitation infra-structure in 177 municipalities in Brazil from 2003 to 2013 and finding only 4 per cent of full implementation within a total or partial success rate of 76 per cent.

Gloppen, Siri (2008), 'Litigation as a Strategy to Hold Governments Accountable for Implementing the Right to Health', *Health and Human Rights: An International Journal*, 10(2), 21–36.

Hoffman, Florian F. and Fernando R. N. M. Bentes (2008), 'Accountability for Social and Economic Rights in Brazil' in Varun Gauri and Daniel M. Brinks (eds.), *Courting Social Justice: Judicial Enforcement of Social and Economic Rights in the Developing World* (Cambridge: Cambridge University Press), 100–145.

IBGE (2005), *As Fundações Privadas e Associações sem Fins Lucrativos no Brasil 2005*, accessed 25 September 2010 www.ibge.gov.br/home/estatistica/economia/fasfil/2005/defaulttab.shtm.

Lopes, José Reinaldo de Lima (2006), 'Os tribunais e os direitos sociais no Brasil – saúde e educação: um estudo de caso revisitado', in José Reinaldo de Lima Lopes (ed.), *Direitos Sociais: teoria e prática* (São Paulo: Método), 221–264.

Ministry of Health, Brazil (2005), *O remédio via justiça: Um estudo sobre o acesso a novos medicamentos e exames em HIV/AIDS no Brasil por meio de ações judiciais* (Brasilia: MoH, Programa Nacional de DST e AIDS).

Nassar, Paulo André Silva (2010), 'Judicialização do Direito à Moradia e Transformação Social. análise das ações civis públicas da Defensoria Pública do Estado de São Paulo', Masters Dissertation (São Paulo: Fundação Getúlio Vargas).

Pepe, Vera Lúcia Edais, Miriam Ventura, João Maurício Brambati Sant'ana, Tatiana Aragão Figueiredo, Vanessa dos Reis de Souza, Luciana Simas and Claudia Garcia Serpa Osorio-de-Castro (2010), 'Caracterização de demandas judiciais de fornecimento de medicamentos 'essenciais' no Estado do Rio de Janeiro, Brasil' [Characterization of Lawsuits for the Supply of 'Essential' Medicines in the State of Rio de Janeiro, Brazil], *Cad. Saúde Pública*, Rio de Janeiro, 26(3), 461–471.

Sager, Lawrence Gene (1978), 'Fair Measure: The Legal Status of Underenforced Constitutional Norms', *Harvard Law Review*, 91(6), 1212–1264.

(2010) 'Material Rights, Underenforcement, and the Adjudication Thesis, [Symposium: Justice for Hedgehogs: A Conference on Ronald Dworkin's Forthcoming Book]', 90 *Boston University Law Review*, 90, 579.

Vieira, Fabiola and Paola Zucchi (2007), 'Distorções causadas pelas ações judiciais à política de medicamentosno Brasil' [Distortions to National Drug Policy Caused by Lawsuits in Brazil], *Revista de Saúde Pública*, 41(2), 214–222.

Wang, Daniel (2009), 'Poder Judiciário e participação democrática nas políticas públicas de saúde', MPhil thesis (São Paulo: University of São Paulo).

Wesson, Murray (2004), '*Grootboom* and Beyond: Reassessing the Socio-Economic Jurisprudence of the South African Constitutional Court', *South African Journal on Human Rights*, 20(2), 284–308.

Yamin, Alicia and Siri Gloppen (eds.) (2011), *Litigating Health Rights: Can Courts Bring More Justice to Health?* (Cambridge, MA: Harvard University Press).

Canada: Systemic Claims and Remedial Diversity

BRUCE PORTER

7.1   Introduction

The success of social rights enforcement strategies should not be assessed solely in relation to the record of enforcement of remedies ordered by courts or tribunals. Readily enforceable judicial remedies may not be effective in remedying certain types of social rights violations. A preference among litigators and courts for claims that are more likely to be successfully enforced may present a more successful enforcement record but deny justice to victims of more systemic social rights violations considered more challenging to enforce. A more fundamental assessment of enforcement strategies in relation to the goals and purposes of the rights claims being advanced and of social rights litigation more generally is in order. Pragmatic issues of what is likely to win cases and achieve remedies in the short term must be balanced with more forward-looking questions about enhancing the role of courts in the realization of all aspects of social rights, not only those aspects which lend themselves to more traditional models of justiciability and enforcement.

A tension between remedies that are most familiar or appealing to courts because of their easy enforceability, and those which are more effective from the standpoint of the violations which claimants seek to remedy is very evident in Canada. What Louise Arbour has described as a "timidity" among both Canadian litigators and courts about advancing social rights claims with complex remedial or enforcement implications has tended to exempt the most egregious violations of social rights from judicial review, and often denied access to justice to the most disadvantaged in society (Arbour, 2005: 7). The problem of enforcement of social rights remedies in Canada is primarily one of effective remedies

Bruce Porter is Executive Director at the Social Rights Advocacy Centre. The author thanks Jaime Mor for his helpful editorial and research assistance and the Social Sciences and Humanities Research Council Community-University Research Alliance for financial assistance with this research (www.socialrightscura.ca).

not being claimed and ordered rather than one of remedial orders being unenforced. Where governments have been given a period of time to remedy a constitutional violation, they have generally done so, though extensions of time have been sought and granted.[1]

The "notwithstanding clause" under the *Canadian Charter of Rights and Freedoms* (the *Canadian Charter*)[2] permits Parliament or provincial legislatures to explicitly exempt legislation from certain *Charter* rights. Fortunately, the notwithstanding provision has been rarely used, only once to avoid enforcement of a judicial decision. In that case, the Parti Quebecois Government of Quebec, with historical motivation to resist the application of the *Canadian Charter* after it was negotiated without Quebec's support, invoked the notwithstanding clause to preserve certain Quebec language laws after the Supreme Court of Canada found them in violation of the right to freedom of expression under the *Canadian Charter*.[3] However, after the UN Human Rights Committee considered the same issue in a complaint filed under the Optional Protocol to the *International Covenant on Civil and Political Rights* (ICCPR) and concluded that the provisions also contravened the ICCPR, a subsequent Quebec government amended the legislation.[4]

The need for more effective remedies for systemic social rights violations, particularly under the *Canadian Charter*, has been identified as a critical issue in Canada by UN human rights bodies. The UN Special Rapporteurs on adequate housing and on the right to food have visited Canada on missions, and each has emphasized the need for institutional mechanisms through which rights to housing and food can be claimed and enforced. They have emphasized that remedial strategies must include coordinated national strategies, involve a range of actors and a variety of legislative and programmatic measures.[5] Similar recommendations have been made by the UN Committee on Economic, Social and Cultural

[1] See, for example, further to the Supreme Court's decision in *Eldridge v. British Columbia (Attorney General)*, [1997] 3 SCR 624 [*Eldridge*], Application for a Stay of the Decision of the SCC of the 9th of October, 1997, Court File No. 24896. Affidavit of Heather Davidson, sworn the 25th day of March, 1998.
[2] *Canadian Charter of Rights and Freedoms*, Part I of the *Constitution Act, 1982*, being Schedule B to the *Canada Act 1982* (UK), 1982, c 11 [*Canadian Charter*], section 33.
[3] *Ford v. Quebec (Attorney General)*, [1988] 2 SCR 712.
[4] *Ballantyne, Davidson, McIntyre v. Canada*, Communications Nos. 359/1989 and 385/1989, U.N. Doc. CCPR/C/47/D/359/1989 and 385/1989/Rev.1 (1993).
[5] United Nations Human Rights Council, *Report of the Special Rapporteur on Adequate Housing as a Component of the Right to an Adequate Standard of Living, and on the Right to Non-discrimination in this Context, Miloon Kothari – Addendum – Mission to Canada (9 to 22*

Rights in reviews of Canada, by members of the Human Rights Council during Canada's Universal Periodic Review, and by parliamentary committees examining problems of poverty and homelessness in Canada.[6]

Governments in Canada have failed to implement these recommendations and have actively opposed interpretations of the *Canadian Charter* that would provide effective remedies to violations of social rights. As repeatedly noted by the UN CESCR, governments in Canada have displayed a pattern of "urging upon their courts an interpretation of the *Canadian Charter of Rights and Freedoms* denying protection of Covenant rights."[7] Governments' arguments against more expansive roles for courts in overseeing the implementation of social rights remedies have not, by and large, been endorsed by the Supreme Court of Canada, but the court has also been timid about clearly affirming positive obligations with respect to social rights and has demonstrated a pattern of avoidance of the most critical social rights issues by declining to hear the important cases.[8] Effective remedies to social rights violations can still be demanded under the *Canadian Charter*, and the struggle of poor people in Canada for access to justice is ongoing. The Supreme Court has been clear that broadly framed rights in the *Canadian Charter*, such as the right to security of the person or the right to the equal benefit of the law, can be interpreted so as to include social and economic rights and has recognized that a broad

October 2007), (Tenth session, 2009) A/HRC/10/7/Add.3 (2009); Office of the United Nations High Commission for Human Rights (OHCHR), "Olivier De Schutter, Special Rapporteur on the right to food: Visit to Canada from 6 to 16 May 2012: End-of-mission statement", www.ohchr.org/EN/NewsEvents/Pages/DisplayNews.aspx?NewsID=12159&LangID=E (accessed 7 August 2014).

[6] For a description of the many recommendations for rights-based housing and antipoverty strategies, see Porter (2014).

[7] United Nations Committee on Economic, Social and Cultural Rights, *Concluding Observations: Canada* (thirty-sixth session, 2006), UN Doc E/C.12/CAN/CO/4 & E/C.12/CAN/CO/5 (2006) at para. 11(b) [Concluding Observations 2006]. A recent example of this pattern is found in the *Factum of the Attorney General of Canada* in the Motion to Dismiss in *Tanudjaja v. Canada* (Ont Sup Ct File no CV-10-403688) (2011) discussed in later pages; http://socialrightscura.ca/documents/legal/motion%20to%20strike/Attorney%20General%20of%20Canada%20Factum%20-%20Motion%20to%20Strike%20(R2H).pdf

[8] See, for example, *Jennifer Tanudjaja, et al. v. Attorney General of Canada, et al.,* 2015 CanLII 36780 (SCC), dealing with obligation to take positive measures to address homelessness (discussed in later pages); *Nell Toussaint v. Attorney General of Canada,* 2012 CanLII 17813 (SCC), dealing with rights of irregular migrants to health care; *Denise Boulter v. Nova Scotia Power Incorporated and Attorney General of Nova Scotia; Yvonne Carvery, Wayne MacNaughton and Affordable Energy Coalition v. Nova Scotia Power Incorporated and Attorney General of Nova Scotia,* 2009 CanLII 47476 (SCC), dealing with access to electricity by households living in poverty.

range of remedies is available to courts (Porter, 2006; Porter and Jackman, 2008). The court has recognized that the overriding principle must be to ensure that remedies are effective in protecting and vindicating the rights at issue and responsive to the circumstances at hand (ibid.). Nevertheless, lower courts have tended to align their interpretation of rights with what they believe they can immediately remedy, granting motions to dismiss claims for more systemic remedies, and legal advocates have tended to follow suit by avoiding claims which demand of courts more robust remedial and enforcement roles that may prompt strenuous governmental opposition and judicial resistance.[9] Traditional assumptions about limited judicial competence and authority to remedy social rights violations in the manner recommended by UN human rights treaty bodies and adopted by courts in some other jurisdictions continue to pose the greatest obstacle to effective social rights litigation in the current legal landscape in Canada.

In Chapter 3, César Rodríguez-Garavito posits a matrix that describes the actual outcomes of ESC rulings by organizing them into four quadrants.[10] Like the assessment proposed in the present chapter, Rogriguez-Garavito's approach measures enforcement outcomes against the goals of realizing the right in question. However, it is helpful in the Canadian context to consider outcomes not only in relation to goals of particular cases but to also consider the extent to which remedies may be effective in realizing the transformative goals of social rights litigation more generally; the ways in which judicial and litigator preferences for traditional paradigms of judicial enforceability may have left key structural violations unchallenged; and whether more expansive approaches to remedies and enforcement might better address these types of violations, even if they also create new challenges in relation to enforceability. Challenges of enforceability in this chapter are considered in relation to three opposing qualities of remedial strategies: immediate and pre-defined as opposed to ongoing

---

[9] Two examples of successful motions to dismiss systemic claims so as to deny access to evidentiary hearings are found in the cases of *Canadian Bar Assn. v. British Columbia*, 2008 BCCA 92 in which a systemic remedy for inadequate civil legal aid had been sought, and *Tanudjaja v. Canada (Attorney General)*, 2014 ONCA 852 (CanLII).

[10] Rodriguez identifies the following four types of outcomes: (1) a "paper ruling" occurs when there is neither meaningful enforcement of the ordered remedy, nor any real positive impact on the rights in question in the aftermath; (2) "winning by losing" occurs when there is no meaningful enforcement of the ordered remedy, but the decision has a positive impact on the situation notwithstanding; (3) "zero-sum litigation" occurs when meaningful enforcement does take place, but the results either hinder, or do nothing to affect a positive impact on the actual rights in question; and (4) "positive-sum litigation" occurs when there is both meaningful enforcement of the remedy, and positive impacts result.

and fashioned through a process (hard vs. soft[11]); discrete (engaging one provision, entitlement or action and one respondent) as opposed to multifaceted (engaging multiple entitlements and/or various actors); and corrective (of a flaw or omission in an existing program, law or entitlement) as opposed to transformative (of existing entitlement systems).

The aim of this chapter is not to derive statistical conclusions about successful enforcement outcomes in Canada. It is too early to assess social rights enforcement strategies in Canada solely on the basis of past outcomes. This might simply reinforce existing systemic patterns of exclusion that operate in Canada's justice system by limiting litigation strategies to those that win by conforming to traditional remedial and enforcement models but which may have excluded the most marginalized claimants and the most important claims. Rather than measuring enforcement outcomes within a justice system that has denied access to justice to many social rights claimants, this chapter provides a broader lens through which to consider effectiveness. Hopefully this perspective can help ensure that the choice of remedial strategies in different circumstances is properly informed by the broader principles of access to justice and inclusiveness and is consistent with transformative goals of social rights practice.

Social rights litigation remains a work in progress in Canada. While it is too early to limit litigation and enforcement strategies to those which have succeeded in the past, or to give up on more transformative models that have failed, it is nevertheless important to continue to learn from our experiences. There is, of course, no universally preferred social rights remedial and enforcement strategy. The choice of strategy must be considered on a case-by-case basis, and the needs and motivation of the rights claimants will always be a critical factor. Social rights claimants do not always aspire to achieve broader structural change or transformative effect. If a claimant requires only a correction to an existing entitlement system in order to secure housing, food, or health care, perhaps qualifying for an already existing benefit, the most effective and appropriate remedy in the circumstances may be one of immediate application, applying to a single entitlement, identifying a single respondent government.[12]

[11] For a parallel discussion of "soft" versus "hard"remedies in international law, see Abbott and Snidal (2000).
[12] An example of this remedial approach is found in the case of *Toussaint v. Canada (Attorney General)*, 2011 FCA 213 (CanLII), http://canlii.ca/t/fm4v6 and *Canadian Doctors for Refugee Care v. Canada (Attorney general)*, 2014 FC 651 (CanLII), http://canlii.ca/t/g81sg where positive obligations to protect the right to life of migrants by providing access to health care were addressed by challenging exclusions from or cuts to an existing program,

In other cases, as in the challenge to homelessness described in later pages, claimants may undertake litigation with clearly transformative aims, identifying multiple entitlements and respondents and demanding the implementation of ongoing strategies with meaningful engagement of stakeholders. It is important to ensure that a range of remedial and enforcement strategies are employed and effective enforcement is in place in all cases.

A potentially unifying concept applicable to both individual claims to discrete benefits and to systemic claims with more transformative goals is the concept of "reasonableness." The concept has been applied in both domestic and international law to assess whether programs and policies, as well as individual decisions regarding particular benefits, are compliant with social rights obligations to progressively realize rights through appropriate budgetary, legislative and policy measures (Porter, forthcoming). The emerging jurisprudence of the Supreme Court of Canada affirms a similar standard of rights-compliant "reasonableness" that can be applied to a range of decisions, laws of policies. As will be explained below, it applies, in different ways, to reasonable limits under the *Canadian Charter of Rights and Freedoms*,[13] to the obligation to reasonably accommodate needs of disadvantaged groups, and to administrative law standards of reasonableness applied to the exercise of discretionary authority and to administrative decisions. While the reasonableness standard raises distinctive enforcement challenges associated with a more contextual, value-informed standard, it will be argued that the risks of this "softer" enforcement model are often outweighed by the transformative potential of a standard of rights-informed decision making that applies to a broad range of actors and policies, and is informed by and consistent with international human rights values and norms.

Litigation designed around remedial and enforcement strategies to address systemic violations of social rights in Canada may result in a less impressive enforcement scorecard than has been the case with the more traditional remedies ordered by Canadian courts. Remedies which engage multiple programs and policies, to be formulated and implemented over

---

the Interim Federal Health Programme. The result of this strategy was a formal win in the case of *Canadian Doctors for Refugee Health Care* but a strategic loss on the question of positive obligations to ensure access to health care. In the case of *Toussaint v. Canada* the claim was unsuccessful at the Federal Court of Appeal and has been submitted as a communication to the UN Human Rights Committee. See *Nell Toussaint v. Canada* HRC No 2348-2014, www.socialrightscura.ca/eng/legal-strategies-right-to-healthcare.html.

[13] *Canadian Charter*, section 1.

time by a range of actors, raise significant challenges for enforceability. Sometimes it will be more practical to avoid these challenges and to aim for more incremental change through discrete and immediate remedies. However, it is important to balance these considerations with the longer-term effect of an ongoing failure to claim remedies that are responsive to the systemic violations of social rights experienced by many of the most marginalized groups. Those who are living in poverty or homelessness in Canada are rarely victims of only one discrete violation of their rights. Identifying effective remedial and enforcement strategies must remain a contextual endeavor that is dependent on the nature of the violation and the claim being advanced and which remains true to the inclusive vision of access to justice that must be a guiding principle of social rights practice.

7.2 Three Dimensions of Remedies and Enforcement

7.2.1 Hard versus Soft

Constitutional remedies that strike down particular legislative provisions, or that "read in" the provision of benefits that were previously denied, fall into the category of "hard" remedies. That is, the remedies ordered by courts in these cases are defined by the court and have immediate effect. These types of remedies have been applied in a number of social rights cases in Canada; generally speaking, they have been effective and have not raised issues with respect to governmental compliance.[14]

"Soft" remedies, by contrast, are those in which courts put in place a process through which the appropriate remedy is to be fashioned in the future. Soft remedial options in constitutional litigation in Canada have relied on declaratory orders of various sorts. In some cases declarations have simply provided guidance to governments about their constitutional obligations, and the courts have left it up to the government to decide if and in what manner to apply the court's guidance. In other cases courts have put governments on notice that one or more rights have been violated, established

---

[14] An example of a striking down remedy, declaring a provision to be of no force and effect, is the case of *Nova Scotia (Workers' Compensation Board) v. Martin; Nova Scotia (Workers' Compensation Board) v. Laseur*, 2003 SCC 54 [2003] 2 SCR 504, in which workers' compensation benefits were extended to apply to those with chronic pain. The best example of a "reading in" remedy in the field of social rights in Canada is the case of *Sparks v. Dartmouth/Halifax County Regional Housing Authority*, (1993), 119 NSR (2d) 91 [*Sparks*], which extended security of tenure protections to residents of public housing. These cases will be discussed soon.

the parameters for what is needed to remedy the violation and provided governments with time to design and implement necessary changes.[15]

Some types of law and judicial roles are limited to softer declaratory remedies. International human rights law is not directly enforceable by courts in Canada if it has not been incorporated by domestic legislation. However, under their jurisdiction to answer questions referred to them by governments, courts in Canada have provided advice to resolve legal uncertainty about international law.[16] Courts may issue declaratory judgments on legal issues for purely extra-judicial purposes, such as to inform political negotiations.[17] More robust approaches are generally applied, however, when constitutional rights have been found to have been infringed by existing legislation and new or revised legislation is necessary to remedy the violation. In these cases, courts have suspended the declaration of invalidity in order to provide the government with time to implement an appropriate remedy before the impugned legislation is rendered of no force and effect.[18] Recent litigation strategies in Canada have also applied tools such as reporting requirements, timetables, monitoring, benchmarks, and designated participatory mechanisms as important components to make suspended declarations of invalidity more effective.[19] Such remedies may be strengthened by the court retaining jurisdiction, assuming a supervisory role to ensure that appropriate processes are implemented and outcomes achieved within a reasonable time.[20]

As will be described below, Canadian social rights litigation has benefitted from softer remedies through which courts provide necessary guidance as to the government's responsibilities and leave time for the remedy to be designed and put in place. The implementation of a process to remedy a violation over a period of time has facilitated more meaningful participation by stakeholders and encouraged the development and implementation of new programs.[21] There is the risk, of course, that softer remedial orders allow governments to implement weaker remedies than the court

---

[15] A good example of a "softer" remedy of this sort is the well-known decision in *Eldridge.*

[16] *Reference re Secession of Quebec,* [1998] 2 SCR 217.

[17] *Manitoba Metis Federation Inc. v. Canada (Attorney General),* 2013 SCC 14 at para 131; *Dumont v. Canada* (Attorney General), [1990] 1 SCR 279 at 280.

[18] *Schachter v. Canada, [1992] 2 SCR 679*; and Roach, (2002) A good example of the use of a suspended declaration in relation to the right to health is the well-known decision in *Eldridge.*

[19] See discussion of *Tanudjaja v. Attorney General (Canada),* 2013 ONSC 1878.

[20] *Doucet-Boudreau v. Nova Scotia (Minister of Education),* at para. 136; Roach, Kent, and Budlender, Geoff (2005); and Roach, (2013).

[21] See the discussion of *Eldridge.*

might have ordered, or preserve structural inequality in the design of new programs that might have been better addressed through an immediate order extending existing legislation or programs to include excluded groups.[22] As will be seen below, this risk has materialized in some cases in Canada. Where weaker remedies have ensued, however, the problem has not been governmental noncompliance with the judgments of courts, but rather a lack of commitment by courts and governments to substantive equality and to democratic participation of marginalized and disadvantaged groups. As will be argued below, there is a need to reconfigure constitutional "dialogue" in Canada, usually conceived as a two-way dialogue between the judicial and legislative branches, into a democratic conversation which meaningfully engages rights claimants and a range of institutional actors in the remedial and enforcement process. Reconfiguring soft remedies to better promote democratic values can play an important role in addressing the democratic deficit that currently exists in Canada.

7.2.2 Discrete versus Multifaceted

A second dimension to be considered in assessing the tension between enforceability and effectiveness is the extent to which remedies engage with more than one piece of legislation or discrete benefit, or more than a single respondent. Even softer remedies that provide a particular government with time to remedy an under-inclusive legislative or benefit scheme may not be adequate to address structural violations of social rights which relate to the interaction of multiple programs and legislative schemes or systemic patterns of administrative decision making. Effective remedies to poverty, homelessness, and social exclusion often need to reach beyond a particular program or piece of legislation to address structural causes. As Amartya Sen's early work on famines discovered, systemic social rights violations are usually rooted in "entitlement system failures" that extend well beyond any single program or entitlement (1988). Effective social rights remedies in Canada will often require comprehensive strategies and broad programmatic reform extending over a number of interrelated program areas such as income assistance, housing subsidy and wage protections (Porter, 2014).

It is also important to consider the unique challenges of federalism and modern systems of governance in designing strategies for

---

[22] See the discussion of *Dunmore v. Ontario (Attorney General)* [2001] 3 SCR1016, 2001 SCC 94.

enforcing social rights in Canada. Many social rights violations involve interdependent and overlapping jurisdiction of federal, provincial/territorial, and municipal levels of government. Social rights claims may not always conform to the traditional "citizen-versus-state" framework – even if that is formally how domestic constitutional or international human rights claims must be structured. Those who are actually assigned the responsibility of ensuring the realization of rights ("dutybearers") may include private actors, nongovernmental organizations, or multiple levels of government spanning local to federal. All of these actors are likely bound together in webs of delegated responsibilities and jurisdictional overlap, whereby their roles become increasingly mixed. Civil society organizations, traditionally tied to rights claimants, have become increasingly engaged in providing or administering services or programs, thus straddling both the claimant and respondent sides of rights claims. The traditional model of judicial remedy in which the court simply orders the state to provide an entitlement that has been denied or to cease an action that has violated a right, is often inadequate. Remedies and enforcement strategies must address the different roles that states play, not only in legislating but also in ensuring that a range of actors behave in a manner that is consistent with the realization of social rights.[23] Courts may be required to design remedies so as to play more of a facilitative role in provoking action by multiple actors and institutions.[24] As will be described, social rights strategies in Canada have recently attempted to address these kinds of challenges by naming multiple respondents and incorporating orders for joint remedial responses by various levels of government. These too, of course, raise unique issues of enforceability.

[23] A connection may be drawn between the notion of "hard" versus "soft" remedies and what Sabel and Simon refer to as "command-and-control" versus "experimentalist" approaches to structural remedies in public litigation. "Command-and-control regulation ... takes the form of comprehensive regimes of fixed and specific rules set by a central authority. These rules prescribe the inputs and operating procedures of the institutions they regulate. By contrast, experimentalist regulation combines more flexible and provisional norms with procedures for ongoing stakeholder participation and measured accountability" Sabel and Simon (2004), at 1019 and 1067–1073. For a discussion of "soft" remedies in the Canadian and South African contexts, see Roach and Budlender (2005).

[24] Abram and Antonia Chayes contend that both governments and the public prefer "treaties with teeth," referring to enforcement models that make use of immediate and coercive sanctions. They contrast this "enforcement model" with their own "managerial model," which tends toward employing "softer," ongoing remedies that may be more novel and less popular, but ultimately more successful in achieving the desired effects. For a discussion of the effectiveness of differing types of remedies, see Chayes and Chayes (1995), chapter 1.

7.2.3   Corrective versus Transformative

Realizing social rights is not simply a matter of changing legislative or benefit schemes so as to ensure access to housing or food as social goods. In
affluent countries such as Canada, where poverty, homelessness, and other
social rights violations are manifestations of increasing inequality and
social exclusion, social rights remedies must also address the marginalization, exclusion, discrimination, and stigmatization that give rise to these
violations of social rights. It is not enough to address unmet needs. Social
rights practice must also address the social construction of need through
inequality and exclusion.

A reaffirmation of human rights values is a critical component of the
creation of a more inclusive social rights architecture, in which access to
justice and the role of the courts in safeguarding and promoting human
rights values must play an important role. The transformative dimension
of remedial strategies extends beyond specific legislative or programmatic
entitlements being claimed to a broader commitment to the struggle to
realize social rights. While transformative strategies tend to be associated
with future-oriented (softer) remedies and multiple actors and entitlements, there may also be transformative dimensions to individual claims
addressing discrete denials, particularly where denials are associated with
discrimination or stigmatization. It is therefore important to also consider
this third axis, assessing whether remedial and enforcement strategies are
able to effect broader social transformations through the claiming and
judicial enforcement of social rights.

7.3   Enforcement Experiences of Social Rights Remedies under the *Canadian Charter*

7.3.1   Negative Rights Claims

Negatively oriented remedies which place limits or invalidate government
action are the most familiar and comfortable forms of remedies for courts
to enforce in Canada. Enforcement challenges are largely circumvented if
courts declare laws or policies invalid or of no force and effect, rather than
finding that some kind of positive action is required. Under the *Canadian
Charter*, negative rights remedies of immediate effect may include reading
down, severance, and declarations of invalidity.

Negative rights remedies of immediate effect are generally more suited to
civil and political rights claims, and the predominance of a negative rights

paradigm for constitutional remedies in Canada has been one of the most serious obstacles to social rights claims. Nevertheless, negative rights remedies have sometimes proven to be effective in generating positive rights outcomes, both through their immediate effect and often, more fundamentally, through advances made in the interpretation of *Canadian Charter* rights. The leading example of this is the Supreme Court of Canada's decision in *R v. Morgentaler*,[25] in which restrictions on abortion services under the *Criminal Code of Canada* were challenged as violating women's right to the security of the person under section 7 of the *Canadian Charter*. The striking down remedy in that case had the immediate effect of ensuring dramatically improved access to safe abortions for and represented a significant advance in challenging systemic discrimination against women in access to health care. The decision also gave a significant impetus to the broader struggle for women's equality rights by securing a rights-based legal victory on a critical issue after years of political mobilization and advocacy. Interpreting the right to security of the person to include access to health care for women was a significant advance in ensuring more expansive interpretations of the *Canadian Charter*. However, the restriction of the remedy to a striking down remedy meant that the court did not address governments' positive obligations to provide services. The legacy of that inadequacy in the remedy remains an issue today, with certain regions failing to provide the services necessary for access to abortions.[26]

In *Victoria (City) v. Adams*,[27] the British Columbia Court of Appeal struck down components of a bylaw prohibiting homeless people from erecting temporary shelters in public parks. The court largely upheld the decision of the B. C. Supreme Court, which had relied on commitments made by Canadian governments to UN bodies to support an interpretation of the right to life and security of the person in section 7 of the *Canadian Charter* consistent with recognition of the right to housing.[28] Although they were only applied in a negative rights framework in this case, the interpretive principles affirmed by the trial judge did establish the connection between

---

[25] *R v. Morgentaler*, [1988] 1 SCR 30.

[26] National Abortion Federation (undated), "Access to Abortion in Canada," www.prochoice.org/canada/access.html.

[27] *Victoria (City) v. Adams*, 2009 BCCA 563; 2008 BCSC 1363 [Adams].

[28] Ibid., para 98; Canada also stated to the United Nations Human Rights Committee that the right to life in the *ICCPR* imposes obligations on governments to provide basic necessities. See United Nations Human Rights Committee, *Supplementary Report of Canada in Response to Questions Posed by the United Nations Human Rights Committee* (March 1983) UN Doc CCPR/C/1/Add.62 (1983) at 23.

the right to housing under international human rights law and the right to security of the person under the *Canadian Charter*. There was, in addition, an indirect positive rights component to the decision. The court ruled that the declaration of invalidity may be terminated if improvements to shelter and housing programs removed the need for homeless people to sleep in parks, such that the bylaws no longer violated section 7 of the *Canadian Charter* – for example, if the City of Victoria could demonstrate that the number of homeless people does not exceed the number of available shelter beds. Although the court recognized that the trial court's ruling would likely require some responsive action by the city to address the inadequate number of shelter beds in Victoria, it declared that: "[t]hat kind of responsive action to a finding that a law violates s. 7 does not involve the court in adjudicating positive rights."[29] The court's reluctance to engage with positive rights meant that the immediate effect of the remedy in *Adams* was simply to permit homeless people to continue to erect temporary overnight shelters in parks. In the longer term, however, the decision may have had some impact in encouraging governments to address the broader systemic issues leaving people to rely on erecting tents or cardboard shelters overnight in parks.

In 2008, the City of Victoria established the Greater Victoria Coalition to End Homelessness, which has added nearly 250 units of permanent, supported housing for people who were formerly homeless (Greater Victoria Coalition to End Homelessness, 2014). The City of Victoria's homelessness initiatives have "now moved towards more permanent housing rather than shelter, and towards attacking the problem of poverty, including the high cost of rental accommodation" (Acker, undated). These initiatives, however, have not kept pace with demand, as rental prices continue to increase, and rental affordability decreases,[30] and shelter use continues to rise in Victoria.[31]

Advocates hoped that the decision in *Victoria v. Adams* might affect positive change in other communities in British Columbia but this does not seem to have been the case.[32] After the release of the decision, the

[29] *Adams*, at paras. 95–96.
[30] Ibid.
[31] In 2010/2011, the emergency shelter occupancy rate was 95 percent compared to 86 percent in 2008/2009 (Greater Victoria Coalition to end Homelessness (2014)).
[32] See Pivot Legal Society (undated). Under the bylaw, any person who sets up a tent or other structure on City property is at risk of receiving a $1,000 fine, unless they apply for a costly permit. See also City of Vancouver (2014). King (undated), *Statement by Douglas King in Personal Email Correspondence*, on file with the author.

legal department of the City of Vancouver reviewed the decision but concluded that the ruling did not apply to similar bylaws in Vancouver.[33] Subsequent litigation is addressing restrictions on constructing shelters on city property in Vancouver (CBS News, 2012). In relation to longer-term goals of access to justice, however, the decision has clearly had some positive effects. Homeless people have become more organized to challenge systemic patterns of discrimination and sought access to justice to challenge such discrimination. The British Columbia Court of Appeal dismissed an appeal from the government of British Columbia of a decision granting standing to an organization, the British Columbia/ Yukon Association of Drug War Survivors, to assert the rights of its members to challenge the grotesque behavior of officials and police in Abbotsford, British Columbia, in forcibly evicting homeless people by spreading chicken manure in the park, using pepper spray in tents, and destroying belongings of the homeless residents. The court held that in these circumstances it is not reasonable to require individual victims to claim constitutional remedies and permitted the case to proceed by way of the organizations' claim for remedies.[34] Combining mobilizing tactics with strategies for access to justice has become an effective empower-ment strategy emanating from the victory in the *Victoria v. Adams* case. The *Adams* decision is an example of how, if rights claims are framed as negative rights restraints on government action, courts in Canada may be more willing to engage with interpretations of the *Canadian Charter* that include rights such as the right to adequate housing and to more directly engage with systemic patterns of discrimination against those who are homeless or living in poverty. These interpretations, in and of themselves, may be helpful in advocating for social rights, both legally and politically. However, there is severe price paid by adopting a nega-tive rights approach. It encourages governments to continue to ignore their positive obligations and rights claimants themselves to conceive of their rights in negative rights terms in a manner that is at odds with the substantive positive obligations of governments to realize rights. There is also a tendency for negative rights remedies to remain tied to particular pieces of legislation or government actions – in this case, to a particular

---

[33] General Manager of Engineering Services (2011); see also Pivot Legal Society (undated), "City by-Laws Must Respect Homeless Rights," www.pivotlegal.org/pivot-points/blog/city-by-laws-must-respect-homeless-rights (accessed 7 August 2014).

[34] *British Columbia/Yukon Association of Drug War Survivors v. Abbotsford (City)*, 2015 BCCA 142. The substantive issue was subsequentlly considered in Abbotsford (City) v. Shantz, 2015 BCSC 1909 establishes that continual displacement of the City's homeless impaired

bylaw – such that a finding in one jurisdiction may not be easy to apply to other jurisdictions.[35]

7.3.2   "Reading In Remedies"

More positively framed social rights claims have been leveraged from courts in Canada when they have agreed to "read in" additional protections or benefits to remedy under-inclusive legislative protections, or social programs that deny disadvantaged groups equal benefits.[36] Correcting unconstitutional exclusions by reading in additional protections is considered the most appropriate remedy when it accords with the "twin guiding principles" of respect for the role of the legislature and respect for the purposes of the *Canadian Charter*. In these circumstances, Canadian courts have been instructed to expand legislative protections or benefits rather than to strike the scheme down so as to be "as faithful as possible within the requirements of the Constitution to the scheme enacted by the Legislature."[37]

"Reading in" remedies provide for immediate and sometimes far-reaching enforcement of judicial orders. In *Sparks v. Dartmouth/Halifax County Regional Housing Authority*, [*Sparks*],[38] security of tenure protection was extended to public housing tenants when the court read protections for this previously excluded group into the applicable legislation. The existing court procedures available to private market tenants contesting evictions became immediately available for an additional 10,000 tenants in public housing. A simple modification to the application of existing legislation had a significant impact on the lives of public housing tenants, altering their relationship with the state from one in which they could be arbitrarily evicted from their homes to one in which their dignity and security was respected. The entitlement that had been denied could be immediately provided by way of an immediate judicial remedy because the institutional structures were already in place for the remedy

---

sleep and caused serious psychological pain and stress and created a risk to their health, violating their right to security of the person under section 7 of the Canadian Charter.
[35] For further discussion of the strategic considerations in the positive–negative rights framing of claims under the Canadian Charter in *Victoria v. Adams* and other cases, see Liew (2012).
[36] Section 15(1) of the *Canadian Charter* states that: Every individual is equal before and under the law and has the right to the equal protection and equal benefit of the law without discrimination and, in particular, without discrimination based on race, national or ethnic origin, color, religion, sex, age or mental or physical disability.
[37] *Schachter*.
[38] *Sparks*.

to be implemented. There was no need to require legislatures to pass new laws or design new institutions, and there was no need for stakeholder participation in designing, monitoring, or enforcing the remedy. The case was precedent-setting, not only for its extension of existing entitlements but also for its recognition of discrimination and stigmatization of poor people and public housing residents. The remedy addressed not only the specific legislative exclusion but also the systemic-structural causes of the exclusion by challenging the discriminatory assumptions about poor people that gave rise to it. The case illustrates how a single entitlement-based claim with an immediate remedy may be capable of leveraging both a positive remedy and transformative effect by challenging prevailing exclusion and stigmatization.

Another positive example of "reading in" remedies is found in the *Vriend* case dealing with under-inclusive human rights protections.[39] The Supreme Court held that a failure to include sexual orientation as a prohibited ground of discrimination under provincial human rights legislation, governing the actions of both private and government service and housing providers as well as employers, violated the equality rights under the *Canadian Charter*.[40] The majority of the court opted to read the missing protection into Alberta's human rights legislation, extending protections from discrimination to a group the legislature had deliberately chosen to exclude.[41] Again, although the claim was framed by the existing human rights protections in Alberta, there was a significant transformative effect achieved by providing protections from discrimination that had previously been denied on the basis of systemic discriminatory patterns of exclusion and stigmatization.

The positive impact of cases like *Sparks* and *Vriend* demonstrate the significant potential of positive remedies that read in additional entitlements or protections so as to have immediate effect. Negative-rights-oriented cases striking down restrictions such as in *Morgentaler* and *Adams* may also have transformative effect, but the absence of positive remedial measures to ensure access to abortion services or adequate housing limited the effectiveness of the remedies in these cases.

[39] *Vriend v. Alberta*, [1998] 1 SCR 493.
[40] Ibid., paras. 65–66.
[41] *Vriend*, at paras. 196–197.

7.3.3   Suspended Declarations of Invalidity

Where remedies to social rights claims have engaged with longer-term obligations of governments to take positive measures to ensure constitutional rights, Canadian courts have chosen to suspend the application of declarations of unconstitutionality in order to provide governments time to develop remedial programmatic or legislative remedies to rights violations. "Suspended declarations of invalidity" are softer remedies than declarations that are of immediate application. In the case of suspended declarations, governments are left with some flexibility to design and implement the appropriate remedy. They therefore raise issues with respect to ensuring the quality of the implementation and enforcement of the court's order. On the other hand, suspended declarations have the advantage of encouraging the courts to engage with positive obligations of governments in areas in which the legislative branch is better placed to design and implement legislative and programmatic measures but where judicial constitutional review is also necessary to ensure that the rights of marginalized groups are not ignored.

A leading example of this remedial approach is found in the well-known case of *Eldridge v. British Columbia*.[42] In that case the applicants, who were deaf, argued that the lack of sign language interpretation services within the publicly funded health care system violated their section 15 equality rights and asked that these services be read into legislation governing health care and hospital services.[43] The court agreed that the failure to provide interpreter services had violated section 15, but rejected the remedy sought by the claimants of reading these services into the existing legislative framework. The court held that it would be more appropriate to give the government time to choose among a "myriad" of options for the best way to provide interpreter services. The government subsequently sought and received an extension of time from the court to consult with affected communities. There was some skepticism within the disability rights and legal communities about whether the claimants would actually secure the remedy to which they were entitled. Ultimately, however, the consultative participatory process proved beneficial.[44] Had the court adopted the "read in" remedy originally requested by the claimants, interpreter services

[42] *Eldridge.*
[43] Ibid.
[44] Zwack, Andrea L. (2010), Counsel for Appellants in *Eldridge v. British Columbia (Attorney General)*, [1997] 3 SCR 624 [Interview by Azin Samani], 15 March.

would have been provided as an individual entitlement as a component of health care and hospital services with services under the direction of medical professionals, preserving a "medical model" of disability. The suspended declaration, on the other hand, resulted in the funding of a nonprofit institute under the direction of a board, most of whose members are deaf, which designed, implemented, and continues to administer appropriate programs in consultation with the deaf community.[45] The remedy that resulted from the suspended declaration of invalidity was significantly more participatory and empowering of people with disabilities, relinquishing a medical model of disability for one which was more compatible with empowerment and social inclusion of people with disabilities. A better remedial and enforcement strategy emerged from the hearing before the court than had originally been proposed by the claimants, who had sought a harder remedy, subject to immediate enforcement.[46]

A less positive example of the enforcement of delayed declarations of invalidity is seen in the events following the appeal to the Supreme Court of Canada in *Dunmore v. Ontario (Attorney General).*[47] In that case, the court ruled that the exclusion of agricultural workers from the *Ontario Labour Relations Act*, denying them the right to organize and to bargain collectively, violated their right to freedom of association under section 2(d) of the *Canadian Charter*. The court held that the government had a positive duty to enact legislation ensuring agricultural workers the ability to meaningfully exercise their right to organize. The court suspended its declaration of invalidity for eighteen months to allow the Ontario government to enact new legislative protections consistent with the *Canadian Charter*. However, the Ontario government's response was considered unsatisfactory by the claimants. Rather than including agricultural workers under the existing legislation, the government enacted a separate legislative regime for agricultural workers which guaranteed only the right to form and join an "employees' association" and to make representations to employers through the association. It failed to protect the right to organize or bargain collectively in a manner that was equivalent to the rights of other workers.

[45] The program is operated by a nonprofit agency, the Western Institute for the Deaf and Hard of Hearing, which is funded by the Provincial Health Services Authority to provide service to communities across British Columbia. It provides interpreter services for most medical appointments including a qualified Sign Language Interpreter for most medical appointments including General Practitioners as well as specialists, psychiatrists, ophthalmologists, patient/ family conferences, gynecology/obstetrics, medical imaging, and hospital stays; see www.widhh.com/services/is_mis.php.

[46] *Eldridge.*

[47] *Dunmore.*

A further constitutional challenge was launched to the government's remedial response but the Supreme Court of Canada found that the new legislation was in conformity with the requirements of the *Canadian Charter*.[48]

These two cases demonstrate the positive and negative aspects of the
delayed declaration of invalidity as a strategy for implementing and
enforcing positive remedies. In the *Eldridge* case, the result was enhanced
consultation and participation of the claimant group and institutional
reform that went further than a simple "reading in" remedy would have
accomplished by recognizing the distinct needs of people with disabilities
and the importance of participatory processes through which to address
those needs. In the *Dunmore* case, on the other hand, agricultural workers were not part of the process of designing new legislative protections.
They would have been better served by a harder remedy of simply reading into the existing legislation an extension of protections accorded to
other workers. In considering the obligations of the government to design
and implement new legislation in *Dunmore*, the Supreme Court failed to
enforce any participatory rights of the claimant group. The claimants were
forced to undertake further litigation within a strictly adversarial framework, which ultimately proved unsuccessful.

7.3.4   Supervisory Orders

The *Dunmore* case demonstrated the need for judicial engagement with
the implementation of longer-term remedies and strategies that require
time to design and put into place. Ongoing judicial oversight of the remedial process with meaningful engagement by the claimant groups would
have significantly increased the chances of a more successful remedial
response without the need for prolonged and costly litigation to test the
constitutionality of the government's remedial response.

There has been some resistance to the idea of courts assuming supervisory jurisdiction in Canada based on the common law principle of
functus officio (according to which the court or tribunal's jurisdiction is
terminated upon the issuance of a binding order). This judicial resistance
to engagement with longer-term remedies plays a significant role in denying effective remedies to social rights claims. The issue was addressed
in the constitutional context in 2003, in the case of *Doucet-Boudreau
v. Nova Scotia*.[49] In that case, francophones in Nova Scotia challenged

---

[48] *Ontario (Attorney General) v. Fraser*, 2011 SCC 20, [2011] 2 SCR 3.
[49] *Doucet-Boudreau v. Nova Scotia (Minister of Education)*.

government's failure to develop adequate French language education based on the right in the *Canadian Charter* to publicly funded minority French language education. The trial judge ordered the provincial government and a council responsible for administering French language education to use their "best efforts" to develop French secondary school facilities and programs by specific dates in various districts. The judge retained jurisdiction to hear ongoing progress reports from the government. The Nova Scotia provincial government appealed, arguing that the remedy exceeded the proper role of the judiciary. The Nova Scotia Court of Appeal upheld the government's appeal, finding that while the *Canadian Charter* provides for a wide range of remedial powers, these do not extend to the power of courts to enforce their own orders.[50] The Court of Appeal held that while the *Canadian Charter* permits the court to order positive remedies to social rights violations, "the Charter does not extend the jurisdiction of these courts from a procedural point of view. Ordering a remedy is one thing. Providing for its enforcement is quite another thing."[51]

The claimants then appealed to the Supreme Court of Canada which, by a narrow majority, reversed the finding of the Nova Scotia Court of Appeal. The Supreme Court affirmed the primacy of the notion of effective and responsive constitutional remedies through which courts fashion, from an array of options, a remedy that is capable of realizing the right:

> A purposive approach to remedies in a Charter context gives modern vitality to the ancient maxim *ubi jus, ibi remedium*: where there is a right, there must be a remedy. More specifically, a purposive approach to remedies requires at least two things. First, the purpose of the right being protected must be promoted: courts must craft responsive remedies. Second, the purpose of the remedies provision must be promoted: courts must craft a remedy which fully vindicates the right.[52]

The majority of the court found that in order to ensure that a remedy fulfills these requirements, the court may play a role in supervising the implementation of remedies. So long as the decision itself is not altered on the basis of subsequent hearings, supervisory jurisdiction may include holding further hearings regarding implementation of the order, as were convened by the trial judge in this case.[53]

---

[50] *Doucet-Boudreau v. Nova Scotia (Attorney General)*, 2001 NSCA 104 (CanLII).
[51] Ibid., para. 37.
[52] *Doucet-Boudreau v. Nova Scotia (Attorney General)*, at para. 37.
[53] Ibid., para. 71.

It is an indication of the continued resistance to this kind of remedy in Canadian legal culture, however, that a significant minority of the Supreme Court of Canada found that the supervisory order exceeded the appropriate role of courts by breaching the separation of powers principle and its jurisdiction in relation to the *functus officio* doctrine. The minority emphasized the importance of separating judicial and political processes, finding that the order in this case led the court to become engaged in political activity by attempting to hold the government's "feet to the fire," noting that "the trial judge may have sought to exert political or public pressure on the executive."[54] While it is the majority decision that is binding on lower courts, the minority view articulated a judicial resistance to the kinds of effective remedial responses to social rights violations which continues to prevail in some lower courts. Governments have attempted to prevent a broader application of the *Doucet-Boudreau* decision by arguing that minority language education rights in the *Canadian Charter* explicitly require positive measures by governments while other guarantees of rights do not, and this argument has, unfortunately, been accepted by some lower courts.[55]

A critical issue which was not explored by either the majority or the minority decisions was the role of a supervisory order in creating a democratic process of meaningful engagement between the government and the affected community in the implementation process. In fact, in this case, it was not the judge who exerted the political pressure, but rather the claimants. The claimant communities relied on the reporting sessions to the court to hold their governments accountable to their constitutional obligations as clarified by the court. The reporting sessions enabled claimants to have their voices heard and to move a cumbersome process along more expeditiously.

In *Doucet-Boudreau*, the ongoing accountability for enforcement was assured by way of scheduled reporting sessions to the court. An alternative remedy, fashioned in a different institutional setting, might have required reporting sessions to some other body that could provide effective oversight. The fundamental principle at stake was not accountability to courts, but rather accountability to rights as interpreted by courts. Courts can play an important role in overseeing the implementation of structural remedies over time. Ongoing jurisdiction of courts does not usurp democratic processes. Rather, it supports and enhances participatory processes that

---

[54] Ibid., para. 131 (per Major, Binnie, LeBel and Deschamps JJ, dissenting).
[55] *Tanudjaja v. Attorney General (Canada)*, 2013 ONSC 1878 at paras. 89–90.

are required to implement responsive and effective remedies to violations of rights in many circumstances.

Under the traditional separation of powers doctrine, courts have the ultimate authority to interpret rights and to determine how they apply in a particular context. This interpretive role must be informed by a dialogue not only with governments, but also with rights holders. Ongoing account-ability mechanisms in the implementation and enforcement process must ensure participatory rights to the groups whose rights have been violated or ignored by legislators (Porter, 2014). In this way, remedial and enforce-ment processes address not only the denial of a specific entitlement, but also the exclusion, marginalization, or discrimination and failures in dem-ocratic accountability that led to that denial.

7.4   The Right to Reasonable (Rights-Informed) Decisions

While it is tempting to lay the blame for inadequate remedial responses to social rights violations in Canada solely on the courts, it is actually the broader legal culture in Canada that finds expression in judicial remedial rigidity. Litigators have demonstrated a propensity to focus on consti-tutional rights claims that seek limited remedies framed within existing entitlement or legislative schemes, and have shied away from asking for programmatic remedies of the kind that was instituted in the *Eldridge* case. The legal culture in Canada has assumed that the role of the court is gener-ally to issue remedies to discrete statutory violations rather than to enforce substantive obligations to take positive measures. A narrow approach to constitutional remedies has been at odds with the transformative aspira-tions that lay behind the adoption of the *Canadian Charter*, described by the Supreme Court of Canada as the creation of a "just society" through an "arduous struggle."[56]

The Supreme Court has laid the foundation for a more transformative approach to remedies, however, in its evolving understanding of reasona-bleness as a constitutional and human rights standard of governmental and administrative decision making in a wide range of circumstances. In a number of cases where claimants have advanced social rights claims within the more traditional framework of statutory entitlement claims, as demands for corrections to legislative omissions or to discrete entitle-ments, the Supreme Court of Canada has instead utilized softer remedies that engage the broader issue of ensuring that decisions are consistent with

---

[56]   *Vriend*, at para. 68.

the realization of rights and the struggle for a "just society." The court has reframed challenges in which the requested remedy was for a discrete entitlement to be added to legislation into softer, more contextual remedial approaches focusing on decisions made in the administration and implementation of programs and on the interpretation of existing statutory entitlements. In cases like *Vriend* or *Sparks*, where no discretion was available to decision makers to extend human rights protections to include discrimination because of sexual orientation or to extend security of tenure protections to include public housing tenants, the specific entitlement had to be read into the legislation. In other cases, however, where the legislation did not explicitly prevent the provision of an entitlement or benefit, the court has preferred, where possible, to frame the remedy as an issue of rights-compliant decision making under the existing statutory regime. The court has relied on a standard of reasonableness to require that conferred decision-making authority be exercised so as to ensure conformity with fundamental rights. While this remedy may seem more conservative because it leaves the legislation unchanged, it is potentially more transformative because it looks beyond the need for a single entitlement toward inclusive, rights-promoting decision making in all areas of governmental authority. The remedy is not limited to the particular entitlement but rather engages the obligations of governmental decision makers to respect and promote human rights. The court has thus laid the groundwork for a more transformative remedial approach based on the right to reasonable policies and decisions consistent with the realization of social rights.

The *Eldridge* decision provides an apt example of the Supreme Court's approach. The applicants' written submissions to the court framed the *Canadian Charter* challenge in that case as an allegation of a discriminatory legislative omission or under-inclusion. They argued that interpreter services should have been explicitly included as a health service in the legislation governing public health care insurance and hospital services. Had the court decided the case in the manner in which the Applicants had framed it, the remedy would have been a simple matter of reading the omitted entitlement into the legislation as an additional health service. However, a different approach was considered at the oral hearing. The court noted that the impugned legislation did not actually preclude supplying sign language interpreters. In its decision, the court therefore rejected the allegation that the legislation itself was unconstitutional.

> [T]he fact that the *Hospital Insurance Act* does not expressly mandate the provision of sign language interpretation does not render it constitutionally

vulnerable. The Act does not, either expressly or by necessary implication, forbid hospitals from exercising their discretion in favour of providing sign language interpreters. Assuming the correctness of the appellants' s. 15(1) theory, the Hospital Insurance Act must thus be read so as to require that sign language interpretation be provided as part of the services offered by hospitals whenever necessary for effective communication. As in the case of the *Medical and Health Care Services Act*, the potential violation of s. 15(1) inheres in the discretion wielded by a subordinate authority, not the legislation itself.[57]

The court held that decision makers are required to exercise their discretion in a manner consistent with the value of full and equal access to health care for the deaf. Moreover, there were many ways in which that result could be achieved, by way of different decision makers. Compliance with the *Canadian Charter* did not actually require that interpreter services be provided as medical services. As noted, the softer remedy ordered by the court allowed for the provision of interpreter services through an independent nonprofit provider under the direction of a board made up of members of the claimant group.

The court's softer remedy in *Eldridge* failed to provide an immediate entitlement, but affirmed that human rights principles and values must be paramount in all decision making emanating from governmental or statutory authority. Moreover, the court ruled that even private actors, generally beyond the reach of the *Canadian Charter*, are subject to it when they have been delegated governmental decision-making authority that impacts upon the enjoyment of constitutional rights. They must exercise authority consistently with the government's constitutional obligations.[58] By disseminating the obligation to conform with the *Canadian Charter* among a broad range of actors, the court provided more flexibility as to how the remedy could be implemented.

The *Canadian Charter* applies to the provincial/territorial and federal governments and to "all matters within the authority" of Parliament and of the provincial legislatures.[59] Rights are "subject only to such reasonable limits prescribed by law as can be demonstrably justified in a free and democratic society."[60] The assessment of reasonable limits under the *Canadian*

[57] *Eldridge*, at para. 34.
[58] *Eldridge*, at paras. 49–52.
[59] *Canadian Charter* s. 1.
[60] Under the "Oakes test" the court considers whether a limitation on Charter right is justified by a pressing and substantial objective and applies standards of rational connection, minimal impairment and proportionality according to the well-known "Oakes test." *R. v. Oakes*, [1986] 1 SCR 103 [*Oakes*].

Charter (section 1) has a dual function of both limiting and protecting rights.[61] In *Eldridge*, having determined that the failure to provide interpretation services violated section 15 of the *Canadian Charter* by denying deaf patients equality in access to and quality of health care, the Supreme Court considered whether the decision not to fund interpreter services was reasonable in the circumstances. The court incorporated the positive duty of reasonable accommodation of disability into its assessment. "Reasonable accommodation, in this context, is generally equivalent to the concept of 'reasonable limits'."[62] The cost of providing interpreter services in relation to the overall provincial health care budget was not found to be significant enough to justify the government's refusal to fund the services. The failure to provide interpreter services by one means or another was therefore not reasonable.[63]

The concept of constitutional reasonableness has thus been developed in the Canadian context primarily through the assessment of reasonable limits. The Supreme Court has established that international human rights law, including the ICESCR, are central to the values that underlie the assessment of reasonableness under section 1. In *Slaight Communications*,[64] the Supreme Court considered whether the order of a private adjudicator appointed pursuant to the *Labour Relations Act*, requiring an employer to provide a positive letter of reference to a wrongfully dismissed employee, was a reasonable infringement of the employer's right to freedom of expression. The court found that the limitation of the employer's right to freedom of expression was reasonable in this case because it was consistent with Canada's positive obligations under the ICESCR to protect the employee's right to work. Chief Justice Dickson held in this regard that:

> Especially in light of Canada's ratification of the International Covenant on Economic, Social and Cultural Rights ... and commitment therein to protect, inter alia, the right to work in its various dimensions found in Article 6 of that treaty, it cannot be doubted that the objective in this case is a very important one ... Given the dual function of s. 1 identified in Oakes, Canada's international human rights obligations should inform not only the interpretation of the content of the rights guaranteed by the Canadian Charter but also the interpretation of what can constitute pressing and substantial s. 1 objectives which may justify restrictions upon those rights.[65]

[61] *Oakes* at 135.
[62] Ibid., para. 79.
[63] Ibid.
[64] *Slaight Communications Inc v. Davidson*, [1989] 1 SCR 1038.
[65] Ibid., paras. 1056–1057.

In the *Baker*[66] case, the Supreme Court took an additional step in linking international human rights values to a standard of reasonableness beyond the framework of *Charter* review and reasonable limits under section 1. In that case, there was no allegation of a *Charter* breach. The court held that for the discretionary authority granted to an immigration officer to review a deportation order on humanitarian and compassionate grounds to be exercised reasonably, it must be consistent with the values entrenched in international human rights law ratified by the Canadian government. The immigration officer should have recognized that the best interests of the child as mandated by the Convention on the Rights of the Child outweighed concerns about the anticipated health care and social assistance costs of reversing the deportation.[67] The deportation decision was therefore reversed by the Supreme Court on the basis that it was unreasonable. The best interests of the child principle were subsequently incorporated into the Act as well as into procedural guidelines for the exercise of all statutory discretion under the Act.[68]

In a more recent case challenging attempts by the Conservative government to shut down a safe injection site ("Insite") for intravenous drug users in the most impoverished area of Vancouver,[69] the Supreme Court of Canada again focused on the right to reasonable decision making, rejecting the claimants' original claim that the governing legislation was unconstitutional. In this case the claimants had argued that the federal *Controlled Drugs and Substances Act*[70] violated the right to life and security of the person under section 7 of the *Canadian Charter* by making it a criminal offense to possess addictive drugs without providing an exception for therapeutic purposes.[71] As it had done in *Eldridge*, the court considered instead whether the impugned legislation did not confer any discretionary authority through which Charter rights could have been ensured. The court noted that the Act conferred executive discretionary authority to provide for exemptions and considered whether the minister

---

[66] *Baker v. Canada (Minister of Citizenship and Immigration)*, [1999] 2 SCR 817.

[67] Ibid., paras. 64–71.

[68] *Immigration and Refugee Protection Act*, SC 2001, c 27 (as per s. 25(1), the Minister may grant permanent residency when he/she is satisfied that it is justified by humanitarian and compassionate considerations when taking into account the best interests of the child directly affected); Government of Canada (May 2013), *OP – 10 Permanent Residency Status Determination*, www.cic.gc.ca/english/resources/manuals/op/op10-eng.pdf, s. 16.1.

[69] *Canada (Attorney General) v. PHS Community Services Society* [2011] 3 SCR 134 [Insite].

[70] *Controlled Drugs and Substances Act*, SC 1996, c 19.

[71] Insite, at paras. 112–115.

of health's failure to grant an exemption for Insite was in accordance with the *Canadian Charter*.[72]

Reviewing the overwhelming evidence of the benefits resulting from Insite's safe injection site and its related health services for those in need, and considering the negative effects of a failure to ensure the continued provision of those services, the court found that the minister's failure to grant an exemption in these circumstances violated the right to life and security of the person, and was not in accordance with principles of fundamental justice. In particular, the court concluded that "The effect of denying the services of Insite to the population it serves is grossly disproportionate to any benefit that Canada might derive from presenting a uniform stance on the possession of narcotics."[73] Based on proper consideration of the evidence and the needs of vulnerable groups the minister was obliged to grant a discretionary exemption to Insite.[74] The court considered the option of issuing a declaratory order and sending the decision back to the minister to exercise discretion in conformity with the *Canadian Charter* but opted instead for a harder mandamus order requiring the minister to grant Insite the necessary exemption "forthwith." The court held that in this case, there was no "myriad" of reasonable options available to the minister as had been the case in *Eldridge*. The only reasonable decision in the circumstances was to grant an exemption so that Insite could continue to provide its critical services to intravenous drug users.[75] Thus, in this kind of case, a reasonableness approach produces a hard and immediate remedy. The minister complied with the court's order and Insite was able to continue to provide its services. The decision has spawned interest in adopting similar services elsewhere in Canada.[76]

In the more recent decisions of *Doré v. Barreau du Québec*[77] and Loyola *High School v. Quebec (Attorney General)*[78] 2015 SCC 12, the Supreme Court revisited the obligation to exercise discretion consistently with the *Canadian Charter* and with human rights principles of reasonableness and considered the relationship between administrative and constitutional

---

[72] Ibid., paras. 127–136.

[73] Ibid., para. 133.

[74] Insite.

[75] Insite, at para. 150.

[76] Initiatives developed in Montreal and Quebec in response to the ruling. Harris (2011), "Following Insite Ruling, Safe-Injection Sites Planned for Montreal and Quebec City," This, http://this.org/blog/2011/11/28/insite-safe-injection-montreal-quebec/ accessed 7 August 2014.

[77] *Doré v. Barreau du Québec*, 2012 SCC 12 [Doré].

[78] *Loyola High School v. Quebec (Attorney General)*, 2015 SCC 12.

standards of reasonableness. The court revised the approach taken in *Slaight Communications* and subsequent decisions following the *Slaight Communications* model, in which the assessment of whether an administrative decision was reasonable and compliant with *Charter Rights* was conducted pursuant to the "reasonable limits" requirements of section 1 of the *Canadian Charter*. The court held in *Doré* that where administrative decision makers are required, as in *Slaight Communications*, to protect *Canadian Charter* rights and human rights values in the context of exercising discretion, judicial review of such decisions may be conducted under an administrative law test of reasonableness, rather than by way of section 1 reasonable limits. Writing for the court, Justice Abella explained that the modern view of administrative tribunals has given rise to a more robust standard of administrative law reasonableness, a standard of reasonableness which incorporates the *Canadian Charter* and human rights law into administrative law standards. A new administrative law standard that is informed by constitutional and human rights values should be applied to provide essentially the same level of protection of fundamental human rights as does the kind of section 1 analysis of reasonable limits and proportionality that was conducted in *Slaight Communications*.[79]

There is a risk that the Supreme Court of Canada's attempt to bring administrative, constitutional, and human rights standards of reasonableness into conformity may lead to greater deference to administrative decision makers than was the case under full-fledged Charter review as conducted in *Slaight Communications* or *Eldridge*. However, the new approach described in *Doré* and further clarified in *Loyola* as affirming a rigorous standard of reasonableness review that "works the same justificatory muscles" as the *Oakes* test for section 1 of the Charter provides strong grounds for insisting that all administrative decision makers consider both *Canadian Charter* rights, including the right to substantive equality obligations and positive measures required to accommodate needs of protected groups, and international human rights obligations (including socioeconomic rights). The challenge of realizing the transformative potential of this new "robust" standard of reasonable decision making will be ensuring that the obligation to consider human rights values is taken seriously by administrative decision makers. As Lorne Sossin and Andrea Hill (2014: 357) note:

> If the principle that discretion should be exercised in a manner consistent with Charter values is incorporated into the guidelines, directives and

---

[79] *Doré*, para. 29.

practices of tribunals, this could have a profound effect on the opportunity
for these adjudicative spaces to advance social rights. By contrast, if such
values turn out not to be relevant in the everyday decision-making of such
bodies, then the Court's rhetoric in Doré will suggest a rights orientated
framework that is illusory.

What is clear is that there is now a foundation in *Canadian Charter* and
administrative law jurisprudence to promote and enforce a broadly
based right to decision making that is informed by and consistent with
fundamental rights under the *Canadian Charter*, Canada's international
obligations under the ICESCR and other human rights treaties and with
a broadly framed standard of reasonableness that incorporates positive duties to address the circumstances and ensure the rights of people
with disabilities and other marginalized groups. Quinot and Liebenberg
(2011: 641) have described a similar convergence of different standards of
reasonableness in South African jurisprudence, which they argue establishes the basis for a coherent model of judicial review "that builds on
the development of reasonableness as a standard in both administrative
justice and socio-economic rights jurisprudence." There is now a basis in
Canadian jurisprudence for enforcing the reasonableness standard proposed by Liebenberg and Quinot under South African constitutional and
administrative law. The question is whether courts and administrative tribunals will apply it.

Reasonableness should be conceived of as more than a standard of judicial review. It is the basis of a positive right to have one's rights properly
considered and ensured when decisions engaging those rights are made.
Enforcing the right to reasonableness is thus not a matter only for courts. It
is a standard of decision making which must be applied by decision makers in a range of settings and which empowers rights holders to claim and
enforce their rights in diverse settings. The wide range of decision making
engaged by the standard is what creates its immense transformative potential, but at the same time raises significant challenges in terms of enforcement. Decision makers must be presented with the evidence needed to
consider all of the relevant circumstances, made aware of how international human rights law and domestic constitutional and human rights
may be engaged, and how statutes can be interpreted consistently with
ESC rights. They must be trained to contextualize social rights in their
areas of expertise and to apply the rights-informed standard of reasonableness affirmed by the Supreme Court of Canada. Enforcing this reasonableness standard before the wide range of administrative, quasi-judicial
and judicial decision makers, ranging from housing tribunals overseeing

eviction, to social assistance tribunals, unemployment insurance arbitrators and administrators of disability programs, is a massive undertaking for stakeholders and civil society organizations. Advocacy organizations able to provide assistance and representation in these areas have been under sustained attack by a right-wing government in Ottawa with traditional governmental sources of funding removed and charitable sources in jeopardy.[80]

The enforcement challenges raised by a more coherent and universally applicable standard of reasonableness, however, are commensurate with its potential. The Supreme Court of Canada has affirmed a right to reasonableness that provides a domestic legal foundation for rights-based advocacy and civil society mobilization engaging with the range of decisions and policies that have created the crisis of poverty, homelessness, and hunger in Canada.[81] The courts can still be called upon to review decisions that are inconsistent with the new standard, so the dissemination of authority for applying human rights norms and values beyond the courts does not suggest an abdication of judicial responsibility for rigorous oversight and review. The risk that courts will apply reasonableness review in too deferential a manner, denying claimants the rigorous standard of correctness review that applies under *Canadian Charter* review is real and must be strenuously resisted. Courts must not abdicate their constitutional responsibility to ensure that administrative decisions are fully consistent with international and constitutional human rights and are properly applied in the exercise of all delegated governmental authority. As noted, effective remedies to structural "entitlement system failures" as Amartya Sen described them, require broadly based strategies to revalue and ensure the rights of people who have been denied their dignity and rights. Strategies will be based on political mobilization, public education and protest in a wide range of areas in which social rights are engaged. In the legal sphere as well, the demand for change must occur at all levels of decision making and engage a wide range of actors. Rights-based strategies as recommended by UN human rights bodies require access to effective remedies at

---

[80] Voices-Voix (2013), "Canada: Voices-Voix Submission to the UN Universal Periodic Review (22 April–3 May 2013)," in *16th Session of the UPR Working Group of the Human Rights Council*, http://voices-voix.ca/sites/voices-voix.ca/files/upr_submission_voices-voix.pdf.

[81] For an example of one initiative to promote and enforce the right to reasonableness, see the resources for claimants and advocates in Ontario at Social Rights Ontario (undated), "Social Rights in Ontario: Adequate Food, Housing and Other Requirements of Dignity," www.socialrightsontario.ca.

all levels of programming and administration. A broadly applied reasonableness standard is the best way to ensure this.

A key issue in the assessment of enforcement strategies is when to rely on courts to ensure compliance with social rights and when to rely on other actors. Judicial remedies that order entitlements in the simplest and most enforceable manner do not tend to address the need for rights-based decision making by nonjudicial actors. They assign the job of interpreting and applying constitutional and human rights primarily to the judiciary. Courts assume sole responsibility for making the decision about what entitlements are required to ensure fundamental rights. This was the paradigm of judicial remedies first proposed by claimants in the *Eldridge* and Insite cases. The claimants sought changes to the legislation to remove any reliance on administrative or executive discretion for the vindication of their rights. The Supreme Court rejected this approach in favor of a model in which the constitution and international human rights function more as a framework for statutory interpretation and decision making. Nonjudicial actors were required to engage in the assessment of what rights actually mean in particular contexts and to make decisions accordingly. Where, in the view of the court, they got it wrong, the court reversed their decisions. Judicial orders reading into the health care legislation at issue in *Eldridge* the explicit right to interpreter services, or reading into the *Controlled Drugs and Substances Act* the right to provide narcotic drugs in the therapeutic context of safe injection, would have been simpler in terms of enforceability. However, such remedies would not have had the same effect of extending the obligation of rights-based decision making beyond courts, disseminating the obligation more widely among other decision makers charged with exercising conferred decision-making authority or empowering rights claimants to demand reasonable decisions and policies in diverse, extrajudicial contexts.

The Supreme Court's remedial focus on ensuring a right to reasonable decisions provides a strong basis for attempting to enforce social-rights-consistent decisions and policies among a range of actors and before multiple adjudicative bodies. Reasonable decisions must situate and apply rights in particular circumstances. The Supreme Court's preferred approach assigns to courts the role of clarifying the principles, rights, and values that ought to inform rights-based decision making, and around which entitlement systems must be designed and administered. Rather than considering whether the *Canadian Charter* or international human rights require that a particular benefit or protection be explicitly provided as a statutory entitlement in every context, this approach focuses on whether the relevant decision maker has the authority to provide the benefit or protection, and on whether the decisions made pursuant to that authority are consistent with fundamental rights. The quality of the decision making is not assessed solely on procedural grounds, but also in light of the substantive obligations of governments to ensure and protect fundamental rights. In its review of particular cases where *Canadian Charter* rights or international human rights were engaged by the exercise of discretion, the Supreme Court has clarified how *Canadian Charter* and international human rights are to be considered and applied by decision makers who must themselves develop the competence to safeguard rights in the exercise of discretion within specialized mandates. Rather than relying on courts or legislatures to resolve every dispute about statutory obligations and entitlements in particular contexts, administrators are required to comply with rights-based standards of reasonableness, with judicial intervention required only when they fail to meet these standards.

7.5 Enforcing the Right to Reasonable Budgetary Allocations: *Newfoundland (Treasury Board) v. N.A.P.E.*

The Supreme Court of Canada has recognized that reasonable policies and programs often involve balancing competing claims on limited resources. As noted, the court held in *Eldridge* that decision makers failed to comply with the *Canadian Charter* when they refused to fund interpreter services, found to be a reasonable expenditure in light of projected costs balanced against the importance of equality for people with disabilities.

A more difficult balancing was necessary in *Newfoundland (Treasury Board) v. N.A.P.E.*[82] – a case in which the Supreme Court of Canada found that decision makers had acted reasonably, in light of budgetary constraints. In this case, the Newfoundland and Labrador Association of Public and Private Employees challenged a provision of the *Public Sector Restraint Act*,[83] to retroactively delay for three years the implementation of a pay equity program. The result of the retroactive delay was to eliminate a preliminary pay equity award of $24 million which would otherwise have been paid to workers in underpaid areas of women-dominated employment. The government argued that the roll-back of the award was made necessary by "a financial crisis unprecedented in the Province's history."[84] The claimants,

[82] *Newfoundland (Treasury Board) v. N.A.P.E.*, [2004] 3 SCR 381 [*N.A.P.E*].
[83] *Public Sector Restraint Act*, SN 1991, c 3.
[84] *N.A.P.E*, para 7.

on the other hand, argued that the rollback constituted sex discrimination, which could not be justified on budgetary grounds. The Supreme Court agreed with the claimants that women's right to equality was violated by the decision to revoke the retroactive award. The court found, however, that the measure was justified in the context of a fiscal crisis which had resulted in across-the-board cuts in government expenditure, including cuts to hospital beds, lay-offs of many employees, and reduced social programs.

The N.A.P.E. decision was seen by many as a setback to women's equality rights, in that no previous decision had found that women's equality rights can be limited by budgetary concerns. However, from the perspective of promoting judicial engagement with substantive social rights claims, it is unlikely (and not necessarily desirable) that courts will consider claims with significant budgetary implications without providing governments or groups defending expenditures on competing needs to provide evidence as to what constitutes reasonable budgetary measures in particular circumstances. Ensuring substantive equality for women and other protected groups under section 15 of the *Canadian Charter* may be more a matter of ensuring that a robust standard of "reasonable budgetary measures" is applied by courts, commensurate with the primacy of human rights and equality, rather than keeping budgetary considerations out of rights adjudication altogether.

An issue which arose in the *N.A.P.E.* case was the quality of the budgetary evidence available to the court. A number of commentators have criticized the Supreme Court's willingness to accept the government's characterization of the fiscal crisis.[85] It is indeed unfortunate that the record available to the Supreme Court of Canada with which to assess the reasonableness of the budgetary decision was limited. The case was first heard before a three-person Arbitration Board as a grievance pursuant to the collective agreement. The evidence put by government before the Arbitration Board in relation to budgetary constraints consisted of an extract from the record of the legislative debate and some budget documents.[86] The government witnesses had not been directly involved in the weighing of different options during the budgetary process.[87]

---

[85] See, for example, a rewritten judgment of the *N.A.P.E.* case produced by the "Women's Court of Canada," a group of feminist/equality Charter activists, lawyers, and academics who rewrite major decisions affecting women's interests – *Newfoundland (Treasury Board) v. N.A.P.E.*, [2006] 1. WCR 327, www.thecourt.ca/wp-content/uploads/2008/06/womenscourt-newfoundland.pdf; see also Mellon (2006), 135.

[86] N.A.P.E., at para. 55.

[87] Ibid.

In assessing whether the Supreme Court's decision in this case accords with evolving international standards of reasonableness in relation to budgeting and available resources, it is important to recognize that the debt-to-GDP ratio in Newfoundland and Labrador at the time was higher than any other Canadian province in the past twenty years (Norris, 2003). Newfoundland and Labrador had the nation's highest unemployment rate at the time the cuts were made, largely as a result of the traumatic collapse of the cod fishery. The province had battled poverty rates among families with children which were the highest in Canada (National Council on Welfare, 1992a). Newfoundland also has a particular political history in relation to debt. The independent Dominion of Newfoundland had lost its independence from Great Britain during the Great Depression because of an unmanageable fiscal crisis and debt was also a factor in the subsequent contested decision to become a province of Canada in 1949 (Reynolds, 2009). This history looms large in the Newfoundland consciousness. It would be difficult in circumstances such as this for an Arbitration Board or a court to reverse a budgetary decision so as to increase by 10 percent the projected budgetary deficit.[88]

A key consideration in a reasonableness analysis must also be whether the needs of the most vulnerable groups are prioritized.[89] Unlike most other provincial governments in Canada, the Province of Newfoundland and Labrador committed to fully protecting social assistance rates of single mothers from any cutbacks during the years of severe restraint, maintaining the highest social assistance rates for single mothers in Canada in real terms (National Council on Welfare, 1992a).[90] The exemption of social assistance rates from expenditure cuts was of critical importance for women living in poverty when the decline and subsequent moratorium of the cod fishery led to widespread lay-offs of women working at low wage, seasonal employment in fish plants. Women relying on social assistance in Newfoundland were in a significantly more precarious and disadvantaged position in the context of austerity measures than the women employed in the public sector who were adversely affected by the revoked retroactive pay equity award.

---

[88] N.A.P.E., at para. 72.

[89] *Irwin Toy Ltd. V. Quebec (Attorney General)*, [1989] 1 SCR 927 at para. 75; Porter 2006; United Nations Committee on Economic, Social and Cultural Rights, *An Evaluation of the Obligation to Take Steps to the "Maximum of Available Resources" under an Optional Protocol to the Covenant* (thirty-eighth session, 2007), UNCESCROR, UN Doc. E/C.12/2007/1 (2007).

[90] Note that in 1999, Newfoundland continues to maintain the highest rates for single parents.

The standard of reasonableness articulated by the Supreme Court in *N.A.P.E* is one which should ensure that courts continue to view governments' budgetary justifications with "skepticism" while recognizing that reasonably balancing competing demands on resources is itself a critical component of rights-compliant decision making. Justice Binnie summarized the court's approach as follows:

> The result of all this, it seems to me, is that courts will continue to look with strong scepticism at attempts to justify infringements of Charter rights on the basis of budgetary constraints. To do otherwise would devalue the Charter because there are always budgetary constraints and there are always other pressing government priorities. Nevertheless, the courts cannot close their eyes to the periodic occurrence of financial emergencies when measures must be taken to juggle priorities to see a government through the crisis. It cannot be said that in weighing a delay in the timetable for implementing pay equity against the closing of hundreds of hospital beds, as here, a government is engaged in an exercise "whose sole purpose is financial." The weighing exercise has as much to do with social values as it has to do with dollars. In the present case, the "potential impact" is $24 million, amounting to more than 10 percent of the projected budgetary deficit for 1991–92. The delayed implementation of pay equity is an extremely serious matter, but so too (for example) is the layoff of 1,300 permanent, 350 part-time and 350 seasonal employees, and the deprivation to the public of the services they provided. (National Council on Welfare, 1992a, para 72)

The standard or reasonableness applied in the *N.A.P.E.* decision is therefore arguably compatible with emerging reasonableness standards internationally. Significantly, the court refused to accept that a deferential standard of review should be adopted in relation to all budgetary decisions. The court firmly rejected the position enunciated by Marshal, J. A. writing the majority decision for the Newfoundland Court of Appeal, suggesting broad deference to governments' budgetary and policy measures based on a more traditional view of the separation of powers between the judiciary and the legislature. Binnie J. responded by elucidating a critical distinction between decisions deemed "reasonable" by legislators, and those which satisfy the rights-based or constitutional standards of reasonableness which the courts are mandated to apply:

> No doubt Parliament and the legislatures, generally speaking, do enact measures that they, representing the majority view, consider to be reasonable limits that have been demonstrated to their satisfaction as justifiable. Deference to the legislative choice to the degree proposed by Marshall J.A. would largely circumscribe and render superfluous the independent

second look imposed on the courts by s. 1 of the Charter. Deference to
the majority view on that scale would leave little protection to minorities.
Marshall J.A.'s proposal, with respect, is not based on fidelity to the text of
s. 1 but to dilution of the requirement of "demonstrable" justification.[91]

Although the court in *N.A.P.E.* found against the claimants and denied
them the judicial remedy they sought, the standard of reasonableness that
was articulated in the decision played an important role in the claimants'
later success in securing this entitlement through political rather than
legal means. Two years after the Supreme Court issued its judgment, with
oil revenues starting to flow into Newfoundland, a lobbying campaign by
women's and labor groups was successful in convincing the government to
make the retroactive payment of $24 million (Baker, 2006). The political
campaign relied heavily on the finding of the Supreme Court that wom-
en's equality rights had been violated and that the austerity measure was
only permissible in the circumstances of a fiscal crisis (Greene, 2010). In
this sense, even in refusing the remedy sought by the claimants, the court
had empowered the group affected to eventually win the entitlement they
sought once the fiscal circumstances changed. The court established a
framework for the assessment of the constitutionality of budgetary allocations which required that fundamental rights, including social rights such
as rights to health care and to work be balanced in a reasonable and fair
manner, with particular attention paid to the needs of vulnerable groups.
In the context of an improved fiscal environment, the N.A.P.E. decision
empowered affected constituencies to lobby for a different result based on
the same standard of reasonable budgetary allocations relative to available
resources and competing social rights obligations.

7.6   *Tanudjaja v. Canada*: Claiming and Enforcing the Right to Adequate Housing

As noted earlier, Amartya Sen (1988), in his early groundbreaking research,
demonstrated that poverty and famine are not generally caused by a scarcity of goods or discrete failures of particular programs, but rather by more
generalized failures of interdependent entitlement systems. Homelessness
in Canada is similarly not a problem of scarcity of housing. The broader
entitlement system of housing subsidies, social housing production,
income assistance, land and property rights, housing laws, land use planning, social programs, wage protections, social security, regulation of

[91] N.A.P.E., para. 103.

private actors (and so on), has, in its cumulative effect, left certain groups without access to adequate housing. The concept of a structural entitlement system failure is thus an accurate characterization of the human rights crisis of homelessness in Canada. There is no single flaw or discrete violation that can be corrected by extending or improving an existing benefit or piece of legislation. An effective remedial and enforcement strategy must address the cumulative and interactive effect of a myriad of laws, policies, and programs that have created a systemic pattern of exclusion, inadequate housing, and homelessness among particular groups.

The concept of a structural entitlement system failure seems particularly apt in the Canadian context where widespread homelessness and hunger have emerged during times of economic prosperity and growing affluence. UN human rights bodies have identified many of the component parts of this entitlement system failure, including inadequate income assistance, low minimum wage, lack of security of tenure, erosion of land and resource rights of Indigenous peoples, insufficient housing subsidy, inadequate funding of social housing, restrictions on unemployment insurance affecting women and part-time workers, lack of housing with support for mental health disabilities, and inadequate human rights protections against increasing stigmatization of people living in poverty or homelessness.[92] None of these failures is justified by the scarcity of resources. On the contrary, the evidence clearly supports the contention that governments would achieve significant net savings in health care, justice and social program costs by taking positive measures to remedy widespread poverty and homelessness (Jackman and Porter, 2014).

In *Tanudjaja v. Canada*,[93] individuals affected by homelessness joined with a network of organizations to ask the courts to engage directly with the ongoing failure governments in Canada to address the human rights crisis of homelessness and inadequate housing through effective

---

[92] United Nations Committee on Economic, Social and Cultural Rights, *Concluding Observations: Canada* (Eighteenth Session, 1993), UN Doc E/C.12/1/Add.31 (1998); United Nations Committee on Economic, Social and Cultural Rights, *Concluding Observations: Canada* (thirty-sixth session, 2006), UN Doc E/C.12/CAN/CO/4 & E/C.12/CAN/CO/5 (2006).

[93] *Tanudjaja v. Canada* (Ont Sup Ct File no CV-10-403688) (2011). Amended Notice of Application (26 May 2010), http://socialrightscura.ca/documents/legal/Amended%20Not.%20of%20App.(R2H).pdf.. *Tanudjaja v. Attorney General (Canada) (Application)*, 2013 ONSC 5410; *Tanudjaja v. Canada (Attorney General)*, 2014 ONCA 852; denied leave to appeal to the Supreme Court of Canada, *Jennifer Tanudjaja, et al. v. Attorney General of Canada, et al.*, 2015 CanLII 36780 (SCC). Further documentation of the case online at http://socialrightscura.ca/eng/legal-strategies-charter-challenge-homlessness.html.

strategies. The claimants in *Tanudjaja* sought to ensure, through an innovative remedial approach including both declaratory and supervisory orders, that governments develop, in consultation with affected communities, joint national and provincial housing strategies. As recommended by UN human rights bodies, these would include effective accountability mechanisms, and set goals and timetables for the elimination of homelessness and the implementation of the right to adequate housing. Claimants requested the court to retain jurisdiction in the same manner as the court in *Doucet-Beaudreau*, to ensure that the strategy would be designed and implemented in a timely manner, with the participation of the affected communities. The innovative remedial strategy designed in the *Tanudjaja* case was developed by a large network of groups and individuals involved with the issue of homelessness.[94] The network looked to the recommendations of international human rights authorities, like the United Nations Special Rapporteur on adequate housing and United Nations Committee on Economic, Social and Cultural Rights (CESCR), which had repeatedly called on Canadian governments to work together to adopt a national rights-based strategy to address homelessness. After many years of governmental inaction in response to these critical recommendations, depriving the fundamental rights under the *Canadian Charter* including rights to life, security of the person, and equality for those affected by homelessness and inadequate housing, stakeholders decided that Canadian courts must play a role in ensuring that these authoritative recommendations are acted upon. In past years, challenges have been advanced in relation to components of the right to adequate housing in Canada, including under-inclusive security of tenure protections,[95] rental qualifications that disqualify low-income tenants,[96] inadequate welfare rates for particular groups,[97] excessive utilities costs for low-income households,[98] and prohibitions on the temporary erection of shelters in parks.[99] International human rights law was employed in these cases to encourage courts to interpret existing

[94] For a description of the civil society organizations and mobilizing accompanying this litigation initiative as well as the legal strategies and evidence, see Social Rights in Canada (2010).

[95] *Sparks.*

[96] *Kearney v. Bramalea Ltd* (1998), 34 CHRR D/1 (Ont. Bd. Inq.), upheld in *Shelter Corporation v. Ontario Human Rights Commission* (2001), 143 OAC 54 (Ont. Sup. Ct.); *Whittom v. Québec (Commission des droits de la personne)* (1997), 29 CHRR D/1 (Que. CA).

[97] *Gosselin v. Quebec* (Attorney General), [2002] 4 SCR 429, 2002 SCC 84.

[98] *Boulter v. Nova Scotia Power Incorporated*, 2009 NSCA 17.

[99] *Adams.*

statutes or constitutional rights in a manner that would advance the right to housing.

Prior to the *Tanudjaja* case, the courts had never considered a constitutional claim to a comprehensive remedy that would actually address the homelessness crisis itself as a violation of rights requiring a multipronged remedial strategy to be implemented over a period of time. No group or individual had put forward a claim that would seek, as a remedy, a coherent response to the problem of homelessness. While asking that homelessness be remedied in a single court case seems ambitious, the claim recognized that the problem of homelessness is eminently solvable in Canada. The solution, however, is not reducible to a single entitlement or policy. The claim did not allege that governments must provide everyone with housing. Rather, it alleged that governments must make decisions and redesign policies and programs in a manner which will reduce and eventually eliminate homelessness. The right to sleep under a box in a park, as had been won in *Victoria v. Adams*[100] is a remedy that is grossly disproportionate to Canada's abundant resources. In *Tanudjaja*, the claimants sought a remedy that more closely conforms with emerging international standards of reasonableness based on available resources.[101]

Rather than trying to identify a specific piece of legislation that could be challenged and asking for a more traditional, statute-based remedy, those developing the claim in *Tanudjaja* asked first what sort of remedy would be effective and contoured the claim to the remedial measures that are required to deal with homelessness. In order to provide coherence and specificity to the alleged violation, the claimants identified the governments' failure to implement a comprehensive strategy to address homelessness and inadequate housing as the central violation. The primary violation alleged in *Tanudjaja*, as in the *Eldridge* case, was government's failure to respond reasonably to the needs of a vulnerable group – a failure to act which led to violations of Charter rights. The failure to adopt a housing strategy has led to violations of the right to life, the right to security of the person and equality rights of disadvantaged groups most vulnerable to homelessness. The claimants asked the court to order the federal and provincial governments to engage meaningfully with stakeholders and to design an effective strategy to implement the right to adequate housing within a reasonable time frame.

---

[100] Ibid.
[101] *Tanudjaja v. Attorney General (Canada)*, 2013 ONSC 1878.

The claimants provided evidence regarding stigmatization and discrimination against the homeless and of the disproportionate effect of homelessness on people with mental and physical disabilities, Indigenous people, women, children, and recent immigrants, thus alleging that the governments' failure to implement a strategy to address homelessness had a discriminatory effect on protected groups. Extensive evidence was provided about the effects of homelessness on life and health. In her Affidavit in support of the claim, Cathy Crowe, a street nurse who has worked with homeless people in Toronto for more than twenty years, describes some of the consequences of homelessness that she has witnessed:

> I saw infections and illnesses devastate the lives of homeless people – frostbite injuries, malnutrition, dehydration, pneumonias, chronic diarrhoea, hepatitis, HIV infection, and skin infections from bedbug bites. For people who live in adequate housing, these conditions are curable or manageable. For homeless people, however, it is much more difficult. The homeless experience greater exposure to upper respiratory disease; more trauma, including violence such as rape; more chronic illness, greater exposure to illness in congregate settings; more exposure to infectious agents and infestations such as lice and bedbugs; suffer more from a greater risk of depression. This is compounded by their reduced access to health care.[102]

The claimants in this case worked with volunteers, experts, and community organizations to assemble a 16-volume record, totaling nearly 10,000 pages, containing 19 affidavits, 13 of which were from experts (including Miloon Kothari, the former Special Rapporteur on Adequate Housing). Only after all of the evidence was filed did the governments of Canada and Ontario bring a motion to dismiss the case without a hearing and without any consideration of the evidence, on the grounds that the claim as described in the Notice of Application served at the commencement of the action is nonjusticiable and has no reasonable chance of success.

After all of the evidence had been compiled and formally served on them, the respondent governments brought a Motion to Dismiss the claim, arguing that it is nonjusticiable. Large coalitions of both international and domestic human rights, antipoverty and housing organizations intervened in the case to defend the justiciability of the claim, emphasizing that rights claims which seek effective remedial strategies to systemic human rights violations should be welcomed, not rejected, by courts

---

[102] Catherine Crowe, "Affidavit for *Tanudjaja v. Attorney General (Canada)*," Ont Sup Ct File no CV-10-403688 (2011) at paras 23–24, www.acto.ca/assets/files/cases/Afd.%20of%20 C%20CROWE,%20Former%20Street%20Nurse%20-%20FINAL.pdf.

because they ensure access to justice for the most marginalized groups in Canadian society.[103]

Sadly, the governments' arguments were accepted both by the Ontario Superior Court and by two of three judges on the Ontario Court of Appeal. The majority of the Ontario Court of Appeal held that the claim is nonjusticiable because an allegation which it described as asserting, in essence, that governments "have given insufficient priority to issues of homelessness and inadequate housing"[104] engages with too many interactive policies and programs to be amenable to adjudication. Rather than requiring governments to justify their failure to implement a coherent plan and strategy to coordinate the interactive programs and policies linked to homelessness, as had been recommended by numerous experts and international human rights bodies, the majority of the Court of Appeal of Ontario simply denied homeless people any hearing on the evidence. Despite a strong dissenting opinion from one of three Court of Appeal judges, the Supreme Court of Canada subsequently denied leave to appeal in this case, leaving the justiciability of claims to effective strategic remedies to homelessness in Canada to be determined by the highest court in some future case that would take years to develop. The claimants, meanwhile, are considering avenues through which to take their claim before international or regional bodies, such as through a communication to the United Nations Human Rights Committee.

A retrospective assessment of the Tanudjaja remedial strategy might consider whether framing the case around a singular benefit would have avoided prevailing prejudices about justiciability. However, such a strategy would be based on a fundamental distortion of the actual cause of homelessness and would force claimants to deny the polycentricity of housing policy simply in order to get through the court room door. Indeed, one of the problems that was evident as the case went forward was that lawyers arguing the case for before the Court of Appeal tended to abandon the original framing of the case as a violation of rights resulting from a failure to implement a comprehensive strategy, and reframed the argument in more traditional negative rights terms focused on discrete actions and denials of benefits – i.e., as a violation resulting from a myriad of governments retrogressive measures and program changes such as welfare cuts and social housing cut-backs. However, asking the court to review the

---

[103] For a list of groups that intervened before the Court of Appeal and copies of their written submissions, see Social Rights in Canada, "Motion to Dismiss – Charter Challenge to Failures to Address Homelessness and Inadequate Housing in Canada."

[104] Ibid., at para 34.

constitutionality of a multiplicity of specific benefit cuts while at the same time recognizing that all of these are inter-related and must be considered together raised more problems than it solved. It was like trying to avoid a positive rights claim in a challenge to the denial of physical access to housing by mobility impaired individuals in a particular building by attempting to identify all of the discriminatory decisions that had been made along the way, by architects, builders, government regulators, and owners of the building. While there is no question that the causes of an inaccessible building extend in many directions to many actors, courts have made these issues justiciable and subject to effective remedy by focusing on the failure of those who are currently responsible for the building to build a wheelchair ramp in response to the needs of current rights claimants. In positive rights claims such as this, the violation and remedy converge. The violation is the failure to implement an identified remedial measure - to build a wheelchair ramp or to implement a housing strategy to address a deprivation of rights. The deprivation is the result of a complexity of previous decisions and current policies and programs but the failure to implement a remedy is a decision that can be subject to judicial review under a reasonableness standard. A remedial focus is critical to make these kinds of claims judicially manageable and capable of securing effective remedies. As the majority of the Court of Appeal noted:

> All agree that housing policy is enormously complex. It is influenced by matters as diverse as zoning bylaws, interest rates, procedures governing landlord and tenant matters, income tax treatment of rental housing, not to mention the involvement of the private sector and the state of the economy generally. Nor can housing policy be treated monolithically. The needs of aboriginal communities, northern regions, and urban centres are all different, across the country.[105]

The question at issue in *Tanudjaja* was whether the complexity of systemic violations of rights renders them non-justiciable. Both the court, and to some extent the lawyers arguing the case for the claimants, failed to recognize that by identifying the violation simply as a failure to take reasonable measures to address a deprivation of rights, complex issues can be rendered judicially manageable. The court need simply have recognized that it is the government that is in the position to address the complex interaction of various programs and to redesign them so as to eliminate homelessness. Adapting the concept of justiciable claims in this fashion is necessary if homeless people are to have access to justice a to protect

---

[105] *Tanudjaja v. Canada (Attorney General)*, 2014 ONCA 852, at para 34.

their rights to life and equality. There is no question that had the court been committed to the protection of these rights, it had the competence to review the evidence produced by the claimants and to consider it in relation to the arguments and any evidence put forward by governments to justify their failures to introduce the recommended strategies. The claimants and interveners quite properly acknowledged that it is not the court's role to itself design and implement the required strategy engaging a wide range of policies and programs. Rather, they relied on the court's competence to consider assessments from experts about whether such a strategy was a reasonable demand to place on governments and whether such a strategy could remedy the violations of the rights of those who are currently homeless. The claim conformed, in structure, to the remedial approach adopted in the *Eldridge* and *Doucet-Boudreaux* cases. The greater complexity of the systemic issue of homelessness corresponds to the more significant numbers affected and the more widespread and egregious violations of rights – a factor which should surely have encouraged the courts to hear the evidence in the case. For courts to deny those affected by these kinds of systemic violations access to hearings even when their right to life is at stake imperils the integrity of Canada's constitutional democracy. At issue is whether victims of the most serious violations of social rights in Canada will have access to effective remedial and enforcement strategies through the courts.

7.7 Conclusion: Addressing Structural Entitlement System Failures and Enforcing Transformative Remedies

In considering the relevance of the Canadian experience to other countries, it is important to recognize that the kind of entitlement system failure that was challenged in the *Tanudjaja* case is not restricted to affluent countries with comprehensive social programs. Sen's research showed that what is most obvious in affluent countries (i.e., that social rights violations relate more to entitlement systems than to scarcity of resources) applies in the context of developing economies as well – only with more severe consequences. In all countries, hunger or homelessness occurs when certain groups are left without access to food or housing because their rights are not prioritized within the existing system of income, property, and other entitlements, be they land and property rights, housing laws, land use planning, social programs, wage protections, social security, international aid programs or regulations of private actors. Therefore, solving hunger and homelessness is not simply a matter of ensuring that governments or charitable agencies provide those in poverty with housing and food, though this is certainly necessary in the short term. The entitlement system that has denied certain groups their dignity, security, and their fundamental rights must be transformed into one which gives priority to the rights of those who have been marginalized, and whose rights have not been properly considered in the design and implementation of programs, laws, and regulations. It is critical that litigation strategies develop enforceable remedies that engage with the need for a transformative social rights project, rather than one that relies solely on discrete judicial remedies framed as corrections to existing entitlements.

Justiciable social rights claims have in the past been conceived of primarily as claiming entitlements to social goods or services that meet certain standards of adequacy, or as protection from being actively deprived of those services or goods. In some cases, such as those involving discrimination or eviction from housing, social rights claims may correspond exactly to these kinds of entitlements, and can be advanced within the framework of traditional judicial remedies and enforcement mechanisms. Such claims can be framed within existing statutory or programmatic obligations by challenging exclusions on the basis of accepted principles of fairness, consistency, nondiscrimination, and minimum standards of adequacy. Entitlement-based claims may involve positive remedies by virtue of extending the entitlement to previously excluded groups, or by demanding positive measures to comply with statutory or constitutional requirements as interpreted by courts or tribunals.

It is now increasingly recognized, however, that if social rights claims are to address the most critical issues of exclusion and deprivation, they must also engage with the strategic or purposive dimension of policy and program design and implementation and with the requirements of progressive realization as articulated in article 2(1) of the International Covenant on Economic, Social and Cultural Rights (ICESCR). Social rights claims addressing this dimension cannot be entirely framed by claims within the existing entitlement system. They must try to implement transformative strategies to reconstruct entitlement systems around social rights and to remedy broader entitlement system failures that extend beyond a single statute or program. Rather than defining the violation and remedy in terms of an unfair deprivation or discriminatory exclusion within an existing statutory or entitlement framework, these claims will seek out structural causes of social rights violations, and create a remedial framework around the transformative project of realizing social rights.

There is clearly a tension between entitlement-based or corrective claims on the one hand, such as those which, as in the *Sparks* or *Vriend* cases, extend existing legislative protections to excluded groups, and cases such as *Eldridge*, *Doucet-Boudreau*, and, most notably, *Tanudjaja* where enforcement of judgments may involve new legislative initiatives and the creation of new institutions and programs through meaningful engagement with rights claimants or stakeholders.

The transformational dimension of social rights remedies and enforcement is most obvious in claims such as the one advanced in *Tanudjaja*. Social rights claims which identify specific exclusions and seek immediate remedies may also have a longer-term transformative effect, however. Claims to entitlements within existing legislative frameworks rely on interpretations of law and of what constitutes reasonable exercise of conferred decision-making authority, both of which are tied to the realization of social rights. Single entitlement-based claims such as those in *Sparks* or *Vriend* may sometimes offer the most strategic approach to challenging the devaluing of the rights of certain groups. In other cases, such as *Eldridge* or *Insite*, interpreting and administering statutes in a manner that is consistent with social rights may be the most effective way to affirm social rights values and engage with broader systemic issues. It is important to recognize the transformative dimension of engagement with courts' interpretive role, since giving meaning to rights in particular legislative contexts is a critical component of transformational rights strategies, whether they rely on legal claims or on broader strategies of social mobilization, public education, and political advocacy.

The success of equality rights litigation on issues of same-sex partnerships in Canada is a good example of the transformative potential of entitlement-based rights claims. Claims advanced by the LGBT community in Canada have consisted largely of challenges to exclusions from existing statutory entitlements or protections. These claims, however, have nevertheless proven to have an immense transformative effect. The inclusion of sexual orientation in human rights legislation and the inclusion of same-sex partners in benefits previously restricted to heterosexual couples, in addition to providing benefits and protections that were previously denied, has helped to redefine discriminatory concepts of family, spousal relationships, and marriage. Challenging discriminatory exclusions within existing entitlement frameworks successfully engaged with systemic patterns of marginalization and discrimination, resulting in a revaluing of the rights of those whose fundamental rights had previously been denied.[106]

---

[106] For an overview of these developments see Smith (2005).

Canadian equality jurisprudence has made important contributions to the understanding of this dialectic between entitlement-based claims and the transformative goals of social rights litigation. Canada's comparatively rich history of substantive equality in early jurisprudence under provincial and federal human rights legislation during the 1970s and 1980s carried over into unique commitments to substantive equality under section 15 of the *Canadian Charter* (Porter, 2006). Canadian courts played a path-breaking role in linking the right to nondiscrimination to positive obligations capable of addressing structural barriers to equality. An early example was the case of *Action Travail des Femmes*, in which a women's organization filed complaints of systemic sex discrimination against the Canadian National Railway. In that case, the remedy granted by the human rights tribunal and upheld by the Supreme Court of Canada included an employment equity program to remedy the under-representation of women and other ongoing effects of systemic discrimination within the industry.[107] Canada was also the first constitutional democracy to include disability as a constitutionally prohibited ground of discrimination, recognizing that nondiscrimination includes positive obligations to reasonably accommodate unique needs of people with disabilities. This legacy remains an important reference point for the notion of substantive equality. While Canadian courts have sometimes retreated from the substantive approach to equality that lay at the centre of historical expectations of the *Canadian Charter* (Porter, 2006; Jackman, 2010), the court's finding in *Eldridge* that conferred decision-making authority must be exercised so as to meet governments' positive obligations to ensure substantive equality remains good law and provides a firm foundation for transformative equality claims under both the *Canadian Charter* and by way of administrative law.

The Supreme Court's jurisprudence suggests, as has been described, a convergence and interdependence of a number of different approaches to reasonableness including proportionality and reasonable limits review under the *Canadian Charter*, administrative law reasonableness review, and the requirement of reasonable accommodation of needs of groups protected from discrimination, including but not limited to persons with disabilities.[108] The court has adopted a rigorous standard of reasonableness review in all of these contexts, which can be applied so as to be compatible

---

[107] *CN v. Canada (Canadian Human Rights Commission)*, [1987] 1 SCR 1114.
[108] For consideration of these convergences, prior to the Supreme Court's decision in *Doré*, see Gratton and Sossin (2011).

with Canada's commitments to international human rights, and with the emerging international standard of reasonableness included in the new Optional Protocol to the ICESCR (Porter, 2009; Griffey, 2011). It is the right to reasonable decisions and policies, informed by international human rights values, which potentially brings together individual entitlement claims and broader structural, transformative claims, mapping out a strategy that moves beyond the enforcement of particular judicial decisions to a strategy for social transformation based on human rights values. The right to reasonable decisions and policies requires not only reasonableness in the administration of statutory entitlements, but more broadly, the design and implementation of reasonable strategies to fulfill social rights.

Many claimants are not in a position to forego individual remedies in the way that the individual applicants in the *Tanudjaja* case chose. In that case the applicants intentionally relinquished any individual claim and sought only systemic remedy in the form of a rights-based strategy to end homelessness and implement the right to adequate housing in Canada. In other contexts it would be preferable to ask the court to order the immediate provision of individual remedies. Strategic litigation aimed at systemic solutions should complement and not displace the vast array of individual claims to particular benefits or challenges to evictions or to discriminatory policies that are critical to housing rights advocacy in Canada and elsewhere. There is ample room for both types of claims.

Modern systems of governance, in which many services and programs are contracted out and complex forms of public–private partnerships abound, demand innovative approaches to social rights remedies and enforcement. New remedial strategies must reflect the multiplicity of actors and the diverse legislative, policy, or adjudicative contexts in which social rights claims must be advanced. State regulation of private actors, whether in the form of contractual obligations or judicial oversight, particularly when they have been delegated governmental responsibilities in relation to social rights, as in the *Eldridge* case, must mean more than restraining them from doing harm. Private actors taking on governmental obligations must also bear positive obligations with respect to the realization of social rights, such as by participating in strategies to fulfill social rights over time. The modern approach to social rights remedies and enforcement must therefore engage with areas of policy, program development and planning that have often escaped human rights scrutiny in the past because of the challenges of enforcing remedies in this context.

Recognizing that multiple actors are involved as duty-bearers does not lessen state responsibility for violations of social rights. Although private actors may be directly responsible for violations, patterns of systemic exclusion and disadvantage are sustained and reinforced by failures of the state to prevent and remedy them through appropriate legislative (and other) means. As the Supreme Court of Canada properly noted in *Vriend*: "Even if the discrimination is experienced at the hands of private individuals, it is the state that denies protection from that discrimination."[109] Protection from discrimination by private actors imposes both negative and positive duties on private actors. The latter include obligations to accommodate the needs of disadvantaged groups and to redress systemic inequality. Similarly, the governments' duty to fulfill social rights through reasonable measures commensurate with the maximum of available resources must be borne by private entities with delegated authority, as in *Eldridge* when nongovernmental hospitals were made to comply with reasonableness standards in the *Canadian Charter*. The intricate links between state policy and the exclusions and inequalities created by the private market challenges litigants to demand a more principled and strategic approach to rights-based policy development, regulation, and legislation. Effective remedies must engage with democratic, institutional, and administrative processes at multiple levels of government and delegated decision making in order to vindicate rights in the context of new forms of governance. A new conversation among governments, stakeholders, human rights institutions, administrative decision makers, tribunals, and courts must be framed around the realization of rights and the interests at stake for rights holders, from which new understandings of duties should emerge.

The expanded role of administrative bodies in relation to rights-based adjudication means that a "robust" standard of reasonableness, articulated in similar terms by the Supreme Court of Canada, by the Constitutional Court in South Africa, and international human rights bodies, can help to initiate these new conversations and guide their outcomes. Reasonableness has become an important framework for the accountability of administrative decision makers and the enforcement of human rights norms and values among a range of decision makers beyond courts. Advocating for and enforcing reasonable, rights-compliant decisions in a wide array of settings places significant demands on under-resourced advocacy organizations and claimant groups. However, the potential benefits of these new approaches, with their broad range of application, must not be disregarded.

[109] *Vriend*, para. 103; see generally Jackman (1998) and Porter (1999).

Claiming social rights must invariably engage with questions about what is reasonable in particular contexts. It does not serve the longer term goals of social rights advocacy to try to avoid "soft" elements tied to contextual decision making in search of hard and fast remedies in every case.

The judicial reticence to engage with broader systemic failures rather than discrete deprivations or exclusions remains a serious obstacle to effective social rights litigation in Canada. The Supreme Court has insisted on leaving undecided the question of whether there is an obligation to put programs and benefits in place *ab initio* in order to ensure social rights.[110] However, the Supreme Court has at the same time recognized that the *Canadian Charter* applies to governments' failures to act within their authority in the same way as it applies to their actions.[111] Ultimately, there is no justification in the context of Supreme Court jurisprudence for the argument that governments have no constitutional obligation to take positive legislative and programmatic measures to ensure rights. Such a position is at odds with Canada's international human rights obligations to adopt necessary legislative measures to implement international human rights, and it is also fundamentally at odds with the court's affirmation that remedies must be responsive and effective. Approaches to remedies and enforcement of rights must catch up with the emerging recognition that the *Canadian Charter* imposes both positive and negative obligations.

The Supreme Court's reluctance to affirm positive obligations under the *Canadian Charter* has meant that courts have sometimes failed to properly engage with the broader purposes of the *Charter* and of international human rights in the design and enforcement of remedies. An early example of this failure was a decision of the Nova Scotia Court of Appeal in an early *Canadian Charter* case on welfare entitlements. After finding that lower welfare rates for single fathers were discriminatory, the court chose to remedy discrimination by lowering the benefits of single mothers to the level of single fathers or "equalizing down" to identical levels of gross inadequacy.[112] The Supreme Court of Canada properly criticized this remedial approach as "equality with a vengeance."[113] In *Vriend*, although the majority of the Supreme Court of Canada ordered "sexual orientation" to be read into Alberta's provincial human rights legislation, it stopped short of holding that there is a positive obligation to enact human rights legislation,

[110] This was the Court's official position in *Eldridge, Vriend,* and N.A.P.E.
[111] *Vriend*, at para. 60.
[112] *Attorney-General of Nova Scotia v. Phillips* (1986), 34 DLR (4th) 633 (NSCA).
[113] *Schachter*.

considering such a finding unnecessary in that case. It was thus open to
one justice, Justice Major, to dissent on the remedy, favoring a declaratory
remedy that would allow the legislature to choose "no human rights Act
over one that includes sexual orientation as a prohibited ground of discrimination."[114] The dissent provided fuel to right wing groups in Alberta
to "enforce" the Supreme Court's decision with a vengeance by demanding
that human rights legislation be repealed.[115] Clearly, a more coherent and
consistent approach to the issue of substantive obligations and remedies is
based on a recognition of positive obligations to enact necessary legislation and programs infusing the design and choice of remedies with values
that move beyond the four corners of a particular statutory entitlement,
toward the goal of substantive realization of rights.

Judicial timidity about positive rights in Canada is often based on a mis-
guided focus on the relationship between courts and legislatures which
leaves out of the equation the rights claimants and the interests at stake.
The expansion of a two-way "dialogue" between courts and legislatures
into a broader engagement with democratic processes to ensure that rights
claimants are heard is thus vital to the effective enforcement of systemic
claims in Canada. A rigid division between the hearing process, in which
claimants' voices are heard, and a remedial process from which they are
too often excluded, is doomed to failure.

Effective participation by rights holders must be incorporated into
standards of reasonable decision making and courts must frame enforcement orders in a way that engages all of the relevant actors in an ongoing,
rights-based process of accountability to substantive rights. Social rights
violations are generally the result of failures of democratic accountability
and inclusiveness; as such, social rights remedies must be enforced in a
manner that will bring about new forms of democratic participation and
accountability, empowering marginalized communities to play a meaningful role in decision-making processes. The struggle for meaningful voice
and democratic empowerment through more effective judicial remedies is
one which advocates and rights claimants in Canada share with their allies
elsewhere, and which will hopefully benefit from advances being made
both at the United Nations and in other domestic and regional systems in
designing more participatory and effective remedies to social rights violations. In all of these spheres, advocates and claimants must at times remain
stubborn in the face of resistance, and insist that prevailing notions of

---

[114] Ibid. para. 196. (Major J dissenting in part).
[115] See, for example, Byfield (1995).

justice and remedial enforcement adapt to the demands of those who have
been too long denied access to justice and effective remedies.

References

Abbott, Kenneth W. and Ducan Snidal (2000), "Hard and Soft Law in International
Governance," *International Organization*, 54(3), 421–456.

Acker, Alison (undated), Statement by Alison Acker in Personal Email
Correspondence, on file with author.

Arbour, Louise (2005), *"Freedom from Want" – from Charity to Entitlement* (Quebec
City: LaFontaine-Baldwin Lecture).

Baker, Jamie (2006), "Pay Equity Cash 'Addresses a Wrong'", *The Telegram (St.
John's)*, http://nlpayequity.cupe.ca/nlpayequity/Article_from_the_St, 24
March, at A3.

Byfield, Link (1995), "The Supreme Court Has Left Alberta No Choice but to Repeal
Its Human Rights Act," *Alberta Report*, 22(26), June 2–3.

CBC News (2012), "Vancouver's Ban on Homeless Street Sleeping Challenged," 22
November www.cbc.ca/news/canada/british-columbia/story/2012/11/21/
bc-homeless-lawsuit.html (accessed 7 August 2014).

Chayes, Abram and Antonia Chayes (1995), *The New Sovereignty – Compliance with
International Regulatory Agreements* (Cambridge, MA: Harvard University
Press).

General Manager of Engineering Services (2011), *Structures for Public Expression
on City Streets* (Standing Committee on Planning and Environment,
Vancouver), http://former.vancouver.ca/ctyclerk/cclerk//20110407/
documents/penv1StructuresforPublicExpressiononCityStreets.pdf.

Gosselin v. Quebec (Attorney General), [2002] 4 SCR 429, 2002 SCC 84.

Government of Canada (May 2013), "OP – 10 Permanent Residency Status
Determination," www.cic.gc.ca/english/resources/manuals/op/op10-eng.pdf.

Gratton, Susan L. and Lorne Sossin (2011), "In Search of Coherence: The Charter
and Administrative Law under the McLachlin Court," in Adam Dodek and
David Wright (eds.), *The McLachlin Court's First Ten Years: Reflections of the
Past and Projections of the Future* (Toronto:Irwin Law inc.).

Greater Victoria Coalition to end Homelessness (2014), "Housing Ends
Homelessness," Greater Victoria Coalition to end Homelessness, http://
victoriahomelessness.ca/get-informed/housing/ (accessed 21 August 2014).

Greene, Shiela H. (2010), *Letter from Shiela H. Greene*, Counsel for Appellants
in *Newfoundland (Treasury Board) v. N.A.P.E.*, [2004] 3 SCR 381 (29
March 2010).

Griffey, Brian (2011), "The 'Reasonableness' Test: Assessing Violations of State
Obligations under the Optional Protocol to the International Covenant on
Economic, Social and Cultural Rights," *HRL*, 11(2), 275–327.

Harris, Megan (2011), "Following Insite Ruling, Safe-Injection Sites Planned for Montreal and Quebec City," *This Magazine*, 11 November, http://this .org/blog/2011/11/28/insite-safe-injection-montreal-quebec/ (accessed 7 August 2014).

Jackman, Martha (1998), "Giving Real Effect to Equality: Eldridge v. British Columbia (A.G.) and Vriend v. Alberta," *Rev Const Stud*, 4(2), 352–371.

    (2010), "Constitutional Castaways: Poverty and the McLachlin Court," in Sanda Rodgers and Sheila McIntyre (eds.), *The Supreme Court of Canada and Social Justice: Commitment, Retrenchment or Retreat* (Markham, ON: LexisNexis Canada); (2010), Supreme *Court Law Review*, 50, 297–328.

King, Douglas (undated), *Statement by Douglas King in Personal Email Correspondence*, on file with author.

Liew, Jamie (2012), "Finding Common Ground: Charter Remedies and Challenges for Marginalized Persons in Public Spaces," 1:1 C.J. Poverty Law.

Mellon, Hugh (2006), "Charter Rights and Public Policy Choices: The Supreme Court and Public Finance," *Forum Constitutionnel*, 15(3), 135–146.

National Council on Welfare, Poverty Profile 1980–1990 (Ottawa, 1992).

Norris, Dave (2003), "The Fiscal Position of Newfoundland and Labrador," Royal Commission on Renewing and Strengthening Our Place in Canada, May, www.gov.nl.ca/publicat/royalcomm/research/Norris.pdf (accessed 7 August 2014).

Office of the United Nations High Commission for Human Rights (OHCHR), "Olivier De Schutter, Special Rapporteur on the Right to Food: Visit to Canada from 6 to 16 May 2012: End-of-Mission Statement," www.ohchr .org/EN/NewsEvents/Pages/DisplayNews.aspx?NewsID=12159&LangID=E (accessed 7 August 2014).

Pivot Legal Society (N.D.), "City by-Laws Must Respect Homeless Rights," www .pivotlegal.org/pivot-points/blog/city-by-laws-must-respect-homeless-rights (accessed 7 August 2014).

Porter, Bruce (1999), "Beyond Andrews: Substantive Equality and Positive Obligations after Eldridge and Vriend," *Const Forum Const*, 9(3), 71–82, www.law.ualberta.ca/centres/ccs/userfiles/9-3porter.pdf.

    (2006), "Expectations of Equality," *Supreme Court Law Review*, 33(23), 23–44.

    (2009), "The Reasonableness of Article 8(4) – Adjudicating Claims from the Margins," *Nordic Journal of Human Rights*, 27(1), 39–53.

    (2014a), "Inclusive Interpretations: Social and Economic Rights and the Canadian Charter," Helena Alviar, Karl Klare and Lucy Williams (eds.), *Social and Economic Rights in Theory and Practice: A Critical Assessment* (London and New York: Routledge), 215–234.

(2014b), "International Rights in Anti-Poverty and Housing Strategies: Making the Connection," in Martha Jackman and Bruce Porter (eds.), *Advancing Social Rights in Canada* (Toronto: Irwin Law 2014), 33–64.

(forthcoming), "Reasonableness in the Optional Protocol to the ICESCR," in Rebecca Brown, Malcolm Langford, Bruce Porter and Julieta Rossi (eds.), *The Optional Protocol to the International Covenant on Economic, Social and Cultural Rights: A Commentary* (Capetown: Pretoria University Law Press).

Porter, Bruce and Martha Jackman (2008), "Canada: Socio-Economic Rights Under the Canadian Charter," in Malcolm Langford (ed.), *Social Rights Jurisprudence: Emerging Trends in International and Comparative Law* (New York: Cambridge University Press), 209–229.

(2014), "Strategies to Address Homelessness and Poverty in Canada: The Charter Framework," in Martha Jackman and Bruce Porter (eds.), *Advancing Social Rights in Canada* (Toronto: Irwin Law 2014), 99–100.

Quinot, Geo and Sandra Liebenberg (2011), "Narrowing the Band: Reasonableness Review in Administrative Justice and Socio-economic Rights Jurisprudence in South Africa," *Stellenbosch Law Review*, 22(3), 639–663.

Reynolds, Neil (2009), "What Newfoundland Can Teach Us," *Globe and Mail*, 27 November, www.theglobeandmail.com/report-on-business/rob-commentary/what-newfoundland-can-teach-us/article793205/ (accessed 7 August 2014).

Roach, Kent (2002), "Remedial Consensus and Dialogue under the Charter: General Declarations and Delayed Declarations of Invalidity," *University of British Columbia Law Review*, 35(2), 211–270.

(2013), *Constitutional Remedies in Canada* (Toronto: Canada Law Book).

Roach, Kent and Geoff Budlender (2005), "Mandatory Relief and Supervisory Jurisdiction: When Is It Appropriate, Just and Equitable," *South African Law Journal*, 122(2), 325–351.

Sabel, Charles F. and William H. Simon (2004), "Destabilization Rights: How Public Law Litigation Succeeds," *Harvard Law Review*, 117(4), 1015–1101.

Sen, Amartya (1988), "Property and Hunger," *Economics and Philosophy*, 4(1), 57–68, reprinted in Wesley Cragg and Christine Koggel (eds.) (2004), *Contemporary Moral Issues* (Toronto: McGraw-Hill Ryerson).

Smith, Miriam (2005), "Social Movements and Judicial Empowerment: Courts, Public Policy and Lesbian and Gay Organizing in Canada," *Politics & Society*, 33(2), 327–353.

Social Rights in Canada (2010), "Charter Challenge to Homelessness and Violations of the Right to Adequate Housing in Canada," April, http://socialrightscura.ca/eng/legal-strategies-charter-challenge-homlessness.html (accessed 7 August 2014).

Social Rights Ontario (undated), "Social Rights in Ontario: Adequate Food, Housing and Other Requirements of Dignity," www.socialrightsontario.ca.

Voices-Voix (2013), "Canada: Voices-Voix Submission to the UN Universal Periodic Review, (22 April–3 May 2013)," in *16th Session of the UPR Working Group of the Human Rights Council*, http://voices-voix.ca/sites/voices-voix.ca/files/upr_submission_voices-voix.pdf.

Zwack, Andrea L. (2010), Counsel for Appellants in *Eldridge v. British Columbia (Attorney General)*, [1997] 3 SCR 624 [Interview by Azin Samani], 15 March.

United States: Education Rights and the Parameters of the Possible

CATHY ALBISA AND AMANDA SHANOR

8.1 Introduction

Despite a complicated political history regarding economic and social rights in the United States and the lack of formal legal protection as a general matter, the right to education is firmly embedded in sub-national constitutions across the country. This exception to the United States' general exceptionalism on economic and social rights is the product of the common schools movement of the mid-nineteenth century and further fueled by achievements of the civil rights movement of the mid-twentieth century. Together those movements have ensured – at least *de jure* – universal access to education for children in the United States from kindergarten through twelfth grade. This achievement is challenged by the push-out crisis in the United States whereby children leave school before high school graduation often due to under-resourced and abusive school environments.[1] Universal access to quality education in the United States is also challenged by deep inequities in school resources and management across the country.

These two challenges are not unrelated. In the United States, education is deeply decentralized – a decentralization that includes school financing, which is generated at the local level most often through property taxes. Consequently, poorer neighborhoods with more limited tax bases provide fewer resources for their schools. Schools receiving the fewest resources are the most overcrowded and tend to have less experienced teachers. The circumstances are often not manageable by students, parents, teachers or administrators. These schools disproportionately engender the most

---

[1] See www.dignityinschools.org.

Cathy Albisa is Director of NESRI.

Amanda Shanor is a Fellow at the Center on National Security and the Law, Georgetown University Law Center.

brutal environments, including severe discipline policies, police in schools and other methods of criminalization of school grounds. Moreover, when extra resources are committed to schools in poorer communities, those resources are often directed toward disciplinary and security, rather than educational ends. It is important to note that although this chapter does not discuss the issue in depth, many of these dynamics are highly racialized and the product – in conjunction with other factors – of a long history of race discrimination in the United States.

This chapter looks at one set of legal interventions to address educational disparities: challenges to school financing schemes at the state level (the United States is a federal system constituted by fifty states) through subnational constitutions. There have been dozens of equity and adequacy challenges to school financing schemes in the last few decades, the legal outcomes of which have been as varied as the on-the-ground impacts of those decisions. This chapter will explore the question of what social conditions and civic engagement beyond a legal challenge itself impact the enforcement of education equity judgments. With a focus on four case studies, this chapter raises more questions than it provides answers. Nonetheless, even this cursory look at a range of impacts makes clear that courts do not operate in a social or political vacuum, and that the level of civil society activity – in particular social movement activity – and commitment before, during and following a judicial decision has a significant, if not dispositive, impact on the effectiveness of a court's decision.

Section 8.1 of this chapter will address the economic and social rights framework in the United States. Section 8.2 will comment on the specific social, legal and political history of the right to education, in particular with regard to two prominent national social movements: the common schools and civil rights movements. Section 8.3 will present four case studies that reveal differences between the enforcement outcomes and civil society activity in four states: Texas, New York, Kentucky and New Jersey. Taken together, these case studies demonstrate that robust social movement activity may be necessary – if not always sufficient – to realizing the right to education. Section 8.4 raises questions regarding what factors are relevant for assessing the role of social movements in the development of legal norms and their implementation. In this section we discuss "the parameters of the possible," by which we mean the factors, social, political, institutional and otherwise, that facilitate or restrict the successful enforcement of a judicial judgment regarding basic rights in a given historical moment. We believe that social movements and certain

actions they take are a large part of – and deeply influence – the parameters of the possible. In addition, favorable social conditions must exist
in order for movements to impact institutions and structures within
society.

8.2   The US Legal Framework for Economic and Social Rights

The United States has a federal legal system with a national constitution
and subnational constitutions for each of the fifty states that constitutes
the union. Despite its abundance of constitutions, however, the United
States generally lacks a constitutional framework for economic and social
rights. While the federal constitution prohibits various forms of discrimination, it contains no minimal economic and social rights guarantees even
to survival rights.[2] It is a constitutional framework premised on negative
rights and generally fails to recognize positive obligations on the government to promote or protect rights.[3] While many state constitutions contain language that either directly protects economic and social rights or
can be interpreted to do so, with few exceptions, state courts have rarely
vigorously enforced those rights, leaving them to legislative fiat and private negotiation. However, as one commentator notes, ironically when US
courts do engage in the economic and social rights sphere they do so in an
unusually expansive and interventionist manner.[4]

Considerable scholarship addresses the lack of positive rights in the US
Constitution, much of it pointing to the Constitution's mid-eighteenth-
century origins and concern of the framers with governmental tyranny.[5]
Nonetheless, there have been efforts to have social and economic rights
recognized as a federal constitutional matter, and there have been important attempts to imbed these rights into the US legislative framework. In
his State of the Union address in 1944, President Roosevelt advocated for a
legislative agenda he termed the "Second Bill of Rights" (Roosevelt, 1944;

---

[2] *Deshaney v. Winnebago County Dept. of Social Services*, 489 U.S. 189, 196 (1989) (stating that
the "Due Process Clauses generally confer no affirmative right to governmental aid, even
where such aid may be necessary to secure life").
[3] One exception is the obligation to abolish slavery found in the 13th Amendment of the US
Constitution.
[4] King (2014).
[5] Judge and scholar Richard Posner, for instance, has famously written that "[t]he men who
wrote the Bill of Rights were not concerned that the federal government might do too little
for the people, but that it might do too much for them." *Jackson v. City of Joliet*, 715 F.2d 1200,
1203 (7th Cir.), *cert. denied*, 465 U.S. 1049 (1983).

see also Sunstein, 2004; Sunstein and Barnett, 2004).[6] Roosevelt urged that: " '[i]f, as our Constitution tells us, our Federal Government was established among other things to 'promote the general welfare,' it is our plain duty to provide for that security upon which welfare depends ... These three great objectives – the security of the home, the security of livelihood, and the security of social insurance – are, it seems to me, a minimum of the prom- ise that we can offer to the American People. They constitute a right which belongs to every individual and every family willing to work" (Roosevelt, 1834). The second bill of rights proposed by Roosevelt encompassed many economic and social rights later included in the Universal Declaration of Human Rights and the International Covenant on Economic Social and Cultural Rights.[7]

Significant US constitutional scholarship debates the degree to which, despite the failure to formally incorporate social or economic rights into the US Constitution, the New Deal era nonetheless fundamentally altered the US Constitutional order around certain social and economic principles. Bruce Ackerman has proposed that the New Deal constituted a "Constitutional Moment" during which "a broad movement of trans- formative opinion has now earned the authority to set major aspects of the political agenda" (Ackerman, 1998: 409). William Eskridge Jr., John Ferejohn and others have likewise suggested that certain framework stat- utes, including the civil rights statutes, have established, beyond the courts, *quasi-constitutional* (or small 'c' constitutional) social and economic rights (Eskridge and Ferejohn, 2010). Ackerman and Jennifer Nou, for exam- ple, argue that "the landmark statute *supersedes* the classical amendment as the form of higher lawmaking most appropriate for modern America" (Ackerman and Nou, 2009: 68).[8] Others have argued that while the New Deal era spurred jurisprudence that conferred constitutional authority on Congress to address economic and social issues, nonetheless it was also "settled that the Constitution does not speak substantively to economic regulation and redistribution, leaving them to the give and take of the political process" (Forbath, 2009: 57).

Whether or not major social legislation in the United States, such as public health insurance for the poor or the subsidized housing scheme, can be considered part of these "super-statutes," one thing remains clear: an

---

[6] FDR's Second Bill of Rights included the right to a living wage, medical care, education, a home, and social security among others.

[7] Universal Declaration of Human Rights, G.A. res. 217A (III), U.N. Doc A/810 at 71 (1948).

[8] Certain statutes "successfully penetrate public normative and institutional culture in a deep way. These last are what we call *super-statutes*" (Eskridge and Ferejohn, 2001: 1215).

economic and social rights consciousness and/or commitment has not penetrated the US judicial system. Not even a minimal range of basic welfare rights is generally understood, by courts or the public, as constitutionally defined or mandated. This has been brought into clear relief during debates over healthcare reform.[9] The key question in all the challenges to the Affordable Care Act (one which had been brought by twenty-six states and resulted in multiple Supreme Court opinions) has been the scope of congressional authority to enact the reforms given that the US federal system allows Congress to act only in areas explicitly defined by the Constitution. Therefore, the courts' role was to determine whether either the Commerce Clause in the US Constitution – which allows Congress to act when interstate commerce is affected – or the Taxing Clause – which empowers Congress to levy taxes – was an adequate foundation for the reforms. Thus, from a constitutional perspective it was a question of congressional authority over commerce and taxes, not a debate over individual rights.

Notably, many of the rights contained in Roosevelt's Second Bill were originally pursued by the African American freedom movement, a strand of which was later termed the Civil Rights Movement (Anderson, 2003). Many highly regarded leaders of that movement supported a human rights strategy inclusive of a full range of economic and social rights. But the combination of entrenched and virulent racism with Cold War hysteria on the question of socialism generated such a profound backlash that the movement ultimately narrowed its goals to the civil and political sphere (ibid.). At the same time, political forces backing these racial divisions and concerns over US sovereignty (Henkin, 1995) led the United States formally to take the position, advocated by Eleanor Roosevelt, that "the United States Government does not consider that economic, social and cultural rights imply an obligation on governments to assure the enjoyment of these rights by direct government action" (Whelan, 2005: 7).

Despite some progressive jurisprudence on the rights of the poor throughout the 1960s and 1970s (Albisa and Schultz, 2009), this basic historical context failed to change and US courts in the aggregate never seriously engaged the question of economic and social rights. The right to education is the most prominent exception; it is recognized by every subnational constitution in the United States. While this broad recognition across the country is very positive, the decentralization of education in the United States leads to wide variations in the contours of the right from state

---

[9] *National Federation of Independent Business v. Sebelius*, 132 S. Ct. 2566 (2012).

to state. Given how education in the United States is currently organized and structured, this is not surprising. There is no national system of education, and states largely do not have fully centralized state-wide systems. Instead, localities run the education system within over 15,000 districts with some oversight provided at the state level (Miller, 2008). Nonetheless, unlike areas such as healthcare or basic welfare, there is a common minimum level required by law in each state: universal access as well as some level of state constitutional protection.

This fragmented rights-based approach is the product of the history of education within the country. As discussed in further pages, the United States' unique relationship to education (unique in two ways at least: deeply decentralized unlike most other countries with similar social and economic profiles but recognized as a right unlike almost all other economic and social issues within the country) is a product of the common schools movement of the early nineteenth century. Subsequent serious changes within education were catalyzed by the US civil rights movement of the mid-twentieth century. Judicial pronouncements and the ability to implement them can only be understood within the context of these social processes.

8.3   History of the Right to Education within the United States

8.3.1   Common Schools

The common schools movement in the early nineteenth century was arguably the first significant US-based movement for a social right in the United States. Colonial America, as other British colonies, was marked by a patchwork of disparate educational systems run by local towns and villages that decided whether to have a school and how to fund it. These schools were neither free nor open to all, funded by a combination of taxes and parental payments. "[T]he amount of schooling a child received was in the last analysis determined by wealth" – and colonial schools generally excluded racial minorities and often girls (or limited their educational opportunities) (Kaestle, 2007).

The common schools movement developed into a national, if still primarily urban-based, network of reformers by the early 1800s, but universal free schooling was far from realized (ibid.). Parents with means continued to send their children to private schools both in the United States and abroad, and free schools – dependent on private philanthropic funding – accommodated the poor. The movement continued to grow,

however, fueled both by the belief that the young country needed an educated citizenry and by a concern over the assimilation of new immigrants
(Taylor, 1836).

In urban centers, the common schools movement sought to integrate
these privately funded free schools into a publicly funded system, and in
rural areas reformers pushed for free schools funded by property taxes
alone (Kaestle, 2007). "[D]uring the 15-year period from 1838 to 1853,
most states in the Northeast ... and the 'old' Northwest (Ohio, Indiana,
Illinois, Iowa, Michigan, and Wisconsin) authorized the position of
state school superintendent and required towns to provide totally free
schools through property taxes" (ibid.). This did not occur without substantial opposition from anti-taxation and limited government activists as well as religious groups, which worried that common schools
would disfavor their beliefs (ibid.). Only after the Civil War were publicly funded schools adopted broadly in the South. Publicly supported
schools were the norm by the early twentieth century throughout the
United States.

However, victories for the movement were secured state by state, without a strong strategy to nationalize education. The institutional model that
resulted in practice was one of local property taxes funding schools with
local control. That model became the basis of today's education system in
the United States (Miller, 2008).

Following the development of this social movement, the right to
education was incorporated into state constitutions in stages. Between
1776 and 1834 roughly half of states had included educational clauses
in their constitutions. Though many "tended to recognize the importance to society of an educated citizenry," during the end of that period
several states placed more concrete obligations upon their state law-
makers regarding the creation and funding of schools (Trachtenberg,
undated: 2). Between 1835 and 1912, many states joined the union and
included education clauses in their initial constitutions. Others already
in the union added education clauses. "This period, clearly the most
active one for state education provisions, was dominated by provisions
that placed far more explicit responsibility on states and their legislatures regarding the establishment, funding and administration of free
common school systems" (ibid.).

While the common schools movement has to be seen as highly successful overall, the fragmented model enabled and facilitated all kinds of
discrimination based on class and race. In the southern United States segregated school systems were the norm up until the landmark case of *Brown*

v. Board of Education in 1954. Understanding the importance of education to equality and freedom, the civil rights movement led by African Americans of the early and mid-twentieth century made integrated education a central demand. By 1954, segregationists were still fiercely defending the system that allowed for inferior and separate schooling for America's black children, but the civil rights movement had changed the American psyche, and polls showed that the majority of whites across the country felt segregation in education should end.[10]

Thus, despite the general vacuum surrounding economic and social rights and repeated refusals by the US Supreme Court to recognize these rights[11] – as well as tremendous resistance by the Southern States to racial integration – the court in 1954 announced that:

> Today, education is perhaps the most important function of state and local governments ... It is required in the performance of our most basic public responsibilities ... It is the very foundation of good citizenship. Today it is a principal instrument in awakening the child to cultural values, in preparing him for later professional training, and in helping him to adjust normally to his environment. In these days, it is doubtful that any child may reasonably be expected to succeed in life if he is denied the opportunity of an education.[12]

Despite this vigorous education advocacy, organizing and legal challenges, the basic framework of local funding and control has not been seriously questioned and schools remained tethered to local property taxes. Consequently, the US educational system was and remains at core severely marred by wealth and race inequities. Moreover, even when inequalities within states are addressed, such as by some of the judgments described in the later pages, the vast majority of inequalities is between states and can only be resolved at the national level (Miller, 2008). These structural issues, which emerged from the social processes of that moment, continue to influence, limit and shape the "parameters of the possible" for realizing the right to education in the United States.

[10] See, *Snapshots in Time: The Public in the Civil Rights Era*, available at www.publicagenda.org/civilrights/civilrights.htm.
[11] See, e.g., *Lindsay v. Normet*, 405 U.S. 56, 74 (1972) ("We do not denigrate the importance of decent, safe, and sanitary housing. But the Constitution does not provide judicial remedies for every social and economic ill. We are unable to perceive in that document any constitutional guarantee of access to dwellings of a particular quality ... Absent constitutional mandate, the assurance of adequate housing and the definition of landlord-tenant relationships are legislative, not judicial, functions.")
[12] *Brown v. Board of Education*, 347 U.S. 483, 493 (1954).

8.3.2 Adequacy of Education Litigation

Litigation since the mid-twentieth century over the right to education in the United States is often discussed as consisting broadly of three waves: cases regarding equity under the federal constitution's Equal Protection Clause; cases regarding equity under state education and equal protection constitutional clauses; and adequacy of education and funding under state constitutional clauses.

The first wave of education litigation challenged per-pupil educational funding disparities under the federal Equal Protection Clause. This strategy was initially successful and in *Serrano v. Priest* in 1971 the California Supreme Court held that right to education as a fundamental interest analogous to the right to vote that was protected by the federal constitution such that only a compelling state interest could justify wealth classifications made by the state that interfered with that right.[13]

In 1973, in *San Antonio Independent School District v. Rodriguez*, the Supreme Court rejected the nascent right to education by upholding a property-tax-based school finance system so long as it did not deprive students of *any* educational opportunity.[14] And in a schizophrenic decision *Plyler v. Doe*, the court emphasized that the right to education was not guaranteed by the federal constitution, while still striking down a state law that excluded undocumented immigrant children from public schooling.[15] Thus under the federal constitution, the right to a "minimally adequate" education is unsettled but if extant,[16] incredibly weak.

Consequently, after 1973 in the second wave, advocates attacked the equity of school finance systems under the equal protection and/or education clauses found in state constitutions. This strategy had mixed success – with state courts upholding the constitutionality of educational financing schemes in nine out of sixteen cases. In the third and current wave of education litigation, which began in 1989, advocates have challenged the adequacy of education under the education clauses of state constitutions – with far greater success. Some commentators have critiqued the third wave claiming that it is an inappropriate role for the courts to define "adequacy"; at the same time others have claimed that it allows for courts to return the issue of concrete financing decisions back to the legislature, unlike the equity cases, which bound the legislatures to much narrower formulas.

[13] 5 Cal. 3d 584, 604–18 (1971).
[14] 411 U.S. 1, 54–56 (1973).
[15] 457 U.S. 202, 221–25 (1982).
[16] *Papsan v. Allain*, 478 U.S. 265, 285 (1986).

8.4   Case Studies: Recent Education Cases in Four States Considered

Almost every state has faced a challenge to the constitutionality of its educational funding scheme – with roughly half of state supreme courts finding those schemes unconstitutional (Kramer, 2002: 6). Economic models indicate that States in which courts found school finance schemes to be unconstitutional have increased spending by 23 percent more than would have absent a judgment (Rothstein, 2000: 73; see also Banks, 1992: 153–154). However, there is continued debate, and conflicting data, as to whether increased court-mandated funding necessarily improved academic achievement.

This section lays out the impact and contours of four of the educational adequacy cases, those in Texas, New York, Kentucky and New Jersey.

8.4.1   Texas

Texas has spawned a great deal of school finance reform litigation, starting as far back as 1973 when plaintiffs in the Edgewood school district first filed a federal equal protection case[17] to address gross funding disparities. They lost that case at the US Supreme Court, which held that under the federal constitution, education is not a "fundamental right or liberty," and rejected any claim unless the "system fails to provide each child with an opportunity to acquire the basic minimal skills necessary for the enjoyment of the rights of speech and of full participation in the political process."[18] Justice Marshall's dissent pointed out that reformers could still seek "review of state educational funding schemes under state constitutional provisions."[19]

Advocates in turn brought *Edgewood Independent School District v. Kirby*[20] challenging the property-tax-based finance system under the Texas constitution. They argued that the financing scheme violated both the education and equal protection clause because of wide disparities in per pupil sending relating to corresponding disparities in property wealth across districts. In fact, the property tax based varied from $20,000 per pupil to $14 million dollars at the high end.[21] The plaintiffs won their initial case at the state Supreme Court; however, enforcement proved

---

[17] *Rodriquez v. San Antonio Independent School District*, 411 U.S.1 (1973).
[18] 411 U.S. at 37.
[19] 411 U.S. at 133 n.100.
[20] 777 S.W.2d 391 (1989).
[21] The Basics of Texas Public School Finance, Texas Association of School Boards, 1996.

complicated and required numerous court interventions. Although the legislature increased funding by \$500 million, the plaintiffs challenged that as inadequate because it left the same tax structure in place ensuring ongoing disparities. In *Edgewood II*,[22] the Texas Supreme Court agreed with plaintiffs and asked the legislature to come up with a new system. The legislature's next attempt – which involved a state mandated property tax distributed on an equal per pupil basis within each district – was challenged by residents of wealthy districts and found unconstitutional in *Edgewood III*[23] on the grounds that the state constitution also required local voter approval of school property tax levies. The third attempt by the legislature was upheld by the court in *Edgewood IV*.[24] The new system was designed to achieve fiscal neutrality. It improved equity and adequacy of school funding by creating a foundation formula guaranteed amount per pupil corresponding to a minimum property rate tax and additional funds for every extra cent of property tax. There was also a cap on wealthy districts implemented through a range of options such as consolidating with poorer districts (Imazeki and Reschovsky, 2003). But the political battle was far from over. In 2001, wealthy districts filed a case under the state constitution challenging state's authority to re-design school financing in this way. In 2003, the Texas Supreme Court remanded the case, *West Orange-Cove Consolidated v. Nelson*,[25] and additional plaintiffs from poor districts intervened claiming that the state's funding scheme was still inadequate.

In a blow to decades of litigation efforts, in 2005, the Texas Supreme Court found the system to be unconstitutional because of limits on state authority to impose state-wide property taxes. The court also found that the system of disparities did not violate the right to education. The court declared that districts must only be "reasonably able to provide all of their students with a meaningful opportunity to acquire the essential knowledge and skills reflected in … curriculum requirements." Despite clear educational deficits in the system, the court relied on controversial standardized test scores to reach its conclusion.

Researchers have undertaken at least two "adequacy" cost studies for Texas, both of which show the need for increased funding.[26] In 2006, the Texas legislature once again re-shaped the tax structure and funding streams for schools, relying on sources like cigarette taxes to fill shortfalls.

[22] 804 S.W.2d 491 (1991).
[23] 826 S.W.2d 489 (1992).
[24] 893 S.W.2d 450 (1995).
[25] 107 S.W.3d 558.
[26] *See* www.schoolfunding.info/states/tx/lit_tx.php3.

There is a consensus among educators that the 2006 reforms to the funding system, while helpful in some ways, were insufficient.

For the five years subsequent to the 2006 legislative restructuring, there was no court action. However, in 2011 in response to the recession, the legislature cut 5.4 billion dollars from the education budget. These cuts, consisting of 8 percent of the education budget, prompted a new coalition of 443 school districts, the Texas Taxpayer and Student Fairness Coalition, and a new lawsuit, *Texas Taxpayer & Student Fairness Coalition, et al. v. Michael Williams, et al.*). In February of 2013, the court found the funding levels to be unconstitutional, specifically stating the funding was inadequate to meet the stated constitutional goal of diffusing general knowledge. The legislature increased funding in May of 2013 by 3.6 billion dollars, but the court once again in August of 2014 found the funding levels still deficient and unconstitutional.

The Texas Supreme Court made its final pronouncement in May 2016 finding the system constitutional.[27] The court noted the torturous path of litigation stating. "[f]or the seventh time since the late-1980s, we are called upon to assess the constitutionality of the Texas school finance system, a recondite scheme for which the word "Byzantine" seems generous."[28] And also noted the insufficiency of a litigation strategy a stating

> Texas's more than five million school children deserve better than serial litigation over an increasingly Daedalean "system." They deserve transformational, top-to-bottom reforms that amount to more than Band-Aid on top of Band-Aid. They deserve a revamped, nonsclerotic system fit for the 21st century.[29]

Nonetheless, emphasizing the Court was not in the role of "super-legislature" it found the system constitutional. It noted some funding increases in its background of the facts, but did not rely on those increases for its conclusion, rather noting that the minimum obligation to ensure a "general diffusion of knowledge' has been met, and that there was no constitutional obligation to adopt "best practices."[30]

---

[27] *Mike Morath, Commissioner of Education, in his official capacity; Glenn Hegar, Texas Comptroller of Public Accounts, in his official capacity; the Texas State Board of Education; and the Texas Education Agency, v. the Texas Taxpayer and Student Fairness Coalition, et al.; Calhoun County isd, et al.; Edgewood isd, et al.; Fort Bend isd, et al.; Texas Charter School Association, et al.; and Joyce Coleman, et al.,* Texas Supreme Court 14-0076 - May 13, 2016.

[28] *Id.* at 1.

[29] *Id.* at 2.

[30] *Id.* at 41.

While there was a Coalition to Invest in Texas Schools formed in 2004, it appears not to have been active for any sustained period of time (perhaps no more than a year). The Texas Taxpayer and Student Fairness Coalition formed afterward appears to be composed of school districts (unlike coalitions in New Jersey and Kentucky which were driven by parents as the case studies detail) and created for purposes of the litigation. Thus, civil society efforts to secure enforcement do not appear to be nearly as visible or vigorous as in the state's discussed. The efforts throughout Texas in fact appeared to be driven primarily by litigation and the research community. Nonetheless, even though the issue has been tangled in the courts for decades cycling between wins and losses, the cases created pressure on the legislature and influenced the 2006 reforms as a response to court inaction and restoration of cuts in 2013. Thus, we might view litigation efforts without broader social movement work as able to increase funds, but unable to create major and sustainable change.

8.4.2   New York

In 1995, in *Campaign for Fiscal Equity v. State of New York*, the state's highest court found that its constitution required it to offer all children a sound basic education consisting of "the basic literacy, calculating, and verbal skills necessary to enable children to eventually function productively as civic participants capable of voting and serving on a jury."[31] As the court noted again in 2003: "We thus indicated that a sound basic education conveys not merely skills, but skills fashioned to meet a practical goal: meaningful civic participation in contemporary society."

The court explicitly stated that achieving this required minimally adequate physical facilities, access to instrumentalities of learning (such as desks, chairs and reasonably current textbooks), and minimally adequate teaching of reasonably up-to-date curricula by sufficient and adequately trained teachers.[32] On remand the trial court determined that New York was violating this standard in New York City. Although the findings were rejected by the appellate court which concluded an eighth grade education was adequate, the state's highest court held that it was indeed in breach of its constitutional duties.[33]

---

[31] 86 N.Y.2d 307, 3016 (1995).
[32] 86 N.Y.2d at 317.
[33] *Campaign for Fiscal Equity v. State of New York*, 719 N.Y.S.2d 475, 491–92 (2001).

New York's highest courts looked at a complex array of inputs and outputs (such as test scores and graduation rates on the output side); however, ultimately the victory for plaintiffs was based on the simple fact that: "Plaintiffs have prevailed here owing to a unique combination of circumstances: New York City schools have the most student need in the State and the highest local costs yet receive some of the lowest per-student funding and have some of the worst results."

Noting a pervasive mismatch between student needs and the flow of resources, including quality teachers, in 2003, the court ordered a three-part remedy: (1) the state must ascertain the "actual cost of providing a sound basic education in New York City"; (2) the state must reform the funding system to ensure that "every school in New York City would have the resources necessary for providing the opportunity for a sound basic education" and (3) the new reforms "should ensure a system of accountability to measure whether the reforms actually provide the opportunity for a sound basic education."[34] This remedy amounted to 1.93 billion dollars of additional funding for New York City schools.

This case was the result of a vibrant and strong campaign with a communications, advocacy, and legal strategy: the Campaign for Fiscal Equity (CFE). Working with a broad-based coalition, CFE turned the litigation's findings and the court's rulings into legislation benefiting public school students throughout New York State: the Education Budget and Reform Act of 2007. CFE worked to ensure enforcement of the judgment. It provided policymakers, the press, and the public with in-depth, fact-based public policy reports for informed decision making on the important policy questions raised by the addition of new operating and capital resources and accountability measures. It also kept the issue visible and relevant from a political perspective. Thus, in 2007, it appeared that this effort had been a success.

However, CFE did not have deep leadership development at the community level or in-depth or broad parent involvement. While parents and youth were mobilized to turn out for marches, it was a coalition model of advocacy where most people involved in decision making and implementation were professional advocates. The accountability strategy was centered around government and the pressure of advocates. As the CFE website notes:

> The long-range impact of the accountability provisions will largely depend on how assertive the Board of Regents, the state Commissioner of

[34] *Campaign for Fiscal Equity v. State of New York*, 100 N.Y.2d 893 (2003).

Education and the New York State Education Department (NYSED) are in
their oversight roles.

CFE did not make parents and students a central part of the implementation and monitoring, but rather they remained in the role of the beneficiaries. And the money may well have been ill spent. Michael Rebell,
the head of Campaign for Fiscal Equity, stated with regard to accountability for the funds: "It's all over the place. There's no way anybody can keep
track of what's going on with that money, whether it's made any difference,
whether it's being used well."

After the crisis of 2008, New York faced, like many States, severe budget
cuts. These cuts to the schools have wiped out most of the resource benefits
gained by CFE, and the issue has not been re-litigated.[35] Thus, the actual
benefit was not felt for very long, and whether or not the shifts in resources
would have improved learning remains an unanswered question. It will
also remain an unanswered question as to whether a deeper social movement process would have stemmed or mitigated the cuts. CFE has been
less active in recent years, and the level of campaign activity it undertook
in the past has not proved sustainable. Having built a broader and deeper
level of community and social engagement could only have been valuable,
however, at a time of austerity imposed through inequitable economic
structures.

8.4.3   Kentucky

Kentucky presents one of the more successful interventions involving a
right to education financing case on the state level. With New Jersey, it is
"generally considered to have the boldest judicial rulings in favor of students' educational rights" even though its constitutional clause on education is "categorized as among the 'weakest'" (Trachtenberg, undated: 3).
New York University political scientist Marilyn Gittell (1998: 237) has
described Kentucky as the "only statewide comprehensive reform resulting from a court decision on equity funding."

The citizen-led work on education reform began far before the complaint
was filed. A great deal of engagement, education and advocacy laid the
groundwork for the litigation itself, the legislation that was produced from
it, and the longer-term work of implementing the judgment and result-
ant statutory scheme. In fact, while the judicial decision issued from the
state's highest court in 1989, the education-focused citizen group that later

[35] See www.cfequity.org.

became an organization entitled the Prichard Committee for Academic Excellence began nearly ten years earlier as a commission of citizens appointed by the Kentucky Council on Higher Education and headed by Edward Prichard. That blue ribbon committee issued a report calling for sweeping changes in Kentucky's education system. Following the failure of either the governor or the state legislature to act on that report's recommendations, the commission's members formed the Prichard Committee as an independent nonprofit organization.[36] That initial group was made up of well-respected members of their communities, and the committee chose its additional members carefully. Those invited were smart, savvy and many had significant political organizing experience on either the state level or national level. For instance, Edward Prichard was a powerful figure in both the Roosevelt and Truman administrations, protégé of Supreme Court Justice Felix Frankfurter, and widely renowned public intellectual, and Dorothy Ridings was president of the national League of Women Voters of the United States from 1982 through 1986. Indeed, in the past twenty years, only one state governor was not at some point a member of the Prichard Committee.[37] Many of the committee's members had a deep expertise with how to effectively organize, create, and sustain a vibrant state-wide network, do clear presentations, and conduct effective research. The committee recruited heavily from the League of Women Voters and other local groups individuals who brought significant skills to the organization.

The Prichard Committee set out to spread information, develop awareness, and build political support for comprehensive change in Kentucky Schools. They planned high-profile events, including a forum for candidates during a governor's race that was broadcast statewide, ran advertisements in 200 newspapers free of charge to reach teachers and inviting them to submit their ideas for education reform (Sexton, 2004: 37). In 1984, the group organized a one-night state-wide town forum, and recruited leaders in each of the state's 176 school districts to do so (ibid.: 39–43). Nearly 20,000 individuals showed up in 145 locations representing each of the school districts, and the governor was asked to introduce it on state-wide television. Those forums gave citizens a chance to speak out and link to others with similar concerns. From those forums, the committee

[36] Interview with Cindy Heine, associate executive director of the Prichard Committee (August 11, 2011) ('Interview with Heine').
[37] Interview with Susan Weston, education attorney (August 11, 2011) ('Interview with Weston').

identified leaders from those who stepped up in each county and trained them further.

In 1982, Edward Prichard and Robert Sexton met with the publishers and editors of two of the state's leading newspapers, who agreed to commit ink to the movement. Three major newspapers all ran lengthy series on the problems in Kentucky's education system, and won a Pulitzer Prize. These produced significant debate prior to the court decision (ibid.: 37–38). Prichard Committee meetings were open to the media and heavily covered by it, and committee members often spoke with the press, leaked stories, and produced editorials – all focused on garnering attention to the education problem and the need for reform, not the committee itself (ibid.: 19–21). The media landscape was also far different at that time, with fewer voices and outlets, such that those inputs were likely more widely heard and respected.[38]

The Prichard Committee developed broad support from the business community, including the prominent Ashland Oil corporation as well as the State Chamber of Commerce, which recognized this economic rational and the importance to the state's economic competitiveness. Ashland Oil spent significant sums running state-wide ads regarding the need for education reform. Polling at the time of the ruling showed that state wide, citizens were willing to pay more in taxes if it meant improvements in the education system.[39] Thus, incredibly significant social and political groundwork was laid prior to the judicial decision.

Robert Sexton, the executive director of the Prichard Committee, also pulled together school administrators, the Catholic conference, education lobbyists, school board members, teachers, business leaders, and others to sit down together for the first time, over a two- to three-year period with the help of a professional facilitator.[40] Those meetings built common ground and a commitment to work together, even through disagreement.[41] That group produced a report, which later went into the legislation adopted by the General Assembly.

During the mid- and late 1980s, Sexton conducted hundreds of presentations across the state and the country, with data regarding the money spent and the message that Kentucky was at the bottom of the country's education barrel.[42] The committee's theory, and Sexton's, was to talk with

---

[38] Interview with Weston.
[39] Interview with Heine.
[40] Interview with Weston.
[41] Ibid.
[42] Interview with Heine.

everyone and never quit.[43] Sexton's message included not only that it was important as a societal matter for Kentucky's children to get a meaningful education, but also that it was economically critical for the state's future because in that future there would be fewer jobs in coal and tobacco. Accordingly, it was important to the state to better educate its children so that they will be able to get good jobs and contribute to ensuring the state-advanced economically, and that the older generation was taken care of as it aged.[44] This message, then, went further than particular parents' interest in their own children's education (Sexton, 2004: 7); it was aimed at, and resonated with, a broader swath of the population as not only right but also important for practical reasons affecting everyone. The committee's aim was at greater development of civic engagement and support of a community-wide cause. It is also noteworthy that these arguments were not framed either solely or perhaps even in the first instance as based in legal right, but instead in broader terms of justice and what values the state and society wanted to invest in for its future. As Robert Sexton described:

> The volunteers and I all had a sense that we were engaged in something that was bigger than improving schools. As activist citizens, we understood that the complex and intractable problems our state faced, like others across the nation, were not to be solved by government action alone. What was needed was a reinvestment by citizens themselves in their civic capital – in weakened communities, institutions, and social organizations. We believed that the solutions required the mobilization of communities and individuals to solve their own problems. The committee's volunteers were comfortable using skills of citizenship and encouraging others to do the same to get people's attention, to take responsibility, and to send a message to those with legal authority that they must also take action. (Sexton, 2004: 24)

In 1985, the committee organized a small group of legislators to speak with a national educational reform advocate over dinner, which spurred the establishment of a legislative subcommittee on school restructuring (ibid.: 51). The committee used the state governor's races to keep education at the fore of political debate, inviting them to a debate broadcast state-wide, starting in 1987.

In 1986, a lawsuit entitled *Rose v. Council for Better Education* was filed by sixty-six school districts seeking more equitable and adequate funding under the state constitution's mandate that the state legislature provide an "efficient system of common schools throughout the state."[45] The plaintiffs'

---

[43] Interview with Weston.
[44] Interview with Heine.
[45] 790 S.W.2d 186 (1989).

attorney, Bert Combs, had formerly been both governor of Kentucky and a federal judge (Adams Jr., 1993). In 1988, the trial judge issued two opinions for the school districts and holding the state school finance system unconstitutional. He defined the meaning of the constitutionally required adequate and efficient school, identifying the type of skills and knowledge required.[46]

Legislative leaders appealed, and the political debate over Kentucky schools further intensified. In June of 1989, the Kentucky Supreme Court upheld the circuit court and went further, finding the entire system of public education unconstitutional. As the court announced:

> Lest there be any doubt, the result of our decision is that Kentucky's entire system of common schools is unconstitutional. There is no allegation that only part of the common school system is invalid, and we find no such circumstance. This decision applies to the entire sweep of the system – all its parts and parcels.[47]

The court went on to define, substantively, what the state constitution required in an "efficient" school system, adopting the trial court's definition in its entirety.

The essential, and minimal, characteristics of an "efficient" system of common schools included equal opportunities for education and adequate funding and oversight.[48] The court found that the state constitution places "an absolute duty on the General Assembly to re-create, re-establish a new system of common schools in the Commonwealth"[49] and ordered the legislature to create, from scratch, a new state-wide system of education no later than the end of the next legislative term on April 15, 1990. In keeping with this mandate, the legislature, with input and pressure from citizens including Prichard Committee leaders, passed the Kentucky Education Reform Act. In the words of the then state secretary of education and humanities, this "represent[ed] the most dramatic restructuring of public education in this century" (Foster, 1999: 5). The law created standards based on accountability and established a new governance which created a shift on the local level in terms of reducing corruption and promoting merit-based school leadership.[50] The law was passed with input from Prichard Committee leaders and the allies they had developed,

[46] *Council for Better Educ. v. Wilkinson*, No. 85-CI-1759, slip op. at 4 (Franklin Cir. Ct. May 31, 1988).
[47] 790 S.W.2d at 215.
[48] 790 S.W.2d at 212–13. See also Foster (1999: 14–15).
[49] 790 S.W.2d at 215.
[50] Interview with Heine.

including the Chamber of Commerce, which supported the tax package. With polling in support for reform as strong as it was, the court's decision also acted as a form of political cover because the legislature was forced to act. No politician lost a seat because of support for the bill.

Since *Rose* and the enactment of the Kentucky Education Reform Act (KERA), by many measures, Kentucky schools have steadily improved, and Kentucky's unusual success – it is far from a wealthy state – has been widely heralded. Indeed, in 1998, the Ford Foundation and Harvard University awarded Kentucky's education system the *Innovations in American Government* Award.

This success was due in significant part to Kentucky's vibrant education movement led by the Prichard Committee. It succeeded not only in catalyzing the litigation through roughly ten years of organizing prior to the decision, but also sustained work to enforce the judgment and implement the legislation through a variety of means. This included recruiting regional coordinators to work across the state and the development community education committees in each of Kentucky's to encourage the implementation of KERA (Sexton, 2004: 84).

The committee additionally made itself available for the media, provided a "research bureau" that helped reporters find data for articles and suggest ideas for stories, and published guidebooks for reporters to explain the law (ibid.: 85). In 1991, the committee helped create the Partnership for Kentucky School reform, which was a project of a nationwide organization of chief executive officers (ibid.: 93–94). The Partnership launched a $1.5 million advertising campaign aiming to explain the changes to the public, and the committee set up a toll-free number to answer the public's questions about the change (ibid.: 85).

They additionally created Parents and Teachers Talking Together, which facilitated discussion between teachers and parents, and served as an opportunity to train hundreds of volunteers to be skilled facilitators (ibid.: 88). In addition, the committee formed the Commonwealth Institute for Parent Leadership to pull together parent mobilizing activities. The institute trained hundreds of parents each year, and graduates became local volunteers, many being elected to positions on school councils and school boards (ibid.: 106–107).

In interviews with activists involved in this effort, several factors were named as relevant to its success. First, the effort was perceived as a unified one. Public discourse was focused on improving the outcomes of all the children in the state. Second, there was a combination of well-respected leaders and skilled organizers who decided they wanted to tackle the problem with the growing body of parent leaders trained through Pritchard. Third, the movement was connected to and committed to open engagement with the media, which developed credibility and built public awareness. Fourth, a wide array of stakeholders was recruited to support the effort – including the business community, which committed significant resources, including to far-reaching advertising campaigns. Finally, the group was committed to rigorous research and consensus built solutions to the education problems they saw in the state. Those interviewed described it as a perfect storm of opportunity to improve education in the state.

The Prichard Committee is still a hub of organizing and advocacy today, thirty years after it formed, and boasts of a center for parent leadership with a self-described "trained army" of 1,500 parent leaders ready to advocate for their schools.[51]

Because Kentucky is a state with a small and more racially homogenous population than many other US states, and with less diversity in wealth,[52] scaling up such an effort elsewhere in more complex social and political environments would involve different and potentially more difficult challenges. As noted by one attorney involved in the Kentucky education litigation, Kentucky's wealthiest districts are among New Jersey's poorest, with 60 percent of children receiving free and reduced rate lunches, rendering the message that these children belong to all of us and all deserve better more perspective.[53] Yet the Kentucky experience still offers insight into what social processes affect enforcement of legal victories on the right to education and deserves ongoing study from a social movement perspective. At the same time, although Kentucky has made significant improvement, it still lags behind States in wealthier regions of the country. The citizen organizing in Kentucky appears to have fundamentally changed the "parameters of the possible" within that state. The question remains, however, whether national disparities require a broader, national solution or instead pervasive local adoption of similar, if locally sensitive, strategies.

---

[51] See www.kde.state.ky.us/KDE/Instructional+Resources/Student+and+Family+Support/ Parents+and+Families/ParentInfo+Archive/20111201ParentInfo.htm; see also www .prichardcommittee.org.

[52] Interview with Weston.

[53] Ibid.

8.4.4   *New Jersey*

In 1973, the New Jersey Supreme Court declared, in *Robinson v. Cahill*,[54] that New Jersey's school funding statute was unconstitutional because it violated the "thorough and efficient education" requirement of the state constitution. The state was slow to implement reforms in the early cases, leading to over a dozen court opinions. The most renowned case in New Jersey is *Abbott v. Burke*. Filed in 1981 representing children from public schools in four cities in New Jersey, *Abbot* challenged the state's education financing scheme as unconstitutional on the grounds that it created unacceptable disparities between wealthy suburbs and poor urban centers, the latter of which could not meet the needs of its students.

In 1985, the New Jersey Supreme Court recognizing the complexity of the case remanded it for specialized administrative review.[55] In 1990, once the facts had been adjudicated the court made an observation similar to its sister court in New York noting that "the poorer the district and the greater its need, the less the money available, and the worse the education."[56] While the court refused to find the entire state-wide financing system unconstitutional (although it left that as an open question which it felt had not been adequately adjudicated), it did uphold the administrative law judge's findings that the Abbot districts (twenty-eight at the time) failed to meet their obligation to provide a "thorough and efficient education."[57]

The court discussed the sheer impossibility of poor districts equalizing funding with the wealthier districts and also noted that given higher needs equalization might not even be the right goal, as higher need students may need greater resources. Consequently, the court ordered the Legislature assure funding for the Abbot districts "substantially equivalent" to the wealthier surrounding districts, and also to ensure adequate supplemental programs targeted to address the extreme disadvantages faced by the urban poor.[58]

Subsequently, New Jersey enacted the Quality Education Act (QEA), representing only a modest increase in funding and nothing resembling parity. Once again, the Abbot plaintiffs litigated the issue now under the 1990 decree, and subsequent to the directive from the New Jersey Supreme

[54] 303 A.2d 273.
[55] 100 N.J. 269 (1985).
[56] 119 N.J. 287 (1990).
[57] Ibid.
[58] Ibid.

Court, the trial court took up the task of developing a full factual record. The trial court concluded that the QEA was unconstitutional in relation to the Abbot districts under the 1990 decree.

In 1994, the New Jersey Supreme Court agreed with the trial court and once again ordered the legislature to create a substantial equivalency and adequate supplemental programs.[59] The second school funding law catalyzed by the Abbot litigation was the Comprehensive Education Improvement and Financing Act or "CEIFA." The New Jersey Supreme Court addressed the question once again in 1997. While deferring to the state's judgment on the question of CEIFA's overall reasonableness, the court found that the state had not considered the special needs and disadvantages of the urban poor living in Abbot districts and thus found CEIFA inadequate to meet constitutional requirements in those specific areas.[60] The court ordered interim relief reaffirming its order to create substantial equivalencies and supplemental programs until those needs could be better assessed.[61]

In addition, at this point, the court took a more directive role and ordered parity in funding leading to an immediate increase in aid of $246 million. Shifting the burden now to the state, this order was to remain in effect until the state could "convincingly demonstrate" that poor urban school children could be afforded an adequate education with less than parity funding.[62] On remand, the trial court was ordered to develop an evidentiary record on the need for supplemental program and for capital improvements in facilities.

Apparently frustrated with the lack of state response, from this point on, the court took a far more active role, ordering specific programs (including early education) and expenditures on school infrastructure.[63] The court also created a process for the individual districts to seek additional funds if they needed greater support.[64] This level of court intervention had been unprecedented in the school finance cases but clearly addressed a number of compelling and unquestionable needs. Moreover, none of the school finance cases addressed the need for targeting those most disadvantaged with additional supports quite in the way that the Abbot decisions did so very directly.

[59] 136 N.J. 444 (1994).
[60] 149 N.J. 145 (1997).
[61] Ibid.
[62] Ibid.
[63] 153 N.J. 480 (1998).
[64] Ibid.

Still, even with the level of specificity and involvement by the court, enforcement proved complicated. Over the next decade the parties returned to the court repeatedly to resolve disputes and disagreements. Some of the interventions involved particular parts of the remedy – such as whether the state was affording the Abbot districts all the components of a quality pre-school program.[65] Similar interventions took place regarding school construction, budget limitations when the state faced fiscal constraints, and how the mediation was undertaken. This can be viewed both as a success and failure from an implementation perspective. On the one hand, the court has been dogged and committed to seeing its rulings applied, on the other it is a cumbersome and adversarial route toward institutional reform.

Perhaps seeking to escape from the court's intense level of involvement, in 2008, the legislature made another attempt to comply with *Abbot* with a new School Funding Reform Act (SFRA). Upon SFRA's enactment, the state sought a finding from the court that SFRA met all constitutional requirements and that previous Abbot rulings regarding implementation were "no longer necessary." After a remand and development of the factual record, the court declared SFRA constitutional for all districts but nonetheless ordered that the new formula be fully funded for three years and thoroughly reviewed by the state to determine whether it was meeting constitutional standards or needed adjustments.[66] With these conditions, the court lifted the requirements of parity and supplemental funding for the Abbot districts.

In 2010, the state reneged on its commitments and cut approximately 14 percent of state aid from the SFRA formula. Once again the court was asked to intervene. On remand, the trail court found that the SFRA formula was underfunding the schools by 19 percent and did not support the needed programs to meet state academic standards. In 2011, the Supreme Court found the cuts to create "instructionally consequential and significant" harm to at risk children and described it as a "real substantial and consequential blow" to the right to education. Once again, the court ordered the legislature to fully fund the formula for 2012 in thirty-one high-need urban areas. More than twenty years from the original filing of the case the enforcement efforts continue.

These vigorous enforcement efforts have not cured all educational deficiencies in Abbot districts. Nonetheless, gaps in achievements have

[65] 163 N.J. 95 (2000).
[66] 199 N.J. 140; 971 A.2d 989 (2009).

narrowed. From 1999 to 2007, math test scores in Abbot and non-Abbot districts narrowed from 31 points to 19 points, as an example.[67] As students got older the impact on the achievement gap becomes increasingly modest (e.g., the achievement gap has not narrowed in high schools), but New Jersey has the highest high school graduation rates for African American males in the country – a group that disproportionately suffers from school push-out.[68] Without question, however, the opportunity gap between poor students and those who are middle class or wealthy (in New Jersey as well as across the country) remains stark and raises serious moral questions about equity and equality in US society.

While presenting a different landscape than Kentucky, New Jersey also represented a vigorous civil society effort to obtain equity in education. The Education Law Center (ELC) has been the litigation arm of civil society in New Jersey for over three decades and is a constant presence ready and willing to go back to court as often as needed to ensure implementation. But that organization is not alone. For example, groups such as the Paterson Education Fund (PEF), the Abbott Leadership Institute (ALI), the statewide Education Organizing Committee (SEOC), with chapters in Newark (One Newark Educational Coalition), and Jersey City (Jersey City Educational Organizing Committee) all work together to support education organizing campaigns in the state. Together, along with ELC, they form the New Jersey Education Organizing Collaborative (NJEOC). The NJEOC supports grassroots efforts for the mandated reforms laid out in the *Abbott* Supreme Court Cases and increase parental and community involvement in educational policy discussions. These organizing and community efforts played a central role in maintaining support for *Abbot* implementation. Paul Tractenbreg, one of the principal Abbot litigators, noted in an e-mail interview:

> Although it's true that there was little organized community participation in the early years, especially the *Robinson v. Cahill* period of 1970–77, Abbott was somewhat different even in its early years and is considerably different now. Five or six years ago, Junius Williams, a long-time community advocate and trustee of the Education Law Center, launched the Abbott Leadership Institute. ALI's program is designed to educate and mobilize the community to support Abbott's implementation, and it has done so with considerable success, including with regard to mobilizing

---

[67] Published in Policy (2009), "New Jersey's Decades-Long School Finance Case: So, What's the Payoff?" Teachers College Columbia University, 19 November, available at www.tc.edu/news.htm?articleID=7240.

[68] Ibid.

young people. More recently, but at least several years ago, the Education Law Center spearheaded the creation of Our Children/Our Schools [NJEOC], a coalition of many community, civic and advocacy organizations. There is a monthly meeting with a lengthy, substantive agenda and lively discussion leading to action commitments. Still, I think it's clear that we need to broaden and deepen community and stakeholder engagement. If our governor has his way ... he may succeed in reshaping the NJ Supreme Court to the point where it is no longer available to provide meaningful constitutional guidance and enforcement of constitutional rights of poor children.

Of special note is the ALI if only because it tracks the Kentucky model of building parent leaders. While having reached fewer parents than Pritchard (about 500), it is still widely perceived as one of the most effective structures in the state for accountability to the constitutional rulings issued by the Supreme Court.

8.5   The Role of Social Movements in Realizing Legal Victories

The cases imply that social movement activity plays a significant, if not dispositive, role in determining the impact of litigation and judgments. Education efforts in Texas, despite initial gains, have fared considerably worse than those in Kentucky, New Jersey and New York, where advocates have devoted more time and resources to mobilization. Kentucky and New Jersey have had the deepest impact.

Thus, it appears that the level and form of social movement engagement largely defined what was possible to accomplish with the courts. Or perhaps, more accurately presented, social movement activity largely influenced the educational outcome, with a part of that activity being litigation. At the same time, particular social and political circumstances were important components to defining what social movement efforts accomplished, and what movement actors sought to accomplish. Advocates in Kentucky strongly felt that the right social and political circumstances were as important as the impressive work they generated, while advocates in New York were in effect slammed with a perfect storm whereby their incredible victory dissipated in the face of the economic crisis. This is in keeping with considerable scholarship regarding the comparatively more politically sensitive nature of the American judicial system (see, e.g., Kagan, 2003). It is also in keeping with more historical examples involving the common schools and civil rights movement. In both of those cases the law followed the growth and acceptance of a powerful social movement.

There is significant legal academic literature in the United States on the role of civil society in evolving constitutional norms, particularly at the national level. Within the legal academy, most of this scholarship focuses on the impact of developing social norms and social movements upon judicial decision-making and constitutional doctrines (Eskridge, 2002; see also, e.g., Balkin, 2005; Goluboff, 2005; Post & Seigel, 2003, Seigel, 2004: 1474–1475; 2006, 2008, 2009). This scholarship highlights the importance of social movements to legal changes, emphasizing the notion of changing constitutional cultures as well as the insight that courts are in general better at responding to social changes rather than tackling the need to create change (Balkin, 2004: 1546). The case studies in this article might be read to lend further support to these theories, although that is not our central aim. In addition, social scientists, including most notably Gerald Rosenberg, have questioned the US Supreme Court's ability (or the ability of social movements by way of litigation) to affect broad or significant social changes, due to constraints such as the limitations of which rights are constitutionally recognized, the court's lack of adequate independence from the other branches of the federal government, and the court's lack of sufficient institutional tools and enforcement powers (namely, that it does not enact legislation, craft budgets, or run governmental agencies) (Rosenberg, 2008). Rosenberg concludes that US courts "can almost never be effective producers of significant social reform" (ibid.: 422) and that court decisions are neither necessary nor sufficient for significant reform.

The case studies mentioned support Rosenberg's finding that the efforts of US courts are constrained (indeed by more factors than he enumerates) and that non-judicial activity is critical to social change on economic and social rights in the United States. However, as Rosenberg's critics have (see, e.g., McCann, 1992: 722–730, 735–737; 1994), we question the extreme conclusion that judicial decisions are as a general matter at best useless or, worse, a distraction for social movement actors – largely because of the difficulty, if not impossibility, of fully disentangling the impact of litigation from other efforts and causes of social change. Rather, we seek to raise questions about the multivalent interplay between movement activity and US courts in promoting social change. Judicial decisions are clearly not made in a social vacuum, and we should consider the variety of factors that influence (both limit and facilitate) the ability of social movement actors to promote, and as a threshold matter seek, recognition of rights that are meaningful and enforced.

From these case studies it appears that there are both key internal and external parameters of the possible, i.e. factors that limit or facilitate rights enforcement. Among internal parameters are social movement infrastructure including robust networks, committees, leadership development and recruitment of skilled and respected members of society, strategy, resources, tactics, rights consciousness and understanding of the social problem, as well as relationship to the media. In this regard, sustained and credible leadership both at the grassroots and higher level appears to be among the most critical of factors, and building both broad and deep leadership among constituents was the one factor both New Jersey and Kentucky had in common. At the same time, those internal parameters are at once constrained and facilitated by external parameters, including the existing social, political, and economic conditions and infrastructure. Key external factors include media structure and response, public receptivity and preexisting understandings of the issue and relevant relationships, ex ante institutional arrangements, the political and economic landscape, and demographic conditions.

In Kentucky, the judicial decision created political space, and political cover, for legislative leaders to more broadly reform the educational system, drew additional support for social movement actors in their call for educational reform, and affected the public discourse on the right to education (through media coverage, town hall events, and corporate sponsored advertisements), supporting the view that judicial decisions, if not sufficient to effectuate social change, may act as one of many elements in evolving norms and rights enforcement. At the same time, the studies support the conclusion that public support and interest, including by many social movement leaders, waned in each state studied after sufficient time following the court decision, if not Rosenberg's stronger thesis that elite support is causally dampened by judicial recognition itself. That is to say, our review demonstrates that the factors supporting enforcement of the right to education, including institutional reorganization, can capture public and social movement actor attention only during a certain window in which a number of internal and external parameters align. In addition, as reflected in the case studies, it is noteworthy that New Jersey, a Northern State with a progressive constitution, a racialized discourse around education and educational system failings that broadly tracked racial and economic divides, and a targeted remedy affecting the most needy children and a Southern State with weak constitutional language, as well as a more racially and economically homogenous populous and a more universal remedy are the two examples in the country with the most in common in terms of sustainable impact on educational outcomes. These differences highlight the complex and multivalent dynamic of internal and external parameters in particular contexts.

Conversely, we might ask why education became the exception as an embraced social right in the United States and why similar movements have not developed around and court decisions have not recognized other economic or social rights. In the first instant, which rights are included both in the federal and state constitutions poses a large constraint upon at least judicial recognition of other economic or social rights. This constraint is further entrenched as far as national social movements and social change are concerned by the unusually difficult manner in which the US Constitution may be amended – either by a vote of two-thirds of both houses of Congress followed by a ratification of three-fourths of all state legislatures or by a constitutional convention called by two-thirds of state legislatures and any amendment ratified by three-fourths of the state legislatures. Political realities render any such amendment likely infeasible for the foreseeable future. This strong constraint explains in part the exceptionalism of the right to education in the United States as well as mobilization around and efforts to enact broad reaching of national legislation on other social and economic rights, most notably the recent passage of the national health care bill. The movement for LGBT equality and marriage rights poses one of the few other exceptions, as that movement has garnered some success in achieving state and federal judicial recognition. In keeping with the educational case studies mentioned, the national LGBT movement built public support for many years prior to the recent judicial successes, garnered skilled, credible, and well-known leaders, and formed and utilized strong ties with the media and corporate actors to promote debate on and change public opinion of LGBT rights, particularly regarding same-sex marriage. However, one parameter that facilitates the success of the movement for same-sex marriage which renders it different from most other struggles for social and economic rights, including education, is that it does not seek to broadly reorganize institutional and economic relations, for example, as school reform and the civil rights movement did and do. Thus, other movements, and their successes and the constraints hemming them in, reinforce the conclusion that a multitude of parameters interact to define the space of possible social change.

In the present moment, the political discourse with regard to the value of economic equality is changing significantly. As the work of sustaining and ensuring enforcement on school finance issues continues at the very minimum, this change in national discourse may add fuel to these efforts. Indeed, it is increasingly not only acceptable but also politically beneficial to discuss economic inequality expressly. Consequently, school finance issues can potentially be engaged within a broader social and political conversation which reinforces the need to successfully restructure how we resource schools – not only within states but between states as well.

Finally, it is important to remember that social movements may also lose battles while still winning the war over the long term. The Texas case study might easily be assessed as a failure within a narrower time window – as might the abolition of the position of state school superintendent in Connecticut in the early 1900s. Likewise, civil rights era initiatives might be understood as a relative failure given the *de facto* resegregation over time and the brutal economic inequalities. Yet, measured over a larger arc of time these may contribute to social trends, norms, and changes toward justice. They lay a foundation for a new structure in education by challenging existing ones, creating political discourse, even demonstrating the cost of failure compared to the benefits of success elsewhere. We believe that while strong social movements are the best route toward vigorous and sustainable enforcement, attempts at enforcement, even those that have failed or been reversed, may also fuel social movements over the long term. These should not be seen as parallel and unrelated universes. Rather, we should ensure that we reflect and act on the potentially synergistic relationship between the two, and avoid strategies that drain social movement energy by relying entirely on litigation strategies without building the long-term capacity of the movements we need.

8.6   Conclusion

The question of how social movement and other civil society activity relate to the successful enforcement of economic and social rights judgment in the United States requires deeper analysis and study than this chapter is able to provide to reach more determinative conclusions. Nonetheless, based on initial consideration of the question, civil society and social movement efforts, which can generate or capitalize on social conditions to improve enforcement outcomes, appear necessary if not sufficient to ensure vigorous enforcement by American courts and other branches of government. Litigation efforts that are not part of – and preceded by – a deeper or broader social effort suffer from lack of support over time, and gains are at greater risk of being reversed and/or not enforced. Simultaneously, while courts have a limited ability to tackle structural change, which the boldest movements seek this as their goal, as Kentucky demonstrates, US courts may play a part in efforts to restructure toward rights, justice, and equity across society, in particular in creating political space and contributing to "moving the needle" of public discourse within the parameters afforded to them by their social context.

As is the case with education reform, even the most sustainable gains by local civil society efforts may be limited by broader structures that are national and global. For instance, greater educational disparities exist between US states than within them. Effective national or global movements may thus be necessary to fully realize certain social and economic rights in the United States. The question then remains, what parameters of the possible must exist in a given historical moment to permit national change, and are those parameters less likely to align, or more difficult to facilitate or predict, than the necessary parameters for sustainable local changes. Regardless, sustained local participation from empowered communities and skilled and well-respected leaders appears to be a necessary component of successful and sustainable realization of social and economic rights in the United States.

References

Ackerman, Bruce (1998), *We the People: Transformations* (Cambridge, MA: Harvard University Press).

Ackerman, Bruce and Jennifer Nou (2009), "Canonizing the Civil Rights Revolution: The People and the Poll Tax," *Nw. U. L. Rev.*, 103(1), 68–148.

Adams, Jacob E. Jr. (1993), "School Finance Reform and Systemic School Change: Reconstituting Kentucky's Public Schools," *J. Edu. Finance*, 18(4), 318–345.

Albisa, Cathy and Jessica Schultz (2009), "The United States: A Ragged Patchwork," in Malcolm Langford (ed.), *Social Rights Jurisprudence; Emerging Trends in International and Comparative Law* (Cambridge: Cambridge University Press), 230–249.

Anderson, Carol (2003), *Eyes off the Prize: The United Nations and the African American Struggle for Human Rights 1944–1955* (Cambridge: Cambridge University Press).

Balkin, Jack. M. (2004), "What Brown Teaches Us about Constitutional Theory," *Va. L. Rev.*, 90(6), 1537–1577.

(2005), "How Social Movements Change (or Fail To Change) the Constitution: The Case of the New Departure," *Suffolk L. Rev.*, 39(27), 27–65.

Banks, Jonathan (1992), "Note, State Constitutional Analyses of Public School Finance Reform Cases: Myth or Methodology?," *Vand. L. Rev.*, 45, 129–160.

Eskridge, William, Jr. (2002), "Some Effects of Identity-Based Movements on Constitutional Law in the Twentieth Century," *Mich. L. Rev.*, 100(8), 2062–2184.

Eskridge, William, Jr. and John Ferejohn (2001), "Super Statutes," *Duke L. J.*, 53, 1215–1276.

(2010), *A Republic of Statutes: The New American Constitution* (New Haven: Yale University Press).

Forbath, William (2009), "Social and Economic Rights in the American Grain: Reclaiming Constitutional Political Economy," in Jack Balkin and Reva Sieget (eds.), *The Constitution in 2020* (Oxford: Oxford University Press), 55–68.

Foster, Jack (1999), *Redesigning Public Education: The Kentucky Experience* (Lexington, KY: Diversity Enterprises Inc.).

Goluboff, Risa, "'Let Economic Equality Take Care of Itself': The NAACP, Labor Litigation, and the Making of Civil Rights in the 1940s," *UCLA L. Rev.* 52, 1393–1486 (2005).

Gittell, Marilyn (ed.) (1998), *Strategies for School Equity: Creating Productive Schools in a Just Society* (New Haven: Yale University Press).

Henkin, Louis (1995), "U.S. Ratification of Human Rights Conventions: The Ghost of Senator Bricker," *Am J. Int'l L.*, 89(2), 341–350.

Imazeki, Jennifer and Andrew Reschovsky (2003), "School Finance Reform in Texas: A Never Ending Story?," www.rohan.sdsu.edu/~jimazeki/papers/TXSchlFin0503.pdf.

Kaestle, Carl F. (2007), "Victory of the Common School Movement: A Turning Point in American Educational History," in US Department of State, *Historians on America* (US Department of State, Bureau of International Information Programs) www.america.gov/st/educ-english/2008/April/20080423212501eaifas0.8516133.html.

Kagan, Robert A. (2003), *Adversarial Legalism: The American Way of Law* (Cambridge, MA: Harvard University Press).

King, Jeff A. (2014), "Two Ironies about American Exceptionalism over Social Rights," *ICON*, 12(3), 572–602.

Kramer, Liz (2002), "Achieving Equitable Education Through the Courts: A Comparative Analysis of Three States," *J. L. & Educ.*, 31(1), 1–51.

McCann, Michael W. (1992), "Reform Litigation on Trial," *Law & Social Inquiry*, 17(4), 715–743.

(1994), *Rights at Work: Pay Equity Reform and the Politics of Legal Mobilization* (Chicago: University of Chicago Press).

Miller, Matt (2008), "Nationalize the Schools (… A Little)!" Centre for American Progress, March.

Post, Robert & Reva Siegel, "Legislative Constitutionalism and Section Five Power: Policentric Interpretation of the Family and Medical Leave Act," *Yale L. J.* 112(8), 1943–2059.

Roosevelt, Franklin D. (1834), "Message to Congress Reviewing the Broad Objectives and Accomplishments of the Administration," Speech, Washington, June 8.

(1944), "State of the Union Message to Congress," Speech, Washington, DC, January 11.

Rosenberg, Gerald N. (2008), *Hollow Hope: Can Courts Bring About Social Change?* (Chicago: University of Chicago Press).

Rothstein, Richard (2000), "Equalizing Education Resources on Behalf of Disadvantaged Children," in Richard Kahlenberg (ed.), *A Nation at Risk: Preserving Public Education as an Engine for Social Mobility* (New York: Century Foundation), 31–92.

Sexton, Robert (2004), *Mobilizing Citizens for Better Schools* (New York: Teachers of College Press).

Siegel, Reva (2004), "Equality Talk: Antisubordination and Anticlassification Values in Constitutional Struggles over Brown," *Harv. L. Rev.*, 117(5), 1470–1547.

(2006), "Constitutional Culture, Social Movement Conflict, and Constitutional Change: The Case of the de facto ERA," *Cal. L. Rev.*, 94(5), 1323–1420.

(2008), "Dead or Alive: Originalism as Popular Constitutionalism in Heller," *Harv. L. Rev.*, 122(1), 191–245.

(2009), "Heller & Originalism's Dead Hand – In Theory and Practice," *UCLA L. Rev.*, 56, No., pp. 1399–1424.

Sunstein, Cass R. (2004), *The Second Bill of Rights: FDR's Unfinished Revolution and Why We Need It More Than Ever* (New York: Basic Books).

Sunstein, Cass R. and Randy E Barnett (2004), "Constitutive Commitments and Roosevelt's Second Bill of Rights: A Dialogue," *Drake L. Rev.*, 53, 205–229.

Taylor, Orville (1836), "Common School Assistant: A Monthly Paper for the Improvement of Common School Education," *Albany*, Vol. 1 (January), *-*.

Trachtenberg, Paul L. (undated), "Education Provisions in State Constitutions: A Summary of a Chapter for the State Constitutions for the Twenty-First Century Project," http://camlaw.rutgers.edu/statecon/subpapers/tractenberg.pdf.

Whelan, Daniel. J (2005), "The United States and Economic and Social Rights: Past, Present … and Future?" Human Rights and Human Welfare Working Paper No. 26, presented at the 2005 International Studies Association Convention, Honolulu, Hawaii, March 5.

India: Compliance with Orders on the Right to Food

POORVI CHITALKAR AND VARUN GAURI

9.1 Introduction

In recent years, there has been a surge in the legalisation of socio-economic rights, in the context of what is often described as a 'rights revolution' from judiciaries (Epp, 1998). During and since the third wave of democratisation around the world, more and more substantive rights have been enshrined in constitutions. Courts around the world have issued far-reaching decisions involving social and economic rights and, in doing so, have at times changed the landscape of policy (Gauri and Brinks, 2008a).

The Indian judiciary is no exception. Since the 1980s it has significantly expanded the ambit of socio-economic rights. The Indian constitution enumerates a number of civil and political rights as justiciable 'fundamental rights' whilst also listing key social-economic priorities as non-justiciable principles to be the goals and duties of the state. These 'Directive Principles of State Policy' were intended to guide legislative and executive action, but they were left non-justiciable so as to give a newly independent state the leeway to balance various priorities according to its economic capacity (Austin, 1966).

In a series of key decisions, Indian courts have transformed these once non-justiciable social and economic rights, such as rights to basic education, health, food and clean environment, into legally enforceable rights. They have done so primarily through the use of Public Interest Litigation (PIL) – a judicial innovation that has allowed citizens to access

Poorvi Chitalkar is Senior Program Officer at the Global Centre for Pluralism. The contents of this paper are the responsibility of the author and do not necessarily reflect the views of the Global Centre for Pluralism.

Varun Gauri is a Senior Economist at The World Bank. Note that the views and findings expressed in this chapter do not necessarily represent the views of the World Bank or its Executive Directors.

courts in a simpler and relatively inexpensive way. Mainly through PIL, Indian courts have adopted an expansive interpretation of the 'right to life', incorporating within its ambit several due process protections for civil and political rights, as well as positive obligations towards social and economic rights.

While the extent of judicial activism of Indian courts has been debated and the practice of PIL extensively studied, the focus of the literature in both spheres has targeted the legitimacy of courts' actions. More recently, there has been some valuable analysis of the effect on judicial decisions on education and health policy (Shankar and Mehta, 2010) as well as enquiries into the beneficiaries of socio-economic rights litigation (Brinks and Gauri, 2014; Gauri, 2011; Rajagopal, 2007). In short, there is as yet relatively little systematic enquiry into the effectiveness of Indian courts' interventions on social and economic rights. To what extent are decisions on social and economic rights implemented? What explains the level of compliance with a decision? Are there particular factors or strategies that facilitate greater enforcement?

This chapter attempts to make a contribution to the literature by focusing on the question of enforcement of Indian courts' decisions on the right to food. Section 9.2 sets the stage with an overview of the challenge of food security in India, highlighting the urgent context in which the courts' interventions took place. Section 9.3 describes the engagement of courts with the right to food. We begin with an overview of Indian public interest litigation on social and economic rights. We then trace early interventions by courts to address food security claims. The most significant decision by the Supreme Court on the right to food has been the *People's Union for Civil Liberties v. Union of India* (the 'right to food' case), which is discussed in greater detail. Section 9.4 discusses the experience with enforcement. Section 9.5 explores the factors that influenced the enforcement of the Supreme Court's decision in that right to food case.

We find that the right to food case represents a turning point on the issue of food security in India. We argue that a combination of factors on the supply and demand side intersected to enable this. On the supply side, the court's approach in this case was starkly different from earlier cases. It adopted a robust approach to compliance monitoring by appointing commissioners to oversee the implementation of its orders, make enquiries, report back in cases of non-compliance, and make recommendations to the court. Further, the court found a significant ally within civil society, which contributed to the legitimacy of the court's actions and, ultimately, to the enforcement of its decisions. In particular, the interlinkage between the litigation, the civil-society-driven 'right to food campaign' and the commissioners appointed by court contributed in great measure to the success of the right to food case. On the demand side, the external environment surrounding the right to food case was a favourable one. The issue of food security received a much greater degree of attention in public opinion and media. This may, at least in part, be a result of the court's dynamism, but also reflected shifting public attitudes and values. The greater visibility of the issue and of the court's decisions likely made non-compliance more difficult. Finally, the prevailing political and economic environment in India also facilitated enforcement of the decisions.

9.2   Hunger and Malnutrition in India

India has witnessed a period of considerable economic growth over the last two decades. Gross National Income per capita (PPP) grew more than tenfold between 1993 and 2012.[1] Domestic food production has also increased 106 per cent between 1951 and 2000 (Caplin, 2008). Despite this, India is one of the most malnourished countries in the world, and the state of food and nutritional security can be described only as a catastrophic failure (Dreze, 2004).

Forty-four per cent of children under the age of five – which is more compared to any other country in the world – are underweight (Caplin, 2008). In 2014, India ranked fifty-fifth of seventy-six in the International Food Policy Research Institute's Global Hunger Index, which combines three equally weighted indicators – undernourishment, children underweight and child mortality. There was a marked improvement in India's performance on this index between 1990 and 1996, when its score fell from 30.3 to 22.6 (a score over 10 is considered 'serious', over 20 'alarming' and over 30 'extremely alarming'). However, progress has since stagnated, and despite a small increase in 2001, the score has now nearly returned to 1996 levels.[2] It may be the case that the poor state of sanitation in India is partly responsible for malnutrition levels.[3]

Paradoxically, India is experiencing hunger amidst plenty. Since the 1970s, the Food Corporation of India (a statutory corporation established by the government of India in 1964 and responsible for procurement and

---

[1] *World Development Indicator* 2013 (2013). Available at http://data.worldbank.org/country/india. India's GNI per capita based on purchasing power parity was 330 in 1993, 1830 in 2003 and stood at 3840 in 2012.
[2] See www.ifpri.org/sites/default/files/publications/ghi12.pdf.
[3] Spears (2012).

storage of food grains in India) has been maintaining buffer stocks of food. While it is required to keep 32 million metric tonnes of rice and wheat as buffer, recent estimates suggest that it has more than 80 million metric tonnes of stockpiles.[4]

The main reason why large stockpiles rot in government warehouses or otherwise fail to reach the poor is because of India's massive but flawed public distribution system (PDS). Since the 1950s, the Indian government has followed an elaborate system whereby it procures food from farmers and provides it to those identified as poor at subsidised rates through a network of state-licensed shops. The central and state governments in India manage PDS jointly. While the centre is responsible for procurement, storage, transportation and allocation, the states are responsible for distribution through fair price shops, identification of families below the poverty line (BPL), supervision and monitoring (Kattumuri, 2011). As a result, there exists substantial difference in the performance of PDS systems between various states.

The PDS was created with three main objectives: to ensure minimum support to farmers to support their livelihoods; to control market price through stocking and controlled release; and to make grain accessible to the poor through subsidised sales in fair price shops (see generally Nayak, 2007). With a network of more than 46.2 million fair price shops, the PDS is the largest distribution network of its kind in the world.

The PDS, however, has suffered from maladministration. In North India, about half of the grain for distribution, which the PDS is meant to distribute to poor households, ends up on the black market. In states such as Bihar and Jharkhand, the number is as high as 80 per cent (Dreze, 2004). In 1997, the government replaced the PDS with a targeted PDS, under which grains were offered at low prices to households whose income and assets were below specified threshold, i.e. BPL. The pitfalls of BPL targeting have also contributed to the inefficiencies of the PDS, as it excludes a large chunk of India's poor due to a low threshold for qualification, coupled with the difficulty of identification. Targeting is also divisive between the 'Above Poverty Line' and BPL groups, thus making what might be a deliberatively identified right into a divisive privilege (Dreze and Sen, 2011).

The failures of the PDS, combined with clientelist governments, pervasive inequities and historically apathetic public opinion, have contributed to starvation and malnourishment. Persistent hunger and starvation

---

[4] Available from: http://fciweb.nic.in.

amidst a situation of plenty suggests that at the root of chronic food insecurity in India is a problem of governance.

9.3   The Indian Judiciary and the Right to Food

Since the 1980s, India's courts have turned social and economic rights, which were constitutionally framed as non-justiciable principles of governance, into legally enforceable rights. This section explores the courts' intervention in defining and enforcing the right to food in particular. We explore early cases (1980s) that constitute attempts by the judiciary to carve out space for a legally enforceable right to food. The impact of these cases was limited. We then explore the turning point for right to food litigation, as well as the right to food movement generally – the PUCL case. However, before discussing these cases, we briefly explain the tool used by the court to entertain socio-economic rights claims, i.e. public interest litigation.

9.3.1   Public Interest Litigation

Soon after India's independence in 1947, a tussle between the executive and judiciary began (Dua, 1983). Early battles involved socialist policies of the Congress government aimed at land reform, equitable redistribution of land holdings and land acquisition for public purposes. The scope of the courts' powers of judicial review was also hotly contested. The Supreme Court finally established its supremacy by holding that the Indian parliament could not alter the basic structure of the Constitution (what constituted basic structure was to be decided by the court).

However, the darkest hour of India's democracy came with the declaration of a national emergency by Indira Gandhi on 26 June 1975. Fundamental rights, including the right to personal liberty, the right to protection in cases of preventive detention and the right to move the courts for enforcement of fundamental rights, were suspended. In extreme deference to the government, the Supreme Court, which had so far strongly struck down arbitrary exercise of executive action, upheld the suspension of fundamental rights by a majority of 4:1 in the landmark case *A.D.M. Jabalpur v. Shivakant Shukla*.[5]

In the post-emergency period, perhaps in an attempt to regain its lost legitimacy, the court became much more accessible, and its doctrinal law

[5]   AIR 1976 S.C. 1207.

more individual-oriented. For this, the court adopted two strategies: First, it re-interpreted the provisions for fundamental rights in a more expansive manner in order to maximise the rights of people, particularly the disadvantaged. Second, it facilitated access to the courts by relaxing the procedural rules of standing, and often acting *suo motu* (Sathe, 2001).

In a number of public interest litigation cases, the courts (including the Supreme Court and the High Courts) expanded the scope of Article 21, the right to life and personal liberty, by holding that the right to life included the right to live with dignity. On this basis, courts subsequently held that the right to livelihood,[6] the right to clean environment[7] and the right to be free from bonded labour[8] are all 'fundamental rights' within the meaning of Article 21 of the Indian Constitution. In the cases discussed in later pages, the court added the 'right to food' to the necessary conditions for a life with dignity and went further to define, explicate and give meaning to the right to food.

Through public interest litigation, courts also adopted a broader scope of remedies. For example, they have relied on 'continuing mandamus' whereby they issue declaratory judgments and at the same time continue to give operative directions on an ongoing basis.[9] Courts have also appointed supervisory mechanisms to oversee the implementation of their orders and report back from time to time.[10] The adoption of these innovative remedies is borne out in the landmark PUCL case.

9.3.2   Early Cases – Right to Food

The first instance of the Supreme Court affirming the right to food as a fundamental right within Article 21 was in *Francis Coralie Mullin v. The Administrator*.[11] The case pertained to the rights of a detainee under preventive detention and in emphasising the fundamental rights of detainees, the court explained that the right to life must mean more than just animal existence. It held that the 'right to life includes the right to live with human

---

[6] *Olga Tellis v. Bombay Municipal Corporation*, AIR 1986 SC 180.

[7] *M.C. Mehta v. Union of India (1998, Delhi Vehicular Pollution Case)*, Supreme Court Writ Petition (Civil) No. 13029/198.

[8] *Bandhua Mukti Morcha v. Union of India*, A.I.R. (1984) SC 802 at 469.

[9] Discussed in greater detail in *Vineet Narain v. Union of India*. The Indian Supreme Court has used this approach in other PILs including, for example, *Bandhua Mukti Morcha v. Union of India* (1984) regarding bonded labour and a number of environmental cases brought by M. C. Mehta.

[10] For example, it appointed commissioners in the *Bandhua Mukti Morcha* case, ibid.

[11] (1981) 2 SCR 516 at 518.

dignity and all that goes with it, namely the bare necessities of life, such as adequate nutrition, clothing and shelter'.[12]

Despite this expansive interpretation by the court, the realisation of the right to food seemed a distant dream in much of the country. The Kalahandi region in Orissa presented itself as a glaring example of failure of drought relief over several years. Plagued by endemic poverty, Kalahandi suffered from drought-induced crises repeatedly in the 1980s. The local and national press, as well as opposition parties, frequently reported the misery that plagued the population of Kalahandi, but this had little impact on the implementation of relief, and starvation deaths continued unabated (Banik, 1998).

The issue arose prominently in 1986, when the case of *Kishen Pattnayak v. State of Orissa* came before the Supreme Court. Two social workers filed a public interest petition against the Congress government in Orissa drawing attention to the extreme poverty of the people of Kalahandi in Orissa, and the failure of the state government to meet its responsibilities specified in the Orissa Relief Code. The petition highlighted the prevailing deficiencies in the welfare safety net of the state- and district-level administrations, which were resulting in predatory money-lenders exploiting farmers and bonded-labour arrangements, amongst other problems.[13] Subsequently, a second petition was filed in 1987 by a public-action group, the Indian People's Front, stating that deaths had occurred in the Kalahandi and Koraput districts due to the callousness and negligence of the state and district administrations.[14] The Congress government, headed by J. B. Patnaik, consistently denied that any starvation deaths had taken place in the districts, and indeed pointed to massive efforts by the government to turn Kalahandi into 'one of the most prosperous districts' of Orissa (Currie, 2000: 179).

In response to the petitions, the Supreme Court appointed a commission to evaluate the condition of distressed persons in Western Orissa and to assess the validity of claims made by the government of Orissa that it was implementing social welfare schemes. The resulting report by a district judge rejected the allegations of the two petitions and ruled overwhelmingly in the government's favour. It even blamed the continuing distress in the region on the 'laziness and lack of ambition' of the poor.[15] However, there was widespread public criticism of the report; as a result,

[12] Ibid. at 529.
[13] *Kishan Pattnayak and Another v. The State of Orissa*, Writ Petition (Civil) No. 12847 of 1985.
[14] *The Indian People's Front v. State of Orissa and Others*, Writ Petition (Civil) No. 1081 of 1987.
[15] Ibid., p. 180.

the Supreme Court chose to distance itself from the findings, holding that the occurrence of starvation deaths could not be ruled out.[16] Despite this, the court failed to initiate any further action, and the case did not catalyse any policy reforms.

As concerns about the inadequacy of government's relief programmes rose, and starvation deaths continued, two further public interest litigations were brought to the Orissa High Court in 1988.[17] Similar to earlier petitions to the Supreme Court, these alleged the exploitation of *adivasis* (tribes) due to the apathy of the administrative machinery. The High Court appointed a retired district judge to conduct an inquiry, and the resulting report confirmed a number of the petitioner's allegations against the state government. Most importantly, the report confirmed that cases of deaths due to starvation, which had thus far been consistently denied by the government, had indeed taken place. On the basis of these findings, in its judgment in February 1992, the Orissa High Court held that five starvation deaths had taken place in Kalahandi and that the state government had failed to fulfil its responsibilities to protect public welfare. Accordingly, the state was ordered to pay compensation to the families of the deceased. The High Court also provided a set of recommendations designed to redress shortfalls in relief and development administration. It highlighted in particular the need for government to be more rigorous in implementing protective legislation designed to safeguard the vulnerable from exploitation, and to provide welfare support and relief during crisis.

The immediate impact of the judicial intervention was a drastic increase in the media attention on Kalahandi. Adverse publicity led the public to vote the Congress government, led by Chief Minister J. B. Patnaik, out of office in 1989 amidst allegations of starvation deaths, sale of children and large-scale government neglect. When the Orissa High Court confirmed starvation deaths in 1992, the new Janata Dal government led by Biju Patnaik blamed the previous government for its failures but ignored judicial recommendations to reformulate guidelines to improve administrative response to starvation (Currie, 2000: 212). This government was also voted out of office in 1995 amidst public concerns regarding corruption and administrative neglect. However, while the judicial decision was repeatedly used to discredit political opponents

---

[16] 1989 Supp (1) *Supreme Court Cases* 258, para 7.
[17] *Bhawani Mund v. The State of Orissa and Others* (OJC 3517/86); *Anukul Chandra Pradhan v. State of Orissa and Others* (OJC No. 525 of 1989).

and led to government change, it had little impact on improving food administration.

As the Court's decision had limited, if any, impact, dire conditions in parts of Orissa continued. Between 1997 and 2006, the National Human Rights Commission held a number of hearings on the *Orissa Starvation Case*, based on reports of several further starvation deaths in the State of Orissa, particularly in the Kalahandi, Balangir and Koraput districts.[18]

9.3.3   The PUCL Case

The People's Union of India (PUCL) Rajasthan commenced Public Interest Litigation in April 2001 before the Supreme Court, following a number of starvation deaths in the State of Rajasthan. At the time of the petition, Rajasthan had been suffering from serious drought conditions for three years. A state government estimate indicated that over 73 per cent of villages were affected by the drought and needed relief; yet close to 50 million tonnes of surplus and undistributed grain lay unused in government warehouses (Birchfield and Corsi, 2010). PUCL argued that the government had not provided the required employment and food relief mandated by the Rajasthan Famine Code, 1962. Initially brought against the government of India, the Food Corporation of India and six state governments, the litigation was later expanded by the court to apply to all state governments.

The petitioner argued that the right to food is implied by the right to life in Article 21, and that the central and state governments had violated the right by failing to respond to the drought situation, particularly by accumulating huge food stocks while people starved (Jaishankar and Dreze, 2005). As relief measures, the petition demanded, amongst other things, the immediate release of food stocks for drought relief, provision of work for every able-bodied person and an increase in the quota of food grains under the PDS (Kothari, 2004).

Since 2001, the Supreme Court's interim orders have served to define, gradually and with increasing detail, India's constitutional right to food (Birchfield and Corsi, 2010). These decisions in the PUCL case have been significant in at least three ways: they have recognised the right to food as a fundamental right within the meaning of the right to life; they have spelled

---

[18] See FAO (2011) and Writ Petition (civil) No. 42/97 filed by the Indian Council of Legal Aid and Advice.

out in detail and made enforceable the entitlements that make up the right to food; and they have created a mechanism for continuous monitoring and reporting of the implementation of the Court's decisions.

Right to Food as a Fundamental Right

By the Order of November 2001, the Court explicitly recognised a right to food enshrined in Article 21.[19] This declaration was indeed a significant step forward in the attempts to establish basic food and nutritional security as matter of right rather than welfare, or merely a moral guiding principle for governments. However, as seen earlier, the idea that a dignified life necessitated access to food was something the Supreme Court had already recognised in earlier cases, including *Francis Coralie Mullin*. Furthermore, India was not unique in this recognition – twenty-two national constitutions explicitly mention a right to food and many others provide for the same through related welfare rights (Vidar, 2006). The true value of this recognition by the court lies elsewhere.

The reason that the PUCL case was significant was that, in addition to declaring the right to food a fundamental right, the court also provided a definition of what the right entailed, who its beneficiaries ought to be, and who was responsible for its enforcement. As Birchfield and Corsi (2010: 718) note, 'what is significant about the Indian example, is that the Supreme Court has taken these general obligations and given them teeth by specifically explicating the right in concrete policy terms and by establishing oversight mechanisms for the enforcement of this specific content'.

Entitlements under the Right to Food

At the time of the PUCL petition, a number of government schemes providing subsidised food-to-poor households and groups already existed. These schemes included:

- Targeted Public Distribution System: To identify BPL households, state governments issued identification cards and were obligated to provide 25 kg of grain to every eligible family every month;

---

[19] In doing so, the Court relied not only on the expansive interpretation of article 21, but also on the harmonious interpretation of fundamental rights and Directive Principles of State Policy. The right to food is enshrined in articles 39(a) and 47 of the Indian Constitution. Article 39(a) states that the state shall strive to ensure that its citizens 'have the right to an adequate means of livelihood' and article 47 states that 'the State shall regard the raising level of nutrition ... of its people ... among its primary duties'.

- *Antyodaya Anna Yojana (AAY)*: AAY card holders (the poorest amongst the BPL category) were entitled to 35 kg of subsidised rice or wheat per month;
- Integrated Child Development Services (ICDS): Governments were to provide take-home rations or cooked meals for adolescent girls, pregnant and lactating women and children under six years of age;
- Mid-Day Meal (MDM) Scheme: Every child in a government-funded primary school was entitled to a cooked school meal.

The Supreme Court converted the benefits of these, and four other already existing schemes (*Annapurna*, National Family Benefit Scheme, National Maternity Benefit Scheme and National Old Age Pension Scheme), into legal entitlements and directed state governments to fully implement the same as per official guidelines. Therefore, it now became possible for beneficiaries to approach the court if their entitlements were not honoured (Guha-Khasnobis and Vivek, 2007). The court went further and gave detailed directions on how these entitlements were to be realised.

For example, with respect to the PDS, it ordered all states to ensure that all closed PDS shops were reopened. Licenses of fair-price shops were to be cancelled if they did not keep their shops open or engaged in black-marketeering of grains. It also ordered that poor families were to be identified immediately, BPL cards issued, and grains supplied to them. In order to address some of the challenges of identifying BPL households, the court also directed governments to frame clear guidelines for proper identification and not to remove any names from BPL lists until the court had deliberated the matter.

The court directed all states to start providing cooked meals in government and government-assisted primary schools. It specified the calorific requirements for the meals – 300 calories and 8–12 grams of protein each day. It asked governments to give preference to Dalits, Scheduled Cases and Scheduled Tribes in the appointment of cooks and helpers and, finally, required that quality safeguards be implemented.

Court-Appointed Commissioners

On 8 May 2002, the court appointed two commissioners to monitor and report on the implementation of the court's orders and suggest ways to promote food security. The commissioners are empowered to enquire into any violation of the court's orders and to demand compliance. They analyse central and state governments' data to monitor the implementation of various food and employment schemes, receive complaints of non-compliance from grassroots organisations and set up enquiry committees for verification purposes. They also work with governments to address obstacles to implementation.[20]

The commissioners are empowered to receive assistance from reliable organisations and individuals. They have appointed advisors in each state who serve as bridges between the commissioners, state governments and various citizens' groups. In addition, as discussed in greater detail in Section 9.4, commissioners have also collaborated directly with grassroots organisations to monitor compliance of decisions and identify gaps.

Overall, the scope of the right to food litigation, which began in 2001, has expanded enormously. Since 2001, there have been more than 382 affidavits filed and 55 interim applications. Although there has yet to be a final judgment on the matter, there have been 44 interim orders by the court to date. The scope of issues covered by this PIL has also expanded significantly. It now covers a wide range of issues related to right to food, including implementation of food-related schemes, urban destitution, the right to work, homelessness, starvation deaths and general issues of transparency and accountability (Jaishankar and Dreze, 2005).

9.4   Implementation of the Court's Orders

The PUCL case is widely regarded as a remarkable success story in the realm of socio-economic rights litigation in India. Reflecting on the past decade of the global right to food movement, the then Special Rapporteur on the right to food, Oliver De Schutter called it the 'most spectacular case of a court protecting the right to food'.[21] However, the available data on the level of compliance with the court's decisions is extremely thin.

A systematic evidence-based measure of compliance with the court's orders was beyond the scope of this research. However, numerous reports of the court-appointed commissioners, state advisors and a number of external reports submitted to the court on a periodic basis provide some indication of the levels of enforcement. On the basis of a review of a sample of these reports, a few key findings emerge: First, there is significant variation in the level of enforcement of the various orders of the court. For example, while commissioners routinely report high levels of enforcement of MDM schemes, pension schemes and the *Antyodaya Anna Yojana*, other programmes such as the Targeted Public Distribution Schemes

---

[20] Available at: www.sccommissioners.org.
[21] *Interim Report of the Special Rapporteur on the Right to Food to the United Nations General Assembly*, A/68/288 (2013, August 7), para. 23.

and the Maternity Benefit Schemes are reported to be in 'dismal conditions' or 'almost non-functional'. Second, there is considerable variation across states in the levels of enforcement, with some states such as Bihar, Jharkhand and Uttar Pradesh repeatedly highlighted for non-compliance. Third, and perhaps an important indicator of the overall value of the court's intervention, the reports indicate a pattern of improvement, both in the implementation of schemes and in the communicative pattern between commissioners and state governments over time. For example, a 2003 report finds that only sixteen out of thirty-three states and territories have implemented the MDM scheme fully or partially but by 2004, the number had increased to twenty-three. Similarly, the commissioners' 2002 report notes a serious lack of response to their communications, but by 2003, they reported that the states and territories were responding more promptly to their queries. Finally, the commissioners' reports also provide the reasons for non-compliance with the court's orders – at times noting the 'complete lack of seriousness shown by State governments to implementation of schemes', and at other times, recognising real constraints hampering implementation. For example, the commissioners report the difficulty of northeastern states to procure food grains from the Food Corporation of India's warehouses due to the prohibitive cost and logistical difficulty of transportation, requesting instead that they be allowed to procure food grains locally.

The MDM scheme, for which data is indeed available, is evidence of the successful implementation of the court's orders, resulting in a positive impact. In a study about the distributive impact of litigating social and economic rights, Brinks and Gauri find that the programme resulted in bringing 2,475,000 girls into school between 2001 and 2006, nearly all of whom were disadvantaged. The program also increased caloric, protein and carbohydrate intake amongst recipients by 49–100 per cent (depending on the micronutrient and the econometric specification used). The study estimates that the scheme benefitted about 60.8 million children between 2001 and 2006 (Brinks and Gauri, 2014). Another study associates the MDM scheme with a 50 per cent reduction in the proportion of girls who are out of school (Dreze and Kingdon, 2001).

In instances where the commissioners have reported the failure of state governments to comply with the court's orders, rather than impose sanctions, the court has sought to encourage enforcement in good faith. Gauri and Brinks suggest that the court has adopted a communicative rationality to move parties from an adversarial mode towards defining a problem and finding its solution – using their orders to assess and encourage the seriousness of official response, rather than as determinate duties to be enforced through sanctions (Gauri and Brinks, 2012). For example, responding to the commissioners' reports of the failure of Bihar, Jharkhand and Uttar Pradesh to fully meet the MDM targets, the court responded by interpreting the actions of the government as an indicator of a 'meaningful beginning' by the states. Similarly, in another order, the court has noted the lack of 'earnestness' on part of the central and state governments, directed them to 'make efforts to comply with the order' or praised them for their 'serious endeavor' to respond to the court's queries.[22]

Thus, the experience of the PUCL case on the right to food has been somewhat different from litigations in India on other social and economic rights, such as education and health (Shankar and Mehta, 2010). Both in terms of implementation of decisions by governments, as well as the broader impact on generating recognition for the right to food, the litigation has made a positive contribution. The following section attempts the explanatory function: What factors influenced the implementation of the court's decisions in the PUCL case? Why was the experience of earlier cases, such as the ones in Orissa, different from PUCL? What lessons does the right to food litigation in India offer for social and economic rights litigation more generally?

9.5 Factors Influencing Enforcement

The PUCL case follows a long line of public interest litigation involving an array of social and economic rights issues in India. However, in many of those cases, the courts' pronouncements have had little impact. Some cases have developed into fraught contests between the judiciary seeking to impose its orders and the executive resisting judicial incursion on policy-making (Chopra, 2009). The right to food case, however, has been different. As seen earlier, the extent of compliance has varied among different decisions by the court but the experience has overall been a positive one.

In this section, we explore some of the factors that influenced enforcement of the court's decisions. We argue that the success of the right to food case has been the result of two broad sets of factors – on the supply side, related to the court's approach in the right to food case, and on the demand side, pertaining to the external environment surrounding the judgment.

[22] See orders dated 17 September 2001; 7 January 2010 and 12 August 2010.

The court's approach in the right to food case was characterised by deliberate choices that served to facilitate compliance with its decisions. The court created its own compliance monitoring institution, in the form of commissioners who were tasked with reporting non-compliance to the court. Further, the court worked in collaboration with allies – activists and civil society organisations through the right to food campaign. These collaborative relationships enhanced the legitimacy of the court's decisions and facilitated their enforcement.

The external environment surrounding the decision was also favourable, and thus facilitated compliance. At the time of the court's engagement, the issue of hunger and malnutrition in India was increasingly receiving attention in media and public opinion. This visibility perhaps made it more difficult for state agencies to ignore the court's decisions. In addition, the broader economic and political environment had changed, and acute malnutrition and starvation in one of the world's emerging powers was increasingly seen as untenable. As one of court-appointed commissioners noted, the right to food 'was an idea of which the time had come' (Saxena, 2012).

9.5.1　Court's Approach

Spriggs (1997) highlights various ways in which courts themselves influence compliance.[23] Because non-compliance is costly to courts, they employ tactics to increase the likelihood of their decisions being obeyed. For example, clarity and specificity of judicial decisions has a positive impact on compliance while unclear standards breed non-compliance (Staton and Vanberg, 2008). Indeed, the Supreme Court's orders in the right to food case were clear, specific and practical, thus avoiding the high rhetoric and low impact of many PIL (Chopra, 2009).

Further, in the right to food case, the court appears to have adopted at least two strategies to facilitate compliance with its decisions: active compliance monitoring and working with allies in civil society.

Compliance Monitoring

Courts around the world rely on different approaches to monitor compliance with their decisions. Some adopt an indirect approach – assuming that if the litigant does not return to the court, the decision has been enforced. In a more direct approach, the executive branch assesses the extent to which

---

[23] For an overview of the discussion, see Kapiszewski and Taylor (2012).

bureaucrats have complied with decisions. Finally, as the Indian Supreme Court did in the right to food case, courts may themselves systematically review compliance with their orders, maintain cases in their dockets after the decision so that implementation can be tracked and initiate *suo moto* proceedings in case of non-compliance (Gauri, Staton and Cullell, 2013).

By actively tracking compliance with its decisions and specifically creating an institutional mechanism in the form of commissioners to monitor the implementation of its rulings, the court took charge of the compliance of its decisions. In its interim order of May 2002, the Supreme Court appointed Dr. N. C. Saxena and Mr. S. R. Sankaran (replaced in 2004 by Mr. Harsh Mander) as 'commissioners' for the purpose of investigating violations of interim orders related to the case and demanding redress. Their mandate includes monitoring the implementation of interim orders by state and central governments, making enquiries into non-compliance and reporting to the court on an ongoing basis.[24]

Court-appointed commissioners were in turn supported by advisers appointed at the state level. The central and state governments were directed by the High Court to provide assistance to the commissioners. They were obliged to appoint assistants to commissioners and Nodal Officers to ensure the implementation of interim orders.

The commissioners have submitted periodic reports to the court on the state of compliance in different states – highlighting issues and concerns regarding the implementation of orders based on their correspondence with state governments, reports of the state advisers, commissioners' interaction with civil society organisations and field visits. The reports include detailed recommendations, which in turn have led to further directions from the court. The commissioners have also drawn the court's attention to related issues of importance, such as homelessness which have since become part of the right to food litigation.

In addition to reporting back to the court, the commissioners have also served as a bridge between the court, civil society and central and state governments, and in doing so helped to build a network of allies that further contributed to effective enforcement of decisions. Despite their roles as monitors, the commissioners have been able to forge partnerships with state government officials and foster political will for implementation of court orders.[25] Therefore, when faced with non-compliance by governments, the commissioners have sometimes opted to seek

[24] Available at: www.sccommissioners.org.
[25] Birchfield and Corsi (2010), based on interviews with the Office of the Commissioners.

resolution without court involvement; that strategy has served the objective of increasing implementation.[26]

The Court's Allies

The enforcement of social and economic rights typically requires a complex support system beyond the litigation itself. In addition to the efforts
of the judiciary, the enforcement of judicial orders often depends on a
number of other actors, including the executive branch and public action
or civil society organisations (Rodriquez-Garavito, 2011: 1692; Vanberg,
2005). The availability of allies, within the constituencies directly responsible for the implementation, as well as those that indirectly contribute
to greater legitimacy and the enabling environment for the realisation of
rights, can greatly facilitate implementation. Thus, the ability of the court
to ally itself with key interest groups or with the public at large in addressing popular causes is a significant factor influencing compliance (Gauri
and Brinks, 2008a; Staton, 2010).

The right parties, such as civil society organisations, can serve as watch-
dogs, monitoring compliance and ensuring that non-compliance results
in legal action (Epp, 1998; Spriggs, 1997: 567). We argue that in the right
to food case, the court found allies within civil society (right to food
campaign) which in turn served as active agents to monitor compliance
and partner with the court's institutional machinery (commissioners) to
report on non-compliance.

The right to food campaign is an informal network of organisations
and individuals that coordinates actions aimed at realising the right to
food in India. It began with the PUCL litigation but grew into a wider
movement following the recognition that legal action without an active
supporting public campaign would not go very far.[27] Various organisations that comprise the campaign have played a significant role, not only
in relation to the (ongoing) litigation but also with advocacy for legislative action, creating accountability and generating public awareness
through local action.

With respect to the litigation, network organisations act as petitioners
who bring claims before the court, as advisors helping the court with evidence to help shape its decisions, and as monitors that report to the court
on implementation (or lack thereof). They frequently file follow-up applications asking the court to clarify, re-iterate, modify, expand or improve

---

[26] Ibid.
[27] *Right to Food campaign* at www.righttofoodindia.org.

its orders. The campaign operates through a wide network of grassroots organisations and has a detailed understanding of how the poor concretely experience government implementation of food-related schemes. As such, it has repeatedly petitioned the court through interlocutory applications to modify government schemes to more appropriately meet the needs of the people. For example, in response to an application filed by the campaign, the court issued an order holding that village communities, self-help groups and *Mahila Mandals* (women's collectives), rather than private contractors, would be relied on for buying grains and preparing meals under the ICDS programme.[28]

The campaign also makes an important contribution by providing the data necessary for supporting the petition before the court. For example, orders of the court in the PUCL case regarding minimum calorific requirements to be provided under the MDM scheme draw on the recommendations of the campaign's research (Birchfield and Corsi, 2010). The campaign's website serves as a valuable repository of information related to various food-related schemes and entitlements, applications made to the court, court orders and commissioners' reports regarding implementation, as well as other resources to enable local and regional calls to action.

The campaign's greatest contribution lies in its work to build the civic base and public pressure necessary for the implementation of the court's decisions and ensuring government accountability.[29] According to Dreze, 'it would be naïve to expect these orders to be implemented without public pressure'. It has organised public hearings, rallies, action-oriented research, media advocacy and lobbying of members of parliament. For instance, on 9 April 2002 it organised a national 'day of action on mid-day meals' which was instrumental in persuading several state governments to initiate cooked MDM in primary schools.[30]

In its important role of ensuring accountability, the campaign has also been assisted by the passage of the Right to Information Act in 2005. The legislation, which allows citizens to access, in public interest, information held by public authorities has enabled civil society organisations, including the right to food campaign, to identify irregularities in the implementation of food schemes and force local authorities to implement or to explain non-compliance (FAO, 2011).

---

[28] Order of 7 October 2004.
[29] Ibid.
[30] Available at www.righttofoodindia.org.

Further, the particular triangular relationship between the case, the right
to food campaign and the commissioners has been especially instrumental
in shaping the ongoing litigation, as well as in the implementation of the
court's orders (Birchfield and Corsi, 2010). The state advisors appointed
by the commissioners – women and men drawn from the right to food
campaign – act as the commissioners' eyes and ears on food security issues
(Hassan, 2011). They rely on grassroots organisations for information on
compliance with court orders, which in turn informs their detailed reports
to the court. The commissioners are also helped in their mandate by the
advocacy and civil society engagement of the campaign, which encourage public awareness of entitlements through publications, public events
such as social audits, and public hearings of complaints and grievances.[31]
In turn, the commissioners respond to complaints from grassroots organisations regarding non-compliance of orders in their jurisdictions, make
enquiries and report back to the court.

Thus, the Supreme Court's approach in the right to food case appears to
have been strategic in that the court began by strongly and clearly declaring the right to food as a fundamental right, and further by defining the
contours of that right in the form of legal entitlements. It then framed
remedies, which, although only re-affirming the existing responsibilities
of governments, clearly detailed milestones to be fulfilled. Most importantly, the court created a robust mechanism for compliance monitoring
when it appointed two commissioners to monitor enforcement of its decisions and report back in cases of non-compliance. It also kept the door
open for litigants to bring follow-up litigation in cases of non-compliance.
As Rodriguez-Garavito argues in this book and elsewhere, the combination of a clear affirmation of the justiciability of the right in question
(strong right), leaving policy decisions to elected branches of government
while laying out a clear roadmap for measuring progress (moderate remedies); and actively monitoring the implementation of the court's orders,
including through follow-up decisions (strong monitoring), is a particularly effective strategy for the enforcement of courts' decisions in socio-
economic rights cases (Rodriquez-Garavito, 2011: 1692).

9.5.2   External Environment

In addition to the success of the court's own approach, the external environment surrounding the litigation had changed. The prevailing political

---

[31] Ibid.

and economic environment in India at the time of the litigation was also favourable, and facilitated success to some measure.

That political calculations are crucial to the implementation of court decisions is now well known. In India, for example, Reetika Khera (2006) provides an acute description of how electoral politics and centre–state political relations influenced drought response in Rajasthan between 2000 and 2003. In the early 2000s, the broader political environment in India was changing. Soon after the 2004 general elections, the newly formed United Progressive Alliance government proclaimed a 'National Common Minimum Programme' – promising rights-based social and economic development policies. It soon established the National Advisory Council – a consultative body largely composed of civil society leaders, to advise the government on social policy issues, including food security, rural employment guarantees, the right to education and the right to information. It seemed as though food security, along with employment and social protection, had become political priorities.

At the same time, the economic environment was also rapidly changing. Following a period of high growth rates, ranging on average near 7 per cent for fifteen years, India came to seen as an emerging power on the world stage. Reflecting the overall sense of optimism, a strong 'India Shining' narrative emerged[32] – highlighting the rise of the middle class, enhanced economic opportunities and openness to business. Contrasted against this booming growth story, India's widespread hunger came to be seen as an uncomfortable and untenable reality. Headlines such as *'If India is booming, why are its children starving?'* sparked debate, as did India's abysmally low ranking on global indices (such as the global hunger index discussed in Section 9.2). India was seeking its seat at the high table of global affairs as an emerging superpower (notably at the UN Security Council), yet it stood below Sudan and Ethiopia on indices of childhood malnutrition. Jean Dreze and Amartya Sen (2011) noted that 'there is probably no other example in the history of world development of an economy growing so fast and for so long with such limited results in terms of broad based social progress'. In these circumstances, the argument that the state lacked the capacity to comply with court's decisions became particularly unacceptable, and financial constraints were no longer accepted by courts as reasons for non-implementation.

---

[32] The term was originally coined in 2004 by an Indian advertising agency as part of a Bharatiya Janata Party election campaign to promote India for business and tourism internationally.

The right to food litigation was also accompanied by a high degree of visibility in public opinion and media, which may have contributed towards compliance. Empirically, scholars have found that transparency facilitates compliance and that, in particular, non-compliance is more likely in cases that are not covered by the media (Staton, 2010). Examining compliance with the decisions of the Constitutional Chamber and the Supreme Court of Costa Rica, Gauri et al. also found that the court's decision to publicise the results of its monitoring programme had demonstrable effects on the timing of compliance with its decisions (Gauri, Staton and Cullell, 2013). The visibility of the court's decision as well as of the right to food issue in India generally was certainly far greater around the PUCL case than they had been before. Writing in 2002, Amartya Sen and Jean Dreze described the nutritional situation in India as a 'silent emergency' – one that received little attention in public debates and democratic politics (Dreze and Sen, 2002). Jean Dreze (2004) notes that between January and June 2000, one of the leading English language newspapers in India, *The Hindu*, published 300 opinion articles, but not a single one of them dealt with health or nutrition.

Dreze and Sen (2013) further described an elite bias in the Indian media and a lack of focus on the 'blind-spots' of grave social and developmental failures.[33] The preoccupations of the media, in turn, cater to those of the privileged parts of society. As a result, they argue that the terms of public engagement are dominated by a relatively small but powerful group of elite Indians, who are the beneficiaries of economic growth, and have little or no need for government-sponsored social safety nets. For these simple political economy reasons, there was no widespread serious discussion of the needs of the underprivileged.

However, the landscape of public opinion appears to be changing. We repeated Dreze's exercise surveying the media and found significantly more attention to the issue since 2001. For example, between 1990 and mid-2012, 118 articles appeared in *The Hindu* on issues related to the right to food. Similarly, a leading English language weekly magazine called *The Outlook* featured 260 articles on issues related to 'right to food', 'food policy', 'PDS' and 'food security'. Finally, a Google search for news articles on 'India' and 'right to food' between 1985 and July 2012 led to 111,000 results, of which an overwhelming 108,000 were from the period 2004–2012.

---

[33] For example, they cite a survey of 315 editors of print and other media in Delhi, which showed that not one belonged to a Scheduled Caste or Scheduled Tribe Chamaria, Kumar and Yadav (2006).

The increased media attention to the issue of food security in India probably reflects a broader shift in public opinion in India. In World Values Survey data from India, strong agreement with the statement that 'incomes should be made more equal' went from 22 per cent in 1990 to 48 per cent in 2001.[34] This shift in public opinion in favour of fighting and reducing inequality in India may indeed have contributed to the greater judicial and media attention to the right to food. It should be noted that public opinion in India continues to be sharply divided between middle class and elite aspirations for growth, and issues of entitlements and rights of the poor. But, ultimately, it is the competition between these narratives and related political contestations that has cemented the hold of the right to food issue.

At the same time, the court's approach in the PUCL case may itself have contributed to the heightened attention to the issue of food insecurity in India, thus serving an important dialogic function. Discussing the legitimacy of judicial review in the context of the Canadian Charter of Rights and Freedoms, Peter Hogg and Allison Bushell (1997) emphasised that one key function of judicial review, and one often ignored in popular accounts, is to generate a dialogue between different branches of the state (in that case, the court and legislature). In their account, dialogic judicial review ultimately strengthens, rather than weakens, democracy. Generally speaking, judicial activism in India has also tended, on many occasions, to generate dialogue, not only with the legislative branch but also in the broader public sphere (Chandrachud, 2009). In the right to food case, the court engaged with a dynamic civil society campaign, directly and through commissioners, on various aspects of the litigation, both within and outside the courtroom, and in this process likely catalysed greater discussion and debate regarding the right to food.

While the importance of media attention and public action surrounding the right to food cannot be overstated, it is important to note that visibility alone is insufficient to ensure compliance in the absence of other conditions being satisfied. For example, Gauri, Staton and Vargas Cullell (2013) cautioned that transparency was likely to influence behaviour when certain other conditions were also met: when parties believed that the court's commitment to monitor and publicise compliance were credible; public officials cared about their reputation; the public attached significance to executive compliance; and bureaucrats were responsive to pressures from their superiors.

[34] Available at www.worldvaluessurvey.org.

This need for supporting conditions may help explain the difference in the experience of the right to food case vis-à-vis early cases. Dan Banik noted that local, regional and English language media routinely covered the starvation deaths in Orissa throughout the 1980s and 1990s without any significant effect (Banik, 1998). Unlike the right to food case, however, the Orissa courts had refrained from adopting robust compliance monitoring. Much of the media also suffered from a perceived lack of independence. Finally, in the absence of the political will to tackle the issue of hunger and malnutrition seriously, the media attention became a tool for political mudslinging without any significant policy change.

9.6 Conclusion

The Indian experience with the right to food litigation presents some important lessons for social and economic rights litigation. Grave situations of starvation deaths, hunger and malnutrition were brought to the Supreme Court in the 1980s and again in 2001. In both instances, the court recognised the right to food as an integral part of the constitutional guarantee of the right to life, and gave directions to governments to address the situations. However, the experience with the enforcement of the courts' decisions was vastly different in the two periods. A variety of factors help explain this difference – some stemmed from the Court's own approach while others were external to it.

First, the court's approach in 2001 was more robust as compared to the earlier cases. In addition to declaring the right to food a fundamental right, it went on to give it meaning by spelling out the specific entitlements provided by the right, and to create an institutional mechanism to monitor compliance with its orders. Unlike earlier cases, the court did not make a final decision but rather remained engaged in the litigation – preferring to continuously explicate the right through a series of interim orders. Importantly, it adopted a robust approach to compliance monitoring by creating institutional machinery in the form of commissioners to monitor enforcement of its decisions, make enquiries into non-compliance and report back to the court with recommendations.

Second, in the PUCL litigation, the court worked collaboratively with key allies in civil society through the right to food campaign. The triangular relationship between the case, the commissioners and the campaign contributed greatly to the implementation of the court's orders. Third, public opinion about the crisis of hunger and starvation in India appears to have undergone a decisive shift in the early 2000s. This shift contributed to, and was influenced by, a shift in media attention. Finally, the prevailing economic and political climate in India at the time of the PUCL case, markedly different from that in the 1980s, had a meaningful effect on the right to food as a priority. The right to food movement helped put the spotlight on a significant social inequality, and contrasted with the dominant narrative of a rising and shining India; this caused introspection and debate in Indian society.

The experience of the right to food litigation and the supporting right to food movement will hopefully provide valuable insight to advocates and activists in designing strategies for social and economic rights claims. Yet, some questions remain. For example, the degree to which each of these factors individually facilitated compliance – by raising the cost of non-compliance or lowering the cost of compliance, and how the various factors interacted with each other is yet unclear. Understanding which factors constitute necessary conditions, and which play a supportive role, may further contribute to effective strategies. We hope to return to these in the future.

The right to food issue remains a lively one in India. Whether encouraged by the litigation, or otherwise, the issue was adopted as a priority by the executive and legislature. The *National Food Security Ordinance* was passed by the executive in July 2013. The Food Security Bill then appeared before the parliament, and was enacted as the *National Food Security Act* in September 2013. There is little doubt that the Act represents a step forward in addressing the issue of food security. Energetic debate about its effectiveness continues. There remain major issues surrounding the Public Distribution System and the methods for targeting. Jean Dreze (2013) offers a humbling perspective: 'The food security bill is a fraction of what is required to tackle India's enormous nutrition problems. The battle for the right to food is far from over.'

References

Austin, G. (1966), *The Indian Constitution: Cornerstone of a Nation* (Oxford: Oxford University Press).

Banik, D. (1998), 'India's Freedom from Famine: Case of Kalahandi', *Contemporary South Asia*, 7(3), 265–281.

Birchfield, L. and Corsi, J. (2010), 'Between Starvation and Globalization: Realizing the Right to Food in India', *Michigan Journal of International Law*, 31, 691–764.

Brinks, D. and Gauri, V. (2014), 'The Law's Majestic Equality: The Distributive Impact of Judicializing Social and Economic Rights', *Perspectives on Politics*, 12(2), 375–393.

Caplin, J. (2008), 'Feeding an Elephant: Malnutrition and the Right to Food in India', *Harvard International Review*, Fall, http://hir.harvard.edu/global-educationfeeding-an-elephant/.

Chamaria, A., Kumar, J. and Yadav, Y. (2006), *Survey of the Profile of the Key Decision Makers in the National Media*, Centre for Study of Developing Societies.

Chandrachud, A. (2009), 'Dialogic Judicial Activism in India', *The Hindu*, 18 July.

Chopra, S. (2009). 'Holding the State Accountable for Hunger', *Economic and Political Weekly*, 33(XLIV), August.

Currie, B. (2000), *The Politics of Hunger in India: A Study of Democracy, Governance and Kalahandi's Poverty* (London: Palgrave Macmillan).

Dreze, J. (2004), 'Democracy and the Right to Food', *Economic and Political Weekly*, 17 (39) (24 April), 1723–1731.

(2013), 'The Food Security Debate in India', *The New York Times*, 9 July.

(undated), Right to Food: From the Courts to the Streets. Available at http://sccommissioners.org/Starvation/Articles/drezecourts.pdf.

Dreze, J. and Kingdon, G. (2001), 'School Participation in Rural India', *Review of Development Economics*, 5(1), 1–24.

Dreze, J. and Sen, A. (2002), *India: Development and Participation* (New Delhi and Oxford: Oxford University Press).

(2011), 'Putting Growth in Its Place', *Outlook*, 14 November.

(2013), *An Uncertain Glory: India and Its Contradictions* (New Delhi: Penguin).

Dua, B. D. (1983), 'A Study in Executive-Judicial Conflict: The Indian case', *Asian Survey*, 4(22), 463–483.

Epp, C. R. (1998), *The Rights Revolution: Lawyers, Activists and Supreme Courts in Comparative Perspective* (Chicago: University of Chicago Press).

FAO (2011), *India: Legal Campaigns for the Right to Food, in Right to Food: Making It Happen* (Rome: FAO).

Gauri, V. (2011), 'Fundamental Rights and Public Interest Litigation in India: Overreaching or Underachieving?' *Indian Journal of Law and Economics*, 1(1), 71–93.

Gauri, V. and Brinks, D. (eds.) (2008a), *Courting Social Justice: Judicial Enforcement of Socio-Economic Rights in the Developing World* (Cambridge: Cambridge University Press).

(2008b), 'Introduction: The Elements of Legalization and the Triangular Shape of Social and Economic Rights', in V. Gauri and D. Brinks (eds.), *Courting Social Justice: Judicial Enforcement of Social and Economic Rights in the Developing World* (Cambridge: Cambridge University Press), 1–37.

(2012), 'Human Rights and Communicative Action', *The Journal of Political Philosophy*, 4(20), 407–431.

Gauri, V., Staton, J. and Cullell, J. V. (2013), 'A Public Strategy for Compliance Monitoring', The World Bank Policy Research Working Paper 6523.

Guha-Khasnobis, B. and Vivek, S. (2007), *Rights Based Approach to Development: Lessons from the Right to Food Movement in India*, United Nations University – World Institute for Development Economics Research.

Hassan, S. (2011), 'Rights, Activism and the Poor in India: Supreme Court and the "Right to Food Case"', Paper presented at International Conference: Social Protection for Social Justice at the Institute for Development Studies, April, United Kingdom.

Hogg, P. and Bushell, A. (1997), 'The Charter Dialogue between Courts and Legislatures (Or Perhaps the Charter of Rights isn't Such a Bad Thing After All)', *Osgoode Hall Law Journal*, 1(35), 75–124.

Jaishankar, Y. and Dreze, J. (2005), *Supreme Court Orders on the Right to Food: A Tool for Action*, October.

Kapiszewski, D. and Taylor, M. M. (2013), 'Compliance: Conceptualizing, Measuring, and Explaining Adherence to Judicial Rulings', *Law & Social Inquiry*, 38 (4): 803–835.

Kattumuri, R. (2011), 'Food Security and the Targeted Public Distribution System in India', Asia Research Centre Working Paper 38.

Khera, R. (2006), 'Political Economy of State Response to Drought in Rajasthan 2000–2003', *Economic and Political Weekly*, 19 (XLI), December 16.

Kothari, J. (2004), 'Social Rights and the Indian Constitution', *Law, Social Justice and Global Development Journal*, 2, online.

Nayak, B. S. (2007), 'The History of Food Security Policy in India with Reference to Orissa and Kalahandi: An Integrated and Universal Approach towards PDS', in B. S. Nayak (ed.), *Nationalizing Crises: The Political Economy of Public Policy in Contemporary India* (New Delhi: Atlantic).

Rajagopal, B. (2007), 'Pro Human Rights but Anti Poor? A Critical Evaluation of the Supreme Court from a Social Movement Perspective', *Human Rights Review*, 3(18), 157–187.

Rodriquez-Garavito, C. (2011), 'Beyond the Courtroom: The Impact of Judicial Activism on Socioeconomic Rights in Latin America', *Texas Law Review*, 89(7), 1669–1698.

Sathe, S. P. (2001), 'Judicial Activism: The Indian Experience', *Journal of Law and Policy*, 6(29), 30–107.

Saxena, N. C. (2012), 'Hunger and Malnutrition in India', *IDS Bulletin*, 43(July, Supplement s1), 8–14.

Shankar, S. and Mehta, P. B. (2010), 'Courts and Socio-economic Rights in India', in Varun Gauri and Dan Brinks (eds.), *Courting Social Justice: Judicial Enforcement of Social and Economic Rights in the Developing World* (Cambridge: Cambridge University Press), 146–182.

Spears, D. (2012). 'How Much International Variation in Child Heights Can Sanitation Explain?', Working paper, Princeton University, www.princeton.edu/rpds/papers/Spears_Height_and_Sanitation.pdf.pdf.

Spriggs, J. (1997), 'Explaining Federal Bureaucratic Compliance with Supreme Court Opinions', *Political Research Quarterly*, 50(3), 567–593.

Staton, J. (2010), *Judicial Power and Strategic Communication in Mexico* (New York: Cambridge University Press).

Staton J. and Vanberg, G. (2008), 'The Value of Vagueness: Delegation, Defiance, and Judicial Opinions', *American Journal of Political Science*, 52(3), 504–519.

Trochev, A. (2011), *Judging Russia: Constitutional Court in Russian Politics 1990–2006* (Cambridge: Cambridge University Press).

Vanberg, G. (2005), *The Politics of Constitutional Review in Germany* (New York: Cambridge University Press).

Vidar, M. (2006), State Recognition of the Right to Food at the National Level, UNU-WIDER Research Paper No. 2006/61.

10

South Africa: Rethinking Enforcement Narratives

MALCOLM LANGFORD AND STEVE KAHANOVITZ

10.1   Introduction

South African jurisprudence on social rights is often promoted as a global model.[1] Whereas attention is beginning to turn towards other jurisdictions due to the comparatively low volume of cases (Alston, 2008) and disappointment with the Constitutional Court's partial deferentialism (Bilchitz, 2007; Pieterse, 2007),[2] South African judgments continue to exert a strong jurisprudential, scholarly and policy-making influence in other parts of the world.[3]

However, the *impact* of these jurisprudential gains in the domain of policy, practice and law is the subject of a growing debate. Accounts of transformative social change are regularly met with scepticism or counter-examples. Part of this dissensus is attributable to methodology. Disparate and varying evaluation methods, case selection and interpretations of court orders, expectations of litigation outcomes and time periods under investigation are evident in the literature.[4] This methodological diversity is compounded by an absence of rigorous mixed methods evaluation (although that is changing[5]). Likewise, the scope of cases under review is also limited. Until recently, most attention has been on two early landmark

---

[1] For a comprehensive overview of these decisions, see Liebenberg (2010).

[2] One clear exception is the area of housing rights where there has been a continued stream of decisions, particularly concerning evictions. There has also been a recent upsurge in cases concerning the right to education, particularly at the High Court level.

[3] See, for example, UK Joint Committee (2004), Porter (2009), Sunstein (2004) and Waldron (2009).

[4] Compare Pieterse (2007), Berger (2008) Robins (2008), Liebenberg (2008), Svart (2005), Heywood (2009), Marcus and Budlender (2008) and Hirschl (2004).

[5] See, for instance, Robins (2008), Berger (2008), and Langford et al. (2014).

Malcolm Langford is Associate Professor in the Faculty of Law, University of Oslo. He is also Co-Director, Centre on Law and Social Transformation, University of Oslo, and former Co-Coordinator, Adjudication Group, ESCR-Net.

Steve Kahanovitz is a Senior Lawyer at the Legal Resources Centre, South Africa.

The authors would particularly like to thank Evan Marcus for research assistance on the cases.

315

decisions of the Constitutional Court in the context of housing and health rights – *Grootboom*[6] and *Treatment Action Campaign*[7] and to a more limited extent, on the specific enforcement challenges posed by social grant cases.[8] And, even if researchers do find consensus on the lack of impact in a particular case, their causal reasons often differ.

If we focus on the slightly narrower question of *enforcement*, we can identify a number of critical narratives that will provide the departure point for this chapter. There is a *descriptive* account that non-implementation of judgments in South Africa is the norm. There is a widespread perception of a culture of non-enforcement even though court orders tend to be limited in scope.[9] Despite the existence of a fairly robust democracy and independent judiciary, all levels of government have come under fire for ignoring court orders or paying 'lip service' to decisions. This critique has been raised across cases covering the full range of remedies (declaratory orders, interdicts against state action, orders for compensation or mandatory orders to revert to a 'status quo')[10] and concerning both positive and negative obligations.[11] However, this narrative appears too simplistic. A

[6] *Government of the Republic of South Africa and Ors v Irene Grootboom and Ors* 2001 (1) SA 46 (CC) [*Grootboom*]. The Court found national housing policy failed to meet the right of access to housing since there was no provision for temporary relief for those most desperately in need.

[7] *In re Min of Health and Ors v Treatment Action Campaign and Ors* 2002 (5) SA 717 (CC) [*TAC*]. The Court found that the failure to roll-out provision of antiretroviral drugs in public hospitals to reduce mother-to-child HIV/AIDS transmission contravened the right to health.

[8] There have been a significant number of judgments dealing with attempts by aggrieved applicants to enforce payment by the state of social security grants: see, for example, *Permanent Secretary, Department of Welfare, Eastern Cape Provincial Government and Another v Ngxuza and Ors* 2001 (4) SA 1184 (SCA); *Khosa and Ors v Minister of Social Development and Ors* 2004 (6) SA 505 (CC); *Cele and Ors v South African Social Security Agency* 2009 (5) SA 105 (D).

[9] The *Grootboom* case is perhaps a classic example of this as the specific rights of the Grootboom community were part of a settlement while the Constitutional Court ruled on the broader obligations of the state: see Liebenberg (2008) and Marcus and Budlender (2008) and contrast with the arguably mistaken interpretation in Berger (2008).

[10] Compare, for example, the weak orders in *Grootboom* (2001) and *TAC* (2002) with the strong orders in *Westville* and *Kate*. This result is interesting given theoretical discussions on whether weak or stronger forms of orders may induce higher levels of compliance. See Berger (2008), Mbazira (2008b) and Tushnet (2008).

[11] In the majority of socio-economic rights cases in South Africa, applicants have focused their claims on interference by public or private actors with their socio-economic rights. However, the distinction is often hard to make as many of these decisions contain positive elements such as reconnecting services, providing compensation or developing plans to address positive obligations. As at 1 January 2014, in the field of urban housing and basic services, numerous Constitutional Court cases have addressed forced evictions and

more reasonable critique or hypothesis may be that non-enforcement is the *immediate* and *default* position for respondents.[12] But over time the picture can arguably change.

This raises the question of why variance might occur. Two dominant *explanatory* narratives of a critical nature are common. Some commentators identify the problem within the judicial sphere: weak forms of judicial review and cautious court orders (Pieterse, 2007) and the lack of effective enforcement mechanisms (Mbazira, 2008a). An alternative is to point to the demand side and focus on the intensity of social mobilisation. This variable is commonly proffered as an explanation for the presumed poor enforcement of the seminal *Grootboom* housing case and the contrary in the *Treatment Action Campaign* (TAC) case. In the latter, the *TAC* merged litigation and mobilisation (including at the post-judgment phase) on the issue of right to healthcare in a compelling manner that placed tremendous pressure on the Mbeki government to overcome its refusal to recognise the link between HIV and AIDS and its sluggishness and obstinacy in facilitating access to medicine to HIV/AIDS patients. The end result was an increase in health budgets, a reduction in the price of medicine and an expansion of healthcare programmes, which contributed to preventing hundreds of thousands of deaths (Heywood, 2009).

This chapter scrutinises both these descriptive and explanatory narratives in order to understand better the levels of implementation and causes of their variance, and to a certain extent identify successful strategies. In

disconnections. Individuals and communities were 'successful' in (1) *Minister of Public Works v Kyalami Ridge Environmental Association* ('*Kyalami Ridge*') 2001 (7) BCLR 652 (CC); (2) *Ndlovu v Ngcobo; Bekker & Another v Jika* [2002]4 A11 SA384; 2003(1)SA113 (SCA); (3) *Jaftha v Schoeman and Others; Van Rooyen v Stoltz and Others* 2005 (1) BCLR 78 (CC) ('*Jaftha*'); (4) *President of RSA and Another v Modderklip Boerdery (Pty) Ltd and Others* 2005 (8) BCLR 786 (CC); (5) *Port Elizabeth Municipality v Various Occupiers* 2005 (1) SA 217 (CC); (6) *Occupiers of 51 Olivia Road, Berea Township, and 197 Main Street, Johannesburg v City of Johannesburg and Others* 2008 (3) SA 208 (CC) ('*Olivia Road*'); (7) *Abahlali baseMjondolo Movement SA v Premier KZN and Others* (2009); (8) *Leon Joseph and Others v City of Johannesburg and Others*, Case CCT 43/09, Date of Judgment: 9 October 2009; and *City of Johannesburg Metropolitan Municipality v Blue Moonlight Properties (Pty) Ltd* [2011] ZACC 33, 2012 (2) SA 104 (CC) ('*Blue Moonlight*'). Only three cases have expressly addressed the provision of housing or services. One was successful (*Grootboom*); one was unsuccessful – *Lindiwe* Mazibuko *and Others v City of Johannesburg and Others Case CCT 39/09* [2009] ZACC 28 ('*Mazibuko*'); and the third lost initially but was later set aside – see *Residents, Joe Slovo Community, Western Cape v Thubeiisha Homes & Ors* CCT 22/08 [2009] ZACC 16 and *Residents, Joe Slovo Community, Western Cape v Thubeiisha Homes & Ors* CCT 22/08A [2011] ZACC 8.

[12] Indeed, follow-up litigation is commonly required: see overview of a range of socioeconomic rights cases in Berger (2008).

other words, we ask what is the actual level of compliance and how is it best explained? These questions are approached through a largely inductive approach. The bulk of the chapter is devoted to a close analysis of six case studies in South Africa concerning the right to housing in urban areas, a field that has been largely understudied. It begins in Section 10.2 with the well-known *Grootboom* case, followed by four other cases in Section 10.3 that also emerged from eviction threats to settlements (*Valhalla, Modderklipp, Ndawoyache* and *Olivia Road*), and a poor individual home-owner evicted for outstanding utility debts (*Jaftha*). In the concluding analytical Section 10.4, these studies are contrasted with literature on the enforcement of a number of cases concerning health and social security rights in order to identify whether the patterns are systemic.

The research method included analyses of selected judgments and court orders, semi-structured interviews with key stakeholders, on-site visits and informal surveys and reviews of policy documents, legislation, secondary literature and mass media sources (primarily undertaken in the period 2010 to 2014). The characteristics of the various cases are summarised in Table 10.1. The table provides not only information on the characteristics of the litigation (complaints, respondents, remedies) but also the related actors (lawyers, *amicus curaie* interveners, external social movement support); whether there was follow-up enforcement litigation; and an assessment of the internal strength or organisation of the complainant. As discussed in the introduction to this volume, these factors may be relevant in assessing the degree of enforcement and thus are set out at this stage of the analysis.

10.2   *Grootboom*

The '*Grootboom* community' consisted of 390 adults and 510 children who originally resided in the Wallacedene informal settlement.[13] Located on the eastern fringe of the Cape Metropolitan Area, the settlement's residents were extremely poor.[14] Heavy winter rainfall had left their part of the set-tlement waterlogged and in September 1998 they moved onto an adjacent vacant property. However, the land was privately owned and earmarked for low-cost housing. On 8 December 1998, the landowner secured a court order for an eviction, despite the community being unrepresented at the

---

[13] Irene Grootboom was the first-named applicant in the case and was the regular contact point between the community and the lawyers and government. She was able to speak both Afrikaans and Xhosa. However, leadership within the community appears to have been shared by a number of individuals.

[14] In 1997, 25 per cent were assessed as having no income at all.

Table 10.1 *Background characteristics of cases*

Case	Year	Nature of complainants	Respondent	Court	Type of remedy	Strength of remedy	Lawyers	Amicus	Follow-up enforcement litigation	Strength of litigant self-organisation	Social movement or external allies
Housing											
Grootboom	2000	Settlement: 900 persons	Municipality province National Government	CC	Declaration (systemic – national) settlement order (litigants)	Weak	Private	Yes	Yes	Medium	No
Rudolph	2003	Settlement: 50 families	Municipality province	HC	Declaration (systemic – regional) injunction (litigants)	Strong	NGO: LRC	No	Yes	Strong	Yes
Olivia Road	2008	Building occupiers: 400 persons	Municipality	CC	Settlement order (litigants) systemic (local)	Strong	NGO: CALS	Yes	No	Weak	Yes
Ndwoyache	2007	Settlement: 10,000 persons	Municipality	HC	Injunction (litigants)	Weak	Private: WW	No	No	Medium	No
Modderklip	2005	Settlement: 40,000	Municipality province	CC	Injunction (litigants)	Medium	Private	Yes	No	Medium	No

(cont.)

Table 10.1 (Cont.)

Case	Year	Nature of complainants	Respondent	Court	Type of remedy	Strength of remedy	Lawyers	Amicus	Follow-up enforcement litigation	Strength of litigant self-organisation	Social movement or external allies
Jaftha	2005	Individual		CC	Injunction/compensation (litigants)	Medium	NGO: LRC		No		
Health											
TAC	2002	Social movement	National	CC	Systemic declaration (national)	Medium	NGO: ALP		Yes	Strong	Yes
Westville		Social movement	Provincial	HC	Mandamus (provincial)	Strong	NGO: ALP		Yes	Strong	Yes
Social security											
Ngxuza/Jaiya/Kate trilogy		NGO	National government province	HC	Mandamus (national/provincial)	Strong/weak/medium	LRC		Yes		Yes
Black Sash		NGO	National government	HC	Mandamus (national)		NGO: Black Sash/LRC		No	Strong	Yes
Khosa		Individual (but test case for all permanent residents)	National government	CC	Systemic declaration (national)	Medium	NGO: CMS		No	Medium	Yes

hearing. The community decided, however, to remain on the land as their previous site in Wallacedene was now occupied and there was no other place to go.

After securing funds to carry out an eviction, the landowner returned to court in March 1999 for a fresh order. This time, the magistrate asked a local private lawyer to represent the community. The result was that of a negotiated agreement with the Oostenburg municipality: the community would vacate the land by 19 May 1999 and the municipality promised that it would seek to identify alternative land. The lawyer was under the impression (falsely it seems) that there was little chance of legal success in fighting the eviction and that the municipality would negotiate in good faith. Oostenburg had earlier and privately concluded that no alternative sites were available. On 18 May 1999, they sent in bulldozers to demolish and burn the settlement. Rendered homeless, the community took shelter on the Wallacedene sports field.

With the encouragement of a former African National Congress (ANC) councillor, the community marched on the local offices of the municipality, controlled by the New National Party. However, the only substantive response was the request by municipality to an ANC politician to 'sort out the problem' (Marcus and Budlender, 2008). During the subsequent discussions with this politician, the community decided that legal action would be taken against local, provincial and national governments. After one further attempt to settle, urgent legal action was launched on 31 May 1999. The applicants requested that the respondents 'provide adequate and sufficient basic temporary shelter and/or housing for the applicants and their children' pending permanent accommodation and that 'adequate and sufficient basic nutrition, shelter, health and care services and social services' be provided to all of the applicants' children in the interim.

After an *in loco* inspection was conducted by Acting Justice Josman, a judgment was delivered by Justice Davis (with Justice Comrie concurring) on 17 December 1999.[15] The rights of the children under Section 28 of the Constitution were upheld and the High Court ordered that 'tents, portable latrines and a regular supply of water' be provided within three months to families. However, no order was given for adults without children: Section 26, which provides that everyone has the right of access to adequate housing, is expressly limited by the requirement of available resources. The municipality appealed the order directly to the Constitutional Court.

---

[15] *Grootboom v. Oostenberg Municipality* 2000 (3) BCLR 277 [25] per Davis J (Comrie J concurring).

The Community Law Centre, which had given some advice to the applicants, and the South African Human Rights Commission joined as *amicus curiae*.

At the start of the hearing, the Constitutional Court issued an order pursuant to an agreement between the parties. The municipality was to provide immediate funding for materials and delivery of temporary toilet and sanitation facilities, as well as materials to waterproof residents' shacks. A unanimous judgment then addressed the broader issues. Writing for the court, Justice Yacoob held that the nationwide housing program fell short of the obligations on the national government under Section 26 of the Constitution. There was a failure by the authorities to take into account or make provision for the immediate temporary amelioration of the circumstances of those in desperate need. A declaratory order was issued to that effect, which stated in particular that Section 26 of the Constitution imposes on the national government obligations to devise, fund, implement, and supervise measures to provide relief to those in desperate need.[16] The High Court's order under Section 28 was struck out as the Court read progressive realisation and the defence of maximum available resources into the provision.[17] In passing, the Constitutional Court also commented that the 'manner in which the eviction was carried out' was a 'breach' of the negative obligation not to forcibly evict enshrined in Section 26 of the Constitution.

Beyond this declaration no further orders were made. The Constitutional Court noted that the second *amicus curiae*, the South African Human Rights Commission (SAHRC), had promised to 'monitor and, if necessary, report in terms of these powers on the efforts made by the State to comply' with its Section 26 obligations in accordance with this judgment.'[18] Whether this statement constituted a formal order is disputed (cf. Berger, 2008; Liebenberg, 2010: 402–403). The SAHRC nonetheless reported on the implementation, and Pillay (2002) and Liebenberg (2010) describe its extensive efforts to monitor local and provincial plans to provide permanent accommodation to the community. Its broad-ranging report to the Constitutional Court on 14 November 2001 describes the dispute

[16] The programme must include reasonable measures such as, but not necessarily limited to, those contemplated in the Accelerated Managed Land Settlement Programme, to provide relief for people who have no access to land, no roof over their heads and who are living in intolerable conditions or crisis situations.

[17] This interpretation has been much criticised from the perspective of children's rights Sloth-Nielsen (2001).

[18] *Grootboom* (2001), para. 97.

between branches of government for responsibility and the lack of clarity over the content of the declaratory order. However, many are critical of the Commission's failure to engage in further monitoring (Berger, 2008: 77).

To turn to the question of compliance, assessing the degree of conformity by the authorities is challenging. A strict interpretation of the orders would mean limiting assessment to the implementation of the settlement order and the adoption and implementation of a national emergency policy (Liebenberg, 2010). A broader interpretation could entail examining whether the judgment led to a halt in forced evictions (Mbazira, 2008b). In any case, the narrow nature of the orders suggests that one also needs to examine impact and not just compliance. Indeed, this is where much of the debate lies even the terminology is often not clear. In other words, it is important to also ask what was the broader effect of the judgment (or the choice to litigate or constitutional rights themselves)? Thus, critics have focused on whether the community obtained permanent housing or housing policy was transformed (Pieterse, 2007).

Our discussion will therefore focus on the implementation of the two orders as well as the broader impacts. This is particularly important as most analysis on this latter dimension is based on research conducted prior to 2005 and a single newspaper article in 2008.

10.2.1   The Settlement Order (and Access to Housing)

Whereas the community secured a settlement agreement on the eve of the Constitutional Court hearing, it was immediately breached by the municipality which took no steps to provide the promised materials, water and sanitation (Berger, 2008). This required a follow-up application to have the agreement made a formal order of court.[19] The materials and facilities were subsequently provided but complaints emerged over the quality of the water and sanitation facilities while overall conditions improved little (Langford, 2003). Community leaders complained of broken pipes, lack of cleaning materials and of being shunted between local and provincial governments when trying to solve maintenance problems.[20] As Pillay (2002: 2) put it, the 'part of the order requiring once-off involvement' was fulfilled but 'other parts of the order, which require continuous

---

[19]   *Grootboom v Government of the Republic of South Africa* (unreported order in Case no. CCt/00), 21 September 2001.

[20]   'Treated with contempt', *Times Live*, 21 May 2004, at www.timeslive.co.za/sundaytimes/article88628.ece.

involvement – like maintenance and the provision of services – have not been'.[21]

At the same time, the agreement facilitated security of tenure for the community. The litigation effectively removed the prior eviction threat and dissolved the community's initial acquiescence to it. In effect, the community had triumphed over the municipality's determined efforts to oust them. It was tacitly agreed amongst the parties that the community could reside on the sports field despite complaints from sporting associations (Liebenberg, 2010). This may appear a marginal victory but its significance at the time cannot be underestimated. Municipalities had commenced eviction drives in many parts of the country after the consolidation of local government in the post-apartheid transition. In 2001, Huchzermeyer (2003) records the eviction of 6,000 households from Alexandria and 10,000 from Bredell.

The focus of commentators though has been the slow progress in the community securing permanent housing (Joubert, 2008; Pieterse, 2007). This frustration was shared in the community. In 2002, its leader despaired that 'We won the championship, but where's the trophy?'[22] But access to permanent housing was not an order of the Court and was not even claimed by the community in their submissions to the High Court. The Constitutional Court even acknowledges, in largely glowing terms, the government's broader efforts in building houses for the poor.[23] Marcus and Budlender (2008: 63) conclude that the community's 'over-inflated expectations and consequent disillusionment' concerning the import of the judgment seem to have arisen from the 'lack of clear communication between the lawyer and his clients about the likely and actual outcomes of the case.'

However, progress on access to permanent housing is worth investigating. The community possesses legitimate medium to long-term expectations of access to housing and addressing this issue helps shed a light on the utility of constitutional rights-based litigation strategies. The South African Constitutional Court has been particularly criticised for failing to

---

[21] It should be noted that the original demand of the community for accessible social services for children was very much lost in the settlement agreement and Constitutional Court's judgment.

[22] Interview with Lucky Gwaza, February 2002 by Malcolm Langford.

[23] 'What has been done in execution of this program is a major achievement. Large sums of money have been spent and a significant number of houses have been built. Considerable thought, energy, resources and expertise have been and continue to be devoted to the process of effective housing delivery': *Grootboom*, para. 53.

focus on alleviating 'the concrete consequences of socioeconomic hardship' and devoting too much attention to the 'coherence, rationality, inclusiveness, and flexibility of legislative or policy measures' (Pieterse, 2007: 811).

The full and entire story of the community's journey towards permanent housing is a complicated one. The initial obstacle was the lack of bureaucratic coordination. The City of Cape Town and the Western Cape provincial government took one year to decide on the 'locus of responsibility' for the implementation of the judgment (Pillay, 2002). Interestingly, their first plan focused on the Wallacedene area – to ensure permanent resettlement for all residents there – *rather* than the required broader reforms to emergency housing policy (which came later). Pillay (2002) is actually critical of the municipality for this decision. But the reverse opinion might be adopted. Despite the court making a country-wide order, the litigation prompted the relevant municipality to direct its attention to the needs of their locality.

The Wallacadene plan involved a series of phased resettlements whereby residents could choose between contractor-built housing (RDP houses) or the Peoples Housing Process. The nearby 130-hectare Blue Ridge Farm was to be purchased for the construction of low-cost housing of 6,800 households while another 2,000 would be developed in existing Wallacedene (LRC, 2002). But, in March, 2002, when members of the *Grootboom* community were presented with the plan, their leader, Lucky Gwaza, expressed sadness: 'relocating his people would only be undertaken during phase three of the development, which could be five or six years away' (ibid.). The plan allowed for ten phases and the *Grootboom* community were slated for Phase 4 (to be completed in 2008). Other sections in the Wallecedene area were deemed to be in greater need. This was clearly a letdown for the *Grootboom* community but at least demonstrates that the principles of the judgment were being followed: the most disadvantaged were being prioritised. One of the other community leaders, Mawethu Sila, acknowledged that the community thought that the ruling was going to be for their community but that they came to accept the need for a broader plan such that the 'judgment, as much as it helped us, it didn't only help us.'[24]

By 2008, the plan was achieved only for half of the community who had chosen the People's Housing Process. Those who choose contractor-built

---

[24] Interview with Mawethu Sila, Wallacedene, 2 June 2012. Carried out by Wilmien Wicomb for the authors.

housing, including Mrs Grootboom, were confronted with delays. While 3,000 of these houses had been constructed in the Wallacedene area (Nicholson, 2008b), progress was stymied repeatedly by a myriad of bureaucratic quagmires, most notably, the cancellation of a contractor's tender due to allegations of corruption. There were also concerns over the quality of construction, type of building foundation, location of houses and availability of alternative accommodation during construction. Thus, in May 2008, when Mrs Grootboom died, she was awaiting relocation (Joubert, 2008). But this group was informed they would be included in the next round and by 2009, the majority had moved into permanent housing. In 2012, Sila advised that 90 per cent had accessed permanent housing although disagreements with contractors and the municipality over quality and location have meant a number of the remainder have refused the offers.

Thus, the vast majority of the community managed to achieve permanent housing and it appears that the judgment accelerated this process by prompting the Wallacedene plan. At the funeral of Mrs Grootboom, tribute was given to her for precisely this. Her sixteen-year-old niece stated, 'She was very loving and would do anything for anyone. She did a lot for the people in the community. If it wasn't for her they wouldn't have houses now' (Nicholson, 2008a). At the same time, the community lived in appalling conditions for many years and it is difficult to calculate by how many years the judgment reduced the likely attainment of permanent housing. But there is a clear causal connection between the judgment and the creation of the plan and potentially its implementation due to the high profile nature of the case.

10.2.2   Emergency Housing Policy

Whereas the community's claim addressed their own situation, the judgment was focused on the broader obligations of the State, particularly towards all those in desperate need. The decision thus carried the potential for catalysing a wider systemic impact. The BBC reported in October 2000, for example, that while the judgment was unclear in 'practical terms', it 'could lead to a total overhaul of the government's housing policy' (Barrow, 2000). With slightly less optimism as to housing policy, the representative for the *amicus curiae* in the case, the LRC, pointed rather towards the judgment's latent destabilising role in housing policy and legal jurisprudence. They noted that the case was a 'watershed moment in our constitutional democracy' by subjecting government policy to judicial review and heralded political change: 'something very fundamental has shifted subtly in South Africa: the power of desperately poor people to leverage assistance from the state' (LRC, 2002: 4). Indeed, eleven years later, the leader of *Grootboom* community affirmed this contribution: 'it was a big breakthrough, because we could see that democracy was taking its full power'; it was 'a way of checking' whether the 'constitution of our country is looking at rich people or poor people'.[25]

As to the actual order, a new policy on emergency housing was adopted. In August 2003, two and a half years after the judgment, the national and provincial ministers approved a new programme called the *Housing Assistance in Emergency Situations*. The programme explicitly acknowledges that it was devised as a direct result of the *Grootboom* judgment as well as the severe floods in Limpopo Province in 2000.[26] It discusses the judgment in some detail noting that the court found that current programmes 'do not satisfy the requirements of the Constitution' and 'suggested that a reasonable part of the national budget be devoted to providing relief for those in desperate need' (LRC, 2002). In April 1994, the policy was incorporated in the National Housing Code and it:

> [D]eals with the rules for exceptional urgent housing situation ... [for] people who, for reasons beyond their control, find themselves in a situation of exceptional and urgent housing need ... The assistance provided consists of funds in the form of grants to municipalities to give effect to accelerated land development, the provision of basic municipal engineering services and shelter.[27]

Exceptional or urgent need was defined as an emergency housing situation (e.g. destruction or major damage to an existing shelter) or a situation that poses an immediate danger to their lives, health and safety, or eviction (or the threat of imminent eviction). Whereas the court referred only vaguely to the provision of adequate budgetary support, the National Treasury Department undertook to allocate a fixed 0.8 per cent in the annual national housing budget to the implementation of the policy. This was gazetted but was not ultimately implemented on the grounds that the Department of Housing was regularly failing to spend all of its existing budget so there would be no need to ring-fence a particular allocation.

[25] Interview with Mawethu Sila, Wallacedene, 2 June 2012. Carried out by Wilmien Wicomb for the authors.
[26] See page 5 of the document.
[27] Section 4 of the *National Housing Act No 107 of 1997* provides for the publication of a *National Housing Code* by the minister of housing.

In 2009, the Programme provided 22,416 ZAR (USD 2,741 at the time) for the repair of existing services and up to the Individual Subsidy quantum amount for the reconstruction of existing houses. For temporary assistance, 4,230 ZAR was provided for municipal engineering services and 47,659 ZAR for the construction of temporary shelters.[28] For temporary settlements, guidelines mandated a maximum level of basic engineering services and shelter requirements as the programme was not intended to constitute provision of formal or permanent housing.[29]

The adoption of policy clearly represents compliance with the judgment. However, implementation of this policy in practice is another story, raising the question as to whether the level of compliance is satisfactory. It has been hampered by numerous problems. Only municipalities (not communities) may apply for funding and only where an emergency situation can be demonstrated. The use of the Emergency Housing Programme by municipalities has been 'minimal' and largely 'ad hoc' (Tissington, 2011b). SHF and Urban Landmark (2010) demonstrated that only six out of the nine provinces had claimed funds and most grants were disbursed for disasters and floods in rural areas, although this does not reflect State-initiated uses of the funds. One of the core problems has been the narrow definition of emergency combined with burdensome institutional procedures, with processes taking up to eighteen months and sometimes leading to questionable rejection (Tissington, 2011b). This possibly confirms Liebenberg's (2010) conclusion that the policy is not fully compatible with the judgment. The constitutionality of the programme was partly raised by applicants in *Nokotyana* before the Constitutional Court in 2010 but only in relation to the standard of temporary sanitation facilities and provision of high mast lighting.[30]

More problematically, when the policy has been deployed in urban areas, the primary purpose has been evictions. Residents are moved to temporary relocation areas (TRAS) or 'transit camps'. Apparently this is to help address housing backlogs but Tissington (2011b: 96) argues that:

> Households are moved from shacks they have occupied, often for many years, to these areas where they are often left indefinitely with no timeline

---

[28] DHS 'Subsidy Quantum – Incremental Interventions,' Part 3, Vol. 4 of the National Housing Code (2009) 4.

[29] Access to water means a water point or tap for every twenty-five families; temporary sanitation facilities may vary from area to area; however, where possible Ventilated Improved Pit (VIP) latrines must be provided as a first option on the basis of one per five families; while high-mast lighting may be provided in special circumstances.

[30] *Nokotyana and others v. Ekurhuleni Municipality* 2010 (4) BCLR 312 (CC) (*Nokotyana*).

of when they will receive permanent accommodation. They are, in effect, off the 'backlog radar' as they are neither informal nor occupants of formal RDP or bond houses. Because of their so-called temporary nature, City officials are unwilling to invest much in infrastructure in these areas and in fact, the Emergency Housing Programme explicitly discourages this.

One of the few exceptions has been the creative use of the policy to provide the basis for in situ slum upgrading. In the *Bardale* litigation, a community agreed to relocate from a settlement adjoining a train track to a new site, and emergency housing funds were used to fund the initial costs of relocation in a flexible means so that the locality and housing could be development incrementally.[31] But in the main, the appropriation of the policy to facilitate 'relocations' has been mostly devastating for urban residents, leaving them worse off than in their original situation (Hunter, 2010).

10.2.3   Indirect Effects

It is perhaps worth mentioning that some of the indirect effects of the judgment were as or more significant.

First, the judgment and the national policy have possibly spurred municipalities to provide temporary services, regardless of access to national funds. In the case of Stellenbosch municipality, there was high awareness of potential litigation against the municipality: in interviews, officials indicated that they adopted a practice of immediately providing water and sanitation points in the mushrooming informal settlements on the edge of the city.[32] However, not all municipalities have been so responsive, particularly in KwaZulu Natal, Eastern Cape and Ekurhuleni in Gauteng. Locating the data to gain precise figures on provision of basic water, sanitation and electricity to informal settlements is not simple but statistics suggest that its provision increased at a faster rate since at least 2008.[33]

Second, there was possibly a contribution to the new informal settlements policy. By 2001, there was widespread recognition that housing policy needed systemic reform. In 2002 and 2003 a government review

---

[31] For a full discussion of this case, see Langford (2014).

[32] Interview with Stellenbosch Local Municipality, February 2008.

[33] 'Below RDP' water services across the whole country was rising more quickly from 2000 than 'above RDP' services. By 2008 this began to taper off as the latter caught up. However, these figures include rural areas and small towns making it difficult to interpret. But anecdotal evidence suggests a move to at least identifying informal settlements, providing services (often rudimentary and varying between settlements and municipalities) and a sketching of plans for the future development.

process identified the problems across the sector, including the housing backlog and the continued growth of informal settlements. The eventual outcome, Breaking New Ground (2004), was more modest than expected but it heralded a new Informal Settlements Programme (included in Chapter 13 of the Housing Code). Informal settlements could be upgraded in situ or relocations could occur in exceptional circumstances.[34] It is likely that the *Grootboom* judgment played a part in influencing the development of the policy given its timing. In a 2009 decision, the Constitutional Court claimed as much, noting that the policy was an attempt by the government to implement the right to housing in the Constitution.[35] While the actual influence was perhaps minimal, since the policy reflected the zeitgeist of the time, the judgment contributed, at least, to legitimatising the existence of informal settlements and their residents as constitutional rights holders. In any case, it is not clear that the policy has led to any significant achievements. Between 2004 and 2010, little upgrading has occurred in major urban areas (Huchzermeyer, 2010) though it has proceeded in some smaller towns. It has been stymied by attempts to evict communities, major breakdowns in the municipality-community relationships, a discursive emphasis on the *eradication* rather than *upgrading* and a complex and decentralised process that contributed to long bureaucratic delays.[36] For the most part, local municipalities seem resistant to the policy and it was largely overshadowed by State's growing of informal settlements. Paradoxically, some of the most promising successes in implementing this policy have emerged from resistance to eviction attempts by municipalities.[37]

Third, the LRC's prediction of the *Grootboom* judgment's importance for constitutional jurisprudence was largely on the mark. All of the key socio-economic rights cases in South African jurisprudence (from housing to health to social security) have largely built on the principles set out

---

[34] Municipalities were to access grants for the four different phases of the upgrading with individual-based (or other) subsidies to be used in the final construction phase.

[35] *Nokotyana* (2010), para. 24.

[36] See Soeker and Bhana (2010).

[37] Given the programme's complexity and decentralised nature the mobilising or creation of local and provincial political will is decisive: Van Wyk (2007). Chapter 13 can only be relied on once the local MEC for Housing has made a decision to upgrade the settlement. Indeed, in *Nokotyana*, the Constitutional Court chastised the MEC for a three-year delay in making a decision, although it permitted a further fourteen months. *Nokotyana* (2010), para. 23. Moreover, the Court stunningly interpreted the programme as not allowing services for the initial phases to be commenced while a final decision was awaited. This was despite such provision being expressly permissible under the policy: Huchzermeyer (2010).

in *Grootboom*. Other NGOs and social movements have indicated their
legal debt to the decision (Marcus and Budlender, 2008: 66). In the domain
of housing rights and evictions, the decision has clearly formed the basis
for an extensive range of jurisprudence.[38] There are instances of judges in
the High Court who subsequently order evictions that do not meet these
constitutional standards (see Huchzermeyer [2003] and discussion of
Makuase case; Wilson, 2006) but Advocate Geoff Budlender SC argues
that over the decade, most urban-based judges have become conscious of
the constitutional principles and the chances of avoiding a forced eviction
through court have improved markedly.[39]

Fourth, perhaps the most significant indirect effect is one that is almost
impossible to measure: the *Grootboom*-proofing of social policy. Senior
officials in departments such as water and social security have acknowledged that the precedent affected policy calculations. If progress was not
achieved fast enough, there was a concern that departments could be
subject to litigation.[40] Marcus and Budlender (2008: 66) found a similar
effect amongst their respondents, concluding that 'the government has
begun factoring these issues into its budgetmaking processes and has
become far more responsive to lawyers'. Interviews with housing officials
in Cape Town and Johannesburg municipalities suggest that they viewed
Grootboom (and some subsequent judgments) as helpfully pushing them
to review the adequacy of policy.[41] Although, there was a strong resistance to any potential ruling that would direct them in their budgetary
allocations.

Fifth, it is not clear how much *Grootboom* and its successors have
impacted the practice of forced evictions. No systemic data is collected.

[38] South African courts entrenched the right to alternative accommodation in cases of eviction, extended constitutional protections against eviction to debt defaulters and occupiers
of private land and housing, set out the minimum standards for alternative accommodation, established a duty of the municipality to meaningfully engage with a community,
provide the right to restoration of shelters and return to land after a forced eviction and
prevent retrogressions in legislative protections against evictions. In some eviction cases,
the *Grootboom* judgment has been proactively used as shield: the absence of an effective
housing programme precluded evictions being granted because people would be left in
desperate circumstances. For a deep analysis of this jurisprudence, see Liebenberg (2010).
[39] Interview with Geoff Budlender S.C. Advocate, February 2010.
[40] See Caspar Human (2006) from the Department of Water Affairs and Forestry and statements he made at the International Conference on Right to Water, Berlin, October 2005.
See also statements by Thabo Rakoloti, chief director of social assistance, Department of
Social Development, at the International Conference on the Right to Social Security in
development, Berlin, 19–20 October 2009.
[41] Interviews in February and March 2010.

But it is relatively clear that the number of large-scale government-initiated evictions has substantially decreased if not disappeared, although small-scale evictions have continued. While evictions are cited as a cause of the service delivery protests since 2004, they are nowhere near the leading cause compared to energy, water and broader housing concerns (see Jain [2010]). The legal, economic and political costs of eviction of large groups has arguably contributed to municipalities now targeting smaller or newer groups of residents or their encouragement of private landowners to take the lead in evicting.[42]

Sixth, the judgment created a tool that could be used in the political arena. The *Grootboom*-proofing of social policy and use of the precedent in subsequent cases is indirect evidence that there has been a shift in broader power relations. However, the case has been more of a background variable in these developments. In this respect, it is easy to accept the argument that the lack of a 'social movement' in this litigation meant there was a lost opportunity to use the judgment to directly and quickly leverage other gains.

Indeed, it is doubtful whether there were any significant recognition or symbolic effects. In 2002, the LRC stated that the judgment had 'changed the debate about social and economic rights – away from discussions about budgetary implications, towards the manner in which government approaches people living in dire circumstances' (LRC 2002: 4). This is true to a certain extent. Within the media, national bureaucracy and some municipalities, *Grootboom* appears to have contributed to a more progressive view on the rights of those living in informal settlements and emergency situations. However, any symbolic victories and other efforts to render informal settlers more visible have run headlong into a counter-discourse, a 'security driven approach to the urban poor': Pithouse (2009: 1–2). Attempts to legislate away housing protections for slumdwellers were foiled by social movements in the Constitutional Court[43] but have coincided with a discourse of criminalisation and attacks on movements such as *Abahlali baseMjondolo* (Amnesty, 2009). The growing jurisprudence on housing rights and evictions appears to have created some backlash itself amongst officials and some ANC leaders (Marcus and Budlender, 2008: 66) and explains attempts to roll back Prevention of Illegal Eviction from and Unlawful Occupation of Land Act 19 of 1998 (PIE Act).

[42] Interview with Advocate Stuart Wilson, April 2011.
[43] *Abahlali baseMjondolo Movement SA v Premier KZN and Others* (2009).

In reflecting on the *Grootboom* decision, the level of enforcement and impact of the judgment was much higher than much of the literature suggests. However, the speedy provision of shelter and then housing to the *Grootboom* community and effective implementation of the emergency housing policy was compromised by bureaucratic malaise and a lack of political and bureaucratic will and consideration. But before asking whether these supply-side constraints could have been overcome by better demand-side strategies (such as greater social mobilisation) or stronger remedies, it is important to compare a number of housing rights cases, many of which began in the same circumstances as *Grootboom*.

10.3   Other Housing Rights Cases

10.3.1   *Valhalla (Rudolph Case)*

The Valhalla or *Rudolph* case built directly on the *Grootboom* precedent. In 2002, the City of Cape Town brought an urgent application to evict and demolish the homes of almost fifty individuals who were living unlawfully in shacks in a public park in the suburb of Valhalla Park. By resorting to 'self-help', the City claimed the respondents had effectively 'jumped the queue' and obtained an unfair advantage over the thousands on the waiting list. The residents and a local civic action group, United Civic Front, opposed the eviction request and responded with a counter-application. They claimed that the City had failed to deliver adequate housing in Valhalla Park and that the City's housing policy did not satisfy the requirements in *Grootboom*.[44] All of the residents faced desperate housing situations: they were mostly unemployed and could not afford to pay nominal rent. Many had also been on the housing waiting list for over a decade.

Justice Selikowitz dismissed the City's urgent eviction application on the basis that it did not meet various pre-requisites under PIE.[45] He also upheld the counter-application, finding that the City had failed to implement a program to address the immediate situation of people in crisis situations. Holding that a declaratory order alone would not suffice, as the City had already failed to comply with *Grootboom*, a structural interdict

---

[44] Valhalla Park United Civic Front Organisation and Environment and Geographical Science Department – UCT (2007).

[45] There was no real and imminent danger of substantial injury or damage to any person or property from the occupation; the balance of hardship did not favour the granting of the order; and there were other effective remedies available to City.

was made. The City was ordered to deliver within four months a report stating what steps it had taken and would take in the future to comply.[46]

The City subsequently delivered four reports but the adequacy of steps taken was contested by the residents. In a subsequent but unreported judgment, Justice Selikowitz found that City had acknowledged, albeit inconsistently, what needed to be done but had failed to implement the necessary measures.[47] In particular, there was no evidence of any program in place intended to deal with those in desperate circumstances, including the applicants. A declaratory order was issued to this effect.[48] However, Selikowitz declined to grant a further structural interdict, as the occupants no longer faced eviction and the City had at least recognised the applicants' rights and commenced taking action.

Interviews with the City in February 2010 indicated that housing policy was partly reformed in the aftermath of the judgment. Moreover, no occupants of Valhalla Park were evicted. The residents took action to improve the condition of the settlement and interviews conducted in 2007 indicated a certain communal pride in this achievement but also frustration that they could not go further.[49] In 2008, the City budgeted for the upgrading of the settlement and began formal low-cost housing development in the area, covering the applicants.

10.3.2   Gabon (Modderklip Case)

In comparison, the Gabon community's struggle against eviction introduced a new factor in the enforcement process: an economic penalty for non-compliance. It proved to be deeply important. In May 2002, a small group (about 400 people) moved onto the Modderklip farm, East of Johannesburg, after being evicted from a larger and overcrowded settlement by the State. By October 2003, the community had grown to approximately 17,000 (and later 40,000) persons. The landowner, Duvenhage, was unsuccessful in attempting to remove the occupiers or in persuading the City Council to expropriate it and so secured an eviction order. But he was unable to enforce it as the sheriff required a deposit of R 1.8 million for

---

[46] *City of Cape Town v Rudolph and Others* 2004 (5) SA 39 (C).

[47] *City of Cape Town v Neville Rudolph & 49 Others*, Unreported judgment, December 2005.

[48] Ibid. The judge noted that the applicants could, of course, always approach the court in the future to assert their rights if they were dissatisfied with the City's compliance and could show an unjustifiable disregard for those rights.

[49] Valhalla Park United Front Civic Organisation and Environment and Geographical Science Department – UCT (2007).

the costs of removing the residents. Duvenage subsequently sued the State in the Pretoria High Court for failing to respect his property rights. The community was not initially included but later joined with a number of NGOs as amicus. Berger (2008: 89) notes that the community were 'led by a larger-than-life, tenacious attorney' while making 'decisions on the basis of consensus-building and inclusivity.'

The eventual judgment in the Constitutional Court found that the State could not fulfil property rights by simply establishing formal mechanisms and institutions. Duvenage's right to the rule of law was infringed as he could not enforce the initial court order. It was unreasonable of the State not to assist when it was impossible for Modderklip to evict such a large group of occupiers whose dire circumstances had to be taken into account. The Constitutional Court held that the authorities should compensate Modderklip for the unlawful occupation and pay rent for the occupiers, which would continue until the occupiers obtained suitable alternative accommodation.

In effect, the judgment halted the eviction order against the Gabon community, and the requirement to pay ongoing compensation provided a 'catalyst' for the municipality to address the community's needs (Liebenberg, 2010: 442). The Department of Housing developed a plan and, in 2006, work began on a new township, Chief Albert Luthuli Extension 6.[50] During this time, the community managed to extract extra concessions, 'basic services – including fresh water and weekly refuse removal' and use of 'a school and clinic in the nearby formal township of Daveyton' (Berger, 2008: 76–77).[51]

The development of permanent housing proceeded at a slightly faster pace than in *Grootboom* – arguably because of the compensation requirement – but it has been also dogged by complication.[52] A first phase of relocations to the new township occurred in 2009 but strangers to the community seized some of the housing. Those carrying relocation papers – but who had been denied a house – had their shacks destroyed and two persons were shot with live ammunition in the process. The community leadership puts much blame on the older leadership for collaborating

---

[50] It would provide 7,278 'housing opportunities' in a mixed-housing environment to Gabon residents and those from neighbouring settlements and on the general waiting list Tissington (2011a).

[51] Although residents in interviews in June 2010 noted the continuing lack of sanitation and were critical of attempts to introduce chemical toilets.

[52] Based on interviews with Gabon residents, June 2010. Attempts to interview municipal officials have been unsuccessful.

corruptly with municipal officials and there were reports that some houses were sold on the private market by council officials.

10.3.3   Makause Settlement (Ndawoyache case)

The *Ndawoyache* case provides an example of a weak remedy. Makause settlement lies halfway between Gabon and Johannesburg in the East Rand and its 10,000 residents live on land that is mostly owned by mining companies, which have ceased operations. In January 2007, drawing on funds from the Emergency Housing Programme, the municipality vaguely announced a relocation plan on the grounds of safety. However, some residents realised that a forced eviction was in the offing, and the Makause Community Development Forum (CDF) was swiftly formed. On 2 February 2007, the date on which the eviction notice was issued, the community sought an urgent interdict (injunction). On 11 February, the High Court found for the residents but the order was *relatively weak*: the municipality could proceed with evictions if, in each instance, residents were interviewed and consented to eviction in front of a third party observer police.[53]

Through a rather dubious process, in which residents signed consent forms represented to be food vouchers, the evictions process commenced despite protests about the process.[54] The first group of residents were moved to the resettlement site 40 kilometres away, but the mere provision of plastic tents on small plots and lack of transport hardened resistance back in Makause. Residents began reading the original court order to security officials and using physical force to resist dispossession. Faced with protest marches, threats of new legal action (with a new lawyer – the earlier and weaker order being blamed on the first lawyer) and a stinging article in a leading newspaper, the municipality relented. The evictions ceased, and of the 3,368 residents who had been evicted by that stage, two-thirds returned permanently while the remainder used the resettlement site only on weekends.

The eviction and counter-mobilisation provided an opportunity for the community to also take steps to improve living conditions and secure tenure. This has been a greater challenge than in other cases discussed. The municipality has been heavily resistant to any informal settlement upgrading (ostensibly on the structural grounds of dolomite and mining

[53] *Mphambo Ndawoyache & Others v. Ekurhuleni Metropolitan & MEC Housing.*
[54] Interview with General Moyo, June 2010.

holes). Nonetheless, the community were able to negotiate better access to water and electricity (although the municipality only provided half the water points and masts agreed upon), created a community centre (mostly for local dispute resolution) and commenced negotiations for direct purchase of the land from the owners. The community formed alliances with other settlements, NGOs and, increasingly, lawyers as they become involved in land negotiations.[55] However, tensions were high after the community largely voted for non-ANC parties in the subsequent local election.

10.3.4   Olivia Road

The Olivia Road presents a similar story of community mobilisation but with some innovations in relation to enforcement strategy. The Inner City Regeneration Strategy in Johannesburg, which sought to stimulate inner urban private sector investment, had led to 10,000 of the 67,000 occupants of 'bad buildings' being evicted by 2006, often without notice and by force, under apartheid-era health and safety laws and regulations (Wilson, 2011). Residents usually found themselves homeless or living in settlements on the periphery of the city (COHRE, 2005). Despite some legal victories in 2003 and 2004,[56] and a growing public debate and criticism by civil society organisations, the eviction campaign accelerated from 2005 onwards.

When the City sought to remove residents from Olivia Road and Joel Street in Berea, a more strategic response was developed by the residents with the Inner City Resource Centre and the legal organisation CALS. They launched a counter-application on behalf of all persons living in such buildings and requested a finding that the Municipality's policy was unconstitutional. The High Court agreed and ordered a halt to the evictions until alternative accommodation was provided. A year later, the Supreme Court of Appeal upheld the appeal of the municipality but ordered the City to provide alternative shelter (consistent with the post-*Grootboom* Housing Code) to those who needed it upon eviction. The occupants appealed but, after hearing argument and before handing down their decision, the Constitutional Court ordered the parties to engage first in a meaningful dialogue. In November 2007, a partial agreement was reached. The occupiers were to be provided with affordable and

---

[55] Interview with General Moyo, March 2011.
[56] *Occupiers of Junel House & Ors v City of Johannesburg (2003); Chancellor House* (2003) and *Park Court* (2004).

safe alternative accommodation in the inner city of Johannesburg, 'secure against eviction' while several policy issues were referred back to the Constitutional Court. The Constitutional Court only addressed some of them. Importantly, it found that the City must engage meaningfully with occupants if an eviction is likely to result in homelessness, and ongoing occupation can be considered illegal only after a court has ordered an eviction. This precedent has subsequently proved critical in other cases.

The judgment was largely implemented for the community: 450 residents were successfully temporarily relocated within City-owned 'communal' housing in one year. An empty building was partly refurbished, with one room per family with shared cooking and sanitation facilities. The rent was subsidised and basic services were provided. However, tensions emerged over the lack of maintenance and the lack of engagement regarding a permanent housing solution. One reason for speedy implementation was identified by the lawyers: a community worker was engaged and employed with the express purpose of negotiating with the municipality the terms and process of the relocation and resettlement.

Despite these advances, broader implementation has been limited. During the Constitutional Court hearings, the City adopted an Inner City Regeneration Charter which would provide 'inclusionary housing' within the inner city but there has been little progress in implementation. Instead, what has emerged is a new eviction strategy driven by owners (often new owners) of these buildings. As Advocate Stuart Wilson has commented, the *Olivia Road* decision compressed the eviction 'balloon' in one place but 'exposed' it in another. This has required a new round of strategic litigation against private owners, which has been so partially successful.[57] It seems one has to wait for the municipality to exhaust all its eviction options before it begins to effectively address inner-city housing issues for low-income residents.

10.3.5   Jaftha

The final case to be examined, *Jaftha*, did not concern informal settlements but rather vulnerable home owners and represents another stream of jurisprudence that has provided protection against various forms of foreclosure. The appellants, Ms Jaftha and Ms Van Rooyen, were poor and unemployed women who suffered from ill-health. With their children,

---

[57] In *Blue Moonlight*, the Constitutional Court found that the City has the same obligations towards poor residents evicted by private owners as it has regarding those evicted from public land. For a discussion of the attempts to ensure full implementation of the decision, see Dugard (2014).

they lived in homes which had been obtained through government sub-sidies. Both women borrowed small sums of money (R250 and R190, respectively) to be repaid in installments to their respective creditors. When they were unable to repay their respective debts, proceedings were initiated against them in the Magistrate's Court, resulting in judgments in favour of their respective creditors and ultimately in the sale in execu-tion of their homes in satisfaction of their outstanding debts. Both women lacked suitable alternative accommodation having lost their homes pursu-ant to sales in execution and were precluded as previous beneficiaries from applying again for State-subsidised housing.

The High Court refused to grant them relief on the basis that if the debtor chooses to vacate the premises, the effective loss of his/her home is caused by the exercise of the debtor's own free will and not by the execu-tion process.[58] In the Constitutional Court, they argued that the legislation was constitutionally overbroad to the extent that it permitted a person's security of tenure, inherent in the right of access to adequate housing under Section 26, to be removed even where it would be unjustifiable to do so. In a unanimous decision, Justice Mokgoro agreed to the extent that it allowed sales in execution in unjustifiable circumstances – for example, where a person could be rendered permanently homeless due to his/her failure to pay a trifling debt – without judicial intervention.

The legislation was declared unconstitutional in that it failed to pro-vide for judicial oversight over sales in execution.[59] In order to 'save' the impugned legislation, Justice Mokgoro read language into it requiring judicial oversight at the point of sale in execution of immovable property of judgment debtors, thereby enabling a court to determine whether to order sale in execution having considered all relevant circumstances.[60] The court also made what appeared to be an order requesting the Western

---

[58] Similarly, the Court held, that if the debtor chooses to remain in occupation, he/she would be 'holding over' and the purchaser would be required to use the provisions of the *Prevention of Illegal Eviction from and Unlawful Occupation of Land Act* to secure eviction, in which case the eviction would be caused by the separate legal proceedings instituted by the new owner and not by the execution process.

[59] It is critical to note that prior to the decision of Mokgoro J in *Jaftha*, default proceedings were overseen simply by a clerk of the court who, in effect, 'rubber-stamped' the default judgment which provided for sales in execution in satisfaction of outstanding debts. The decision in *Jaftha*, however, drastically altered the nature of default proceedings by expressly requiring oversight by a judicial officer prior to granting default judgment.

[60] This included the circumstances in which the debt was incurred; any attempts made by the debtor to repay the debt; the financial situation of the parties; and the amount of the outstanding debt.

Cape Law Society to investigate the behaviour of the lawyers for the creditors in the case.

Following the decision, although not ordered to do so by the Court, the
Minister of Justice established a task team to draft new legislation setting
out a procedure to govern the sales in execution process; to date, however, despite multiple drafts, no such legislation has been passed. Indeed,
it would appear that there are variable practices in the High Court and the
Magistrate's Court, as well as disparate practices within these courts in different jurisdictions.[61] Interviews with officials in the Western Cape High
Court and with the National Sheriff's Office indicated that the judgment
may have been simply proceduralised: Lawyers representing creditors submit an affidavit indicating why eviction was justified in the circumstances
and, given that home owners often did not file legal defences, executions
simply proceeded.

The evidence that the practice continues is evident in a public hearing
conducted by the South Africa Human Rights Commission in Gauteng.[62]
After complaints from residents in Katorus, Ennerdale and Lawley (and
later from the Eastern Cape) and public hearings with different stakeholders, the Commission found that 'although many of the role players
are following the letter of the law, more can be done'. The Sheriffs and the
South African Police Service 'acknowledged that illegal evictions are taking place' and the Commission was particularly critical of the Department
of Housing, for only focusing on 'low-income first-time homeowners' and
not also evictions. It also criticised the private sector and 'unscrupulous
buyers', with allegations that law enforcement and local government officials were involved.

The Commission made an enormous range of recommendations
to different actors indicating the potential complexity in addressing
the problem, and in effect that the reading-in order, a favourite of the
Constitutional Court, might not have been appropriate. In our view, a
broader policy and legislative effort might have been catalysed by a court
ruling requiring an effective state response by a certain deadline. More
importantly, it appears the issue has been largely overlooked by NGOs and
social movements. However, in a number of subsequent cases, occupants

---

[61] In the absence of such a unified procedural framework and in light of a number of subsequent court decisions dealing with the procedure relating to applications for default judgments and the issuing of warrants for attachments of immovable property in pursuance
thereof, some procedural aspects remain confusing; see Smith and Van Niekerk (2010).

[62] South African Human Rights Commission (2008), *Report on the Public Hearing on Housing,
Evictions and Repossessions*, Pretoria.

who had been dispossessed of ownership in a manner contrary to the required by the Constitutional Court decision in *Jaftha* have successfully reviewed court proceedings and had their ownership reinstated – despite the transfer to innocent third parties who had purchased in the interim through the judgment creditor.[63]

10.4   Analysis

10.4.1   *Housing Rights Cases – Degree of Compliance*

If we reflect on the six cases discussed, it is clear that enforcement is challenging but not elusive. We can summarise the outcomes as follows:

- There are markedly varying levels of enforcement amongst the cases, particularly once a period of three to five years has elapsed since judgment.
- Partial implementation is common.[64] Many decisions contained a number of orders or were directed to a range of beneficiaries. It is not uncommon to find one part of the order fully implemented and another not.
- In a significant number of cases, the depth and breadth of implementation improved over *longer time periods* (e.g., in *Grootboom* and *Valhalla*). In *Grootboom*, the order was formally implemented after the elapse of four years and helped catalyse access to a permanent housing solutions for the community after eight years. This is at least a decade earlier than could have been reasonably expected given the crisis in housing policy and the growth of informal settlements.
- In recent cases (such as *Olivia Road* and *Moddderklipp*), the orders relating to litigants were implemented in a very short space of time, often beyond the terms of the order.

10.4.2   *Causation in a Broader Perspective*

As to causal narratives, these findings on housing rights provide some but limited support to the idea that strong judicial review promotes better compliance. The case with the least impact, *Makause*, was characterised by very weak procedural protections against forced eviction while a

---

[63] See *Nxazonke and Another v ABSA Bank Ltd Ltd and Others* (18100/2012) [2012] ZAWCHC 184 (4 October 2012).
[64] See discussions of *Grootboom* and *Jaftha* in particular.

strong and detailed order in *Olivia Road* was correlated with a relatively successful resettlement process (although this was also the result of a settlement). However, the pace of access to permanent housing solutions does not always correlate in such a fashion. Stronger mandatory orders in the *Valhalla* case did not seem to speed implementation in comparison to the non-existent orders in *Grootboom*. In the *Jaftha* case, the remedy was strong – the constitutional and statutory protections against forced evictions were read into debtor legislation – but its influence in practice has been muted. In this case, a more dialogical and deferred remedy that required a government response– spurring a more effective policy change and legitimating the decision at the same time - may have been much more appropriate.

The findings provide significant support to the social mobilisation hypothesis. In examining the variance in results across these housing rights cases, the extent of social mobilisation by different communities appears critical. The litigants in *Olivia Road* and *Gabon* in particular were able to combine a mix of strong internal mobilisation, links with NGOs and lawyers and skilful use of the media at various points in the struggle. It also affirms the standard distinction between implementation levels in *Grootboom* and *TAC*. The Treatment Action Campaign faced the same problems with enforcement on the right to health but, with strong legal and political pressure, was able to overcome them relatively quickly and ensure that compliance, at least at the policy level.[65] Indeed, Treatment Action Campaign attributes its temporary failure to enforce the Nevirapine order due to its attention being diverted by other issues. Berger's (2008) review of other socio-economic rights cases generally supports the thesis on the primacy of civil society pressure.

However, caution needs to be exercised in pressing either of these explanations too far or too narrowly, particularly if used as a strategic template. There are four important variations on these themes.[66]

---

[65] Note that there is not full implementation of the decision or a permeation of its empirical findings. Jones (2009) notes that at the local, misperceptions on the value of antiretrovirals persist amongst many local communities and health officials.

[66] These observations are not meant to be exclusive. Some social security cases (see Berger, 2008) and health cases (e.g., *Nyathi*) appear to be driven by individuals with a clear sense of injustice beyond the individual material deprivation. The trilogy of security cases in the Eastern Cape – *Ngxusa, Jayiya, Kate* – are partly attributable to this factor as well as a responsive judiciary on the question of enforcement.

Unpopular Litigants

First, there is a challenge of replicating such litigation for highly stigmatised groups. It is not clear whether social mobilisation is always possible
or fully effective in these situations or whether mandatory injunctions will
compel the necessary action. A most striking example is complementary
litigation by the TAC concern prisoners. In the *Westville* prison case concerning access to HIV medicines, prison officials refused to provide anti-
retroviral medicines to prisoners despite repeated orders by a High Court
in Durban. Despite this case being subject to some of the strongest judicial
orders seen in South Africa and the target of the most powerful national
social movement, TAC, prison officials and their lawyers remained obstinate. This suggests that strategies for enforcement need to be open to creative forms of enforcement. One possible road forward is the adoption of
orders that create economic incentives for compliance. This appeared to
have a particularly strong effect in the *Gabon* case. The municipality was
forced to pay compensation to the landowner for the informal occupation
until it provided residents with a housing solution that was consistent with
the principles of *Grootboom*. Similarly, the *Nyathi* litigation on enforcement of monetary claims (in that case concerning medical negligence at a
hospital) is also a good example.[67] The Court permitted litigants to execute
enforcement against assets of the state.

Bureacratic Contingency

Second, it is important not to underestimate the degree of bureaucratic
contingency (Epp, 2009). One surprising finding in the discussion above
was how quickly some authorities were able to adopt new policies in
response to these judgments or litigation. Litigation in these cases catalysed the adoption of at least four new national and local housing policies,
some exhibiting a high degree of complexity. The rub comes, however, in
the implementation of those very policies. Here there is considerable variance. This reflects in many ways the underlying problem with the state in
South Africa: implementation across almost all sectors.

In some instances, an order may be simple to implement since it just
extends a current and relatively successful programme. In 2004, *Khosa*
and *Mahlaule* Constitutional Court cases[68] granted permanent residents

---

[67] *Nyathi v Member of the Executive Council for the Department of Health Gauteng and Ors*
    2008 (5) SA 94 (CC) (*Nyathi*).
[68] CCT12/03 (*Khosa & Others v Minister of Social Development & Others*) (Pretoria High
    Court 2003) and CCT13/03 (*Mahlaule & Another v Minister of Social Development &
    Others*) (Pretoria High Court 2003).

the same rights as citizens to government child support grants and old age pension grants.[69] What is noticeable in the various housing rights cases is that orders that relied on the coordination of multiple government actors as well as private sector tendering were particularly likely to face delays and problems in implementation. This suggests that litigants and courts need to be careful with simply seeking to enforce a top-down and complex housing model, which is only partly appropriate in South Africa at this time. Legislatively we have the example of Brazilian laws that permit slum dwellers themselves to initiate slum upgrading processes with the backing of administrative courts. But can constitutional litigation help support a move towards a more community-centric rights-based approach that permits space for in situ upgrading? Some evidence is available. The settlement in the *Bardale case* sparked the creative use and combination of existing emergency and upgrading policies to provide a relocation site for in situ upgrading.[70] Moreover, in the final Joe Slovo case, the Constitutional Court acknowledged that the parties had since adopted an in situ upgrade program rather than persist with the eviction and set aside its own eviction order.[71]

Another approach can be the development of particular alliances with government. If one government actor is particularly motivated then the chances of success appear higher. For example, Black Sash took the Department of Social Development to court in order to force it make back payments to social grant recipients who had waited for long periods before receiving their grants, which resulted in people being paid from the date of application rather than the date of approval. This led to more than R2 billion (US$250 million) being attached from the budget to ensure implementation (Goldblatt and Rosa, 2014). Respondents suggested that one of the reasons for the positive response was that the Minister for Social Affairs was willing to push the issue within the cabinet in the face of contrary views from the Minister for Finance.

---

[69] According to Polzer Ngwato and Jinnah Polzer Ngato and Jinnah (2013), the case was 'very effective in significantly improving the socio-economic standing of this specific group by enabling access to an important welfare net, especially given that most beneficiaries of the case live in rural areas where high levels of unemployment mean there are few livelihood options other than government grants.' It also established the principle of non-discrimination regarding the constitutional right to social security, even though it emphasised that permanence of residence in the country was a relevant criterion for reasonably apportioning rights, thereby including permanent residents but leaving the interpretation regarding other categories of non-nationals uncertain.

[70] See analysis in Langford (2014).

[71] See note 10.

Internal Mobilisation and External Alliances

Third, the role of different civil society actors should not be conflated. The degree of mobilisation of broader social movements may affect broader enforcement but the role of *internal mobilisation* amongst litigants and *types of alliances* in enforcement should not be overlooked – particularly in more focused cases. There may be different incentives and costs for the applicants to continue pressing enforcement. Additionally, applicant communities often experience different levels of organisation and unanimity. For example, highly-organised communities facing eviction in the *Modderklipp, Bardale, Olivia Rd, Valhalla* and *Joe Slovo* cases have been able arguably to achieve more than the more divided *Grootboom* community. These communities worked closely with lawyers and social movements and appeared to have well-organised, representative and hard-working governance structures.

In the *Grootboom case*, while it could be said that the judgment only partly empowered the community – their 'power to' in Gaventa's (2006) terms – it was here that the particular circumstances of the case came into play. The community seemed to have missed the chance to expand their 'power with' and 'power within'. They quickly lost access to their private lawyer, Julian Apollos: he merged his small law firm with a larger firm that represented the municipality, thus creating a conflict of interest. The LRC attempted to assist the community negotiate with the authorities, but Marcus and Budlender (2008: 63) argue that there seems to be a 'lack of effective leadership in the community which made the process extremely difficult'.[72] The community was able to form alliances with civil society organisations such as Development Action Group and the housing-oriented Community Organisation Resource Centre (CORC) and played an active part in the Wallacedene leadership which developed in response to the new housing plan. But the cooperation did not always last and the community were not part of broader and emerging urban movements. Likewise, the constellation and calibration of social movements and NGOs in a particular case can also be decisive. Sometimes, it is not a question of *more* civil society but *better* civil society.

---

[72] This was confirmed in the interview with Sila who also identified some of the causes: 'There was fighting among the leadership. Irene decided to leave Wallacedene because of the fighting. I wanted to insist that she stay where we fought. She came back and then built a shack close to me ... The problems started when more and more people got involved. They saw our success and they moved here. Every time the City of Cape Town looked, there were more numbers. Irene was not happy with this.'

Different Rights, Different Contexts

Finally, singular causal comparisons across different rights could be problematic. The ability to mobilise for some rights may be more difficult due to their localism (e.g., housing) or remoteness (e.g., rural land and labour). For example, while health litigation has largely been driven by national movements, almost all housing rights cases have been commenced by local and impoverished communities. This localism is not unsurprising given the particularism of most housing struggles and the lack of national housing rights social movements in South Africa. While social movements focused on housing have emerged, they remain largely locally based and it is not clear yet whether they can exert the same influence on national policy as their counterparts in health and social security.[73] In the case of social security, the early litigation was often commenced by individuals but its quantitative and national character has lent itself to the engagement of national NGOs and movements, and later litigation has often been driven by civil society actors. These differences suggest that strategies for improving compliance should take account of these power differentials. Thus, it is arguable that stronger and ongoing remedies – such as supervisory jurisdiction by a court - might be more justifiable in cases where rights-holders lack strong social movement backing.

10.5   Conclusion

The state of compliance with socio-economic rights judgments in South Africa should be met with neither pessimism nor optimism. Examining six housing rights cases in the context of the broader empirical scholarship on social rights judgments, we find that any descriptive or explanatory narrative requires nuance. The picture of enforcement varies dramatically between judgments and across time. Some litigants were able to enforce orders and catalyse broader policy change while others were left with little to show for their turn to the courts.

Likewise, the findings cast some doubt on the idea that the strength of remedies or accompanying social mobilisation are always the principal factors in explaining levels of enforcement. Part of the *causal* story is the nature of remedies but it is hazardous to believe that mandatory supervision of compliance is always the answer. We argued that dialogical remedies such as deferred declarations of invalidity could also have been used

---

[73] Although, the potential threat of one urban movement, *Abahlali baseMjondolo*, has led to severe repression by some arms of government (Amnesty, 2009).

to spur more appropriate and legitimate policies and practices (e.g., *Jafta*) while creative approaches that incentivise compliance or raise the cost of non-compliance (such as in the *Gabon*) deserve greater consideration. This is particularly salient in an environment when many but not all judges evince a reluctance towards the use of mandatory supervision.

Equally, social mobilisation explains much of the difference in levels of implementation but it is unrealistic to expect an emulation of the well-known *TAC* campaign in every case. It is important to identify practical means by which highly marginalised litigants can build sufficient but effective alliances with social movements, NGOs, journalists, trade unions, churches, bureaucrats and politicians. More ambitiously, these alliances have the potential to morph into broader pro-compliance and advocacy coalitions (Dugard and Langford, 2011). But this will only occur if civil society organisations see judgments as a place to develop or strengthen advocacy platforms.

Most importantly, when cases involve highly marginalised and stigmatised groups, an obstinate defendant or require complex coordination between different actors, the question of enforcement is brought into sharp relief. Strong as well as responsive, unorthodox and creative methods will be essential and judicial and civil society actors will need to be highly alert to the question of implementation.

References

Alston, Philip (2008), 'Foreword', in Malcolm Langford (ed.), *Social Rights Jurisprudence: Emerging Trends in International and Comparative Law* (Cambridge: Cambridge University Press), ix–xiii.

Amnesty (2009), *South Africa: Failure to conduct impartial investigation into Kennedy Road violence is leading to further human rights abuses*, Public Document AI Index: AFR 53/011/2009, 16 December.

Barrow, Greg (2000), 'South African Squatters Win Battle', *BBC News Online* http://news.bbc.co.uk/2/hi/africa/956507.stm.

Berger, John (2008), 'Litigating for Social Justice in Post-apartheid South Africa: A Focus on Health and Education', in Varun Gauri and Daniel Brinks (eds.), *Courting Social Justice: Judicial Enforcement of Social and Economic Rights in the Developing World* (Cambridge: Cambridge University Press), 38–99.

Bilchitz, David (2007), *Poverty and Fundamental Rights: The Justification and Enforcement of Socio-Economic Rights* (Oxford: Oxford University Press).

COHRE (ed.), (2005), *Any Room for the Poor? Forced Evictions in Johannesburg, South Africa* (Geneva: COHRE).

Dugard, Jackie (2014), 'Beyond Blue Moonlight: The implications of judicial avoidance in relation to the provision of alternative housing', *CCR* 5, 265–279.

Dugard, Jackie and Langford, Malcolm (2011), 'Art or Science? Synthesising Lessons from Public Interest Litigation and the Dangers of Legal Determinism', *South African Journal on Human Rights*, 26(3), 39–64.

Epp, Charles (2009), *Making Rights Real: Activists, Bureaucrats, and the Creation of the Legalist State* (Chicago: University of Chicago Press).

Gaventa, John (2006), 'Finding the Spaces for Change: A Power Analysis', *IDS Bulletin*, 37(6), 26–33.

Goldblatt, Beth and Rosa, Solange (2014), 'Social Security Rights', in Malcolm Langford, Ben Cousins, Jackie Dugard and Tshepo Madlingozi (eds.), *Socio-Economic Rights in South Africa: Symbols or Substance?* (Cambridge: Cambridge University Press), 253–274.

Heywood, Mark (2009), 'South Africa's Treatment Action Campaign: Combining Law and Social Mobilization to Realize the Right to Health', *Journal of Human Rights Practice*, 1(1), 14–36.

Hirschl, Ran (2004), *Towards Juristocracy: The Origins and Consequences of the New Constitutionalism* (Cambridge, MA: Harvard University Press).

Huchzermeyer, Marie (2003), 'Housing Rights in South Africa: Invasions, Evictions, the Media, and the Courts in the Cases of Grootboom, Alexandra, and Bredell', *Urban Forum*, 14(1), 80–107.

(2009), 'The struggle for in situ upgrading of informal settlements: A reflection on cases in Gauteng', *Development Southern Africa*, 26(1), 59–74.

(2010), 'Pounding at the Tip of the Iceberg: The Dominant Politics of Informal Settlements Eradication', *Politikon*, 37(1), 129–148.

Human, Caspar (2006), 'The Human Right to Water in Africa: The South African Example', in Eibe Riedel and Peter Rothen (eds.), *The Human Right to Water* (Berlin: Berliner Wissenschafts Verlag), 83–93.

Hunter, M. (2010), *Case Study: The Difference that Place Makes: Some Brief Notes on the Economic Implications of moving from an Informal Settlement to a Transit Camp* (Department of Geography, University of Toronto).

Jain, Hirsh (2010), *Community Protests in South Africa: Trends, Analysis and Explanations* (Community Law Centre: Local Government Working Paper Series No. 1).

Jones, Peris (2009), *Aids Treatment and Human Rights in Context* (London: Palgrave Macmillan).

Joubert, Pearlie (2008), 'Grootboom Dies Homeless and Penniless', *Mail & Guardian*, 8 August http://mg.co.za/article/2008-08-08-grootboom-dies-homeless-and-penniless.

Langford, Malcolm (ed.) (2003), *Litigating Economic, Social and Cultural Rights: Achievements, Challenges and Strategies* (Geneva: Centre on Housing Rights & Evictions).

(2014), 'Housing Rights Litigation: *Grootboom* and Beyond', in Malcolm Langford, Ben Cousins, Jackie Dugard and Tshepo Madlingozi (eds.), *Symbols or Substance? The Role and Impact of Socio-Economic Rights Strategies in South Africa* (Cambridge: Cambridge University Press), 187–225.

Langford, Malcolm, Ben Cousins, Jackie Dugard and Tshepo Madlingozi (eds.) (2014), *Socio-Economic Rights Strategies in South Africa: Symbols or Substance?* (Cambridge: Cambridge University Press).

Liebenberg, Sandra (2008), 'Socio-economic rights under South Africa's transformative constitution', in M Langford (ed.) *Socio-economic rights jurisprudence: Emerging trends in international and comparative law* (Cambridge: Cambridge University Press), 75–101.

(2010), *Socio-Economic Rights: Adjudication under a Transformative Constitution* (Claremont: Juta).

LRC (2002), *Annual Report for the Period 1 April 2000 to 31 March 2001* (Johannesburg: Legal Resources Centre and Legal Resources Trust).

Marcus, Gilbert and Stephen Budlender (2008), *A Strategic Evaluation of Public Interest Litigation in South Africa* (Hamilton: Atlantic Philanthropies).

Mbazira, Christopher (2008a), 'Non-Implementation of Court Orders in Socio-economic Rights Litigation in South Africa', *ESR Review*, 9(4), 2–7.

(2008b), *You Are the 'Weakest Link' in Realising Socio-economic Rights: Goodbye – Strategies for Effective Implementation of Court Orders in South Africa* (Research Series 3; Cape Town: Community Law Centre, University of the Western Cape,).

Nicholson, Zara (2008a), 'Foreign Shopkeepers: Tensions Run High', *IOL News* www.iol.co.za/news/south-africa/foreign-shopkeepers-tensions-run-high-1.414475#.VK0II3bKxaQ.

(2008b), 'Hundreds Say Farewell to Housing Heroine', *IOL News*, 10 August www.iol.co.za/news/south-africa/hundreds-say-farwell-to-housing-heroine-1.411865.

Pieterse, Marius (2007), 'Eating Socioeconomic Rights: The Usefulness of Rights Talk in Alleviating Social Hardship Revisited', *Human Rights Quarterly*, 29(3), 796–822.

Pillay, Karisha (2002), 'Implementation of Grootboom: Implications for the Enforcement of Socio-Economic Rights', *Law Democracy and Development*, 6, 255–277.

Pithouse, Richard (2009), 'A Progressive Policy without Progressive Politics: Lessons from the failure to implement 'Breaking New Ground''', *Town Planning Journal*, 54, 1–14.

Polzer Ngato, Tara and Zaheera Jinnah (2014), 'Migrants and Mobilisation around Socio-Economic Rights', in Malcolm Langford Ben Cousins, Jackie Dugard and Tshepo (eds.), *Symbols or Substance? The Role and Impact of Socio-Economic Rights Strategies in South Africa* (Cambridge: Cambridge University Press), 389–420.

Porter, Bruce (2009), 'The Reasonableness of Article 8(4) – Adjudicating Claims from the Margins', *Nordic Journal of Human Rights*, 27(1), 39–53.

Robins, Steven (2008), *Revolution to Rights in South Africa: Social Movements, NGOs and Popular Politics after Apartheid* (London: James Currey).

SHF and Urban-LandMark (2010), *An Investigation into an Apparent Increase in Evictions from Private Rental Housing* (Johannesburg: SHF and Urban-LandMark).

Sloth-Nielsen, Julia (2001), 'The Child?s Right to Social Services, the Right to Social Security, and Primary Prevention of Child Abuse: Some Conclusions in the Aftermath of Grootboom', *South African Journal of Human Rights*, 17(2), 210–231.

Smith, Christo and van Niekerk, S.J. (2010), 'Execution against Immovable Property: Negotiating the Tightrope of s 26', *DeRebus* (January/February), 32–33.

Soeker, Ardiel and Bhana, Kailash (2010), 'Hangberg: A Question of Land Denied', *Pambazuka News*.

Sunstein, Cass (2004), *The Second Bill of Rights: FDR's Unfinished Revolution and Why We Need It More Than Ever* (New York: Basic Books).

Swart, Mia (2005), 'Left Out in the Cold? Crafting Constitutional Remedies for the Poorest of the Poor', *South African Journal of Human Rights*, 21, 215–224.

Tissington, Kate (2011a), 'Demolishing Development at Gabon Informal Settlement: Public Interest Litigation Beyond Modderklipp', *South African Journal of Human Rights*, 27(3), 192–205.

   (2011b), *A Resource Guide to Housing in South Africa: Legislation, Policy, Programmes and Practice* (Johannesburg: SERI).

Tushnet, Mark (2008), *Weak Courts, Strong Rights: Judicial Review and Social Welfare Rights in Comparative Constitutional Law* (Princeton: Princeton University Press).

UK Joint Committee on Human Rights of the House of Lords and House of Commons (2004), *Report on the International Covenant on Economic, Social and Cultural Rights*, (Twenty First Report of Session 2003–2004, 20 October).

Van Wyk, J. (2007), 'The Complexities of Providing Emergency Housing Assistance in South Africa', *TSAR*, 1, 35–55.

Waldron, Jeremy (2009), 'Socio-Economic Rights and Theories of Justice', in Thomas Pogge (ed.), *Freedom from Poverty as a Human Right*, Vol. 2 (Paris: UNESCO), 21–50.

Wilson, Stuart (2006), 'Judicial Enforcement of the Right to Protection from Arbitrary Eviction: Lessons from Mandelaville', *South African Journal on Human Rights*, 22(4), 535–562.

   (2011), 'Litigating Housing Rights in Johannesburg's Inner City', *South African Journal on Human Rights*, 27(3), 127–151.

11

The African Human Rights System and Domestic Enforcement

FRANS VILJOEN

In this chapter, some reflections are provided about the domestic 'enforcement' (or 'implementation') of the recommendations of the African Commission on Human and Peoples' Rights (African Commission) and the orders of the African Court on Human and Peoples' Rights (African Human Rights Court) in respect of socio-economic rights (together, referred to as 'regional orders'). Although states' obligations in respect of these rights are often associated with the fulfillment of rights, the obligations to respect, protect and promote also come into play. Initially, a brief overview of these obligations of states under the African regional human rights system is provided.

This chapter then proceeds to question, on the basis of an earlier study dealing mostly with 'civil and political' rights, whether the factors predictive of compliance or implementation identified in that study also apply to cases largely dealing with socio-economic rights. By postulating a number of hypotheses, adjusted from the earlier study, it suggests a number of factors (related to the relevant oversight body or tribunal, the domestic legal framework, the 'victims', the nature of the respondent state, civil society and community involvement, and the role of the international legal framework) as possible predictors of domestic enforcement. It identifies and discusses the extent of 'compliance' in four 'communications' (here referred to as 'cases') in which the African Commission directed recommendations in respect of socio-economic rights to states. Against this background, but while not endeavouring to formally or statistically test the validity of the hypotheses, given the limited number of cases surveyed, this chapter explores the resonance of the identified hypotheses in understanding enforcement in the four cases.

Compliance, understood as the fulfillment of a state obligation under a treaty, is distinguished from the much broader issue whether an individual

Frans Viljoen is a Professor at the Centre for Human Rights, Faculty of Law, University of Pretoria.

is 'fully enjoying' treaty rights (Green, 2001: 1086). Even if it is used in this narrow sense, compliance should be clarified further, to indicate whether the obligation at stake is extensive (e.g., to 'give effect' to treaty rights) or circumscribed (e.g., to give effect to a remedial order). In this chapter, the focus falls on *compliance with regional remedial orders*.

Adopting this focus is clearly limited and limiting. Restricting the focus on remedial orders as the frame of analysis implies a violations-based approach. Particularly in the context of 'socio-economic' rights, it may well be asked if such an approach, rather than a wider 'progressive realisation' approach, is not more suitable.

11.1   Socio-economic Rights under the African System

It is usually understood that the 'African regional human rights system' consists of three treaty institutions that may make findings or take decisions in respect of African Union (AU) member states: the African Commission, the African Human Rights Court and the African Committee of Experts on the Rights and Welfare of the Child (African Children's Rights Committee) (Viljoen, 2012).

Operating since November 1987, the African Commission has for almost three decades been finalising 'communications' related to the African Charter on Human and Peoples' Rights (African Charter).[1] By mid-2016, all AU member states had for some time been party to the Charter. The Charter has been celebrated for including 'socio-economic' rights alongside other ('civil and political' and 'peoples'') rights, without any distinction as to the justiciability of these rights.[2] Over time, the Commission clearly accepted the justiciability of all these rights, and emphasised that all rights – including 'socio-economic' rights – impose the obligation on states to respect, protect, promote and fulfil.[3] According to the African Commission, the duty to respect requires that

[1] While the emphasis in this contribution falls on the Commission's protective (individual complaints) mandate, its promotional mandate, comprising the examination of state reports and the elaboration of thematic studies by special mechanisms such as the Commission's Working Group on Economic, Social and Cultural Rights, is also of some importance.
[2] See in particular arts. 16 and 17 of the African Charter on Human and Peoples' Rights, adopted 27 June 1981, OAU Doc. CAB/LEG/67/3 rev. 5, 21 I.L.M. 58 (1982), *entered into force* 21 October 1986. The term 'socio-economic' is here used as has become customary in respect of the African Charter. However, the term is problematised later in this chapter.
[3] See the articulation of the three-layered obligations in the *Ogoniland* case (Communication 155/96, *Social and Economic Rights Action Centre and Another v Nigeria* [2001] AHRLR 60 [ACHPR 2001] [15th Annual Activity Report]), paras 44–47.

the state refrain from interfering with the enjoyment of these rights, for example, by respecting the use of resources, and the duty to protect entails the protection of rights-holders against other subjects.[4] The duty to promote entails ensuring an environment that enables individuals to exercise their rights (such as creating and maintaining an effective legal environment, promoting tolerance and raising awareness); the duty to fulfil to some extent overlaps with the 'promotional duty', but further entails a 'positive expectation' that the state would 'move its machinery towards the actual realisation of rights', for example, through the 'direct provision of basis needs'.[5] However, the Commission has not made it clear in its jurisprudence whether positive obligations in respect of socio-economic rights have to be realised immediately or progressively (Chirwa, 2008). The limited list of these rights in the Charter,[6] a fact admitted by the drafters,[7] prompted the Commission subsequently to extend the catalogue of 'socio-economic' rights. Applying the 'implied rights theory', the Commission found that the right to shelter/housing and food/nutrition may be derived from the explicit provisions of the Charter,[8] and found a violation of 'the right to shelter' and 'the right to food'.[9] However, it subsequently did not take up the invitation to expand the list, by including the right to water as an 'implied right', as such.[10] Instead, the Commission used its competence under article 60 and 61 of the Charter to draw interpretive guidance from a wide array of international human rights sources to interpret an existing Charter right (the right to health) as including access to water as one of its 'underlying determinants'.[11] To give more detailed content to the 'socio-economic' rights in the Charter, the Commission in 2012 adopted 'State Party Reporting Guidelines for Economic, Social and Cultural Rights in

[4] *Ogoniland* case, supra n. 3, para 46.
[5] *Ogoniland* case, supra n. 3, paras 46 and 47.
[6] The only rights that clearly impose an obligation to fulfill are the rights to education and to health; in addition, the Charter also includes the right to equitable conditions of work and protects the right to property.
[7] The drafters of the Charter considered a minimalist approach to the inclusion of socio-economic rights as the most appropriate approach to follow at that time (see Viljoen, 2004:320).
[8] *Ogoniland* case, supra n. 3, paras 60, 65 and 66.
[9] *Ogoniland* case, supra n. 3, paras 62 and 66.
[10] Communications 279/03; 296/05, *Sudan Human Rights NGO and Centre on Housing and Evictions v Sudan*, 28th Activity Report of the African Commission www.chr.up.ac.za/images/files/documents/ahrdd/theme02/african_commission_28th_activity_report.pdf (2009) AHRLR 153 (ACHPR 2009) (28th Activity Report) (*Darfur* case), para 126.
[11] *Darfur* case, supra n. 10, paras 206–212.

the African Charter on Human and Peoples' Rights' (Tunis Reporting Guidelines).

In addition to its competence to hear cases based on the African Charter, the African Commission also has the competence to adjudicate communications alleging violations of the Protocol to the African Charter on the Rights of Women in Africa (African Women's Protocol) against state parties to this Protocol. The African Women's Protocol not only reinforces the socio-economic rights in the Charter by detailing their relevance to the lives of women,[12] but it also formalises the Commission's jurisprudential extension of the scope of the Charter to include, as far as women are concerned, the rights to housing and food.[13]

Despite its broad substantive scope, the Commission's protective mandate is constrained by the generally accepted perception that its quasi-judicial determinations (findings) are recommendatory only. With the election of the first eleven judges of the African Human Rights Court in 2006, the protective mandate of the Commission was enhanced by the possibility of binding judicial pronouncements (judgments).[14] The Court has jurisdiction over the African Charter, the African Women's Protocol and the African Charter on the Rights and Welfare of the Child (African Children's Charter), as well as other human rights treaties ratified by the states concerned.[15] By mid-2015, the Court had delivered three judgments on the merits, none with particular relevance to socio-economic rights.[16]

---

[12] See, e.g., arts. 12–19 of Protocol to the African Charter on Human and Peoples' Rights on the Rights of Women in Africa, adopted by the 2nd Ordinary Session of the Assembly of the Union, Maputo, CAB/LEG/66.6 (13 September 2000); reprinted in 1 Afr. Hum. Rts. L.J. 40, entered into force 25 November 2005.

[13] Ibid., arts. 15 ('food security') and 16 ('adequate housing').

[14] The Court was established by way of a Protocol to the African Charter on the Establishment of an African Court on Human and Peoples' Rights, 1998, which entered into force in 2004, and by mid-2016 counted thirty state parties.

[15] On the Court's expansive contentious jurisdiction, see art. 3(1) of the African Human Rights Court Protocol. Arts. 27 and 31 of the Protocol, read together, provided jurisdiction to both the African Commission and African Court. Reading art. 27 as providing exclusive jurisdiction to the Court would be an absurd interpretation, as it would allow complaints under the Protocol only to individuals in state that had made an art. 34(6)-declaration. Art. 27 should be read as adding the Court as a forum to which complaints can be directed, in addition to the Commission, which would automatically, as the institutional arm under the original treaty, also be competent to hear cases on a normative supplement to the charter.

[16] African Court on Human and Peoples' Rights, *Tanganyika Law Society and Another; Mtikila v Tanzania*, Applications 9/2011, 11/2011 (joined), 14 June 2013; *The Beneficiaries of the Late Norbert Zongo and Others v Burkina Faso*, Application 013/2011, 28 March 2014; *Konaté v Burkina Faso*, Application 4/2013, 5 December 2014.

The African Commission may refer an instance of non-implementation of any of its findings to the African Human Rights Court. Under its 2010 Rules of Procedure, a state is given an initial period of 180 days to indicate what measures it has taken towards implementing the Commission's decision, and if the state does not respond, it may be given a reminder to do so within further 90 days.[17] If the Commission 'considers that the State has not complied or is unwilling to comply', it may refer the case to the Court.[18] So far, the Commission has not referred any case to the Court on this basis.[19]

In the application of its mandate to consider 'communications', the African Children's Rights Committee may also have reference to the 'socio-economic' rights included in the African Children's Charter.[20] In the first of its three findings thus far, the Committee found that the denial of and restrictions placed on Nubian children's right to nationality and registration at birth constituted discrimination. However, the Committee also found violations of the right to health and education as 'consequential' to the finding of discrimination.[21] In effect, the Committee found that the right to equality not only gives rise to the obligation to respect, protect, and promote, but also to fulfil.[22] The Committee's findings in the *Children of Northern Uganda* case did not deal with socio-economic rights.[23] In its third finding, concerning the *talibés* (children attending Qur'anic schools who were forced to beg) in Senegal,[24] the Committee concluded that the state's failure to effectively regulate these schools violated the children's right to survival and

---

[17] Rules 112(2) and 112(4) of the Commission's 2010 Rules of Procedure.

[18] Rule 118(1) of the Commission's 2010 Rules of Procedure.

[19] The Commission has, however, referred cases on non-compliance with provisional measures to the Court; see the Court's decisions in *African Commission v Libya*, Order of Provisional Measures, Application 4/2011, 25 March 2011; *African Commission v Kenya*, Order of Provisional Measures, Application 6/2012, 15 March 2013; *African Commission v Libya*, Order of Provisional Measures, Application 2/2013, 15 March 2013.

[20] See, e.g., arts. 11 and 14 of the African Children's Charter.

[21] Communication 2/2009, *Institute for Hunan Rights and Development in Africa (IHRDA) and Open Society Justice Initiative (on behalf of Children of Nubian descent in Kenya) v Kenya*, 22 March 2011, at www.acerwc.org/communications (accessed 18 August 2015).

[22] Ibid., para 58.

[23] Communication 2/2009, *Hansungule and Others (on behalf of children in Northern Uganda) v Uganda*, decided at the Committee's 21st ordinary session (15–19 April 2013) (the right to education and health [arts. 11 and 14 of the African Children's Charter] were found not to have been violated).

[24] Communication 1/2012, *Centre for Human Rights and la Rencontre Africaine pour la Defence des Droits de l'Homme (RADDHO) (on behalf of Senegalese Talibés) v Senegal*, 15 April 2014.

development, education, and health. Its remedial 'order' directed the state not only to take measures aimed at non-repetition (such as adopting laws and policies to set minimum standards and to integrate these schools into the formal education system), but also to adopt measures with clear 'fulfillment' implications (such as ensuring that the children are 'taken back … to their families' and that 'free and compulsory basic education' is provided).[25]

Even if there is clarity about the three institutions that make up the core of the 'African human rights system', the greater involvement of judicial institutions operating under the aegis of Regional Economic Communities (RECs) in human-rights-related matters calls for their inclusion within a redefined scope of the term. It is the weaknesses of the regional system, in its traditional guise, which inspired individual recourse to the sub-regional courts. The extended understanding of the term 'regional human rights system', as including the sub-regional level, is especially pertinent in the Economic Community of West African States (ECOWAS), as the ECOWAS Court has explicit jurisdiction to hear human rights cases on the basis of the African Charter. In two other RECs, the East African Community (EAC) and the Southern African Development Community (SADC), the sub-regional courts have decided cases related to human rights, but the legal basis of their findings is the provisions of the treaties founding the RECs.[26] The SADC Tribunal has subsequently become defunct, and is likely to re-emerge as an exclusively inter-state court. While a number of decisions of the ECOWAS Court are relevant to 'socio-economic' rights,[27] none of the decisions of other REC Courts relate specifically to socio-economic rights.

Against this background, it is fair to claim that the African regional human rights system holds the explicit promise that 'socio-economic' rights would be vindicated.

---

[25] Ibid., para 82.

[26] See *James Katabazi and Others v Secretary-General of the EAC and Attorney-General of Uganda*, Reference 1 of 2007, East African Court of Justice, 1 November 2007; (2007) AHRLR 119 (EAC 2007); and *Mike Campbell (Pvt) Limited and Others v Republic of Zimbabwe*, Case SADCT 2/07, SADC Tribunal, 28 November 2008; (2008) AHRLR 199 (SADC 2008).

[27] See *Registered Trustees of the Socio-Economic Rights & Accountability Project (SERAP) v Nigeria* (2009) AHRLR 331 (ECOWAS 2009) (*SERAP* 2009 case) and ECOWAS Court, *SERAP v Nigeria*, judgment no ECW/CCJ/JUD/18/12, 14 December 2012, www .courtecowas.org/site2012/pdf_files/decisions/judgements/2012/SERAP_V_FEDERAL_ REPUBLIC_OF_NIGERIA.pdf (*SERAP* 2012 case).

11.2. Enforcement of 'Socio-economic Orders'

The focus of this book on the enforcement (or 'implementation') of 'socio-economic judgments' prompts the following question as a point for preliminary consideration: Is there anything peculiar about the implementation of socio-economic rights judgments, as opposed to or as distinct from judgments in respect of the violation of all other rights (and in particular, 'civil and political' rights)?

Before attempting to answer this question, another threshold issue presents itself: What are the 'socio-economic' rights under the African Charter? 'Socio-economic' rights are often considered to be self-evident. However, on closer inspection of the provisions of the African Charter, this notion of self-evidence may rightly be questioned. Most commentators would accept that the right to health and education are 'socio-economic' rights. But what about the Charter provisions dealing with the right to work 'under equitable and satisfactory conditions', the right to property, or the protection of the family?[28] Even if all these provisions have social and economic dimensions, they entail different obligations on the state. The mere mention of 'work' in my mind does not make for a meaningful categorisation of this right as 'socio-economic'. What about the right to a 'general satisfactory environment'? On what basis should it be categorised as a 'socio-economic' right?

In all likelihood, proponents using 'socio-economic' as a category have in mind those rights that have traditionally been associated with the obligation on states to promote and in particular *fulfill* rights, rather than merely respect or protect them. While it is clearly correct that *all* rights may – depending on the circumstances – impose *all* four layers of obligations on states, it is also true that 'socio-economic' rights have more strongly been associated with the state obligation to make resources available to realise rights (in other words, the 'fulfillment' obligation). However, as the cases discussed in this chapter illustrate, socio-economic rights give rise to other obligations as well.

The layered nature of 'socio-economic rights orders' often makes it very difficult, when assessing compliance or implementation, to disentangle the various parts of an order. It is inaccurate to refer to a 'judgment' or an 'order' in a particular case as imposing one particular obligation (such as the obligation to fulfil) on a respondent state. Findings of the Commission and judgments of courts, and the ensuing remedial orders, do not deal

---

[28] Arts. 15, 14 and 18 of the African Charter, supra n. 2.

in an either/or fashion with 'socio-economic' rights. Rather, one remedial recommendation in a finding may consist of a number of distinct
and distinguishable 'orders', in respect of both 'civil and political' and
'socio-economic rights', and imposing different kinds of obligations on
states. To illustrate this point: In the finding of the Commission in which
the respondent state's obligation to fulfil has probably been most clearly
articulated, *Purohit and Another v The Gambia (Gambian Mental Health
case)*,[29] the Commission recommends ('orders', if that word is used generously) that the 'Lunatics Detention Act' should be replaced, that a review
body should in the meantime be appointed to review the position of all
detainees, and that the government should '*provide adequate medical and
material care* for persons suffering from mental health problems in the territory of The Gambia'.[30] The legislative amendment and reconsideration of
the detainees' cases speak to the arbitrary nature of their detention (a 'civil
and political' right), and could be viewed as placing an obligation of the
government to *respect* the victim's rights (or, perhaps, as facilitation, which
is part of the obligation to fulfill). The obligation to provide 'medical and
material care' *unequivocally* speaks to the obligation to *fulfill*.

The distinction between the enforcement of 'civil-political' and 'socio-
economic' rights, which is implied by the notion of 'socio-economic judgments', therefore seems to be unimportant. There is nothing peculiar about
the enforcement of 'socio-economic' rights, as such. The right to property,
which is sometimes understood as a 'socio-economic' right,[31] frequently
gives rise to the obligation to respect (for example, in eviction cases). The
right to work under equitable conditions imposes a clear obligation to protect on states. As will be more fully explained, a study of the implementation of findings of the African Commission by Viljoen and Louw (and
other papers in this publication) suggests that the legal characterisation of
a case or judgment as either 'socio-economic' or 'civil-political' is also not
a significant factor in predicting state compliance. The reason must, in the
light of the argument so far, be obvious: The characterisation of a case or
communication as 'civil-political' or 'socio-economic' is just not significant in and of itself. Rather, as far as the 'right' is concerned, compliance
or implementation is related to the nature and extent of the obligation
imposed by a right under a particular set of circumstances. In any event,

[29] Communication 241/2001, *Purohit and Moore v The Gambia* (2003) AHRLR 96 (ACHPR
2003) (16th Annual Activity Report) (*Gambian Mental Health* case).
[30] Ibid., para 85 (emphasis added).
[31] See, e.g., Fons Coomans (2003) 'The Ogoni case before the African Commission on Human
and Peoples' Rights', *International and Comparative Law Quarterly*, 52 (3), 749–760 at 450.

the study mentioned revealed that there there the major potential predictors of compliance are not 'rights'-related, but are the political situation prevailing in or nature of the respondent state; and the involvement of mass mobilisation/a social movement around the case and its implementation. This contribution investigates the extent to which these factors also impact on compliance with 'socio-economic' orders.

Attempts to focus on enforcement of socio-economic orders are in my mind aimed at serving as a reminder that rights are indivisible and that all 'judgments' (containing remedial orders) need to be enforced. The aim of this book should thus be understood not so much as demanding a focus on the enforcement of 'socio-economic orders', but rather as a call for the inclusion of socio-economic rights in the existing enforcement/implementation discourse. Zooming in on the enforcement of 'socio-economic orders' is thus a plea not to neglect the complexities arising from the enforcement of all rights – including those about which some controversy had traditionally existed because they imposed obligations on states to fulfil, and not only to respect, protect, and promote.

11.3 Previous Study Identifying Factors Indicative of State Compliance

In this section of the chapter, reliance is placed on a study on 'state compliance' by states with the recommendations of the African Commission, which provides some support to the contention that the categorisation of cases along legal features is not decisive in predicting compliance.

In order to address the lack of information about the compliance by states with the African Commission's recommendations, Louw conducted a doctoral research study consisting of desk studies, media reviews and interviews with authors of communications, commissioners, and state representatives, to ascertain what the extent of compliance is (Louw, 2005). Restricting her scope to the period 1987–2003, she found that there was 'full implementation' in only six cases out of a total of forty-four finally decided against state parties on the merits (representing 14 per cent of the finalised cases). 'Non-implementation' was recorded in 13 cases (30 per cent of the cases); and 'partial' implementation in 14 cases (32 per cent of the finalised cases). 'Situational' compliance occurred in 7 (or 16 per cent) of the cases. 'Full' compliance denotes the implementation of all aspects of the remedy indicated; 'non-compliance' is used if a state did not implement any of the recommendations; 'partial' compliance indicates that a state implemented some but not all elements of the recommended remedy;

and 'situational' compliance denotes implementation that came about as a result of changed circumstances and not from a respondent (or erring) government's response to an order, as such. In other words, the term 'situational' compliance is used to refer to implementation occasioned by a far-reaching change in circumstances, such as a change of government.

On the basis of this data, a further study was undertaken to identify the factors that most influence compliance (Viljoen and Louw, 2007; Viljoen, 2010). A number of hypotheses were formulated and tested on the basis of the data. These hypotheses relate to the following: (1) the way in which the treaty body (the African Commission) executes its mandate, such as the quality of its reasoning, the precision of its remedial 'order', and its involvement in follow-up activities; (2) the nature of the case (communication), for example, whether it deals with a 'civil and political' or 'socio-economic rights'; (3) the complainant, and his or her involvement in follow-up activities; (4) the system of government and political stability at the level of the respondent state; (5) the involvement of civil society actors (in particular NGOs), for example, in the submission and follow-up of a communication; and (6) the existence of international pressure. Hypotheses formulated as part of the study may be divided into those that speak to relatively narrow legal factors, and those touching on the socio-political context. The first two factors, pertaining to the Commission and the communication, are predominantly 'legal' in nature, while the other factors are more attuned to a broader extra-legal context. The hypotheses were tested by juxtaposing the six cases of 'full compliance' with the thirteen cases of 'non-compliance'. The correlation between the hypothesis and the category of case was assessed, and the statistical significance of this correlation established. Fisher's Exact Test was used to determine the statistical significance of each of the factors as a predictor of compliance or non-compliance. It was considered statistically appreciably significant if the relationship between a factor and compliance or non-compliance is on the 10 per cent level of significance (that is, where p is equal to or smaller than 0.1) (Viljoen and Louw, 2007).

The factors found most likely to influence compliance, according to our study, are non-legal. The three hypotheses that found the most unequivocal statistical data-based support are the following:

- A stable, open, free and democratic system of government is conducive to compliance.
- Involvement of non-state actors such as NGOs in 'following up' cases make compliance more likely.
- Involvement of NGOs in submitting cases make compliance more likely.

Table 11.1 *Factors and Probability*

FACTOR	PROBABILITY (p) (of most significance $p \leq 0-0,1$; less significance $p \leq 1$)
Type of government (free/non-free)	0.0029
NGO involvement in follow-up	0.0116
NGO involvement in case	0.1093
Scale of violation (single/massive)	0.2776
Commission's involvement in follow-up	0.3498
Nature of state obligation (respect/ fulfill)	0.5439
Formulation of remedy (vague/ precise)	0.7892
Reasoning by Commission (brief/ substantial)	0.9999

While these were the only factors that met the test for statistical significance (a p value around 0.1 or less), the study revealed that the next most important predictor of compliance was the scale of the violations found in the case (with a p value of 0.2776). Cases categorised as involving single or multiple victims tended to lead to greater compliance than cases dealing with violations on a 'massive scale', involving much bigger groups of complainants (Viljoen and Louw, 2007: 19–21). It is important to note that none of the instances of full compliance in the study relates to violations categorised as 'massive'.

The study findings in Table 11.1 may be summarised as follows.

Little support could be found to uphold the strictly legal hypotheses. The extent (or 'quality' measures on a scale of 'brief' and 'substantial') of legal reasoning in a particular finding was, for example, found not to correlate with greater compliance. Resulting in a p score of more than 0.99 on the Fisher Exact Test, the hypothesis that 'well-reasoned findings are more likely to be implemented' found no support in the available data (Viljoen and Louw, 2007). On the very limited available data, the premise that the violations of 'civil and political' rights would more likely lead to compliance than violations of 'socio-economic' rights could also not be substantiated (Viljoen and Louw, 2007: 18). Similarly, the state obligation imposed by the right also did not prove to be a decisive factor predicting compliance.

However, it should be borne in mind that the number of 'socio-economic' rights cases was quite limited, and that only one case in the sample was categorised as imposing a predominantly 'fulfilment' obligation. The finding in respect of the nature of state obligations was therefore not well substantiated by the available data.

It should be pointed out that methodological difficulties may detract from the accuracy and reliability of some of the conclusions in the study. As far as the empirical aspect of the study, the collection of evidence by way of desk review and interviews, is concerned, the following factors to some extent hampered the research: communication difficulties, reluctance of governments to engage on the issue by way of interviews, insufficient and inaccessible records, inability to trace victims and authors of communications, lack of quality and discontinuity in state representatives attending the Commission's sessions, divergent views about compliance by those involved in the process, and the lack of media coverage. Also, the limited number of communications finalised by the Commission – and the small number of cases used for the statistical analysis – did not allow for optimal statistical analysis of the data. Even if the factual circumstances surrounding compliance could be established with some accuracy, the data still needed to be analysed and categorised as 'full', 'partial', or 'non-compliance'. A major factor complicating attempts at such categorisation is the lack of precision in the formulation of recommendations. If it is not clear what exactly the state was required to do, it is difficult to know if the state actually did what was required (that is, whether there was 'enforcement' or 'implementation'). The only solution in such instances is to derive a specific remedial order from the facts of the case and the judgment as a whole.

Even if it should be obvious, it bears repeating that although the presence of the identified factors may be 'predictive of compliance', their presence holds no guarantee for actual compliance or 'enforcement'.

11.4   Towards Identifying Factors Indicative of Implementation by States of 'Regional Socio-economic Rights Orders'

On the basis of the results of the study on state compliance with the African Commission's findings, a number of hypotheses that have been shown to be of statistical significance are here identified as being of potential relevance to the 'enforcement' of 'socio-economic judgments'/'regional orders'. Although these conclusions have been derived almost exclusively from the analysis of 'civil and political' rights cases, invoking the government's obligation to 'respect', it is anticipated that these factors would also have a bearing on the enforcement of recommendations pertaining to 'socio-economic' rights. The hypotheses of the previous study are thus restated and adjusted.

In addition to these 'adjusted hypotheses', further hypotheses are formulated and postulated as being of potential relevance specifically in the context of states' obligations in respect of socio-economic rights. In devising these hypotheses, the point of departure is that where there would be overlaps and similarities with the hypotheses in the earlier study, these would be restated and tested in this context. However, there are also important differences, informed by factors pertinent to 'socio-economic' rights, based on their particular relevance in the context of 'socio-economic' rights and the types of obligations mostly associated with these rights.

The findings of the study referred to earlier relates to the findings of a supra-national body, the African Commission. The question may be posed to what extent the implementation of judgments by supra-national human rights courts differs from the implementation of judgments by national courts. In so far as the factors in the prior study relate to recommendations of a supra-national (or 'international') body, they may also be relevant in respect of judgments of national courts. While a number of the hypotheses mentioned in the pages that follow are therefore aimed specifically at the supra-national (and more particularly, regional/continental) level, some others should be as relevant to the supra-national as to the national level. In any event, although the hypotheses are all framed as relating to the implementation of 'regional orders', they could often also find application at the national level.

The hypotheses do not as a rule distinguish between the quasi-judicial 'recommendations' of the African Commission (and African Children's Rights Committee), on the one hand, and the legally binding 'orders' of the African Human Rights Court, on the other. Instead, the shorthand 'regional order' is used to encompass both. However, one specific hypothesis postulates that the Court' (binding) orders are likely to be better implemented than the (non-binding) recommendations of the Commission and Committee.

These hypotheses are divided into those pertaining to (1) the treaty body or Court; (2) the domestic legal framework; (3) the 'victims'; (4) the state; (5) civil society and community involvement; and (6) the international legal framework. This is obviously not a list with a claim to be comprehensive.[32]

11.4.1   Hypotheses Related to the Treaty Body (African Commission, Children's Rights Committee) or Court (African Court, REC Courts)

The clarity and precision of a socio-economic rights order increases the likelihood of compliance. The rationale for this contention is that a clear order speeds up and facilitates the process of domestic implementation. Orders aimed at states' obligation to fulfill, in particular, are often framed in open-ended terms, so as to leave some margin to the states in its choice of concrete measures. This hypothesis departs from the premise that precise and clear orders (for example, stipulating time frames) reduce the manoeuvring space of states, and therefore empower civil society to lobby for implementation measures; and enhance accountability.

The greater the involvement of the treaty body or Court in the follow-up to its finding or decision is, the greater the likelihood of enforcement of socio-economic rights orders becomes. A 'structural interdict', in terms of which the adjudicating body remains involved in the supervision of enforcement, is, for example, assumed to enhance implementation through the treaty by continuous prodding of the body or court.

A binding order by the African Court or REC Courts is more likely to be complied with than a recommendatory order by the African Commission or Committee. This hypothesis is based on the prevailing perception, at least among member states, that the remedial 'orders' issued by the Commission are recommendatory, while the Court's order enjoy clear and unambiguous binding legal status. The importance of factors such as the nature or the politics prevailing in the respondent state, and the presence of a social movement rather than factors such as the legal status of the finding or order, may militate against this hypothesis. In any event, at the time of writing, the African Court has yet not decided any case related to

---

[32] Other possible categories include 'hypotheses related to the Intergovernmental Organisation (IGO)', which would assess the reaction and actions taken at the political level in respect of each specific order in each separate instance. This line of inquiry is premised on the inclination that the more decisive the action supporting enforcement taken by the AU (or the relevant REC) is, the better the chances of enforcement become. The lack of any decisive action by the AU, thus far, renders this a hypothesis less likely to yield any insights. While the role of international civil society is touched upon in one of the hypotheses in the study, the role of international mobilisation (including the role of the media) is not fully canvassed here. While this is potentially a very important factor (see, e.g., Simmons [2009]), the available data did not justify its inclusion here.

socio-economic rights. However, there are some relevant decisions and orders by the ECOWAS Court.

Socio-economic rights orders issued by sub-regional courts are more likely to be enforced than orders issued at the continental level. This hypothesis departs from the premise that greater political or economic pressure is likely to be brought to bear on a state within a closely knit regional arrangement based on a relationship of proximity or 'clearly evident bonds of mutuality' (Claude, 1984). As yet, due to the absence of relevant case law from the African Human Rights Court, this hypothesis can be tested only by juxtaposing the REC Courts, and in particular the ECOWAS Court, with the African Commission. Owing to the issues arising from the perceived non-binding nature of the Commission's findings, this may be an unfair comparison: It would be more appropriate to compare the enforcement of the binding decisions of the ECOWAS Court with those of the African Court.

11.4.2   Hypotheses Related to the Domestic Legal Framework

The likelihood of enforcement is enhanced if socio-economic rights are included as justiciable guarantees in a country's constitution.[33] This factor relates to the linkage between the domestic and regional legal regimes. It departs from the premise that communications dealing with 'socio-economic rights' would be considered by the Commission or Court if there is no available domestic legal remedy, that is, these rights are not justiciable in that legal order. (They may be Directive Principles of State Policy, or examples of judgments of relevance to socio-economic rights based on 'civil and political rights', but these do not constitute unequivocal legal acceptance of these obligations.) Even if that would be possible for the Commission (or Court) to waive the requirement of exhausting local remedies, the hypothesis postulates that if such a case is decided by the Commission or Court, the implementation of the eventual finding may be problematic due to the absence of explicit socio-economic rights, understood to impose fulfillment obligations on the state, in the domestic system.

Enforcement of a socio-economic rights order is more likely in a state following the monist legal tradition. Although there are indications that the

---

[33] Another possible hypothesis, namely, that the likelihood of successful enforcement of a regional order to fulfill increases if national legislation or a national mechanism allowing for the domestic enforcement of international decisions exists, is not pursued here due to the general absence of such mechanisms in Africa.

theoretical divide between 'monist' and 'dualist' states loses its signifi-cant in practice, it is still, as a matter of constitutional theory, postulated that a state following the monist legal tradition, in that international law is automatically part of the country's legal framework, is more likely to enforce socio-economic rights orders, issued by regional bodies or courts. However, implementation prospects for a dualist state in which effec-tive domestication is the norm would largely correspond with those in a monist state.

11.4.3   Hypotheses Related to 'Victims'

Socio-economic rights orders relating to cases brought on behalf of a single or small groups of individuals are more likely to be enforced than cases brought by collectives ('peoples') or groups consisting of a significant number of indi-viduals. This hypothesis builds on the finding in the earlier study that the likelihood of state compliance with decisions of the African Commission was greater for cases of a single or a few victims than for massive violations involving significant groups of victims. This hypothesis is of particular res-onance in the context of the African Charter, which allows for collective rights, such as peoples' right to development. The collective nature of these Charter rights makes allowance of the *actio polularis* almost inevitable.

11.4.4   State-Related Hypotheses

States are more likely to enforce socio-economic rights orders related to a cause of action that arose under a previous political dispensation (than one related to a cause of action arising during its own term of governance).[34] In the study discussed, the transition from an undemocratic or repressive to a more open and democratic system of government, referred to as 'situ-ational compliance', was identified as a significant factor contributing to the probability of enforcement (Viljoen and Louw, 2007: 6–7). A newly

---

[34] Other state-related hypotheses, not canvassed here, may focus on the resources, for exam-ple, postulating that a state is more likely to comply if it has resources available, in terms of its budgetary allocation, to enforce the order to fulfill; that richer states are more likely to comply with regional orders to fulfill than poorer states; that states in which budgets are adopted in an open, transparent and participatory ways are more likely to enforce fulfill-ment orders; that a state is more likely to comply if it has resources available, in terms of its budgetary allocation, to enforce the order to fulfill; and that an order in line with the budg-etary policies and priorities of the state is more likely to be enforced that an order at odds with existing policies and priorities. It may also be worth investigating whether countries that depend on aid are more likely to comply with enforcement orders to fulfill.

installed government may find it politically opportune to distance itself from the previous regime, and to present itself as holding the promise of a clean slate. Expunging the wrongs committed under the watch of the previous regime, and enforcing regional orders related to these 'wrongs' may be ways of doing so. While the doctrine of 'continuity of state responsibility' weighs in support of the hypothesis, the burden that fulfillment obligations may bring could mitigate against its validity. A transitional or post-traumatised government may see it as inimical to its interests to devote significant state resources to redress the illegal conduct of the previous regime. While the moment the cause of action arose seems to be the most relevant temporal marker, the time when the case was submitted or when the decision was given may also be relevant. For example, the current regime may find it politically expedient to enforce an order arising from a decision in respect of which the previous regime took a negative stance – a position those currently in government had earlier openly criticised.

Open and democratic states adhering to the rule of law are more likely to enforce socio-economic rights orders by regional bodies. This hypothesis was shown to have been of relevance in the previous study. As indicators of what an 'open and democratic state' is, emphasis should be placed on the de facto situation rather than the de jure position. A number of institutions provide quantitative data analysis per country, which may be of use here: (1) Is the country categorised as 'free', 'partly free', or 'not free' by Freedom House?[35] (2) What is its score in the World Justice Project Rule of Law Index?[36] (3) What is its 'rule of law' score in the Mo Ibrahim Index of African Governance?[37] (4) What is the country's score for the 'rule of law' in the World Bank's Worldwide Governance Indicators (WGI)?[38] This hypothesis is adjusted from the earlier study. Although that study mostly involved the state's obligation to respect, the assumption is that this factor would be of significance in respect of all state obligations – including the obligation to fulfil.

11.4.5   Hypotheses Related to Civil Society or Community Involvement

Involvement of non-state actors, such as civil society organisations, and of the community, in 'following-up' to influence states, makes enforcement

---

[35] www.freedomhouse.org/report/freedom-world/freedom-world-2013.
[36] http://worldjusticeproject.org/rule-of-law-index.
[37] www.moibrahimfoundation.org/downloads/2012-IIAG-summary-report.pdf.
[38] See http://info.worldbank.org/governance/wgi/index.asp.

more likely.[39] This factor was one of the most significant in explaining compliance by states with findings of the Commission, in general. Experience at the domestic level in countries such as South Africa suggests that this factor would be equally relevant in predicting the enforcement of orders imposing on states the distinct obligation to fulfil.

The involvement and mobilisation of transnational (subregional/regional/global) civil society or social movements around the case and its implementation is likely to enhance the prospect of enforcement. This is an adjunct to the hypothesis related to national civil society, contextualised in the framework of the international community.

11.4.5   Hypotheses Related to the International Legal Context

A state that subscribes fully to the relevant global (UN) human rights instruments is more likely to comply with socio-economic rights orders. Establishing adherence to 'relevant' human rights standards may lead to the following questions, related to the 'socio-economic' rights standards within the UN: Did the state ratify the ICESCR? Did the state accept the Optional Protocol to the ICESCR? However, answers to these two questions may not yield great insights in an Africa context, because almost all states are party to the ICESCR,[40] and only three to the Optional Protocol.[41] Ratification of the Optional Protocol to the ICESCR should in the African context be viewed with circumspection, because all AU member states already accept the compulsory jurisdiction of the African Commission, and half of them already accept the jurisdiction of the African Court, over some 'socio-economic' rights. To this should be added the jurisdiction of the ECOWAS Court, to which aggrieved parties may already bring these cases even *without exhausting local remedies.* The question may thus be posed as to what the 'added value' would be of ratifying the Optional Protocol, and a cynic would be able to argue that ratifying the Protocol would create a less invasive route, that could deflect challenges away from

---

[39]   The media evidently also have an important role in the process of enhancing the prospects of implementation. A related hypothesis, namely, that the greater the attention by the media to the hearing of the case, the decision, and the need for or resistance to enforcement, the greater the likelihood of domestic enforcement, is not interrogated here, but is left to those equipped with the expertise and research capabilities relevant to media and cultural studies.

[40]   The exceptions are: Botswana, Comoros, Mozambique, Sao Tome e Principe and South Sudan.

[41]   By August 2015, of the twenty-one state parties, three (Cape Verde, Gabon and Niger) were from Africa.

the regional and sub-regional Courts. More relevant question related to global (UN) human right standards could be: (1) how frequently a state reports under the ICESCR; and (2) whether a state has accepted the UN's (other) optional complaints mechanisms and inquiry procedures.[42] If this factor is accepted, a correlation is postulated between implementation of judgments to fulfil, on the one hand, and adherence with the core ICESCR obligation of periodic reporting and the acceptance of global complaints and inquiry mechanisms, on the other.

A state that subscribes fully to the African regional human rights system is more likely to comply with regional socio-economic rights orders. This hypothesis is informed by the contention that even if states are human-rights-minded and accept international obligations because they expect to be compliant, remedial orders still 'add value' as source of external legitimation and by serving as a 'domestic focal point' (Hillebrecht, 2014: 34). As all states have become party to the Charter, to provide comparative insights, the indicators of 'fully subscribing with the African regional human rights system' must relate to other human rights treaties or institutions than the Charter or the Commission, leading to the following as questions serving as the basis of indicators: (1) Did the state ratify all three the core AU human rights treaties (African Charter; African Children's Charter; Women's Protocol)? (2) Did the state ratify the Court Protocol? (3) Did it make a declaration under Article 34(6) of the Court Protocol? (4) Did the state accept, and did it undergo an examination under the African Peer Review Mechanism (APRM)? Although these questions may seem to lack immediate relevance to the issue of enforcement of orders,

---

[42] Such as the Optional Protocol to the International Covenant on Civil and Political Rights (OP-ICCPR), G.A. res. 2200A (XXI), 21 U.N. GAOR Supp. (No. 16) at 59, U.N. Doc. A/6316 (1966), 999 U.N.T.S. 302, *entered into force* March 23, 1976; art. 14 of International Convention on the Elimination of All Forms of Racial Discrimination (ICERD), G.A. res. 2106 (XX), Annex, 20 U.N. GAOR Supp. (No. 14) at 47, U.N. Doc. A/6014 (1966), 660 U.N.T.S. 195, *entered into force* January 1969; art. 22 of the Convention against Torture and Other Cruel, Inhuman or Degrading Treatment or Punishment (CAT), G.A. res. 39/46, [annex, 39 U.N. GAOR Supp. (No. 51) at 197, U.N. Doc. A/39/51 (1984)], *entered into force* June 26, 1987; Optional Protocol to the Convention on the Elimination of Discrimination against Women (OP-CEDAW), G.A. res. 54/4, annex, 54 U.N. GAOR Supp. (No. 49) at 5, U.N. Doc. A/54/49 (Vol. I) (2000), *entered into force* 22 December 2000; First Optional Protocol to the International Convention on the Protection and Promotion of the Rights and Dignity of Persons with Disabilities (OP-CRPD), G.A. Res. 61/106, Annex II, U.N. GAOR, 61st Sess., Supp. No. 49, at 80, U.N. Doc. A/61/49 (2006), *entered into force* 3 May 2008; art. 31 of the International Convention for the Protection of All Persons from Enforced Disappearances E/CN.4/2005/WG.22/WP.1/Rev.4 (2005), which was adopted but not yet in force.

they underscore the (potential) interplay between various treaties, treaty monitoring procedures, and other review mechanisms. The multiplicity of these institutions is increasingly becoming part of the reality of life, and fulfilment must be seen as embedded in layers of obligations both potentially duplicating and mutually reinforcing.

11.5   Selected Cases: Status of Implementation

Against the background of the hypotheses presented, this chapter explores compliance in four communications where the Commission dealt prominently with 'socio-economic' rights. The four selected decisions are cases in which the Commission made findings that are generally considered as 'socio-economic rights', and that also entail, albeit to varying degrees, an obligation in the remedial 'order' on the respondent states to 'promote' or 'fulfill' those rights.[43] In this part, the status of implementation is ascertained, based on reports by various entities, and occasionally, on interviews.

11.5.1   Ogoniland Case

The first and most celebrated of these cases is the *Ogoniland* case, in which the Commission dealt with a collective communication, brought in the name of the 'Ogoni people' of the Niger Delta region of Nigeria in 1996.[44] This case was brought against Nigeria principally for the harm caused by the Nigerian National Petroleum Company (NNPC), a state-owned company, with Shell Petroleum as a minority shareholder. The NNPC's oil exploration and gas flaring in the area had a destructive effect on the

---

[43] These are not the only decisions in which the Commission found violations of 'socio-economic rights'. Two other prominent cases are: *Malawi African Association and Others v Mauritania* (2000) AHRLR 149 (ACHPR 2000) (13th Annual Activity Report) (*Mauritanian Widows* case) and *Free Legal Assistance Group and Others v Zaire* (2000) AHRLR 74 (ACHPR 1995) (9th Annual Activity Report) (*Zairian Mass Violations* case) (see, e.g., Chirwa 2008: 331). Although the Commission in the first case found that the right to health had been violated by the state not providing adequate food, blankets and hygienic conditions to prisoners (para 122), and that the same right was violated in the second case due to the 'failure of the government to provide basic services such as safe drinking water and electricity and the shortage of medicine' (para 46), in neither of these cases did the Commission make any remedial recommendation related to this (or any other 'socio-economic') right.

[44] Communication 155/1996, *Social and Economic Rights Action Centre (SERAC) and Center for Economic and Social Rights (CESR) v Nigeria* (2001) AHRLR 60 (ACHPR 2001) (15th Annual Activity Report).

Ogoni people, causing the Commission to find that their right to health and a clean environment had been violated. Acts of resistance by the Ogoni people, and the formation of the Movement for the Survival of the Ogoni People (MOSOP), lead to retaliation by the government in the form of indiscriminate killing, and the destruction of the Ogoni peoples' homes and crops. Violations found by the Commission include the right to property, health, a satisfactory environment, and the right of a people to freely dispose of its wealth and natural resources.

In an unprecedented and unusually elaborate remedial recommendation,[45] delivered in October 2001, the Commission makes five distinct orders. The first is an appeal to the government to 'stop all attacks on Ogoni communities' and to permit citizens and independent investigators free access to the territory'. The second is to 'conduct an investigation into the human rights violations' and to prosecute those responsible. Third, the state was to provide 'relief and resettlement assistance to victims of government sponsored raids, and undertaking a comprehensive clean-up of lands and rivers damaged by oil operations'. Fourth, the Nigerian government had to ensure that 'appropriate environmental and social impact assessments are prepared for any future oil development' and that effective and independent oversight bodies for the petroleum industry are put in place. Fifth, it had to provide 'information on health and environmental risks and meaningful access to regulatory and decision-making bodies to communities likely to be affected by oil operations'. Although these recommendations are couched primarily as requirements of conduct (for example, to conduct investigations, prepare impact assessments, and put regulatory bodies in place), a requirement of outcome is to some extent implied in the recommendations that *relief be provided,* that *comprehensive clean-up* be conducted, and that oversight bodies are *effective.*

What does not explicitly appear from the *Ogoniland* case is the reality that the Niger Delta state, generally, and the Ogoniland area, more specifically, had for long suffered from severe underdevelopment and levels of impoverishment, particularly if compared with the other regions of Nigeria. For many years, the inhabitants of these regions have not benefited from the rich oil resources of the Niger Delta.

It is important to note that the *Ogoniland* case was submitted, and speaks to events that occurred and a situation prevailing during the

---

[45] Up to that point, the Commission largely adopted very brief and open-ended recommendations, for example, calling on the government to 'take the necessary steps to bring its law into conformity with the Charter' (*Media Rights Agenda and Others v Nigeria* (2000) AHRLR 200 (ACHPR 1998), para 93.

dictatorship of General Sani Abacha, which lasted from 1993 to 1998. After 1998, the new civilian government under President Obasanjo set in motion a process of institutional reform that indirectly responded to the Commission's remedial recommendations. (These processes were continued subsequently under Presidents Yar'Adua [2007–2010] and Goodluck Jonathan [2010–2015].) This case illustrates how a change of government may spearhead policy changes. In such a context, it is unsurprising that measures are taken to 'correct' the prevailing situation, even in respect of a pending case, as an acknowledgement of the inappropriate action of the previous regime. The 'remedial action' taken by the government under these circumstances pre-empts the Commission's decision and formal recommendations, which were formally adopted only in October 2001. Some year earlier, in October 2000, the new Nigerian government as part of its submissions on the merits presented a *note verbale* to the Commission in which it admitted 'the gravamen' of the complaint and described the 'remedial measures' the new administration was taking.[46]

In its response, the government highlighted the establishment of a number of institutions that would be in a position to ensure that the situation in the affected area is rectified. The first institution is the Federal Ministry of the Environment; the second is the Niger Delta Development Commission (NDDC); and the third, the Judicial Commission of Enquiry to investigate human rights violations, is of a more ad hoc nature (Ohaeri, 2012). In its eventual finding, the Commission urges the government to keep it informed of the 'outcome' of the 'work' of these institutions. However, there is no indication, subsequently, of this information being provided to the Commission.

These institutions were aimed at addressing many of the concerns raised in the *Ogoniland* case, even if not explicitly mandated to do so. In 2000, President Obasanjo established the NDDC as a federal governmental agency mandated to develop the Niger Delta so as to ensure greater autonomy to the Ogoni people over the resources of the region in which they live. The objectives of the NDDC are at least in part aimed at accomplishing some of the measures recommended by the Commission.[47] However,

[46] Reported in the Commission's finding in the *Ogoniland* case, para 30.
[47] The NDDC aims at 'assessing and reporting on any project being funded or carried out in the region by oil and gas companies and any other company, including non-governmental organizations, as well as ensuring that funds released for such projects are properly utilized' and at 'tackling ecological and environmental problems that arise from the exploration of oil mineral in the Niger Delta region and advising the Federal Government and the member states on the prevention and control of oil spillages, gas flaring and environmental pollution' (www.nddc.gov.ng/about%20us.html) (accessed 28 May 2012).

while the Commission's recommendations are framed in terms requiring the government to 'ensure' that compensation and relief is granted, that clean-up is undertaken, and that impact assessments are undertaken, the response has been to create these three and other institutions capable of doing what is required, and not indicating that the required or desired measures, as such, have been taken. In this period, the federal government also adopted the Environmental Guidelines and Standards for the Petroleum Industry 2002, and established the Environmental Standards and Regulation Enforcement Agency.[48]

Later on, in 2008, some seven years after the Commission's finding, under the then President Yar'Adua, the institutional framework was further strengthened when a Niger Delta Ministry was formed, with the NDDC as a parastatal under its auspices. The new ministry has a minister of state in charge of development of the Niger Delta area, and a minister of state in charge of youth empowerment. The National Oil Spill Detection and Response Agency (NOSDRA) was also established.[49] Although it would be difficult to link the establishment of the these institutions causally to the submission of or finding in the *Ogoniland* case, they may be viewed as a result of these concerns and as an attempt to improve the lot of the delta's population. Much has also been invested in youth development, and the Niger Delta Minstry was well resourced.

A number of independent reports shed light on the implementation of the *Ogoniland* recommendation. In 2009, Amnesty International released its report 'Nigeria: Petroleum, Pollution and Poverty in the Niger Delta'.[50] This report reveals a lack of effective measures in response to the *Ogoniland* decision, and calls for the implementation of the African Commission's recommendations.[51] In 2011, the government-initiated United Nations Environment Programme (UNEP) report, 'The Environmental Assessment of Ogoniland'[52] (Ohaeri, 2012), was released. This report highlights that the oil contamination and degradation in the Niger Delta started as far back as the 1950s. Although oil exploration officially ceased in 1993, its consequences are still present in a myriad of forms. The disturbing findings of this report contradict any contention

---

[48] Through the Environmental Standards and Regulation Enforcement Agency (Establishment) Act 2006.

[49] Through the National Oil Spill Detection and Response Agency (Establishment) Act 2006.

[50] www.amnesty.org/en/library/asset/AFR44/017/2009/en/e2415061-da5c-44f8-a73c-a7a4766ee21d/afr440172009en.pdf.

[51] Supra n, page 82.

[52] http://postconflict.unep.ch/publications/OEA/UNEP_OEA.pdf (28 May 2012).

that the Nigerian government had adequately responded to the plight of the Ogoni, and complied with the recommendations in the *Ogoniland* case – in particular as far as outcomes are concerned. The fact that there is no reference whatsoever to the *Ogoniland* case underlines how peripheral human rights in general, and the Commission's decisions specifically, are to the way in which these issues are approached in Nigeria, and also how the human rights and environmental discourses have developed and exist in isolation from each other. This report recommends the establishment of a new series of institutions, including the Environmental Restoration Authority, to oversee implementation of this study's recommendations, and an Environmental Restoration Fund, with an initial capital injection of USD 1 billion. As this report was handed to the president only in 2012, its implementation is still pending.

A case concerning factual circumstances largely overlapping with that of the case under discussion, subsequently decided by the ECOWAS Court, also suggests limited implementation of the *Ogoniland* decision. This case, *Socio-economic Rights and Accountability Project (SERAP) v. Nigeria,*[53] was submitted some eight years after the Commission had rendered its finding, and was decided on 14 December 2012. Since the ECOWAS Court has an explicit mandate to adjudicate human rights cases, based in part on the alleged violations of the African Charter, the *SERAP* decision is to a large extent a reconsideration of the *Ogoniland* case. In fact, the applicant placed explicit reliance on the African Commission's finding in the *Ogoniland* case, in particular as far as a possible violation of the right to food is concerned.[54] However, the ECOWAS Court in its decision steers clear of the applicant's main contention (based on potential violations of the right to an adequate standard of living and sustainable development) and does not place explicit reliance on the African Commission's jurisprudence. Instead, it finds a violation of only Articles 1 (the obligation to give effect to the rights in the Charter) and 24 (the right to a general satisfactory environment) of the Charter. The Article 1 violation is based on the finding that despite the adoption of laws, the establishment of agencies, and 'the allocation to the region of 13 per cent of the resources produced there', the government did not live up to its obligation of due diligence in that it did not ensure 'additional and concrete measures to prevent the occurrence of damage and ensure accountability'.[55] The Article 24 violation is based on the 'continued

---

[53] *SERAP* 2012 case supra n. 20.
[54] *SERAP* case supra n. 20, para 64.
[55] *SERAP* case supra n. 20, para 105.

environmental degradation of the region'.[56] In its remedial order, the Court focuses on the need for effective measures to restore and prevent damage to the environment and to hold perpetrators accountable.[57]

There is some evidence of the African Commission's continuing engagement with the implementation of this decision. In its Concluding Observations adopted after examining Nigeria's periodic state report in 2008, the Commission expressed concern that, 'despite decisions by regional and domestic institutions on the activities of trans-national corporations operating in the Niger Delta', there was little evidence of any change in their operations with respect to the right to food, shelter and the environment of the people in that region, 'therefore pointing to a lack of effective monitoring mechanism by the Government'.[58] The Commission recommended the establishment of an 'effective monitoring mechanism for the implementation of decisions of regional and domestic bodies on violations of the rights in the Niger Delta'.[59] In the overview of its activities on the occasion of its twenty-five years' celebration, the Commission noted the Nigerian government's establishment 'in compliance with the decision of the Commission in the *SERAC v Nigeria* case' of the Federal Ministry of Environment and the Niger Delta Cooperation as an example of 'evidence of willingness on the part of Member States to cooperate with the Commission'.[60]

Even if the Commission acknowledged the government's 'willingness to cooperate', it can hardly be contended that the finding in the *Ogoniland* case had been fully implemented. However, the main impetus of this decision was to frame the issue (also) as a human rights issue; to legitimate and draw attention – during a period of repressive and stifling dictatorship – to the plight of the Ogoni people through the submission of this case to the primary supranational human rights body; to mobilise the people of Ogoni, other Nigerians, and concerned individuals and groups worldwide; and to build domestic 'socio-economic rights' jurisprudence (Morka, 2011; Ohaeri, 2012). It also set in motion a train of litigation,[61]

---

[56] *SERAP* case, supra n. 20, para 104.
[57] *SERAP* 2012 case, supra n. 20, para 121.
[58] Concluding Observations and Recommendations on the Third Periodic Report of the Federal Republic of Nigeria, 10–24 November 2008, para 25.
[59] Ibid., para 40.
[60] Combined 32nd and 33rd Activity Report of the African Commission on Human and Peoples' Rights, 21–25 January 2013, Au Doc EX.CL/782(XXII) Rev. 2, para 27.
[61] In addition to the ECOWAS case, the Nigerian High Court also decided the *Gbemre v Shell Petroleum Development Company and Others* (Suit no FHC/B/CS/53/05, Benin City, 14 November 2005 (*Gas flaring* case), in which it restrained Shell and the NNPC from flaring

which kept prominently on the national agenda the issue of the environmental impact of the oil industry, and in particular the government's role
in effective and swift reaction, investigation, and regulation.

11.5.2   Gambian Mental Health Case

The second communication, *Purohit v. The Gambia* (*Gambian Mental Health*
case),[62] was submitted in 2001 by two non-Gambian mental health advocates
on behalf of a group of anonymous persons who had under existing legislation been 'condemned' to indefinite institutionalisation. In its 2003 decision,
the Commission found violations of the detainees' fair trial rights, their rights
to equality, and their right to liberty and security. On the basis of inadequate
treatment, including the provision of insufficient resources and therapeutic
programmes, the Commission also found that their right to health had been
violated. It recommended that the Gambian government 'repeal' the Lunatics
Detention Act (adopted in 1917 and last revised in 1964) and replace it 'as
soon as possible' with legislation in line with the Charter and other relevant
international law. In the interim, the government was required to 'create an
expert body to review the cases of all persons detained under the Act and
make appropriate recommendations for their treatment or release'. Finally,
in a recommendation related to both conduct and outcome, it called on the
government to 'provide adequate medical and material care for persons suffering from mental health problems in the territory of The Gambia'.[63] The
Commission also requested the government to report back, in its next periodic state report to the Commission, about the measures taken to comply
with the recommendations in this case.

Tracking the implementation of the *Gambian Mental Health* case provides little insight about state compliance, but the litany of difficulties
encountered in the research process provides some useful insights into
the methodological and practical pitfalls when conducting qualitative
research on implementation.[64]

---

gas in the particular community, and ordered the attorney general to set in motion legisla-
tive changes to the Associated Gas Regulation Act. Although both the applicant and the
Court refer extensively to the African Charter (and the African Charter on Human and
Peoples' Rights (Ratification and Enforcement Act), no reference is made to the African
Commission's *Ogoniland* decision.

[62] Supra n. 26.

[63] Ibid., para 68.

[64] These insights are based on interviews and observations by Nicholas Orago, an alumnus
of the LLM (Human rights and Democratisation in Africa), presented by the Centre for
Human Rights, University of Pretoria, in collaboration with a number of Law Faculties

The first difficulty is the inaccessibility of government officials. While it may in many states be problematic to access and interview government officials, especially highly placed civil servants and ministers, this problem is more pronounced in the Gambia. In a context of a very small civil service administration under the complete personal dominance of President Jammeh, senior civil servants and members of the executive are conscious that they serve in their positions at the pleasure of the president. A general reluctance or unwillingness to be interviewed was noted on the part of the relevant officials, namely the minster of health, the permanent secretary of health, and the director of medical services. It is an open secret that members of the Gambian executive and senior administrators are regularly dismissed at short notice. In a closed society characterised by fear and secrecy, being interviewed is viewed with great suspicion and is avoided for fear of exposing oneself to unnecessary risk. During 2011, reluctance to be interviewed was further exacerbated by upcoming presidential elections (which took place in November 2011). Sensitivity about the topic increased in early 2011, when a CNN documentary on Kenya's decaying mental health system, 'Locked up and forgotten', was shown.[65] It appeared that the documentary provoked a wide response and resonated in many Commonwealth African states, including in the Gambia,[66] where similar conditions prevail. After considerable efforts and many delays, the Permanent Secretary of Health and Director of Medical Services were interviewed. However, the former mostly feigned ignorance, while the latter was uncooperative.

Another difficulty hampering the research about implementation is the frequent 'rotation' of senior government officials, leading to very high turnover and very weak institutional memory within government departments. When an interview with the Minister of Health was requested, it was reported that she had been in that position for only two weeks and would consequently not be able to assist. The high turnover rate is exacerbated by very limited record-keeping, and a reluctance to share available documents.

across Africa, who spent six months in the Gambia as a visiting lecturer at the University of the Gambia, in 2011, and as my research assistant, as well as on my own personal observations over many years, attending sessions of the African Commission on Human and Peoples' Rights in the Gambia.

[65] www.youtube.com/watch?v=gM4meNCLYAA&feature=player_detailpage (accessed 18 May 2012).

[66] The Gambia had long been a member of the Commonwealth, but withdrew from it in 2013.

While the formal requirement of prior research clearance may legitimately be raised in many states, the rigid requirement of an Ethics Research
Certificate from the Ethics Committee seems to be used by the director of
medical service (the highest official directly responsible for mental health
issues) in an attempt to thwart any attempt at making any inquiries, and of
obtaining a copy of the draft of Mental Health Policy.

The inaccessibility of and inability to establish contact with the complainants also proved to present considerable difficulties. The complainants were not resident in the Gambia, but reportedly live in the
United Kingdom. Attempts to get in touch with them proved futile, as
the Commission's files do not contain their phone numbers or an email
address. This factor not only negatively affects efforts to assess the status of
implementation, but also plays an important role in the extremely low level
of awareness of the Commission's finding in the *Gambian Mental Health*
case, and in the complete lack of any local effort to create some momentum towards the implementation of the recommendations in this case.

In the particular context of this case, one last difficulty is the inaccessibility of mental health institutions, which a member of the public is not
able to freely visit and inspect.

In so far as they were allowed and undertaken, observations and investigations revealed that little if any dissemination or awareness-raising of
the case happened at the local level, resulting in most of those potentially
involved in the finding's implementation, such as NGOs, academics, and
the Law Reform Commission, being unaware of the finding. The permanent secretary of Health had no knowledge of the case; from the surrounding circumstances, it may be assumed that the minister also did not;
playing a cat-and-mouse-game, the director of medical services did not
confirm or deny knowledge about the case.

As far as the reform of the 'Lunatics Detention Act' is concerned, investigations at the Law Reform Commission and Government Printer indicated that no such reform has been undertaken, no reform initiatives have
been undertaken or are pending, and that no reform is envisaged in the
near future. Efforts to interview the permanent secretary of the Ministry
of Health, to obtain more information about this aspect, did not bear fruit.

Two measures taken provide some indication of movement in the
direction of the recommendations in this case. In one identifiable positive development, the 'mental hospital' was moved from the Royal Victoria
Hospital in Banjul to a new facility (the Tanka Tanka Psychiatric Hospital,
with a capacity of one hundred, opened in 2009) some distance outside
the city of Banjul. According to available information, it is better equipped

in terms of space and other resources including staff than the previous mental section of the Royal Victoria Hospital. Another positive development took place in respect of the provision of legal aid: The government has established a National Association for Legal Aid (NALA), under an Act of Parliament. NALA aims to provide legal aid and legal representation services to indigent litigants. However, the legal aid scheme is still in its infancy and is not properly funded and staffed to enable it undertake its duties effectively. Whether or not it will be useful in the amelioration of the conditions of the mentally ill in the Gambia is open to conjecture. Apparently, the government is working on revising the 2007 National Mental Health Policy, which reportedly is at an advanced stage. However, any progress has to be framed by the fact that less than 1 per cent of the health budget is reportedly dedicated to mental health.[67]

11.5.3 Endorois Case

In the third matter, the *Endorois* case,[68] submitted in 2003, the Commission in November 2009 found that the displacement of an 'indigenous' community in Kenya, the Endorois, from their long-standing place of residence and survival, to make place for a national game reserve, and to subsequently have allowed for mining in that area, amounted to numerous violations of their rights under the African Charter, including the right to property, education, and development. The recommendatory 'order' of the African Commission may be divided into four categories. First, the Commission made a general order for 'compensation', which is potentially associated with all violations of rights. Second, the obligation to respect appears from the Commission's order to 'recognise rights of ownership to the Endorois', grant them unrestricted access to Lake Bogoria and surrounding sites, and to 'grant registration to the Endorois Welfare Committee'. Third, the Commission called on the government to 'engage in dialogue with the Complainants for the effective implementation' of its recommendations.[69] Last, a number of its orders engage the obligation to fulfill: the government

---

[67] 'Mental health in the Gambia', *The Point*, 25 September 2012, http://thepoint.gm/africa/gambia/article/mental-health-in-the-gambia.

[68] Communication 276/03, *Centre for Minority Rights Development (Kenya) and Minority Rights Group (on behalf of Endorois Welfare Council) v Kenya* (2009) AHRLR 75 (ACHPR 2009) (27th Activity Report) (publication of finding in February 2010, after adoption of activity report).

[69] Ibid., para 298(2): 'The African Commission avails its good offices to assist the parties in the implementation of these recommendations'.

must restitute ancestral land to the Endorois; and to 'pay royalties to the Endorois from existing economic activities and ensure that they benefit from employment possibilities within the reserve'.[70] Carving out for itself a role in the follow-up process, the Commission requested that the government report to it on the implementation of these recommendations 'within three months from the date of notification'.

The recommendations in the *Endorois* finding have not yet fully been complied with. Despite numerous efforts from many role players, there still is 'no evidence of a structured approach to the negotiations, and so far there has been no official, binding communication from the government stating its position regarding the decision and its implementation' (Ochieng Odiambo, 2012: para. 4.2).

In response to the finding, the government has committed itself to the implementation of the recommendation, or, stated differently, the government never explicitly refused to implement this finding. The minister for lands was not only present as guest of honour at a public community celebration of the decision in March 2010, organised by the Endorois Welfare Council (EWC) and supporting partners, and attended by some 10,000 people, but also publicly proclaimed the government's willingness to implement the decision (Claridge, 2011). The minister undertook to prepare a cabinet memorandum to this effect. At the African Commission's session in November 2010, the state delegation further indicated its commitment to the implementation of the recommendations.

However, the government also posed some unnecessary obstacles and took some ambiguous actions. Insisting, as the very same minister for lands did, that the Commission's finding has no official status, and requiring the formal delivery of an original, sealed copy of the judgment, is both churlish of obstructionist (Ochieng Odhiambo, 2012). Despite having subsequently been availed of a copy, there is little publicly accessible indication that the minister has started the process of preparing a cabinet memorandum to set into motion the process of domestic implementation. Without consulting the Endorois community, the government in 2012 embarked on the process of having Lake Bogoria proclaimed as a UNESCO heritage site.

The mainstay of the government's substantive response relates to the complexity of the possible restoration processes. This response should be understood against the background of the post-electoral violence period, during which a government of national unity has been put in place and the

[70] Ibid., para 298(b).

process of adopting a more inclusive Constitution was undertaken. It is indeed so that the 2010 Constitution accommodates minority rights and indigenous groups. In particular, the state is compelled to adopt 'affirmative action programmes' to advance the rights of 'minorities and marginalised groups'.[71] 'State organs and all public officers' are further under an obligation to 'address the needs of vulnerable groups within society' including 'members of minority or marginalised communities' and 'members of particular ethnic, religious or cultural communities'.[72] While the concept 'minorities' is not defined, a 'marginalised community' is defined as including 'an indigenous community that has retained and maintained a traditional lifestyle and livelihood based on a hunter or gatherer economy'.[73] The government's contention is that the need for a comprehensive and holistic approach to the protection of the rights of a multiplicity of groups makes it difficult for it to take measures to protect the rights of a particular group.

The involvement of civil society organisations has been crucial in both the pre-judgment and post-judgment phases. From as far back as 2002, Minority Rights Group International (MRG) played an important role in the preparation of and awareness-raising about the case (Claridge, 2011). With the EWC and CEMIRIDE, it embarked on a project 'A Solution to the Forced Displacement of the Endorois in Kenya: Working towards the Implementation of the African Commission on Human and Peoples' Rights' Judgement'.[74] Acknowledging that the implementation phase of the litigation entails a shift from the legal to the political, one of the main objectives of this project was to build the capacity of locally based EWC to be the principal interlocutor with the Kenyan government. While this aim has largely been achieved, the limited technical expertise within the EWC would necessitate a continuous role for CEMIRIDE and MRG. A coalition of human rights and environmental advocacy groups, which assisted EWC in organising the 2010 celebration, subsequent to the event, formed a Civil Society Stakeholders Forum to work towards the implementation of the *Endorois* decision (Ochieng Odhiambo, 2012).

---

[71] The Constitution of Kenya, 27 August 2010, art. 56: The State shall put in place affirmative action programmes designed to ensure that minorities and marginalised groups (1) participate and are represented in governance and other spheres of life; (2) are provided special opportunities in educational and economic fields; (3) are provided special opportunities for access to employment; (4) develop their cultural values, languages and practices; and (5) have reasonable access to water, health services and infrastructure.

[72] Ibid., art. 21(3).

[73] Ibid., art. 260.

[74] This was a three-year project supported by the Baring Foundation.

Although no formal 'implementation meeting' has yet been held between the government and the complainants, strategies have been developed to build capacity and prepare the community for an eventual dialogue or negotiation with the government, enabling Endorois leaders and representatives to bring a well-developed proposal for reparations to the table. Local and international civil society organisations collaborated in this process. ESCR-Net, MRG, Socio-Economic Rights Institute (SERI), Norwegian Centre for Human Rights, University of Oslo, with CEMIRIDE, for example, hosted a 'Strategy Meeting on the Implementation of the Endorois Decision' on 12 November 2012, in Nairobi. A multiple strategy was devised, including undertaking a mapping exercise to identify the ancestral lands of the Endorois, and working out the modalities for the compensation for loss suffered and benefit from economic activities. Another option considered was an advisory opinion by the Kenyan Supreme Court. Article 163(6) of the Kenyan Constitution empowers the Supreme Court to give an advisory opinion 'at the request of the national government, any State organ, or any county government with respect to any matter concerning county government'. Such a request would have to be lodged by a state body such as the Kenya National Commission on Human Rights or the Gender and Equality Commission (whose statute obliges it to monitor state compliance with international treaties touching on inter alia, marginalised communities and groups). The Gender and Equality Commission (as well as the Commission on Administrative Justice) has expressed some support for the implementation process in the *Endorois* case.[75]

In relation to the 'reparations' element, complex issues arise pertaining to the reparation process, the form reparation should take, calculating the amount, and identifying the recipients. For this reason, the EWC partnered with Dejusticia and the ESCR-Net Adjudication Working Group, in 2013, organised a one-and-a half-day workshop on reparations for violations of the rights of indigenous communities in Nakuru, Kenya, from 23 to 24 July 2013, with the active support of the Minority Rights Group (MRG), Norwegian Center for Human Rights and Ford Foundation.[76]

International mobilisation has been a salient characteristic of the implementation strategy. MRG and the EWC have used opportunities in international fora, including the UN Permanent Forum on Indigenous

---

75 Communication (email) from Korir DSingOei, legal counsel to CEMIRIDE, 25 January 2013 (on file with author).
76 www.escr-net.org/node/365247 (accessed 6 August 2013).

People, to raise awareness about the *Endorois* case and the status and need for implementation. In addition to MRG, ESCR-Net, other international civil society organisations such as Human Rights Watch drew attention, through its advocacy campaigns, to the fact that the Commission's ruling in the *Endorois* case had not been carried out.[77]

One of the recommendations emanating from Kenya's 2010 Universal Periodic Review (UPR) called on the government to 'implement the recommendations and decisions of its own judicial institutions and of the African Commission on Human and Peoples' Rights, particularly those relating to the rights of indigenous peoples'.[78] During the mid-term (2013) assessment, the state mentions the Constitution of Kenya 2010 (as strengthening indigenous peoples' personal and collective rights), the development of the National Community Land Bill (to provide a legal framework for the protection of community land in accordance with constitutional imperatives), and the draft national policy and action plan on human rights (aimed at adopting legislative and affirmative action to ensure that minorities and marginalised groups realise all their rights). However, with regard to the *Endorois* judgment, specifically, the state concedes that 'the Attorney General of Kenya and the Ministry of Lands are currently working on the necessary modalities to implement the judgment'. The civil society response noted that, as of February 2012, 'not one meeting between the community, its representatives and government officials has taken place'. The Kenya National Commission on Human Rights also concluded that the decision remains unimplemented.[79]

Some influential individuals, such as the MP for Turkana Central (1998–2013), Ekwe Ethuro, was also instrumental in foregrounding the need for implementation. Ethuro posed a parliamentary question to the Minster for Lands about the implementation status of the Endorois recommendations.

The importance of political context cannot be discounted. In the period during which the communication was considered (first on admissibility, and later on the merits), from 2003 (when the matter was declared admissible) to November 2009, the political environment in Kenya underwent significant changes. In elections at the end of 2002, the National Rainbow Coalition (NARC) defeated the Kenya African National Union (KANU), which had been the governing party since independence in 1963. The

---

[77] www.hrw.org/africa/kenya (accessed 6 August 2013).
[78] Report of the Working Group of the UPR: Kenya, U.N. Doc A/HRC/15/8, 15 June 2010, para 110.114.
[79] www.upr-info.org/followup/assessments/session21/kenya/MIA-Kenya.pdf.

new government's 'embrace of human rights and democratic principles evidenced by the introduction of a raft of institutional reforms and the opening up of democratic space' (Ochieng Odhiambo, 2012) did not immediately translate into cooperation with the African Commission in respect of the consideration of the *Endorois* matter. From December 2003 to April 2005, the Commission to no avail directed numerous requests to the government to submit its arguments on admissibility.[80] However, the government failed to do so, and the Commission reached its admissibility decision without the benefit of any inputs from the Kenyan government. Subsequently, from May 2006, the government participated more effectively, including engaging in an unsuccessful attempt to reach an amicable settlement. While the initial lack of cooperation may in all likelihood be ascribed to the slow pace with which civil service and the administration of governance changes to become aligned to new political perspectives, a similar explanation cannot be offered to justify the government's reluctance and non-committal in the post-judgment period, from early 2010, when the decision was made public, to the present. Different forces were at play: After the 2007 election, and the post-election violence of 2008, the coalition government in place in 2010 was based on 'a marriage of convenience' of political rivals. As Odhiambo contends, in this context, the minister for lands may have been undermined by 'different (and opposing) coalition partners' holding portfolios that are key to the process of implementing the *Endorois* decision (Ochieng Odhiambo, 2012: para 3.2).

Subsequent to issuing its decision in the *Endorois* case, the African Commission remained engaged with the plight of the community, and with the follow-up of the decision. The issue of implementation was explicitly placed as an item on the agenda of its fifty-first session.[81] The African Commission's Working Group on Indigenous Populations/Communities in Africa, for example, undertook a mission to Kenya from 1 to 19 March 2010. In its report, adopted by the Commission at its session in November 2011, the government of Kenya is called upon to implement the ruling of the African Commission in the case of the Endorois people, and to 'return their ancestral land and respect their right to unrestricted access to Lake Bogoria'.[82] At the same session, the Commission also reacted positively to the information provided to it about the inscription of Lake Bogoria on the World Heritage List without the involvement

---

[80] *Endorois* case, supra n. 31, paras 27–41, 60.
[81] Combined 32nd and 33rd Activity Report of the African Commission on Human and Peoples' Rights, 21–25 January 2013, Au Doc EX.CL/782(XXII) Rev. 2, para 21.
[82] Ibid., para 14.

of the Endorois in the decision-making process by adopting a resolution on this issue. In the resolution, the Commission noted that the failure to obtain their free, prior, and informed consent of the Endorois 'contravenes the African Commission's Endorois Decision'.[83] The Commission remains engaged with the issue, as reflected in its adoption of the report of the Commissioner rapporteur on the implementation of this case.[84]

One of the options open to the Commission is referral to the Court, which could see its recommendatory finding potentially being 'converted' into a binding decision. However, although Kenya has, by mid-2015, had some six years to implement the *Endorois* decision, the Commission has not yet referred the case to the Court. Arguably, the Commission's decision not to refer the case has been informed by the political changes brought about by the introduction of the 2010 Kenyan Constitution, the elections of 2013, the views of the complainants, and the government's somewhat cooperative stance. However, indications are that the Commission is running out of patience. It held a confidential oral hearing during its session in April 2013, to which it invited the complainants and government to discuss the issue of implementation. There, it transpired that only one part of the remedial order, namely, the requirement to register the EWC, had been implemented.[85] The government subsequently reneged on its commitment to produce an interim implementation report within ninety days, and a more comprehensive roadmap at the Commission's November 2013 session. At that session, in its boldest resolution concerning implementation to date, the Commission implored Kenya to 'immediately transmit to the Commission, a comprehensive report, including a roadmap for implementation'.[86]

This pressure may be one of the primary reasons why President Kenyatta in 2014 established a Task Force on the Implementation of the Decision of the African Commission Contained in Communication

---

[83] Resolution 197: Resolution on the Protection of Indigenous Peoples' Rights in the Context of the World Heritage Convention and the Designation of Lake Bogoria as a World Heritage site, 5 November 2011.

[84] 'The Report of the Commissioner rapporteur on the implementation of Communication 276/03 (Final Communiqué of the African Commission's 56th ordinary session, May 2015, para 34(iv).)

[85] See ACHPR, Final Communiqué of the Workshop on the Status of the Implementation of the Endorois Decision of the African Commission on Human and Peoples' Rights, 23 September 2013, para. 5; available at www.achpr.org/news/2013/10/d96/ (accessed 18 August 2015).

[86] Resolution 257: Resolution Calling on the Republic of Kenya to Implement the Endorois Decision; available at www.achpr.org/sessions/54th/resolutions/257/ (accessed 5 August 2015).

276/2003.[87] It is chaired by the solicitor general and consists of four further members: principal secretary, Ministry of Lands, Housing and Urban Development; principal secretary, Ministry of Sports, Culture and Arts; secretary, Kenya National Commission on Human Rights; and the county secretary, Baringo County. The Task Force is mandated to 'examine the practicability of restitution of Lake Bogoria and the surrounding area to the Endorois Community taking into account that Lake Bogoria is classified as a World Heritage Site by UNESCO'; and to 'assess the amount of compensation payable to the Endorois Community for losses suffered and for settlement of royalties owed from existing economic activities on and around Lake Bogoria'.[88] In more general terms, its stated aims are to 'study the Decision', 'provide guidance on the political, security and economic implications of the Decision', and to 'examine the potential environmental impacts on Lake Bogoria and the surrounding area because of the implementation'. By mid-2015, the Task Force had met a number of times, also with civil society groupings including the parties who brought the case, but has made very little progress towards actual implementation.

11.5.4   Darfur Case

In the fourth case, the *Darfur* case,[89] which was decided in May 2009 and relates to the situation in Darfur, the Commission found Sudan in violation of numerous provisions of the Charter, based on the government's complicity in and failure to prevent indiscriminate killings, torture, poisoning of wells, forced displacement, and destruction of property of civilians in Darfur. As far as socio-economic rights are concerned, the Commission found that the right to property, health, and development has been violated. The majority of the remedial orders relate to the obligation to 'respect and protect'. In this respect, the Commission recommended that the Sudanese government 'conduct effective official investigations into the abuses' and to prosecute those responsible for the human rights violations; to 'undertake major reforms of its legislative and judicial framework in order to handle cases of serious and massive human rights violations'; and to 'ensure that the victims of human rights abuses are given effective remedies, including restitution and compensation'.[90] The government

---

[87] Government Gazette 6708, 14 September 2014.
[88] Para 1 of the Gazette.
[89] Communication 279/2003–296/2005, *Sudan Human Rights Organisation & Centre on Housing Rights and Evictions (COHRE) v Sudan* (2009) AHRLR 153 (ACHPR 2009) (28th Activity Report) (*Darfur* case).
[90] Ibid., para 229.

was further required to establish a National Reconciliation Forum to address the 'long-term sources of conflict, equitable allocation of national resources to the various provinces, including affirmative action for Darfur, resolve issues of land, grazing and water rights, including destocking of livestock'; desist from adopting amnesty laws for perpetrators of human rights abuses; and consolidate and finalise pending Peace Agreements. A positive obligation is clearest derived from the recommendation that the government should 'rehabilitate economic and social infrastructure, such as education, health, water, and agricultural services, in the Darfur provinces in order to provide conditions for return in safety and dignity for the IDPs and Refugees'.[91]

Of relevance, too, is the fact that the *Darfur* case consists of two separate communications, which have been joined by the Commission. The one case was submitted by the Sudan Human Rights Organisation (based in London), the Sudan Human Rights Organisation (based in Canada), the Darfur Diaspora Association, the Sudanese Women Union in Canada, and the Massaleit Diaspora Association. The second communication was submitted by an international NGO, the Centre for Housing Rights and Evictions (COHRE), based in Washington DC in the United States. In other words, none of the complaints in the Darfur case were local NGOs with a direct link to the affected communities.

COHRE, in its 2010 submission to the Universal Periodic Review, contended that 'Sudan has failed to take the steps necessary to end the human rights violations in Darfur or facilitate safe and dignified return of those displaced by those violations' (COHRE, 2012). The government did not respond to this contention; in fact, it made no reference to the case in its submission at all. Its reliance on a 'new strategy encompassing peace, security and development in Darfur with components for the return of internally displaced refugees to their homeland'[92] is an implicit concession that the government had not yet adequately addressed the situation in Darfur, and, by necessary implication, the circumstances giving rise to the *Darfur* case.

On the occasion of its twenty-five-year celebrations in 2012, the Commission noted with regret that the conflict in the region was on-going, and continued to 'destroy livelihoods and infrastructure, trigger mass displacements of whole populations creating internally displaced persons

[91] Ibid., para 229.
[92] Report of the Working Group on the Universal Periodic Review Sudan, para 42, A/HRC/ 18/16, 11 July 2011.

(IDPs), refugees and asylum seekers'.[93] Although the Commission refers to issues in Darfur as concerns in its Concluding Observations adopted after examining Sudan's reports in 2009 and 2012, no mention is made of the *Darfur* case and its recommendations.

11.5.5   Extent of Compliance and Categorisation of Four Cases

All four cases defy any unequivocal conclusions about the issue of domestic enforcement or implementation. In two cases, the *Gambian Mental Health* case and the *Darfur* case, there are strong indications of 'no' enforcement or implementation, and in two, the *Ogoniland* and *Endorois* cases, there are indications of 'partial' enforcement or implementation.

In the *Gambian Mental Health* case, there is very little indication of enforcement. Although not required in the recommendation, as such, a new hospital for the mentally ill has been constructed and opened. Any further insight about this or any other aspect of enforcement is blurred by the failure of government officials to cooperate, as manifested by a lack of transparency and inaccessibility. This case suggests strongly that an undemocratic quasi-dictatorial regime not only limits the prospects of enforcement, but is also likely to restrict access to knowledge of implementation. The continuing instability in the Darfur region of Sudan reduces the likelihood of enforcement in the *Darfur* case. Despite government rhetoric about improvements and changes in some international fora, there still is no indication that the actual living conditions of people in Darfur have improved.

As far as the other two cases are concerned, the available data paints a picture of limited enforcement: In *Ogoniland*, the main problem is the difficulty of establishing a causal relationship between the finding and measures taken by the state. However, the main contribution of the decision seems to be its impact on the awareness of the relevant issues among ordinary people, the government at various levels, and the broader international community. All these factors impacted on the various steps adopted by the government. Although these steps have not resulted in the eradication of the underlying social problems, they have generated broader benefits to the affected communities, also in respect of its fulfilment obligation. Kenya implemented unequivocally at least one element of the Commission's recommendatory order in the *Endorois* decision (the

---

[93] Combined 32nd and 33rd Activity Report of the African Commission on Human and Peoples' Rights, 21–25 January 2013, Au Doc EX.CL/782(XXII) Rev. 2, para 28.

registration of the Endorois Welfare Council). Although constitutional and other changes affecting indigenous communities have been adopted in the aftermath of this decision, the government has been reticent to give full effect to the other recommendations.

11.6 Selected Cases: Factors Affecting Compliance

In this chapter, some hypotheses are formulated that could be useful in the pursuit to better shed light on the conditions that enhance enforcement of 'regional orders' in cases where socio-economic rights feature prominently. While the focus here is on the interrelationship between the international and national dimensions of human rights protection, many parts of this discussion may still be of relevance to the enforcement of similar orders of national courts. Given the limited data set of four cases, conclusive testing of the validity of the stated hypotheses is not attempted here. However, some exploratory insights about the hypotheses are drawn from the available data, and tentative findings are made about the likelihood of certain factors being more predictive of implementation than others. In the process, the validity of the insights gained from hypotheses in the previous study, which did not focus on positive obligations arising from socio-economic rights cases, referred to earlier, are interrogated.

11.6.1 Relevance of Treaty Body or Court

As far as the Commission as treaty body is concerned, there is a definite indication that its involvement in following up findings is a relevant factor in predicting state compliance. In the two instances of 'no enforcement', on the one hand, the Commission did not engage in any follow-up measures specifically related to the findings. In both instances of 'partial enforcement', on the other hand, the Commission remained engaged in at least some follow-up, through state reporting (in the *Ogoniland* case), on-site visits (such as the one undertaken by the Commission's Working Group to Kenya subsequent to the *Endorois* case), the adoption of subsequent resolutions (for example, in respect of the implementation of the *Endorois* case), and holding private 'implementation hearings' (in respect of the *Endorois* case).

The instance of greatest subsequent engagement by the Commission (the *Endorois* case) is also the case in which it was most explicit about follow-up actions in its 'remedial order'. In that case, the government was required to report to the Commission about implementation within three months after having been notified of the decision. Although there is no indication that Kenya has produced the required information officially to the Commission, its declarations from the floor during public sessions of the Commission represent some form of 'reporting'. The three-month period has in the Commission's 2010 Rules of Procedure been adjusted and formalised as a requirement to report within six months (180 days).[94] Predating the adoption of these Rules, it is unsurprising that the Commission's practice with regard to the inclusion of explicit follow-up measures in its recommendations varies across the four cases. In two, the *Ogoniland and Darfur* cases, no specific follow-up measures were taken or timelines set. In the two other cases, two different measures were adopted. While Kenya was required to report back directly to the Commission, in the *Gambian Mental Health* case, the Commission required the Gambian government to report to the Commission about the implementation when it next submits its state report. However, the Gambia did not submit a state report under the African Charter since this case had been decided – its last report was submitted and examined in 1994. Although Kenya was not required to include information about follow-up in its subsequent period reports, this process could also have contributed to enhance the Commission's engagement with the state on the issue. Kenya has submitted one report since the *Endorois* finding, covering the period 2008–2014. However, this report, scheduled for examination in November 2015, does not contain any mention of the *Endorois* decision.[95]

   As the Commission has not referred any of the four cases to the Court, there is no data allowing for the juxtaposition between the recommendatory findings of the Commission and the binding decisions of the African Human Rights Court. None of the cases could have been submitted directly to the Court, because none of the states has made the declaration accepting individual access directly to the Court. Indirect referral is possible in respect of the three states that have ratified the Court Protocol (the Gambia, Kenya, and Nigeria). Only Sudan is not a state party to the Court Protocol, rendering indirect referral to the Court impossible. As discussed, the *Endorois* case is the most likely to be referred to the Court. The *Endorois* case was decided in 2009, and Kenya became a state party to the Court Protocol on 18 February 2005. While the cause of action and the

---

[94] Albeit with an extended timeframe: 2010 Rules of Procedure of the African Commission, Rule 112(2), in terms of which a respondent state must within six months inform the Commission of the steps it is taking to implement a decision against it.

[95] www.achpr.org/files/sessions/57th/state-reports/8th-11th-2008–2014/kenya_state_report_eng.pdf (accessed 5 August 2015).

submission of the case pre-date this, the Commission decided the matter subsequent to Kenya's ratification of the Protocol, and the violations are arguably of a 'continuous' nature. The *Ogoniland* case had been decided in 2001, some five years before the Court Protocol entered into force in 2004. To advance an argument that the violations are 'continuous' is complex, but may succeed. The *Gambian Mental Health* case was decided in 2003, and the same observation applies.

While the enforcement of the ECOWAS decision in the 2012 *SERAP* case may be juxtaposed against the implementation of the *Ogoniland* case, further research is called for to verify the explanatory leverage of the hypothesis that the binding nature of the ECOWAS Court's decision enhances the prospect of enforcement. In the absence of a comparable decision by the African Court, the hypothesis that the orders of sub-regional courts are more likely to be enforced than those of a regional court cannot yet be tested.

11.6.2 Relevance of Domestic Legal Framework

As for the domestic legal framework, the two categories of cases may also be clearly distinguished as far as the constitutional inclusion of justiciable socio-economic rights is concerned. In the 'no enforcement' countries, there is little basis to argue that socio-economic rights are justiciable under domestic law. Neither the 1996 Constitution of the Gambia, nor the 2005 Interim National Constitution of Sudan contains justiciable socio-economic rights. Instead, these 'rights' are placed in non-justiciable chapters dealing with 'guiding principles and directives'. In the two 'partially enforcing' countries, the situation is not so clear-cut, and in both there are some indications that socio-economic rights may be regarded as justiciable. While the Kenyan Constitution did not contain justiciable socio-economic rights at the time when the *Endorois* case was submitted and decided, such rights have subsequently been included in Kenya's 2010 Constitution, which provides for an extensive array of justiciable socio-economic rights.[96] Implementation debates therefore take place in a legal context in which the justiciability of socio-economic rights is accepted. The position in Nigeria is more ambiguous. While the 1999 Constitution relegates socio-economic rights to non-justiciable guarantees (in Chapter II, as 'Directive Principles of State Policy'), the African Charter – including

---

[96] Constitution of Kenya, 2010, art. 43; see also 56(e) (affirmative action for minority and marginalised groups, including access to water, health services and infrastructure).

its justiciable socio-economic rights provisions – has been domesticated, and in the view of the Court of Appeal in *Fawehinmi v Abacha* enjoys a status superior to national legislation.[97] The African Commission seems to accept that these rights are non-justiciable.[98] It should, however, be kept in mind that the domestic legal regime is framed by the supra-national level, in respect of which socio-economic rights provided for under the African Charter are justiciable and can be brought to the ECOWAS Court,[99] and to the African Commission and Court.

The available data allow much less support for the relevance of monism/dualism as a factor. The Gambia is a classically dualist state, in which domestication of international treaties is exceptional; Nigeria is a dualist state, but has domesticated the African Charter. Kenya has moved from a dualist to a de jure monist state, with international human rights treaties being recognised as 'part of the law of Kenya' under the 2010 Constitution.[100] The Interim Constitution of Sudan stipulates that 'international human rights treaties, covenants and instruments' ratified by Sudan 'shall be an integral part' of the Bill of Rights.[101] From this, it appears that it may be more useful to look at the actual (legislative and judicial) practice than having reference to the formal (constitutional) position on monism/dualism, as suggested in the formulated hypothesis.

11.6.3   Relevance of Victims (Scale of Violation)

It is not possible to test the validity of the hypothesis related to the number of or 'victims' (which also relates to the scale or extent of the violation), because all four cases involve significant numbers of 'victims': The *Ogoniland* case was brought on behalf of the Ogoni people, the *Endorois* case on behalf of an indigenous people, the Endorois, numbering some 60,000 people, and the *Darfur* case on behalf of the 'people' of Darfur. Although the precise number of victims in the *Gambian Mental Health* case is not known, and while it is correct that the scale of the violation is more restricted than in the other three cases, the victims are also numerous and do not make up an

---

[97] (1996) NWLR (Pt 475) 710; see also the Supreme Court's decision in *Abacha and Others v Fawehinmi* (2001) AHRLR 172 (NgSC 2000).

[98] Concluding Observations and Recommendations on the Third Periodic Report of the Federal Republic of Nigeria, 10–24 November 2008, para 13.

[99] *Registered Trustees of the Socio-economic Rights and Accountability Project (SERAP) v Nigeria* (2009) AHRLR 331 (ECOWAS 2009) paras 17–19.

[100] Constitution of Kenya, 2010, art. 2(6).

[101] Interim Constitution of Sudan, 2005, art. 27(3).

enumerated list. Given that all four cases of inadequate compliance under discussion share this feature, the extensive scale of the violations may well be a factor that informs a lack of implementation, more generally.

11.6.4   Relevance of State

An analysis of the four cases supports the hypothesis that states are more likely to enforce orders to fulfill related to a cause of action that arose under a previous political dispensation. The experience in the four instances illustrates the relevance of changed political circumstances, most clearly manifested in a change of the government, or the transition from one political order to another, to domestic enforcement. On the one hand, Nigeria and Kenya in the *Ogoniland* and *Endorois* cases showed some willingness to enforce the Commission's order. In both instances, this willingness came about in the context of political change. In Nigeria, the facts relate to the conduct of the Abacha regime, which was replaced by a democratic government against which the case was submitted and the 'order' directed. In Kenya, the conduct complained about relates to the KANU government, which lost its hold on power in 2002. In the other two communications, on the other hand, the respondent states (the Gambia and Sudan) did not show any readiness to implement the Commission's recommendations. In both these instances, the undemocratic and deeply repressive nature of the political power remained unchanged after the Commission issued its orders, rendering enforcement of regional orders very unlikely.

Some indicators used in this study support the contention that states observing the 'rule of law' are more likely to enforce regional orders pertaining to socio-economic rights. Using the Freedom House categorisation for 2013,[102] the Gambia and Sudan are 'not free', while Kenya and Nigeria are 'partially free'. In fact, Sudan was among the seven countries given the survey's lowest possible rating for both political rights and civil liberties. Other indicators draw a smaller distinction between Kenya, Nigeria, and the Gambia. While the Gambia performs better than Kenya and Nigeria in the overall 2012 Ibrahim Index of African Governance, on the 'rule of law' yardstick the scores are as follows: Kenya 53, Nigeria 43, and the Gambia 37.[103] The World Justice Project indicators are not very useful

---

[102] www.freedomhouse.org/report/freedom-world/freedom-world-2013.

[103] www.moibrahimfoundation.org/downloads/2012-IIAG-summary-report.pdf, p. 20 (Sudan was, due to the political transition into dual statehood, not included). See also the World Bank Worldwide Governance Indicators (WGI) (http://info.worldbank.org/governance/wgi/index.asp), in which the Gambia is ranked higher than Kenya and Nigeria in respect of the rule of law.

for the purposes of this study, as only Kenya and Nigeria are included. Another possible conclusion, more related to the general trend towards non-implementation among the four states, is that (even) these two states are not performing very well in terms of 'rule of law', with a ranking that compares unfavourably to surveyed countries in region.[104]

11.6.5   Relevance of Civil Society and Community Involvement

Civil society and local community involvement enhance implementation prospects. There has been little civil society or domestic actor involvement in the submission and follow-up of the *Gambian Mental Health* case. The case has been brought by two health professionals acting on behalf of anonymous victims. The health professionals were not based in the Gambia, and did not involve themselves in the process of follow-up. The preparation and follow-up of this case was never embedded domestically and did not benefit from the involvement of local civil society actors. Similarly, there is little indication that the *Darfur* case has generated interest and involvement by an – admittedly very weak – Sudanese civil society. Such lack of domestic attention is clearly linked to the fact that the case was – already from the submission stage – not locally embedded, as the case was brought by NGOs based in London, Canada, and elsewhere in the diaspora.

In contrast, the *Ogoniland* and *Endorois* cases were submitted with the full involvement of prominent and profoundly committed and implicated local civil society organisations (SERAC in Nigeria, and CEMIRIDE and the Endorois Welfare Council in Kenya). The implementation of these cases was firmly inscribed into the agendas of these organisations. International NGOs (particularly, the Social and Economic Rights Action Center in respect of the *Ogoniland* case, and MRG, ESCR-Net, and Dejusticia in the *Endorois* case) provided further support and, through their involvement, also ensured some much-needed donor funding.

11.6.6   Relevance of International Legal Context

There is some indication that fuller adherence to the UN human rights system is aligned with better enforcement. As far as state reporting is

---

[104]   http://worldjusticeproject.org/rule-of-law-index.

concerned, there is very little difference in the frequency of reporting between the four states. The Gambia, which shows the least commitment, has not submitted a report under ICESCR in thirty-five years; Sudan submitted two reports in twenty-seven years;[105] Nigeria submitted one in ten years; and Kenya submitted two reports in forty-one years. However, as far as acceptance of complaints processes and inquiry procedures accepted under UN human rights treaties is concerned, the Gambia and Sudan had only accepted one such procedure each, while Nigeria accepted six and Kenya two. The juxtaposition of the two categories of countries ('no' vs. 'partial' enforcement) lends at least some support to the hypothesis that meaningful adherence to the UN human rights system aligns well with enforcement of regional socio-economic rights orders.

As far as full adherence to the AU human rights system is concerned,[106] it is noted that none of the four states has made a declaration under Article 34(6) of the Court Protocol. As far as ratified treaties are concerned, Sudan and the Gambia fared worst: Sudan has accepted only two of the three core treaties; it did not accept the jurisdiction of the African Human Rights Court; and although it signed on to the APRM, it has not yet allowed for a visit of this mechanism. Although the Gambia accepted all three core treaties and the Court's jurisdiction, it did not accept the APRM process. In contrast, Kenya and Nigeria had ratified the core treaties, the Court Protocol and had not only accepted but had also been subjected to an APRM visit.

11.7   Conclusion

A juxtaposition of the cases of 'no' (*Gambian Mental Health* and *Darfur* cases) and 'partial' implementation (*Ogoniland* and *Endorois* cases) provides support for the validity of five of the hypotheses formulated. First, the involvement of the treaty body (the African Commission, who finalised all four these cases) in the follow-up of its orders seems to be aligned with greater prospects of implementation. Second, there are strong indications that implementation is enhanced by the continuous engagement by and involvement of domestically located and embedded NGOs and community groups, acting with the support of international civil society. Third, the likelihood of implementation seems to increase if the government responsible for implementation is not the same as the government

[105]   Data from http://tbinternet.ohchr.org/_layouts/TreatyBodyExternal/Countries.aspx.
[106]   Data from www.au.int/en/treaties.

responsible for the violation and for redressing it. In other words, a fundamental change in the political dispensation seems to be predictive of greater implementation. Fourth, there is some support for the hypothesis that the more committed states are to the UN and AU human rights systems, the more likely they are to implement regional socio-economic rights orders. Fifth, there is at least some evidence to back up the hypothesis that the inclusion of justiciable socio-economic rights in a state's constitution corresponds with higher rates of implementation of regional socio-economic rights orders by that state.

In the previous study, discussed earlier, the first three factors have also emerged as predictors of implementation; the last two were not specifically tested in that study. It therefore appears that the factors predictive of compliance or implementation largely overlap in respect of civil and political rights and socio-economic rights.

A further rather obvious conclusion in respect of assessing the implementation in the four cases is that none of these four 'orders' have been fully adhered to. This conclusion invites the identification of those features mostly strongly present in *all* four cases as factors that inhibit full implementation. From this analysis, it appears that two factors are strongly predictive of non-implementation: (1) States lacking an open democratic political culture characterised by the presence of the rule of law are not likely to give full implementing effect to regional socio-economic rights orders. (2) Socio-economic rights orders are less likely to be implemented if these orders relate to mass-scale violations. Both these insights are also consonant with the findings of the previous study, and further confirm the tentative conclusion that there largely is correspondence between factors enhancing and detracting from the implementation of civil and political rights, on the one hand, and socio-economic rights, on the other.

Perhaps it should not be surprising that regional and other international orders are not regularly enforced. These orders suffer from the impediment that they lack direct and immediate political backing to secure or support enforcement. Although there may also be resistance against national court orders, at least there are measures available within the national legal system to ensure enforcement, for example, in extreme cases, contempt of court proceedings. Also, the counter-majoritarian nature of judicial orders plays out differently in the international sphere. The contention that judges are unelected is exacerbated, in that, although international judges may in fact be elected, these elections are by intergovernmental organisations in which the particular state only has one (or a limited) vote among many. Owing to the restricted membership of international monitoring bodies or courts, it may often be the case that a particular state is not represented at all. In fact, in the African Human Rights Court, national judges are barred from being part of the panel deciding a case against that particular state. In addition, the charge that courts lack expertise and specific understanding of the issues involved in abiding by fulfilment obligations is aggravated by international judges' remoteness, their lack of knowledge of the specific legal system involved, and the nuances and subtleties derived from a sustained engagement with local circumstances. In the absence of the rigorous testing of a hypothesis that enforcement of socio-economic rights orders at the national level is likely to be better than at the international level, these observations remain conjectures. One can but hope that, as the number of socio-economic rights judgments at both the national and international level increases, sufficient data will in the near future become available to allow this hypothesis to be tested.

References

Chirwa, Danwood Mzikenge (2008), 'African Regional Human Rights System: The Promise of Recent Jurisprudence on Social Rights', in Malcolm Langford (ed.), *Social Rights Jurisprudence: Emerging Trends in International and Comparative Law* (Cambridge: Cambridge University Press), 323–338.

Claude, Inis (1984), *Swords into Ploughshares* (New York: McGraw-Hill).

COHRE (2012), *Submission to the Universal Periodic Review concerning Sudan*, November 2012, accessed 18 May 2012 http://lib.ohchr.org/HRBodies/ UPR/Documents/Session11/SD/COHRE_TheCentreonHousingRightsand Evictions-eng.pdf.

Coomans, Fons (2003), 'The Ogoni Case before the African Commission on Human and Peoples' Rights', *International and Comparative Law Quarterly*, 52(3), 749–760.

Green, Maria (2001), 'What We Talk About When We Talk About Indicators: Current Approaches to Human Rights Measurement', *Human Rights Quarterly*, 23, 1062–1097.

Hillebrecht, Courtney (2014), *Domestic Politics and International Human Rights Tribunals: The Problem of Compliance* (New York: Cambridge University Press)

Louw, Lirette (2005), 'An Analysis of State Compliance with the Recommendations of the African Commission on Human and Peoples' Rights', unpublished LLD thesis (University of Pretoria).

Morka, Felix (2011), 'The Social and Economic Rights Action Centre and Center for Economic and Social Rights v Nigeria – Matters Arising', presentation delivered on 24 June 2011, Interights/Open Society Justice Initiative Conference on 'The Implementation of Human Rights Judgments: the Litigator's Perspective', London (abstract on file with author).

Ochieng Odhiambo, Michael (2012), 'A Solution to the Forced Displacement of the Endorois in Kenya: Working towards the Implementation of the African Commission on Human Rights' Decision (November 2008 – October 2011): Report of Final Evaluation' (Minority Rights Group International: Nakuru), 11 August 2015 www.minorityrights.org/download .php@id=1099.

Ohaeri, Victoria (2012), 'Regional Courts' Decisions and the Enforcement Challenge: Lessons from the Ogoni Case', paper presented at Africa Regional Workshop on Social Rights Litigation, Johannesburg, South Africa, 12–14 March 2012, co-organised by the International Network for Economic, Social and Cultural Rights (ESCR-Net) Socio-Economic Rights Institute of South Africa (SERI) and the Norwegian Centre on Human Rights (PowerPoint on file with author).

Simmons, Beth (2009), *Mobilising for Human Rights: International Law in Domestic Politics* (New York: Cambridge University Press).

Viljoen, Frans (2004), 'The African Charter on Human and Peoples' Rights: The Travaux Préparatoires in the Light of Subsequent Practice', *Human Rights Law Journal*, 25, 313–326.

(2010), 'State Compliance with the Recommendations of the African Commission on Human and Peoples' Rights', in Mashood Baderin and Manisuli Senyonjo (eds.), *International Human Rights Law: Six Decades after the UDHR* (Aldershot: Ashgate), 411–430.

(2012), *International Human Rights Law in Africa*, 2nd edn. (Oxford: Oxford University Press).

Viljoen, Frans and Lirette Louw (2007), 'An Assessment of State Compliance with the Recommendations of the African Commission on Human and Peoples' Rights between 1993 and 2004', *American Journal of International Law*, 101(1), 1–34.

12

Reproductive Rights Litigation: From Recognition to Transformation

LUISA CABAL AND SUZANNAH PHILLIPS

12.1 Introduction

Litigation strategies have been used increasingly to advance reproductive rights at the national, regional, and international levels, and have led to groundbreaking judicial decisions. This chapter evaluates how some of these landmark decisions have been successfully implemented, identifying key factors – institutional design, the nature of the remedies awarded, public attention to the case, and the social, political, and cultural environment – that enhance or hinder implementation of these decisions by national, regional, and international bodies.

Based on an analysis of eight reproductive rights decisions, we examine both compliance with individual orders and the broader transformative changes that motivate reproductive rights litigation. Evaluating implementation in the context of reproductive rights litigation, requires a broad conceptualisation, one that encompasses not only direct compliance with judicial orders, but also the transformative effect that can result from a positive judicial decision, even where implementation of specific remedies is incomplete or absent. Our conclusions suggest that governments are more likely to implement individual than general remedies of non-repetition

Luisa Cabal is a Lecturer-in-Law at Columbia Law School. Former Vice-President of Programs and Director of Global Program at the Center for Reproductive Rights.

Suzannah Phillips is Senior Legal Advisor for Women Enabled International and former Legal Adviser for International Advocacy, Center for Reproductive Rights.

The authors would like to thank their former colleagues at the Center for Reproductive Rights – Lilian Sepúlveda, Vice President, Global Legal Program, Melissa Upreti, Regional Director for Asia, and Christina Zampas, former Regional Director for Europe – for their feedback and insight on initial drafts of this chapter; Dante Costa and Lara Shkordoff, former Global Legal Program Interns, who contributed significantly to this chapter through research and drafting assistance; and Payal Shah, Senior Legal Adviser for Asia, Juan Sebastián Rodriguez, Legal Fellow for Latin America and the Caribbean, and Johanna Fine, former Deputy Director, Global Legal Program for providing updated information for later drafts.

but that transformation of the social and cultural environment together with political commitments can occur under certain conditions.

Reproductive rights cover a range of previously defined human rights, including economic, social, and cultural (ESC) rights, such as the right to health, the right to education, and the right to benefit from scientific progress. Accordingly, the realisation of reproductive rights encounters many of the same obstacles as the realisation of other ESC rights, including resource allocation and the political will necessary to strengthen health systems.

Unlike other ESC rights, however, recognition and acceptance of reproductive rights as human rights is constantly questioned. This recognition is an essential factor in ensuring that reproductive rights decisions are implemented. Generally, ESC rights – such as the rights to health, work, and housing – are expressly codified in the International Covenant on Economic, Social and Cultural Rights (Economic, Social and Cultural Rights Covenant).[1] In contrast, while the core components of reproductive rights – the rights to reproductive autonomy and reproductive healthcare – are articulated in the Convention on the Elimination of All Forms of Discrimination against Women (CEDAW),[2] and reproductive rights are increasingly affirmed in concluding observations, general recommendations, and other interpretive documents from United Nations treaty monitoring bodies,[3] reproductive rights are constantly challenged and sidelined in political arenas. The 1994 International Conference on Population and Development's Programme of Action (ICPD Programme of Action) marked a paradigmatic shift with respect to the recognition of reproductive rights as fundamental human rights.[4] This consensus agreement marked the first time that the two core pillars of reproductive rights were framed as basic human rights issues, almost thirty years after the Economic, Social and Cultural Rights Covenant was adopted and opened for signature and ratification. While the ICPD

---

[1] For more discussion on how the right to health, as initially codified in the Economic, Social and Cultural Rights Covenant, excluded women's reproductive health, see Cabal and Todd-Gher (2009: 120–121).

[2] Convention on the Elimination of All Forms of Discrimination against Women, G.A. res. 34/180, 34 U.N. GAOR Supp. (No. 46) at 193, U.N. Doc. A/34/46, entered into force 3 September 1981('CEDAW'), arts. 12, 14, 16(1)e.

[3] For a comprehensive review of UN treaty body observations on how reproductive rights abuses violate UN human rights treaties, see Center for Reproductive Rights (2008).

[4] See paragraph 7.3 of the ICPD Programme of Action (*Programme of Action of the International Conference on Population and Development*, Cairo, Egypt, 5–13 September 1994 Ch. VII, U.N. Doc. A/CONF.171/13/Rev.1 (1995)).

REPRODUCTIVE RIGHTS LITIGATION

Programme of Action was pivotal in acknowledging on the international plane that women's reproductive rights are grounded in existing human rights norms, this acknowledgment was in the form of soft norms, rather than binding legal obligations, and it remains an ongoing struggle for women's rights groups to ensure that these principles are reaffirmed in similar political spaces.[5] Thus it has been the role of reproductive rights advocates to solidify recognition of reproductive rights as human rights by transforming existing human rights principles into concrete protections for reproductive rights.

Realising reproductive rights, then, requires a strengthening of human rights norms to better recognise and respond to reproductive rights violations. Accordingly, while reproductive rights litigation pursues individual remedies in the form of reparations for the victims and general remedies in the form of normative or structural changes to redress systemic violations, these cases also seek symbolic or transformative remedies: recognition of these violations as fundamental human rights violations, a shift in the public discourse around the issues, and stronger, better-defined national, regional, and international standards on human rights as they relate to reproductive health. Positive rulings in reproductive rights cases may be a catalyst for normative or policy changes through the direct implementation of judicial orders, but they may also facilitate normative or policy changes through more indirect means by reshaping the legal and political discourse around reproductive health and rights at the national, regional, and international levels. Thus, these broader objectives of reproductive rights litigation need to be part of the evaluation of whether and how well reproductive rights judgments have been implemented, rather than looking more narrowly at the implementation of specific judicial orders.

It is worth noting that positive rulings in reproductive rights in the context of highly polarised political environments can generate a backlash and energise the opposition, potentially jeopardising gains achieved through litigation. Given the potential backlash to positive judicial rulings, reproductive rights litigation cannot be an isolated tactic, but should rather take place in the context of a broader advocacy strategy aimed at promoting and advancing reproductive rights and fostering an environment where the political, social, and cultural institutions that systemically

---

[5] The Millennium Development Goals, for instance, excluded reproductive health and rights entirely from the initial document. It was only five years later that a goal pertaining to reproductive health was inserted as a target goal.

restrict women's reproductive rights can be transformed.[6] In this context, the goals of reproductive rights litigation may change over time according to the needs or stage of the broader advocacy strategy. Earlier in the advocacy strategy, for instance, when international standards around a particular issue have not been fully developed, one of the primary goals of litigation, aside from individual reparations, is recognition by courts or human rights bodies that the violation in question is in fact a human rights violation. Accordingly, earlier suits might be filed in fora where positive decisions are more likely to shape the contours of human rights standards with respect to reproductive rights at the regional or international level, even though full compliance with the general remedies may be more challenging to achieve. Once international standards around the issue have evolved, advocates may pursue follow-up lawsuits in fora better suited for the implementation of comprehensive structural reform. What constitutes successful implementation of a given decision, then, should also be considered within the context of the overarching advocacy and litigation goals.

This chapter evaluates the implementation of key reproductive rights decisions relying on this broader conceptualisation of implementation. Section 12.2 provides a brief overview of reproductive rights as human rights. Section 12.3 presents several reproductive rights case studies that the Center for Reproductive Rights (the Center) has litigated or helped litigate with its local and regional partners around three thematic areas – coercive sterilisation, access to abortion, and maternal mortality – and identifies the degree to which the different remedies – individual, general, and transformative – resulting from the final outcome have been implemented. Drawing on the Center's experience with these case studies, Section 12.4 then discusses the factors that enhance or hinder implementation of the individual, general, and transformative remedies that arose out of these decisions.

---

[6] We rely here on Nancy Fraser's concept of misrecognition as status subordination, whereby the goal of recognition is to "overcome[ ] subordination by establishing the misrecognized party as a full member of society, capable of participating on par with the rest" (2000: 113). In the context of reproductive rights, this misrecognition occurs at two levels: first, through the institutionalisation of socio-cultural norms that infringe women's reproductive rights, and second, through the historical exclusion of women's rights, including reproductive rights, from mainstream human rights movements. Goals of recognition through reproductive rights litigation, then, are bi-fold; transformative or symbolic remedies seek on the one hand to challenge or dismantle the socio-cultural underpinnings of reproductive rights violations and on the other to garner greater recognition of reproductive rights as human rights.

12.2   Reproductive Rights as Human Rights

Since the 1994 ICPD Programme of Action recognised reproductive rights as fundamental human rights central to development and population policies, a number of countries around the world have strengthened the protection of reproductive rights, for instance, by recognising these rights in national constitutions,[7] liberalising laws around contraceptive and abortion access,[8] and developing national plans and policies aimed at improving maternal health. At the same time, despite the fact that reproductive rights have been increasingly and consistently reaffirmed by adjudicatory bodies at the national, regional, and international level, reproductive rights remain highly contested politically, due in large part to competing religious and moral views around contraception and abortion. As a result, reproductive rights violations are widespread.

Reproductive rights is broadly defined as 'the basic right of all couples and individuals to decide freely and responsibly the number, spacing and timing of their children and to have the information and means to do so, and the right to attain the highest standard of sexual and reproductive health'.[9] These two core pillars of reproductive rights – the rights to reproductive self-determination and to sexual and reproductive healthcare – rest on a host of fundamental human rights enshrined in regional and international human rights treaties and in national laws. These rights include both ESC rights and civil and political rights, including, inter alia, the right to life, the right to health, the rights to equality and non-discrimination, the right to information, the right to be free from torture or cruel, inhuman, or degrading treatment, the right to privacy, and the right to be free from gender-based violence.

The right to health underlies governmental obligations to respect and ensure reproductive rights and provides a useful frame for understanding reproductive rights as human rights, as the primary components of the right to health mirror the core pillars of reproductive rights. The Committee on Economic, Social and Cultural Rights (ESCR Committee)

---

[7] For example, Nepal, Kosovo, Ecuador, Bolivia, and Kenya have all recently adopted new or interim constitutions that strengthen protections for reproductive rights. Interim Constitution of Nepal, Art. 20 (2007) (Nepal); Constitution of the Republic of Kosovo, Art. 26 (2008) (Kosovo); Constitución de la República del Ecuador [C.P.], art. 66 (2008) (Ecuador); Constitución Política del Estado de Bolivia [C.P.], arts. 14, 15, 45, 66 (2009) (Bol.); Constitution, arts. 26(d), 43 (2010) (Kenya).

[8] Between 1994 and 2014, thirty-five countries liberalised their abortion laws, while only four countries increased legal restrictions on abortion (Center for Reproductive Rights, 2014).

[9] See paragraph 7.3 of the ICPD Programme of Action.

has explained that the right to health encompasses both freedoms – which 'include the right to control one's health and body, including sexual and reproductive freedom' – and entitlements, including 'the right to a system of health protection which provides equality of opportunity for people to enjoy the highest attainable level of health'.[10] Whereas the right to health, as with other ESC rights, is subject to progressive realisation, the ESCR Committee has noted that States have an 'immediate obligation [to] guarantee that the right will be exercised without discrimination of any kind'.[11]

Gender-based discrimination with respect to the right to health can be seen not only in unequal access to healthcare and health services, but also in a State's failure to ensure essential health services catering to women's biological differences and distinct health concerns (Cook and Howard, 2007: 1046–1047). As the CEDAW Committee has explained, achieving substantive equality requires 'a real transformation of opportunities, institutions and systems so that they are no longer grounded in historically determined male paradigms of power and life patterns'.[12]

Governmental obligations to remedy systemic gender-based discrimination in the healthcare setting are twofold. First, states must ensure adequate provision of the health services that women need because they are women, including having the means and information to decide the number, spacing, and timing of their children free from discrimination, coercion, or violence and access to appropriate pregnancy, childbirth, and post-natal health services, including emergency obstetric care, safe abortion, and post-abortion care. To that end, CEDAW explicitly provides that member states have an obligation to ensure to women 'the information, education and means' to make decisions about reproduction and to ensure special healthcare treatment for women 'in connection with pregnancy, confinement and the post-natal period'.[13] Similarly, the ESCR Committee includes 'reproductive, maternal (pre-natal as well as post-natal) and child health care' among the core obligations of the right to health.[14]

In addition, states have an obligation to eliminate legal, economic, social, and cultural barriers to reproductive health services. In this

[10] Committee on Economic, Social and Cultural Rights (ESCR Committee), *General Comment 14: The Right to the Highest Attainable Standard of Health (Art. 12)* (Twenty second session, 2000), U.N. Doc. HRI/GEN/1/Rev.9 at 78 (2008) ('General Comment 14') para. 8.

[11] Ibid., para. 30.

[12] Committee on the Elimination of Discrimination against Women (CEDAW Committee), *General Recommendation No. 25: On Temporary Special Measures* (Thirtieth session, 2004), U.N. Doc. HRI/GEN/1/Rev.9 at 365 (2008) para. 10.

[13] CEDAW arts. 12(1) and 16(1)(e).

[14] General Comment 14 para. 44(a).

context, the CEDAW Committee has explained that '[i]t is discriminatory for a State party to refuse to provide legally for the performance of
certain reproductive health services for women'.[15] The ESCR Committee
has similarly articulated States' obligations to 'refrain from limiting access
to contraceptives and other means of maintaining sexual and reproductive health, from censoring, withholding or intentionally misrepresenting
health-related information, including sexual education and information'
in order to fulfil the right to health without discrimination.[16]

Government commissions and omissions in the area of reproductive
health services – including sterilisation of women without their informed
consent, imposition of barriers to accessing safe and legal abortion, and
failure to address preventable maternal mortality – violate the right to
health and other fundamental human rights. These human rights issues
were at the core of the reproductive rights litigation strategy of the Center
and are the basis for the case studies presented in the following section.

12.3 Reproductive Rights Case Studies

Reproductive rights litigation can transform overarching human rights
norms into concrete protections for reproductive rights. Litigation of individual cases can be used to hold governments accountable for their international human rights commitments by seeking redress for specific rights
violations and mandating legislative and policy changes to prevent similar violations from occurring in the future. Litigation can also help define
and shape the content of broader human rights principles as they apply
to reproductive rights and can reshape the public discourse around contentious issues, such as abortion. The Center for Reproductive Rights, in
partnership with local nongovernmental organisations, has pioneered the
use of national, regional, and international reproductive rights litigation
over the past two decades, as part of a comprehensive legal and advocacy
strategy, to advance these dual objectives of redress on the one hand and
international norm building on the other.[17] This section examines specific
case studies that the Center has litigated or directly supported around
coercive sterilisation, access to abortion, and maternal mortality, laying
out the details of the case and offering a critical review of the successes and

---

[15] CEDAW Committee, *General Recommendation 24: on Women and Health (Art. 12)*,
    (Twentieth session, 1999), U.N. Doc. HRI/GEN/1/Rev.9 at 358 (2008) para. 11.
[16] General Comment 14 para. 34.
[17] For more information on norm entrepreneurship, see Hannum (2004), Charnovitz (2006),
    and Keck and Sikkink (1998).

challenges in implementing the judicial orders, as well as the larger implications these decisions have had for the Center and its partners' broader advocacy efforts.

12.3.1   Involuntary Sterilisation

Surgical sterilisation is a permanent contraceptive method that, where voluntary, can be an effective means of preventing future unwanted pregnancies. In contrast, sterilisations that are performed without the patient's voluntary and informed consent cause tremendous physical and psychological harm. Involuntary sterilisations can either be coerced, where an individual agrees to be sterilised as a result of incentives, misinformation, or intimidation, or forced, where an individual is sterilised without his or her knowledge, for example, during another surgical procedure such as a caesarean section. Involuntary sterilisations are a global phenomenon, and marginalised populations – including racial or ethnic minorities, women living with HIV, and persons with disabilities – are often targeted by involuntary sterilisation policies or practices because they may be deemed to be 'unfit' to bear children.

María Mamérita Mestanza Chávez v. Peru

Under President Alberto Fujimori's government, Peruvian officials systematically sterilised thousands of poor and indigenous women without their consent.[18] María Mamérita Mestanza Chávez, a thirty-three-year-old woman from Cajamarca, Peru, was among the women targeted by government officials for sterilisation. Healthcare workers threatened Mestanza that she and her husband would be imprisoned and fined if she did not agree to undergo surgical sterilisation. In response to repeated harassment and threats, Mestanza underwent a sterilisation procedure, which was performed without any prior medical examination. After being released from the hospital, Mestanza experienced serious complications but was denied follow-up care, and within a few days of the surgery, she died from a post-surgery infection.[19] In 1999, the Center partnered with several

---

[18] The Peruvian Ombudsman has documented at least 2,074 cases of involuntary sterilisation between 1996 and 2000, though unofficial estimates indicate that the actual number of cases may be much higher. See, e.g., Ángel Páez, 'Perú: CIDH exige justicia para esterilizaciones forzadas', Inter Press Service (November 2011).

[19] For a more detailed account of the facts of this case, see the friendly settlement agreement, *María Mamérita Mestanza Chávez v. Peru*, Case 12.191, IACHR, Report No. 71/03 OEA/ Ser.L/V/II.118 Doc. 5 rev. 2 (22 October 2003) (*María Mamérita Mestanza Chávez v. Peru*).

other non-governmental organisations[20] to litigate Mestanza's case before the Inter-American Commission on Human Rights (Inter-American Commission).

In October of 2003, the government of Peru signed a friendly settlement in *María Mamérita Mestanza Chávez v. Peru*, agreeing to individual and general reparations.[21] The state admitted its international responsibility for the human rights violations that occurred, namely the rights to life, physical integrity and humane treatment, equal protection under the law, and freedom from gender-based violence. The settlement also provided for individual reparations to Mestanza's family, in the form of financial compensation and a thorough criminal and administrative investigation into the violations of Mestanza's rights. In addition, the Peruvian government agreed to reform its domestic laws and policies to strengthen protections of the rights of healthcare patients and to improve accountability mechanisms for human rights violations.

The Peruvian government is currently in partial compliance with the terms of this friendly settlement agreement. Peru has paid Mestanza's husband and children the financial compensation agreed upon. In addition, Peru's Ministry of Health issued guidelines on sexual and reproductive health that articulated, among other things, the right of patients not to be subjected to any family planning procedures, which includes surgical sterilisation, without their free, voluntary, and informed consent.[22] It is unclear whether these guidelines have been implemented in full at the healthcare facility level, but the involuntary sterilisation campaigns did come to an end. The promised criminal investigation languished and was eventually dismissed on the grounds that the statute of limitations had run (IACHR, 2009: 751). However, sustained legal and advocacy strategies helped generate widespread awareness and remembrance of these human rights violations, which have had lasting symbolic and transformative effects. In Peru's 2011 presidential election, candidate Keiko Fujimori was haunted by her father's involuntary sterilisation campaigns, and it has been suggested that her weak response to the sterilisation

[20] The Center partnered with the Latin American and Caribbean Committee for the Defense of Women's Rights (CLADEM), the Study for the Defense of Women's Rights (DEMUS), the Association for Human Rights (APRODEH), and the Center for International Law and Justice (CEJIL) to present Mestanza's case to the Inter-American Commission.
[21] *María Mamérita Mestanza Chávez v. Peru.*
[22] Ministerio de Salud (Ministry of Health, Peru), Guías Nacionales de Atención Integral de la Salud Sexual y Reproductiva (National Guidelines on Integrated Sexual and Reproductive Health Care), Modulo VIII: Planificación Familiar (Module 8: Family Planning) 1–2 (2004).

campaigns may have cost her the presidency.[23] In addition, following the change of government in July 2011, Peru's new government announced in October 2011 that it would begin treating the involuntary sterilisation cases as crimes against humanity,[24] and in November 2012, the government reopened its investigation into the cases, including Mestanza's case (IACHR, 2015: 271). As yet, however, there has not been a satisfactory resolution to the criminal investigation; a complaint has been filed against two health officials, but the culpability of public authorities has not been established (IACHR, 2015: 272). Furthermore, any impact the sterilisation campaigns may have had on Keiko Fujimori's 2011 campaign does not seem to be affecting her current lead in the polls for Peru's upcoming 2016 presidential election.[25]

A.S. v. Hungary

A.S., a Hungarian woman of Roma origin, was taken to a public hospital because she was experiencing labour pains; her amniotic sac had ruptured; and she was haemorrhaging. Upon admittance to the hospital, A.S. learned that she had miscarried and would have to undergo an emergency caesarean section. Minutes later, in a state of shock and dizzy from blood loss, A.S. was on the operating table and was asked to sign a statement of consent to the caesarean. Unbeknownst to A.S., the statement also contained an illegible handwritten note using the Latin word for sterilisation. A.S. learnt only later that she was sterilised during the surgery, when she asked the physician when she would be able to try to conceive again.[26]

A.S., represented by the European Roma Rights Centre and the Legal Defence Bureau for National and Ethnic Minorities, filed a petition before the CEDAW Committee,[27] and the Center supported the petition by submitting a technical opinion. A.S.'s complaint alleged that sterilisation is

---

[23] See, e.g., Natalia Sobrevilla Perea, 'Peru's sterilization victims still await compensation and justice', *The Guardian*, 17 June 2011.

[24] Associated Press, 'Peru reopens probe of forced sterilizations', *Miami Herald*, 28 October 2011.

[25] Gustav Cappaert, 'Peru's Keiko Fujimori leads a familiar cast of 2016 presidential hopefuls', *Latin Correspondent*, 24 July 2015.

[26] For more information on the facts of the case, see the final decision by the CEDAW Committee, *A.S. v. Hungary*, CEDAW Committee, Communication No. 4/2004, U.N. Doc. CEDAW/C/36/D/4/2004 (2006) (*A.S. v. Hungary*).

[27] A.S. presented her claim to the CEDAW Committee with assistance from the Legal Defense Bureau for National and Ethnic Minorities (NEKI) and the European Roma Rights Centre (ERRC).

never a life-saving medical intervention such that it would need to be performed without informed consent, and that by failing to obtain her fully informed consent Hungary had violated her rights to information on family planning, to health, and to decide freely on the spacing and number of children.[28]

In August 2006, the CEDAW Committee issued the first judgment from an international human rights body recognising that failure to obtain fully informed consent for a reproductive health procedure violates fundamental human rights. The CEDAW Committee recommended both individual and general measures as reparation for the violation of A.S.'s rights. In particular, the Committee ordered indemnification of A.S. 'commensurate with the gravity of the violations of her rights'.[29] Initially Hungary refused to give the CEDAW Committee's views due consideration, stating that the payment of compensation was not feasible because domestic courts had not found any violation of A.S.'s rights. According to the CEDAW Committee, however, domestic decisions 'could never relieve a State of its obligation to implement the recommendation of the Committee', and it urged the state to comply with its recommendations in concluding observations.[30] After sustained advocacy from the petitioners and the Center, as well as repeated follow-up by CEDAW Committee members, Hungary complied and paid compensation to A.S.[31] In addition to individual reparations, the CEDAW Committee recommended that the State take general measures to bring its domestic legislation on informed consent into conformity with international human rights and medical standards. However, despite amendments to its domestic laws following the decision, Hungary's Public Health Act still allows for sterilisation without consent on the basis of 'health reasons'.[32] In its most recent concluding observations, the CEDAW Committee expressed concern over the fact

---

[28] CEDAW arts. 10(h), 12, and 16(1)(e).

[29] A.S. v. Hungary, para. 11.5.

[30] CEDAW Committee, Summary record of the 801st meeting of CEDAW (Chamber A): Consideration of reports submitted by States parties (Hungary) (thirty-ninth session, 2007), U.N. Doc. CEDAW/C/SR.801 (A) at 4 (2007) ('Summary Record of the 801st Meeting of CEDAW').

[31] Letter from the Permanent Mission of the Republic of Hungary to the Office of the United Nations High Commissioner for Human Rights (20 July 2009) (on file with the Center for Reproductive Rights).

[32] CEDAW Committee, Consideration of the reports submitted by States parties under article 18 of the Convention on the Elimination of All Forms of Discrimination against Women: Combined seventh and eighth periodic reports by States parties (Hungary), para. 75, U.N. Doc. CEDAW/C/HUN/7–8 (22 September 2011).

that Hungary's law still permits sterilisation of certain individuals without their free and informed consent.[33] By establishing that governments can be held accountable for failing to provide information necessary for making informed decisions regarding reproductive health-related medical procedures, the CEDAW Committee's decision has also had transformational effects, and has been cited in current litigation and advocacy efforts to push other bodies, in particular, regional human rights bodies, to strengthen standards on informed consent.[34]

12.3.2   Access to Abortion

Two critical barriers inhibiting women's access to safe and legal abortion are restrictive laws criminalising abortion in all or most circumstances and regulatory and practical barriers to abortion where it is legal. Given the highly contentious nature of abortion, the Center's litigation strategy on access to abortion has been to denounce the harmful impact that such bans have on women's lives and to push for an incremental recognition of abortion rights. This section focuses on cases addressing access to abortion where it is legal, as these are the only cases at the international level that are in the implementation stage.

Tysiąc v. Poland

Alicja Tysiąc, a Polish woman, suffered from severe myopia. Pregnant for the third time, she consulted three ophthalmologists who concluded that carrying the pregnancy to term constituted a serious risk to her eyesight. After some difficulty, Tysiąc finally obtained a referral for an abortion, a requirement for obtaining a therapeutic abortion under Polish law. Even with this referral, though, the head of the gynaecology and obstetrics department of a clinic in Warsaw denied Tysiąc's request, stating that there

---

[33] CEDAW Committee, *Concluding Comments of the Committee on the Elimination of Discrimination against Women: Hungary* (U.N. Doc. CEDAW/C/HUN/CO/7–8 at 8–9 (2013).

[34] See, e.g., *Case of V.C. v. Slovakia*, App. No. 18968/07, ECHR, para. 84 (2011) (citing to CEDAW documents referencing *A.S. v. Hungary* among relevant international materials in a case where the Court held that the government had violated the applicant's rights to be free from torture and to privacy by sterilising her without her informed consent); *I.V. v. Bolivia*, Case 12.655, IACHR, Report No. 72/14 (15 August 2014) (citing *A.S. v. Hungary* in the case of a woman who was sterilised during a caesarean section surgery to support findings that informed consent requires a process of communication between a provider and patient and should not be sought when a patient is under surgical stress); *F.S. v. Chile, P-112-09*, IACHR, Petitioner's Brief (on file with the Center for Reproductive Rights).

were no medical grounds for a therapeutic abortion. No procedures were available to appeal the doctor's decision, and Tysiąc had no option but to carry her pregnancy to term. As predicted, after the delivery her eyesight seriously deteriorated, qualifying her as a significantly disabled person under Poland's social welfare system.[35]

With representation from Interights and Polish attorneys, Tysiąc brought her case to the European Court of Human Rights (European Court) in 2003. The Center acted as a third-party intervener (amici) in the case. The European Court held that the State had violated Tysiąc's rights to privacy and to an effective remedy. The Court ordered financial compensation to Tysiąc for the violations she suffered. In addition, the Court mandated the establishment of an effective appeals mechanism to review cases when there is a disagreement as to whether the conditions for legal abortion are met. The Court laid down four key elements of the appeals mechanism for Poland to satisfy its obligations: the review must be conducted by an independent body, the views of the pregnant woman must be considered, the decision must be in writing, and a decision must be made within a reasonable amount of time under the circumstances.[36]

Poland paid the financial compensation in full. In 2009, Poland also adopted legislation on patients' rights to object to a doctor's decision before a medical board, claiming that this legislation brings it into compliance with the *Tysiąc* judgment. However, while the revised law, on its face, meets three of the main conditions of the decision – an independent Commission must hear the pregnant women's views and issue decisions in writing – the efficiency and accessibility of the mechanism was deemed insufficient for the timeliness required of a decision pertaining to therapeutic abortions and pre-natal testing (Committee of Ministers, 2015: 161). Accordingly, the Committee of Ministers, the body that oversees compliance with European Court decisions, continues to monitor implementation of the judgment. The Center and its local partner, the Federation for Women and Family Planning in Poland, developed targeted advocacy strategies to strengthen compliance, including by providing technical opinions on the new law to the Committee of Ministers. In addition, and as a result of these advocacy strategies, the UN Special Rapporteur on the Right to Health issued a report on the right to health in Poland in 2010, which addressed the status of abortion and criticised

---

[35] For a more detailed account of the facts of the case, see the final judgment of the ECHR in *Case of Tysiąc v. Poland*, App. No. 5410/03, ECHR (24 September 2007) ('*Tysiąc v. Poland*').
[36] Ibid., 117–118.

the State's failure to implement the general measures in the *Tysiąc* judgment.[37]

Paulina del Carmen Ramírez Jacinto v. Mexico

Paulina del Carmen Ramírez Jacinto, a thirteen-year-old girl from Mexico, was raped during a burglary. Paulina became pregnant as a result of the rape, grounds for legal abortion under the penal code in Baja California, the Mexican state where Paulina and her family lived. Paulina reported the rape to the Public Prosecution Service in order to obtain the necessary authorisation for a legal abortion. However, after she was admitted to the hospital for the abortion, hospital employees delayed the procedure and used a variety of tactics to pressure Paulina to not have an abortion. When she persisted in her desire to terminate the pregnancy, the hospital staff provided Paulina and her mother with misinformation about the physical dangers of undergoing an abortion, and ultimately frightened her into carrying her pregnancy to term.[38] The Center, along with local partners,[39] presented Paulina's case to the Inter-American Commission, and in 2006, the parties reached a friendly settlement agreement.

In the friendly settlement, the Mexican government agreed to individual and general remedies. The State agreed to issue a public acknowledgement recognising that it had violated Paulina's human rights by failing to facilitate access to legal abortion.[40] The settlement agreement also provided for financial compensation to Paulina and required Mexico to take general measures to prevent similar violations from recurring.[41]

The Mexican government has paid the financial reparations to Paulina. The secretary of health issued a circular pushing all Mexican states to ensure access to abortion when legal to ensure compliance with the *Paulina* settlement (IACHR, 2009: 681). It is unclear to what extent this

---

[37] OHCHR, *Report of the Special Rapporteur on the right to the highest attainable standard of physical and mental health: Mission to Poland* (Fourteenth session, 2010), U.N. Doc. A/HRC/14/20/Add. 3 (2010) 11–12.

[38] For a full account of the facts of this case, see the friendly settlement agreement in *Paulina del Carmen Ramírez Jacinto v. Mexico*, Case 161-02, IACHR, Report No. 21/07, OEA/Ser.L/V/II.130 Doc. 22, rev. 1 (29 December 2007) ('*Paulina del Carmen Ramírez Jacinto v. Mexico*').

[39] The Center partnered with Mexican nongovernmental organisations Alaíde Foppa and Information Group on Reproductive Choice (GIRE) to present Paulina's claim to the Inter-American Commission.

[40] See statement published in the Official Journal of the Government of the State of Baja California (*Public Acknowledgment of Responsibility: Paulina Ramirez Jacinto*, P-161/02 (10 February 2006)).

[41] *Paulina del Carmen Ramírez Jacinto v. Mexico*.

circular has been implemented at the state level, but in at least one case, authorities in the Mexican state of Sinaloa granted a twelve-year-old rape victim a legal abortion to avoid another *Paulina* case (GIRE, 2005: 9). Also, in response to the settlement agreement, Baja California enacted a regulation to facilitate access to abortion for rape victims, but the regulation was never formally published and its impact is unclear. Despite the lack of clarity on the impact of these regulations, the Inter-American Commission considers that the Mexican government has fully complied with the agreement (IACHR, 2015: 88).

The friendly settlement in the *Paulina* case has also led to transformative effects beyond the specific facts of the case. The *Paulina* case is largely credited with reshaping the public discourse around abortion in Mexico, an effect that contributed significantly to the decriminalisation of abortion in Mexico City in 2007 (GIRE, 2008: 12–14). It is worth noting, though, that this transformative effect has not been entirely positive. The renewed debate around abortion and the decriminalisation of abortion in Mexico City also contributed to a backlash against abortion in a number of Mexican states. The backlash led to the passage of constitutional amendments protecting life from conception, which were aimed at precluding liberalisation of those states' abortion laws (Cook, 2010: 1).

Both the *Tysiąc* and *Paulina* cases had transformative impact on legal discourse outside of their own countries, as well. Both were used to support the decision of the Supreme Court of Nepal in the case of *Lakshmi Dhikta v. Nepal*, which held that the government has an obligation to guarantee women's access to safe and affordable legal abortion.[42] *Tysiąc* has also been instrumental in framing what an appropriate redress mechanism would look like for women who have been denied legal abortions, and was cited for this purpose by the CEDAW Committee in its 2011 decision in the case of *L.C. v. Peru*.[43]

K.L. v. Peru

K.L., a seventeen-year-old girl from Peru, was several months into her pregnancy when her foetus was diagnosed with anencephaly, a grave foetal abnormality incompatible with life outside the womb. Continued pregnancy posed risks to K.L.'s life and physical and mental health, and her physician recommended that she terminate the pregnancy. Despite

[42] *Laksmhi Dhikta v. Government of Nepal*, 2007 Writ No. 0757, 2067 Supreme Court of Nepal.
[43] *L.C. v. Peru*, CEDAW Committee, Communication No. 22/2009, U.N. Doc. CEDAW/C/50/ D/22/2009 at 8.17 (2011).

these risks and her doctor's recommendation, hospital authorities denied K.L. access to a legal therapeutic abortion,[44] and she had to carry the pregnancy to term. After she gave birth, hospital staff made K.L. breast-feed her anencephalic child for four days until, as anticipated, the infant died. K.L. suffered severe psychological consequences as a result of these events.[45]

The Center and its local partners[46] presented K.L.'s case before the Human Rights Committee. In the first decision by an international human rights body on abortion, the Human Rights Committee held that by deny-ing her access to legal abortion, Peru had violated K.L.'s rights to freedom from torture or cruel, inhuman, or degrading treatment, to privacy, and to special protection as a minor. In its recommendations, the Human Rights Committee called for indemnification of K.L., along with general meas-ures to prevent similar violations from occurring in the future.[47]

For some time Peru did not comply with the Human Rights Committee's recommendations. The recommendations do not specify an amount for financial compensation and attempts to negotiate compensation right after the decision came down stalled. Peru's proffered amount was well below international standards for the rights violations suffered, and K.L. was reluctant to accept the offered compensation without larger structural change. Accordingly, the offer was rejected, and, at the time, no financial compensation was paid. Furthermore, even where there was willingness among high-level health officials to address the structural problems high-lighted in the Human Rights Committee's decision, there were orders not to move forward.[48]

Despite these setbacks in implementation, the Center and its local partners continued to engage in legal and advocacy strategies seek-ing full implementation of the *K.L.* judgment, and Peru is finally taking steps to comply. In 2014, Peru adopted technical guidelines on therapeu-tic abortion, which ostensibly will prevent violations similar to the one

---

[44] Peru's Penal Code permits abortion where necessary to preserve the life or health of the pregnant woman. Decreto Legislativo No. 635 [Legislative Decree No. 635], Código Penal de Perú, art. 119.

[45] For more information on the facts of the case, see the final communication by the Human Rights Committee in *K.L. v. Peru*, Human Rights Committee, Communication No. 1153/2003, U.N. Doc. CCPR/C/85/D/1153/2003 (2005) ('*K.L. v Peru*').

[46] The Center partnered with DEMUS and CLADEM to present K.L.'s complaint to the Human Rights Committee.

[47] *K.L. v. Peru*, para. 8.

[48] This assessment is based on conversations that the Center and its partners have had with the Secretariat of the Human Rights Committee and government officials.

experienced by K.L. and should facilitate access to legal abortion (as called for in the CEDAW Committee's decision in *L.C. v. Peru*,[49] a follow-up case that the Center and its partners filed as part of the legal advocacy strategy). However, the impact of these guidelines at the health facility level remains to be seen. In addition, in September 2010, local advocates submitted a complaint to push for national-level implementation of the Human Rights Committee's recommendations, and in January 2015, and a Peruvian court issued a decision in this case finding that Peru was legally bound by the Human Rights Committee's decision.[50] The Court's decision requires the state to provide financial compensation to K.L., publicise the Human Rights Committee's decision in the case, and ensure implementation of the guidelines on therapeutic abortion. This decision paves the way for financial compensation to K.L. and further implementation of the general remedies called for in the Human Rights Committee's recommendations.

Moreover, the standards set in the *K.L.* decision have had significant transformative effects, having been cited in key decisions liberalising abortion laws or upholding liberalised abortion laws around the world.[51] The decision has also reshaped the dialogue around abortion within the human rights community. In 2007, for instance, Amnesty International moved from its previously neutral stance on abortion to one that views restrictive abortion laws as human rights violations.[52] The organisation's reports addressing total abortion bans cite to *K.L.* to support their stance that international human rights law encourages liberalisation of abortion laws (Amnesty International, 2014: 23; 2015: 104).

12.3.3   Maternal Mortality

Preventable maternal mortality has been recognised increasingly as a human rights issue in recent years by a number of international and regional human rights bodies, including through concluding observations

---

[49] *L.C. v. Peru*, CEDAW Committee, Communication No. 22/2009, U.N. Doc. CEDAW/C/50/D/22/2009 (2011).

[50] 9° Juzgado Constitucional [Juzg. Const.] [Constitutional Court], 21/1/2015, 'Noelia Karin Llantoy Huaman v. Ministerio de Justicia y Ministerio de Salud / Acción de Amparo' (Per.).

[51] *K.L. v. Peru* was cited in decisions by the Constitutional Court of Colombia and the Constitutional Court of Slovakia on liberalisation of abortion laws. Corte Constitucional de Colombia [Colombian Constitutional Court] (2006), Sentencia C-355/06 (10 May 2006); Constitutional Court of the Slovak Republic (2007), PL. ÚS 12/01-297 (4 December 2007).

[52] Cahal Milmo, Amnesty's abortion stance splits grassroots support, *The Independent* (1 September 2007).

issued by UN treaty monitoring bodies,[53] several groundbreaking resolutions by the UN Human Rights Council,[54] and a recent report by the
Inter-American Commission (IACHR, 2010). Building on the momentum generated by these developments, advocates have begun to litigate
individual cases over the past decade to give meaning to constitutional
and international human rights protections relevant to maternal mortality. Given that this is a relatively new strategic approach, there have not
been many final decisions handed down. The case studies selected for this
section include cases for which there is a final decision, including one case
where interim orders led to a tangible impact before the final decision was
issued.

Domestic Litigation on Maternal Mortality in India

India accounts for almost one-fifth of all maternal deaths worldwide
(WHO, 2014: 1). The Indian government has developed national policies
aimed at reducing maternal mortality and morbidity by improving access
to and quality of maternal healthcare, but these policies have not been
adequately implemented. In an effort to highlight the systemic nature of
the problems, local advocates with legal representation from the Human
Rights Law Network (HRLN), and with technical support and third-party
interventions from the Center, have been implementing a targeted public
interest litigation (PIL) strategy since 2007. This strategy has grown into
a robust reproductive rights litigation initiative with more than forty PIL
cases filed, including a number that addresses maternal healthcare.[55]

As a result of this strategy, in 2010, the High Court of Delhi handed
down a landmark joint decision in the cases of two women who were
denied access to maternal healthcare due to a variety of factors, including an inability to pay hospital fees.[56] Experiencing an intrauterine death,
Shanti Devi was turned away from four hospitals and forced to carry her
dead foetus around for five days before she finally received emergency

---

[53] For a comprehensive review of UN treaty body observations on preventable maternal mortality, see Center for Reproductive Rights (2008).

[54] H.R. Council Res. 11/8, U.N. Doc. A/HRC/11/L.16/Rev.1 (16 June 2009); H.R. Council
Res. 15/17, U.N. Doc. A/HRC/15/L.27 (27 September 2010); H.R. Council Res. 18/11, U.N.
Doc. A/HRC/18/L.8 (23 September 2011); H.R. Council Res. 21/6, U.N. Doc. A/HRC/21/
L.10 (21 September 2012); H.R. Council Res. 27/11, U.N. Doc. A/HRC/27/L.19/Rev.1 (24
September 2014).

[55] For more details on the HRLN's Reproductive Rights Initiative, see http://hrln.org/hrln/
reproductive-rights/the-initiative.html.

[56] High Court of Delhi, *Laxmi Mandal v. Deen Dayal Hospital and others*, W.P.(C) 8853/2008
and *Jaitun v. Maternity Home MCD, Jangapura and others*, W.P.(C) 10700/2009.

obstetric care. Shanti Devi never received follow-up care or counselling, soon became pregnant again, and died during unassisted childbirth. Fatema, a homeless woman suffering from epilepsy and anaemia, was ultimately forced to give birth unattended under a tree, after being turned away from the hospital while in labour.

The Court's decision affirms that maternal mortality and morbidity are human rights issues, and that the government has an obligation to remove barriers to access to maternal healthcare. The Court awarded individual reparations to the petitioners, as well as general measures aimed at strengthening the implementation of maternal and child health benefits schemes to facilitate greater access to maternal healthcare for poor women. Financial compensation has been paid in full. The general remedies, which would facilitate implementation of cash incentives schemes to promote pre-natal and delivery care for pregnant women living below the poverty line, have yet to be implemented. However, the Court continues to monitor implementation of these remedies, and in 2013, ruled against the government in a contempt hearing for its failure to adequately implement these schemes.[57] HRLN continues to file follow-up cases to push for implementation of the schemes.[58] In addition, the Court's decision that the denial of maternal healthcare violates fundamental constitutional and human rights set an important precedent – both legal and symbolic – for ensuring that maternal mortality is legally actionable. Several months after its decision in these cases, the Delhi High Court initiated a *suo moto* proceeding to address discrimination and denial of medical care to homeless women, and pregnant and lactating women in particular, and issued interim orders to the Delhi government to establish shelters to provide adequate medical assistance and other services to destitute pregnant and lactating women.[59]

The case of *Sandesh Bansal v. Union of India and others* is another such example. Madhya Pradesh faces the worst maternal mortality rates in India, and local advocates sued the state to push for structural change.[60] While the litigation was still pending before the High Court of Madhya

---

[57] For more information on the contempt hearing, see http://hrln.org/hrln/ reproductive-rights/pils-a-cases/1210-delhi-high-court-orders-union-of-india-and- nct-of-delhi-and-to-provide-entitlements-to-below-poverty-line-women-within-6- weeks-finds-the-governments-stand-unacceptable.html.

[58] See, e.g., High Court of Delhi, *Bilkis and Anr versus Govt of NCT of Delhi and others*, W.P. (C) 4200/2015, filed in April 2015.

[59] High Court of Delhi, *Court of its own Motion v. U.O.I.*, W.P. (C) 5913/2010.

[60] *Sandesh Bansal v. Union of India and others*, W.P. No. 9061/2008.

Pradesh, the Court conducted an inquiry into the implementation of public health standards and issued interim orders. Even before a final decision was issued in the case, the state began to implement the general remedies called for by the interim orders, approving a license for a long-awaited hospital blood bank and constructing a water tank to help bring a primary health centre in compliance with the applicable standards.[61] In 2012, the Court issued a final decision in the case, calling for the government to take specific steps to address preventable maternal mortality, including through ensuring availability of trained health care providers around the clock, improving basic infrastructure to provide uninterrupted water and electricity, ensuring access to emergency transportation for local communities, providing vaccines to pregnant women and newborn children, and tracking patient records.[62] In contrast to the other case studies included here, *Sandesh Bansal* focused exclusively on structural change, and not on an individual woman's case, and accordingly, the Court's decision only provides for general remedies, not financial compensation. Although the general remedies have not been fully implemented, the Court continues to monitor implementation. In 2013, HRLN filed a follow-up complaint to push for full implementation of the Court's orders,[63] and this complaint is currently pending before the High Court of Madhya Pradesh.

Alyne da Silva Pimentel v. Brazil

Alyne da Silva Pimentel, a poor Brazilian woman of African descent, died from preventable pregnancy-related causes after she was denied timely emergency obstetric care. Alyne first sought care when experiencing severe symptoms of pain and nausea during her sixth month of pregnancy. Without being admitted or examined, she was sent home with only anti-nausea medication and vitamins. Two days later she returned to the hospital, where providers discovered there was no foetal heartbeat. After a fourteen-hour delay – in contradiction to medical standards requiring immediate surgery – providers operated on Alyne to remove the dead foetus. Alyne began haemorrhaging after the surgery, her condition worsened, and after more delays and neglect on the part of the healthcare providers, Alyne died.[64]

[61] For more information on the implementation of these and other maternal mortality cases being litigated in India, see Center for Reproductive Rights and Human Rights Law Network (2011).

[62] *Sandesh Bansal v. Union of India and others*, W.P. No. 9061/2008.

[63] *Sandesh Bansal v. Union of India and others*, W.P. No. 11860/2013.

[64] For more detailed facts of the case, see the case overview by the Center for Reproductive Rights, available at http://reproductiverights.org/en/case/alyne-da-silva-pimentel-v-brazil-committee-on-the-elimination-of-discrimination-against-women.

In November 2007, the Center and Citizens' Advocacy for Human Rights (ADVOCACI), its local partner, presented Alyne's case before the CEDAW Committee, alleging violations of Alyne's rights to, inter alia, life and health. *Alyne da Silva Pimentel v. Brazil* marks the first case brought before a UN human rights body framing maternal mortality as a human rights violation and seeking government accountability for a systematic failure to prevent maternal deaths. In a landmark decision, the CEDAW Committee established that Brazil violated Alyne's rights to health, to be free from discrimination, and to access to justice, and called for compensation for Alyne's family, in addition to general remedies to ensure women's right to safe motherhood and affordable access to adequate emergency obstetric care, to provide adequate professional training for health workers, to ensure that private healthcare facilities comply with national and international standards on reproductive healthcare, and to ensure that penalties are imposed on health professionals who violate women's reproductive rights.[65]

Even before a final decision was issued, the Center and its partners had engaged in a complementary advocacy strategy to heighten international attention to the issue; strengthen international standards, including pushing for the above-mentioned Human Rights Council resolutions; and to lay the groundwork in Brazil for successful implementation in the event of a positive decision. As a result of this strategy and targeted follow-up, Brazil has implemented several components of the ruling since the decision was issued in 2011. Specifically, in March 2014, Brazil paid financial compensation to Alyne's mother and publicly acknowledged the state's responsibility in Alyne's death. Shortly after this, the Maternal ICU in a newly inaugurated hospital was named after Alyne, bearing the following plaque: 'The Alyne da Silva Pimentel Maternal ICU: Symbolic reparation and acknowledgment of her preventable death. For improvement in the quality of care for women's health.' The Brazilian government is not yet in full compliance with the general remedies outlined in the CEDAW Committee's decision. However, the state has taken some steps to address maternal mortality in the country through the adoption of a plan referred to as the Rede Cegonha, for which implementation began in 2011.[66]

---

[65] *Alyne da Silva Pimentel v. Brazil*, CEDAW Committee, Communication No. 17/2008, U.N. Doc. CEDAW/C/49/D/17/2008 (2011).

[66] See the Center for Reproductive Rights' *Interim Report for the Fifty-Seven (57th) Session of the CEDAW Committee, on the Concluding Observations of the CEDAW Committee to the*

As the first international decision addressing maternal mortality as a human rights issue, the case has also had a transformative impact on the discourse around maternal mortality. As one legal scholar explained, the decision 'has led to a shift in understanding of maternal deaths as a matter of social injustice that societies are obligated to remedy', as opposed to something that can 'be explained away by fate, by divine purpose or as something that is … beyond human control' (Cook, 2013: 109). By reframing maternal mortality as a human rights imperative, rather than as a public health concern, states now have legal obligations to address preventable maternal mortality, and they can be held accountable for the failure to take the necessary steps to do so.

12.4.   What Factors Enhance or Hinder Implementation?

The judgments in each of the case studies presented above have been partially implemented when taken as a whole, but some remedies have been fully implemented, some partially, and others not at all. This section analyses some of the key factors that enhance or hinder implementation of reproductive rights judgments, namely the design of the adjudicatory body issuing the decision, the nature of the remedies awarded, public attention to the issue, and the social, political, and cultural environment.

12.4.1   Institutional Design

Variations in the structure and procedural mechanisms of adjudicatory bodies can have a significant impact on the degree to which the bodies' judgments are implemented. Several elements of institutional design may enhance implementation of direct remedies, such as individual reparations or systemic reform, while others aid in the far-reaching impact of transformative remedies.

At the supranational level, mechanisms that facilitate direct engagement with the State party can enhance implementation of the final outcome. Where a State has participated in negotiations and signed a final agreement, it may be more likely to view the outcome as legally binding and thus more inclined to abide by it.[67] The Rules of Procedure of the

---

Brazilian State during its Fifty-First (51st) Session for more information on Brazil's implementation of its Rede Cegonha program on maternal health.

[67] A review of state compliance with different types of remedies in the Inter-American Commission on Human Rights found that financial compensation awarded through friendly settlement agreements had an implementation rate of 88 per cent, compared to an implementation rate of 58 per cent for monetary reparations awarded through a decision,

Inter-American Commission, for instance, empowers the Commission to facilitate negotiations between the petitioner and the State party with the consent of both parties. If both the State and the victim can reach a friendly settlement agreement 'based on respect for the human rights recognized' in the regional treaties, the Commission will adopt a report with an overview of the facts of the case and the final outcome.[68] The European Court has a similar process by which the victim and the State party can enter into negotiations in an effort to reach a friendly settlement.[69] In contrast, most UN treaty monitoring bodies do not have mechanisms in place to facilitate settlement negotiations.[70] In addition, a negotiated settlement may result in more specific individual remedies, which, as discussed in the pages that follow, can also facilitate greater compliance.

Of the case studies presented in this chapter, two cases – *María Mamérita Mestanza Chávez v. Peru* and *Paulina Ramírez v. Mexico* – were concluded with friendly settlement agreements. Both settlement agreements provide a range of remedies, including financial compensation for the plaintiff, general measures to prevent future violations, and recognition that the State violated the victim's human rights. In both instances, the State has paid the petitioner the full settlement agreement and the State acknowledged that it had violated the victim's human rights. With respect to general measures agreed to in both settlements, Mexico is considered to be in total compliance, while Peru is in partial compliance. In the case of *Paulina*, a regulation to facilitate access to legal abortion was enacted in Baja California, the state where the violations took place, though this regulation was never formally published. In addition, the secretary of health issued a circular pushing all Mexican states to ensure access to abortion where legal to ensure compliance with the *Paulina* settlement. Following the settlement of the *Mestanza* case, guidelines on sexual and reproductive health were disseminated, but their longer-term effect in protecting patients' rights is harder to assess.

---

supporting the assertion that States are more likely to implement remedies when they have been involved in direct negotiations (Baluarte and De Vos, 2010: 66).

[68] IACHR, *Rules of Procedure of the Inter-American Commission on Human Rights*, art. 40, 137th Session (13 November 2009).

[69] European Court of Human Rights (European Court), *Rules of Court*, at 36 (1 April 2011).

[70] One exception is the Optional Protocol to the International Covenant on Economic, Social and Cultural Rights, which does include a clause providing for friendly settlement agreements, but the Optional Protocol only entered into force in May 2013, so the efficacy of its friendly settlement clause has yet to be evaluated.

Another element of institutional design that may enhance implementation is the existence of monitoring or follow-up mechanisms. Stronger mechanisms for monitoring and evaluating compliance can strengthen implementation of reproductive rights judgments. PIL mechanism in India is one example of how ongoing monitoring can aid in the implementation of judicial orders in ESC rights cases. PIL was intended not as an adversarial judicial mechanism, but was instead designed to 'promote and vindicate' the rights of economically and socially disadvantaged persons (Center for Reproductive Rights and Sood, 2006: 24). Because PIL judgments are primarily aimed at correcting systemic problems to prevent future abuses, PIL cases will often lead to a series of interim orders that enable the presiding judge to keep the case open and continuously monitor the degree to which the government has complied with the decision (Center for Reproductive Rights and Sood, 2006: 28). As a former Supreme Court Justice in India has explained, this strategy enables judges to 'keep a case open and direct the authority to perform and report, so you are constantly breathing down the neck of that authority' (Center for Reproductive Rights and Sood, 2006: 28). In the case of *Sandesh Bansal v. Union of India and others* described earlier, the Court issued interim orders that facilitated the construction of a hospital blood bank and a water tank even before the Court had issued a final decision in the case. The ability of the Court to keep the case open and closely monitor compliance with interim orders had a significant impact on the implementation of these structural changes, and may even make it easier for the Court to push for compliance, as evidenced by the fact that the structural changes called for in the final decision in the case have not yet been fully implemented.

Regional human rights bodies also make use of follow-up mechanisms to promote implementation of final decisions. Implementation of judgments issued by the European Court is monitored by the Committee of Ministers, a political body within the Council of Europe that is also imbued with the authority to oversee membership of the Council of Europe, among other responsibilities. The Committee of Ministers engages in ongoing review of European Court judgments until the State is deemed to have fully complied with the order and the case is closed (Committee of Ministers, 2009: 20). Notably, the Rules of the Committee of Ministers for the supervision of execution of judgments expressly provide for the participation of civil society and national human rights institutions in monitoring implementation of European Court decisions.[71] In the case of

---

[71] Council of Europe Committee of Ministers, *Rules of the Committee of Ministers for the supervision of the execution of judgments and of the terms of friendly settlements*, 9(2) (10 May 2006).

Tysiąc v. Poland, the State has argued that a new law allowing patients to appeal decisions regarding medical treatment complies with the European Court's decision. The Center and its partner have submitted background information to the Committee of Ministers demonstrating why the law does not meet the terms of the Court's judgment, and the Committee of Ministers continues to keep the case open until the State can demonstrate that all four elements of the appeals mechanism called for by the European Court have been met.

The Inter-American Commission is directly responsible for overseeing State compliance with its recommendations. In its capacity of overseeing friendly settlement agreements, as well, the Commission acknowledges its role in following-up and monitoring compliance with each component of the negotiated agreement,[72] which it monitors through periodic submissions by both parties and through working groups meetings. For instance, in the *Mestanza* case, both parties are required to submit reports to the Commission every three months to report on compliance, and the Commission includes updates on implementation in its annual reports.[73] In addition, the Inter-American Commission has convened working group meetings with both parties to follow up on the status of, and to discuss obstacles to, implementation of its decisions and settlement agreements. Unlike the Committee of Ministers, the Inter-American Commission lacks the weight of a political body to enforce its recommendations; it does, however, have the power to refer cases to the Inter-American Court of Human Rights (Inter-American Court), whose judgments are legally binding.

The UN treaty monitoring bodies, in contrast, do not have any direct follow-up mechanisms to enforce the decisions they have issued, and follow-up procedures vary between the different committees. Compliance with these decisions can be formally addressed during the State's reporting to the relevant committee, which generally occurs every few years.[74] The Human Rights Committee has a permanent rapporteur delegated to oversee implementation, and the Office of the High Commissioner on Human

---

[72] *María Mamérita Mestanza Chávez v. Peru*, para. 18(2); *Paulina del Carmen Ramírez Jacinto v. Mexico*, para. 27(2).

[73] *María Mamérita Mestanza Chávez v. Peru*, para. 18(2).

[74] For example, Rule 73 of the CEDAW Committee's Rules of Procedures provides that the Committee may request states parties to include information in their state reports on any action taken in light of the Committees views and recommendations on individual communications. CEDAW Committee, *Rules of Procedure of the Committee on the Elimination of Discrimination against Women*, U.N. Doc. CEDAW/C/ROP (2001) 25.

Rights has an individual communications branch that can facilitate meetings between claimants and the State party to discuss implementation of treaty monitoring body recommendations, while the CEDAW Committee assigns different committee members to serve as follow-up rapporteurs on an ad hoc basis.[75] However, the decisions by treaty monitoring bodies are generally not seen as legally binding and there is no significant consequence when a State party fails to comply with the decision (Baluarte and De Vos, 2010: 125). The lack of enforcement mechanisms, among other factors, can undermine the effectiveness of these international bodies to ensure implementation.

Although international bodies may lack enforcement mechanisms or may not be seen as legally binding, the impact of positive decisions by international bodies may be farther reaching than those of regional or national-level bodies. International bodies help define human rights standards at the global level, and such standard setting impacts all signatories to the relevant treaty and can influence judicial decisions at the national and regional levels. In the *K.L.* case, for instance, although the Peruvian government has only just begun to implement the judgment, the Human Rights Committee's decision has had a far-reaching effect outside of Peru in the decade since it was issued. The case was cited in the Colombian[76] and Slovakian[77] Constitutional Court decisions to liberalise and uphold the countries' abortion laws respectively, and was referred to by Mexican Supreme Court Justices in oral hearings to determine whether or not to uphold a Mexico City law decriminalising abortion during the first trimester. In addition, regional human rights bodies rely on the international norms developed by international bodies when issuing judgments.[78]

---

[75] See, e.g., CEDAW Committee, *Report of the Committee under the Optional Protocol on follow up to views of the Committee on individual communications*, para. 2 (Forty-second session, 2008) *in* Report of the Committee on the Elimination of Discrimination against Women, U.N. Doc. A/64/38 at 110 (2009).

[76] *Corte Constitucional de Colombia [Colombian Constitutional Court]* (2006), Sentencia C-355/06 (10 May 2006) ('*Colombian Constitutional Court*').

[77] *Constitutional Court of the Slovak Republic* (2007), PL. ÚS 12/01-297 (4 December 2007) ('*Constitutional Court of the Slovak Republic*').

[78] The European Court, for example, relied extensively on the text of CEDAW, as well as CEDAW Committee decisions, general recommendations and concluding observations in its decision in *Opuz v. Turkey*, App. No. 33401/02, ECHR, paras. 73–77, 9 June 2009. Similarly, the Inter-American Court cites to the *K.L.* case – among other individual decisions, general comments, and concluding observations by the Human Rights Committee – to provide guidance on right to life protections in its recent decision in the *Case of Artavia Murillo, et al. v. Costa Rica*, Inter-Am. Ct. H.R. (ser. C) No. 257, ¶ 317 (28 November 2012).

12.4.2 Nature of the Remedies

In addition to the institutional design of the body issuing the judgment, the types of remedies awarded and the specificity of the remedies are also key factors that have affected the enforceability of the reproductive rights judgments discussed here. Putting aside the symbolic importance of a decision finding a reproductive rights violation, thus strengthening standards on the issue, the remedies awarded in the cited case studies fall broadly into two categories: individual reparations[79] and general reparations that seek to prevent similar rights violations in the future. Financial compensation has been paid in full in almost all of the cases in which there is a final decision, with the exception of *K.L. v. Peru*. When the *K.L.* decision was first issued, Peru offered to pay a nominal sum to the petitioner for her emotional suffering. However, the offer was well below international standards for the rights violations suffered, efforts to negotiate fair compensation stalled, and the petitioner was reluctant to accept the offered financial compensation without implementation of larger structural changes. Accordingly, the offer was rejected, and no financial compensation was paid. However, following a Peruvian court's decision holding that the government is legally bound by the Human Rights Committee's decision and calling for indemnisation of K.L., we anticipate that compensation will have been paid by the time of publication.

General measures, in contrast, have been partially, but not fully, implemented in the majority of the cases. This may be due to the fact that general measures, particularly those requiring legal reform, may be more cumbersome for States to implement, as such reforms often require political will and sophisticated coordination among government bodies. This observation is consistent with evidence from the Inter-American system that states are less likely to take action to implement general measures.[80] In general, steps have been taken to revise public policies or Ministry of Health regulations to respond to

---

[79] Individual reparations may take the form of both financial compensation and non-monetary remedies for the individual victim. In the present case studies, however, non-monetary reparations were not uniformly awarded. Accordingly, our discussion of individual remedies in this section looks exclusively at financial compensation.

[80] According to a study looking at implementation of decisions by the Inter-American Commission and Court, 'the more common response by states to general measures is inaction. ... [S]tates make no effort to implement approximately 75 percent of such orders' (Baluarte and De Vos, 2010: 70).

the rights violations, but the efforts have fallen short in one respect or another. As mentioned earlier, the structural remedies agreed to in *Mestanza v. Peru* and *Paulina Ramírez v. Mexico*, and as an outcome of the legal advocacy strategies following the decision in *K.L. v. Peru*, resulted in the development of some relevant regulations, but in each of these instances, the direct impact of these regulations at the health facility level is unclear. In *A.S. v. Hungary*, Hungary revised its Public Health Act following the CEDAW Committee's decision, but the revised act still permits sterilisation without informed consent for 'health reasons', and so does not adequately address the problem highlighted in the *A.S.* decision. Similarly, in *Tysiąc v. Poland*, Poland enacted a new law on patients' rights, which the State claims brings it into compliance, but the new law does not meet all four requirements for a procedural safeguard that the European Court laid out in its decision. The case of *Sandesh Bansal v. Union of India and others* is one positive exception. While the general remedies called for in the recent final decision in the case have yet to be implemented, the state has constructed a water tank and licensed a blood bank as required under the Court's interim orders. For almost a decade, *K.L. v. Peru* was another exception, but on the other end of the spectrum. When the decision first came down, the Ministry of Health drafted a protocol to facilitate access to legal abortion to remedy the structural problems highlighted in the Human Rights Committee's decision, but the protocol was prevented from going into effect by conservative political forces and the Catholic hierarchy. Despite the delayed implementation, however, the case strengthened the basis for national and sub-national advocacy to push for greater access to legal abortion. As a result of these sustained advocacy efforts, the Peruvian government recently issued technical guidelines on therapeutic abortion, and a recent judicial decision found that the government was legally bound by the Human Rights Committee's decision and ordered broad implementation of the technical guidelines on therapeutic abortion.[81]

---

[81] The case has further served as a catalyst for leading legal scholars and medical experts to advocate for implementation of the decision through improved access to legal therapeutic abortions in Peru (Abad Yupanqui, 2008; Ayala Peralta et al., 2009), as well as for a coalition of national, regional, and international organisations to push for a broad interpretation of therapeutic abortion throughout Latin America (Alianza Nacional por el Derecho a Decidir et al., 2008).

The specificity of the remedy may also impact its implementation. With respect to financial compensation, when the judgment calls for a specific sum to be paid to the victim, it is easier for the State to comply, as in the case of *Tysiąc* before the European Court[82] or the friendly settlement agreements in *Mestanza* and *Paulina* before the Inter-American Commission.[83] The UN treaty monitoring bodies do not specify the financial compensation to be awarded, but instead, as in the case of *A.S. v. Hungary*, provide for compensation 'commensurate with the gravity of the violations of her rights'.[84] This lack of specificity can lead to disagreements over what constitutes fair compensation and thereby delay or prevent implementation, as in the *K.L.* case. Similarly, specificity with respect to the general measures necessary to bring the State into compliance with its human rights obligations can facilitate implementation. In the *Tysiąc* case, for instance, the European Court laid out four specific requirements for establishing a procedural mechanism to protect women's right to access legal abortion. Any legislative changes that do not meet those four minimum requirements, then, can be deemed to have fallen short. Similarly, the interim orders in the case of *Sandesh Bansal v. Union of India and others* included specific recommendations related to the licensing of a blood bank and the construction of a water tank, both of which were implemented following the ruling. The Human Rights Committee in the *K.L.* case, in contrast, merely issued the view that Peru 'has an obligation to take steps to ensure that similar violations do not occur in the future' without specifying what those steps might look like.[85] Judgments that issue concrete recommendations to the State, then, can make it easier for States to implement the decision because there is a clear course of action to be taken. Specific recommendations also make it easier for both adjudicatory bodies and civil society to monitor the government's implementation of the decision.

---

[82] The European Court also mentions a specific timeline for repayment, generally mandating that individual reparations be paid within three months of the issuance of the final judgment (European Court, *Rules of Court*, *supra* note 65, at 71).

[83] It is worth noting that when the Inter-American Commission makes a decision on the merits, it cannot specify the financial compensation to be paid. Friendly settlement agreements and decisions by the Inter-American Court of Human Rights, in contrast, typically specify the exact sum to be paid to the victim.

[84] *A.S. v. Hungary*, para. 11.5(I).

[85] *K.L. v. Peru*, para. 8.

12.4.3   Public Attention

The extent to which the media and other key public actors engage in dialogue around the issue being litigated or the case itself may also influence implementation of a decision, particularly the transformative remedies of a decision. Litigation can provide a personal narrative of a particular issue that can help sensitise and mobilise key actors – such as policymakers and prominent academics – to the underlying human rights issue, and reshape the public dialogue around contentious issues, such as access to abortion. In the case studies discussed, the Center's national-level partners have played a significant role in mobilising public attention to these issues through strategic use of the media, coalition building, and other awareness-raising strategies.

The *Paulina* case is one such example. The compelling circumstances around Paulina's need for a legal abortion, and the shocking manner in which authorities coerced a thirteen-year-old rape victim into carrying a pregnancy to term, mobilised the media and other public figures and policymakers around the issue. Elena Poniatowska, a well-known Mexican author and journalist, published a book, *The Thousand and One… (Paulina's Wound)*, on the facts of the case (2000), and Paulina's story was widely covered in the press both domestically and internationally, with prominent figures across Mexico weighing in on the case and generating significant public attention. As the director of GIRE, one of the Center's local partners in the litigation of the case, explained, 'We didn't take the streets; we took the media' (GIRE, 2008: 37). GIRE has credited this strategy of mobilising the media and other prominent figures with movement around the issue, noting that '[t]he attention that the government of Baja California gave to the Paulina case would surely have been different if the media had not followed the case, not only reporting, but *defending* an otherwise helpless victim' (GIRE, 2005: 11). The mobilisation of political, academic, and journalistic elites not only impacted the direct effect of the *Paulina* case; it also had a transformative effect. The public debate around the case provided a new lens with which to view abortion. The question was no longer limited to whether or not abortion was a crime or a sin. Access to abortion could now also be discussed as a human rights issue, and as a result of the friendly settlement agreement, the Mexican government publicly acknowledged that by denying Paulina access to a legal abortion, it had violated her fundamental rights. As Adriana Ortega Ortiz, the director of Gender Equity at the Supreme Court of Justice in Mexico, has noted, 'The "Paulina" case, as it is known in Mexico, was of paramount importance in changing the debate about abortion rights in Mexico. ... Subsequent legal developments ... can all be attributed to the awareness that the Paulina case raised among several public and private actors' (2007), and the resulting transformation in the public discourse was a key factor contributing to the decriminalisation of abortion in Mexico City (GIRE, 2008: 12–14).

At the same time, however, the public debate around abortion and decriminalisation of abortion in Mexico City may have contributed to a backlash in Baja California, resulting in an amendment to Baja California's state constitution protecting a right to life from the moment of conception. It is unclear what effect, if any, this constitutional reform might have on the existing exceptions to Baja California's restrictive abortion law, and thus implementation of the general measures agreed to in the *Paulina* friendly settlement agreement.

Similarly, in the case of *Mestanza*, extensive media coverage and grass-roots mobilisation spearheaded by the Movimiento Amplio Mujeres, helped bring to light the widespread nature of Peru's coercive sterilisation policies under Fujimori, and helped prompt an investigation into the violations by the Ombudsman's office,[86] whose findings and recommendations formed the basis for the legislative and policy changes agreed upon in the friendly settlement agreement in the *Mestanza* case.[87] As discussed, this sustained effort to raise awareness and remembrance of these human rights violations is said to have had a significant impact on the outcome of the 2011 presidential election in Peru, and in November 2012, the government reopened its investigation into the cases (IACHR, 2015: 271).

12.4.4   Social, Political, and Cultural Environment

One of the primary challenges to implementing reproductive rights judgments is religious, political, or cultural opposition. Opponents of reproductive rights are quick to deny that reproductive rights are human rights, and this challenge highlights why recognition is crucial to implementing reproductive rights decisions at the national, regional, and international level.

Political, religious, and cultural opposition to abortion in particular is unwavering, and has been the primary hurdle to implementing structural remedies in the Center's cases on access to safe and legal abortion. Soon

---

[86] Defensoría del Pueblo de Perú [Peruvian Ombudsman] (2002), Resolución Defensorial N° 031-2002/DP (23 October 2002).

[87] *María Mamérita Mestanza Chávez v. Peru*, para. 14(11).

after the decision in *K.L. v. Peru* came down, for instance, the Ministry of Health drafted a protocol to help facilitate access to legal therapeutic abortion, which would have brought the State into compliance with the Human Rights Committee's recommendations. However, the ministry's attempt to issue and implement the protocol was stymied by the Catholic hierarchy in Peru. Similarly, even where laws and policies are consistent with international or regional human rights standards, discrimination or opposition on the part of individual healthcare practitioners can prevent laws and policies from being implemented. In the *Paulina*, *Tysiąc*, and *K.L.* cases, the countries in question permitted abortion on the grounds for which the women were seeking them, but hospital staff denied them access to abortion.

Political will to improve the situation of women's reproductive health is another key challenge to implementing reproductive rights judgments, particularly in the context of maternal mortality. While there is certainly a correlation between poverty and deficient reproductive health services – 99 per cent of maternal deaths occur in developing countries (WHO, 2014: 22) – poverty alone is insufficient to explain high rates of maternal mortality; there are a number of low-cost interventions that States can take to significantly reduce maternal mortality where they have the political will to do so, such as revising restrictive laws and policies on reproductive health services, including abortion, improving access to contraceptive information and services, and training mid-level health workers to provide quality pre-natal, delivery, and post-natal care. Getting human rights adjudicatory bodies and States to recognise preventable maternal mortality as a human rights issue can be an integral part of overcoming political inertia on maternal health. To this end, advocacy carried out even before the CEDAW Committee had yet to issue its final decision in the case of *Alyne v. Brazil*, which has been having a significant transformational effect. Since filing the case, the Center and local partners have engaged in a targeted advocacy strategy to improve recognition of maternal mortality as a human rights issue by hosting a seminar in Brazil for stakeholders from different disciplines to raise awareness of the case and to identify key recommendations for improving maternal health policies; obtaining statements from UN Special Rapporteurs; and lobbying the Human Rights Council to strengthen international standards and political commitments on the issue. The seminar, in particular, was instrumental in identifying key allies at the national and local level and in building consensus across disciplines on the most strategic approach for implementing a decision in the *Alyne* case. The Center continues to engage with seminar participants in the follow-up to the CEDAW Committee's decision. The Center also enlisted the support of influential organisations and institutions in providing technical information to the CEDAW Committee to support the resolution of the *Alyne* case. For example, the International Commission of Jurists, Amnesty International, and the Latin American Committee for the Defence of Women's Rights (CLADEM) all submitted technical opinions emphasising that addressing maternal mortality in Brazil is not only a public health issue, but also a human rights imperative. These strategies have helped to lay the groundwork for the implementation of the CEDAW Committee's decision.

Recent developments in the *Mestanza* case similarly highlight the importance of political will in pushing for implementation. For a number of years, the Peruvian government excused the languishing criminal investigation called for in the friendly settlement on the grounds that the statute of limitations had run (IACHR, 2009: 751). After Peru's 2011 presidential election, however, the new government recognised the mass involuntary sterilisation campaigns as crimes against humanity, exempting these cases from the previously applicable statute of limitations, and reopened the investigations.

The political, social, and cultural environment, then, can be a crucial, and in some cases determinative, factor in implementing reproductive rights decisions.

12.5 Conclusion

As these case studies demonstrate, governments have generally complied with individual reparations. The bigger challenge has been in ensuring full implementation of general remedies. The design of adjudicatory bodies and the nature of the remedies awarded can play a role in improving the likelihood of implementing general measures, by allowing for settlement negotiations, improving the specificity of the remedies awarded, and strengthening the capacity for follow-up. However, based on the Center's experiences, transforming the social, political, and cultural environment to gain greater acceptance of reproductive rights as human rights and to strengthen political commitment is essential to paving way for the implementation of general measures. To that end, litigation of reproductive rights should be developed and considered within the broader advocacy efforts, ideally with collaboration between grassroots, national, and international organisations, to achieve these transformative effects.

In earlier stages of advocacy and litigation on reproductive rights, litigation can be seen as a tool to amplify the voice of those whose rights have been violated and as a norm-building tool, seeking transformative remedies – recognition of reproductive rights as human rights, stronger international standards, and heightened public awareness of reproductive rights – in addition to seeking reparation for the individual victim. Positive rulings in reproductive rights cases, while contributing to positive symbolic remedies, can also lead to additional hurdles, including political backlash and an energised opposition. The potential for backlash is one reason that it is essential to be aware of the social, political, and cultural environment in which the strategic litigation efforts are taking place, and why impact litigation strategies must be formed within larger advocacy strategies that seek to foster a social, political, and cultural environment conducive to implementing positive judicial decisions. Partnerships between local and international organisations are crucial at this stage of the litigation and advocacy strategies to play on the different strengths of each to, for instance, mobilise media, policymakers, and other key stakeholders at the national level and engage UN experts and other key actors at the international level.

The *K.L. v. Peru* case is an example of this early advocacy around the issue of access to legal abortion. *K.L.* was the first case on access to legal abortion to be litigated at the supranational level, and a primary goal was to strengthen international human rights norms around the issue. The Human Rights Committee's decision did just that. Despite the fact that the Peruvian government is only now effective in its efforts to implement the individual and general remedies that came out of the decision, the transformative effect of the case internationally has been far reaching. This case has been cited in several key national decisions to liberalise or uphold liberal abortion laws.[88] For example, the Colombian Constitutional Court held that Colombia's blanket ban on abortion was unconstitutional, citing the Human Rights Committee's holding that a failure to provide access to therapeutic abortion violated a woman's right to be free from cruel, inhuman, or degrading treatment.[89] Furthermore, the Colombian Constitutional Court explained that 'women's sexual and reproductive rights have finally been recognized as human rights, and, as such, they have become part of constitutional rights, which are the fundamental basis of all democratic states'.[90]

[88] See, e.g., *Constitutional Court of the Slovak Republic.*
[89] *Colombian Constitutional Court.*
[90] Ibid.

The *K.L.* decision has played a key role in shifting political will and public discourse around abortion in Peru, and through a sustained legal advocacy strategy stemming from this groundbreaking decision, local organisations were finally able to push the government to take effective measures to comply with the Human Rights Committee's decision in the case.

At the same time, the elements necessary for the successful implementation of reproductive rights judgments should be part of the advocacy strategy before litigation is even initiated. Indeed, each of the key factors influencing enforcement of reproductive rights judgments discussed – institutional design, nature of the remedies, public attention, and the social, political, and cultural environment – are elements that can, and should, be part of the calculus in determining whether, when, and where to litigate. Strategic litigation is one component of an advocacy plan to promote and protect reproductive rights, and thus needs to be undertaken and evaluated within the context of this broader advocacy plan. In many instances, in the Center's experience, the transformational impact of having filed a case in conjunction with a well-laid advocacy plan could be felt even before a final decision in the case was handed down.

By crafting an impact litigation strategy in accordance with the larger advocacy goals and by taking into consideration the key factors that impact implementation before a case has even been brought, advocates can lay the necessary groundwork to strengthen the possibility that a positive ESC rights decision will be implemented and will have a transformative impact on women's lives worldwide.

References

Abad Yupanqui, Samuel B. (2008), *Validez constitucional del aborto terapéutico en el ordenamiento jurídico peruano* (Lima: Centro de Promoción y Defensa de los Derechos Sexuales y Reproductivos [PROMSEX]).

Alianza Nacional por el Derecho a Decidir and Anis-Instituto de Bioética, Direitos Humanos e Gênero et al. (2008), *Causal Salud: Interrupción legal del embarazo, ética, y derechos humanos* (Bogota: La Mesa por la Vida y la Salud de las Mujeres and Alianza Nacional por el Derecho a Decidir).

Amnesty International (2014), *On the Brink of Death: Violence against Women and the Abortion Ban in El Salvador* (London: Amnesty International).

— (2015), *She Is Not a Criminal: The Impact of Ireland's Abortion Law* (London: Amnesty International).

Ayala Peralta, Félix, Santiago Cabrera Ramos et al. (2009), *Interrupción terapéutica del embarazo por causales de salud* (Lima: Centro de Promoción y Defensa de los Derechos Sexuales y Reproductivos [PROMSEX]).

Baluarte, David C. and Christian M. De Vos (2010), *From Judgment to Justice: Implementing International and Regional Human Rights Decisions* (New York: Open Society Foundations).

Cabal, Luisa and Jaime M. Todd-Gher (2009), 'Reframing the Right to Health: Legal Advocacy to Advance Women's Reproductive Rights', in Andrew Clapham and Mary Robinson (eds.), *Realizing the Right to Health* (Zurich: rüffer & rub), 120–138.

Center for Reproductive Rights (2008), *Bringing Rights to Bear* (New York: Center for Reproductive Rights).

(2014), *Abortion Worldwide: 20 Years of Reform* (New York: Center for Reproductive Rights).

Center for Reproductive Rights and Avani Sood (2006), *Litigating Reproductive Rights: Using Public Interest Litigation and International Law to Promote Gender Justice in India* (New York: Center for Reproductive Rights and Avani Sood).

Center for Reproductive Rights and Human Rights Law Network (2011), *2011 Update: Maternal Mortality in India: Using International and Constitutional Law to Promote Accountability and Change* (New York: Center for Reproductive Rights).

Charnovitz, Steve (2006), 'Nongovernmental Organizations and International Law', *The American Journal of International Law*, 100(2) (April), 348–372.

Committee of Ministers (2010), *Supervision of the Execution of Judgments of the European Court of Human Rights: Annual Report 2009* (Strasbourg: Council of Europe)

(2015), *Supervision of the Execution of Judgments of the European Court of Human Rights: 8th Annual Report of the Committee of Ministers 2014* (Strasbourg: Council of Europe).

Cook, Rebecca (2010), 'Interpreting the "Protection of Life"', www.gire.org.mx/publica2/SeminarioAborto_300810_Cook_eng.pdf.

(2013), 'Human Rights and Maternal Health: Exploring the Effectiveness of the Alyne Decision', *Journal of Law, Medicine & Ethics*, 41(1), 103–123.

Cook, Rebecca and Samantha Howard (2007), 'Accommodating Women's Differences under the Women's Anti-Discrimination Convention', *Emory Law Journal*, 56(4), 139–192.

Fraser, Nancy (1997), *Justice Interrupts: Critical Reflections on the 'Postsocialist' Condition* (New York: Routledge).

Fraser, Nancy (2000), 'Rethinking Recognition', *New Left Review*, 3 (May–June), 107–120.

Grupo de Información en Reproducción Elegida (GIRE) (2005), *Paulina: Five Years Later* (Mexico City: GIRE).

(2008), *The Process of Decriminalizing Abortion in Mexico City* (Mexico City: GIRE).

Hannum, Hurst (2004), *Guide to International Human Rights Practice*, 4th edn. (Ardsley: Transnational Publishers).

IACHR (Inter-American Commission on Human Rights) (2009), *Annual Report of the Inter-American Commission: Status of Compliance with the Recommendations of the IACHR*, OEA/Ser.L/V/II. Doc. 51, corr. 1.

(2010), *Access to Maternal Health Services from a Human Rights Perspective* (Washington, DC: Organization of American States).

(2015), *Annual Report of the Inter-American Commission on Human Rights* (Washington, DC: Organization of American States).

Keck, Margaret E. and Kathryn Sikkink (1998), *Activists beyond Borders: Advocacy Networks in International Politics* (Ithaca: Cornell University Press).

Ortega Ortiz, Adriana (2007), *Mexico: 'Paulina' Case Settlement & Impact* (email on file with the Center for Reproductive Rights [April 18, 2007]).

Poniatowska, Elena (2000), *Las mil y una … (la herida de Paulina)* [The Thousand and One … (Paulina's Wound)] (Barcelona: Plaza & Janés Editores).

World Health Organization (WHO) et al. (2014), *Trends in Maternal Mortality: 1990–2013: Estimates by WHO, UNICEF, UNFPA, the World Bank, and the United Nations Population Division* (Geneva: WHO).

International Housing Rights and Domestic Prejudice: The Case of Roma and Travellers

ANDI DOBRUSHI AND THEODOROS ALEXANDRIDIS

13.1 Introduction

For all their cultural and linguistic differences, the majority of Roma and Travellers in Europe[1] experience all too similar housing conditions. Segregated settlements in remote locations, unfit for habitation with poor access to public utilities, and constantly under the threat of eviction are often the norm, a phenomenon caused and compounded by endemic racism and discrimination. This harsh reality for Roma and Travellers has not gone unnoticed. Almost all European Union (EU) or Council of Europe (CoE) Member States have acknowledged that the situation must be addressed and there is no shortage of action plans or ad hoc measures aimed at alleviating their living conditions.

Nevertheless, these initiatives have failed in bringing about a measurable and lasting improvement in their daily lives. Reviewing the implementation of the 2003 OSCE *Action Plan on Improving the Situation of Roma/Sinti within the OSCE Area*,[2] the OSCE (2008: 29) concluded that Roma/Travellers continued to face rampant discrimination and highly substandard housing conditions. Five years later, the same body found that only 'some' positive changes had been effected, primarily in the allocation

---

[1] For practical purposes, all reference to Roma/Travellers in the present chapter should be understood as extending to other groups such as Sinti, Kale, Manouche, Gens de Voyage and so forth. Wherever necessary, particular reference will be made to the self-ascribed ethnic identity of the persons in question.

[2] OSCE (2003), *Action Plan on Improving the Situation of Roma/Sinti within the OSCE Area*, available at www.osce.org/odihr/17554.

Andi Dobrushi is Director of the Open Society Foundation for Albania.

Theodoros Alexandridis is Legal Counsel for Greek Helsinki Monitor (GHM) and Albanian NGO Res Publica.

The opinions expressed in the chapter are those of the authors and do not necessarily reflect the official policy of the respective organisations.

of additional funding and the implementation of (largely piecemeal) housing programmes for Roma (OSCE, 2013: 32). The principal challenges remained largely unaddressed (ibid.). In the same vein, and somewhat more candidly, the CoE's Parliamentary Assembly (PACE) noted in 2010 that:

> Besides the appalling rise of violence against Roma, the Assembly observes that the process of Roma integration has not reached its objectives over the last 20 years ... Assembly Recommendation 1557 (2002) on the legal situation of the Roma in Europe already stressed that the aims set out in its Recommendation 1203 (1993) on Gypsies in Europe had been achieved only to a limited extent. The Assembly now notes with great concern that the present situation is virtually unchanged, if not worse. This is a shamefully poor record considering the amount of paper – and money – dedicated to improving the situation of Roma at all levels.[3]

Echoing these concerns, the CoE's Commissioner for Human Rights noted:

> At a number of key moments, member states have rendered European-level calls to tackle Roma and Travellers' exclusion hollow, by openly flouting those expressions of concern ... Roma and Travellers throughout Europe follow these developments closely, and are keenly aware that, when push comes to shove, force currently prevails over international concern. Deep scepticism over whether there exists even the possibility of positive change for Roma and Travellers – a sentiment already widespread among Roma throughout the continent – is continually strengthened when international institutions fail to have a real impact on abuses by states and others. (Council of Europe, 2012: 221)

The Commissioner's remarks provide a backdrop for the two principal interrelated questions this essay seeks to tackle: How have international judicial and quasi-judicial bodies treated strategic litigation housing cases concerning Roma and Traveller groups, and why have the respondent States appeared so reluctant in implementing the relevant decisions handed down by these bodies?

In our view, strategic litigation is instrumental not only in securing redress for the victims of housing rights violations – and, increasingly, in preventing such violations from taking place – but also in expounding legal norms on housing. Recent decisions by the quasi-judicial UN human rights treaty bodies, the European Committee of Social Rights Committee (ECSR) and the European Court of Human Rights (the Court or ECtHR)

---

[3] Council of Europe's Parliamentary Assembly (PACE) Resolution 1740 (2010), 'The Situation of Roma in Europe and Relevant Activities of the Council of Europe', 22 June 2010, available at: http://assembly.coe.int/nw/xml/XRef/Xref-XML2HTML-en.asp?fileid=17875&lang=en sections 5–6.

attest to a gradual shift to an approach more receptive to the particular problems Roma/Travellers face. This shift does not, however, appear to be equally reflected in the implementation phase of these decisions, a phase that remains largely outside the purview of the international judicial and quasi-judicial bodies. While States generally pay Roma and Traveller applicants the damages and costs and expenses awarded to them, they appear unwilling to bring their law and practice in line with the *ratio* or principles of these decisions and to implement orders (whether explicit or implicit) for measures of a general or wide-ranging nature. The consequence is that the CoE's Secretary General noted that some ECSR and Court decisions regarding the Roma had yet to be fully implemented and observed that many member states lacked the requisite political will to implement both national and CoE standards (Council of Europe, 2014:47).

The ostensible causes of this reticence vary. In some cases, it can be attributed to no more than simple bureaucratic inertia or the overall inefficiency and lack of coordination between the State's executive and administrative machinery. However, in most cases the main reason behind this persistent and recurring failure is arguably none other than the very ethnic identity of the applicants. Their membership of a marginalised and often despised social group, a group that has no economic or political clout to directly demand compliance or build alliances with other social groups and political forces must be foregrounded in any analysis. Indeed, the Secretary General attributed this lack of will, amongst other reasons, to the hostile public opinion toward Roma integration as well as entrenched stereotypes and prejudice against them(Council of Europe, 2014: 47).

This unpalatable reality obviously casts a shadow on the premise that strategic litigation is a catalyst for change in the legal and policy fields.[4] Yet, we contend that even in the face of non-compliance, favourable judicial decisions from international tribunals might provide Roma and Travellers with modest protection as well as inflect the domestic political and legal agenda, particularly on account of the normative status that such decisions enjoy and the wide-ranging publicity they attract. Ultimately, strategic litigation cannot constitute the 'handmaiden of change'; it cannot, on its own, reshape the political and social consensus at the domestic level that would be necessary for Roma and Travellers to have their human rights respected

---

[4] This apparent contradiction has not gone unnoticed. According to Goldston and Adjami (2008: 42), 'At one level, public interest litigation on behalf of Roma has had enormous success to date ... And yet, at the same time, it would be hard to conclude that the situation on the ground for most Roma has markedly improved – let alone, that public interest litigation can claim any credit.'

and ensured. In this context, strategic litigation is primarily a rear-guard battle: no matter how successful, such skirmishes do not win wars. That requires a broader, offensive strategy.

The present chapter consists of four sections. In the first three, the factual background of seminal Roma and Travellers housing cases brought respectively before UN bodies, the ECSR and ECtHR is presented, followed by an assessment of their implementation to date. Our initial intention of presenting a sample of both successful and less so instances of execution proved to be an impossible task. In the vast majority of cases reviewed, implementation by the states concerned was deficient, sometimes by a very large margin, thereby raising legitimate concerns regarding both the commitment of the states in question to abide by their international obligations as well as the supervising authority's (more often than not a political body) determination to ensure a timely and effective implementation of the decisions in question. For the purposes of the chapter, the authors considered it important to eschew a lengthy legal analysis of the various monitoring and implementation mechanisms (with the qualified exception of the respective European mechanisms in light of the extensive jurisprudence developed under these two instruments) and focus on the tangible results, if any, that they might have yielded. By way of conclusion, we put forward our analysis on the reasons behind the reluctance and ultimately the failure of States to adequately implement decisions by international tribunals relating to Roma and Travellers' housing and offer some suggestions as to the way forward for NGOs and legal advocates active in the field.

13.2   Roma Cases before UN Treaty Bodies

Individual complaint mechanisms have been established for a range of international human rights treaties. Complainants must usually exhaust domestic remedies and meet a range of other admissibility criteria before their cases on the merits are considered by the relevant treaty monitoring committee. In this section we consider cases from the Committee against Torture, Committee on the Elimination of Racial Discrimination and Human Rights Committee.

These quasi-judicial bodies are empowered to provide an assessment (called 'Views' or 'Opinions') on whether a state is in compliance followed by a recommendation. However, the committees increasingly solicit follow-up information on whether their views have been complied with, while the issue might also be examined in the context of assessment of the pertinent periodical report submitted by the state party in question. For a number of reasons, the UN bodies monitoring mechanisms and procedures are slightly less robust than those established under the European Social Charter and clearly the European Convention on Human Rights but even with these limitations, these decisions undoubtedly have considerable moral authority (see OSJI, 2010: 52, 118, and 125).

13.2.1   Hajrizi Dzemajl et al. v. Yugoslavia (Committee against Torture)

The alleged rape of a non-Romani girl by two Romani youths in April 1995 in the town of Danilovgrad in Montenegro sparked a pogrom by several hundred non-Roma citizens of the town against the local Roma community.[5] With the acquiescence of the municipal authorities and the police, the mob destroyed the Roma settlement, amidst slogans calling for their extermination. The Roma managed to flee, but their homes and personal belongings were ultimately burned or otherwise destroyed, and the debris were subsequently cleared away, together with all traces of the settlement. In fear for their lives, the Roma fled the town and became were effectively internally displaced persons (IDPs), settling in the outskirts of Podgorica where they lived in appalling conditions. Following a largely pro-forma criminal investigation into the attacks, judicial authorities closed the case for lack of evidence while both the civil and labour law proceedings launched by the Roma remained pending at the time the UN CAT (Committee against Torture) issued its decision in November 2002.

In its decision, the CAT held that 'the burning and destruction of houses constitute, in the circumstances, acts of cruel, inhuman or degrading treatment or punishment'. It also considered the presence of some Roma in the settlement when the events were taking place, together with the racist motivation behind them, as aggravating factors. In the operative part of its decision, the Committee called upon the Montenegrin authorities to launch an effective investigation into the events and provide adequate redress to the victims.

In their Initial Report to the CAT submitted in 2006, the Montenegrin authorities informed the Committee that an out-of-court settlement had been reached with seventy-four Romani victims whereby an award of almost one million euro had been paid to them for pecuniary and

---

[5] *Hajrizi Dzemajl et al. v Yugoslavia*, CAT Committee, Complaint No. 161/2000, U.N. Doc. CAT/C/29/D/161/2000 (2002).

non-pecuniary losses. The authorities were reluctant to launch fresh criminal proceedings and conduct a new investigation into the 1995 events, invoking the prescription of the offences and lack of new evidence.[6] Although the damages award might appear rather low, it is worth noting that the Montenegrin authorities adopted the relevant decision rather promptly (within seven months of the handing down of the decision by the Committee) and tried to provide full redress to the victims.[7] Considering that questions regarding the implementation of the Committee's decision do not feature in any subsequent exchange between it and the Montenegrin authorities, the Committee has presumably held that its views have been taken into account and adequate redress has been afforded to the victims.

13.2.2   L.R and Others v. Slovakia (Committee on the Elimination of Discrimination)

This seminal case originated in a resolution, adopted by the Municipal Council of the town of Dobšiná in Slovakia, approving a housing policy for the local destitute Roma community and calling on the mayor to take all the necessary operative measures to that end.[8] Following the adoption of the resolution, however, local non-Roma residents petitioned the municipality not to proceed with the housing plan, as it would lead to 'an influx of inadaptable citizens of Gypsy origin'. Upon receiving this petition, the Municipal Council adopted a new resolution, revoking the resolution and effectively abandoning the housing project for the Roma.

In its March 2005 opinion, the Committee on the Elimination of Racial Discrimination (CERD) noted that the initial resolution of the Municipal Council constituted an important policy initiative and a concrete step towards the realisation of the right to housing, constituting an integral component of it. In the words of the Committee,

> [I]t would be inconsistent with the purpose of the Convention and elevate formalism over substance, to consider that the final step in the actual implementation of a particular human right or fundamental freedom must occur in a non-discriminatory manner, while the necessary preliminary

[6] CAT, *Consideration of Reports submitted by States Parties under Article 19 of the Convention, Initial Reports of States Parties due in 1999*, UN. Doc, CAT/C/MNE/1 (2008) paragraph 142.

[7] See ERRC (2003), 'Montenegrin Government Agrees to Pay 985,000 Euro in Compensation to Pogrom Victims', available at: www.errc.org/cikk.php?cikk=330.

[8] *L.R. and others v. Slovakia*, Communication No. 31/2003, U.N. Doc CERD/C/66/D/31/2003 (2005).

decision-making elements directly connected to that implementation were
to be severed and be free from scrutiny.[9]

The subsequent revocation of the first municipal resolution was found to
be racially motivated and in violation of the state's obligation to ensure that
all authorities, national and local, exercise their functions in a non-racially
discriminatory manner. Furthermore, the CERD held that the petitioners
did not have at their disposal an effective remedy that would enable them
to challenge their discriminatory treatment.

Regarding the nature of redress that should be provided to the authors
of the communication, the CERD held that the authorities should effectively reinstate the previous status quo and proceed with the housing plan
as laid down in the first municipal resolution.

In terms of implementation, it should be noted that the Government
of Slovakia continuously stresses its will to tackle the problems the country's Roma community faces. Slovakia was a member of the Decade of
Roma Inclusion 2005–2015 (launched shortly before the issuing of the
CERD Opinion) and drafted an ambitious Roma Action Plan[10] as well as
a comprehensive national Roma Integration Strategy in the framework
of its obligations as an EU member state.[11] Both policy documents contain extensive provisions on projects and policies aimed at addressing
the housing predicament of the Roma. Both central and local authorities,
however, have exhibited a marked reluctance in abiding by the conclusions
of the CERD opinion. In an exchange of correspondence with the CERD,
the Slovak government considered that the annulment of the second resolution (not accompanied, however, by the re-introduction and adoption
of the first resolution), together with the assumption of some rather vague
undertakings regarding the eventual provision of low-cost housing to the
Roma of Dobšiná and the launching of criminal proceedings against
the authors of the petition, afforded adequate reparation to the victims.
The municipality also tried to downplay the gravity of the problem, effectively questioning the premise, if not the rationale, of CERD's Opinion. In
the meetings with the European Roma Rights Centre (ERRC), the Deputy
Mayor of Dobšiná stated that according to his interpretation of the CERD's

---

[9] Ibid., 10.7.

[10] Member States to the Decade were required to draft and implement an Action Plan addressing the problems Roma are facing in the fields of education, employment, health and housing. The Slovakian Action Plan is available at www.romadecade.org/cms/upload/file/9296_
file25_sk_action_plan_2011_eng.pdf.

[11] The Slovakian Roma Strategy is available at http://ec.europa.eu/justice/discrimination/
files/roma_slovakia_strategy_en.pdf.

Opinion, the latter did not call for the provision of low-cost housing to Roma, with the Mayor adding that the living conditions of the Roma in his city were not that 'dramatic' in comparison with those of non-Roma inhabitants.[12]

The CERD revisited the issue of implementation in its February 2010 consideration of Slovakia's periodic report. Members of the CERD requested additional information regarding the measures the Government had taken in order to conform to the decision.[13] The Slovak delegation's submissions apparently failed to impress the CERD. In its Concluding Observations, the Committee confined itself to taking note of the Slovak government's commitment to address the housing situation of the Roma of Dobšiná and recommended that Slovakia ensure the 'effective and timely' implementation of its recommendations.[14]

In their response to the CERD's observations, the Slovak government subsequently informed it that, as of February 2011, work had not yet started on the construction of housing but that the municipality had included a housing project for the Roma among its priorities; and rather cryptically, the then recently elected Municipal Council 'might assumingly be more inclined towards the construction of lower-standard rental flats'.[15]

This did not transpire. Once again, CERD took up the issue of implementation and in its opinion in 2013, expressed its concern over the State's failure to exercise control over local authorities' decisions limiting Roma access to housing in general, and calling once again upon Slovakia to address the housing predicament of the Roma community of Dobšiná as well as provide updated information towards that respect in particular.[16] In their reply the next year, the Slovak government declined to address the CERD's concerns or to provide the follow-up information requested, and

[12] CERD, *Report of the Committee on the Elimination of Racial Discrimination* (Seventieth and Seventy-first sessions, 2007), U.N. Doc. A/62/18 (2007), page 155 et seq.
[13] CERD, *Consideration of reports, comments and information submitted by States Parties under article 9 of the Convention, Sixth to Eighth periodic reports of Slovakia* (Summary Record of the 1975th Meeting), U.N. Doc. CERD/C/SR.1975 (2010), paragraphs 42 and 51.
[14] CERD, *Concluding Observations of the Committee on the Elimination of Racial Discrimination: Slovak Republic* (Seventy-sixth session, 2010), U.N. Doc. CERD/C/SVK/CO/6-8 (2010), at paragraph 20.
[15] CERD, *Information received from the Government of Slovakia on the implementation of the concluding observations of the Committee on the Elimination of Racial Discrimination* (Eightieth session, 2012), U.N. Doc. CERD/C/SVK/CO/6-8 (2011), paragraphs 21-22.
[16] CERD, *Concluding Observations of the Committee on the Elimination of Racial Discrimination: Slovak Republic* (Eighty-second session, 2013), U.N. Doc. CERD/C/SVK/CO/9-10 (2013), at paragraph 16.

merely referred to the various legislative measures they were planning on adopting.[17] Similarly, in their recent periodic report to CERD, submitted in July 2016, the Slovak government appear to have forgotten to respond to the part of the relevant CERD recommendation regarding the implementation of CERD's Opinion, as they stressed once again the principle of the autonomy of municipalities.[18]

The inertia of the Slovak authorities to abide by their obligations flowing from the CERD opinion prompted two international NGOs (the European Roma Rights Centre that had represented the Roma before the CERD and the Centre on Housing Rights and Evictions) together with a Slovak NGO (the Milan Šimečka Foundation) to launch fresh domestic proceedings, initially before the Slovak Equality Treatment Authority (the Slovak National Centre for Human Rights). In 2006, they requested an informative legal opinion regarding the Slovakian authorities' failure to implement the CERD's decision and examine whether this failure was in breach of the domestic anti-discrimination law. By a rather surprising and tersely worded decision, the Slovak National Centre effectively ignored the CERD's opinion and held that a right to provision of public housing was not recognised under Slovak law and hence it did not fall within the remit of anti-discrimination law while it also considered that the refusal at the time of the town of Dobšiná to take any measures to comply with the CERD opinion did not violate the equal treatment principle.[19] With the assistance of the three NGOs, Roma from Dobšiná have launched judicial proceedings in which they effectively call upon the authorities to conform to their obligations flowing from the CERD opinion.

To summarise, more than eleven years after the handing down of the CERD's Opinion and despite the Slovak government's professing of political will to tackle the housing problems of the Roma, the Roma of Dobšiná have yet to witness even a meagre improvement in their everyday lives.

---

[17] CERD, *Concluding Observations on the combined ninth and tenth periodic reports of Slovakia* – Addendum: Information received from Slovakia on follow-up to the concluding observations [date received: 27 February 2014], U.N. Doc. CERD/C/SVK/CO/9–10/Add.1 (2014), at paragraphs 18–21.

[18] CERD, *Consideration of reports submitted by States Parties under article 9 of the Convention*, Combined eleventh and twelfth periodic reports of States parties due in 2016 Slovakia. U.N. Doc. CERD/C/SVK/11-12, 11 August 2016 (Date received: 18 July 2016), paragraphs 200–203.

[19] Slovak National Centre for Human Rights, letter dated 18 October 2006, on file with the authors.

13.2.3   *Georgopoulos and Others v. Greece (Human Rights Committee)*

Already the victim of an unlawful eviction in the summer of 2006 and unable to find an apartment to house his family with a meagre allowance provided by the municipality of Patras, Greece, Mr. Georgopoulos and his family of seven moved into his father's small shack made of wooden planks in the settlement where they had lived for many years.[20] However, he was soon forced to look for a housing alternative, as living conditions in his father's shack became severely overcrowded. He therefore started, in September 2006, erecting a new shed, adjacent to his father's. This did not escape the attention of local residents who had been calling for the Roma community's eviction for a number of years and immediately alerted the police and the local municipality. Officials from both agencies arrived at the scene shortly thereafter and threatened Mr. Georgopoulos with arrest should he resist the demolition of his home. Mr. Georgopoulos relented and his half-assembled shack was promptly destroyed. Rather fortunately for him, however, on that very same morning and only hours after his eviction, the CoE's Commissioner for Human Rights visited the settlement and witnessed its aftermath: Mr. Georgopoulos's family belongings had been placed on their pick-up truck whose back end had been configured to serve as an impromptu sleeping place for the family of eight while the bulldozer's tracks, still visible on the soft ground, led to a pile of smashed wooden planks. Indeed, the very existence of this pile belied the contentions of two deputy mayors who informed the Commissioner that only a cleaning operation (a euphemism used by local authorities in Greece when referring to the demolition of Roma shacks) and no eviction had taken place that morning.

Before the Human Rights Committee (HRC), the authors claimed that there were no effective remedies at their disposal to challenge their double eviction. Furthermore, they emphasised that their evictions had not been ordered by a court – on the contrary, when in the past the municipality had sought to evict them by legal means, they had successfully challenged them before the competent court which ruled that their eviction would be abusive and stayed their eviction pending their relocation into adequate housing. Finally, the Roma noted that they had also filed a criminal complaint but that the investigation launched into their allegations was characterised by significant delays.

---

[20] *Georgopoulos and Others v. Greece*, Human Rights Committee, Communication No. 1799/2008, U.N. Doc. CCPR/C/99/D/1799/2008 (2010).

The HRC found that the authors' consecutive evictions were in violation of the Covenant and called upon Greece to provide the authors with an effective remedy as well as adequate reparation, including compensation. It also reminded Greece of its obligation to ensure that no similar violations take place in the future.[21] The Greek state was mandated to inform the HRC within six months of the measures it would undertake towards implementing the HRC's decision.

In terms of implementation, the authors' request for an out-of-court award in damages is currently pending before the competent state authorities while following communication of the decision to the prosecutor's office of Patras by the authors' representatives (as the state authorities' failure to *ex officio* transmit the HRC decision to the prosecutor's office), the case was reopened and criminal proceedings for breach of duty were instituted against the then incumbent mayor of Patras and two deputy mayors, as well as the unknown officials that took part in the authors' eviction. In the end, the mayor and the two deputy mayors were acquitted, prompting the filling of another communication with the HRC, this time over the failure of the domestic authorities to properly execute the HRC opinion and in particular the failure to hold responsible the public officials who sanctioned the eviction. Apart from these developments, however, the Greek state has failed to take any additional measures such as, for example, adopting a legislative framework on forced evictions, in order to conform to the HRC opinion. Greece's failure to implement the HRC's opinion led the latter to suspend the follow-up dialogue after reaching a finding of unsatisfactory implementation of its recommendation.[22]

13.3   Collective Complaints on Roma/Travellers Housing under the European Social Charter

The European Committee of Social Rights (ECSR) is a quasi-judicial body entrusted with monitoring the compliance by state parties of the European Social Charter and the Revised European Social Charter. It carries out its functions first by reviewing reports submitted by the Contracting States (in which they set out the measures adopted towards implementing the Charter's provisions) in accordance with a reporting cycle and adopting conclusions as to a state's compliance with the Charter and, second, by

---

[21] Ibid., paragraph 9.
[22] HRC, Follow-up progress report on individual communications, adopted by the Committee at its 112th session (2014), U.N. Doc. CCPR/C/112/3 (2014), at page 17.

reviewing collective complaints submitted to it and adopting decisions regarding the conformity or not of the allegations with the Charter.[23] In its decisions regarding the collective complaints alleging violation of *inter alia* the housing rights of Roma/Travellers submitted to it,[24] the ECSR has both acknowledged the housing predicament they experience in a number of countries (namely Greece, Italy, Bulgaria, France, Portugal, Ireland and Belgium)[25] as well as fleshed out the contours of the right to housing.

A finding of a violation of the Charter by the ECSR does not signal the conclusion of the collective complaint proceedings, as the ECSR's report is then transmitted to the Committee of Ministers, which comprises the Foreign Affairs Ministers of all the CoE member states, or their permanent diplomatic representatives. The Committee of Ministers cannot overrule the ECSR's verdict yet it can severely undermine its significance and impact. Thus, should the Committee of Ministers be presented with

[23] For a more detailed description of the ECSR's monitoring mandate see www.coe.int/t/dghl/monitoring/socialcharter/Presentation/FAQ_en.asp#5._How_does_monitoring_work.

[24] See the ECSR decisions on the merits in relation to the following collective complaints on Roma and Travellers housing (in brackets the dates when the decisions on the merits were adopted): *ERRC v Greece, Collective Complaint 15/2003* (8 December 2004), *ERRC v. Italy, Collective Complaint No. 27/2004* (7 December 2005), *ERRC v. Bulgaria, Collective Complaint No. 31/2005* (18 October 2006), *International Movement ATD Fourth World v. France, Collective Complaint No. 33/2006* (5 December 2007), *European Federation of National Organisations Working with the Homeless (FEANTSA) v. France, Collective Complaint No. 39/2006* (5 December 2007), *ERRC v. France, Collective Complaint No. 51/2008* (19 October 2009), *International Centre for the Legal Protection of Human Rights (INTERIGHTS) v. Greece*, No 49/2008 (11 December 2009), *Centre on Housing Rights and Evictions (COHRE) v. Italy, Collective Complaint No. 58/2009* (25 June 2010), *ERRC v. Portugal, Collective Complaint No. 61/2010* (30 June 2010), *International Federation of Human Rights (FIDH) v. Belgium, Collective Complaint No. 62/2010* (21 March 2012), *Centre on Housing rights and Evictions (COHRE) v. France, Collective Complaint No. 63/2010* (28 June 2011),*European Roma and Travellers Forum (ERTF) v. France, Collective Complaints No. 64/2011*(24 January 2012) *Medecins du Monde- International v. France Collective Complaint No. 67/2011* (11 September 2012), *ERRC v. Ireland, Collective Complaint No. 100/2013* (1 December 2015). Another collective complaint on Roma housing has been declared admissible and is pending at the time of writing: a *ERTF (European Roma and Travellers Forum) v. the Czech Republic, Collective Complaint No. 104/2014*. All decisions are available at: www.hudoc.esc.coe.int/eng/#.

[25] To date there has been no case of a collective complaint (even in the cases of repetitive ones) in respect to which the Committee found that the situation was in conformity with the Charter: this in turn is a serious indictment of the Roma housing policies adopted by the states in question. It is also very likely that the conclusions of the Committee would be similar in relation to other countries with a sizeable Roma population such as Romania, Hungary and Slovakia, none of which (as of September 2016) have signed (in the case of Romania) or ratified (in the case of Hungary and Slovakia) the relevant provisions of the Revised European Social Charter or the collective complaints Protocol that would allow for the lodging of collective complaints against them.

an ECSR decision holding that a State has violated the Charter, then following a two-thirds majority of the Committee of Ministers members entitled to vote (namely the ministers of those states that have ratified the European Social Charter or the Revised European Social Charter), it ought to adopt a recommendation addressed to the state in question. Should this quorum not be met, then the Committee adopts a resolution whose operative part is usually couched in exhortatory or neutral terms. It should be noted in this respect that resolutions are also adopted when the ECSR has previously ascertained that the allegations do not amount to a violation of the Charter. The Committee of Ministers has in fact adopted a recommendation in relation to a collective complaint only once, in a case against France relating to the professional rights of certain categories of tour guides. In its recommendation, the Committee of Ministers prescribed a series of concrete measures that the French State ought to implement in order to bring the situation in conformity with the Charter.[26]

For the purposes of this chapter, our analysis will be limited to the consecutive collective complaints lodged against Greece and France that not only highlight the failure of the respective governments to bring their Roma housing policies in line with the findings of the ECSR but also the rather passive role of the institution tasked with monitoring the implementation of the ECSR's decisions, namely the Committee of Ministers, in the face of repetitive and particularly serious violations of the European Social Charter.

13.3.1   Collective Complaints against Greece

Overview of Decisions

In its decision regarding the first collective complaint filed against Greece in 2003 *ERRC v. Greece*,[27] the ECSR found in 2004 that Greece had violated Article 16 (right of the family to social, legal and economic protection) of the European Social Charter on three distinct grounds, namely the insufficiency of permanent dwellings provided to the Roma, the lack of temporary stopping facilities and the numerous forced evictions and other sanctions that the Roma were subjected to. The ECSR was particularly

---

[26] Council of Europe, Committee of Ministers, Recommendation RecChs(2001)1 on Collective complaint No. 6/1999, *Syndicate national des Professions du tourisme* against France, 31 January 2001, available at hudoc.esc.coe.int/eng/#.

[27] Collective Complaint No. 15/2003.

critical of the Greek state's lack of institutional means to either encourage or ultimately compel local authorities to undertake action in order to improve the living conditions of the Roma. A welcome development during the proceedings before the ECSR was the repeal of the explicitly racist 1983 Sanitary Regulation providing for the relocation of "athinganoi" (a pejorative term used to refer to Roma) to organised settlements that, under the terms of the regulation, ought to be set up outside inhabited areas and 'at a capable distance' from the urban plan or the last contiguous houses of a town/community.

Apart from repealing this regulation, Greece failed to implement any effective measures towards substantively addressing the findings of the ECSR. This prompted the latter to conclude in its 2006 conclusions, concerning the report submitted by Greece regarding *inter alia* steps undertaken to comply with its obligations flowing under Article 16, that the decision regarding the collective complaint had not been implemented and that Greece continued to violate Article 16 on the three grounds named in the decision.[28]

The persistent failure of the Greek state in taking even nominal steps in the field of Roma housing prompted the filing of a second complaint by INTERIGHTS in 2008; the Greek government contested the admissibility of the complaint, arguing among others that the complaint brought forward by INTERIGHTS was in fact containing the same allegations as the previous one filed by ERRC and to which the Committee of Ministers had adopted a resolution, thereby effectively concluding the proceedings. In the alternative, the Greek government argued that the implementation of the ECSR's decision regarding the first collective complaint was under the supervision of the Committee in the framework of the regular reporting procedure envisaged by the Charter and hence a new complaint was devoid of purpose. The Greek government further argued that the filing of a new complaint on the same subject only three years following the adoption by the Committee of Ministers of their resolution constituted an abuse of procedure. In its admissibility decision, the ECSR held that it was not precluded from entertaining the complaint filed by INTERIGHTS on the grounds advanced by the Greek government and proceeded to declare it admissible.

In 2009 the ECSR adopted its decision on the merits of the complaint, finding once again that Greece was in violation of Article 16. Reiterating

---

[28] European Committee of Social Rights, *Conclusions XVIII-1 (Greece): Articles 1, 12, 13, 16 and 19 of the Charter* (2006) 13 available at hudoc.esc.coe.int/eng/#.

its earlier findings, the ECSR held that the Greek state had failed to take into account the particular situation of the Roma when taking measures towards ameliorating their living conditions. It also found, in effect, a 'continuing violation' of Article 16,: Roma continued to be subjected to forced eviction and the available legal remedies were not effective.

The ECSR would once again reach similar conclusions in 2011 following the assessment of Greece's periodical report on Article 16: regarding the follow-up to the first collective complaint, the ECSR held that the prevailing situation was still not in conformity with Article 16. In relation to the second collective complaint, the Committee held that as the decision was adopted at the end of the reference period, an examination of its follow-up was premature and called upon the Greek government to include comprehensive and updated information regarding the implementation of the Committee's decision in its next periodic report. Considering, however, the almost identical nature of the two collective complaints, one could well assume that but for the procedural reason advanced by the ECSR, the latter would have found that the Greek government had also failed to adequately (if at all) implement the second decision.[29]

Implementation

In relation to the first collective complaint lodged by ERRC against Greece, the Committee of Ministers declined to adopt a recommendation, confining itself in its 2005 resolution to taking stock of a series of policy measures announced by the Greek government.

Even if this passive approach was warranted, pursuant to the principle that states should be afforded with a wide margin of appreciation when devising and implementing resource-intensive policies in the social and economic fields, it is more difficult to account for the failure of the Committee of Ministers to confront the full-frontal assault launched prior to the adoption of the resolution by the representative of Greece against the ECSR and ultimately against the European Social Charter itself, excerpts of which are worth quoting at length. While acknowledging that the Greek government were faced with some 'inadequate situations, which are mostly related to the local level [sic]', Greece's representative also cautioned the Committee of Ministers that

[29] European Committee of Social Rights, *Conclusions XIX-4 (2011) (Greece): Articles 7, 8, 16, 17 and 19 of the Charter* (2012) 15 available at www.coe.int/t/dghl/monitoring/socialcharter/Conclusions/State/GreeceXIX4_en.pdf.

[W]e [the Greek government] are increasingly alarmed at what seems to us to constitute an increasing trend: that of the overambitious or exaggerated, if not false, interpretations of these texts [i.e. the European Social Charter]. Such interpretations are neither legitimate nor constructive, nor do they encourage those member states that have not signed and ratified them – especially the Additional Protocol, whose provisions only thirteen member states have accepted – to do so.

Bearing this in mind, and reiterating our commitment to the values enshrined in the Charter, we should like to encourage the European Committee of Social Rights to remain close to the text of the Charter and to avoid the perhaps natural temptation to transform it into to an all-inclusive vessel that can be applied to everything and anything under the sun.

As far as the opinion of the European Committee of Social Rights on the specific collective complaint is concerned, we should first of all like to remind the Committee that this is a problem which all European countries with a Roma population face. It is not particular or exclusive to my country.[30]

The Committee of Ministers also declined to adopt a recommendation regarding the second collective complaint launched against Greece. Notably, it is to be recalled that the ECSR had effectively twice (first in its conclusions regarding Greece's report under Article 16 and second with its decision in the collective complaint brought by INTERIGHTS) held that the Greek government had failed to ensure an adequate implementation of the ECSR's first decision. Nevertheless, in its 2011 resolution, the Committee of Ministers simply confined itself once again to taking cognizance of a new spate of policy measures announced by the Greek government as well as welcoming the (primarily legislative in nature) steps already undertaken to that effect as well as the (self-professed) commitment demonstrated by the Greek government in bringing the situation in conformity with the Charter.

To conclude, in four instances in the span of seven years, the ECSR has concluded that the housing situation of Roma in Greece was in violation of Article 16 of the Charter. Moreover, in two of these instances, it reached its findings in the context of quasi-judicial proceedings and following the submission of comprehensive information by both parties. It is difficult to see on what grounds the Committee of Ministers could effectively

---

[30] Council of Europe Committee of Ministers, *Intervention of the permanent representative of Greece to the Council of Europe ambassador Constantin Yerocostopoulos*, item 4.1.a 'Collective Complaint No. 15/2003: European Roma Rights Center v. Greece', 924th CM Meeting, 20 April 2005 available at https://wcd.coe.int/ViewDoc.jsp?Ref=CM/Notes/929/4.3c&Language=lanEnglish&Ver=original&Site=CM&BackColorInternet=C3C3C3&BackColorIntranet=EDB021&BackColorLogged=F5D383.

substitute the ECSR's assessment for its own and blunt the ECSR's incisive findings, depriving them of any meaningful impact. The authors find even more worrying the Committee of Ministers' failure to take a stand against the malicious and hostile fulmination against the ECSR and the Charter by the Greek government which aimed *inter alia* at trivialising and relativising the housing predicament of the Roma. Although one cannot but speculate as to whether the adoption of a recommendation or a more sternly worded resolution by the Committee of Ministers would have forced the Greek government to rise from its inertia and meaningfully address the housing plight of Roma, one would hardly expect that the tepid wording of the two resolutions would have any impact on the Greek government's lack of resolve to do so.

13.3.2 Collective Complaints against France

Overview of Decisions

During the past few years, France has repeatedly been the object of successive collective complaints regarding the housing situation of Travellers and Roma migrants. The first collective complaints on *inter alia* the housing situation of the *Gens du Voyage* (Travellers) to be lodged against France were filed by the International Movement ATD Fourth World (No. 33/2006) and the European Federation of National Organisations Working with the Homeless (FEANTSA) (No. 39/2006). Both organisations raised similar complaints regarding the housing situations of Travellers in France and particularly the lack of an adequate number of halting sites and the increased danger of forced evictions they incurred by not having access to enough authorised sites to park their caravans on. In its decision on the merits regarding both complaints adopted in 2007, the ECSR found a violation of Article 31 of the Revised Charter (right to housing) and underlined that both central and local authorities had for a long time failed to adequately address the housing situation of Travellers.

Some of these allegations were also raised in the collective complaint lodged by the ERRC against France in 2008 (No. 51/2008). In addition to allegations regarding the inadequate number of halting sites, the ERRC contended that the prevailing living conditions on many of the sites in operation were very poor; and it also pointed out that the French state's policies failed to take into consideration the increasing adoption of a sedentary or semi-sedentary lifestyle by many Travellers that in turn called for the adoption of more culturally sensitive housing policies. The ERRC found that the French state had failed to adopt comprehensive measures to provide housing to the numerous Roma immigrants from other CoE countries while it also disputed the conformity with the Charter of the wide-ranging eviction powers that did not include the provision of alternative accommodation or the eviction following a judicial decision. By its decision adopted in 2009, the ECSR found that the situation was not in conformity with the Charter and held that France had violated *inter alia* Articles 31 (right to housing), as well as Article 16 (right of the family to social, legal and economic protection) of the Charter in conjunction with Article E (the non-discrimination clause of the Charter), as well as Article 19 (right of migrant workers to protection and assistance).

The next collective complaint to be filed against France was lodged by the Centre on Housing Rights and Evictions (COHRE) in 2010 (No. 63/2010). The complaint primarily focused on the massed collective evictions of Roma migrants from their impromptu settlements and their subsequent expulsion from France to their countries of origin on public order and security grounds, under a veneer of legitimacy provided by the payment of an allowance to the Roma towards securing their 'consent' to their expulsion. In one of its most sternly worded decisions to date, which is worth quoting at length, the ECSR vocally criticised the actions of the French government and held that

> 53. Having regard to the adoption of measures, which are incompatible with human dignity and specifically aimed at vulnerable groups, and taking into account the active role of the public authorities in framing and implementing this discriminatory approach to security, the Committee considers that the relevant criteria (COHRE v. Italy, Complaint No. 58/2009, decision on the merits of 25 June 2010, § 76) have been met and that there was an aggravated violation of human rights from the standpoint of Article 31§2 of the Revised Charter. In reaching this conclusion, the Committee also takes into consideration the fact that it has already found violations in its decision of 19 October 2009 on the merits of Complaint No. 51/2008, European Roma Rights Centre (ERRC) v. France.
>
> 54. The measures in question also reveal a failure to respect essential values enshrined in the European Social Charter, in particular human dignity, and the nature and scale of these measures set them apart from ordinary Charter violations. These aggravated violations do not simply concern their victims or their relationship with the respondent state. They also pose a challenge to the interests of the wider community and to the shared fundamental standards of all the Council of Europe's member states, namely those of human rights, democracy and the rule of law. The situation therefore requires urgent attention from all the Council of Europe member states (Centre on Housing Rights and Evictions (COHRE) v. Italy,

Complaint No. 58/2009, decision on the merits of 25 June 2010, § 78). The Committee invites them to publish its decision on the merits, once it has been notified to the parties and to the Committee of Ministers. Turning more specifically to the respondent Government, the finding of aggravated violations implies not only the adoption of adequate measures of repara-tion but also the obligation to offer appropriate assurances and guarantees of non-repetition and to ensure that such violations cease and do not recur.

In its recent decision on the merits in relation to Collective Complaints No. 64/2011 and 67/2011, brought respectively against France by the European Roma and Travellers Forum (ERTF) and Médecins du Monde – International, the ECSR effectively reiterated its previous findings adopted in relation to the aforementioned collective complaints. It also noted that although more and more sites and parking place were becoming avail-able for Travellers and that the State had committed adequate financial resources to that end, the overall timeframe of implementation of the government initiatives was characterised by significant delays, making Travellers more prone to forced evictions without provision of alternative accommodation. Furthermore, the ECSR ascertained that forced evic-tions of Bulgarian and Romanian Roma continued to take place, in viola-tion of the Charter.

Implementation

In its resolutions regarding the first three collective complaints (namely nos. 33/2006, 39/2006 and 51/2008) the Committee of Ministers merely took note of the ECSR's decisions and called upon the French govern-ment to both adequately implement the measures it had in the meantime announced as well as keep the Committee regularly informed regarding all pertinent developments. In sharp contrast to the Greek government, the French delegation presented to the Committee of Ministers a wealth of information regarding the concrete policy measures it had already or was in the course of adopting in order to conform to the ECSR's findings, while it was also much more deferential in its criticism of the ECSR. Moreover, the ECSR's decisions came at a moment when the French state was put-ting through its paces a groundbreaking piece of legislation, namely the Enforceable Right to Housing (Loi DALO).[31] It was therefore rather logi-cal that the French government be provided with some breathing space in order to overhaul its housing policies and legislation, including *inter alia* in the field of housing of Roma/Travellers.

[31] Law No. 2007–290 of 5 March 2007, known as Loi DALO (Droit au Logement Opposable; Law on Enforceable Right to Housing).

What was, however, rather surprising (although admittedly rather foreseeable) was the Committee of Ministers' failure to adopt a recommendation or voice its concern regarding the collective complaint filed by COHRE, particularly the mass evictions and resulting expulsions of Roma migrants from France. Moreover, considering the strong terms employed by the ECSR (that characterised the violations as an 'aggravated violation of human rights'), it would legitimately have been expected that the Committee of Ministers would have reflected at least some of the ESCR strong criticism of the French state's overtly discriminatory policies in its resolution. Instead, the Committee of Ministers once again merely took cognisance of the ECSR's report and called upon the French authorities to inform it at a forthcoming meeting of the measures undertaken to address the ECSR's findings. It should therefore come as no surprise that the Committee of Ministers also failed to adopt a recommendation in relation to the two subsequent collective complaints (nos. 64/2011 and 67/2011). Summarising, the resolutions of the Committee of Ministers regarding Greece and France gives the impression that the Committee seems to downplay, if not actually ignore, the findings of the ECSR. And while clearly its composition, if not its very name, should be enough in order to lower one's expectations regarding its potential as an effective implementation monitoring mechanism, this state of affairs also undermines the effectiveness of the European Social Charter itself and ultimately constitutes a disincentive for member states to comply with their obligations under the Charter.

13.4 European Court of Human Rights: Housing Jurisprudence

The ECtHR is the final arbiter of the compliance of a member state with its obligations flowing under the European Convention of Human Rights. Nevertheless, until the coming into effect of Protocol 14 that introduced wide-ranging changes to the Convention, the supervision of its judgments was the exclusive prerogative of the Committee of Ministers – the same body that adopts resolutions in respect of collective complaints under the European Social Charter/Revised European Charter referred to earlier – to which member states had to submit outlines of the individual and general measures they intended to adopt and implement in order to address the Court's findings in its judgements and ensure that similar violations do not occur in the future. In contrast to the proceedings before the Committee of Ministers under the European Social Charter, applicants and their advocates have a role, albeit limited, to play, namely by providing input to the Committee as to the effectiveness of the measures adopted by the respondent state, thereby allowing for a more comprehensive exchange of information and the forming of a better picture of compliance. Until recently, the most practical as well as publicly visible way the Committee could express its dissatisfaction with the measures undertaken towards the execution of a judgment was the issuing of an interim resolution criticising and urging the receiving member state to duly undertake all the necessary measures to that end. While it is true that the Committee of Ministers has to this date avoided issuing interim resolutions in any of the Roma housing cases referred to in the pages that follow (but has threatened to do so in one case, a much promising and welcome development), it has kept them open for review thereby at least exerting some pressure on member states. Following the entry into force of Protocol 14, the Court can now also be brought to bear in the implementation phase: the Committee might, following a two-thirds vote of its representatives, either seek an interpretative ruling regarding the terms of a judgment or launch infringement proceedings against a state if it considers that it has failed to abide by its obligations in executing a judgment (OSJI, 2010: 48–49).

Turning to the development of the Court's approach to Roma/Travellers housing cases, its jurisprudence cannot be considered without discussing the early string of cases brought by Gypsies and Travellers against the United Kingdom. An overview of the Court's jurisprudence is therefore apposite before embarking on the presentation of the two case studies concerning other states. Moreover, as the European Convention on Human Rights does not provide for a right to housing, it is useful to discuss the Court's derivation of a qualified housing entitlement, which was made possible only through persistent litigation as well as by the adoption by the Court of a more comprehensive and contextual approach to the issue of housing in general and for Roma and Travellers in particular. This incremental approach ultimately led to the seminal case of *Winterstein and Others v. France*, where the Court found among others a violation of Article 8 on grounds of lack of availability of culturally adequate housing.[32]

13.4.1   *The UK Gypsy and Travellers Cases*

The Court was first seized of the housing problems faced by Roma/ Travellers in the United Kingdom. Although all (save one) applications

---

[32] Appl. no. 27013/07 ECHR 17 October 2013.

were ultimately rejected, they nevertheless constitute evolutionary milestones in the Court's approach to Roma and Travellers' housing cases.

The first applications to reach the Court were those of *Jones v. the UK*[33]
and *Smith and Others v. the UK*.[34] In the former, the Commission (as it
then was) found that the authorities' refusal to grant planning permission
to the applicant to station his caravan on a plot of land he owned constituted a legitimate and proportionate interference with his rights, particularly so in light of the view that the competent authorities had proceeded
to a careful examination of this request and adduced cogent reasons for
their decision. In the latter, the applicants complained over the paucity of
adequate Gypsy sites in the area where they lived and the lack of effective
remedies to challenge this. The Commission held that while in principle
the traditional lifestyle of a minority attracts the protection afforded by
Article 8, the applicants' complaints touched upon questions of policy and
public administration, issues that the Commission was rather ill-suited to
address. In view of the due deference that should be had to the authorities' discretion in addressing such issues, together with evidence that the
authorities had taken into consideration the applicants' situation, the
Commission held that these allegations were ill-founded.

Subsequent applicants fared no better,[35] but their applications gave the
Court the opportunity to further elaborate on its approach to Gypsy and
Travellers' housing issues. Thus the Court reaffirmed in these cases that
caravans stationed without the requisite planning permission constituted
homes for the purposes of Article 8 and therefore came within its protective ambit. The Court also considered that states are under an obligation to
facilitate the 'Gypsy way of life'.[36] It also intimated that it will be willing to
review its jurisprudence on themes where a pan-European consensus can

---

[33] Appl. no. 14837/89 ECHR 7 May 1990. There was in fact an even earlier case which the
Court, following the applicant's withdrawal from the proceedings owing to the granting of
a planning permission he sought in the meantime, struck the case off its list. See *Drake v the
U.K.*, Appl. no. 11748/85 ECHR 7 May 1990.

[34] Appl. no. 14455/88 ECHR 4 September 1991.

[35] See *Chapman v. United Kingdom*, Appl. no. 27238/95; *Beard v. United Kingdom*, Appl.
no. 24882/94; *Coster v. United Kingdom*, Appl. no. 24876/94; *Lee v. United Kingdom*, Appl.
no. 25289/94; *Jane Smith v. United Kingdom*, Appl. no. 25154/94. All five cases were joined
by the Grand Chamber that delivered its judgment on 18 January 2001.

[36] *Chapman v. United Kingdom*, paragraph 96: '... As intimated in *Buckley*, the vulnerable
position of Gypsies as a minority means that some special consideration should be given to
their needs and their different lifestyle both in the relevant regulatory planning framework
and in reaching decisions in particular cases ... To this extent, there is thus a positive obligation imposed on the Contracting States by virtue of Article 8 to facilitate the Gypsy way
of life.'

be held to have emerged.[37] A very important (and often overlooked) aspect of these judgments relate to the Court's holding that in cases of eviction, the availability and provision by the authorities of alternative accommodation are countervailing factors that should be taken into account when assessing the proportionality of the interference,[38] thereby suggesting that an eviction not accompanied by provision of alternative accommodation might run counter to Article 8. The Court has reaffirmed this approach in subsequent Gypsies and Travellers cases.[39]

Turning to the in-depth case studies, we have opted to present first two Roma/Travellers housing cases that sit at the opposite ends of the spectrum, both in terms of the gravity of the violations ascertained by the Court as well as the breadth and scope of the implementation measures that were called for under the Court's judgments. This analysis is followed by a discussion of the recent *Yordanova and Others v. Bulgaria case* which arguably draws together many of the threads in this chapter.

13.4.1   Security of Tenure of Gypsies/Travellers in Local Authorities' Sites

The first successful Gypsy/Traveller case to be brought before the Court was that of *Connors v. the UK.*[40] The applicant, a Gypsy, was evicted from a local authority site on which he and his family resided for many years, under a summary eviction procedure that was not conditional on the prior securing of a judicial decision on the merits of the case but was essentially automatic in certain cases prescribed by law. The Court commenced by

---

[37] Ibid., at paragraph 70.
[38] *Chapman v. United Kingdom*, paragraph 103: 'A further relevant consideration, to be taken into account in the first place by the national authorities, is that if no alternative accommodation is available the interference is more serious than where such accommodation is available. The more suitable the alternative accommodation is, the less serious is the interference constituted by moving the applicant from his or her existing accommodation.' The Court ultimately held that alternative sites were available to the applicant and that she had failed to adduce before the Court any special considerations that prevented her from availing herself of them.
[39] See *Codona v. United Kingdom*, Appl. no. 485/05 ECHR 7 February 2006. For a similar case regarding French Travellers (Gens du Voyage), see *Gabriel Louis Stenegry et Mme Sonia Adam c. France*, Appl. no. 40987/05 ECHR 22 May 2007. In both cases, the Court held that the authorities had in fact provided the applicants (a British Gypsy and French Travellers respectively) with adequate alternative accommodation following their eviction and as a result no violation of Article 8 arose, even though the accommodation provided did not fully satisfy their needs for culturally adequate housing.
[40] Connors v. United Kingdom, (Application no. 66746/01), ECHR 27 May 2004.

noting that the applicant and his family did not enjoy any security of tenure (under domestic law applicable to Travellers living on such sites, as they were considered as licensees rather than as tenants). It then added, that had Mr Connors been living in any other form of housing his eviction would require a judicial sanction, and yet no justification was put forward for this difference in treatment. The Court held that the applicant's eviction was not attended by any due process safeguards and was therefore in breach of Article 8's procedural limb.[41]

To turn to the implementation of the *Connors* judgment, it was only in April 2011 and only in relation to England that the relevant legislation (in the form of Section 318 of the Housing and Regeneration Act 2008) brought the legal status of local authority sites in line with similar forms of housing (namely homes covered under the Mobile Homes Act 1983), a proposal already made by the Parliamentary Joint Committee of Human Rights in 2005 (Joint Committee on Human Rights, 2007: chapter 7). Section 318 would come into effect in relation to Wales on 10 July 2013.

In 2013, the Committee of Ministers closed its supervision of the implementation of the *Connors* case, noting that it would continue supervision of its execution vis-à-vis Wales in the context of the *Buckland* judgment (for all intents and purposes, a case identical to *Connors* but concerning the eviction of a Traveller in Wales);[42] Thus, in the end, it would be only in November 2013 that the Committee of Ministers would effectively fully conclude its supervision of the execution of the *Connors* judgment.[43] In other words, it took the UK government a full nine years to adopt the necessary (and relatively straightforward) measures to comply with the Court's findings in *Connors* whereas for more than two years Travellers in Wales were afforded with a lower level of protection to that of Travellers in England.[44] Even worse, one has reason to suspect that it would have taken

---

[41] Appl. no. 66746/01, 27 May 2004. The Court placed significant emphasis on the fact that the applicant was living in a lawfully established site, thus distinguishing the case from the previous 'Gypsy' cases where the applicants had settled on a plot of land in full knowledge that they were in breach of planning regulations.

[42] App. no. 40060/08, ECHR 18 September 2012.

[43] Resolution CM/ResDH(2013) 237, adopted on 20 November 2013, available at: http://hudoc.echr.coe.int/.

[44] In all fairness, it should be noted that some other measures were instituted in the meantime; thus, for example, following legislative amendments the courts could stay the enforcement of an eviction order for up to twelve months. As the Court found in *Buckland* however, this did not constitute an effective (and Article 8-compliant) remedy insofar as it did not allow the applicant to challenge the proportionality of the eviction order but merely suspended one's eviction. App. no. 40060/08, ECHR 18 September 2012, at paragraph 68.

longer had it not been for the active and persistent lobbying and advocacy by Travellers' organisations and their supporters (Johnson et al., 2010).

13.4.2 The Romanian Roma Pogrom Cases

These cases concern the virulent anti-Roma pogroms that took place in the early 1990s in Romania, resulting in the killing of Roma and widespread destruction of their houses and possessions.[45] For present purposes these cases can be divided into two groups: the first comprises cases that were concluded by means of a friendly settlement[46] or were struck out by the Court on the basis of a unilateral declaration by the Romanian government[47] acknowledging multiple violations of the Convention, and the second consists effectively of a sole case that was examined by the Court following contentious proceedings.[48] In the latter, the Court found *inter alia* violations of Articles 3 and 8 of the Convention on grounds of the appalling living conditions and discrimination experienced by the applicants[49] following the destruction of their houses by an angry mob, with the acquiescence of the police. In relation to all cases, the Romanian government undertook to implement a number of general measures, in order to both provide full redress to the applicants and to ensure that similar incidents would not take place in the future.

In order to discharge their obligations under the judgment in the *Moldovan 1 and 2* cases, the Government devised a socio-economic action plan entitled 'Program for the Community Development of Hădăreni 2006–2008' (commonly referred to as the 'Hădăreni Program') while a

---

[45] For a more personal account of the immediate aftermath of the 1993 events as well as the Romanian government's persistent failure to provide adequate reparation to the victims, see interview by human rights activist István Haller entitled 'Destroyed houses a lot of confused people', available at: www.errc.org/blog/destroyed-houses-and-a-lot-of-confused-people/67.

[46] *Moldovan and Others v. Romania* (No.1, friendly settlement), Appl. nos. 41138/98 and 64320/01 ECHR 5 July 2005.

[47] *Kalanyos and Others v. Romania* (striking out), Appl. no. 57884/00 ECHR 26 April 2007, *Gergely v. Romania* (striking out), Appl. no. 57885/00 ECHR 26 April 2007, *Tănase and Others v. Romania* (striking out), Appl. no. 62954/00 ECHR 26 May 2009.

[48] *Moldovan and Others v. Romania* (No.2), Appl. nos. 41138/98 and 64320/01 ECHR 12 July 2005.

[49] Ibid., paragraph 113: 'In the light of the above, the Court finds that the applicants' living conditions and the racial discrimination to which they have been publicly subjected by the way in which their grievances were dealt with by the various authorities, constitute an interference with their human dignity which, in the special circumstances of this case, amounted to "degrading treatment" within the meaning of Article 3 of the Convention.'

similar program was to be implemented in the framework of execution of the *Gergely, Kalanyos et al* and *Tănase and Others* judgments. The programs encompassed a series of initiatives, ranging from the promotion of economic development, awareness-raising and anti-discrimination activities for public officials and non-Roma communities, to the provision/ rehabilitation of housing and infrastructure construction.

To turn to the most emblematic of the cases and the more ambitious program to be implemented, namely the Hădăreni program, it is safe to say that the original program that was scheduled to be concluded in 2009 failed to meet even its most basic objectives due to a combination of bureaucratic inertia and inefficient management rather than due to lack of funding. As a result of its palpable failure, amply documented in successive submissions filed by the ERRC and the Romanian Roma NGO Romani CRISS before the Committee of Ministers,[50] the program was repeatedly revised. Only in March 2016 did the Committee of Ministers conclude that the Romanian Government had fully implemented the Court's judgments.[51] It is interesting to note that in reaching its assessment, the Committee of Ministers carried out an in-depth evaluation of the different measures implemented by the Romanian Government. It also paid particular attention to the establishment by the Romanian Government of an ad hoc supervisory mechanism tasked with monitoring and assessing the effectiveness of the numerous on-going initiatives to the benefit of the Roma undertaken by the authorities in the fields of employment and conflict prevention, as well as the involvement of civil society in these monitoring activities. It would therefore appear that the Committee of Ministers decided to close the supervision of the implementation of the judgments only when it was convinced that the Romanian Government had fully assumed the ownership of the domestic program by adopted a well thought-out Action Plan and setting up a monitoring mechanism.

This sudden outburst of activity on the part of the Romanian Government sits ill at ease with the rather relaxed approach it has adopted in the past. We believe that the main reason behind this shift can be traced back in December 2014, when the Committee of Ministers condemned in very harsh terms the Romanian government's sluggishness; in particular,

---

[50] For an overview of the domestic proceedings as well as an updated evaluation of the government's initiatives see the two NGOs latest Memorandum submitted to the Committee of Ministers in June 2015, available at https://search.coe.int/cm/Pages/result_details .aspx?Reference=DH-DD(2015)600.

[51] Resolution CM/ResDH(2016) 39, adopted on 10 March 2016, available at: http://hudoc .echr.coe.int/.

the Committee 'deplored the significant and persistent delay' in the effective execution of the judgments and issued an ultimatum to the Romanian government, instructing the Committee's Secretariat that in the absence of 'concrete substantial progress' until the next review in June 2015, the latter should prepare a draft of the interim resolution. Such interim resolutions are adopted when the Committee of Ministers wants to express its concern or make suggestions regarding the execution of a judgement.[52] Although, as discussed, the Committee of Ministers ultimately concluded in March 2016 that the Romanian Government had fully executed the judgments and hence the interim resolution was not put to a vote, let alone adopted, such displays of assertiveness by the Committee towards recalcitrant members states cannot but be welcomed even if they are rare.

13.4.3   Yordanova: A Paradigmatic Case

Yordanova and Others v. Bulgaria[53] is a truly groundbreaking case which conceptually brought together different normative and interpretative strands and approaches from all the judgments referred to earlier and concerned the pending eviction of a Roma community that had settled in a locality of Sofia, Bulgaria, in the early 1960s. Squatting on municipal property, the Roma had proceeded to build their houses without first securing the necessary town planning permissions and which, as a result, were not connected to the public utilities networks. The local municipality decided to evict them, and following an unsuccessful judicial challenge by the applicants, the latter lodged an application with the Court.

In what was in itself a very important development, the Court ordered interim measures under Rule 39 of the Rules of the Court and requested them to suspend the execution of the final domestic court decision authorising the eviction of the applicants, pending the proceedings before the Court. This was in fact the first time that the Court made use of its power to grant interim relief under Rule 39 in a housing and evictions context.[54] It is worth noting here that this development was echoed by other international judicial/quasi-judicial bodies: on 15 November 2010, the

---

[52] Council of Europe, Committee of Ministers, 1214DH meeting of the Ministers' Deputies, 4 December 2014, Decision cases no. 15, Moldovan group against Romania, available at www.coe.int/en/web/execution/home.

[53] Appl. no. 25446/06 ECHR 24 April 2012.

[54] Rule 39 measures are usually indicated in cases of pending extradition/expulsion to countries where the applicant might be tortured or even killed.

Inter-American Commission on Human Rights (IACHR) granted precautionary measures and called upon the Haitian authorities to refrain from forcibly evicting IDPs from their camps as well as to provide adequate shelter to those who had already been evicted.[55] Similarly, on 8 July 2011, the UN HRC requested from the Bulgarian government to desist from forcibly evicting the Dobri Jeliazkov Roma community, pending examination of the communication to the Committee.[56] Moreover, when the local authorities attempted to coerce the Roma into vacating their settlement by cutting off their water supply, the Committee issued on 9 May 2012 an additional interim injunction, by which it reminded the Bulgarian authorities of the previous one and directed them to re-establish the supply of running water to the community.[57]

To return to the *Yordanova and Others* case, the Court in its judgment highlighted the plight and the vulnerable position of the applicants and noted that despite the housing policy measures and initiatives adopted by the Bulgarian government towards improving the life of the Roma in Bulgaria, the applicants had not benefitted from such programmes. This weighed heavily in the Court's finding that their eviction would have been disproportionate and in violation of Article 8. In its judgment, the Court also referred to a previous collective complaint lodged by the *European Roma Rights Centre v. Bulgaria* (Coll. Compl. No. 31/2005), in which the ECSR had noted among others that the simple guarantee of equal treatment as the means of protection against discrimination does not suffice and that the integration of the Roma minority requires the adoption of positive action measures. Although the Court, in line with its jurisprudence, refrained from explicitly holding that Article 8 also included an entitlement to be provided with housing, it nonetheless held that such an obligation could arise, in exceptional cases, when it was necessary to secure shelter to 'particularly vulnerable individuals'. The Court was also

---

[55] For a summary of the case and the interim relief granted, see case *PM 367-10 – Forced Evictions from Five Camps for Displaced Persons, Haiti*, Inter-American Commission on Human Rights, 15 November 2010.

[56] The Committee's Interim Measure is available here: Human Rights Treaties Division, Letter to Mr Thiele and Ms Mihailova, 8 July 2011, http://globalinitiative-escr.org/wp-content/uploads/2012/05/Human-Rights-Committee-intervention-Interim-Measures.pdf. The authors would like to express their thanks to Bret Thiele, Global Initiative for Economic, Social and Cultural Rights co-executive director and co-representative of the petitioners before the Committee for sharing background information as well as his insights on this case.

[57] Human Rights Treaties Division Letter to Ms Mihailova and Mr Thiele 9 May 2012, available at http://globalinitiative-escr.org/wp-content/uploads/2012/05/Human-Rights-Committee-intervention-Access-to-Water.pdf.

highly critical of the authorities' failure to adopt a more proportionate approach in the context of the case: the authorities had, for example, failed to examine whether alternative accommodation could be provided to the applicants, whether they could have been provided with social housing or whether any of the Roma houses could be regularised. Of particular interest was the Court's holding under Article 46, in which it called upon the Bulgarian authorities to either repeal the final domestic decision calling for the applicants' eviction or to suspend it pending their housing rehabilitation.

A sociological analysis and interpretation of the Bulgarian government's arguments (for they clearly could not be considered as valid, or at least tenable, legal arguments) in the case of *Yordanova and Others* bears stark testimony to the reticence of the Bulgarian government to abide by its international obligations and of the deep marginalisation of Roma in Bulgaria. Despite the manifold commitments of the Bulgarian government to improve the housing conditions of the Roma and the need to adopt affirmative measures to that end (as highlighted by the ECSR in its 2006 decision on the collective complaint No. 31/2005 *European Roma Rights Centre v. Bulgaria*), the Government did not find it incongruous to claim before the Court that adopting positive action measures in favour of the Roma would amount to 'privileged' treatment (notwithstanding that, for example, the regularisation of illegal dwellings was also foreseen for ethnic Bulgarians) and would amount to discrimination against the majority population. The Bulgarian government also unequivocally expressed themselves in favour of the local non-Roma residents (who had repeatedly called for the Roma's eviction and engaged in typical anti-Roma invective, accusing them collectively of various infractions and requesting that they be sent back where they came from), noting that the case before the Court was effectively a dispute between the lawful residents of the neighbourhood and the applicants who trespassed on municipal land and 'whose way of life is in contradiction with public norms and rules and in this sense generates tensions in society'.[58] The Bulgarian government would go even further than that, calling upon the Court to take into consideration in its deliberations that a finding of a violation of the Convention would send 'a wrong message' to the rest of the Bulgarian society which expected the law to be applied to all equally.

Although one can only speculate at this point in time, the preceding arguments clearly suggest that the Bulgarian government will only

---

[58] Appl. no. 25446/06 ECHR 24 April 2012, at paragraph 97.

grudgingly, if at all, fully implement the Court's judgment, primarily because they do not appear convinced of the need, let alone of their moral duty, to integrate Roma into mainstream society by *inter alia* addressing their housing conditions, something that would necessitate the combating of racist stereotypes and prejudice against Roma that are present in Bulgarian society. Thus even after the *Yordanova* judgment, evictions of Roma under conditions and circumstances similar to the ones obtaining in *Yordanova* have continued unabated[59] amidst a virulently anti-Roma public discourse in the run-up to the local elections,[60] forcing NGOs to turn once again to the European Court with a Rule 39 request for the suspension of the evictions.[61]

Indeed, a cynic would observe that in terms of a purely Machiavellian political cost-effectiveness calculus, the Bulgarian government (or any other government for that matter) would incur more losses if they try to abide by their obligations regarding unpopular groups such as the Roma rather than by flouting international tribunals' rulings issued against them. This is all the more the case if one bears in mind that Roma are not simply an unpopular minority group; they are *the* most unpopular minority group. According to the 2015 Pew Research Survey, Roma continue to be the most despised minority, with 86 per cent of Italians polled holding an unfavourable view of them.[62] One need to contrast this with the Italian

---

[59] See Romea Cz article: 'Bulgaria: Roma blockade demolition of their homes, riot police intervene', dated 22 July 2014, available at www.romea.cz/en/news/bulgaria-roma-blockade-demolition-of-their-homes-riot-police-intervene, BBC article: 'Bulgaria tensions lead to Roma home demolitions', dated 21 July 2015, available at www.bbc.com/news/world-europe-33597660. See also Bulgarian Helsinki Press Release, 'Leaving Garmen families homeless is a racist campaign that breaches three international treaties ratified by Bulgaria', 3 July 2015, available at: www.bghelsinki.org/en/news/press/single/press-release-leaving-garmen-families-homeless-racist-campaign-breaches-three-international-treaties-ratified-bulgaria/.

[60] Roma Cz article: 'Bulgaria: Nationalists exert political pressure to override suspension of Romani home demolitions', 22 July 2015, available at www.romea.cz/en/news/world/bulgaria-nationalists-exert-political-pressure-to-override-suspension-of-romani-home-demolitions.

[61] *Aydarov and Others v. Bulgaria*, appl. no. 33586/15. On 10 July 2015, the European Court addressed a letter to the Bulgarian authorities, informing them that unless they provided alternative accommodation to the vulnerable members of the Roma community in question, then it would grant applicants' Rule 39 request and suspend the eviction. The letter is on file with the authors. It would appear that the authorities decided to disregard the Court's injunction and proceeded with the evictions: see Amnesty International Urgent Action Appeal *Bulgaria: Hundreds of Roma at risk of forced eviction*, dated 30 July 2015, available at www.amnesty.org/en/documents/eur15/2199/2015/en/.

[62] Pew Research Center, *Faith in European Project Reviving*, 2 June 2015, chapter 3, available at: www.pewglobal.org/2015/06/02/chapter-3-anti-minority-sentiment-not-rising/.

public's perception of the LGBT community; in the recent judgment of *Oliari and Others v. Italy* on legal recognition of same-sex relationships, the Court took into consideration the popular acceptance of homosexual couples in Italian society as well as the support for their recognition and protection.[63] It will be quite some time before the Court will be in a position to reach similar findings in relation to Roma in Italy.

13.5   Conclusion: From Strategic Litigation to Total (Legal) War?

With this cursory look at compliance with the decisions of international tribunals concerning Roma and Travellers housing, the following salient points appear to emerge. First, the groundbreaking jurisprudential developments render it beyond any doubt that at least under particular circumstances and in relation to certain vulnerable groups, the social right to housing is fully justiciable while various civil rights also incorporate various housing rights.

Second, only rarely will states invoke purely financial reasons as responsible for the failure to adequately implement housing policies for the Roma; neither Greece nor France, for example, attributed before the ECSR the lack of progress in securing adequate housing for the Roma/Travellers to the dearth of funds; if anything else, their submissions are replete with references to past and projected expenditures that are presented as evidence of their commitment in tackling the issue. To this, one should add that EU member states can also draw significant funds from relevant EU budget lines, thereby easing the pressure on domestic budgets: following the recent (2010) amendment of the European Regional Development Fund (ERDF) regulation, more EU funds are now available for housing and infrastructure of marginalised Roma communities (Europa, 2010) while recently the EU Commission stated rather self-assuredly that 'The amount of EU funding available for Roma inclusion will not be a constraint' (EU Commission, 2015: 7). And although clearly addressing the housing predicament of Roma and Travellers is a resources-intensive and time-consuming undertaking (all the more against the backdrop of the present economic crisis), it should not be forgotten that even countries that face severe financial hardship are enjoined under international law to adopt relatively low-cost-targeted programmes for the most vulnerable members of society in order to meet the bare minimum obligation

---

[63] [GC], Appl. nos. 18766/11 and 36030/11 ECHR 21 July 2015, at paragraph 181.

of providing basic shelter/housing – an obligation incumbent on the state regardless of their financial resources. Such measures could simply consist of abstaining from certain practices and facilitating 'self-help' for affected groups.[64]

If respecting, protecting and fulfilling the housing rights of the Roma/ Travellers is therefore a legal and justiciable obligation incumbent on states that can be achieved in a financially viable manner, one could legitimately inquire as to why states appear to be reticent to do so; all the more so since CoE member states as a general rule tend to more readily comply with the European Court's judgments issued against them (OSJI, 2010: 52), even when there are awards for significant damages on account of pecuniary and non-pecuniary losses. Could it be that states are concerned that their compliance with the international tribunals' decisions regarding Roma and Travellers housing might adversely affect their other interests and if so, what could these interests be or how deeply seated are they, to the degree of leading a state to disregard decisions handed down by international courts?

In our view, the real operative reason behind this persisting failure is none other than the social unpopularity of and deeply entrenched prejudice against the Roma and Travellers in virtually all the CoE member states. Although clearly Roma and Travellers are far from being the only unpopular ethnic/national minority groups in the EU/CoE and while judgments handed down concerning the rights of other unpopular ethnic/national minority groups (such as, for example, the Turks and Macedonians in Greece, the Kurds in Turkey or Macedonians in Bulgaria) are also characterised by rather low rates of implementation (Grozev, 2009; Sitaropoulos, 2011), what is striking is that virtually all the judgments and decisions regarding Roma/Travellers referred to earlier contain ample evidence that institutional or institutionalised racism and prejudice, present in all countries against which judgments were issued and particularly virulent at the local government level, against the Roma. They are not forcibly evicted or persecuted from the homes primarily because they are squatting or trespassing but because they are Roma and not members of any other ethnic group that is tolerated, if not favoured, by the domestic societies.

In the case of Greece, for example, the authorities have for a number of years been implementing a highly successful program for the housing of Greek repatriates from the former USSR. Nevertheless, the equivalent

---

[64] See Committee on Economic, Social and Cultural Rights, *General Comment 3, The nature of States Parties obligations* (Fifth session, 1990) U.N. Doc. E/1991/23 (1991).

program for the Roma has been palpably ineffective, although it has been generously funded. The authors contend that the causes of the program's failure outlined by the ECSR (for example, the refusal of local authorities to implement housing projects for the Roma) are in effect not the real causes of its failure but the symptoms of a deeply-entrenched discriminatory public (and ultimately espoused by the authorities) perception against the Roma who are not viewed as equal members of the Greek society (as the Greek repatriates are) but rather as foreigners who do not really have a claim to protection by the State.[65]

The findings of a joint research by the EU's Fundamental Rights Agency (FRA) and the United Nations' Development Programme (UNDP) on Roma/Travellers exclusion in 11 EU member states, encompassing both old and new EU members (FRA, 2012), amply corroborate the aforesaid. In the words of one of the leading researchers, 'EU membership *per se* is no recipe for success. Roma are similarly excluded in new and old Member States. Significant variations between countries exist but the difference between "successful" and "unsuccessful" doesn't run along a new-old member states divide. The practical implication is clear: Roma inclusion is an EU-wide priority.'[66] Echoing these remarks, the European Commission, after taking stock of the national action plans adopted and implemented by EU Member states, noted in 2016 that despite some positive trends, the measures implemented did not manage to forestall a further deterioration of the living conditions of Roma or check the 'widespread hostility of majority societies'. The European Commission identified the lack of commitment to Roma integration at the local level as one of the main reasons behind the lack of real progress and called for a "political recommitment to Roma integration" (EU Commission, 2016:20).

Should this be taken to mean that strategic litigation in this as well as similar fields is a rather pointless, purely academic exercise? The answer

---

[65] As noted by a senior member of the Greek Ombudsman's office, 'It is interesting here, to consider that the generous housing, land, work and loan programs directed to Greek Pontians from the ex USSR have never been provided to this extent also for thousands of Roma, formally Greek citizens, the living conditions of whom till today represents a "social emergency". This fact insinuates that there is not a very visible but implicit indicator for planning public policies, the "Greekness", which practically serves as a subjective instrument of social classification.' See Pavlou, Miltos (2002) 'Greek state policy from "irredentism" to "home-coming"/"immigration": the case of two repatriated kin minority groups', available in English at www.kemo.gr/gr/index.asp.

[66] See article UNDP Voices from Eurasia (2012), 'Roma Excluded from Society: Q&A with Andrey Ivanov', Blog, available at http://europeandcis.undp.org/blog/2012/05/24/roma-excluded-from-society-qa-with-andrey-ivanov/.

to that question will depend on one's expectations regarding the goals that can be achieved by means of litigation before international bodies. Empirical research on the implementation of European Court of Human Rights judgment suggests that the adoption of judgments by the Court (and especially in relation to unpopular groups, such as LGBT individuals or unpopular ethnic/national minorities) (Grozev, 2009; Sitaropoulos, 2011) cannot by itself produce legal and policy change at the domestic level unless domestic actors, sometimes for their own and very divergent reasons, are determined to make effective use of all the means at their disposal, including international court judgments, as instruments to that end (Çalı and Wyss, 2009: 27; Helfer and Voeten, 2011). In the absence of such a consensus among domestic actors, international litigation has indeed rather little to offer in terms of reshaping public perceptions but will continue to constitute the only means of last resort available to Roma and their advocates to safeguard and defend their housing rights, if not by promoting them (in the sense of ensuring the provision of adequate housing) then at least by preventing the further degradation of their living conditions. The post-*Yordanova* increasing number of interim measures indicated by international tribunals requesting states to suspend the eviction of Roma[67] or non-Roma[68] applicants pending review of their complaints suggests that legal advocates are becoming increasingly aware of these tools and do not hesitate to use them. In light of this, the authors consider that the need has arisen to shift from focusing on a select few strategic litigation cases – all the more since the relevant standards have already been set out and elaborated upon in landmark cases such as *Yordanova* and *Winterstein*. Rather, what is required is the

---

[67] In addition to the cases already referred to above, see UN HRC, *Cultural Association of Greek Gypsies Originating from Halkida and Suburbs "I Elpida"* No. 2242/2013 (in the context of which communication the UN HRC issued four interim injunctions), UN HRC *Kosturi and Others v. Albania* No. 2438/2014, UN HRC *Shabani and Others v. Albania*, No. 2444/2014 and Mr. Stylianos Kalamiotis, No. 2242/2013. All communications are currently pending, Additionally, the European Court recently granted another two interim requests asking for the suspension of eviction of Roma in Italy and Romania. See the relevant ERRC press releases, "European Court issues emergency measure to stop Italy from evicting Roma family", dated 25 March 2016, available at: www.errc.org/article/european-court-issues-emergency-measure-to-stop-italy-from-evicting-roma-family/4468 and "In Second Emergency Order in a Week, European Court Temporarily halts Eviction of Roma", dated 31 March 2016, available at: www.errc.org/article/in-second-emergency-order-in-a-week-european-court-temporarily-halts-eviction-of-roma/4469.

[68] See *Raji and Others v. Spain* (dec), appl. no. 3537/13 ECHR 16 December 2014, *A.M.B. c. Espagne* (dec), appl. no. 778412 ECHR 28 January 2014, and *Ceesay Ceesay and Others v. Spain*, appl. no. 62688/13, pending.

undertaking of a veritable legal campaign consisting of the launching of as many legal proceedings on housing as possible, before both domestic and international tribunals, with a view to 'carpet-bombing' (if another military metaphor can be excused) states with cases. It is interesting in this respect to note that even the European Commission has acknowledged that 'Real change often requires a critical mass of cases'[69] while the UN Special Rapporteur on minority issues recently observed that, considering the significant disadvantages and marginalisation experienced by Roma in Europe, there are relatively few cases brought before the European Court.[70] Perhaps the adage that quantity has a quality all of its own is apposite also in this context.

References

Çalı, Başak and Alice Wyss (2009), 'Why Do Democracies Comply with Human Rights Judgments? A Comparative Analysis of the UK, Ireland and Germany', United Kingdom Economic and Social Research Council Project on the 'Legitimacy and Authority of Supranational Human Rights Courts: A Comparative Analysis of the European Court of Human Rights', Grant No: RES-061-25-0029.

Council of Europe (2012), *Human Rights of Roma and Travellers in Europe* (Strasbourg: Council of Europe).

(2014), *State of Democracy, Human Rights and the Rule of Law in Europe: Report by the Secretary General of the Council of Europe (Strasbourg: Council of Europe).*

Europa (2010), 'EU Adopts New Measures to Improve Housing Conditions of Roma Communities', Press Release, Brussels 20 May http://europa.eu/rapid/press-release_IP-10-589_en.htm.

European Commission (2016), *Communication from the Commission to the European Parliament, the Council, the European Economic and Social Committee and the Committee of the Regions*, COM (2016) 424, Brussels 27 June http://ec.europa.eu/justice/discrimination/files/roma-report-2016_en.pdf.

(2015), *Communication from the Commission to the European Parliament, the Council, the European Economic and Social Committee and the Committee of the Regions: Report on the Implementation of the EU Framework for National*

[69] European Commission, *Commission Staff Working Document – Annexes to the Joint Report on the application of the Racial Equality Directive (2000/43/EC) and the Employment Directive (2000/78/EC)*, SWD (2014)5 final, 17 January 2014, available at: http://ec.europa.eu/justice/discrimination/files/swd_2014_5_en.pdf, page 7.

[70] Report of the Special Rapporteur on minority issues, Rita Izsák, *Comprehensive study of the human rights situation of Roma worldwide, with a particular focus on the phenomenon of anti-Gypsyism*, U.N. Doc. A/HRC.29/24 (2015), available at: www.ohchr.org/Documents/Issues/IEMinorities/ProtectionRoma/A-HRC-29-24.doc, page 19.

Roma Integration Strategies 2015, Brussels 17 June http://ec.europa.eu/justice/discrimination/files/roma_communication2015_en.pdf.

FRA (2012), 'Widespread Roman Exclusion Persists, Finds New Survey', Press Release, 23 May http://fra.europa.eu/en/press-release/2012/widespread-roma-exclusion-persists-find-new-surveys.

Goldston, James A. and Mirna Adjami (2008), 'The Opportunities and Challenges of Using Public Interest Litigation to Secure Access to Justice for Roma Minorities in Central and Eastern Europe', Preliminary Draft, Subject to Revision, prepared for Vienna, World Justice Forum, 2–5 July.

Government of Wales (2012), 'The Implementation of Section 318 of the Housing and Regeneration Act 2008', Press Release, Welsh Government, 10 April.

Grozev, Yonko (2009), *Supranational Rights Litigation and the Domestic Impact of Strasbourg Court Jurisprudence on Rights of Ethnic Minorities*, Comparative Report (Sofia: Centre for Liberal Studies), http://www.eliamep.gr/old/eliamep/content/home/research/research_projects/juristras/state_of_art/en/index.html.

Helfer, Laurence and Erik Voeten (2011), 'Do European Court of Human Rights Judgments Promote Legal and Policy Change?', Working Paper http://papers.ssrn.com/sol3/papers.cfm?abstract_id=1850526.

Johnson, Chris, Andrew Ryder and Marc Willers (2010), 'Gypsies and Travellers in the United Kingdom and Security of Tenure', *ERRC Periodicals: Roma Rights 1, 2010: Implementation of Judgements*, www.errc.org/en-research-and-advocacy-roma-details.php?page=6&article_id=3613.

Joint Committee on Human Rights (2005), *Fourteenth Report* (London: UK Parliament).

OSCE, Office for Democratic Institutions and Human Rights (2008), *Implementation of the Action Plan on Improving the Situation of Roma and Sinti within the OSCE Area: Status Report 2008* (Warsaw: OSCE).

(2013), *Implementation of the Action Plan on Improving the Situation of Roma and Sinti within the OSCE Area: Status Report 2013* (Warsaw: OSCE).

OSJI, Open Society Justice Initiative (2010), *From Judgment to Justice: Implementing International and Regional Human Rights Decisions* (New York: Open Society Justice Initiative).

Sitaropoulos, Nicholas (2011), 'Implementation of the European Court of Human Rights' Judgments Concerning National Minorities or Why Declaratory Adjudication Does Not Help', Conference Paper Series, Conference Paper No. 4/2011, European Society of International Law, http://papers.ssrn.com/sol3/papers.cfm?abstract_id=1968186.

Part III

Concluding Perspectives

Solving the Problem of (Non)compliance in Social and Economic Rights Litigation

DANIEL M. BRINKS

Winning is not everything. In fact, winning a judgment from a court may just be the opening salvo in a prolonged campaign to bring economic, social and cultural rights (ESCR) to bear on the realities of a particular group or individual. On the other hand, winning is not nothing, as some skeptics have suggested. The chapters in this book present a mixed record of compliance with judicial decisions in ESCR cases around the world. The cases represent a fascinating cross-section of the sorts of demands that fall under this category, and may be used to generate some hypotheses about the conditions under which compliance is more or less likely. Table 14.1 in the appendix summarizes many of the cases discussed in the various chapters, and identifies the main contribution of these experiences to the discussion in this chapter. In what follows I will use a simplified framework to organize the variables identified as important in each of the chapters and construct a unified scheme for understanding the challenges and opportunities litigants face in making their hard-won ESCR judgments effective.

The subject matter of these cases certainly poses compliance challenges. ESCR judgments are perhaps not the hardest case for compliance – judgments that threaten the political survival of powerful political actors, among others, may be harder – but they pose nontrivial challenges to courts. They often, though not always, as Viljoen (this volume) reminds us, involve complex affirmative orders requiring governments to do difficult things they have thus far been unwilling to do, to spend money they had perhaps slated for other priorities, all, perhaps, on behalf of marginalized groups or to address a problem that has been festering for a century. They might require a government to take on a problem – such as the contamination of the Riachuelo watershed (Morales et al., this volume) – that has been two hundred years in the making, and has stymied governments for decades. The challenges of fulfilling ESCR would likely be daunting for

Daniel M. Brinks is an Associate Professor at the University of Texas at Austin.

a single bureaucracy seeking to order its own priorities and supervise its own lower ranks, let alone for one bureaucracy – the courts – seeking to reorder the priorities of another, and supervise the latter's performance.

Whether we think courts are "effective" in this context largely depends on our prior expectations. It is clear from the chapters that they are accomplishing something; it is also clear that they are accomplishing less than what ESCR advocates would like; and yet, in some ways, what is remarkable is that courts in many instances succeed at all. My goal here is not to proclaim that courts are or are not the right way to make ESCR effective but rather to offer a framework to organize the many different variables that could affect the likelihood their judgments will be implemented, including variables that are not discussed in this volume. This conceptual framework may not prove which one variable might be most important to a theory of compliance, but it should be helpful to litigators who wish to increase the likelihood that their hard-won judgments will actually make a difference, and it may be helpful to academics who are grappling with the difficult theoretical issues surrounding compliance with judicial decisions.

My starting point for a theory of compliance is loosely rationalistic, with one important exception, as we will see. The descriptions in the chapters suggest we should emphasize the decision calculus of the target of the litigation, and consider that the target will comply not out of a general conviction that compliance is the right thing but because the net cost of compliance is less than the net cost of noncompliance – or, to say the same thing in another way, because the net benefits of compliance outweigh the net benefits of noncompliance: COMPLY IF $C_c < C_d$, where C_c is the expected net cost of compliance and C_d is the expected net cost of defiance.

There are, of course, costs and benefits on both sides of the scale, so the target will be required to do a cost-benefit analysis for each side, and then weigh the net results against each other. Moreover, it may be that the target will be balancing apples and oranges – the costs and benefits of compliance and noncompliance are not necessarily symmetrical, either in the sense that we would find similar things on both sides of the scale, or in the sense that the costs to the target are equal to the benefits to the proponent. All of this suggests that the targets of litigation may not always be performing an exact, conscious calculation. Still, it seems likely that something like this is actually going on – people who lose a case in court often seem to ask themselves what it will cost to comply, and what might happen if they do not.

Compliance is the counterpart, typically, of enforcement, and many of the chapters use the terms interchangeably. Theories of systems of

social control distinguish between first-, second- and third-party-based enforcement, depending on whether the impetus comes from the obligated party (whom I will call the target), the beneficiary (herein called the proponent) or a third-party enforcement mechanism, whether state or nonstate (Brinks and Botero 2014). First-party theories of compliance tend to emphasize norm-based, voluntary compliance, or self-enforcing schemes (in which violating the rule brings its own punishment). These theories lead us to identify as the primary motors of compliance such variables as the legitimacy and features of the court (Gibson and Caldeira 1995; Gibson et al. 1998), or of the process (Tyler and Rasinski 1991), or even of meta-norms of compliance (Bergman 2009), which make it more likely that actors would voluntarily comply with an order. Second-party enforcement would focus our attention on the ability of the proponent to impose costs directly on the target, say through a boycott, or by mobilizing a political opposition to a noncomplying public official. Third-party enforcement, meanwhile, pushes us to look for mechanisms of enforcement that are external to the immediate relationship between proponent and target – say, the intervention of an ombudsman or prosecutor in a domestic system, or of another member state in an international system, or of a global "naming and shaming" community, for failure to comply.

The experiences related in the chapters of this book make clear that, in the context of ESCR judgments, there is very little unmediated first- or third-party enforcement. If the judgment is to be effective, the second party – the proponents – will have to do or threaten to do much of the work. There are a couple of instances of what we might call expansive compliance that look quite voluntary, and thus could be classified as first-party enforcement – the Costa Rican health service extended medical care to all people living with AIDS after an individual judgment, for example, and established democracies tend to comply with human rights judgments of the European Court of Human Rights even in the absence of any visible coercive pressures. While these look like voluntary compliance or first-party enforcement, we will see in the sections that follow how they too can be seen as the product of a cost-benefit analysis based on the anticipated reaction of others. The anticipated reaction can either be the reaction of the affected second parties themselves, or of third parties at the urging of the affected parties.

In addition, there is occasionally the possibility that a prosecutor (a classic, state-based, third-party enforcement agent) might file criminal charges against a noncomplying public official – see the chapters on Costa Rica, again, Brazil and Argentina. But there is little evidence that these third-party mechanisms have worked in most of the cases described in this volume, and in any event it is clear that they are triggered only if the second party motivates them, thus blurring the distinction between third- and second-party mechanisms. Compliance, at least in the costly, high-profile cases that are the primary subject matter of this book, is mostly the product of what is at best a mediated version of second-party enforcement: the rights-bearers who benefit from the judgment must be prepared to generate costs of noncompliance for the first parties, sometimes by engaging with third-party mechanisms. When the first party appears to comply voluntarily (albeit after refusing to comply and being sued initially), it seems likely to be the product of an implicit cost calculus that still depends on the possibility that the second (occasionally, the third) party will be able to bring pressure to bear on the target.

Kapiszewski and Taylor have arranged the various factors producing compliance into a framework that distinguishes attributes of the case, of the regime or the state, of the court and of the ruling (Kapiszewski and Taylor 2013). This seems useful in cataloguing the variables, but such a taxonomical framework is not meant to address the mechanism that might be at work or why the individual variables might be important. For these reasons, it seems more useful to organize our discussion here around a more dynamic framework that can help put the different variables in conversation with each other, suggesting the ways in which one sometimes trades off against another, or conditions the impact of a third, in something that resembles a cost-benefit calculus.

This simple cost-benefit model should be understood as a heuristic simplification, in order to render visible some recurring patterns that affect the likelihood of compliance, rather than as a traditional formal model or a purely rationalist, materialist, self-interest-based model. The chapters indicate that political actors' calculations typically include financial and political costs, which we could capture with a purely rationalist model. But in many cases, it seems clear that the calculations can also include an ideological or normative cost that is a function of the substantive commitments and prejudices of the actors in question, and thus something that is not a standard part of rationalist models of political behavior.

To speak of normative or ideological costs comes close, as we will see, to a more normative theory of compliance, but the narratives in the chapters suggest that it is more helpful to include these normatively grounded impulses to comply (or to defy) in the ultimate cost-benefit calculus. The case studies suggest that a meta-norm of compliance, when it exists, or a normatively rooted desire to comply with rulings that advance a particularly favored interest or group, or an ideologically based resistance to the rulings of foreign and international courts, is just one of many factors that are traded off against one another. In the various chapters, actors can sometimes be seen weighing their normative preferences against the financial or political costs of noncompliance. An exceptionally high fiscal or political price may well override the impulse to comply even for the most human rights- or rule-of-law-oriented actors. Moreover, affect can color and determine the weight of the other costs – a million dollars spent on housing for members of the dominant group may carry a lower political cost than a single dollar spent on the despised Roma. The decision whether or not to comply, then, is a function of a complex mix of often mutually interacting and crosscutting considerations.

For this reason, the case studies in this volume suggest that compliance is best understood not as a more or less automatic action, the product of a meta-norm of compliance, or habituation, for example. In fact, the case studies suggest that the dominant considerations, especially in important structural ESCR cases, are case-specific rather than the product of diffuse support for a court (Caldeira 1986; Gibson et al. 1998), the accumulated legitimacy of a court (Epstein et al. 2001) or a generalized expectation by the public that it should back the court (Carrubba 2009). This is not to deny that some societies may have such a meta-norm, whatever its origin, or that some courts may be more costly to defy given their level of public support. Rather, it is to recognize that even in such societies and for such courts there is variation in compliance across cases and over time, which seems to be the product of a decision-making process that looks a lot like the balancing of competing considerations I describe here. Such meta-variables and meta-calculations, then, are best understood within the framework I propose, as making it easier or harder to generate costs for noncompliance, rather than as a separate paradigm altogether.

I use the language of costs, simply because it seems more intuitive in the context of judicial orders which are expected to require costly compliance. But of course, as noted, there are both costs and benefits of both compliance and defiance, and what we are searching for is really the balance between the net cost (benefit) on each side of the equation. What is less clear is how different circumstances affect that cost-benefit calculus, and how advocates can strategically increase the likelihood of compliance. The introduction to this volume identifies a number of variables – characteristics of the legal, civil society and political environments – that might affect one or the other side of this inequality. I will use the more particularized findings and arguments from the chapters to explore which factors matter in which contexts, and why, with an eye to exploring what litigants can do to raise the cost of noncompliance or lower the cost of compliance without compromising on their goals. To see whether we can expect compliance in a particular case, we would have to weigh each of these factors, as applicable in that case, on both sides of the scale, and see what the calculus produces. In what follows, I do not do this for any one case. Rather, I discuss the variables separately, to highlight what and how much they might contribute to the calculus in a particular case.

At its most basic, then, the problem of compliance with judicial orders can be reduced to the simple inequality laid out earlier: we should observe compliance only if the target of the order considers that compliance would be less costly than noncompliance. COMPLY IF $C_c < C_d$. The inequality, as abstract as it is, should make one point absolutely clear for activists seeking to use the courts to change rights on the ground: The greater the "cost" of the relief requested, the more litigants must be prepared to invest in enforcement; the resources available for enforcement should be considered in deciding how costly, in political, financial and ideological terms, a remedy to ask for.

14.1 Types of Costs

The first step, of course, is to define what we mean by cost. Here, the findings in the various chapters are very useful, helping define and catalogue the types of costs, already briefly identified, that affect the compliance decision. The costs and benefits of compliance or noncompliance in these cases appear to have at least three dimensions, a purely financial or material one, a political one and what we might call a normative one, for lack of a better term. In this section I explore some of the less obvious implications of considering each of these classes of costs separately.

Financial costs: What I mean by financial costs is conceptually obvious, although it might be hard to measure empirically in particular cases, but can still use some elaboration. Sometimes the cost is self-evident, and acts as the primary motivation. A recurring objection to certain right to health awards is that the medications in question are too expensive. Surely at least one reason the Brazilian government has resisted Interamerican Court orders that would prevent construction of the massive Belo Monte dam is the anticipated loss of the expected financial benefits of building the dam. One reason individual cases in Argentina generate greater compliance than complex structural cases (Sigal et al., this volume) is because they are cheaper to satisfy. It is evidently not true, as Viljoen and Çali and

Koch forcefully argue, that ESCR cases always entail greater financial out-lays than Civil and Political Rights cases. But many ESCR cases will require great outlays of resources that targets had undoubtedly intended to des-tine for other uses. Alternatively, as in the Belo Monte case, various open-pit-mining cases, or the controversy over building a highway through the TIPNIS preserve in Bolivia, a judgment may require a government to forego the expected economic benefits of great projects, in deference to the rights of local populations to a clean environment, or to ancestral rights to land.

Moreover, not all dollars spent weigh the same. Opportunity costs mean that a dollar in fat years is not the same as a dollar in lean years, just as a dollar in New York is not the same as a dollar in Mississippi or India. The clearest example of this is the year-to-year variation in compliance with education rights rulings. Initial compliance in New York faded once an economic crisis required state governments to trade off spending on vari-ous other priorities (Shanor and Albisa, this volume). Similarly, the pro-vincial government resisted paying a multimillion-dollar award favoring women, in the NAPE decision of the Canadian Supreme Court, in years of straitened budgets, but an easing of the budgetary crisis and contin-ued political pressure led to an eventual payment (Porter, this volume). Finding the opportune moment to litigate may be as important as the actual outlay compliance would entail – although, of course, it may well be that one must litigate precisely when resources are most strained because that is when budgets are cut and social programs curtailed.

While there is, within the ESCR category, a great deal of variation in the potential expense of compliance that cannot be controlled, activists would be well advised to take into consideration ways in which they might reduce the material cost of compliance for the target of the litigation, without compromising on their goals. In Brazil's health rights litigation, plaintiffs wittingly or unwittingly ease the pain of compliance by joining local, state and national authorities as defendants, even though the former may be the only ones technically charged with providing a particular health service.

Perhaps more importantly, many of the chapters discuss the courts' occasional use of more open-ended, dialogical or deliberative orders, in which the target plays a part in designing the actual mode of compliance. There has been a great deal of debate, reflected also in the pages of this vol-ume, regarding whether dialogic, open-ended judgments aid or hamper compliance. One of the ways in which they might help with compliance is that they could allow the target to design more efficient, lower-cost ways to achieve the goals of the litigation than could be designed by a court with limited experience and information in the policy area.

One strategy many litigants and courts have employed is raising the financial costs of noncompliance, rather than trying to reduce the cost of compliance. US courts have levied fines on noncomplying agencies in prison reform litigation, for example. Among the case studies in this volume, the reality or threat of sanctions appears in several chapters. In Costa Rica, bureaucrats are subject to fines or criminal penalties for noncompliance in their individual capacity; this may be one reason why the career civil servants who are charged with spending public money on court orders appear to comply at a fairly high rate – a personal cost balanced against a cost to the state offers an easy choice (Wilson and Rodriguez, this volume). In Argentina, on the contrary, as we will see, these fines do not appear to work at all – individual bureaucrats turn over too quickly to be held personally responsible, and perhaps for the same reason do not seem to care when their agency is subject to fines (Sigal et al., this volume). The effectiveness of fines – whether personal or on the state – seems to be conditional on the existence of a stable, professionalized bureaucracy, which provides someone to actually bear the cost of the fine.

It seems reasonable to suggest that in many cases compliance with these judgments can save money over the long term. Structural decisions improving health and education outcomes should have a long-term positive impact on the economy. Some of the lower court decisions in the Texas education litigation have made this point explicitly. Many of the demands pressed by advocates and described here could be recharacterized as investments in human capital. But there is little indication in the chapters collected here that policymakers are willing to accept that argument when it comes from a court.

This suggests that proponents may well have an advocacy task to perform even before securing a judgment. It is hard to imagine a purely financial cost-benefit analysis that would favor compliance with a judgment that prioritizes the cultural rights of a minority group over the vast wealth expected from many of these mega projects, or the environmental rights of small rural communities over the many projects governments sometimes imagine funding through a mining boom. For this reason, it may well be that the first task for many groups anticipating such a judgment will be to educate and persuade the relevant decision makers to include a wider array of costs into their calculus. As we will discuss in the next section, changing normative commitments can change how decision makers weight different considerations, so that environmental or multicultural commitments can begin to have some intrinsic weight. Similarly, broadening the calculus, say, to sustainable development or to human development may allow proponents to place other and longer-term considerations on the scale. And, of course, changing the politics of the issue on a national scale may well upend the calculus.

Normative costs: By normative costs (benefits) I mean the clash (congruence) between the objective of the litigation and the proclaimed goals and values of the organization or actor in question – the inclination of a "green" company to comply with an environmental ruling, or the objection of a libertarian party to a ruling requiring the expansion of social protections, for instance. The product of this normative cost (benefit) is the resistance (desire) to do something, which results from normative or ideological commitments, from prejudice or sympathy, and which cannot be reduced to the financial cost of changing course, the political cost of doing something unpopular, or even the political cost of appearing hypocritical. Normative and ideological considerations can have intrinsic weight, or they can give positive or negative valence to judgments and radically change the weight of financial and political considerations.

It is likely that normative costs can be distinguished from both financial and political costs. It is one thing to force a social democratic party to provide a better health service, and another to force a libertarian party to do so even if they would both face the same consequences at the polls; it is one thing to prod a left-liberal party to offer state benefits to immigrants, another to order a right-wing anti-immigrant party to do so, regardless of public support for such measures. For a bureaucrat or a judge, we can imagine some claims that are more consistent with their practices and training, and others that appear to run against the grain of their craft. In part this is a consequence of the differential political costs each would suffer from complying or defying – parties must cater to their bases, bureaucrats must justify their actions after the fact, judges must be seen as applying the law. But some of the findings in this book suggest that there is an intrinsic normative cost to actions that contradict an actor's ideological or normative commitments and prejudices.

There are multiple reasons why this normative cost might matter. If the goal of the litigation is clearly consistent with the expressed goals and values of the targets, it will simply be easier to secure compliance once the initial resistance is overcome. In this case, the litigation can simply adjust the means, or the timing, or the priorities of a target, rather than changing its very goals. The litigation may serve to provide political cover, the litigants may actually find allies inside the organization or the target may decide simply to claim credit for the outcome it was forced to provide. Normative considerations also color how the other classes of costs are processed: If the case or issue has broad normative support among the population, noncompliance will more easily trigger mobilization in support of the claimants, media coverage and other vehicles for the eventual imposition of political costs. Similarly, financial costs and the trade off with other public policy goals will be seen as justified. In short, for a number of reasons, compliance should be less costly, and noncompliance more costly, for a target that has proclaimed itself to be for whatever was being litigated, than for an actor that has publicly defined itself as an opponent.

Noncompliance carries similar normative costs. In many emerging democracies there are some politicians who define themselves by reference to the rule of law, so that resisting a court order, regardless of its content, can generate political and ideological costs. The same, of course, is true for large corporations, which might, as in the case of antiretrovirals in South Africa, decide to provide the remedy or stop the violation in order to avoid appearing callous. Politicians and corporations alike might adopt a specific posture that is more or less congenial with ESC rights – witness the various corporations with "green" messages, or corporations committed to defending intellectual property rights. The former should pay a heavier ideological cost for defying court rulings that direct them to fulfill their express commitments, while the latter should resist complying with rulings that limit patent protections.

Examples of the normative cost of compliance are scattered throughout the volume. In several cases (*TAC* and *Westville*, in South Africa, *Verbitsky*, in Argentina) politicians had staked out a very visible position against the policy the court required. In all these cases, as expected, the government resisted compliance even if public opinion was in favor of the court ruling (so there was actually a net political cost to defiance). It is difficult to separate the normative from the political costs in the Roma cases in Slovakia and the Czech Republic, but in Greece at least it seems the politicians themselves were ideologically committed to removing the Roma from their communities. These cases create problems for politicians that fall on the border between political and ideological costs.

Clearly, normative costs can trump or transform financial concerns. Dobrushi and Alexandridis describe how municipal governments pay reparations to the Roma but are unwilling, when it becomes a public matter, to adopt policies that might encourage "an influx of inadaptable citizens of Gypsy origin" (this volume, p. 443). The issue is not the cost, but rather, as these authors suggest, the fact that the proponents belong to a despised social group. Similarly, Latin American governments that resist the very notion of reproductive rights have rather quickly paid individual reparations to plaintiffs in these cases, but have strongly resisted policy changes that would strengthen reproductive rights (Cabal and Phillips, this volume).

By the same token, cases with positive valence strongly color the financial cost of compliance/noncompliance. Essentially the same claims in housing rights litigation in South Africa lead to compliance in some cases and defiance in cases involving stigmatized plaintiffs. Spending on education triggers less resistance than spending on Roma housing. It is difficult, in Brazil, to deny medications to individuals who need them, no matter what the cost, while structural responses, which lack the sympathetic individual plaintiff but could save money in the long run, are unsuccessful (Ferraz, this volume). In the long-term strategy to bring Western medicines to bear on the HIV epidemic ravaging South Africa, litigants could have first asked for funding to prevent and treat infections among men who have sex with men, or intravenous drug users or sex workers, but they chose pregnant mothers and their children. Cost was an important part of the government's objection to the demands, and the cost might have been much the same in all those cases, but clearly, it was best to begin with the prevention of mother-to-child transmission of HIV, with its innocent victims and sympathetic claimants.

Separation of powers concerns fit under this rubric too. Brazilian judges resist issuing structural judgments that would infringe on their notion of legislative prerogatives, and bureaucrats may well resist such orders, even though the cost of individual litigation is clearly exorbitant for both courts and public health budgets. European governments find it more difficult to accept the orders of a nonnational court than the orders of their own courts or the policy decisions of their own legislators, regardless of their content. Nationalist governments find it harder to comply with international court orders than governments that do not employ nationalist rhetoric. Essentially the same order might have very different valence, depending on normative considerations about who properly should exercise policymaking authority on a subject. In the case of African Commission decisions, governments find it easier to comply with judgments that are based on violations by predecessor governments, than with those that are grounded in their own violations (Viljoens, this volume). All of these distinctions seem driven by normative or ideological considerations, not cold-blooded rational calculations, but it is also clear that these normative considerations are but one of the elements to be placed on the compliance scale.

Crucially, for many publicity is positively associated with compliance – presumably because it makes it possible to impose political costs for non-compliance (Staton 2010), as discussed in the following section. These findings, however, suggest a caveat: In cases with strong negative valence, publicity can kill compliance by increasing its political cost. The Municipal Council of the town of Dobšiná in Slovakia seemed poised to pass a housing policy that would help the Roma, but did an about-face when it became known and the public objected (Dobrushi and Alexandridis, this volume).

There is some debate and disagreement in this volume regarding the perceived strengths and weaknesses, advantages and disadvantages, of so-called soft, dialogic or open-ended remedies. They seem to work in some cases but not in others. For some advocates they are the preferred result, for others they are weak outcomes – nearly akin to a loss – because they offer little purchase with which to wage a compliance campaign. If compliance depends on monitoring, and the specificity of the order provides the metric by which to measure compliance, then these vague orders should be more difficult to enforce (Staton and Vanberg 2008). The difference between these outcomes may well be attributable to the normative valence of the cases in question. Soft remedies may work best (only?) in high positive valence cases: These remedies are hard to monitor; they don't offer benchmarks and clear moments of noncompliance that could help coordinate political costs; but they do give a willing defendant the flexibility to find the most efficient way to comply, thus reducing resistance to the order. If this is true, then advocates should seek more concrete and directive orders in negative valence cases like the Roma discrimination cases, and more open-ended soft orders in positive valence cases like the Right to Food cases in India.

Political costs: Often both financial and normative costs are processed through politics. Indeed it is hard to imagine political costs that are not driven by the financial and normative dimensions of the case in question. The politics of an issue or court are not determinative – just as popular politicians can sometimes afford to challenge and ignore courts, so too can popular politicians sometimes afford to comply with unpopular rulings by courts – but all the chapters make it clear that the politics of compliance are central.

By political costs I mean the burden of public disapproval and its attendant negative consequences for public officials, bureaucrats or businesses, as well as the burden of disapproval of a more specific political principal, such as the executive, for a judge, or a political appointee, for a bureaucrat. A corporation or politician defying a popular and public court order should expect to incur some loss of public support (Staton 2010). It may also be that, regardless of the subject matter, politicians might pay a price for defying the order of a popular court, which is not the same thing (Gibson and Caldeira 1995). We often focus on the more extreme versions of this cost – whether a politician will lose an election, a bureaucrat his or her job – but targets are susceptible to more subtle expressions of disapproval as well. Negative public opinion can affect business enterprises by the loss of what is sometimes called "good will," the intangibles that affect the decision to purchase products from a particular source or with a particular brand, even in the absence of a coordinated boycott. It can affect bureaucrats or government agencies, even formally autonomous ones who nevertheless depend on political support for funding and often on public support for some measure of real autonomy from politicians. And it can affect politicians electorally – the equivalent of a boycott – or by depressing their public opinion ratings – the equivalent of good will.

A boycott, of course, is more effective but requires a higher level of coordination and investment. Similarly, elections are blunt and relatively ineffective instruments for producing compliance in individual cases. Certainly there are no examples in the pages of this volume of politicians who were unseated for failing to comply with the order of a domestic or international court. Still, it is clear that targets are attuned to the political implications of a decision to comply with or defy a court order. For example, when there are more potentially responsible parties, so that responsibility is diffuse and hard to pin on any one actor, compliance declines (Morales, Sigal and Rossi, this volume). Judges in Brazil, attuned to the political repercussions of structural rulings, stick to individual cases (Ferraz, this volume). This finding is consistent with earlier arguments that courts can be most effective when they are backed by a powerful political actor – the executive, the legislature or the organized public (Brinks and Gauri 2008: 345–349). And it is congruent with arguments that posit that intra-electoral societal accountability, in which social groups join legal and political action, can be effective at moving elected officials (Smulovitz 2003; Smulovitz and Peruzzotti 2003; Peruzzotti and Smulovitz 2006).

Less democratic governments, naturally less subject to domestic political pressures, are less likely to comply (Viljoen, this volume). Some experiences shared at the conference that originated this volume, but not included here, confirmed the effect of civil and political rights on the likelihood of compliance. When such rights are denied – either because the regime is authoritarian, as in Mubarak's Egypt, or because the proponents are effectively denied political rights within a nominally democratic regime, as in the case of Palestinians and Israeli Arabs in Israel – compliance was much more difficult to secure. Similarly, when the litigants are poor, excluded from the political process, or otherwise less capable of exerting political pressure, we should expect a lower likelihood of compliance regardless of the cost of compliance, simply because these plaintiffs have less collective political capital. The Roma clearly suffer from this disability – they are often politically irrelevant, if not a liability, they have few if any allies within the administration and bureaucracies, and thus have very little leverage to move public officials. Clearly a robust measure of civil and political rights is often a necessary component for a group attempting to secure compliance with economic, social and cultural rights.

Several chapters make clear that collective action issues strongly condition the ability of proponents to impose political costs. Morales et al. (this volume) show how the cases that targeted a medium-sized, geographically concentrated population – neither individuals nor broad societal interests – were the ones that generated the most compliance for the leading public interest litigation group in Argentina. When the beneficiaries are one or a few individuals, they can exert very little political pressure, so compliance is weak, even if the overall cost of compliance is low. But as the number of beneficiaries grows, and when they are part of an organized neighborhood, their political capital grows faster than the cost of compliance. In these cases, in the end politicians compete to claim credit for solving the problems of the community. As the number of beneficiaries continues to grow, however, collective action problems make it harder to bring costs to bear. Meanwhile the cost of compliance continues to grow (this is the case, paradigmatically, of so-called "diffuse" interests, where by definition it is difficult to identify the direct beneficiaries). This is why, paradoxically, we have problems of noncompliance at both ends of the spectrum.

The problem is exacerbated in test case litigation or in contexts with a strong norm of precedent. Here, the direct beneficiary may be a single individual, but the target fully expects that the cost of compliance will go well beyond that plaintiff. Unless the proponents are able and willing to mobilize on behalf of the entire affected community, one would expect a great deal of resistance on the part of the target. This seems to be at least part of what is going on in the reproductive rights cases (Cabal and Phillips, this volume). Whenever the case only directly involves a small number of individual plaintiffs but the goal is structural reform, as in *Tysiąc v. Poland*, compliance is more difficult. For purposes of compliance and in calculating the level of organization that will be needed even in the event of a positive judgment, therefore, proponents need to treat these cases as collective cases, regardless of who the named plaintiffs are. When the proponents in international fora do not have a strong organizational base in the target country, it seems unlikely that any real change will take place, even if the named plaintiffs obtain their individual remedies.

Indeed the one variable that comes up in nearly all the chapters is one that critically affects political costs by solving the collective action problem: The organizational capacity of the proponents. If there is unanimity among the authors in this volume on any one issue, it is on this. Thus the variation across US states in compliance with education rights litigation is largely a function of the capacity of the proponents to sustain political pressure over time: Litigation without broader social movements, as in Texas, is not unhelpful, but does not lead to major changes, while litigation campaigns that are supported primarily by professional organizers can turn rulings into legislated policy, as in New York; and campaigns that can count on deep-rooted and long-lasting political campaigns can lead to the most significant change, as in Kentucky (Shanor and Albisa, this volume). The primary variable to explain the varying degrees of compliance with housing rulings in South Africa is organizational – well-organized coordinated groups, with strong leadership and staying power secure the greatest benefits from their wins in the courtroom (Langford and Kahanovitz, this volume). Cabal and Phillips (this volume) argue that, in the context of reproductive rights cases from international courts, "national level partners [can play] a significant role in mobilizing public attention to these issues through strategic use of the media, coalition-building, and other awareness-raising strategies."

Another proposed solution to the problem of noncompliance can also be seen as an aid to the proponents in imposing political costs. Many advocates and some courts have decided that one way to ensure compliance is to maintain jurisdiction and monitor performance. Rodriguez-Garavito, Morales et al., Porter, Langford and Kahanovitz, Dobrushi and Alexandridis, and Cabal and Phillips all describe some experiences with continuing supervision by the adjudicatory body. When this works – in Colombia, Argentina, Canada, and South Africa, for example – it is because the affected groups were able to use the process as a focal point and platform for continued organized political activity. Thus, in Colombia, the monitoring phase allows the representatives of the affected parties to develop information, produce proposals (and ultimately solutions) that are most likely to succeed, while allowing a periodic reexamination of compliance and publicity and the imposition of costs for delays and failures to comply. And after the *Doucet-Boudreau* decision in Canada, "the claimant communities relied on the reporting sessions as democratic accountability mechanisms to ensure the timely implementation of their fundamental rights, such that the judicial remedy operated to enhance democratic accountability" (Porter, this volume).

When continued monitoring failed, most notably in the Roma cases, it is because the monitoring entity was weak if not complicit, and thus the affected community was unable to create political opportunities out of a supervised compliance process. The European Committee of Social Rights found a violation of Roma housing rights on the part of Greece. The Council of Ministers, which is supposed to be the monitoring/implementing entity for the ECSR, failed to take any real action to follow up on the ruling, and Greece consequently failed to make any real changes to its policies beyond repealing the most offensive of the regulations in question (Dobrushi and Alexandridis, this volume). Continued monitoring also failed in some instances in South Africa, when the affected community lacked the organizational resources to capitalize on continued court involvement in their plight (Langford and Kahanovitz, this volume). On the other hand, in Canada it was the court's continued supervision which itself seemed to trigger some resistance (Porter, this volume). It seems likely, therefore, that continued compliance monitoring by a court would work best for proponents with some organizational capacity, in a political context in which it is possible that politicians could suffer costs for failing to attend to the needs identified in the litigation.

Plenty of studies and theories of enforcement place the political costs of *non*compliance at the center of the analysis (Weingast 1997; Vanberg 2001; Carrubba 2009; Staton 2010). But the variety of cases and claimants in this volume suggest that politicians can pay dearly for *compliance* as well. The southern politicians in the United States who feared to comply with *Brown v. Board of Education* knew this. This is what motivated the municipal authorities of Dobšiná to backtrack on their proposed accommodation of Roma demands for housing, as described by Dobrushi and Alexandridis. Friendly settlement agreements between Mexico and the Interamerican Commission on Human Rights that were seen as enhancing abortion rights led to a backlash in several states in that country, as politicians sought to capitalize on opposition to the agreement and to a Mexican Supreme Court decision approving the decriminalization of abortion in Mexico City (Cabal and Phillips, this volume). Depending on the issue, then, a deeply unpopular ruling or a directive from an easily vilified court can lead political leaders to conclude that there are net gains to be earned from flamboyant noncompliance.

14.2   Costs to Whom?

Thus far, for simplicity, I have proceeded as if all targets are exposed to more or less the same costs. In reality, the first task is to determine on whom the burden of compliance will fall, and to identify the sorts of costs to which they are susceptible, from the three categories identified. In general, in ESCR cases, we can find four sorts of targets of litigation. Scholars often overlook the fact that many targets are private commercial enterprises (in our survey of health and education litigation across the developing world, for example, the defendants included pharmaceutical companies, mining companies, individual physicians, teachers, unions, private school administrators, soft drink bottling companies, public transportation enterprises and more)(Gauri and Brinks 2008). In many cases, however, litigation targets elected politicians. To take just three examples, this is true in Colombia, when the courts required the legislature to find solutions to an unconstitutional state of affairs; in Costa Rica, when legislation was necessary to formalize the outcome of gender equality decisions; and in the Roma cases in which Greek or Slovak officials had to legislate new housing policies. The group that is perhaps the paradigmatic defendant in these cases is made up of bureaucrats who are responsible for implementing government programs. Occasionally, there is a fourth group, judges who must apply the standards set forth in human rights rulings, for example, when victims of rape in Mexico seek permission to have an abortion. Each of these groups is subject to different sorts of costs, and poses special challenges for compliance.

In the chapters in this book the majority of the targets are public officials, and many but by no means all of these are bureaucrats. When the cases are politically important and involve deeply contested issues, it is safe to assume that these bureaucrats respond to the same dynamics that would move their more politically sensitive superiors. The housing cases in South Africa, the education cases in the United States, the Roma cases in Greece or Slovakia can likely be analyzed as though elected officials were making the key compliance decisions. In fact, sometimes the volume of litigation, or the scandal of repeated noncompliance, is such that policymakers may make a global compliance/noncompliance decision, even if no individual case rises to a level that would warrant attention at the highest levels of the political sphere. In many cases, then, we may consider that bureaucrats and politicians are subject to similar incentives.

Sometimes, however, the decision truly is made by a faceless, nameless bureaucrat who simply has to decide whether to attend to something ordered by a court, or to whatever else happens to land on her desk at about the same time. This is clearest in the Costa Rican, Colombian or Brazilian health cases, which simply require a bureaucrat to provide a health-related service or good of a particular type or to a particular individual or group. In Argentina as well, the targets of much of the litigation have been mid-level bureaucrats who make routine decisions about the allocation of health or education services to the shantytowns around the capital. These cases have slightly more salience, but only after the proponents mobilize to make it happen. In Canada, the decisions that "read in" groups into existing policies, or that require local agents to allow homeless people to erect shelters in public spaces, also target bureaucrats.

Epp (2009) also suggests the key players in the United States and the United Kingdom are often bureaucrats who have different interests than elected officials. For Epp, it is more the embarrassment of a negative finding than the actual financial impact of liability that is at work in motivating bureaucrats. It is not clear whether this is what is at work in all the cases described in this book, but the key insight holds: Often it will be important to consider what might motivate a bureaucrat to comply, independently of the electoral politics of an issue. When the decisions are not particularly salient, compliance theories and strategies have to focus on relatively faceless individuals, who respond very remotely and imperfectly to political appointees or to politicians themselves and thus to ordinary political costs. In these cases, the lack of a clear political strategy suggests a focus on the things that matter to individual bureaucrats – budgets, personal liability, routines, the prestige of their agency and the logic of their craft. In fact, there are times when these more personalized strategies seem to work.

It may well be the apparently real threat of personal civil and criminal liability that leads to such a high level of compliance on the part of the officials of the public health system in Costa Rica or Brazil. Wilson's chapter suggests that ordinary civil servants in relatively more autonomous institutions are more likely to comply routinely than is the personnel of the various ministries. Bureaucrats in these agencies are expected to simply carry out their legal mandate, and likely are not particularly concerned whether the mandate comes from the courts or from the legislature, so long as it does not disrupt the operation of their agency.

Similarly, once the courts decide that a certain medication should be part of the regular course of treatment for one plaintiff, public health bureaucrats in Brazil often extend that ruling to similarly situated plaintiffs. Presumably, this is at least in part an acknowledgment that similar patients should be treated similarly. Some of this respect for the logic of the craft is also apparent in the HIV/AIDS litigation in South Africa, where the proponents often found allies either within the public health bureaucracy or at the policymaking level for the scientifically sound argument that HIV/AIDS should be treated with Western medicines.

But the mechanisms for personalizing accountability that appear to work in Brazil or Costa Rica do not work in Argentina, where the courts use them too timidly, and where the targeted heads of agency experience such a high turnover that compliance can always become the problem of a successor, who would then also have to be threatened with personal liability, and who could in turn leave the problem to a successor. The high turnover also means that individual administrators are insensitive to fines against the state or agency itself. In these cases, then, it seems very little can compel compliance. To make the obvious explicit, the professionalism and responsibility of bureaucrats can only be counted on where there are professionalized and responsible bureaucracies.

Moreover, it is clear that the logic of equality is not universally applied even within the same government. Retiring employees in Costa Rica are often forced to re-litigate the same issues the Constitutional Court has decided thousands of times before, because the agencies continue to deny them judicially recognized rights to severance and pension pay, even though their peers in public health seem to rather readily universalize individual court decisions. The Wilson and Rodriguez chapter does not offer enough information to ascertain exactly why there might be such a difference between the way health and employment cases are treated in Costa Rica. We can speculate, however, that, while by 1997, the year of the health care order, it was standard medical practice to treat HIV positive people with antiretrovirals, there is no similar "human resources consensus" supporting a certain level of severance and retirement benefits. In short, for reasons traceable to what I have called normative costs, professional bureaucrats are more likely to voluntarily comply when the judgment embodies conclusions that are seen as valid and sound, or even compelling, by the professionals in question.

Finally, it is clear that the impact of a decision on an agency's budget and its plans is important to many bureaucratic defendants. Many of the arguments presented by these defendants in court hinge on the fact that the demands are too costly or would exhaust budgets that contemplate something else altogether. One of the ways in which courts and litigants have tried to address this concern (as well as a concern about the limitations of courts' remedial powers and separation of powers) is through dialogical and open-ended rulings that set goals but do not prescribe specific means. It seems plausible, and some of the case studies support the idea, that an agency that has had a hand in designing the solution to the problem identified in the litigation will be more likely to implement that solution rather than resist it. Çali and Koch describe such a deliberative process that leads to greater compliance in the case of ECHR judgments. Similarly, Shanor and Albisa show how education reform efforts are more likely to succeed when courts destabilize the status quo (as suggested by Sabel and Simon 2004) but give local officials a role in designing the reforms. As discussed, however, it seems clear that this works only in the context of a strongly positive normative or political balance in favor of the ultimate goal of the litigation.

The experiences captured in this book suggest that a remarkably high percentage of claims will have to be satisfied by elected legislators themselves. Thus the ECHR judgments and the education reforms in the United States required legislated changes. Similarly, the IDP case described by Rodríguez Garavito, the Costa Rican gender equality decisions identified by Wilson and Rodriguez, the decisions of the African Commission on Human and Peoples' Rights, the Roma/Travelers' housing measures and the reproductive rights remedies secured through the Interamerican Commission on Human Rights all require a legislated response.

Over and over in these cases we see that when the order targets a legislative body, the compliance issue is exacerbated – legislatures have difficulties enough passing legislation initiated from within, let alone responding to an order from without. Thus victims of reproductive rights violations receive individual remedies with some reliability, but legislated structural responses are rare if not nonexistent, as shown in the Cabal and Phillips chapter. While individual bureaucrats in decentralized institutions respond quite readily in Costa Rica, the elected officials and their appointees in the various ministries do not. Even more clearly, the description of the gender equality litigation in Costa Rica, by Wilson and Rodriguez, shows bureaucrats complying with individual decisions but legislators failing to respond for years. Of all the orders in this book, the ones directed at elected policymakers seem to have the worst track record for compliance.

The reason for this emerges from the balance of costs analysis. On the noncompliance side, the cost to any individual legislator of failing to legislate in response to the decision of a foreign or domestic court is surely minimal. This is all the more true when the decision might be unpopular with the legislator's specific constituency. Legislators are not subject to fines, or personal civil or criminal liability, for failing to legislate in response to a court order. The multiplicity of potentially responsible parties itself diffuses responsibility. In the absence of focused, sustained and intense mobilization, the odds that any single member of a legislature would suffer electorally for failing to comply with a decision – even if it is a popular one – is negligible.

Moreover, on the cost of compliance side, elected officials incur many normative and ideological costs that bureaucrats do not. Whereas bureaucrats in general carry out other people's mandates, and so may not have much personally invested in making policy on an issue, legislators have a vested interest in retaining control over policymaking – this is what they do. Legislators in general may be more sensitive to the loss of power implied when courts enter the policymaking arena, appearing to exceed the bounds of traditional judicial roles in a separation of powers arrangement (cf. Ferraz, and Çali and Koch, this volume). Legislators in more nationalistic countries are especially wary of rulings that favor minority groups, and European legislators in general have a strong preference for policymaking and decisions by their own national courts and legislatures (Çali and Koch, this volume). Indeed, the high normative cost of rulings in favor of stigmatized groups such as the Roma or unpopular rights like abortion rights provide entrepreneurial politicians in Slovakia, Greece, France, Romania and Mexico the opportunity to make political hay out of *resisting* a court order.

In short, it appears that in most cases the presence or absence of a court decision does not alter the balance of costs for legislators by very much, and compliance is, in general, less likely when the judgment requires legislative coordination and intervention. If anything, once we factor in the normative costs of compliance, the prospect of a negative balance seems quite likely, so it is not surprising that so many judgments directed at politicians produce few if any real world effects. The opposite is true, of course, when a judgment simply modifies the legislation by fiat, as when a statute is declared unconstitutional. At times, the courts themselves can legislate affirmatively by modifying the legislation themselves – thus Canadian and Colombian courts "read in" changes to legislation. Other judgments simply veto or redact offending legislation, and courts can sometimes re-interpret existing legislation to meet demands. In all these cases, it is the legislative body that must bear the costs of coordinating to overcome the court's ruling, and the record of success is much higher.

The balance seems to shift for legislators when they consider that building up or complying with the court is itself part of a legislature's interest. Thus, Çali and Koch argue, the national legislatures of established EU
states tend to comply with ECHR judgments because they perceive it to be
in their interest to set an example for less established states. This is especially likely when the "deliberative" nature of the order reduces the loss of
sovereignty costs by permitting them to design the specifics of the policy.
In turn, the legislatures of less established or aspiring EU states comply
because they perceive it to be in their national interest to show that they
are or could be good citizens of the EU, even at the expense of losing on the
specific policy issue. There may be instances, in short, when broader interests render legislators more sensitive to the orders of particular tribunals
than bureaucrats would be.

One lesson from these examples is that, while for bureaucrats the costs
and benefits are largely circumscribed to their personal interests and those
of the agency, and perhaps the merits of case itself, for elected officials
the particulars of the case may well be subordinated to broader concerns.
Strategic litigators would do well to consider these broader concerns, and
the greater difficulty of securing compliance from legislators, when deciding how to frame the litigation, where to bring it and what sort of remedy
to request.

But what about judgments that target other judges – whether lower
court judges within the same system, or national judges who must comply with the rulings of international courts? In many Civil Law systems,
lower court judges consider it an affront to their independence to submit to the rulings of even a superior court, unless it is in the context of a
direct appeal. Even so, when a court order is directed at an inferior court,
the problems of compliance are minimized. It is possible that lower courts
will dissent, but unlikely that they would succeed in defying a direct order
for long – in most if not all systems, judicial superiors hold many tools to
bring a recalcitrant lower court judge into compliance. This is true even
in the many Civil Law systems that expressly deny any erga omnes effects
of high court decisions. Clearly, in these cases, the financial and political
costs of compliance are relatively minimal – although there may be high
ideological costs – while the cost of noncompliance is very real, and measured in terms of careers, assignments, pay, loss of collegiality and the like.

The situation of international tribunals addressing national courts is
more complicated. In many cases the local tribunals appear to be willing
to ally themselves with their supranational peers – the Argentine courts
have repeatedly adopted the jurisprudence of the Interamerican Court,

and European courts have often done the same. Occasionally, however, domestic courts resist. The Brazilian courts have followed the lead of their elected officials in resisting the rulings of the Interamerican Court in the Belo Monte dam case, and in the case of amnesties for past human rights violations. As noted by Çali and Koch, this seems to be a function of the domestic politics of each country, and the relative weight assigned to, on the one hand, the political costs potentially imposed by an international audience, and on the other, the normative cost of ruling contrary to an important domestic policy decision, at the behest of a "foreign" court. In the case of the Brazilian courts in particular, it seems likely that the costs are more ideological/normative than actual political costs, since these courts are quite well insulated from politics, and not at all reluctant to rule on behalf of ESCR, at least in individual cases (Ferraz, this volume).

The volume unfortunately includes no examples of private targets from which to derive conclusions, but it seems likely that a similar cost-benefit calculus animates the compliance decisions of market actors. Producers and retailers are sensitive to the threat of boycotts, the loss of a brand's good will or the possibility of third-party punishment through regulation or prosecution. Moreover, the basic mechanisms – concerted action, sustained mobilization and publicity, engagement with state enforcement mechanisms are quite similar. And the resources proponents must bring to bear to raise the costs of noncompliance should be approximately the same. As a result, we would expect to find similar dynamics and concerns at work in the enforcement of judgments against private actors, as we see against market actors.

14.3   Strategies

Clearly, there are strategic decisions that have a global effect on the cost of compliance. We note in our work (Gauri and Brinks 2008), for example, that individual cases are easier to win than huge collective cases. But the record of compliance is more mixed at both ends of the numeric spectrum, as we have seen. As discussed, this is because, in most cases, the budgetary costs of compliance are much lower in individual cases, but so is the political cost of noncompliance. Absent exceptional circumstances, dragging bureaucratic feet in response to an individual court order awarding a particular medication to a particular plaintiff is unlikely to generate headlines and demonstrations. It is even unlikely to draw individual sanctions, unless the litigant has the support of well qualified and resourced attorneys. Conversely, complex collective cases will draw more sustained attention from advocates and publics, but are typically much more expensive for the target and thus justify much greater resistance.

One way to affect the political cost of compliance, then, might be to begin with individual cases until a right is well established and accepted by the public – that is, to use compliance in low-stakes cases to change the valence of an issue. One can use narrow, targeted orders and the threat of small court-ordered penalties aimed at lower-level bureaucrats to raise the cost of noncompliance in the initial cases. Then, once the right is broadly accepted, and the discourse around a topic has changed (see Rodriguez-Garavito, this volume) one can attempt a more important collective case with a far higher budgetary cost, trusting that publicly defying a well-established right in an important instance can generate much higher political costs, especially if it is coupled with political mobilization.

Similarly, one can reduce the normative costs of an order by engaging in a more dialogical process during the course of the litigation. If the target of the litigation is involved in the process of finding a solution to the problem, it is more likely that the ultimate order incorporating that solution will, regardless of its actual budgetary impact, find people willing to carry it out. The trade off may be a remedy that is less comprehensive or absolute – or even less transparent, which can detract from compliance – than what was originally sought, but it may be well worth it, in exchange for the willing compliance of the litigation's target. One can also reduce the financial cost of an order by finding ways to insert the requisite response in the existing state structure – seek remedies that can be met out of existing state structures, and the budgetary and normative costs of compliance should be reduced.

Finally, there are some things proponents themselves can do, with the cooperation of the courts, to increase the costs of noncompliance. They can ask for intermediate measures, prior to a final judgment, that change the politics and valence of an issue. In some of the cases discussed in this book, proponents have secured court orders that generate new information about the plight of the victims of a human rights violation. In Argentina, the court has ordered epidemiological studies and other surveys of the populations affected by the horrendous pollution in the Riachuelo basin. In Colombia, the court has done the same with the millions of internally displaced people. In both cases, public hearings generate attention and press coverage. Periodic reports by the targets of litigation provide opportunities to highlight just how far short they are still falling. One can litigate explicitly to generate the conditions that make it possible to increase the costs of noncompliance, producing information and opportunities that did not exist before.

14.4 Conclusion

The few more theoretical works done so far on compliance have tended to focus primarily on the public response to judicial orders and the consequent political costs of noncompliance (Vanberg 2001; Staton 2004). Others might add a consideration of the salience of the issue to the other branches of government (this is akin to what I would call the normative costs of compliance) (Epstein et al. 2001). These works do not, however, go into any detail on the strategies civil society might implement to affect the compliance cost-benefit analysis, nor do they examine systematically the relative importance of each factor. Here I have tried to draw lessons from the academic literature and the chapters in this volume, with an eye to exploring what litigants can do to raise the cost of noncompliance or lower the cost of compliance without compromising on their goals.

Compliance, this volume makes clear, is often a greater challenge than winning a judgment. The academic literature has made some important contributions but we still know too little about what will produce compliance in particular cases. The experiences collected in this book offer an important cross-section of experiences with compliance around the globe. They add invaluable information, allow us to derive some hypotheses, and prompt even more questions for further research. In addition, they offer advocates some important lessons and examples that might help in devising new strategies and in shaping new litigation. As these contributions make clear, ESCR litigation is changing the face of politics around the world, and better understanding its effects, including the likelihood of compliance, is the new challenge for advocates and academics alike.

References

Bergman, Marcelo (2009), *Tax Evasion and the Rule of Law in Latin America: The Political Culture of Cheating and Compliance in Argentina and Chile* (University Park, PA: Pennsylvania State University Press).

Brinks, Daniel M. and Varun Gauri (2008), 'A New Policy Landscape: Legalizing Social and Economic Rights in the Developing World: Chapter 8', in Varun Gauri and Daniel Brinks (eds.), *Courting Social Justice* (New York: Cambridge University Press), 303–352.

Brinks, Daniel M. and Sandra Botero (2014), 'Inequality and the Rule of Law: Ineffective Rights in Latin America', in Daniel M. Brinks, Scott

Mainwaring and Marcelo Leiras (eds.), *Reflections on Uneven Democracies: The Legacy of Guillermo O'Donnell* (Baltimore, MD: Johns Hopkins University Press), 214–239.

Caldeira, Gregory (1986), 'Neither the Purse nor the Sword: Dynamics of Public Confidence in the Supreme Court', *American Political Science Review*, 80(4), 1209–1226.

Carrubba, Clifford (2009), 'A Model of the Endogenous Development of Judicial Institutions in Federal and International Systems', *Journal of Politics*, 71(1), 55–69.

Epstein, Lee, Jack Knight, and Olga Shvetsova (2001), 'The Role of Constitutional Courts in the Establishment and Maintenance of Democratic Systems of Government', *Law & Society Review*, 35(1), 117–164.

Gauri, Varun and Daniel M. Brinks (eds.) (2008), *Courting Social Justice: Judicial Enforcement of Social and Economic Rights in the Developing World* (New York: Cambridge University Press).

Gibson, James L. and Gregory A. Caldeira (1995), 'The Legitimacy of Transnational Legal Institutions: Compliance, Support, and the European Court of Justice', *American Journal of Political Science*, 39, 459–489.

Gibson, James L., Gregory A. Caldeira, and Vanessa A. Baird (1998), 'On the Legitimacy of National High Courts', *American Political Science Review*, 92, 348–358.

Kapiszewski, Diana and Matthew Taylor (2013), 'Compliance: Conceptualizing, Measuring, and Explaining Adherence to Judicial Rulings', *Law & Social Inquiry*, 38(4), 803–835.

Peruzzotti, Enrique and Catalina Smulovitz (eds.) (2006), *Enforcing the Rule of Law: Social Accountability in New Latin American Democracies* (Pittsburgh: University of Pittsburg Press).

Sabel, Charles and William Simon (2004), 'Destabilization Rights: How Public Law Litigation Succeeds', *Harvard Law Review*, 117(4), 1015–1101.

Smulovitz, Catalina (2003), 'How Can the Rule of Law Rule? Cost Imposition through Decentralized Mechanisms', in José María Maravall and Adam Przeworski (eds.), *Democracy and the Rule of Law* (Cambridge: Cambridge University Press), 168–187.

Smulovitz, Catalina and Enrique Peruzzotti (2003), 'Societal and Horizontal Controls: Two Cases of a Fruitful Relationship', in Scott Mainwaring and Christopher Welna (eds.), *Democratic Accountability in Latin America* (Notre Dame: University of Notre Dame Press), 309–332.

Staton, Jeffrey K. (2004), 'Judicial Policy Implementation in Mexico City and Mérida', *Comparative Politics*, 37(1), 41–60.

——— (2010), *Judicial Power and Strategic Communication in Mexico* (Cambridge; New York: Cambridge University Press).

Staton, Jeffrey and Georg Vanberg (2008), 'The Value of Vagueness: Delegation, Defiance, and Judicial Opinions', *American Journal of Political Science*, 52(3), 504–519.

Tyler, Tom R. and Kenneth Rasinski (1991), 'Procedural Justice, Institutional Legitimacy, and the Acceptance of Unpopular US Supreme Court Decisions: A Reply to Gibson', *Law & Society Review*, 25(3), 621–630.

Vanberg, Georg (2001), 'Legislative-Judicial Relations: A Game-Theoretic Approach to Constitutional Review', *American Journal of Political Science*, 45(2), 346–361.

Weingast, Barry R. (1997), 'The Political Foundations of Democracy and the Rule of Law', *American Political Science Review*, 91(2), 245–263.

Table 14.1 *Summary of cases, variables and balance of costs*

Case	Key variables	Balance of costs analysis	Compliance
ECHR judgments (Çali and Koch)	Domestic versus international courts; deliberative enforcement process; general support for human rights in the population of target states.	The deliberative process of compliance allows the target to define the means in such a way as to reduce the normative and financial cost of complying with a "foreign" court order. Positive affect for human rights decisions means target is looking for ways to comply with minimum cost, rather than loopholes to avoid substantial compliance. Perceived cost of setting bad example for new states leads established EU states to comply; desire to belong leads new/aspiring EU states to comply.	High
Colombian Constitutional Court IDP case (Rodríguez-Garavito)	Dialogic activism: strong rights, moderate remedies, and continued monitoring	The monitoring phase allows affected parties to develop information, proposals, and ultimately solutions that are most effective, while allowing a public reexamination of compliance and publicity and imposition of costs for failure to comply	High
Costa Rica Sala IV decisions in individual cases (Wilson and Rodríguez)	Personal liability for noncompliance; immediacy of the order; nature of the target agency – the closer the agency is to power/ politics, the lower the level of compliance	Individual bureaucrats balance personal cost of noncompliance, with state-borne costs of compliance.	High (conditional on monitoring)

Costa Rica public sector right to strike (Wilson and Rodriguez)	Organized workers, clear orders	Well-organized public unions can impose costs for noncompliance	High
Gender equality (Wilson and Rodriguez)	Well-placed, organized plaintiffs and interested persons; legislators versus bureaucrats as targets	Compliance by bureaucrats (low cost) was immediate; legislative action to formalize the outcome in legislation more costly, and took years	High and low, depending on target
Medical services for patients living with AIDS in Costa Rica (Wilson and Rodriguez)	Unpopular plaintiffs; nature of the agency	Original 1992 case treated as individual – no expansive compliance. The 1997 case treated as universal – high compliance despite much greater cost (although the cost of treatment had dropped quite dramatically between the two decisions), but also larger constituency. The 1997 case is hard to explain. It benefits more individuals, so compliance could be seen as driven by their political capital, but as late as 1998, the government was denying gay activists the right to organize, and making public antigay statements. The group seems to have had more support from legal elites, although not from the general public, by 1997	Initially low, then high

(cont.)

Table 14.1 (cont.)

Case	Key variables	Balance of costs analysis	Compliance
Argentina: medium N cases, affecting the *villas*; structural cases, affecting all incarcerated people; all people living in the *Riachuelo* watershed; all disabled persons using a certain railroad (Morales, Sigal and Rossi)	Number, organization (presence of CSOs) and dispersion of proponents, together with the ability to claim credit for improvements on the other side. Magnitude of the challenge. Threats of personal fines and criminal charges (not successful – possibly because of their timid and inefficient use). Fines on the state are useless in this context.	Focus in this chapter is still on the judge. But it's clear that there is a difference between the impact of the litigants in the medium N cases, who are said to be present in the courtroom and able to identify exactly the consequences of the failure to comply	Individual and medium N cases are usually complied with; Structural cases only if the court acts affirmatively
Brazil right to health cases (Ferraz)	Individual versus collective cases	Separation of powers concerns inhibit judges from issuing rulings to enforce the right to health, possibly anticipating resistance	Compliance in individual cases; "noncompliance" in collective ones

Canadian structural remedies (Porter)	Nature of the order: orders directed at the legal framework that are entirely in the control of the courts are easier versus orders directed at structural features of the state, which are more difficult	"Reading in" groups is easy – extend existing programs to a new group; eliminate discriminatory exclusions; "negative rights" reading of ESCR – allow the homeless to build shelters on public property. In more structural decisions (e.g., *Doucet-Boudreau*), he says "The claimant communities relied on the reporting sessions as democratic accountability mechanisms to ensure the timely implementation of their fundamental rights, such that the judicial remedy operated to enhance democratic accountability"	High in less structural cases.
N.A.P.E. multimillion-dollar award for women against Newfoundland (Porter)	Lobbying campaign by women's and labor groups; fiscal context	In the context of scarcity, opportunity costs led to nonpayment. Once there was more money, and strong political pressure, payment	High
US education litigation (state level) (Shanor and Albisa)	Presence of broader social movement are helpful in some ways; nature of the political campaign (e.g., professional organizers versus grassroots). Fiscal crisis	Open-ended rulings that destabilize the status quo but allow the legislature to re-create the school system, coupled with a deep political movement, leads to significant school reform in some cases. Some gains short lived, as politics faded and fiscal crises arose	Mixed compliance as a function of mobilization and opportunity costs

(cont.)

Table 14.1 (cont.)

Case	Key variables	Balance of costs analysis	Compliance
South African housing (Langford and Kahanovitz)	Community organization; stigmatized plaintiffs	In contrast to US education cases, here compliance improved over time – a function of continuing political mobilization. But when there is a stigmatized or poorly organized group, less compliance	Mixed compliance depending on the nature of group and CSO presence
African Comm'n on Human and Peoples' Rights (Viljoen)	Factors that do not seem to matter: Immediacy, clarity of decision, nature of right, massive violations. Factors that do seem to matter: stable, free, democracy, NGO involvement; size of proponent group (single or small group of complainants less likely to produce compliance), violation by prior government rather than current one	Political costs seem to be driving the decision to comply. Thus a change in government reduces the political cost of acknowledging the commission of a violation; democracy makes it easier to impose costs, and more organized proponents succeed more often	Low/no compliance except in cases of political change

Roma/Travelers cases versus Slovakia, Greece, France, Romania, and the United Kingdom (Dobrushi and Alexandridis)	Stigmatized group; supervision by adjudicatory body (ECSR) didn't work	States pay damages, but don't address the underlying problem by complying with policy because of opposition to measures that are seen as favorable to the Roma. Lack of organization and political resources. Resistance is not really based on financial costs, since much compliance could be based on EU funds, or allowing them self help, so the key seems to be normative costs: "the real operative reason behind this persisting failure is none other than the social unpopularity of and deeply entrenched prejudice against the Roma and Travellers in virtually all the Council of Europe member States"	Low
Reproductive rights – forced and involuntary sterilization; abortion rights; maternal mortality (Cabal and Phillips)	Individual reparations versus structural remedies; organizational capacity of proponents; continuing oversight	Key factor is ability to impose political costs: when a single NGO uses a couple of individual plaintiffs to pursue structural reforms, compliance is more difficult. Mobilizing media helps: "National level partners have played a significant role in mobilising public attention to these issues through strategic use of the media, coalition-building, and other awareness raising strategies," especially when there is some ongoing oversight. But negative affect makes it easy for politicians to defy the court, sometimes leading to backlash campaigns	Compliance primarily with individual awards, not structural ones

CASE INDEX

THEMATIC INDEX

Lightning Source UK Ltd.
Milton Keynes UK
UKHW020000300719
347062UK00014B/179/P